Building Brand Equity and Consumer Trust Through Radical Transparency Practices

Elena Veselinova
Goce Delčev University of Štip, Macedonia

Marija Gogova Samonikov
Goce Delčev University of Štip, Macedonia

A volume in the Advances in Marketing, Customer Relationship Management, and E-Services (AMCRMES) Book Series

Published in the United States of America by
IGI Global
Business Science Reference (an imprint of IGI Global)
701 E. Chocolate Avenue
Hershey PA, USA 17033
Tel: 717-533-8845
Fax: 717-533-8661
E-mail: cust@igi-global.com
Web site: http://www.igi-global.com

Library of Congress Cataloging-in-Publication Data

Names: Veselinova, Elena, 1985- author. | Samonikov, Marija Gogova, 1984- author.
Title: Building brand equity and consumer trust through radical transparency practices / by Elena Veselinova and Marija Gogova Samonikov.
Description: Hershey, PA : Business Science Reference, [2018]
Identifiers: LCCN 2017001154| ISBN 9781522524175 (hardcover) | ISBN 9781522524182 (ebook)
Subjects: LCSH: Brand name products--Management. | Product management. | Branding (Marketing)
Classification: LCC HD69.B7 V47 2017 | DDC 658.8/27--dc23 LC record available at https://lccn.loc.gov/2017001154

This book is published in the IGI Global book series Advances in Marketing, Customer Relationship Management, and E-Services (AMCRMES) (ISSN: 2327-5502; eISSN: 2327-5529)

British Cataloguing in Publication Data
A Cataloguing in Publication record for this book is available from the British Library.

All work contributed to this book is new, previously-unpublished material. The views expressed in this book are those of the authors, but not necessarily of the publisher.

For electronic access to this publication, please contact: eresources@igi-global.com.

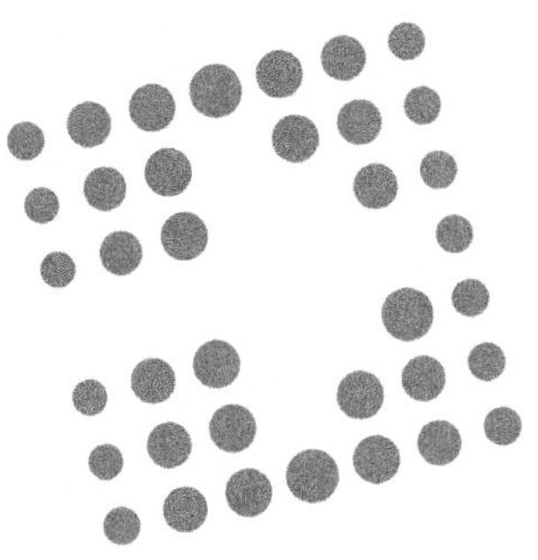

Advances in Marketing, Customer Relationship Management, and E-Services (AMCRMES) Book Series

Eldon Y. Li
National Chengchi University, Taiwan & California Polytechnic State University, USA

ISSN:2327-5502
EISSN:2327-5529

Mission

Business processes, services, and communications are important factors in the management of good customer relationship, which is the foundation of any well organized business. Technology continues to play a vital role in the organization and automation of business processes for marketing, sales, and customer service. These features aid in the attraction of new clients and maintaining existing relationships.

The Advances in Marketing, Customer Relationship Management, and E-Services (AMCRMES) Book Series addresses success factors for customer relationship management, marketing, and electronic services and its performance outcomes. This collection of reference source covers aspects of consumer behavior and marketing business strategies aiming towards researchers, scholars, and practitioners in the fields of marketing management.

Coverage

- Social Networking and Marketing
- Database marketing
- Electronic Services
- E-Service Innovation
- Data mining and marketing
- B2B marketing
- CRM in financial services
- Mobile services
- Customer Retention
- Ethical Considerations in E-Marketing

IGI Global is currently accepting manuscripts for publication within this series. To submit a proposal for a volume in this series, please contact our Acquisition Editors at Acquisitions@igi-global.com or visit: http://www.igi-global.com/publish/.

The Advances in Marketing, Customer Relationship Management, and E-Services (AMCRMES) Book Series (ISSN 2327-5502) is published by IGI Global, 701 E. Chocolate Avenue, Hershey, PA 17033-1240, USA, www.igi-global.com. This series is composed of titles available for purchase individually; each title is edited to be contextually exclusive from any other title within the series. For pricing and ordering information please visit http://www.igi-global.com/book-series/advances-marketing-customer-relationship-management/37150. Postmaster: Send all address changes to above address.

Titles in this Series

For a list of additional titles in this series, please visit: www.igi-global.com/book-series

Strategic Marketing Management and Tactics in the Service Industry
Tulika Sood (JECRC University, India)
Business Science Reference • copyright 2017 • 393pp • H/C (ISBN: 9781522524755) • US $210.00 (our price)

Narrative Advertising Models and Conceptualization in the Digital Age
Recep Yılmaz (Ondokuz Mayis University, Turkey)
Business Science Reference • copyright 2017 • 360pp • H/C (ISBN: 9781522523734) • US $205.00 (our price)

Socio-Economic Perspectives on Consumer Engagement and Buying Behavior
Hans Ruediger Kaufmann (University of Applied Management Studies Mannheim, Germany & University of Nicosia, Cyprus) and Mohammad Fateh Ali Khan Panni (City University, Bangladesh)
Business Science Reference • copyright 2017 • 420pp • H/C (ISBN: 9781522521396) • US $205.00 (our price)

Green Marketing and Environmental Responsibility in Modern Corporations
Thangasamy Esakki (Nagaland University, India)
Business Science Reference • copyright 2017 • 314pp • H/C (ISBN: 9781522523314) • US $180.00 (our price)

Promotional Strategies and New Service Opportunities in Emerging Economies
Vipin Nadda (University of Sunderland, UK) Sumesh Dadwal (Northumbria University, UK) and Roya Rahimi (University of Wolverhampton, UK)
Business Science Reference • copyright 2017 • 417pp • H/C (ISBN: 9781522522065) • US $185.00 (our price)

Strategic Uses of Social Media for Improved Customer Retention
Wafaa Al-Rabayah (Independent Researcher, Jordan) Rawan Khasawneh (Jordan University of Science and Technology, Jordan) Rasha Abu-shamaa (Yarmouk University, Jordan) and Izzat Alsmadi (Boise State University, USA)
Business Science Reference • copyright 2017 • 311pp • H/C (ISBN: 9781522516866) • US $180.00 (our price)

Analyzing Children's Consumption Behavior Ethics, Methodologies, and Future Considerations
Jony Haryanto (President University, Indonesia) and Luiz Moutinho (Dublin City University, Ireland)
Business Science Reference • copyright 2017 • 278pp • H/C (ISBN: 9781522509936) • US $165.00 (our price)

Handbook of Research on Leveraging Consumer Psychology for Effective Customer Engagement
Norazah Mohd Suki (Universiti Malaysia Sabah, Malaysia)
Business Science Reference • copyright 2017 • 374pp • H/C (ISBN: 9781522507468) • US $230.00 (our price)

701 East Chocolate Avenue, Hershey, PA 17033, USA
Tel: 717-533-8845 x100 • Fax: 717-533-8661
E-Mail: cust@igi-global.com • www.igi-global.com

Table of Contents

Preface

There are universal questions for which we tirelessly search answers: Who are we? What are we committed to? What do we want to be? In times of rapid technological change, global agendas and changing market conditions finding the right answers to these classical issues has become significantly more difficult, and equally important. The attempts of the companies to create more, achieve more, earn more... are more and more intense. Even when this becomes far more difficult, additional efforts are being made to achieve the desired goal. Perhaps this is logical.

Nowadays, it is not difficult to measure one's success; it is difficult to define the manner of its achievement. On the one side, there are companies for which it is enough to hear the name (brand) and without hesitation to acknowledge they are successful companies and, on the other side, quite the contrary, although we strive to remember the brand, associations are just missing. These assumptions underline the cause and motive for the thematic coverage of this book. A summary indicator of the overall performance of the companies is precisely the brand. Is it necessary to wait for the results of the ratio analysis of the financial statements of the Coca-Cola Company or it can be immediately concluded that it is a company with millions in profits? Is it necessary to discuss whether Nike and Adidas can hire the best designers of sports equipment? Anyone doubting the quality of the BMW and Toyota cars? In a word, literally, the brand could reveal everything the company is and everything it does.

The main reason for the stressed actuality of the idea of driving brand equity with radical transparency as a source of sustainable competitive advantage and companies' profitability lies in the fact that in the long run there is no other alternative but to be better than the competition. To win and retain this position companies ought to demonstrate superior qualities against their competitors in many different ways. The common denominator of the superiority of one company over others is exactly the value of its brand, measured through different attributes and this could be done only when all involved stakeholders have access to all important information.

The brand equity has the privilege of dichotomous nature. It is a goal for itself. Companies invest heavily in its construction. Simultaneously, it is also a resource to achieve other goals, of course more important, therefore, financial. The title of this book is based on the second meaning of the brand equity - it is a source of sustainable competitive advantage. One thing is certain, the powerful brand does not remain obliged, it returns. The importance of the brand equity, symbolically and literally, is more than clear. In addition, this book is another attempt to elaborate the brand equity role as a source of sustainable competitive advantage through unique and thoughtful practices, using the concept of radical transparency and how to transform the company into a 'brand company' which grows together with its shareholders. The spatial framework for proving the idea could be local and global, independently.

The companies around the globe are permanently faced with two eternal categories: complexity and variability. The process of building and managing the brand equity with radical transparency enables dynamic development of companies through time and space along with the successful confrontation with problems arising from the above two categories.

The focus of this book is the importance of brand equity for long-term companies' profitability, taking into account the complexity of the environment as a resultant factor that increasingly complicates the process of creating new value and its effectuation in stable profitability. This implies the need of using new, prosperous practices such as the concept of radical transparency in business. The pragmatism of the idea is proved by establishing the brand equity with radical transparency: generating consumers' awareness of the brand, improving the level of the perceived quality of products / services, building unique associations of the brand and strengthening the consumers' loyalty to the brand.

The significance of the brand equity, and especially its creation and improvement, according to modern theorists in the field of strategic marketing management on the one hand, and by the practical knowledge of top managers of major corporations around the world on the other hand, is a topic that intensely occupies the advanced scientific and practical interest. The book analyzes the question whether the sustainable source of competitive advantage derives from the emphasis of the internal strengths and the elimination of internal weaknesses or it is the result of successful manipulation with the opportunities in the environment and avoidance of external threats. Despite the efforts of numerous authors supporting the second, the modern scientific thought in the field of strategic management emphasizes the first variant. So, the analysis of the hypothesis of intangible resources and their mobility as a necessary condition for sustainable competitive advantage follows as a logical sequence. Thus, the idea of the brand equity as a sublimate of all typical resources and capabilities of the company is put in the core of the book and its creation and maintenance leads towards the desired competitive advantage. But, today's world scrutiny asks for a transparent explanation of how and what companies do. So, exactly the concept of radical transparency could be that typical, different 'thing' that leads from competitive advantage to sustainable competitive advantage. This thesis is proved through the prism of the VRIO concept.

The domain in which the brand equity, perceived as a source of sustainable competitive advantage for companies, has a scientific contribution is illustratively demonstrated through the construction of rounded theoretical basis in the book, emphasizing the brand equity as a symbol of: higher value, higher quality, greater market share, higher price, more loyal consumers, i.e. a symbol of everything that provides higher profitability, which enhances the need for practical affirmation of this idea. The realization of the above hypothesis is supported by the concept of radical transparency in every activity the company performs. The most obvious confirmation of these findings is the diametrically different levels of success of companies that consciously create and manage their brand equity versus those unrecognizable 'survivors' far from the top.

The book elaborates the phenomenon of branding and the related process of creating additional value, and thus profitability. The arguments support the thesis that the usage of radical transparency practices, while building and managing the brand equity, leads towards achieving greater market share, creating entry barriers for new competitors, achieving product and market expansion, providing premium price, attracting quality workforce, ensuring customer loyalty and stimulating innovation.

The acceptance of the idea of driving brand equity with radical transparency stimulates the efforts to build the brand pentagon with radical transparency practices: completing the rise, definition, articulation, measurement and expansion of the brand together with all relevant stakeholders.

Furthermore, the justification of all theoretical and practical knowledge of radical transparency in business is verified through the evaluation of the brand. This thesis is elaborated through several variants: using the brand equity as a measure of the value of the brand, financial approaches for evaluating brands with(out) radical transparency, integrating finance and marketing through the 'best practice' approach and constructing the value chain of the brand with radical transparency. In this way, the efforts for understanding, applying and evaluating the brand equity through the concept of radical transparency are rounded, which opens the door for new, alternative ways of striving for sources of sustainable competitive advantage.

The companies' opportunity to commit to building a brand equity that will be a differentia specifica is not a choice among several possibilities, but acknowledged necessity. Therefore, this book highlights the need of top management to create or strengthen the vision of the brand and to spread and share it throughout the company and around it. Any further activity would be undertaken with one common goal: to achieve the vision.

Taking into account the need for simultaneous possession of theoretical and practical knowledge and experience in building and managing the brand equity, the contribution of the book is validated through the need of creating a critical mass of successful examples of companies which enjoy the benefits of implementing the concept of driving brand equity with radical transparency practices. The number of companies that are committed to building a brand, that, as a whole, would represent transparency, security, openness and collaboration with all relevant stakeholders (which is by itself an original source of sustainable competitive advantage) is limited until now, thus the strengthening and promotion of this book's purpose is a further challenge.

At the end, the conclusions in the book systematize the findings in order to complete the process: from idea to realization of the concept of driving brand equity and consumer trust through radical transparency practices, which should strengthen the answer to the most essential question in economics: how to achieve more?

Chapter 1
Defining the Concept of Brand Equity With Radical Transparency

ABSTRACT

Every company must seek the formula that works best for its particular culture and industry. There is no one right way to transform a conventional company into a value driven company. But all the authentically responsible companies subscribe to a set of principles about: the mission, vision, transparency, working, responsibility, openness, authenticity and innovation – all this put in an agenda for value driven companies which are prepared for the challenges we all face. This chapter analyses how the transformational forces: the tangible worth of intangible assets, the war for top-grade talent, the impressive power of inspired employees, the transparent supply chains, the global impact of NGOs, the informed global consumer reshape the business landscape. The insurgent companies that seize on these drives will create real value and increase their long-term profitability. The concept of radical transparency in business gives the companies the opportunity to win the battle for success differently from the competitors, which would ensure the company's sustainable growth and profitability, arousing from the well-shaped relationships with the stakeholders who provide value for the company. The company's brand would be a synonym for those connections.

INTRODUCTION

The tangible worth of intangible assets, the war for top-grade talent, the impressive power of inspired employees, the transparent supply chains, the global impact of NGOs, the informed global consumer – all these transformational forces reshape the business landscape. The insurgent companies that seize on these drives will create real value and increase their long term profitability.

The concept of radical transparency lays in the basics of a vision of a better business, one that operates in greater harmony with its environment and offers a more exciting and meaningful place to work. The vision blends principles and practices—like understanding the challenges that come with creating

DOI: 10.4018/978-1-5225-2417-5.ch001

a sense of purpose and what it takes to integrate that mission into an enterprise's day-to-day work. The key is to keep building capability along dimensions, increasing genuine commitment and the skills to deliver on that commitment.

A small number of corporations are starting to internalize the truly strategic implications of the changes that are looming, but even these few leading enterprises are far from truly integrating an expansive business mission into their daily operations. The following two things can shift this state of affairs: a different vision of the future that is more inspiring than the actual status quo, and a new consensus on what it will take to move toward it.

Every company must seek the formula that works best for its particular culture and industry. There is no one right way to transform a conventional company into a value driven company. But all the authentically responsible companies subscribe to a set of principles about: the mission, vision, transparency, working, responsibility, openness, authenticity and innovation – all this put in an agenda for value driven companies which are prepared for the challenges we all face. Responsible companies believe that what they stand for their purpose and values are far more important than the products they make or services they sell. For them, advocacy is a synonymous with strategy – the industry needs a reform and they aim to fix it. When companies stand for something big, something that truly matters to people, they sharply differentiate themselves from their competitors.

In the future, companies will fight a battle for brand dominance. Investors will recognize the brand as the most important asset of companies. This is a critical concept. This is a vision of how to develop, manage, strengthen and define the business. It will be more important to own markets than to own resources. And the only way to own the market is to have a dominant brand. The concept of radical transparency in business gives the companies the opportunity to win the battle for success differently from the competitors, which would ensure the company's sustainable growth and profitability, arousing from the well-shaped relationships with the stakeholders who provide value for the company. The company's brand would be a synonym for those connections.

ADOPTING THE IDEA OF RADICAL TRANSPARENCY IN BUSINESS

History has shown that the world has faced many challenges in many different ways. The economy has put a lot of people out of work in different part of the world in different time interval. But the difficulties people suffered are always the same. The extraction and usage of resources has led and, yet, leads to growing climate crisis and changes with catastrophic possibilities, and the costs for the current lifestyle that the future generations will bear are incredibly huge. As dramatic as the past has been, it only announces the economic, social, political and environmental turbulence yet to come. According to the World Wildlife Fund, if China alone were to reach the rate of U.S. consumption, in terms of natural resources extracted and ecosystems impacted, we would need the equivalent of two Earths. The consequences of such excess and the resultant degradation disproportionately increase the unequal distribution of wealth worldwide. Today, on the one side, half of world's wealth is in the hands of 1% of the population (*The Guardian*, 2017, January 16) and on the other, approximately one billion people do not have reliable access to clean drinking water. Clearly, the world is still away from reducing the enormous economic, social and environmental imbalances. And yet, after the entire recent crisis, the everyday business discussions are about how the get the economy back to 'normal' as it was. Although growing numbers of leaders in all sectors are starting to sense the depth and breadth of the challenges that lie ahead, we still assume a return to business-as-usual, albeit with some necessary adjustments.

All of this leaves us profoundly ambivalent about the future. On the one hand, we long for real change. Few among us want to live in a way that generates enormous amounts of waste and pollutants, depletes precious resources more rapidly than nature can replenish them and destroys ecosystems. On the other hand, we fear that a future fundamentally different from the past is not truly possible. Consequently, we have little collective will to follow a better path. Insofar, as the business is one sector that must help and take a lead in building a better future, the burgeoning corporate social responsibility movement gives us a reason to hope. But it, too, has been mired in this same ambivalence. Many executives now concede that companies that focus narrowly on their own business and ignore all larger social and environmental impacts invite activists' ire and put their profits at risk. Consequently, more and more multinational corporations are turning out glossy CSR reports and are creating senior staff positions dedicated to corporate responsibility. Then again, most people doubt that the present CSR programs are the grand success story of businesses transformation. Despite these efforts, for the most part, we still make and use the wrong products, powered by the wrong energy, driven by the wrong business models.

A small number of corporations are starting to internalize the truly strategic implications of the changes that are looming, but even these few leading enterprises are far from truly integrating an expansive business mission into their daily operations. The following two things can shift this state of affairs: a different vision of the future that is more inspiring than the actual status quo, and a new consensus on what it will take to move toward it.

The need to fundamentally shift from 'profit-driven' to 'value-driven' businesses was mentioned by the management guru, Peter Drucker, who believes that 'every social and global issue is a business opportunity just waiting for the right kind of inventive entrepreneurship, the right kind of investment, the right kind of collective action,' (Drucker, 2001, p.42). Today, this visionary statement is more than accurate and steadily enters the mainstream business thinking. Two critical actions serve as an evidence of the above claim, coming from the foremost champions of conventional capitalism: Bill Gates, the cofounder of Microsoft, and Lee Scott, the ex-CEO of Wal-Mart. In 2008, the former CEO made special commitments to reduce the company's energy use and to improve working conditions in the whole supply chain. At the same time, at the World Economic Forum in Davos, Switzerland, Bill Gates stated: 'more people can make a profit, or gain recognition, doing work that eases the world's inequities.' (Gates, WEF, 2008, Switzerland). These actions simply underline the economic and social pressures and opportunities that force the companies to reconfigure their business models into new which include a better business purpose. Furthermore, in 2007 McKinsey, the global consultancy, published a report which contained a result form a survey that more than 90% of the interviewed CEO are trying more to build strategies which include an environmental and social component than they did five years ago (McKinsey, 2007).In 2005, *The Economist*, stated in an article: 'corporate responsibility and radical transparency are booming and only few big companies can afford to ignore it' (*The Economist*, 2005, January 20). Later, the statement will alter to 'corporate responsibility and radical transparency are part of everyday activities of companies and no one can afford to ignore it'. Even *Forbes Magazine*, the so-called 'capitalist tool', asked: 'Do corporations exist solely to maximize their profit? We do not think so.' (*Forbes Magazine*, 2016, May 9).

There are several reasons why radical transparency and corporate responsibility are gaining such importance:

- With history full of crisis and turnovers, the companies must work harder to protect their brand and brand equity;
- The global brands which compete to win markets all over the world are expected to perform better and better and this includes taking into account the welfare of all relevant stakeholders;
- The customers, thanks to the advanced technology, are more informed and powerful than ever before. They have the power to scrutinize the companies' activities and 'to punish' them when see signs of misbehavior;
- The employees today expect from companies to set purposes greater than the goal for profit and exactly the value driven companies are those which attract the best talents;
- The nongovernmental organizations (NGOs) are growing exponentially and are relentlessly pushing companies to contribute to society;
- The stakeholders are pressuring the shareholders and institutional investors to adopt strong principles of governance and responsible investment strategies.

These arguments have turned into key drivers that make responsible and transparent corporate behavior to be an imperative. They are not only persistent; they are predominant and will endure for decades. The next generation of leaders and entrepreneurs will light the match and play the role of accelerants. They need to remake the business practices and construct sustainable business models that will stop the current consumption of what our children's children should inherit. These pioneers need to prepare to meet the global threats and opportunities in order to stay competitive, to undertake activities that will protect the company's most valuable asset – the brand equity, which represents around 75% of the total value of the average business in U.S. In a world where more than 50% of the consumers (Transparency International's Corruption Perceptions, 2009) believe that the business sector is dishonest, the only true asset to stand up in the fight against the odds is the brand equity.

The new transparent way of doing business will be a powerful magnet for great talents. Just as the Google cofounder Larry Page has proclaimed 'Talented people are attracted to Google because we empower them to change the world.' (*Time*, 2013, May 1). When traditional business models are used, most employees have no bigger ambition than hitting the numbers, which is not such a stimulant for the great minded. Regardless of the industry, the company's desire to create something that matters to the world is a powerful lure for smart people who thrive to 'crack the code' of the problems that bother the world. The companies that are organized around an inspirational mission not only attract the best human capital, they yield the best results, because they summon their employees to extraordinary contributions and inspire them to use all of their imagination and inventiveness to work each day. Just as Howard Schultz opined: 'Ultimately, Starbucks cannot flourish and win customers' hearts without the passionate devotion of our employees.' (Schultz, 1999, p.25) A true conformation that supports this claim is the fact that in the period between 1997 and 2007, the companies which were listed as the 'best place to work' achieved more than twice of the annual return of the S&P 500 Index.

Transparent managers will earn a 'license to manage' from relevant, critical external stakeholders. This does not mean that the business would meet or exceed a set of necessary legal and regulatory requirements. It involves the need to transform the entire company into a value seeker with actions that produce benefit for the society as a whole. Maybe a little late, but still, Wal-Mart understood this request and struggled to win community approval for the location of the new stores. Google, also, got it – the giant is investing hundreds of millions of dollars in developing renewable energy technologies. It is more than clear - the customers reward the companies that contribute to the society.

The businesses which embrace the concept of radical transparency recreate the relationships with their suppliers. When the activists around the world stood up against the persistent health, safety and child-labor violations in the overseas factories of some of the U.S. most famous apparel brands, the targeted companies reacted as expected – they complied a 'procedure list' for their suppliers and regularly sent representatives to check how much they respect the rules. This was a step forward to accepting corporate responsibility. Gap Inc. acted even more transparently. The company proudly announced that it had terminated the contracts with 136 factories that failed to meet the company's standards. However, recently, the company admitted that the internal monitoring cannot solve the supply chain problems and gain the public's trust. So, in 2006, Gap surprised the business world by publishing on its website the list of all the contract factories which were part of the supply chain of the company. Even more, Gap and Nike started to collaborate with the union and NGO representatives in order to become a more sustainable and desirable place to work. These two companies understood that when contract factories invest in people and threat their workers well they tend to improve efficiency and product quality, which grows their business and, at the end, improves their customers' (in this case Gap and Nike) business results.

As the example above, the companies that accept the idea of radical transparency in every activity do not fear to cooperate with one of the today's most powerful 'regulatory' force – the NGO. NGOs have grown to become big as the eight largest economy in the world, numbering in millions and with annual operating budgets of more than $1 trillion. They grow with accelerated proliferation and spread their influence everywhere in the world. Recently, Wal-Mart viewed the NGO sector with outright hostility. But painfully learned that it cannot hide from them. When the retailing giant finally conceded that it needed a sustainable strategy it turned towards the previous critics. The former CEO, Lee Scott, acknowledged that NGOs were an essential stakeholder which urges the company to innovate and contribute to the society. Once outsiders who challenged the system, now the NGOs act increasingly as insiders – an important part of the system they are trying to change. They stimulate the companies' transformation into conscientious businesses which helps them to be better equipped to successfully deal with the robust new conscience of the marketplace.

A new kind of responsible and transparent managers is evolving. They have the desire for a new, responsible era in the business. The number of individuals who demand change by rewarding the companies that meld economic growth with social justice is growing every day. The customers, also, have grater expectations. They, particularly the younger generations, are moving toward a different way of judging the business. 'They celebrate companies and brands that share their value, rather than have the most muscle' (Thorson&Duffy, 2012, p.16). It may be difficult for the bigger and older brands to emulate this new generation, but can and must if they want to succeed in the selling to today's informed and empowered consumers.

The tangible worth of intangible assets, the war for top-grade talent, the impressive power of inspired employees, the transparent supply chains, the global impact of NGOs, the informed global consumer – all these transformational forces reshape the business landscape. The insurgent companies that seize on these drives will create real value and increase their long term profitability.

The concept of radical transparency lays in the basics of a vision of a better business, one that operates in greater harmony with its environment and offers a more exciting and meaningful place to work. The vision blends principles and practices—like understanding the challenges that come with creating a sense of purpose and what it takes to integrate that mission into an enterprise's day-to-day work. The key is to keep building capability along dimensions, increasing genuine commitment and the skills to deliver on that commitment. For example, Triodos Bank N.V. was the bank which increased its income for 25% and its loan portfolio for the same margin during the Great Recession in 2009 while the biggest players on Wall Street almost brought down the global economy. The bank is based in Netherlands, with network offices throughout Western Europe and a working capital of € 3.7 billion. This bank succeeded to achieve those excellent results due their policy to finance only sustainable businesses and projects, which include more than 9.000 economically, socially and environmentally beneficial initiatives only in 2008. Despite the company's history and background, if the project does not positively contribute to the society or the environment, the company does not fulfill the conditions to obtain a loan from Triodos. The idea of supporting truly responsible and transparent businesses presents the bank as one of the pioneers in driving the economy to a regular sustainable direction. And what must be emphasized, the profit always grew even if it is not the primary goal of the bank. Triodos has never recorded a quarterly loss in the three decades since its founding. Certainly, the bank tends to maximize the shareholders returns, but with a different kind of a business model which puts sustainability on the first place (Hollender&Breen, 2010).

Putting values before profit is a basis which does not fit into the conventional business models. To many managers, the idea of radical transparency is an upside down way of building strategy and a direct threat for sales and revenues. But, the emerging examples, such as the Dutch bank, give the skeptics a relevant reason to start believing that building the business on the principles of economic and social equilibrium can lead to stable long term profitability. The constantly positive performance of Triodos bank is a prominent piece of evidence that corporate responsibility and radical transparency are entering the business world slowly but surely. This is going to be a change that is as revolutionary as it is evolutionary. The obvious signs for these changes are the increased number of value-driven companies and the new generation of value-driven leaders who leave the thesis that 'the only business of business is business.' The implementation of radical transparency practices in business will determine how companies organize, strategize and compete. It will reconfigure the sources of competitive advantage and growth.

The idea of transparency in every action is an idea that most businesses embrace in principle but find terrifying in practice—for good reason. A company that reveals its demerits as well as its merits opens itself up to a never-ending and invariably humbling journey of examining facts, listening to others' views, reflecting, and learning. Those companies that do it well build a culture that embraces high levels of self-criticism and a willingness to challenge management's most cherished beliefs including its privilege to make decisions behind closed doors. Such a culture inevitably extends to all members of the organization and beyond, including those who are neither employees nor experts in the business.

A company that benefits society as well as shareholders require leaders who never stop reflecting on who they are and who they want to be; who can blend their own personal vision with those who see the world differently; who tell the truth about obstacles and recognize their own personal responsibility in creating them; and who know there are no final answers or formulas. Building a responsible company takes, literally, forever.

The concept of radical transparency can be a powerful tool to transform ordinary businesses into more responsible, conscious and profitable entities. Radical transparency is required for a business to succeed in today's environment of stakeholders' scrutiny. Information technologies let everyone to see everything anyone does. Even though, at first sight, it might look like that sharing information for all the company's activities puts the company to open critics, but at the end, the company would have more friends than prosecutors. The radical transparency practices create long-lasting partnerships with all relevant stakeholders and in this way it becomes the first step towards overcoming the weaknesses and threats and securing the strengths and opportunities of the company, which, ultimately, leads to achieving a sustainable competitive advantage and long-term profitability.

The forms of radical transparency are various and spring from each activity the company performs. For example, a business can willingly disclose all of its product ingredients, or it may disclose all the sources and operations in the supply chain. The knowledge of the product / service creates loyal customers. Knowing that a company is willing to share detailed information allows the customer to trust the company. A trustworthy management team will personally communicate the message with both, employees and customers, regardless of the content of the message, whether it is about the successes or failures of the company. If there is trust in the brand, then there is loyalty. And where is loyalty there are sustainable revenues and long term profitability. Nurturing a positive relationship with customers is good for the company's profitability and it creates a unique connection that can be the basis for a competitive advantage that competitors could not overcome. Or even more, if one company can do it, then others will try to, at least, copy it, which would create a chain reaction of companies engaging in similar business practices. Ultimately, this will utter the competitive conditions to an upper scale and provide several benefits for the entire community. Transparent companies may voluntarily provide the public with sustainability reports, including all aspects of corporate responsibility towards the: customers, employees, investors, suppliers, competitors, public groups and the society as a whole.

Radical transparency should start internally, with the attempts of the company to share information with its employees, not just with their customers or other external stakeholders. This relationship directly affects the company culture and the values it creates. The company would benefit from creating a culture of trust, loyalty and commitment in the workplace. It is important for each employee to be informed, thus, empowered, thus motivated and satisfied. This kind of employee would be the most effective and efficient input in process of generating value for the company. Even more, he/she would be the most trusted mouthpiece the company could have. At the end, fostering the sense of doing good work would result in doing great work.

It is more that obvious that the social pressure has a big impact on the way the business is conducted. Many previously successful brands are now in danger of becoming tainted in our minds as customers are demanding but failing to get information about what is in the products they are using and how their purchases are impacting the world. Today customers seek value and engage with companies, expecting to be informed of both the pros and cons of the business. The social media can be a useful marketing tool but they should be used for much more than promotion. They could be a powerful tool in disclosing relevant information for the customers on time, so the radical transparency will minimize the risk from misunderstandings due to uninformed customers, which may lead to losing the trust and loyalty to the brand and spoil the hardly gained brand equity.

The traditional forms of transparency are always necessary. Company's transparency via social media is important but so is the ability for customers to easily reach for any information at the other end of a product inquiry. It is more than important to make it easy and pleasant for the customer to contact an individual in the company, as well as, allowing all individuals (employees at the first place) to tell and discuss scores and results about the company. This will help the company build a corporate culture of appreciation and esteem and everyone would feel proud to share how much they respect their customers and, at the end, how much the customers respect the company. Customers should have the opportunity to get information about their purchase and this information must be clear, believable and easy to understand. The more customers try to get the answers, the less credibility and trust the business will have. All other efforts invested in the brand equity maintenance will be fruitless.

No matter what form of transparency a company takes, it is always a wise decision to be open about what goes on behind the scenes. The radical transparency concept is more than using the proper resources and reducing the usage of the limited, informing the customers over the product details, building sustainable relations with suppliers, donating to charities, supporting health programs or solving selected society problems. It's about reconfiguring companies from inside: innovating new ways of working, instilling a new logic of competing, identifying new possibilities for leading and redefining the vision and mission of the business. The radical transparency should become part of the realms of strategy, leadership and management. This concept would change the industry structure and alter the competitive conditions to a new level of priorities. But to fully understand and feel the benefits of the idea of driving brand equity and sustainable profitability with radical transparency practices it is mandatory to turn theory into practice and build entities that receive revenues by contributing to the greater good. In order to transfer the primary goal of profitability to a goal of generating value for all stakeholders, companies ought to change - change their priorities, the way they organize, the way they operate, how they compete, and the way they interact with the world. Some companies would take the pioneers role and would be the first to light the torch for this concept and others will follow because they want to or because they have to. The reason will be the huge number of informed consumers, values-driven employees, conscious investors and intelligent competitors. The time has come to turn exceptions into a trend.

Even the skeptics now admit, as positive examples emerge, that sustainable companies often enjoy a distinct competitive advantage over their profit-fixated competitors and continue to deliver outsized financial results. Here is some evidence. Between 1995 and 2007, socially responsible investments assets increased by 324%, sharply outpacing growth in the broader world of investments, which increased by less than 260% over the same period. Cheryl Smith, the chair of the Social Investment Forum Board, declared: 'social investing is thriving as never before' (Social Investment Forum [SIF], (2010). Even during the Great Recession, the investments in socially responsible funds grew 'at higher rates than ever' to an estimated $ 2.7 trillion(Social Investment Forum [SIF], 2016).Clorox, which built its brand on chemical bleach, bought natural-based Burt's Bees for $ 950 million, a multiple of more than five times of the company's sales in 2007. Within two years, Burt's grew into a heavyweight, ranking among the top U.S. 'green brands' in 2009. Then, there is the renewable energy industry. Revenue growth in biofuels, wind power and solar photovoltaic expanded by 50% in 2008, even though tightening credit began to squeeze markets. The future for renewable looks even brighter. The research company Clean Edge estimated that the three benchmark technologies will leap from $ 115 billion in 2008 to $ 325 billion within a decade. Companies that compete outside of this industry are also moving in the same direction. A survey by the consulting group A.T. Kearney found that companies committed to corporate sustainability and radical transparency practices achieved above average performance in the financial markets during the tough recession in 2008, which can be translated as an average of $ 50 million in incremental market value per company. In the retail industry, a Boston Consulting Group survey which included 9000 consumers in developed countries came with a result that more shoppers 'systematically' purchased green products in 2008, when the global economy was plummeting, then in 2007.' And finally, even the 'wolfs of Wall Street' sometimes take the sustainability and transparency seriously. In 2008, Goldman Sachs created a task force with many of the world's largest financial houses to help the industry put social, ethical and environmental issues at the heart of the investment analysis. Goldman analysts concluded that such a perspective leads to a 'good overall proxy for the management of companies relative to their competitors', which directly signalizes their chances of long term success. This eye-opening finding motivated the companies, especially in the period after the recession. The companies that were leaders in leveraging corporate governance, social and environmental considerations for sustainable competitive advantage outperformed global stock funds by 25%.

When they realized that corporate responsibility and radical transparency can help them build and sustain a unique competitive advantage and flourish their brands, companies lined up to proclaim their values and visions by presenting positive messages to their web sites, annual reports and advertising. For example, more than 52.000 company web sites highlight that corporations are beginning to account for their social and environmental impacts in addition to their traditional focus on profitability. Representatives from more than 4.700 companies in 130 countries have signed the UN Global Compact, committing to follow its 10 principles concerning human rights, labor, and the environment and anti-corruption efforts. A growing number of CEOs from the biggest companies in the world take part at corporate responsibility and radical transparency conferences to pronounce their passion for improving the labor standards worldwide, to expound their company's new commitment creating value without waste etc. It is more than clear – many executives now see corporate responsibility and radical transparency as a source of sustainable competitive advantage, or, at a minimum, as an inescapable priority. This is why it can be expected that a fairly large number of companies will master the corporate responsibility and radical transparency practices. The future belongs to these revolutionary companies that not only bring out the best in employees and other relevant stakeholders, but also build their market share by committing to a boarder vision for the business.

Every company must seek the formula that works best for its particular culture and industry. There is no one right way to transform a conventional company into a value driven company. But all the authentically responsible companies subscribe to a set of principles about: the mission, vision, transparency, working, responsibility, openness, authenticity and innovation – all this put in an agenda for value driven companies which are prepared for the challenges we all face. Responsible companies believe that what they stand for – their purpose and values are far more important than the products they make or services they sell. For them, advocacy is a synonymous with strategy – the industry needs a reform and they aim to fix it. When companies stand for something big, something that truly matters to people, they sharply differentiate themselves from their competitors.

Truly responsible and transparent companies are not littered whether the eyes of the consumers or NGOs are on the company and follow each move. On the contrary, they invite them to do so. The transparent company preempts the critics and takes the first step towards collaboratively fixing the problems. It is ready to publicly share the impacts it makes on the society and environment. Just as the Danish pharmaceutical Novo Nordisk, the world's largest producer of insulin, revealed its forays into such controversial topics as animal testing, stem-cell research and gene technology. However, in the long run, more eyes do not literally mean more advocates - it means fewer difficulties and less problems.

The time has come to change the old business models which were based on hierarchy: the management team delivered the strategy and the employees executed it. Today, transparent companies work as a community. Talented people, motivated by the company's sense of purpose, provide the power for generating breakthrough ideas and spread them around the world. When the employees are let to set their own strategic direction they act less like employees and more like entrepreneurs. When organizing the company as a community it catalyzes people's capacity to create and share. The companies that implement the radical transparency concept believe in the premise that 'two heads are always smarter than one'. So, the more heads get into the game, the better the chance they would make a real difference in the market and in the world. For example, IBM is full of 'Mensa members' but it does not rely solely on them. It listens to the customers' voice and other outside stakeholders. Today, to interact is more than important, yet, only few companies dare to put customers at the very heart of their innovation process. But when they do so, they leverage people's power by giving up the full control.

Promoting responsibility through advertising and marketing campaigns is not enough. When a company is declared as sustainable, responsible and transparent it includes these attributes in every activity it performs. For example, in the lobby of its London headquarters, the British retailer Marks&Spencer uses a giant electronic ticker to broadcast its performance against 100 social and responsible initiatives. The message is clear: M&S is genuinely committed to 'doing good' and considers itself accountable for the results. A truly responsible and transparent company aligns its words with its actions.

To truly incorporate the responsibility and transparency concept into everything it does, the company should construct a collective view of what it should be. This requires the development of a high degree of clarity about what matter the most to the company and then to acquire the necessary knowledge for the important strategic decisions. The company must stimulate a sharper awareness to the way it works and what it seeks to accomplish. All this should start with asking the right questions, because the questions we ask shape the answer we get. For example, if we ask, 'What can we do to increase the market share?' we will get a very different answer form the answer to the question 'What can we do to build a more sustainable economy?' Questions like the last should motivate the companies to explore how they can best respond to the enormous challenges and the boundless opportunities that wait around the world.

ANALYZING THE BRAND EQUITY ASSETS WITH RADICAL TRANSPARENCY

In the future, companies will fight a battle for brand dominance. Investors will recognize the brand as the most important asset of companies. This is a critical concept. This is a vision of how to develop, manage, strengthen and defend the business. It will be more important to own markets than to own resources. And the only way to own the market is to have a dominant brand. The concept of radical transparency in business gives the companies the opportunity to win the battle for success differently from the competitors, which would ensure the company with sustainable growth and profitability, arousing from the well-shaped relationships with the stakeholders who provide value for the company. The company's brand would be a synonym for those connections.

There are several factors that contribute to the increased interest in brand equity and generally in branding. First, the companies are willing to pay more for their brand development because the development of new, alternative (competing) brands is almost impossible or too expensive. Second, companies are feeling significant pressure from the continued emphasis on price reduction by exaggerated promotions or desperate attempts to reduce costs, ultimately resulting in disruption in the industry structure and turning all products / services into consumer goods for daily needs. This is why it takes more resources to be used in activities related to branding, in order to develop significant points of differentiation. The need to develop a sustainable competitive advantage based on non-price competition is already recognized. The problem is that the efforts dedicated to building and managing the brand equity, opposed to price promotions, have little tangible impact on sales in the short term. Third, managers are captured by the need to fully exploit the resources in order to maximize business performance. Despite all efforts, all this looks quite fragmented. Some employees are responsible for one thing, another for other, managers are 'stuck' in their functions, investors in financial results and it looks like no one can see the wood from the trees. The idea of applying radical transparency to reinforce the brand equity is a way of uniting all activities in and around the company.

The brand equity is a set of assets and liabilities associated with the brand, its name and symbol that contribute to the value of a product / service of a company and its customers (Keller, 2007). For an asset or liability to be part of the base of the brand equity, it must be associated with the name or symbol of the brand. If the name or symbol of the brand is changed, some or even all assets and liabilities may be affected or lost and eventually transferred to a new name or symbol. The assets and liabilities on which the brand equity is based vary from context to context. However, generally, they can be grouped into the following five categories (Aaker, 1991):

- Brand loyalty.
- Brand awareness.
- Perceived quality.
- Brand associations.
- Other proprietary assets - patents, trademarks, distribution channels, etc.

The five categories of resources are the basis of the brand equity. The brand equity requires permanent investment and disappears over time if not properly maintained, Figure 1.

- **Brand Loyalty:** For any business, it is relatively more expensive to get new customers and cheaper to retain the existing, especially if the existing customers are satisfied with and even love the

Figure 1. The brand equity model

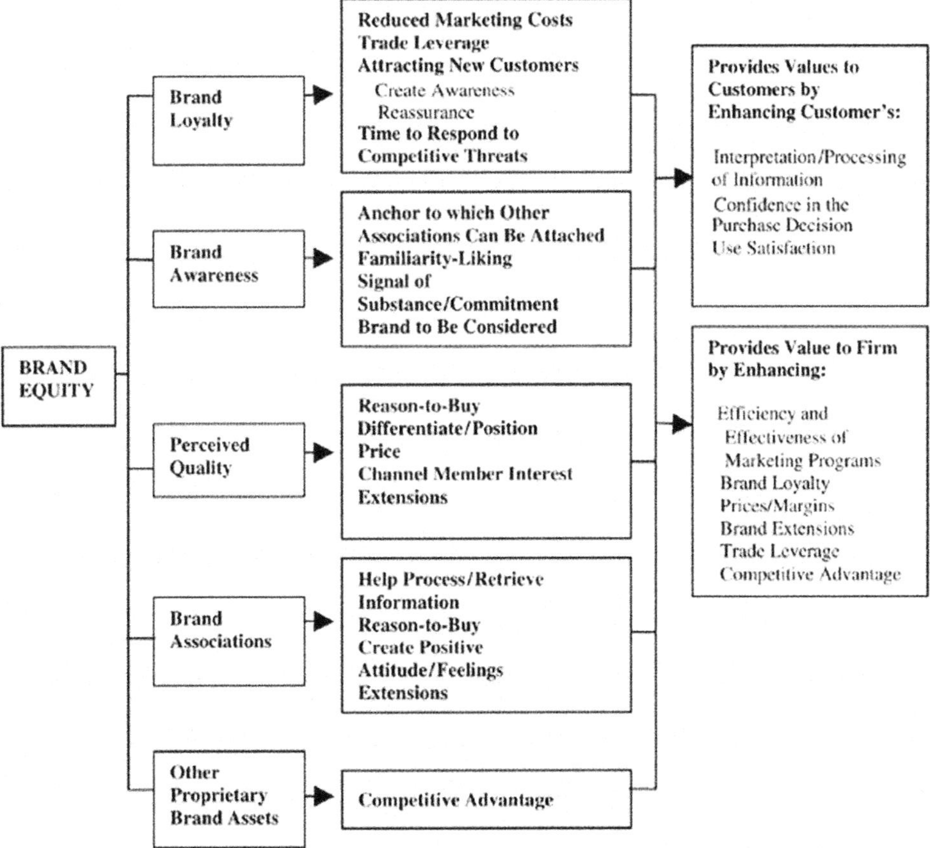

brand. In fact, in many markets customers have certain inertia, even if there are low switching costs and low customer commitment to existing brands. Thus, the installed base of customers is an investment from the past. Furthermore, at least some of the existing customers provide brand exposure and brand confirmation for the potential customers. Customer loyalty reduces the vulnerability to competitors' actions. Competitors may be discouraged from spending additional resources to attract satisfied customers. Also, higher loyalty means higher trade leverage because the consumers expect that the product / service will always be available (Aaker, 1991). The usage of radical transparency practices in the process of building and strengthening the brand loyalty as one of the key assets of brand equity will increase the customers switching costs and retention ratio; easily attract new customers; lower the company's marketing costs and provide the company with additional time to react to competitors moves. Ultimately, these advantages would secure the customers trust in the brand, i.e. the company and the last is a direct driver of stable revenues and sustainable long term profitability.

- **Brand Awareness:** People often buy a familiar brand because they feel comfortable and secure. In addition to this claim goes the assumption that the brand, which is known, is reliable and offers reasonable quality. So, the recognizable brand will always be preferred over the unknown. The awareness as a factor is particularly significant in the sense that the brand must first enter the consideration zone (to be taken into account) – it should be one of the brands that are assessed. Providing the customers (and other relevant stakeholders) with detailed information for what happens 'behind the scene' is the first step in the path towards transforming the company into a 'brand company' that would radiate openness and security. These attributes can be the basis for additional differentiation of the company which would support the sustainable competitive advantage at the long run.
- **Perceived Quality:** In order to connect the brand with the perception of quality in general, the company should necessarily provide information, knowledge and understanding of the detailed specifications for each relevant stakeholder. The perception of quality gets different forms in different industries. The perceived quality means one thing for Hewlett Packard or IBM and another for Procter&Gamble or Henkel. However, it will always be a measurable, significant feature of the brand and the more customers are informed over the brands features, the higher the perceived quality would be. The perceived quality directly affects the purchase decision and the brand loyalty, especially when the customer is not able or motivated to do a detailed analysis of the brand. But, if all the necessary information for the brand is available to her/him, then the thought of having the opportunity to be well informed strongly influences the strengthening of perceived quality and brand equity as a whole. The high perceived quality allows premium price, which in turn creates a larger margin that can be reinvested in the brand equity. Furthermore, the perceived quality may be the basis for brand expansion, but, once again, the likelihood of its success would be greater while using the radical transparency practices.
- **Brand Associations:** The potentiate brand value is often based on a specific set of associations connected to the brand. An association as 'a great birthday party' can create a positive attitude or feeling towards the brand McDonalds. An association for 'the context of use', as the link between aspirin and prevention of heart attack can be a reason for buying the product / service and affect the purchase decision. So, the company ought to demonstrate readiness to be here for the customers for every additional explanation they need. The lifestyle of customers or a personal association can change the experience of the product/service usage. For example, associations related to

driving a BMW car generates an experience of driving a 'different' car. This is directly connected with the information the company provides for its customers and other relevant stakeholders. Companies' transparency can influence the creation of such unique association that it could never be copied from any other competitor. This is a direct driver of brand equity and long lasting competitive advantage. The strong association can also be the basis for brand expansion. If the brand is well positioned in relation to a key attribute of the product/service (for example, technological superiority) which is very familiar to the customers, the competitors can hardly attack the brands position. If they attempt a frontal assault, claiming superiority in this dimension, they will have a problem with credibility. For example, it is difficult for any department store to gain credibility for the statement that it is stronger than Nordstrom in additional services. Competitors are forced to find another, perhaps inferior basis for competition. Thus, associations can be a barrier for competitors particularly when radical transparency practices are used to communicate with the customers.

- **Other Proprietary Assets:** This category includes other proprietary brand assets such as patents, trademarks and relationships in distribution channels. The resources of the company are the most valuable when they limit or prevent competitive erosion of the customer base and their loyalty. These assets take several forms. A trademark can protect the brand equity from competitors who want to confuse customers by using a similar name, symbol or package. The patent, if sufficiently strong and relevant to customer's choice can prevent direct competition. The distribution channels can be controlled by the brand, because of the historical performance of the brand. The usage of radical transparency practices while managing the other proprietary assets will secure each category of the brand equity, the connections among them and the brand equity as a whole.

The concept of creating brand equity through radical transparency, in parallel creates value for the company and for the customers.

- **Providing Value for Customers:** The brand equity assets, basically, add or subtract value for customers. They may assist in processing, interpreting and storing large amounts of information about products / services and brands. They also affect the level of confidence when making the purchase decision (thanks to past experience or knowledge of the brand and its characteristics). This is the reason why radical transparency can strengthen the brand equity base. Potentially, the fact that perceived quality and brand associations can enhance customer satisfaction through the experience of use is equally important. When the customer knows that the product is from 3M, it can affect the experience of its usage: the user may feel safer and satisfying.
- **Providing Value to the Company:** The other role of the brand equity, when managed with radical transparency, is its potential to provide added value for the company by generating marginal cash flows in several ways:
    - First, it can reinforce programs for attracting new and retaining old customers. For example, the launch of a new flavor or a new use of a product will be more effective if the consumer is not skeptical about the quality of the product or service.
    - Second, the other categories of brand equity reinforce the loyalty to the brand. The perceived quality and associations can support the reasons for purchase decision and can affect the level of satisfaction. Even if the brand is not the market leader, when perceived quality and unique associations are formed with the usage of radical transparency, they certainly

reduce the consumers' motives to try products / services from other competing brands. The increased loyalty to the brand is particularly important for 'buying time' for an answer when competitors have innovation and product improvement. It can be freely noted that the brand loyalty, as one of the brand equity assets, affects and is being affected by the brand equity at the same time. The potential impact of the other assets of brand equity on loyalty, when managed transparently, is so important that this intercourse is explicitly listed as one of the ways in which the brand equity provides value for the company. Furthermore, there are similar relationships between the other dimensions of brand equity. For example, the perceived quality can be affected by the awareness, associations and/or loyalty. Only one transparent activity from the company (sometimes just one statement) could change the links and interrelations among the brand equity assets. Therefore, under certain conditions, it is important to treat the brand equity dimensions not only as inputs, but also as outputs of the process of building and managing the brand equity.

- Third, the usage of radical transparency for driving brand equity enables realization of higher margins through premium prices and reduced frequency of price promotions. In many situations the brand equity assets, when properly combined, stimulate a premium price policy. On the contrary, a brand with dysfunctional or incomplete brand equity will have to invest more in promotional activities, just to maintain its position.
- Fourth, the transparently managed brand equity can provide a platform for growth through brand extensions. For example, Unilever expands its brand to several products claiming openness and sustainability, creating successful business areas in which it would be much more expensive to get into without such a move.
- Fifth, the brand equity provides leverage in the distribution channel. As consumers, retailers also feel more confident in trading with proven brand that has already achieved recognition and positive associations. The transparent brand has an advantage in winning the shelves and can easily cooperate in the implementation of the business plan.
- Finally, the achievement of a unique combination of the brand equity assets with radical transparency provides a sustainable competitive advantage for the company which can be a serious barrier for competitors. Only one association, for example, Ariel – the family washing powder for 'heavy impurities', can set a condition for success in a given market segment. It may be difficult for another brand to compete with Ariel in the mentioned segment. The strong position of well perceived quality is a competitive advantage that is not easy to 'shoot down' – it is really difficult to convince customers that another brand has achieved superior quality. Achieving parity in brand awareness is extremely expensive for a brand with a lack of awareness.

CONCLUSION

The tangible worth of intangible assets, the war for top-grade talent, the impressive power of inspired employees, the transparent supply chains, the global impact of NGOs, the informed global consumer – all these transformational forces reshape the business landscape. The insurgent companies that seize on these drives will create real value and increase their long term profitability.

The concept of radical transparency lays in the basics of a vision of a better business, one that operates in greater harmony with its environment and offers a more exciting and meaningful place to work. The vision blends principles and practices—like understanding the challenges that come with creating a sense of purpose and what it takes to integrate that mission into an enterprise's day-to-day work. The key is to keep building capability along dimensions, increasing genuine commitment and the skills to deliver on that commitment.

Every company must seek the formula that works best for its particular culture and industry. There is no one right way to transform a conventional company into a value driven company. But all the authentically responsible companies subscribe to a set of principles about: the mission, vision, transparency, working, responsibility, openness, authenticity and innovation – all this put in an agenda for value driven companies which are prepared for the challenges we all face. Responsible companies believe that what they stand for – their purpose and values are far more important than the products they make or services they sell. For them, advocacy is a synonymous with strategy – the industry needs a reform and they aim to fix it. When companies stand for something big, something that truly matters to people, they sharply differentiate themselves from their competitors.

The concept of radical transparency can be a powerful tool to transform ordinary businesses into more responsible, conscious and profitable entities. Radical transparency is required for a business to succeed in today's environment of stakeholders' scrutiny. Information technologies let everyone to see everything anyone does. Even though, at first sight, it might look like that sharing information for all the company's activities puts the company to open critics, but at the end, the company would have more friends than prosecutors. The radical transparency practices create long-lasting partnerships with all relevant stakeholders and in this way it becomes the first step towards overcoming the weaknesses and threats and securing the strengths and opportunities of the company, which, ultimately, leads to achieving a sustainable competitive advantage and long-term profitability.

The forms of radical transparency are various and spring from each activity the company performs. For example, a business can willingly disclose all of its product ingredients, or it may disclose all the sources and operations in the supply chain. The knowledge of the product / service creates loyal customers. Knowing that a company is willing to share detailed information allows the customer to trust the company. A trustworthy management team will personally communicate the message with both, employees and customers, regardless of the content of the message, whether it is about the successes or failures of the company. If there is trust in the brand, then there is loyalty. And where is loyalty there are sustainable revenues and long term profitability. Nurturing a positive relationship with customers is good for the company's profitability and it creates a unique connection that can be the basis for a competitive advantage that competitors could not overcome. Or even more, if one company can do it, then others will try to, at least, copy it, which would create a chain reaction of companies engaging in similar business practices. Ultimately, this will utter the competitive conditions to an upper scale and provide several benefits for the entire community. Transparent companies may voluntarily provide the public with sustainability reports, including all aspects of corporate responsibility towards the: customers, employees, investors, suppliers, competitors, public groups and the society as a whole.

A company that benefits society as well as shareholders require leaders who neverstop reflecting on who they are and who they want to be; who can blend their own personal vision with those who see the world differently; who tell the truth about obstacles and recognize their own personal responsibility in creating them; and who know there are no final answers or formulas. Building a responsible company takes, literally, forever.

In the future, companies will fight a battle for brand dominance. Investors will recognize the brand as the most important asset of companies. This is a critical concept. This is a vision of how to develop, manage, strengthen and defend the business. It will be more important to own markets than to own resources. And the only way to own the market is to have a dominant brand. The concept of radical transparency in business gives the companies the opportunity to win the battle for success differently from the competitors, which would ensure the company with sustainable growth and profitability, arousing from the well-shaped relationships with the stakeholders who provide value for the company. The company's brand would be a synonym for those connections.

There are several factors that contribute to the increased interest in brand equity and generally in branding. First, the companies are willing to pay more for their brand development because the development of new, alternative (competing) brands is almost impossible or too expensive. Second, companies are feeling significant pressure from the continued emphasis on price reduction by exaggerated promotions or desperate attempts to reduce costs, ultimately resulting in disruption in the industry structure and turning all products / services into consumer goods for daily needs. This is why it takes more resources to be used in activities related to branding, in order to develop significant points of differentiation. The need to develop a sustainable competitive advantage based on non-price competition is already recognized. The problem is that the efforts dedicated to building and managing the brand equity, opposed to price promotions, have little tangible impact on sales in the short term. Third, managers are captured by the need to fully exploit the resources in order to maximize business performance. Despite all efforts, all this looks quite fragmented. Some employees are responsible for one thing, another for other, managers are 'stuck' in their functions, investors in financial results and it looks like no one can see the wood from the trees. The idea of applying radical transparency to reinforce the brand equity is a way of uniting all activities in and around the company.

For an asset or liability to be part of the base of the brand equity, it must be associated with the name or symbol of the brand. The assets and liabilities on which the brand equity is based vary from context to context. Generally, they can be grouped into the following five categories:

- Brand loyalty.
- Brand awareness.
- Perceived quality.
- Brand associations.
- Other proprietary assets - patents, trademarks, distribution channels, etc.

The concept of creating brand equity through radical transparency, in parallel creates value for the company and for the customers.

REFERENCES

Aaker, D. (1991). *Managing Brand Equity*. The Free Press.

Drucker, P. (2001). *Management Challenges for the 21st Century*. Harper Collins Publishers Inc.

Gates, B. (2008). *World Economic Forum, Switzerland*. Retrieved from http://www.gatesfoundation.org/media-center/speeches/2008/01/bill-gates-2008-world-economic-forum

Gustin, S. (2013, May 1). TIME Tech 40: The Most Influential Minds in Tech. *Time*. Retrieved from http://business.time.com/2013/05/01/time-tech-40-the-ten-most-influential-tech-ceos/slide/larry-page-google/?iid=sr-link5

Hollender, J., & Breen, B. (2010). *The Responsibility Revolution: How the Next Generation of Businesses Will Win*. John Wiley and Sons Inc.

Keller, K. (2007). *Strategic Brand Management*. Pearson Education.

McKinsey. (2007). *Insights and innovations for social impact*. Author.

Pontefract, D. (2016, May 9). Should Companies Serve Only Their Shareholders Or Their Stakeholders More Broadly? *Forbes Magazine*. Retrieved from https://www.forbes.com/sites/danpontefract/2016/05/09/shareholders-or-stakeholders/#3972accd13d2

Schultz, H. (1999). *Pour Your Heart Into It: How Starbucks Built a Company One Cup at a Time*. Hyperion.

Social Investment Forum (SIF). (2010). *US SIF and US SIF Foundation Annual Sustainability and Financial Report*. Author.

Social Investment Forum (SIF). (2016). *The Impact of Sustainable and Responsible Investment*. Author.

The Economist. (2005, January 20). The good company. *The Economist.* Retrieved from http://www.economist.com/node/3555212

The Guardian. (2017, January 16). World's eight richest people have same wealth as poorest 50%. *The Guardian*. Retrieved from https://www.theguardian.com/global-development/2017/jan/16/worlds-eight-richest-people-have-same-wealth-as-poorest-50

Thorson, E., & Duffy, M. (2012). *Advertising Age: The Principles of Advertising and Marketing Communication at Work*. South-Western Cengage Learning.

Transparency International. (2009). *Transparency International's Corruption Perceptions*. Author.

Chapter 2
Driving Brand Equity With Radical Transparency

ABSTRACT

The main purpose of this chapter is to analyze the categories of brand equity assets through the prism of radical transparency. The results reveal that the brand equity requires investment and disappears over time if not maintained consistently with the selected business model and the company's values. The chapter is dedicated to systemize the theoretical and practical findings over the brand equity elements. Brand loyalty is the first element of the brand equity model. The benefits for the company which uses the radical transparency practices can be simply synthesized into one big advantage - satisfied and loyal customers who generate stable revenues and profits for the company in the long term. Radical transparency has a major impact on stimulating brand awareness as a factor that is particularly important in the sense that the brand must first enter into the considerations set. The company should be ready and open for cooperation with all interested parties and provide positive feedback whenever necessary. This enhances the perceived quality of the brand and the trust. The application of the radical transparency concept in the overall operation of the company enables the creation of a special set of brand associations that create long-lasting relationships with consumers, mixed with positive emotional mix that seals the success in the long term.

INTRODUCTION

When the need for building sustainable brand equity is more than obvious, then it is inevitably to raise the question of the efficiency and effectiveness of that process. The pragmatism starts through the establishment of the brand equity. This chapter focuses on the analysis of generating brand awareness through radical transparency practices; additional advancing of the level of perceived quality of products / services of the company by means of radical transparency and the analysis of a completely new idea for building and strengthening the brand associations as one of the most specific brand equity assets through radical transparency practices; as well as strengthening the customer loyalty to the brand, while using these practices. Besides the elaboration of the concept of creating brand equity through appropriate

DOI: 10.4018/978-1-5225-2417-5.ch002

application of radical transparency in reinforcing the specific elements of the brand equity, this chapter, quite logically, includes the strategic analysis of the factors affecting the brand equity through the prism of radical transparency.

GENERATING AWARENESS OF THE BRAND

The brand awareness represents the ability of potential customers to recognize and remember the brand present in a particular market or industry. It involves creating a link between the brand and the category of the product or the company. The use of a balloon that marked the name Levi's can make the name prominent, but this does not unconditionally support the awareness of the brand. However, if the balloon is made in the form of jeans, it ensures the connection with the activities of the company and strengthens the effectiveness of this measure to create and enhance the brand awareness of the brand Levi's. The brand awareness includes a continuum within the range form the uncertain feeling that the brand is recognizable until the belief that it is the only one in the particular industry. As shown in Figure 1 this continuum consists of three different levels of brand awareness.

The importance of brand awareness for brand equity depends on both the context and the level of brand awareness. The lowest level, the brand recognition, is usually determined with the usage of a 'recall test'. The respondents are offered a set of brands from a certain category of products or industry and asked to identify those they have heard of. The radical transparency practices directly support the most critical level of brand awareness – the brand recognition. If the company shares all important information with its customers, than the customers will easily remember the brand even from the first contact, or, at least can recognize it among others. At this level, although there should be a link between the brand and the category of the product or the industry, it is still not strong enough. The brand recognition is a minimum level of brand awareness. At this level, it is particularly important that the customer decides to buy the product / service from the particular brand. When the company is responsible and transparent in every activity it performs than this level is quickly exceeded because most of the customers can easily recall the brand that is open for collaboration and is different from the other competitive brands.

Figure 1. The brand awareness pyramid

The next level is the *brand recall* level. The brand recall level can be determined when consumers are asked to list the brands of a particular category of products or services. This is considered to be an 'unsupported recall' - without the help of listed alternatives, as is the case with the first level of awareness. The unsupported recall is significantly more important than the recognition, because it provides a better position for the brand. Individuals with support can think of many more things than without support. As it was mentioned above, using radical transparency when communicating with consumers and with other relevant stakeholders is the way to easily climb the steps of the brand awareness pyramid. The access to information about the company and the brand generates confidence among customers, and that sense of security directly affects the level of memory, i.e. the interest the customers have for the brand. Moreover, many customers are often aware of the brands they do not like. Just one bad experience with the brand, whether in the form of bad quality, poor service, lack of transparency for the production process, disregard for the environment or society, can affect the level of awareness of the brand, but in an extremely negative way, for example, its avoidance. This is an important opportunity for the newly emerging brands that may face low level of awareness of the brand - exactly the absence of negative experiences with the brand as the old conventional brands have is a significant advantage that needs to be quickly used through sharing all necessary information with customers and empowering employees to do so, which will lead to increased levels of brand awareness. It is interesting that these first positive experiences can create an unforgettable specific set of associations for the brand in the consumers' minds and particularly the mingling of the elements of the brand equity is a key source of sustainable competitive advantage and long-term profitability for the company. Therefore, enabling customers to gain a positive experience with the brand even form the first contact allows the company to strengthen this element of the brand equity to the highest level. The firstly stated brand with unsupported brand recall has reached the so-called 'first in mind' awareness, i.e. a special brand position. In the true sense of the word, this brand is ahead of everyone else in the mind of a potential customer.

An even stronger position, which is not shown in Figure 1, is the one of a dominant brand – the most of the respondents can recall only one brand. Let's take for example the American renowned brands: Arm & Hammer, the baking powder (which has a market share of 85% in the US market and enjoys a level of 95% brand recognition), Band-Aid, the company for medical bandages, Jell-O for gelatin, Crayola - chalks, Lionel - trains, Philadelphia - melted cheese and so on. In any case, the Americans can hardly recall any another brand in each of the categories. But, the potential new brands in some of these industries should not be afraid of failure. The idea of full transparency in every activity is so affordable for the stringent consumers that it can provide a position for the brand that no other brand in the industry has ever achieved. Possessing a dominant brand is one of the strongest competitive advantages. This means that when customers make the purchase decision, they do not take into account any other brand. The application of the concept of radical transparency in generating brand awareness is the first critical step in strengthening the brand equity as a source of value for the business.

How the application of the concept of radical transparency in generating brand awareness helps the brand? The use of radical transparency in driving brand awareness as a brand equity asset revives the four ways that Aaker (1991) considers to be important in generating value for the business.

The radical transparency causes brand awareness to turn into an anchor to which other brand associations are attached. The brand recognition is the first step in brand communications. It is usually futile to try to communicate the attributes of the product / service until a name that will be connected to those attributes is not established. The name is a separate folder in the mind of customers which can be filled with facts and feelings associated with it. Without a specific 'place of storage' in the memory, facts and feelings are lost and cannot return when they are needed. One metaphor can be used about the importance of brand awareness as an anchor associated with the brand McDonald's. Think of the brand as a ship on open seas. Associations (smaller boats), such as: the golden arches, Ronald McDonald, children, entertainment and Big Mac are connected to McDonald's through chains (links to memory). The chains may be thicker and stronger or thinner and weaker. Also, the structure can be enhanced with links between the associations. But, this brand can also be connected with associations as: unhealthy food, errors in the supply chain, dissatisfied employees etc. Such associations are intertwined with the previous and create a mix that is variously accepted by different customers. For someone, the positive moment may prevail, but for others - the negative. However, it is too risky for a brand, especially with a presence on the global market, to allow interlocking of series of positive and negative associations related to the brand awareness. The largest and oldest brands have built strong brand equity, which may possibly withstand certain shocks and provide time for the company's adequate response to the requirements and behavior of customers, but the reactive behavior towards the environment is a way of functioning that does not lead to radical successes. In the future, this approach, in general, will not be able to generate success. The prevention of negative associations connected with the brand awareness can be critical for the success of the lesser-known brands. Therefore, the application of radical transparency in the daily operations of the company, without extra efforts to build the brand equity, will cause extremely rare brand associations to be associated with the brand awareness in a way that they cannot be replicated by any other competitor. This is the basis for long-term success of the company.

Every company is particularly concerned about gaining familiarity of its brand. Virtually every model that tries to predict the success of a new product / company has the brand recognition as the initial element. A purchase without recognition can occur only by accident. Furthermore, the introduction to the features and benefits of the product / service is difficult without the achievement of brand recognition. With an established level of recognition, the task turns down to a simple attachment of a new association as a feature of the product or the company. Therefore, radical transparency is particularly important at this point of building and managing the brand equity. It enables a faster and easier overcome of the level of brand recognition and stimulates an efficient rise up the pyramid of brand awareness through the addition of positive associations.

Radical transparency provides familiarity and connection with the brand. Recognition provides, in a sense, brand familiarity, and people just want familiar things. The radical transparency implies companies' openness towards all relevant stakeholders, an approach that provides a sense of proximity and connection with the company. Especially in sectors with products for final consumption that require little involvement, familiarity is crucial for the purchase decision. In the absence of motivation for evaluation of the attributes of the product / service, the brand familiarity is more than enough. This is the reason why the company has to provide the necessary information for customers when they need it in order to gain confidence and achieve a connection and a sense of familiarity and proximity. Once this point is reached, consumers rarely or less evaluate the brand. However, consistency and transparency in the company's activities and cooperation with the environment should always be on the list of company's prerogatives. Otherwise, the acquired familiarity and connection to the brand can break down like a house of cards. Numerous studies have shown a positive relationship between the number of exposures and the connection with the brand when as incentives are used: images, names, music, almost everything... When the company uses the radical transparency practices to increase the brand exposure the consumers' connection with the brand may be more intense and long lasting. Interestingly, studies show that the repeated exposure of the brand can affect the connection even when the level of recognition is intact. The explanation is that the effect of recognition (or familiarity) can exist below the measure of recognition.

Radical transparency enables connection and commitment to the brand. The brand awareness signals the presence, commitment and connection with the brand – attributes which are very important for both industrial buyers and the consumers. The logic is that if the name is known there must be a reason for that, such as: the company works well, it is a long time in this business, it is widely spread; it is successful, the products / services are with good quality, the company takes care of customers, it acts responsibly in the environment and is open for cooperation, it is not afraid of criticism, it is ready to adopt changes and so on. These assumptions are not necessarily related to knowing specific facts about the brand. Even if someone has not been exposed to advertising connected to the brand and knows very little about the company, the brand awareness can still lead to an assumption that the company is successful and supports the brand. Sometimes, even in case of major purchase decisions that require considerable customer involvement, the brand awareness and the brand perceptions for connection can make a significant difference. If there is no clear winner after an extensive analysis, for example, which computer to be bought or which consulting company to be engaged, then the power of the brand awareness has a pioneering role. It is therefore very important to leave a good impression at the first contact with the potential customers, because such good first impression affects the customers' assumptions for the brand. Do not forget the good old rule that the first impression is the most important. Furthermore, if the customers' assumptions for the brand turn into a positive experience then the brand awareness will remain sealed forever. Moreover, the level of recognition can move up from the recall level to the so-called "first in mind" brand. The application of radical transparency in the brand equity management, despite the impact on the other assets of the brand equity, has an undeniable importance in providing connection and commitment to the brand. This is a necessary condition for advancing the other dimensions of the brand equity. Without strengthening the awareness of the brand other efforts would have no positive effect.

Radical transparency affects the consideration set. The first step in the purchase process is selecting a group of brands that will be considered – the consideration set. When choosing a consulting house, a car or a computer in principle, three to four alternatives are being analyzed. The buyer, usually, is not exposed to many brands during the purchase process. Thus, the brand recall may be critical for the brand to enter to the consideration set. For example, who produces computers? The first companies that will come up the mind would have an advantage. The company which lacks a brand recall is likely to miss the opportunity to get into this set. The role of the brand recall is also crucial for the frequently purchased products for final consumption. In some industries, however, there are so many alternatives that overwhelm the consumer (e.g. cereal flakes). In this case, it is not only important to have a brand the consumer has thought of, it may take to be the first in mind brand so the sale would be realized. If the company operates on the principles of transparency and openness for cooperation and sharing information then it would be much easier to achieve the desired level of awareness and the brand will always enter the consideration set. For example, if the company sells cereals and transparently and clearly explains the production process, the ingredients, the activities of the supply chain, the responsibility towards the community, etc., then consumers would quickly and easily decide to buy that product, rather than one for which the information is simply missing. The once gained trust in the brand, especially if the consistency in this principle of transparent operations is maintained, allows the brand to be always included in the consideration set and even be the first brand in mind, which ensures the future revenues and provides long-term profitability for the company.

Basically, if the brand is not at least at the recall level, it will not be included in the consideration set. But people also remember the brands they do not like. Studies have proved the link between the first in mind awareness level and the attitudes / behavior of customers during the purchase process. One such study of six brands in three categories (fast food, soft drinks and banking services) showed differences in preferences and the willingness to buy, depending on whether the brand is ranked on the first, second or third place on the list for unsupported recall (Wilson &Gilligan, 2005). Therefore, it is necessary to properly exploit the opportunities offered by the concept of radical transparency. The benefits of its application will take the form of positive experiences among customers that would strengthen the level of awareness and interweave with the other elements of brand equity in a way that cannot be imitated by competitors. This is the ultimate goal and value for the business.

The strength of the brand according to Landor. Landor Associates has developed a measure of the brand strength which is determined based on a survey of 1,000 US brands (Ryan, 2008). Two dimensions are being measured. The first, called the share-of-mind score is a measure for the brand recognition. The other, named esteem is a measure of the positive opinion that people have for the companies and brands they know. The results are used to calculate an average to determine the total measure of the strength of the brand - the Image Power. The results of the Landor study prove the high correlation between the brand awareness and the brand esteem. Of course, the correlation is due to the fact that people are aware about the brands they love; however, it reflects the fact that well-known brands are commonly appreciated. Of course, there are exceptions: Playboy and Warner Bros have a high rate of recognition, but not so high level of esteem. Others, such as Rolls-Royce, Hilton, Harley-Davidson and Rolex are in the opposite situation - they face the intriguing opportunity to capitalize from the brand esteem by building brand awareness. Using the same technique in Japan and Europe, Landor emphasizes its potential to identify the relative success of the companies while establishing the brands. Indeed, by integrating data from all three studies, Coca-Cola is one of the most famous brands followed by IBM, Sony, Porsche and McDonald's (Wong et al, 2006). But the brands that are on this list still face the challenge of implementing radical transparency in their activities. Despite the high result of the brand awareness and the high positive correlation with the esteem, there are customers who are not satisfied from the experience with these brands. For example, Coca-Cola is still hiding the secret ingredients and method of preparation for one of the most famous drinks around the world. This, in turn, opens a series of unanswered questions about whether the drink is harmful for the consumers' health or not? Or, Porsche's unwillingness to answer the request from the daughter of the Hollywood star Paul Walker for the cause of his death in a car accident while driving the car from this brand. Now the company is facing a lawsuit from his daughter. Even if it is proved that there was nothing wrong with the car, the missing transparency and unwillingness to cooperate with a customer expands worldwide as the influenza infection. It does not matter whether the customer is right or not, the company that practices the principle of transparency in every activity will address the "spiked views" in order to prevent them. This is the essence of the concept of radical transparency. When stakeholders are well informed about the company's operations, they are friends of the company, so the company does not have to invest additional efforts to manage relations with specific groups or stakeholders, since they are all equally treated, but it can focus on other important issues about everyday operation. This creates the magical circle of trust in the brand.

The strength of old brands. Of course time as a factor adversely affects the acquired level of brand recognition, especially when it comes to first in mind brand awareness. However, there is a noticeable phenomenon - when the brand becomes really well recognizable with a high level of brand awareness among potential customers, the recognition remains at this level a long period of time, even if the advertising support is missing. One of many is a study on the brand awareness among manufacturers of blenders conducted in the 1990s. When the respondents were asked to remember all the possible brands of blenders, their responses have resulted in a second place for General Electric and this company does not produce blenders for more than 20 years. In 2009 a study for the brands recognition among households in US was conducted. Several thousand housewives have been asked to name as many different brands as they can remember and have been motivated for that with an incentive for each name they would mention (Bogart and Lehman, 2009). On average, 28 different brands have been mentioned and 15% of respondents counted more than 40 brands. Half of the named brands were the brands of companies that produce food. The age of the mentioned brands is very significant, as shown in Table 1, more than 85% of the brands are older than 25 years and 36% are older than 75 years. Can this discourage the new brands? Of course not. The analysis of the durability of the brand awareness in the mind of consumers can only be beneficial for new brands. Yes, it is true that the old brands have already built a level of brand awareness which fluctuates in the range from brand recognition to the first in mind brand, providing time for maneuver, but, as previously mentioned, consumers are aware of the brands they do not like.

What is particularly important is the brand awareness to be associated with positive associations and this will influence the purchase decision. If the company achieves to make this connection then the success is guaranteed. The application of radical transparency in building brand equity is a way that increases the likelihood of connecting the brand awareness with the brand associations and this relationship is crucial to maintain and increase the revenues in the long term. Another older but remarkable study by Boston Consulting Group made a comparison of the leading brands in 1925 with those in 1995, in 22 different industries. In 19 industries the market leader was the same. In the other three, the leader still had a good market position (Wurster, 1995).

The strength of old brands is incredible. This is partly based on the high levels of recognition, which in turn are based on thousands of brand exposures over the years. Which are the implications? First, the establishment of a strong brand which is supported by a high level of recognition creates an asset with tremendous value. Furthermore, the asset is strengthened over the years, as the brand exposure and the positive customer experience increase. This is a critical moment. As a result, it is difficult to fight for a position in the customer's mind, especially for a new brand, regardless of the size of the marketing budgets and the superiority of the product / service.

There is a widespread belief that with enough advertising and a good product the new brand can win, even in mature, saturated markets. This is easier to be said than done. In particular, with the expansion of the social corporate responsibility and the creation of a climate for radical transparency acceptance by a growing number of world famous brands, the ability to fight a "smart Goliath" is shrinking. In

Table 1. The age of the famous brands

Brand Age	% From 4.923 Brands
over 100 years	10
75 to 99 years	26
50 to 74 years	28
25 to 49 years	4
15 to 24 years	4
under 14 years	3

some mature industries to be the leading brand means to have been born so. The actual application of the concept of care for the stakeholders and the society and environment in general assures that position. This is not a hypocritical axiom. Instead, suggestions move towards the direction that if you want to challenge a known and recognized brand, especially in an old industry, the most suitable way is to do that is to take over and revitalize an existing brand, rather than entering the market with a new name. If the choice is, however, to enter with a new brand, then the likelihood of success is greater within the companies from similar industries.

How to Achieve Brand Awareness

Achieving awareness, either recognition or recall, implies two tasks: achieving brand identity and its connection to the category of product / service or industry. For a new brand - both are needed. Otherwise, in another context, the one is already accomplished, what makes the task different. How to achieve, sustain and improve brand awareness by applying the practices of radical transparency? The best approach depends on the situation, but there are some useful guidelines that arise from combining formal studies of numerous companies which have successfully passed the creation and maintenance of brand awareness level of their brands (Aaker, 1991) and the new ideas for implementing transparency while managing the brand equity.

- **Different and Memorable:** The message for awareness should provide a reason for observation and should be easy to remember. There are several tactics, but the simplest is to be different and unusual. Many companies have a similar approach in the brand communications and it is difficult to separate one from the others. For example, many advertising messages for perfumes, cars, drinks and so on, have similarity which inhibits the task of the message to achieve recognition. Almost all advertisements for perfumes point out that you would feel very special if you use the perfume and, usually, a celebrity assures you for that. But if, unlike the others, you explain how you produce the perfume, it will be a different approach from the competitors. Of course, there should be a connection between the company, product / service and the brand in order to achieve the goal. For example, if you put a car on top of the mountain everyone will notice, but most would not know which car, if you do not mention. So, the idea of applying radical transparency in the communications with consumers is revolutionary. You tell everything about you, what you are doing and why you do it. If others do not do it, then you are unique. Everyone will notice it. This will provide a competitive advantage for the first mover. If competitors start to imitate your strategy, which, in the worst case, can lead to a competitive parity, which is very rare, because the relationships that are created between the elements of brand equity are so special and they almost cannot be imitated. If we add the acquired trust from customers and other relevant stakeholders from the environment than the sustainability of the competitive advantage is guaranteed. All the company has to do is be really accountable and transparent.
- **Included Slogan or Jingle:** The slogan and jingle can significantly contribute to the recall. They are a kind of recognition stimulus. The brand associations are reinforced through them and the combination of the brand equity assets results in higher impact on brand awareness. Yet, again, the creation and prominence of the slogan or jingle indistinguishable from the other will not cause a significant change in the level of brand awareness. Consumers are overwhelmed with promises of quality, offers of pleasure and enjoyment, the best they need and many of them are ignorant to

such messages. A slogan or jingle which reminds that the company exists to create value for the customers and contributes to a better world in the true sense of the word is one that will be remembered, because customers will check the credibility and if the test is passed, the brand awareness will not only be increased among wider range of customers - it will climb up a higher level.

- **Exposed Symbol**: The development of a specific symbol which marks the brand, such as the castle of Walt Disney, the apple of Apple or the circles of Audi, could play a key role in the process of creating and maintaining brand awareness. The symbol is a visual image that is much easier to be remembered and recognized, rather than a word or a phrase. Moreover, there are many creative ways of exposing the symbol different from the classic ads and relatively cheaper. For the success of this tactic, it is particularly important to practice the previously described methods for generating brand awareness transparently and responsibly. The frequent use of the symbol will play the role of catalyst for the brand value, but it is particularly important that the brand remains engraved in the customers' memory as a brand that cares about stakeholders, society and the environment. Only this way, the tactic can increase the level of brand awareness, and even more, to influence the purchase decision. Investing in the brand symbol exposion in various expensive or cheaper forms will bear no result if the company does not practice the radical transparency in its daily activities. On the contrary, this measure may erode the brand equity if the company does not act transparently and with accountability. In that case, the exposed symbol will only remind customers that it is the company that does not meet their expectations. In fact, the ways to increase brand awareness are mutually intertwined and their common denominator is the usage of radical transparency in the company's activities.
- **Publicity:** Advertising carries the primacy in generating brand awareness, as it allows the message to be 'tailored' according to the crowd - it is an effective way for brand exposure. However, it sometimes lacks credibility, especially if the company is not yet sufficiently transparent and opened for cooperation with the environment. Meanwhile, publicity can, as well, do the job and costs far less. People more often want to hear a new story than to see a new advertisement. Therefore, it is important to ensure that events associated with the brand are having a dimension of novelty. The ideal situation arises in cases where the product is inherently interesting, such as the concept of a new model of a car that does not pollute the environment, a PC performance and new materials that are not harmful to the environment and so on., However, it is not necessary to improve the product and make it a novelty, so the good publicity can function. The shortage may be supplemented by a symbol, event and so on. For example, the Ben & Jerry's 'cow mobile' – a mobile ice cream shop is a hit which runs across the US for years, especially in smaller places (Randall, 2006). The concept of applying radical transparency in generating brand equity is, actually, publicity in every moment of the company's operations - the company carries all relevant information to all relevant stakeholders whenever they need it. Even more interesting is the fact that if the company decides to accept radical transparency as a way of doing business, then the satisfied customers alone will influence the spread of positive publicity for the company. This double effect undoubtedly strengthens the brand equity, not only by increasing the brand awareness, but, more importantly, by combining the elements of brand equity which leads to enhanced competitive advantage and, thus, to sustainable long-term profitability.
- **Sponsoring Events:** The main purpose of sponsoring events is exactly the creation and increase of brand awareness. This tactic combined with the concept of radical transparency can have a strong positive impact on brand awareness, as well as creating a series of positive associations

connected with the brand awareness (previously discussed). This ensures increased brand exposure in front of the spectators, regardless whether on television or in person, before, during or after the event. So, many world famous brands like: Coca-Cola, Pepsi, Rolex, Budweiser and many others, regularly sponsor: tournaments, sports competitions or charity events with the sole purpose of maintaining and increasing the visibility of the brand. But the temporary demonstration of corporate social responsibility does not meet the customers and other relevant group strict requirements. The real improvement of the brand equity takes company's consistent behavior in the daily operations without exceptions. If the company selectively practices the principle of transparency and accountability in the operation, then the sponsorship as a way to raise brand awareness can play its role, but in a completely negative connotation - customers will remember the brand as untrusted, this will break the loyalty, it will cause amplification of negative associations to the brand, and with two demolished key elements of brand equity everything is falling into the water.

- **Brand Extensions:** To ensure a higher level of brand recognition, the usage of the same brand for all products / services of the company is suggested. This is always practiced by the Japanese companies as: Sony, Honda, Toyota, Mazda, Mitsubishi, Yamaha, Canon, Nikon etc., which use the benefits of the various promotional efforts for the brand. For example, the ubiquitous Mitsubishi brand with three diamonds symbol appears on more than 25,000 products, including: cars, financial products and mushrooms (Keller, 2000). Of course, there is always a compromise. Although the brand recall can be increased with the widespread use of one name, the different names of brands (brands for products) offer the possibility of developing different associations for each brand. However, the synergistic effect of the use of a brand can be achieved only if the company is perceived as transparent, responsible and willing to cooperate, otherwise the brand extensions will not result in increased sales in the categories of products that use the same brand. In fact, the basic idea is that the strengthening of the brand equity as a whole is only possible if radical transparency is used in managing all the assets of the brand equity. If the company is not consistent in its activities the expansion of the brand can play a more negative than positive role. But if the company accepts the idea of value rather than profit, then the brand expansion is more than recommended - it will strengthen not only the awareness of the brand, but also the other components of brand equity. Companies that are driven by value and which have accepted the concept of radical transparency in their operations without major difficulties could expand with new products or appear in new markets, because they will never have a problem with credibility and will easily overcome the obstacles arousing from the brand extensions.
- **The Usage of Signs:** Signs are always welcomed in the campaign aimed to increase brand awareness. One of them which is commonly used is packaging, because it is a stimulus that the potential customer directly faces. Famous celebrities are engaged very often. For example, Novak Djokovic as a very successful athlete, but modest, responsible and always willing to help may be engaged in a campaign for sports equipment and clothing and the awareness and credibility in that brand will instantly increase. But if the company does not practice such behavior (positive) as the person who promotes the brand, then the positive effects will quickly disappear and they will be replaced with disappointment and lost customers' trust. Moreover, the cooperation between the public figure with credibility and social responsibility and the company which inadvertently practices the radical transparency may adversely affect the celebrity's reputation. The consumers are aware for the existence of this moral hazard in advance, and therefore gain trust in the brand more easily, relying on the assumption that a famous person would not have done it if it considers that its hardly

gained reputation would be lost in a second. Sometimes the signs are used on the package to remind customers of other previously used propaganda. For example, a picture with the girl from the Nesquick advertisement with the cat that turns into a tiger is being set on the Nesquick packages to remind consumers and to provide a higher level of recognition, as well as to awaken more positive associations. But again, if the company Nestle is ready to share all relevant information about their products with consumers as a key stakeholder of the company (especially products intended for the youngest and dearest), then the positive connection between the brand associations and the brand awareness will disappear, such tactics will not affect and strengthen the brand equity. The challenge is not only in front of this company but also in front of many others. Once the company decides to implement the concept of radical transparency, not only in the management of the brand equity, but in all the activities the company performs (in fact, one cannot be done without the other) it may face difficulties that would cause tectonic shifts in the company, but after changing the business model, the future will be significantly brighter. An interesting analogy – the caterpillar hardly turns into a butterfly, but when it does the sight to the world and from the world towards it is amazing.

- **Recall Requires Repetition:** Developing recall is much harder than developing recognition. The brand must be prevalent and the connection between the brand, the company and the product has to be as strong as possible. Recognition persists, even if it is based on only few brand exposures, while recall disappears over time. Analogous to recognizing people – we remember the face, but we cannot remember the name. The recall is difficult; it requires long-term experience or frequent repetitions. The first on mind awareness, of course, requires even more. For Coca-Cola or Budweiser to have primacy in brand awareness, they invest enormous sums in regular exposure of the brand. To emphasize again, the sustainability of the level of brand awareness is associated with repetition, but repetition should arise from a positive experience with the brand, otherwise the level of brand awareness may be high, but it will be an awareness of a brand that the customers do not like. As long as the company is transparent and responsible for its operations, the risk of causing high negative brand awareness simply does not exist. On the contrary, all the activities aimed to boost brand awareness (previously described) will only affect the brand in a positive direction.
- **Recall Bonus:** Achieving and maintaining high brand awareness through constant brand exposure not only strengthens the awareness of a particular brand, but it inhibits the development of awareness for competing brands. A series of studies confirmed that when consumers are offered several alternatives and asked to add a few more brands from the particular industry, they, in average, list less than in case they are asked to do the same but without support in the form of a list with brands (Alba and Chattopadhyay, 2006). The companies which are pioneers in the application of radical transparency have a unique opportunity to create brand awareness associated with positive and genuine associations that will block or reduce the awareness of competing brands. This is crucial to the success of companies in future, and the logic is still the same – the first movers will achieve maximum benefit.

IMPROVING THE PERCEIVED QUALITY

Perceived quality can be defined as the customer's perception of the overall quality or superiority of a product / service or company, taking into account its purpose, compared to alternative products or companies (Aaker, 1991). Perceived quality is primarily a customer's perception. In this sense, it differs from concepts such as factual and objective quality - the extent to which the product / service or the company provides superior value; product quality; production quality. Perceived quality, in fact, cannot be objectively determined, because it basically involves personal perception and assessment of what is important for the customers. The perceived quality is the basic feeling someone has about the brand. However, it is based on highlighted dimensions, for example, the characteristics of the product to which the brand is attached. To fully understand the perceived quality, the identification and measurement of significant dimensions is required, but the perceived quality itself is a total, global construction.

How the application of radical transparency while managing the perceived quality of the brand can generate value for the business? It can be achieved in several ways (Aaker, 1991):

- **Reason for Purchase:** In many contexts, the perceived quality of the brand provides primary reason for buying, influencing the involvement of the brand into the consideration set and the specific customers choice. The customer often lacks the motivation to acquire and sort all the necessary information leading to the delineation of the real quality. Or simply information can be inaccessible. Or the customer does not have the ability and resources to obtain and process the information. In such situations, the company can offer additional information, support, openness, a clear description of the company's activities, the method of production of products, or, simply, a visible concern of the company for the environment and society can be a direct demonstration of real quality that consumers will notice as such and, quite possibly, consider it a key element when making the purchase decision, regardless the product or service. Simply, by applying the radical transparency in the everyday activities, the companies allow customers to gain trust and proximity to the brand and have a general feeling of acceptance, approval and brand preference over other competitors in the industry. Therefore, perceived quality is a central category. Having in mind that perceived quality is linked to the purchase decision, it can make all the components of brand equity or of any marketing program more effective. If the perceived quality is on a high level, then promotion and advertising are likely to be more effective. Otherwise, it is difficult to overcome the low levels of perceived quality. It requires a lot of extra effort with unpredictable result. If customers due to a specific reason, such as: lack of information about the product / service, unwillingness for cooperation by the company, improper care for particular stakeholders, shortcomings in the operation and the like, felt cheated, then everything will collapse like a house of cards. Gaining positive customer's opinion, as well as employees', or the general impression for the perceived quality of the brand can turn into mission impossible, or at least, into a long and expensive process. The application of radical transparency in maintaining the perceived quality of the brand is based on the good old rule: 'It is better to prevent than to cure'.
- **Differentiation / Positioning:** The basis of brand positioning is its position in relation to the dimension of perceived quality. The usage of radical transparency in managing brand equity, especially when many companies still do not do it, creates such a difference compared to competitors which is a direct source of competitive advantage. The originality of the everyday work and the attitude towards the stakeholders will be a feature of the company that is difficult to be copied by competitors, especially if the company has played a pioneering role in practicing radical transparency consistently and continuously. The positioning based on the rule of openness and transparency is an original choice for positioning which leads to gaining a market position that has not yet been acquired by any competitor. At first glance, this may seem to be an expensive and risky

alternative. But there is nothing more expensive than lost dissatisfied customer. Once the company decides to change the business model, then, after the installation of the radical transparency practices, openness, sharing information (and resources) and principles will lead to a direct reduction in operating costs. Such a trend in the long run will contribute the increase in the company's profitability in two ways: on the one hand, by increasing sales revenues due to favorable market position, and on the other, by reducing the cost of operations, due to the elimination of errors.

- **Premium Price:** The advantage of the high level of perceived quality allows premium price. It increases profits and / or provides resources for reinvestment in the brand. Additional investments can be realized in activities which build the brand equity, such as strengthening the awareness or associations; or in research and development, improvements in the production range of the company or alike. Apart from the additional profits and resources, the premium price affects the retroactive increase in the perceived quality. Until recently, the premise "you get what you pay for" was particularly important in the case of lack of information about the product / service or the company. But modern consumers are not willing to pay without knowing what they pay for. Thus, the premium price may be applied only to the brand that demonstrates exactly why the price is a premium. The application of radical transparency, not only to strengthen the brand equity, but in every activity of the company provides appropriate feedback to customers about the product / service or the company. Indeed, an openness show what the company does which allows it to achieve a premium price - how it generates quality that deserves a premium price. Instead of a premium price, the customer can be offered a superior value at a competitive price. This kind of added value should result in an expanded customer base and / or greater purchase frequency, higher loyalty to the brand and more efficient and effective marketing programs. Perhaps, at first glance, margins in this case are limited, but this strategy of stable profitability in the long term can cumulatively generate better results than any other alternative of fast growth that can cause disruption of the brand equity elements, and thus a decrease in the trust and loyalty of customers, so the net effect of this alternative in the long run can be far worse than the first one.
- **Interest for the Channel of Distribution:** Perceived quality is also significant for wholesalers, distributors and other participants in the channel of distribution, thus contributes to providing better distribution. The image of the participant in the channel of distribution is influenced by the products / services included in its assortment. If the company has accepted the radical transparency practices it means that the associates (distributors) involved in the sale chain are part of that system and expand the change towards openness and readiness for cooperation. Furthermore, the distributor which is part of the channel can affect the increase in the level of perceived quality which will ultimately attract consumer demand. In any case, participants in the distribution channel are motivated to trade products from brands that tend to have high levels of perceived quality, i.e. brands that are preferred by customers. This leads to success and satisfaction of all parties involved.
- **Brand Extensions:** Additive, the perceived quality generated by the application of radical transparency could be exploited by presenting brand extensions when using the familiar name for entry into a new product category or industry. The strong brand, in terms of perceived quality, can develop extensions and there is a higher probability for success compared to any inferior brand. A study of 18 potential extensions of several world famous brands, including Unilever, Procter & Gamble, Nike and Toyota found that the perceived quality of the brand is an important indicator for the evaluation of extensions (Aaker and Keller, 2008).

- **The Results of the PIMS Analysis:** The PIMS database (Profit Impact of Market Strategy) includes ten variables such as ROI, perceived quality, market share and relative prices for more than 3,000 businesses and for some of them information is provided since 1970. One of the most important results from this research is connected to the role and importance of quality. "On the long-term, the most important single factor affecting the performance of the business is the company's quality of products / services over that of competitors" (Buzzell and Gale, 1987, p.163). Figure 2 summarizes the main effects of the relative perceived quality through the analysis of ROI and ROS (Return on sales) as a function of the position of quality. Thus, companies with inferior relative quality (about 20%) realize an average 17% return on investment, while those with superior relative quality (in the interval 20% - 80% and more) earn nearly twice as much.

The detailed examination of the relationship between perceived quality and other key strategic variables, in addition to ROI, conducted by Jacobson and Aaker (1997), provides information on how perceived quality creates profitability:

1. Perceived quality affects market share. Ceteris paribus, companies that have products with better quality are preferred and achieve greater market share.
2. Perceived quality affects the price. Greater perceived quality allows the company to charge a higher price. This directly improves profitability and gives the businesses the chance to improve the quality additionally and thus create higher barriers for current and potential competitors. Even more, the higher price retroactively affects the strengthening of perceived quality, acting as a seal of quality.
3. The perceived quality has a direct impact on profitability, regardless of the impact on the market share and price. Improved perceived quality on average increases profitability, even if it has no impact on the market share and the price. The retention costs for the existing customers decrease with the quality increase and the competitive pressure reduces when quality improves. In any case, there is a direct relationship between quality and the rate of return on investment.

Figure 2. Relative perceived quality and return on investment

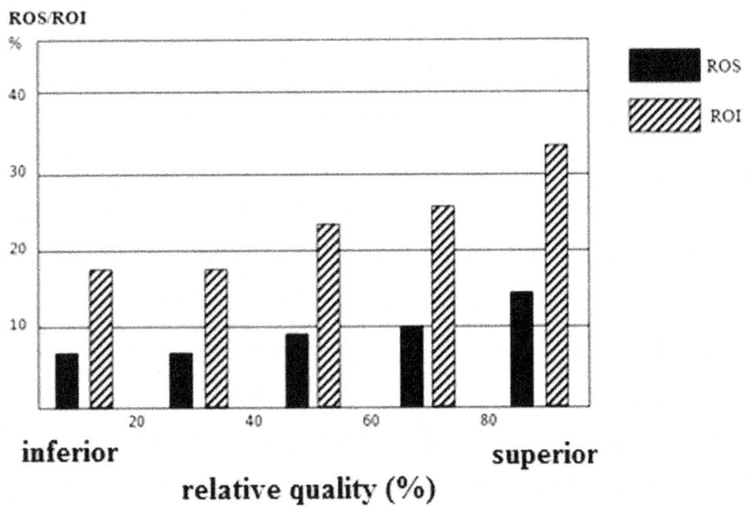

4. Perceived quality does not adversely affect costs. In fact, according to some authors, it does not affect the costs at all. The opinion that there is a natural (logical) association between the strategic option of high quality and high costs is not reflected in the research data. The improved quality leads to reduced defects and decreased manufacturing costs.
    a. **Perceived Quality and the Business Performance:** Another perspective on the importance of perceived quality in the field of competitiveness comes from a survey of 248 different industries (Aaker, 2001). The key managers of the companies in each industry were asked to identify the sustainable competitive advantage of their business. The summary list presented the "reputation for high quality" at the first place, emphasized by more than 40% of respondents. The next most mentioned sustainable competitive advantage - "service for customers, product support" won 32% of the votes. When the survey was narrowed to three large groups of industries: companies dealing with high technology, service companies and manufacturing companies, the perceived quality was the most frequently mentioned competitive advantage in each of the groups. One is for sure - perceived quality is considered an important factor for the long-term success of the business. The third most mentioned sustainable competitive advantage was another dimension of brand equity: name recognition and high reputation, followed by the installed base of customers which is directly related to the brand equity. All of the just mentioned categories: perceived quality, reputation, customer service, support, image and customer base can be precisely promoted with the application of radical transparency and these are the factors that define the company's profitability.

What affects the perceived quality? To understand and manage the perceived quality, especially through the prism of radical transparency, it is necessary to analyze what affects the perceived quality. The dimensions underlying the assessment of perceived quality depend on the context. For example, for the household appliances important are: the quality of food processing, functionality, cost of maintenance and repair, design and alike. To find out the relevant dimensions in a given context, it is often necessary to implement a certain research. Then, the relative importance of each discovered dimension should be assessed and ranked. We can distinguish two main contexts that generate a set of dimensions that illustrate the complexity of the concept of perceived quality and provide a useful starting point for developing rankings in a given context (Keller, 2007).

Dimensions of perceived quality: the product context. When it comes to product quality, seven dimensions of quality stand out: performance, functionality, compliance with specifications, reliability, durability, servicing and the final effect (Garvin, 1984). Dimensions of perceived quality: the service context. A series of studies on the consumers' perceptions about the quality of service by Parasuraman, Zeithaml and Berry, (1990) involving companies from industries such as: service of machines and appliances, commercial banking, telephone and telecommunications services, brokerages and insurance companies, resulted in the identification of several dimensions of service quality. Few of them are similar to those in the context of product: competence, visibility and safety. The other five dimensions are associated with the personal contact between the service company and the user. These include: responsibility, empathy, credibility, trust and kindness, which in principle oscillate depending on the nature of interactions among the service users and the company's employees.

Delivering high quality. The first step towards improving the perceived quality is developing the ability to deliver a high-quality product / service. Usually, it is in vain to convince customers that the quality is excellent when it is not, unless their experience is not consistent with the position for product / service quality. Of course, the delivery of high quality depends on the context. For example, the company Xerox has given itself to the issue of quality by improving product design - designing products that are much more reliable, even if the high-speed operation could be "sacrificed". Conversely, banks, especially after the great crisis in 2007 are trying to improve quality by focusing on interactions between employees and customers (Doyle and Stern, 2009).

Studies on how to achieve excellence in quality consistently observe the following several dimensions (Knapp and Hart, 2000):

1. **Commitment to Quality:** Achieving and maintaining quality over time is not an easy task. If this is not one of the top priorities of the company, then it is impossible to be fulfilled. The missions of Federal Express, Nordstrom and Toyota are conceived in a way that they clearly express what they do to deliver high quality. This is not just demagogy; there is no compromise for quality.
2. **Culture Based on Quality:** The commitment to quality should be reflected in the company's culture, values, symbols and norms of behavior. Simply, in the trade-off relationship between quality and cost, the quality needs to win. This is a simple decision. There are companies that will show the right direction.
3. **Customers' Needs:** Ultimately, customers define quality. Managers are often wrong in their assumptions about what is important for the customers. For example, the managers in the General Electric subsidiary for household appliances overestimated the need for superb functionality of the devices and underestimated the need for easy cleaning and the look of the appliances. Just as the credit card users in the US were concerned about their security and protection against loss / theft more than the managers of the commercial banks thought. It is necessary to provide accurate and timely information about consumers demands. The frequent contacts between managers and customers on a regular basis are a great approach. IBM appoints top managers as managers for key clients and Disneyland expects their top managers to regularly appear on stage in the parks. Many Japanese companies practice to hire one person who is in charge to collect, systematize and summarize the problems customers have encountered or complained throughout the day. And, what is even more important, this problems are solved in a daily basis. Quality in every activity cannot wait.
4. **Measuring / Goals / Standards:** The difference between the declaration of quality and its achievement is often located in the installed goals that are measurable and tied to the system of remuneration. If the goal related to quality is vaguely noted it can easily become ineffective. The goals and standards related to quality should be understandable and set as priorities. Too many purposes without priority will have the same effect as not having any purpose.
5. **Providing Incentives for Employees:** Japanese companies often show how employees, working as a team, provide a very effective approach to improving quality. These teams are not only sensitive to the problems, but also in a position to implement and support a perspective solution. Another perspective for this dimension comes from the research by Zeithaml (Kirmani and Wright, 2009). The key insight here is that quality problems in services are often caused by the lack of control on employees during the process of service delivery. Employees often lack flexibility in dealing with customers, so they blame the system rather than themselves. Companies, however, often respond to this problem by regulating the quality through an "according to the book" access, rather than "according to the client" access.

6. **Customers' Expectations:** Perceived quality can also be deficient because of the high expectations of customers. Thus, Holiday Inn has developed a "no surprises" system once the company understood that their guests believe that consistent quality is that which prevents unpleasant surprises. This system is based on operational management without any errors.
   a. **Signals of High Quality:** Achieving high quality is not enough, real quality should be turned into perceived quality. This is a direct effect from the application of radical transparency in brand equity management. But in many situations the dimensions of quality that are considered most risky are the most difficult for evaluation. For example, when buying a car, the endurance (durability) can be considered a key attribute of the quality of the car, but simply there is no good enough method to check it. With extra efforts, information on the previous experience of others can be provided, but sometimes the time and the additional effort can be a limiting factor and the value of knowledge of past experience may prove insufficient and irrelevant. The solution lies in determining a signal or an indicator for a particular dimension of quality. For example, if the company is open to share any information about the process of production and offers a long warranty for the product, the consumer may assume that the company is confident in its quality and is ready to stand behind it. In addition to the information on the characteristics of a particular product (internal signs) numerous other associations for the brand can be used, such as: the scope of the promotion, the brand name or the price (external signs) that may affect the perceived quality. The basic prerequisite for the quality signals to be visible to customers is the company's willingness to cooperate with them.
   b. **The Price as a Sign of Quality:** The variable which can be used as a significant sign of quality is exactly the price. The analysis of 36 studies, most of which involved frequently purchased, relatively cheaper products for final consumption, consistently demonstrated that the price is a strong sign of quality, nearly as strong as the brand name (Akshay and Monroe, 2008). The significance of price as a sign of quality depends on the availability of other signs of quality. The price will be considered an important sign of quality if other signals are not visible. But if the price is not a direct and real sign of quality, then after the first experience with the product / service the trust in the brand may be lost. Therefore, the application of radical transparency reinforces the importance of price as a sign of quality. It allows consumers to verify the price as an index of quality and when that relationship is confirmed, and then loyalty to the brand is imminent. When internal and / or external signs are present, consumers rely less on price. The use of price as a sign of quality differs depending on the industry. In industries where it is more difficult to value the products, the price as a sign of quality will be used more, while for products with small variations in price, it is not a sign of quality (Randall, 2006).However, the application of radical transparency allows the brand to achieve as high price as possible, regardless of the industry, and to bind it with the perceived quality of the product / service, as well as with the trust in the brand in the long run. The price will be a stronger sign of quality where major differences in perceived quality in products / services exist. In one classic study, Leavitt asked respondents to choose between two brands in four different categories and the only information offered was the price (Leavitt, 1957). The percent of respondents who chose the more expensive brand is associated with the perceived differences in quality. It represented 57% and 30% within the two different product groups, and 24% and 21% within the similar products.

i. The results from the PIMS analysis show that the relationship between the relative perceived quality and relative price associations is a "two way street" (Buzzell and Gale, 1987). Higher prices on average lead to a higher perceived quality. This relationship is consistent with the notation that in the absence of complete information, the price is used as a sign for quality. However, the other explanation is that the companies which are able to charge higher prices have greater opportunities to improve the quality of the product / service because it includes large initial costs and risks.

c. **Connecting Perceptions with Real Quality:** Achieving high level of quality is not enough. The company must create or change the customers' perceptions. One way to fulfill this task is to manage the signals of quality, such as the price level or the employee's skills and commitment. Both provide signs for customers. Another way is to simply convey the message for quality. The problem in this case is that consumers are accustomed to hear statements such as "we are the best". For example, it takes 5 years in the automotive industry to perceive the changes in quality, so that it would affect positively on sales (Balmer and Greyser, 2003). The challenge is how to establish credibility by explaining why the quality is superior – exactly with the application of radical transparency.

BUILDING AND MANAGING THE ASSOCIATIONS

Brand associations are everything in the memory associated with the brand. Associations not only exist, but they also have a level of intensity (Keller, 2007). The connection to the brand will be much stronger if it is based on many positive experiences or frequent exposure to communications. It would-be also stronger if supported by a network of other connections. Thus, if the relationship between children and McDonald's is based only on advertisements depicting this relationship then it would be a much weaker link than the one which includes mental network of experiences from birthday parties at McDonald's; games and toys from McDonald's and so on. The brand image is a set of associations usually organized with a certain meaning. Thus, McDonald's is not just a set of strong and weak associations; on the contrary, associations are organized into groups that have meaning. There may be a group of associations related to children, service or type of food, mental images that come to mind when you mention McDonald's, as the symbol of the golden arches or simply fast food - hamburgers and fries. Associations and image, both represent the perceptions that may or may not have to reflect the objective reality. For example, the image of competence could be based on the appearance of the doctoral office and the way employees treat patients much more than on objective measures of the health of treated patients. The positioning of the brand is closely linked with the associations and the concept of brand image but it implies a certain reference which is usually connected to the competition. The focus is put on a particular association or image (set of associations) defined in the particular context of an attribute or a competitor. A well-positioned brand will have a competitive, attractive position backed up by strong associations. It would rank high on the basis of the desired feature or would take a position different from competitors. The brand position reflects how people perceive the brand. However, the strategy of positioning can reflect how the company tries to be perceived.

How associations create value for the brand by applying radical transparency? Accented brand value is usually represented by a set of associations. The associations constitute a basis for the purchase decisions and loyalty to the brand. There are a number of possible ways in which associations can provide value for the brand (Aaker, 1991):

- **Assistance in Providing / Processing Information:** Associations can serve to summarize facts and specifications that could otherwise be difficult for the customers to process and evaluate, and very expensive for the company to communicate. The association may create compact information that will help the customer to overcome such situations. For example, a number of facts related to Nordstrom can be summarized in a relatively strong position compared to competitors. The associations may also affect the interpretation of facts. Furthermore, associations can influence the reminders of information, especially during the process of purchase decision. For example, the symbol of the Travelers umbrella or the circles of Audi encourage you to think about the experience with the brand, which would not occur in the absence of the symbol. Therefore, it is important that each contact the customer has with the brand causes creation and / or strengthening of positive associations. By applying an open approach to sharing information, looking after the stakeholders and the environment, the possibility of creating a wrong relationship with any group of stakeholders, and thus negative associations is reduced to a minimum. Simply, nurturing the philosophy of working with transparency and openness for cooperation provides original position for the brand and such a level of connection with consumers through a set of strong positive associations, which few competitors could achieve.
- **Differentiation:** The association may constitute an important basis for differentiation. In some industries such as, for example, production and sales of wine, perfume and clothes, many brands are not distinguished by a large number of consumers. Associations linked to the brand name can play a critical role in distinguishing one brand from the others. For example, the care for the environment is Henkel's point of differentiation that the company has been working on for a long period, and it is difficult to be imitated by most competitors because it requires large investments in technology, knowledge, processes, and human resources and so on. Moreover, building a specific set of associations through application of radical transparency in operations requires implementation of a new business model that will be based on new values and broad objectives. In this way, associations which cause differentiation can be a key competitive advantage. If the brand is well positioned, based on a key feature, it will be very difficult for the competitors to attack the brand's position.
- **Reason for Purchase:** Many brand associations include characteristics of the products / services or benefits to consumers which represent a specific reason for buying a specific brand. They represent a basis for the purchase decisions and the brand loyalty. Thus, Colgate provides clean and white teeth and Mercedes status for its users. But if these companies fail the trust of customers through operations that demonstrate disregard for any components of the environment, the associations can convert to a reason for not buying the products from these brands. Therefore, the application of radical transparency is the foundation that strengthens associations in the direction of gaining loyal customers who have only one choice when making the purchase decision- their favorite brand that does not cheat. Associations influence purchase decisions by providing credibility and confidence in the brand. When the champions of Wimbledon use a certain brand of sportswear or professional stylists recommend specific products for hair care that have no harmful substances, then consumers feel much more comfortable when buying and using products from these brands.

- **Creating Positive Attitudes and Feelings:** Some associations are linked and stimulate positive feelings transmitted to the brand. Engaging celebrities in promoting a certain brand stimulates the emergence of feelings and likeability of the brand. Sympathetic characters can also be used to reduce the incidents and objections of the public in terms of the context in which the company operates. Some associations create positive feelings during the use of the product / service, turning the experience into something different. Once again, the acceptance of the concept of radical transparency stimulates positive feelings and attitudes about the brand.
- **The Basis for Expansion:** The association can provide the basis for expanding the brand by creating a sense of harmony between the brand and the new product or by providing a reason for purchase. In this way, Honda has successfully completed the expansion in the bike segment, although it previously covered only the car segment.

Types of Associations

A significant number of associations may be relevant for anyone. Managers are primarily interested in those associations that directly or indirectly affect consumer behavior. Their focus is not only to identify brand associations, but whether they are strong and shared among many or weak and different from person to person. The diffuse image involves a very different context from the consistent image. Eleven types of associations are described in addition. The application of radical transparency in managing this component of brand equity directly affects the brand image, the consumer behavior, the purchase decision and, ultimately, the sales revenues and profitability of the company.

- **Product Features:** Probably the most used positioning strategy is based on associations related to the attributes and characteristics of the product / service. It is quite effective to develop such associations, because when the attribute is significant the association can directly turn into a reason for (not) buying. It is important to transparently send the message on the characteristics of the products to all target consumers and affected stakeholders. But the credibility and consistency of the product must be primary. Otherwise, a sense of disbelief can evolve which may cause negative associations and brand avoidance. For example, Colgate became the leader in sales of toothpaste by providing strong association - caries control, which was supported by the American Dental Association. It is estimated that 40% of Colgate's market share in the US is a result of the development of this association (Clark, 2004). In other product categories or industries different brands are associated with different attributes. For example, Volvo underlines the durability of their vehicles, BMW highlights the performance of their cars, Jaguar, meanwhile, offers performance and elegance, and Mercedes through the "car from the top engineers" emphasizes luxury and durability, while Hyundai with the statement "a car with sense" provides a price advantage (Balmer and Greyser, 2003). It may be noted that each of these brands has chosen a different feature of the product as the basis for brand positioning. The basic problem in positioning is to find such a characteristic that is important for consumers from a segment that is not grounded from another competitor. The identification of any unresolved consumers problem or need may lead to a discovery of an attribute that has previously been ignored by competitors. The efforts to connect the brand with several features simultaneously which would not ignore a single argument or a market segment are a big challenge. The problem is partly linked to a lack of motivation and ability of the public to process the message which includes multiple dimensions. The use of several attributes can work well when they complement each other. Interestingly, the concept of radical transparency in any operation causes a synergetic connection among multiple characteristics, regarding not only the product, but also the performance of the company as a whole, leading towards creation of original market position and greater trust and loyalty from customers.

- **Invisible Dimensions:** Companies want to compare brands. They engage into "a match of squabbling", trying to convince others of the superiority of their brand through one or two key dimensions. A fight for being: faster, lighter, smaller, more durable, more nutritious, which has fewer calories… is going to infinity. Companies on average compare to their competitors in terms of a list of more than 30 features. There are several problems with this process of proof (Aaker and McLoughlin, 2010). First, the position which is based on a particular specification is vulnerable to innovation. There will always be someone who will suddenly become faster, more durable, more nutritious or whatever it is. Second, when companies engage in "a match of squabbling" they lose credibility. In a short time nobody will trust the manufacturer of aspirin which claims that exactly his product is the most effective. Consumers encounter conflicting and contradictory statements so often that at the end they reject them all. Third, consumers do not always base their purchasing decisions on a particular specification. Many believe that small differences in certain features are not important or consumers have no motivation or ability to process information on a detailed level.

McKenna, (1996), emphasizes that invisible factors are much more effective associations than a specific feature. The invisible factor is a general attribute such as perceived quality, technological leadership, perceived value, healthy product and so on, which serves to sum up most individual attributes in one set. The concept of radical transparency reinforces the phenomenon: "a feeling that the brand is good" among consumers. Unlike many specific attributes, the invisible attribute is harder to reach and win. The brands that have associations connected to invisible attributes are not so vulnerable to competitive attacks. The corporate brands like: Samsung, HP, IBM, Apple or Toyota include set of associations that result in a general feeling of acceptance by consumers. Consumers' perception for these companies is that they have good products. Such companies can develop associations connected to perceived quality and innovation, supporting all products under one corporate umbrella.

- **Benefits for Consumers:** Since most of the product features provide benefits to consumers, there is usually a correspondence between the two. Thus, the caries control is a characteristic of the Colgate products as well as a benefit for consumers. Whether the dominant association derives from a characteristic or a benefit it can have an important role in the development of the association. It is useful to distinguish between rational and psychological benefits. Rational benefits are closely linked to the characteristics of the products and part of a rational purchase decision. The psychological benefits are a consequence of the formation of an attitude and connect with the feelings that appear in the purchase process or during the use of products / services. Snickers is an example of a brand that has expanded associations from a chocolate with caramel and peanuts to reward at the end of the day. Psychological benefits follow rational benefits, but at the same time they are very different. Psychological benefits can be a stronger type of association even for products such as computers. Furthermore, psychological benefits would be more effective if accompanied by rational benefits. The openness to stakeholders significantly impacts the unification of rational and psychological benefits for consumers. This creates a general sense of security and confidence in the brand which guarantees its success.

- **Relative Price:** One of the product's attributes - the relative price is so useful and important it deserves to be analyzed individually. In many product categories there are about five well-developed price levels. The positioning in relation to the relative price can be quite complex. Brand's position should be clearly defined in one of the price categories. Then it should be determined what will be offered, and will differ from competitors within the specified price level. One way is to connect the offer to one from the higher price level. For example, Suave is a line of shampoos that Helen Curtis successfully introduced in the market at significantly lower price than the price of competitors. The brand positioning with a relatively higher price and a brand upgrade can be a major pitfall. For example, Sears is trying to offer designer clothes in their stores. However, consumers may remain confused whether Sears enters the premium segment or remains the place that provides maximum value for the price (Clifton and Simmons, 2004). With the application of radical transparency as a way of the everyday functioning of the company, the right information to consumers about price / quality ratio can be provided. This approach secures value for money, which is one of the most important dimensions in the purchase decision for many strict modern consumers. With the application of radical transparency, consumers gain trust in the brand and the value it offers in general, which is a basis for loyalty in the long run.
- **Use:** Another approach is to connect the brand with the use of the product / service. A study of the market for coffee found nine relevant contexts for the use of coffee (Urban et al, 1994) - at the start of the day, between meals alone, between meals in company, after lunch, after dinner, at night with guests, in the evening in front of TV, at night to stay awake or in cafes with friends. This study found significant differences in the choice of the brand of coffee, depending on the type of use. Brands can certainly have multiple strategies for positioning; however, the proliferation involves obvious difficulties and risks. Often, the positioning strategy based on the use of the product is a secondary or tertiary brand position, which is a position that is deliberately trying to expand the market for the brand. The company may try to communicate with the consumers openly and to suggest ways of using its products that can motivate consumers to an increased frequency of use. Again, we emphasize that the reliability of the brand offer should at no time be put into question. For example, if the brand proclaims that the drink meets the consumers' needs in the morning, as well as in the afternoon, independently, or in company, then such a relationship should be a fact, not praise.
- **Users:** Another approach to positioning is to connect the brand with the type of user, i.e. the consumer. When the positioning strategy based on users works, it is very effective because it can connect with the strategy of segmentation. The role of positioning based on users can be illustrated with the example regarding the cosmetics industry in the US in the 90s. During that period, Revlon was considered the market leader with about 25% market share and associations connected with more sophisticated women. Maybelline, however, barely had 15% market share and lagged due to the lack of a strong image – a recognizable set of associations. Then it was decided to strengthen the brand and it was repositioned in a cosmetic line for women with style, leaving a print of a modern company with an assortment of products for modern women (Collins and Porras, 1994). The problem that occurs when using a strong association, especially an association related to users is that it limits the possibility of market expansion. The radical transparency concept offers a double benefit for the company. It not only provides trust and loyalty from customers, but with such open communication, consumers are encouraged to bring their demands directly to

the company, and the company to respond by meeting them. Nowadays it is very difficult to know exactly what consumers want in order to offer a product / service that leads to a purchase decision.

- **Celebrity:** Hiring a celebrity almost always provides strong associations to the brand. A significant feature for the brand is to develop a technological competence - the ability to design and manufacture products that would be promoted by famous persons. It is very difficult to convince people that your product, whether it is a pair of sports shoes or a soft drink, is superior to competing products. The challenge is not just in creating a credible argument, but to attract people to hear that argument and to believe in it, facing similar statements by competitors. But it is much easier to believe in such arguments, if they are supported by celebrity. Convincing goes in the direction that this person would not have promoted the product or service if he / she does not consider that it is superior to competing products, because otherwise this would have violated his/her public image. In the mid 90-ies Nike for the first time faced the challenge from Reebok who intended to take over the first place in the market for sports shoes (Murray, 1996). The answer from Nike to this threat was the engagement of Michael Jordan and the introduction of a new line Air Jordan. The innovation which was included in the new models of sports shoes consisted of patented air pockets under pressure in the sole of the shoes that worn by the rebel of gravity, the legendary Michael Jordan, guaranteeing imminent success. In the first year of sales, the models from the Air Jordan line delivered sales of $ 100 million. Since then, until today, this line of sport shoes and sportswear is still one of the most popular in the world and Nike has been and remains the market leader in this domain. The person who is used as an association for the brand does not necessarily have to be a famous public figure. It can be a fictional character and even a cartoon character. What is important is to achieve and maintain credibility.
- **Lifestyle:** Every individual has a personality and lifestyle that are complex, colorful and, of course, different. The brands, even those for machines such as cars, are also described with characteristics similar to those of the personality and lifestyle of the people. A survey conducted by the company Pepsi which included 17 different groups of loyal consumers of Pepsi or Coca-Cola resulted in knowledge of the personality of these two brands (Enrico, 2009). Basically, the Coca-Cola consumers are traditional, family people throughout the United States. By contrast, Pepsi fans are younger, exciting and innovative entertainment seekers and risk takers. Based on these findings, Pepsi decided to exploit and enhance its image. Since then, Pepsi constantly engages around the motive: "Dare for more". It is important for the company to build a way of communication with consumers through which it will receive and deliver relevant information which will strengthen the relationship and support consumers' lifestyle through appropriate products / services from the company. The benefits from such a relationship are mutual.
- **Product Group:** Some brands have to include a critical decision for positioning which involves associations connected to the product group. For example, some margarine manufacturers position their products in terms of butter; or brands relating to milk powder position their brand regarding true milk. Some manufacturers of cereals are trying to position their products as substitutes for bread, wanting to expand their business. In any case, the application of radical transparency in the process of decision making regarding the brand positioning in relation to other products in the product group provides an original position that consumers recognize and value.
- **Competitors:** Within many positioning strategies one or more competitors occur as a frame of reference (explicit or implicit). In some cases the reference competitors may be the dominant aspect of the positioning strategy. It is useful to take into account the competitors when selecting

the brand position for two reasons. First, a competitor may have a solid, clearly crystallized image, developed through time, which can serve as a bridge to communicate another image associated with it. Second, sometimes it is not important how much the consumers think a brand is good, but how much they think it is better than the competing brands (Kapferer, 2008). Perhaps one of the most famous strategies of this type is that of the car rental company, Avis, with its campaign "we are in the second place and therefore we try more". The main purpose of the message was to show that the market leader - the company Hertz is so great that it did not have to work. The strategy was Avis to get closer to the leader Hertz as the only alternative to renting cars, above all others (Adamson and Sorrell, 2007). The brand positioning in relation to a particular competitor is justified, taking into account the characteristics of the product, especially the price / quality ratio. If further, the brand positioning is supported by an approach of openness and collaboration, a specific market position in relation to any competitor in the field can be achieved.

- **Country / Geographical Origin:** The country of origin can be a powerful symbol and association, because there is a close link to the products, materials and capabilities. Thus, Germany is associated with high quality cars and beer, Italy with shoes, clothes and pizza and France with perfumes. This kind of associations can be exploited by connecting the brand with his country of origin. There may be sharp differences in consumers' perceptions of brands depending on the country of origin. One study in the US was conducted to analyze the manufacturers of televisions and cars (Han and Terpstra, 1999). Subjects were asked to rank the different models that previously were described with emphasis on the country of origin. In the both product groups Japan was ranked the highest, followed by Germany, the third place was for the United States, and then followed the other developed European countries and the developed countries from Asia. Another study that involved 13 product categories, 21 product features from 15 different countries suggests that the impact of the country of origin would significantly vary depending on the context. For example, French believe, regardless of the type of product, that the superior products come from France, Japan and US. Canadians and Britons thought superior products come from the United States (Papadopoulos and Avlonitis, 2002). The issues regarding associations related to the country of origin are becoming more complex and more important due to the efforts of companies to develop global strategies and compete in markets worldwide. Radical transparency should not tackle the country of origin of products, but rather to explain it. The supply chain and manufacturing processes of products worldwide ample with activities implemented in different countries around the world. We are witnessing the frequent abuse of the country of origin. The application of radical transparency solves the problem of distrust in the declarations and product labels. It implies that the company is open to convey any relevant information to any stakeholder, which is the basis for building long-term trust and loyalty to the brand.

Measuring Brand Associations

There are several approaches for determining the intensity of associations linked to a brand. The simplest is the direct way when people are directly asked what they think about the brand. This access is commonly implemented with a detailed discussion of the brand from individual consumers or focus groups. With the usage of this open access, most relevant information on the consumers' opinions and associations for the brand can be obtained, but the unwillingness of respondents to directly transfer their opinion and attitude can occur as a potential trap. However, the use of open, friendly relationship within every interaction with consumers will affect the confidence and freedom in expressing the opinion, which undoubtedly would be associated with positive associations about the brand if radical transparency is correctly implemented in any activity.

- **Indirect Approaches:** Although direct approach is quite useful to understand the perceptions, often it is viable to take into account the so-called indirect methods, although some of them at first seem strange. These indirect approaches are supported by the assumption that the respondents might be unwilling or unable to reveal their thoughts, feelings and attitudes in response to direct questions. For example, they might be aware that the real reason for the purchase of designer jeans is to feel socially accepted when wearing them, and would respond through rationalization that seems logical: they buy those jeans because of the quality craftsmanship, price or design, although these arguments are actually a secondary motive. Or respondents are simply not able to provide expert information because they buy something for themselves not knowing the real reason. So a board range of indirect approaches is being used (Aaker, 1991):
- **Free Associations:** Associations with words are one way to overcome limitations in the minds of respondents. The procedure is to have a list of specified brands and ask respondents to list all the words that come to their mind regarding the specific brand. The aim is to avoid thinking and evaluation, but to generate words as quickly as possible. After completing the list, a discussion follows on why certain associations occur. This technique is especially good to examine the potential effects of a new brand or a slogan. The result of the associations in words is usually a list of hundreds of words and ideas. In order to quantitatively assess the relative importance of each, a representative sample of the targeted segment should be formed and each respondent should to be asked to rank the words that suit the brand. This approach is also useful when measuring the associations applied for competing brands. One variant of this technique - associations in words is completing a started sentence. Respondents are asked to complete the sentence according to their opinion. For example, "People like Apple, because ...", "Audi symbolizes ..." etc. Respondents are encouraged through an open and friendly attitude to respond with the first words that come to their minds.
- **Picture Interpretation:** Another approach is to ask the respondents to freely interpret an image depicting a scene which includes the brand. In one study respondents were shown an image of a man who lists the catalog of products from the supermarket and his wife standing beside him. Respondents were asked to list any comments they think his wife gives. The use of the image is a way that allows respondents to express how they really feel, using characters from a scene to communicate their personal views and feelings. It may be uncomfortable to admit feelings of power and prestige when driving BMW, but it is not difficult to attach these feelings and attitudes to an unnamed character in an image. In such conditions, even feelings and attitudes for which the respondent was unaware can occur. At first glance, this way of measuring associations may seem impractical and complicated, but through direct communication with consumers and other stakeholders, important information about the brand image can be obtained. More importantly, the company can discover possible deficiencies that are not immediately visible; new ideas for innovation in the process or within the relationship among the brand and consumers can be born. It is important not to forget the consistency in the application of this open approach in order to achieve trust and positive attitude among consumers that they will not be let down by the brand.
- **If the Brand was a Person:** There are three components of the image of the brand (Plummer, 1998): product attributes, customer benefits and the brand personality. It is often argued that in

many product groups or industries the personality of the brand is the key element for understanding the choice of brand. In a study of Y&R the respondents were asked to describe the offered brands with a selection of words from a list which included 50 words that represent the personality. The results of the technique explicitly demonstrated that different brands are perceived differently. For example, Holiday Inn has been described as: cheerful, friendly, casual, practical, modern, reliable and honest, while Oil of Oley has been described as: gentle, sophisticated, mature and mysterious. Ernest Dichter, the father of qualitative research, routinely applied psycho drama where people were asked to act out the product: "Imagine you are the washing powder Ariel ... Are you a man or a woman ...? What kind of person are you...? What kind of magazines you read? What do you do in your free time? "(Bartos, 1996, p. 17). The results lead to a detection of a wide range of associations for the brand. Another variant of this approach is to ask respondents to draw figures for the typical user of the brand (Miller and Tsiantar, 1998). Thus, in one study dedicated to two manufacturers of cakes in the US, Pillsbury and Duncan Hines, which involved hundreds of participants, users have drawn Pillsbury as lady in years that resembles their grandmother while users of Duncan Hines were represented by the profile of a modern housewife (Thomas, 2007). These innovative techniques allow achieving closeness to customers and send a simple message that it is important for the company what customers think and what they want. The demonstration of care by evaluating the hidden relationship between the consumer and the brand with indirect methods, in order to measure the associations, further strengthens the invisible links between the brand and the consumers. The application of radical transparency leads to building complex associations that consumers have about the brand, and even if they could not explain them, they mean them. This close relationship that each company wants to achieve is shown through the consumers' statements: "I simple like it." It is, in fact, the ultimate goal which guarantees success in the long term.

- **Animals, Activities and Magazines:** Sometimes, when discussing brands, people have difficulty in articulating their perceptions. They tend to use the obvious, common descriptors to which they are used. But the challenge is to strengthen and enrich the answer. A useful approach is to ask consumers to connect the brand with other objects, such as animals, cars, magazines, trees, movies or books. The questions that can be used are: If the detergent Ariel was an animal, what animal would it be? Why? Which features of the animal remind you of the brand? If Bank of America was a car, what model would it be? If British Airways was a magazine, which magazine would it be? The marketing agency Young & Rubicam often uses this productive approach. One study gave participants a list of 29 animals and asked them to choose one animal to describe the 29 brands. Among the participants there were representatives of 35 professions and 21 nationalities. The main goal was to learn about the symbols used to associate brands. For example, Kentucky Fried Chicken was associated with zebra (because of packaging associations with black and white lines). The results were rich descriptions of the brand that suggested which associations should be developed and which avoided (Plummer, 1998). This technique can detect the sincerest associations and customer opinions about the brand expressed through the characteristics of the animal or object that describes the brand. While applying this technique it is of particular importance not to interrupt the process after receiving the first information, but to make efforts to systematize descriptions and to obtain purified image from the brand associations, which will ultimately lead to strengthening the positive and avoiding negative associations. Of course, this takes time and dedication. Associations cannot change overnight, but they can be modified. The application of radical transparency in the indirect approaches in order to measure associations contributes significantly to filtering the right brand image.

- **Usage Experience:** Instead of asking respondents which brands they use and why, the discussion can focus on the experience of use. The discussion of the specific historical experience of using a certain brand allows respondents to recall and communicate their feelings in a context that reflects the experience of use. So, a summary, purified image of the brand can be set. Again, we emphasize that the application of radical transparency allows the company to get relevant information from customers over their real opinion about the brand, and this is an important starting point for building brand equity in the long term.
- **Purchase Decision:** Another approach is to monitor the process of making an individual purchase decision. When the process of making a purchase decision is dissected, it reveals the impact of various brand associations, which may not be part of the total picture individuals have for the brand. Associations can be very subtle. Let's analyze, for example, the process of making a purchase decision for a portable computer. We can start by discovering the brand that is the cheapest, so choosing to focus on Dell. Or whose battery is serving the longest, so in the focus appears Toshiba; which brand has a contemporary design – Apple or which one is the best-selling and to finish with choosing Lenovo. The process of analyzing alternatives awakens different associations for different brands and the most dominant lead to finalizing the decision-making and choosing one alternative. The openness and readiness for support and cooperation from the company, not only in analyzing consumer opinions, but primarily in offering value for money or in building a relationship with customers is the key to building positive and original brand associations. The application of radical transparency in measuring associations should be just a new episode in the company's business model and the main content is quality in all activities which leads to a customer's purchase decision.
- **The User of the Brand:** Axelrod, (1995) through his experiments and experience confirms that only two issues are important in order to understand the preferences of consumers. First, focusing on the user, the question is how a consumer of one brand differs from a consumer of another. In fact, how the needs and motivations of the users of both brands vary. When the focus is on the user of the brand, rather than the brand, respondents are more likely to respond above the rational logic for their choice of brand. The differences in the described profiles reveal important information, in particular, if during the test users feel free and motivated to respond.
- **Differences Between Brands:** The second important issue, according to Axelrod is how one brand differs from other (Axelrod and Wybenga, 1995). The perceived difference between brands can even be the color of the package, although very few respondents believe that packaging is crucial in their purchase decision. However, as to act as an insignificant factor, the focus on the differences between brands causes irrelevant dimensions to get meaning. This approach is implemented by offering a list of brands and request from respondents to state how they differ.
- **From Product Characteristics, Through Consumer Benefits, to Personal Values:** This model suggests that it is useful to induce respondents to think above the characteristics of the product towards the consumer benefits and personal values (Reynolds and Gutman, 2004). The essence of the concept is that personal values represent the desired end state and should therefore be included. Personal values can be externally oriented (a feeling of importance and acceptance) or can relate to the way the individual sees himself / herself (self-esteem, happiness, security). The characteristics of the product as "kilometers per liter", "strong taste", "saving money" etc. represent

things that lead to achieving the desired end state. This approach can be illustrated by an example of the airline industry. The process begins with a request from consumers to indicate preferred airline. Then, with the technique of expansion ("why") consumers are asked to describe why it is their choice. The possible answers are: "physical comfort", "getting more for the money" and finally "feeling better about myself."

- **Interpreting Qualitative Research:** Much of the heretofore described is qualitative research (including projective techniques and small samples). It can provide a close contact between managers and customers, because it is fast, relatively cheap and includes respondents. The most important thing is that this provides an opportunity to acquire counter intuitive insights that lead to improved brand strategy. The key is the interpretation of the research. The following suggestions may be used as a guide (Aaker, 1991): to think of the ultimate goal, not to limit the observations, to detect the brand signals, discover symbols and discover connections. Ideas for brand associations and position can be born when using qualitative research and the same can be tested by checking the respondents' reactions. The growing number of companies worldwide which accept the concept of radical transparency in every operation confirms that its application leads to strengthening specific and unparalleled brand associations that affect all other elements of the brand equity. Finally, these connections between the brand equity assets provide original market position and profitability in the long run.

Selecting Associations

The choice of associations drives all strategic efforts of the company. Let's suppose that we are entering into a new business - electronic cinema, where users choose movies and receive them in a special e-mail. Possible associations of this business would be: comfort, speed, wide choice, friendly operators etc. Which would be the primary and which secondary associations? The answers lead to the generation of the name and symbol of the brand and the design of the details in the operation. Such decisions for positioning determine not only the short-term success, but the long-term viability, because associations should support the competitive advantage, and it should be sustained and convincing. For example, on the long run, the friendly culture, open access and readiness for cooperation may be more difficult to be imitated than the delivery of movies. There are numerous suggestions, advices and guidance, summarized in three considerations that greatly assist while analyzing and selecting the decision to reposition the brand through the prism of radical transparency:

- **Self-Analysis:** Before positioning the brand, it is important to conduct trials or "blind tests" among company employees whose results should ensure that the brand delivers what it promises and that is compatible with the proposed image. It is completely unnecessary to create a position different from what the brand delivers. This could be very damaging to the company's strategy, since it would undermine the basis of the brand equity - consumers will be skeptical of the value of the brand and will lose credibility and trust. The brand perceptions are, actually, more important than the actual product or service, especially if connected with a strong, known name and a positive consumer experience with the brand. It is therefore important to ensure that the nature and strength of existing associations is well known. It is usually very difficult to change the present, particularly strong associations. In general, the best solution is to build new associations over current than to change or neutralize existing associations.

- **Associations for Competitors:** Knowing the associations of competing brands is the second key element when making the decision for the brand positioning. For most brands, in almost any context, it is an imperative to develop associations that represent a certain point of differentiation against competitors. If there is nothing different about the brand, there is no reason for consumers to choose, even to notice it. The research on new product launches shows that the best single predictor of the success of a new product and its ability to foster awareness are the points of differentiation. It is a fatal error to enter the market with the premise "and we too." The application of the concept of radical transparency in circumstances when most are being skeptical about the success of the new business model is the primary point of differentiation. In this way several similar associations with a point of differentiation can be developed. For example, the PC clones of IBM. These models emphasize that they are the same as all models of IBM regarding the basic performance, but are cheaper, faster, smaller, more accessible, offer better service etc. However, radical transparency, itself, enforces access of openness not only to consumers but also with all other stakeholders, allowing all points of brand diversity over competitors to be easily detected and taken into account. This will create a comprehensive picture of the different performance of the brand leading to a general association - the brand is good. The co-option of the main associations is important for two reasons. First, these associations are critical to users. Without them, consumers would not choose the brand. Second, communicating the associations is relatively easy. Instead of presenting all the details about the product, specifications, etc., it is sufficient to highlight the differences (Ulrich and Smallwood, 2007).
- **Targeted Market:** The third dimension of the analysis involves the targeted market. The point of the "game" is to develop associations: which build and develop the strength of the brand and its attributes, provide a point of differentiation and to which the targeted market will respond. The application of radical transparency under the motto "being different" will help the brand recognition, and even more in building a stronger position that creates reason for purchase and / or adds value to the product / service.
- **Association that Create Reason for Purchase:** One of the roles of radical transparency is to create an association that would create a reason for purchasing the brand. Thus, the associations connected with the product / service often provide a clear reason for buying the brand, for example, Xerox printers offer superior value. The reason for the purchase must be sufficiently influential to be really attractive for consumers. The concept of the unique selling proposition - USP, developed and practiced by Rosser Reeves, one of the creative giants in strategic marketing focuses on the reasons for purchase and includes specific and genuine benefit to the consumer which is important enough to cause a reason for buying the brand. For example, "Colgate refreshes your breath while it cleans your teeth" or "M&M melt in your mouth, not in your hands." Rosser Reeves alluded to the fact that once you formulate a good USP, it should be maintained without any changes. There is even an anecdote for defending this view. One of his clients, Anacin, spent more than $ 85 million for 10 years, repeating an original commercial, for which the production cost were 8,200 dollars. When once asked what his 1,000 experts in the agency do while media show the same ad for 10 years, Reeves replied: "They try to convince the client not to change it" (Weilbacher, 1993, p. 148). Such is the logic behind the use of radical transparency. Once the business model is changed, it should be continually practiced.
- **Association that Adds Value:** An association can "touch" you indirectly, not through the explicit reason for purchase, but by the added value it creates. Therefore the concept of radical transpar-

ency is important because it creates a close relationship with customers, strengthens and builds unforgettable associations that connect the brand with consumers in the long run, and this is the key to success. The association does not have to generate a rational reason for purchase which can easily be verbalized. Rather, it may involve a sense associated with the brand and the experience of its use. The association may be created through a special advertising message or even more, passed through the experience of use or during the use. In any case, such a sentiment, that may be subconscious and difficult to express in words, creates added value for the brand. Let's analyze, for example, a gift from Tiffany. For many people, opening a box of jewelry from Tiffany creates a specific feeling - intense and special. Moreover, wearing jewelry from Tiffany can influence an individual to feel more attractive and more confident. Associations for quality actually change the experience of use and add value to the brand. The associations for Tiffany that add value are generated during a long period of time. Tiffany's vision with which they open the stores every morning has not changed in the past 153 years ... It is absolute commitment to classic beauty. It connects everything that the company creates.

Creating Associations

Associations can be created by anything related with the brand. Of course, the characteristics of the product / service and the benefits to consumers, along with packaging and channels of distributions are central to the brand image. Furthermore, the name, symbol and slogan of the brand are among the most important tools for positioning. Of course, advertising efforts are a direct contributor. However, there is a wide range of approaches to generate associations that need to be considered. Some, such as promotion and publicity, are visible and also significant. Others are more subtle and complex and require an understanding of the signals used by consumers to form perceptions.

- **Identifying and Managing Signals:** Consumers often overlook or do not believe in actual information. Even worse, they lack the interest and ability to process them, so they are never truly exposed to them. Consumers deal with the situation by using signals or indicators - an attribute or association implies another. For example, a health-conscious consumer perhaps is unwilling or unable to "digest" all the nutritional information that a box of cereals has. Instead, the consumer requires signals that enable the creation of perception without an extensive processing of information. Thus, the signal for healthy cereals can be the presence of oats and/or the absence of sugar in its composition. In this case, radical transparency is a key element - in absence of time and/or detailed interest by the consumer, the approach of openness to share important (necessary) information directly influences the purchase decision and gains trust and loyalty to the brand. It is important to know which associations will be created. The signals of high quality were previously discussed. Consumers typically lack the ability to value the actual quality of products / services. As a result, signals of quality become very important. The perceived quality is not the only association influenced by the signals. A set of associations can be found in that role. As much as such associations are different and specific, that much the company's market position relative to competitors will be better.
- **Understanding Unanticipated Signals**: Sometimes negative connotations that cause unanticipated signals for negative associations are created for the features that bare significant benefit for consumers and are highlighted as advantages for the company's product. It is critical to under-

stand the subtle interpretations of the brand associations. For example, when Pringle's appeared in 1968, the chief executives planned to win a dominant market share of at least 30% at the fragmented market for chips in the United States. They had, as they thought, a brilliant product with excellent taste, consistent form and quality, not a single burnt piece, mild salted, packed into a cylindrical canister which will prevent damage and always in stock in stores. All these dimensions area real advantage for consumers. In addition, Pringle's was advertised on national television channels, with distribution throughout the country, thus providing significant economies of scale. But the combination of these elements of the product caused unexpected signs of "artificial", "processed", "made from low quality ingredients" and "tasteless." Most consumers considered that the product did not deliver the value it promoted, although the "blind tests" proved that the Pringle's potato chips was indeed better than that of competitors. But, supermarket consumers are not "blindly" exposed to the products. Something was lacking. In terms of competitors, Pringle's looked inferior. The brand performance was disappointing. The advertising support was immediately withdrawn and the chief executives began to think about scaling the faith of this product. But in short term, negative signals started to disappear. Positive associations began to dominate and demand to grow. It is indeed difficult to discuss tastes. Today Pringle's is one of the leading brands of chips worldwide and the primary associations connected with the brand are the same which were forced during its launching (Clark, 2004). Did the company lack credibility because consumers lacked confidence in their brand? Quite likely. Despite all the efforts there was that "something" in the mind of consumers that created skeptical and disloyal customers. But, imagine if you are ready at any moment of the process of creating value of the product to explain what are you doing and why, even to show. Very often, kind words are not enough. It is necessary to get closer to stakeholders in every aspect –to every employee of the company, through every activity they undertake. That is the essence of radical transparency. This way you can influence the elimination of unanticipated signals, or influence the creation of positive signals of quality that will create associations which lead to a purchase decision and brand loyalty in the long run.

- **The Role of Promotion:** Sales promotion provides a short-term motive for purchase decision. The promotions are often quite effective in influencing sales, but carry the risk of increasing price sensitivity and reduce consumer loyalty. The promotions that simply offer a discount or free of charge products or samples can make the brand look cheaper and negatively affect its image. However, there are ways of practicing promotions that will enhance rather than damage the brand image. The key lies in the fact that when developing promotional activities a component from the brand equity has to be included in order to prevent the promotion to damage the brand equity. In other words, promotional activities through the idea of radical transparency should be used to highlight another advantage of the brand - an element of the brand equity, such as positive association, perceived quality, loyalty or a combination. In contrast, the common practice is to assume that promotions have their own agenda - to stimulate sales, and are frequently selected and evaluated accordingly. But this is a mistaken approach that could disrupt the brand equity in the long run. The role of promotion should be only to "announce" the other elements of brand equity that will be built through the activities of the new business model.
- **Strengthening Associations and Brand Awareness:** One way in which promotions can support the brand equity is through the reinforcement of key associations and brand awareness. Examples are found in the leather luggage tags provided by American Express to its customers with club cards, the velvet pouch from Ralph Lauren for each bought perfume or the Levi's promotional ac-

cessories for each pair of purchased jeans. In each of these cases, promotional activities reinforce associations and awareness of the brand. The offer of accessories that highlights a certain key association is a suggestion for all car dealers, especially in the last period of struggle fueled by price discount. The approach to look at the promotion as a brand itself is very useful. The promotion should develop awareness and associations, and that creates a bond with the brand. The promotion which clearly outlines the crucial elements of the brand equity reinforces its power - it attracts the attention of those who are not regular customers of the brand.

Promotions that enhance loyalty. The promotions can be used as a reward for existing customers; thereby they increase their loyalty to the brand. The promotion should be seen as a way to strengthen relationships with core customers of the brand and also to attract new customers. For example, Visa Gold is convening such promotional activities –the company allows its users to have a free shopping after a certain number of transactions or limit used.

Promotions that enhance perceived quality. Sometimes a relatively inexpensive way to upgrade the image of the brand is to use promotions that enhance strong associations compatible with the high perceived quality of the product. "Quality" promotion, presented in an appropriate manner, suggests a quality product. The brands with quality cannot afford "cheap" promotion. Numerous studies conducted in the United States confirm that the quality of promotion affects the perceived quality of the brand (Gaeth et al, 2009).

- **Added Value**: The promotions that offer bonuses that add value to the product will prevent the damage of the brand equity, rather than those that simply offer a price discount. Thus, BMW instead of engaging in price discounts could include navigation built in every car. Moreover, the premium should have an adequate quality and the brand image will inevitably be improved. So the question implied is: which kind of premium to choose? A study conducted by experts from Walter Thompson compared premiums associated with different product categories (Tuck and Harvey, 2008). Combinations included premiums that are directly related to the product and such which are not. The results showed that the cleaning products premiums associated with the product are much more effective than those that are not linked with the product, while dairy products and shampoos for hair care premiums associated with the product have been less effective than the unrelated premiums. In this case unrelated premiums are attractive because they add an element of extravagance. Thus, it is difficult to predict the nature of the premiums that work best only by following the rule: the connection with the product.
- **The Role of Publicity:** Creating associations and gaining brand recognition is not necessarily expensive. In fact, paid advertising is sometimes extremely difficult and expensive because it lacks credibility and interest for the value. Radical transparency combined with well thought-out publicity can provide both. For example, sometimes it happens an athlete dressed in sportswear from Adidas to appear on the cover of Sports Illustrated, so the managers in charge from Adidas can respond with a letter of gratitude and a symbolic financial prize to the photographer who "caught" the brand image. Then, the company can attract the attention of consumers, using the cover as a motive for a purchase decision. For publicity to be most effective, it needs an event or activity that has a dimension of innovation, particularly if it is unusual. But the company should ensure consistency in its actions in order not to damage the credibility and consumers' confidence in the brand, as well as all other stakeholders.

- **Including the Consumer:** The strongest associations are those that involve the consumer to the extent they intertwine in his / her life. For example, many wineries wine tours worldwide are the heart of their efforts in building the brand equity. Those consumers who perceive the experience of a wine tour or tasting are not only directly exposed to the product, but with reliable information about the background of the story, they enjoy this experience, which will be translated into a range of associations that strengthen the brand equity in the long term.

Maintaining Associations

Often, associations are much harder to maintain than to create, taking into account the marketing program of the company and the effect of external factors. Guidelines on the application of the concept of radical transparency include: being consistent over time; to be consistent with the marketing program and to use the organization to protect the brand equity.

- **Consistency Over Time:** Indeed it is possible, sometimes even necessary to change the associations. But it should be recognized that such a task is often difficult and costly. Changing associations - the repositioning of the brand is often a delicate matter. When existing associations are inconsistent with the repositioning, the problems are born. First, the existing associations could prevent repositioning efforts. Second, they can be significant for a large segment, which could become distant with the repositioning. It is clear that considerable effort is required, which costs dearly, taking into account all operations of the company, in order to overcome previous strong associations that have been generated for years. This certainly involves significant risk. Changing associations is in vain when it allows the associations that were groomed for a long time to fade away by emphasizing the new association. Let's take for example the investment and value of the association for hydration associated with the brand Dove. Let's suppose that the company believes that hydration is not significant and that another association should carry the message of the brand. Association for hydration, a huge asset to this brand will gradually be lost.

According to many, the set of associations is the result of the overall marketing effort behind the brand. Specifically, if the promotion, packaging and quality support both consistent strategy of positioning over time then the brand will be strong. Take, for example, the consistent messages on brands like: Nivea, Apple, BMW, Toyota and many others. Conversely, if the positioning changes, the investments in advertising messages that preceded the change lose its value. Sometimes companies are bothered "to stick" to a strategy of positioning and will endeavor to make a change. However, the brand image is like that of humans –it evolves over the years and the value of consistency for a long time cannot be neglected. Some of the most successful campaigns with enormous budgets last for 10, 20, even 30 years, while some of the least effective change each year. A common mistake is the underestimation of the task of creating a new set of associations. Another mistake is the belief that consumers can be bored from the existing brand position and it is necessary to "refresh" the brand (Balmer, 2001). Regardless, the installed set of brand associations should carefully be maintained over time, and any change should be gradually implemented.

- **Consistency With Elements of the Marketing Program:** One of the threats to the brand equity is the potential change in the marketing program, which isolated has the fullest sense, but analyzed as a whole, can cause a negative impact on the brand associations. The message is simple: you have to be consistent. Changes in price up to a certain level can be tolerated, but the brand image is facing a real problem in dealing with inconsistent marketing mix. This kind of changes cause the need to change the perceptions of consumers and that, ultimately, can confuse and alienated them from the brand.

- **Using the Organization as Protection for the Brand Equity:** There is always a great pressure on managers to generate short-term results, even at the expense of the company's assets, such as the brand equity. Promotional activities and distribution channels can be a specific threat. Short, sharp improvements are often accomplished through visible promotions. Expansion of distribution to increase sales is another method for a dramatic jump in short-term results. However, new channels of distribution, if not carefully selected, can create new associations that are bad enough to weaken key associations which are the basis of the brand equity.
- **Organizational Factors:** The mechanisms used by most companies to protect the brand from damage by short-term pressures include continuous involvement and oversight by top management. With regular involvement and revision of plans, initiatives that are risky for the long-term health of the brand can be marginalized or eliminated. Such supervision opens two problems. First, the top managers are those who push for short-term financial results and attempts to defend the brand are conflicting in terms of demand for results. Ultimately, all other managers and employees in the company would not know which the priority is. The concept of radical transparency in every operation is not an idea for change overnight. It requires commitment on the long run and does not leave a room for occasional maneuvers. Second, supervision is commonly practiced ad hoc and therefore offers no guarantee that all plans and programs will be revised in time. Again, the acceptance and ultimately the success of the new business model require changes in the mindset of senior management who will not allow random decisions and behaviors. One partial solution which is practiced by the world famous brands is to hire a special manager for brand equity (a privilege of the large companies). He / she will have the responsibility to continuously monitor and measure the brand equity in order to detect signals indicating erosion of the brand equity assets and also to approve various programs proposed from other managers, which have the potential to affect the elements of the brand equity (especially associations). The smaller companies remain with the alternative to align well the short-term and long-term goals on behalf of the long-term success. The full acceptance of the model of radical transparency eliminates such problems and costs, because it allows only one type of behavior and actions - open, with principle and justified. Thus, the probability of intervention regarding brand equity threats can be brought down to zero.

STRENGTHENING THE LOYALTY

The customer base loyalty is often the core of the brand equity and the main purpose of the concept of radical transparency. If consumers are indifferent to the brand and actually buy products depending on their characteristics and based on price and availability, with little attention to the brand name, then the brand equity is at a very low level. On the other hand, if consumers continue to buy the brand even if faced with competing products / services with superior features, price and availability, the brand holds considerable value. Brand loyalty is a measure of the consumers' commitment to the brand. It reflects how likely it is a consumer to switch to another brand, especially if the brand has changed in terms of price / features. As the loyalty increases it reduces the vulnerability of the customer base on competing activity. This is an indicator of brand equity which is directly linked to future profits, for brand loyalty translates into direct sales.

- **Levels of Brand Loyalty:** There are several levels of brand loyalty shown in Figure 3. Each level is a different challenge for the management and exploitation of different assets. Not all occur in a specific product category or market. At the bottom of the pyramid are the disloyal customers who are completely indifferent to the brand or any brand is perceived as adequate and the brand name has a negligible role in the purchase decision. Anything that is available can be selected. These consumers can be named as eclectic buyers or price sensitive buyers. The second level includes consumers who are satisfied with the product / service or at least are not dissatisfied. In fact, there is no such a dimension of dissatisfaction sufficient to stimulate change, especially if the change involves additional effort. These consumers may be designated as habitual buyers. This segment is quite vulnerable to competitors that can create tangible benefits from switching. However, it is difficult to win these customers because they have no reason to seek alternatives.

The third level consists of those consumers who are also satisfied, but additionally have switching costs: time, money or performance risk associated with the transfer. Perhaps they have invested in understanding a system that is associated with the particular brand or maybe there is a risk that another brand may not work so well in the circumstances. To attract these customers, competitors need to overcome switching costs by offering incentives for switching or big enough benefit as compensation. This group of consumers is named as loyal consumers with switching costs. The fourth level consists of consumers that really like the brand. Their preference may be due to a specific association, such as the symbol, experience from use or high perceived quality. Consumers in this segment can be called friends of the brand, because there is an emotional connection. And at the top level are the dedicated consumers. They feel proud of the discovery and use of the brand. The brand is very important for them, functionally or as an expression of what they are. Their confidence is at such a level that they recommend the

Figure 3. Pyramid of loyalty

brand to others. The value of dedicated consumers is not only in the income they generate, but rather in the influence of others on the market. An extremely dedicated consumer is the driver of the Harley Davidson that bears the symbol of the Harley-shaped tattoo on his arm; or a Macintosh user who visits their presentations and spends considerable time to persuade his acquaintance that he / she should not buy the dominant Microsoft software. The brand that has a significant group of extremely dedicated and involved consumers can be named as a charismatic brand. Certainly, all brands do not achieve to be charismatic, but when you reach that aura, it really pays off (Aaker, 1991).

These five levels of loyalty are stylized, they do not always appear in pure form, and also, others can be conceptualized. For example, there may be consumers that occur as a combination of some of these levels - consumers who love the brand and have switching costs. Others may have a profile different from the one described above - those who are dissatisfied, but have significant switching costs and continue to buy the brand. However, these five levels provide a sense of the different forms that loyalty can have and how it affects the brand equity.

Measuring Brand Loyalty

To clearly understand the brand loyalty and manage it through the prism of radical transparency, it is useful to discuss the methods of its measurement. When thinking over the several ways to measure the brand loyalty, additional information about its size and shades, as well as a practical tool for its construction and connection to profitability can be provided. One approach is to consider the current behavior. Other approaches are based on the drivers of loyalty, including: switching costs, satisfaction, connection and commitment.

- **Behavioral Measures:** A direct way of determining loyalty, especially within the habitual behavior, is to consider the buying habits. These measures include (Keller, 2008):
  - The rate of purchase: how many of the last 10 purchases are purchases of a specific brand?
  - The rate of repurchase: which percentage of car owners of a particular brand buy again a car from the same brand?
  - Number of purchased brands: which percentage of customers purchases only one, two, three brands?

Consumers' loyalty can vary within different product categories, depending on the number of competing brands and the nature of the product. For example, the percentage of consumers who buy only one brand is more than 80% for products such as spices for cooking, hygiene and beauty products and pet food; and under 40% for: fuel, tires, canned food and plastic products (Alsop, 2009). Data on behavior, although objective, have limitations. It can be difficult and expensive to obtain and provide limited diagnostics for the future. Furthermore, when using data about the behavior, it is difficult to distinguish those individuals who have changed the brand which and are part of a family or an organization. Thus, the apparent switch from IBM to Compaq may be simply because one organization is loyal to IBM, another to Compaq.

- **Switching Costs:** The analysis of switching costs can provide knowledge about the extent to which they represent the basis of loyalty to the brand. If it is too expensive or risky for a company or an ordinary consumer to change the supplier, then the rate of leaving the customer base will be lower. Radical transparency endeavors to achieve proximity to customers and gain their trust in a way that will trigger the creation of switching costs and ensure consumer loyalty. The most obvious type of switching cost is the investment in a particular product or system. Thus, if the default operating system is the one from Misrosoft, then it is hard to make the switch to another operating system. Another type of switching cost is the risk from change. If the current system works, even with the problems, there is always a risk that the new system could be even worse. There is often a reluctance to fix something unless it is demonstrably broken. Operationally, consumers may not be able to recognize the risks associated with the change. They therefore need to be well informed –to know what they are getting and what they may lose if they leave the brand. In fact, the purpose of the application of radical transparency in every operation is to create such a relationship with customers and other stakeholders that will cause the loyalty to rise up to a higher level on the pyramid of loyalty (previously described), which directly translates into stable profitability at the long run. Every company needs to evaluate the advantage of switching costs that it enjoys. History shows that companies that do not follow this maxim are somewhere in history. Moreover, companies need to increase the consumer reliability on the product / service.

- **Measuring Satisfaction:** A key diagnostic for the level of brand loyalty can be provided when measuring the level of satisfaction and, perhaps more importantly, the level of dissatisfaction of consumers. What problems do consumers have? Witch are the sources of irritation? Why do some consumers switch? Which are the reasons for complaints? A key premise at the second and third level of loyalty is the absence of dissatisfaction or it should be kept low enough not to trigger a decision for switching. It is important every measure of consumer satisfaction to be ongoing, representative and sensitive. To ask customers to fill out and return a written statement about their satisfaction with the product / service (or by phone) is neither representative nor sensitive. By 2007, with such measures, the insurance companies were described as excellent, with 95% approval by the customers and at the same time in California a proposal to reduce the amount of insurance rates by 20% was voted (Ind and Bjerke, 2007).

The change in the modus operandi by introducing radical transparency should eliminate all possibilities for "bureaucratization", slowdown and disinformation of all individuals in the story behind the brand.

The business model which includes radical transparency in any activity minimizes the discontent of consumers in several ways:

1. Consumers are informed about all dimensions of the product / service and know what they get for their money;
2. Deviations in product quality are minimized and negative impacts on the perceived quality are avoided;
3. Relationships of proximity and trust which cause positive brand associations are built;
4. After-sales service is optimized;
5. Rapid and precise actions / reactions to consumer demands are taken.

In fact, the philosophy of this concept lies in the attitude that "it is better to prevent than to cure."

- **Brand Connections:** The fourth level of brand loyalty includes connection which creates barriers to entry for new competitors. It is very difficult to compete against a general feeling of liking,

rather than a specific characteristic. The connection is reflected in the additional price that consumers are willing to pay for the product / service and the price advantage that competitors need to generate before they can attract a loyal customer. There are several ways to estimate the premium price that supports the brand, however, the simplest is the metric, i.e. the question: how much the buyer would pay to get his / hers preferred brand? As previously mentioned, the purpose of the concept of radical transparency is to affect the level of customer loyalty, which affects the success of the company, even more - on the one hand it stimulate sales revenues, and on the other, operating costs are minimized, because mistakes are avoided.
- **Commitment:** When there is a significant level of commitment, it usually manifests itself in many ways. One key indicator is the level of interactions and communications relating to the product / service. Another indicator is the level to which the brand is important for the individual in terms of its activities, or personality. High value for both standards is achieved only by those brands that are consistent in the "presentation" of their story (in this case it would be improper to say "selling").

The Strategic Value of Brand Loyalty

Brand loyalty is a strategic asset that, if properly managed, has the potential to provide value in several ways (Aaker, 1991):

- **Reduced Marketing Costs:** The set of consumers who are loyal to the brand reduces the marketing costs. Simply, it is easier to retain than to win new customers. Potential new customers typically lack the motivation to change the brands they are currently buying, so their contact will be expensive, in part because they do not make efforts to detect alternative brands. Even when they are exposed to alternatives, they will require a significant reason to risk to buy and use the product / service from another brand. In contrast, existing customers are usually relatively easy to maintain, if they are not dissatisfied. The familiar is comfortable and safe. Often, with significantly less cost, existing customers can be hold satisfied; the reasons for switching reduced and new customers can be attracted in order to increase brand loyalty. Of course, the greater the loyalty, the easier it is to maintain existing customers.
- **The Loyalty of Existing Customers is a Significant Barrier to Entry for new Competitors:** To enter a market where existing customers are loyal and satisfied with the existing brands and have no reason to switch means that the competitor will require significant additional resources. With this, the profit potential of new entrants decreases. The barrier to be more effective, potential competitors need to know about it, they should not be permitted to "enjoy the delusion" that consumers are vulnerable. In this regard, it is useful to send signals of the strong customer loyalty to potential competitors, such as propaganda and advertising messages that document the customer loyalty, product quality and so on.
- **Trade Leverage:** Brand loyalty provides trade leverage. Strong customer loyalty to brands like Procter & Gamble and Dove, for example, ensures the preferred shelf space because the managers of the supermarkets know that consumers have these products on their lists for purchase. In extreme cases, brand loyalty may dominate the decision when choosing the store. For example, if a supermarket does not have the Budweiser beer in its range, some consumers may not buy from there. The trade leverage is particularly important when introducing new sizes, new variants or new products as brand extensions.

- **Attracting New Customers:** The customer base which consists of satisfied consumers who love the brand can convince potential customers, especially if the purchase is, in a sense, risky. In this case, the purchase would not be an adventure in hopes of making the right choice. Using existing customers to increase sales to new ones rarely occurs automatically, usually it requires an explicit program. The relatively large customer base provides brand image in the form of accepted success, confidence in getting the necessary service and achieve production improvements. In many industries where the aftersales service is necessary and important, such as computers and cars, two of the most common concerns of buyers are: is the company "healthy" and committed enough –will it be available when needed and whether its products are accepted on the market. In this sense, the company Dell aims to expand its customer base by 100,000 new customers each year (including corporate clients from the list of Forbes), retaining existing ones, but motivating potential customers (Berry, 2004). Brand awareness can also be generated through the customer base.
- **Time to Respond to Competitive Threats:** Brand loyalty provides the company time to respond to competitive moves - "breathing space." If a competitor develops a superior product, loyal customers provide the company time to achieve or surpass production improvements. For example, high-tech markets have many customers who are attracted to the latest products at the moment, i.e. there is little brand loyalty. Conversely, loyal, satisfied customers would not demand new products, so would not have found out about the improvements. Furthermore, they would have a weak incentive to switch, even if exposed to the new product. According to some authors, companies with a high level of brand loyalty can afford the luxury of practicing the less risky strategy of followers.

Maintaining and Strengthening Loyalty

In many situations it is difficult to "get rid" of consumers - to get them to switch to competitors' brands. For example, in the period 1995-2005in the US, General Motors, according to nearly all valid standards, had inferior cars. Logically, GM's market share in the US market should have fallen to almost zero, but still it was maintained at around 30% (Temporal, 2009). The argument in favor of this is that consumers, in general, do not like to change. However, some companies very quickly expel their customers. Changing the brand requires considerable effort, especially if the decision involves additional investment and therefore risk. Furthermore, positive opinions about the existing brands (previously developed) only reinforce the primary choice. People actually do not want to admit they were wrong - it is much easier to rationalize the initial decisions. In truth, the customers purchase decisions have a huge inertia. The familiar is comfortable and secure. In addition to this, is the example of The Coca-Cola Company - when they introduced the new variants Coca-Cola Light and Coca-Cola Zero a large part of the enormous mass loyal consumers of the brand rebelled, approving only the good old formula (even though the majority could not spot the difference between Coca-Cola and Pepsi in the blind tests) (Hollis, 2010). Ultimately, it is good to highlight that there are ways to keep consumers (Aaker, 1991):

- **Good Treatment of Customers:** When the director of Maytag (now part of the group Whirlpool), Tom Peters, was asked for "the secret of their success," he replied: "We deliver washing machines that work" (Keller, 2002). The point is that the product or service which operates as expected provides loyalty - the reason for not switching. Consumers need a reason to change the selection. The key to ensure positive experience for customers is training and culture. In Japan the training is intense and detailed, cultural dimensions strict and so, and it is a rarity to meet a consumer with a bad experience. Simply, negative interactions are not allowed. This is the basic prerequisite for building the brand equity through radical transparency successfully.

- **Familiarity with Customers:** Companies that have developed strong organizational culture find a numerous ways to be close to customers. Even top executives, for example, in IBM and Microsoft have contacts with key, even smaller customers and bear responsibility for their satisfaction. The aim is to realize that real people, with real care depend on others alike. The act of encouraging contacts with consumers sends signals to everyone in the company and to all customers that the customer is worth.
- **Measuring / Managing Customer Satisfaction:** Regular surveys of (dis) satisfaction of consumers are especially helpful to understand what consumers think about a particular product or company. Such research should be timely, responsive and understandable to allow the company to understand and learn how consumer satisfaction changes. In order to have an impact, measures of consumers' satisfaction should be integrated in the management of everyday activities in companies. One way to ensure the application of the research results to increase customer satisfaction is to connect them to the system for rewarding employees.
- **Creating Switching Costs:** One way to create switching costs is to discover a solution to a consumers' problem which may include a redefinition of the business. For example, in the United States there has been a long speculation of the distribution of drugs and traders were allowed to set retail prices. Ten years ago, one of the largest retail distributors of drugs across the United States, McKesson, installed computer terminals for each dealer and all computers were networked into an integrated system. Suddenly the records of stocks, orders and prices were very easy to be set and controlled. This caused a significant positive reaction among consumers and they wanted to buy drugs only from pharmacies within this chain. This step has changed the distribution of drugs in the United States (Clark, 2004). Another approach is the direct reward of loyalty. Forming the so-called clubs of privileges and discounts for existing customers is widely spread, regardless of the activity of the company. In any case, the additional benefits for consumers create switching costs.
- **Additional Services:** It often happens the consumers to change their behavior from tolerance to enthusiasm when the company provides some additional, unexpected services. The explanation for a particular procedure, free installation, copy, gift, ornament or just a nice word can leave an incredible impression on consumers. The US chain of department stores Nordstrom is a typical example of enhanced services provided for its customers that the competition cannot even imagine (Aaker, 2011). Companies should not necessarily copy these examples, in contrast, they can find their own original solutions and implement them successfully.
- **Selling the Product to Existing, Rather Than New Customers:** Perhaps the most common mistake that companies make is trying to grow by attracting new customers. In addition, they often prepare aggressive marketing campaigns. The problem is almost always the same – it is difficult to attract new customers. In contrast, it is very profitable to retain existing customers, especially as programs for customers' retention are relatively cheaper. If the company can reduce the migration of customers to other competitors, then growth will naturally appear. New customers will come without additional effort, influenced by existing customers. The customer base is like a container with holes in which you pure liquid - it is better to close the holes than to constantly add more liquid. What is important here is to reduce the rate of dissatisfied customers who are motivated to shift and increase switching costs for those who are satisfied.

- **Customer Retention Analysis:** How to introduce a good program to retain customers? How will it affect the future profitability? The answers to these and similar questions can be found in the systematic analysis of customer retention through sharing information with all stakeholders in the company who are involved in the everyday process of building the brand equity. One approach in this analysis is to assess the relationship between the level of customer retention and profitability (Reichheld, 1990). Taking the current annual level of customer retention as a basis, how much will the marginal profit change if the annual rate of customer retention increases or decreases by 1, 5 or 10 percentage points? Figure 4 illustrates this analysis.

In a certain interval, the dominant concerns are the involved variable costs. Affecting only the variable costs, high leverage will be created associated with the level of customer retention. The annual profit realized due to the change in the rate of retention should be converted in net present value. In fact, the annual profit projected in the future should be discounted at the cost of capital and the rate of retention simultaneously. Thus, with the cost of capital of 15% and rate of retention of 90%, the annual profit of $100 from the next year, this year would be $100 x 0,85 (cost of debt) x 0,90 (retention rate), or $ 76.5. The analysis in US showed that the increase in the retention rate by 5 percentage points causes a dramatic increase in profitability (Reichheld and Sasser, 2009). The rising profits depend on the industry. For example, companies dealing with servicing cars, where the rate of loyalty is low, can reach an estimated 30% increase in profits and companies which develop software - up to 35%. In industries where there is a higher level of loyalty, as commercial banks, the increase in the profitability can go up to 75%.

CONCLUSION

The analysis of the categories of brand equity assets through the prism of radical transparency reveals that the brand equity requires investment and disappears over time if not maintained consistently with the selected business model and the company's values.

Brand loyalty is the first element of the brand equity model. It is relatively expensive for any business to get new customers and cheaper to retain existing ones. In fact, in many markets, consumers have

Figure 4. The customer retention analysis

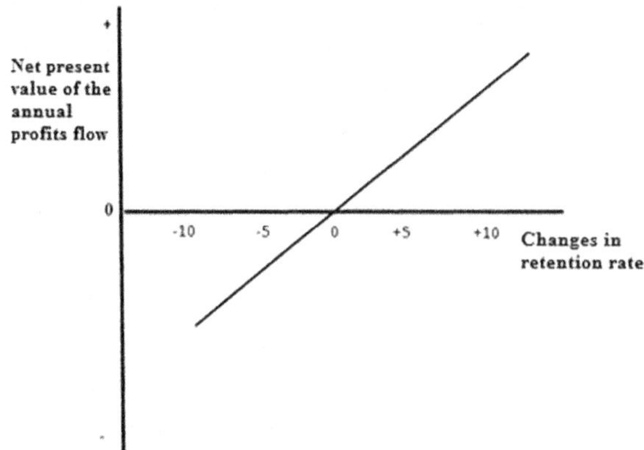

certain inertia, even if there are low switching costs. If we add the approach of radical transparency to this, then the benefits for the company can be simply synthesized into one big advantage - satisfied and loyal customers who generate stable revenues and profits for the company in the long term. Thus, the installed customer's base is an investment from the past that should be maintained and increased. Consumer loyalty reduces the company's vulnerability to competitors' actions. Also, the higher brand loyalty means higher trade leverage.

Brand awareness. People often buy a familiar brand because it feels comfortable and secure. In addition goes the assumption that the brand which is known is reliable and offers reasonable quality, because good brands are created with the intention to last for long. Radical transparency has a major impact on stimulating brand awareness as a factor that is particularly important in the sense that the brand must first enter into the considerations set–it should be one of the brands that are assessed and taken into account in the purchase decision. If the company is here for consumers and other stakeholders to provide additional information, services or simply cares about their needs, then brand awareness quickly spreads in width - among many consumers, as well as in depth - at the higher level of brand awareness, striving to reach the level of "top of mind." This, again, strengthens the company's position in the market in the long term.

Perceived quality. The brand connects to a perception of quality in general, not necessarily based on knowledge and understanding of the detailed specifications. However, the company should be ready and open for cooperation with all interested parties and provide positive feedback whenever necessary. Thus enhances the perceived quality of the brand and enhances the trust. The perception of quality gets different forms in different industries. Perceived quality directly affects the purchase decision and brand loyalty, especially when the customer is not able or motivated to do a detailed analysis, but relies on his/her current "feeling" about the brand. Perceived quality also supports premium price and may be the basis for brand expansion.

Set of associations. The most sophisticated factor affecting the value of brand is often associated with specific brand associations. The strong association can be the basis for brand expansion. If the brand is well positioned in relation to a key attribute of the product / service in the industry, then competitors can hardly attack. If they attempt a frontal assault, claiming superiority in this dimension, they will have a problem with credibility. Competitors are forced to find another, perhaps inferior basis for competition. Thus, associations can be a barrier for competitors. The application of radical transparency in the overall operation of the company enables the creation of a special set of brand associations that create long-lasting relationships with consumers, mixed with positive emotional mix that seals the success in the long term.

It is impossible to use one universal formula - model for radical transparency suitable for any company, because companies are too different, even within the same industry, and even more in different sectors. However, we can synthesize the so-called strategic factors of brand equity that determine the relationships within and around the brand. A key premise for the maximization of the positive effects of these factors is the support of senior management and nurturing an approach of continuous improvement. The more factors are implemented, the greater the benefits for the company.

REFERENCES

Aaker, D. (1991). *Managing Brand Equity*. The Free Press.

Aaker, D. (2001). *Developing Business Strategies*. HBS Press.

Aaker, D. (2011). *Brand Relevance: Making Competitors Irrelevant*. John Wiley and Sons.

Aaker, D., & Keller, K. (2008). Consumer Evaluations of Brand Extensions. *Journal of Marketing*, *34*, 2–22.

Aaker, D., & McLoughlin, D. (2010). *Strategic Market Management: Global Perspectives* (9th ed.). John Wiley and Sons.

Adamson, A., & Sorrell, M. (2007). *Brand Simple: How the Best Brands Keep it Simple and Succeed*. Macmillan.

Akshay, R., & Monroe, K. (2008). The Effect of Price, Brand Name and Store Name on Buyers' Perceptions of Product Quality: An Integrative Review. *JMR, Journal of Marketing Research*, *26*, 351–357.

Alba, J., & Chattopadhyay, A. (2006). Salience Effects in Brand Recall. *JMR, Journal of Marketing Research*, *107*, 363–369.

Alsop, R. (2009, February 23). Brand Loyalty Is Rarely Blind Loyalty. *The Wall Street Journal*, p. 48.

Axelrod, J., & Wybenga, H. (1995). Perceptions That Motivate Purchase. *Journal of Advertising Research*, *110*, 27–31.

Balmer, J. (2001). The three virtues and seven deadly sins of corporate brand management. *Journal of General Management*, *27*(1), 1–17. doi:10.1177/030630700102700101

Balmer, J., & Greyser, S. (2003). *Revealing the corporation: perspectives on identity, image, reputation*. Routledge. doi:10.4324/9780203422786

Bartos, R. (1996). Ernest Dichter: Motive Interpreter. *Journal of Advertising Research*, *12*, 15–20.

Berry, J. (2004). *Tangible Strategies for Intangible Assets*. McGraw-Hill.

Bogart, L., & Lehman, C. (2009). What Makes a Brand Name Familiar. *JMR, Journal of Marketing Research*, *33*, 17–22.

Buzzell, R., & Gale, B. (1987). *The PIMS Principles*. The Free Press.

Clark, K. (2004). *Brandscendence: Three Essential Elements of Enduring Brands*. Dearborn Trade Publication.

Clifton, R., & Simmons, J. (2004). Brands and Branding. *The Economist*, pp. 256-272.

Collins, J., & Porras, J. (1994). *Built to Last*. Harper Business.

Doyle, P., & Stern, P. (2009). *Marketing management and strategy*. Pearson Publishing.

Enrico, R. (2009). *The Other Guy Blinked*. Bantam Books.

Gaeth, G., Levin, I., Chakraborty, G., & Levin, A. (2009). *Consumer Evaluation of Multi-Product Bundles: An Information Integration Analysis*. Working Paper, The University of Iowa.

Garvin, D. (1984). Product Quality: An Important Strategic Weapon. *Business Horizons*, *27*(3), 31–44. doi:10.1016/0007-6813(84)90024-7

Han, M., & Terpstra, V. (1989). Country of Origin Effects for Uninational and Binational Products. *Journal of International Business Studies*, *17*, 242.

Hollis, N. (2010). *The Global Brand: How to Create and Develop Lasting Brand Value in the World Market*. Macmillan.

Ind, N., & Bjerke, R. (2007). *Branding Governance: A Participatory Approach to the Brand Building Process*. John Wiley & Sons.

Jacobson, R., & Aaker, D. (1997). The Strategic Role of Product Quality. *Journal of Marketing*, *63*, 31–44.

Kapferer, J. N. (2008). *The New Strategic Brand Management: Creating and Sustaining Brand Equity Long Term* (4th ed.). Kogan Page.

Keller, K. (2000). *Building and managing corporate brand equity*. Oxford University Press.

Keller, K. (2007). *Strategic Brand Management*. Pearson Education.

Keller, K. (2008). *Strategic Brand Management: Building Measuring, and Managing Brand Equity*. Prentice-Hall.

Kirmani, A., & Wright, P. (2009). Money Talks: Perceived Advertising Expense and Expected Product Quality. *The Journal of Consumer Research*, *16*(3), 344–353. doi:10.1086/209220

Knapp, D., & Hart, C. (2000). *The Brand Mindset: Five Essential Strategies for Building Brand Advantage throughout Your Company*. McGraw-Hill.

Leavitt, H. (1957). A Note on Some Experimental Findings about the Meaning of Price. *The Journal of Business*, *27*(3), 205–210. doi:10.1086/294039

McKenna, R. (1994). *The Regis Touch*. Addison-Wesley.

Miller, A., & Tsiantar, D. (1998, April 14). Psyching Out Consumers. *Newsweek*, 46-47.

Murray, T. (1996, November 10). The Wind at Nike's Back. *Adwa's Marketing Week*, pp. 28-31.

Papadopoulos, H., & Avlonitis, G. (2002). *Does County Of Origin Matter?* Working paper. Marketing Science Institute.

Plummer, J. (1998). How Personality Makes a Difference. *Journal of Advertising Research*, *24*, 27–31.

Randall, G. (2006). *Branding: a practical guide to planning your strategy*. Kogan Page Ltd.

Reichheld, F. (1996). *The Loyalty Effect*. Harvard Business School Press.

Reichheld, F., & Sasser, E. (2009). Zero Defections: Quality Comes to Services. *Harvard Business Review*, *64*, 105–111. PMID:10107082

Reynolds, T., & Gutman, J. (1994). Advertising Is Image Management. *Journal of Advertising Research*, *25*, 29–37.

Ryan, M. (2008). *Assessment: The First Step in Image Management*. Tokyo Business Today.

Temporal, P. (2009). *Advanced Brand Management: Managing Brands in a Changing World*. John Wiley & Sons.

Thomas, A. (2007). *Strategies for Branding Success*. eBookIt.com.

Tuck, R., & Harvey, W. (2008). *Do Promotions Undermine the Brand?*. ADMAP.

Ulrich, D., & Smallwood, N. (2007). *Leadership Brand: Developing Customer-Focused Leaders to Drive Performance and Build Lasting Value*. Harvard Business School Press.

Urban, G., Johnson, P., & Hauser, J. (1994). Testing Competitive Market Structures. *Marketing Science*, *3*(2), 83–112. doi:10.1287/mksc.3.2.83

Weilbacher, W. (1993). *Brand Marketing: Building Winning Brand Strategies That Deliver Value and Customer Satisfaction*. NTC Business Books.

Wilson, R., & Gilligan, C. (2005). *Strategic Marketing Management: planning, implementation and control* (3rd ed.). Elsevier Butterworth-Heinemann.

Wong, L., Sim, D. F., & Siu Hui, L. T. (2006). *Brand Think: a guide to branding*. Trafford Publishing.

Wurster, T. (1995). *The Leading Brands: 1925-1995*. BCG Perspectives.

Chapter 3
Radical Transparency and Brand Equity as Key Factors for Successful Business Strategy

ABSTRACT

This chapter analyzes the phenomenon of branding and the related process of creating new value, and thus a sustainable competitive advantage through recognition of the concept of radical transparency. The brand equity is a common denominator of all tangible and intangible resources of the company, the amount of its abilities, of any activity indicating a slightly higher value, any attempt to be better and to achieve more. Therefore, in addition the brand equity is elaborated as a source of value for the business. This chapter examines the role of brand equity in providing greater market share, creating entry barriers for new competitors, achieving production and market expansion, providing a price premium, attracting quality workforce, ensuring consumers loyalty and stimulating innovation. For the brand equity to truly provide value it should be more than the company's image or position of the product – the brand should be a unifying force across the company, providing the business with direction and purpose.

INTRODUCTION

This chapter analyzes the phenomenon of branding and the related process of creating new value, and thus a sustainable competitive advantage through recognition of the concept of radical transparency. The brand equity is a common denominator of all tangible and intangible resources of the company, the amount of its abilities, of any activity indicating a slightly higher value, any attempt to be better and to achieve more. Therefore, in addition the brand equity is elaborated as a source of value for the business. Here we examine the role of brand equity in providing greater market share, creating entry barriers for new competitors, achieving production and market expansion, providing a price premium, attracting quality workforce, ensuring consumers loyalty and stimulating innovation. For the brand equity to truly provide value it should be more than the company's image or position of the product – the brand should be a unifying force across the company, providing the business with direction and purpose.

DOI: 10.4018/978-1-5225-2417-5.ch003

Brand strategy is more than marketing. Traditionally, the brand is seen as a tool to achieve marketing goals such as increase in the market share or increased repurchase. Consequently, branding is primarily treated as a marketing discipline. Of course, the brand can play these roles, but the brand strategy is more than marketing. Compiling a successful brand equity and functional brand strategy should ensure that all relevant business activities support the position of the brand and that they are carried out openly, transparently and consistently.

Brand strategy is more than communication. To communicate means "to impart information or ideas."[1]In business, it is the well-known, old-fashioned art of persuasion. This logic applies for brands and often with great success. These are the basics of branding: building an image that resonates with consumers putting in their mind what they should buy. However, the brand strategy is more than a plan for the brand image, building a strong brand requires more than communication. The brand strategy ensures that what the company says is what the company does. This is, precisely, the logic of the new business model.

Brand strategy is more than effectiveness and efficiency. The imperative to ensure profit growth led to an increase in operational efficiency in all areas of business. Of course, any well managed business will force efficiency in all areas of its operations: the elimination of losses is essential to maintain competitiveness, and when times are tough, it may be the only way "to survive." However, the efficiency - to do something good, is not itself a strategy.

Brand strategy is more than effectiveness. Achieving an increase in some specific indicators (measures of the success of the brand) may be an indicator that the strategy is on track, but it is not the primary strategic objective of the business. For example, a promotional campaign can lead to a rise in sales, but also can undermine the long-term competitive position of the company. The brand strategy must place a credible difference over competitors. Such competitive difference (advantage) must be sustainable in the long term. The use of radical transparency provides this advantage. Efficiency and effectiveness, of course, are essential, but they are one of the most useful indicators of short-term performance of companies and rarely indicate something more about the long-term trends. With some military terminology and metaphor, efficiency is about how to win the battle and brand strategy with radical transparency about how to win the war.

Brand strategy is more than positioning. It is always important to gain a sustainable competitive advantage over competitors. This question is often interpreted as positioning: Art in finding "a place in the minds of consumers." The positioning means clearly differentiating the brand from those of the competitors. This can, certainly, easier and better be achieved with a transparent and consistent performance - every day, with each activity. The positioning is a useful way of thinking about branding, so much that positioning and branding have become almost synonymous with each other. Usually, when discussing branding, the focus is on the points of difference – the competitive advantage. However, branding is more than creating a single position.

Brand strategy is business strategy. Each brand strategy should answer the following four questions (Miller and Muir, 2004): 1. Who are the customers? 2. Which products / services are offered? 3. How will it perform against competitors? 4. Which resources and capabilities are required? For example, the general articulation of the brand strategy of Southwest Airlines can be stated as something like this: "We will offer flights to short haul, without waiting, with lower prices for customers who want fast, affordable and acceptable air transport. Our highly motivated employees enable faster, cheaper and better service than competitors, working as a highly effective team with a sense of fun." In this sense, the brand equity has become a principle for organizing the business – the radical transparency "lubricates" the company's efforts behind the company's offer (Ind, 2007). The role of brand strategy is to create value for the business by bringing together all the activities with the offer for the consumers. With a clear, strong brand strategy, the company can offer products and services in a number of different sectors. Some of these decisions can be very difficult. Sometimes, they include 'no' to the possibility of short-term earnings. But as Michael Porter reminds us: "The essence of strategy is choosing what not to do" (Porter, 1996, p.181).

PRESENTING THE BRAND EQUITY AS A SOURCE OF VALUE FOR THE BUSINESS

The brand equity can create value for the business in different ways - from maintaining and increasing market share, to attracting and retaining talented employees. There are several potential sources of business value that can be provided by strong brands (Miller and Muir, 2004):

- Brand equity provides market share. The strength of the brand is correlated with the market share, and this is closely linked to profitability. Furthermore, brands allow self-reinforcing of the market share.
- Brand equity creates barriers to entry for competitors. The brands may have a defensive role: the costs related to the establishment of a strong brand in a particular industry can often deter potential competitors which want to enter the market.
- Brand equity can expand the business into new areas. Brands provide opportunities for business growth through brand extensions. This can open up access to new sources of revenue or to assist the business in response to market changes.
- Brand equity can provide entry into new markets. Foreign markets can be an important source of potential revenue for strong brands, ensuring proper balance between global consistency and local sensitivity.
- Brand equity provides lower price elasticity. Brands can support the price the buyer is willing to pay – a strong brand can increase the price of the product / service with no significant loss in sales volume.
- Brand equity can make a price premium. Brands can enable companies to charge a premium; sometimes customers want to pay more - a higher price creates a reassuring sense of superior quality.
- Brand equity can deal with market disruption. Brands can help companies keep their performance in time of uncertainty, if they accept a flexible and open approach to the future.
- Brand equity can attract and retain talent. The brands create competitive advantage by attracting and retaining talented employees. This can also reduce the significant costs associated with recruitment and re-recruitment.

- Brand equity is a source of trust. Brands can foster trust between stakeholders - ultimately it is the source of real value to a company. True confidence comes from having a clear brand strategy and its continuous compliance over time.
- Brand equity stimulates innovation. Brands can create new ideas for products and services, providing the research and development activities of the company with an integrated market orientation.

In addition, each of these potential sources of value to the business is discussed in more details and with case studies.

THE BRAND EQUITY ENSURES MARKET SHARE

Building and maintaining market share is the goal of any business. There is a direct relationship between market share and profitability. Various researches show that, on average, brands with a market share of 40% generate three times higher return on investment from brands with a market share of only 10%, Figure 1 (Miller and Muir, 2004). Building and maintaining the market share, and thus profit is the main reason for the existence of any brand. Strong brands mean high profits. Moreover, applying radical transparency, stability and profitability is maintained in the long term.

Defining market share. For marketers, the market is defined as all potential buyers for a particular product / service. Then, the market share of a brand is that part of the total sales of a particular product / service which represents product sales from the particular brand. Of course, every business wants to sell as much as possible products to as many people as possible: it is tempting "to cast the net wide." However, market definition is a key strategic issue and sometimes it involves placing some clear boundaries.

The strength of the brand is correlated with the market share. The acquisition of market share and its retention is often seen as the "raison d'être" branding. From the perspective of most marketers, the business is a battle for territory on the market and it seems that most successful businesses are the ones

Figure 1. The relationship between market share and profitability

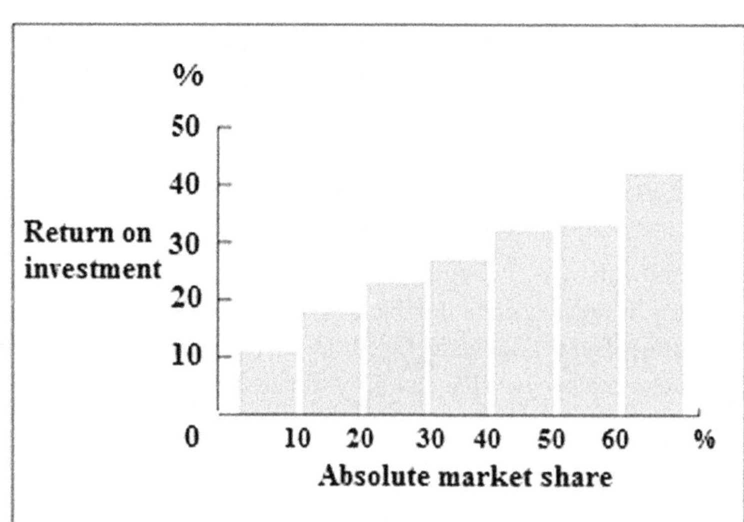

with the strongest brands. The brief overview of the correlations between measures of the strength of the brands and their market share confirms that strong brands really determine market share, Table 1 (Miller and Muir, 2004).

The Role of Brand Equity to Build Market Share: The Case of Intel

In 1989, when Intel set a goal to build a strong brand for the end user, the company faced considerable skepticism. The industry for semiconductor chips was treated as a commodity market for industrial consumption. Competition was based on cost and performance. Most people who bought computers do not even know that there is a chip inside. Since the birth of the industry of personal computers in the late 1970s, the market was dominated by computer sellers, such as IBM, Apple and Compaq, and software publishers, such as Microsoft. The idea to communicate with customers for a small part of the computer was radical. Many doubted the need for such access. After the campaign, Intel was already the market leader, with an impressive 56% market share. Despite its lead, Intel could not take its competitive position "for granted" - a strong brand was needed that would separate Intel from the whole package. In 1991, Intel began their landmark program "Intel Inside" worldwide, and by 2001, the company invested around 5.5 billion US dollars in it. Available to all computer manufacturers, the program offered a cooperative share of the costs of the advertising which included the brand Intel. This was widely accepted, with around 2,000 partners; nearly 90% of all computers in 2001 had the "Intel Inside" logo. The decline in prices of personal computers in the mid-1990s further stirred the demand and the consumer base expanded into the mainstream market. Many first-time computer buyers considered the respected Intel brand as a guarantee of quality. This, combined with the long-standing policy of low margin, in order to maintain the "market price", was effective enough to provide the dominant market share: in 2001, the market share of Intel was 86% (Beverland, 2009).

Market Share Can Become Self-Reinforcing

Brands with high market share are often more popular because they are popular. Strong brands are signaling low risk and high acceptance: buyers feel a sense of safety in numbers. In the case of Intel, the strong market position of the brand became self-reinforcing. When the mainstream PC market was still young consumers were seeking guidance and reliability. In other words, everyone wanted a PC with a

Table 1. Correlation between measures of brand strength and market share

Industry	Coefficient
Airline	0,911
Banking	0,937
Brewery	0,958
Pet food	0,852
Hotels	0,758
Newsletters	0,939
Sports equipment	0,872

processor from Intel, because everyone else had one. This effect can be seen in many industries, even in those in which it can be assumed that the decision-making process is very rational, such as within the pharmaceutical brands. Studies on prescription practices of doctors showed that the market share has a significant impact on the choice of brand (Wreden, 2005). Each brand that has achieved a leading market share may consider its position consolidated in this way, intensifying the challenge for the smaller brands.

THE BRAND EQUITY CREATES ENTRY BARRIERS FOR NEW COMPETITORS

If a business generates a healthy profit in a particular industry, usually new companies would like to enter the market and take advantage of the high profit margins. Over time, this usually lowers the profitability of all companies in the industry, but also may erode the market share of "old players." The defense against new competitors is a strategic priority for businesses growth. The investment in the brand equity can be part of a strategy for creating barriers to entry for potential competitors. The specific characteristics of the industry often prevent new competitors to freely enter the market. For example, the minimum level of production that will be effective can be higher than the level of sales the new participant expects. Strong brands can act as an effective barrier to entry for potential competitors. This can function in two ways.

1. **Brand Advertising is a Sunk Cos:** It is cheap to produce soap, using low technology. So why there are no new competitors to appear in the market for soaps for a longer period of time? Current brands spend a lot on advertising, just in order to create a barrier to entry for new competitors. If a new brand of soap is eager to attract consumers, it would need to spend at least as much as existing brands spend. In the UK, the cost of advertising when launching a new brand for soaps is estimated at 10 million British pounds, and this is considered a sufficient amount to prevent entry of new competitors (Randall, 2006). Advertising is known as a sunk cost. For example, if you choose to pay 2 euro to go to the movies, you probably will not get your money back if you do not like the movie. If the price of the tickets is very high, let's say 20 euro, you are very unlikely to go, unless you are very sure that you will enjoy it. Similarly, if a company has to spend a large amount on advertising in order to enter the market, it is unlikely to do so unless it is very certain that it will succeed.

An additional effect further strengthens the entry barriers. New competitors, of course, want to compensate for the cost of entry. But the presence of a new player in the market usually results in pressure for lowering the price. Existing competitors, freed from the need to recover the costs of entry, will be able to reduce the cost without significant loss of margin - they will probably win every price war.

2. **The Brand as an Exclusive Position:** There is another way that brand equity can create barriers to entry. In some industries, one brand is so dominant that consumers use the brand name when referring the product or service. In these cases, it is really very difficult for the potential competitors to make any impact. This can clearly be seen within those companies that have developed brands of products which are actually part of another product for final consumption, such as for example: Dolby, Intel, Nutra Sweet, Teflon and Lycra (Post and Post, 2007). This "branding ingredient" has a double effect: it stimulates the demand for "the brand steward" and therefore grows sales volume, while simultaneously extrudes the potential entry of new competitors.

THE BRAND EQUITY PROVIDES PRODUCTS AND MARKET EXPANSION

The brand which has established itself in one business area can be extended to other, by launching new products / services under the same brand. Brand extensions can create value for the business in several ways: through access to new sources of income by revitalizing the brand in the eyes of consumers or helping the business to respond to significant changes in the market (Davis et al, 2002).

- **Brand Extensions Maintain the Brand Contemporary:** Established brands face a particular challenge. If the brand is not maintained over time, then it risks losing its relevance and importance. On the other hand, if the brand is not consistent if it moves too far and too fast, if the company does not do what it proclaims, then it risks to damage the relationship of the brand with the existing customers. Determining the balance between change and consistency is an ongoing problem for all existing brands and the launch of the brand expansion is one way to address this issue. The corporate brand of the company Pond, a company for products for skin care, maintains this balance for more than 150 years. As one of the oldest brands for beauty products in the world, Pond had to adapt to changing attitudes of women towards beauty, while "keeping" the brand firmly based on deeply rooted values. Pond uses the brand extensions to keep the brand "fresh" (Schmitt and Simonsen, 2009).
- **The Expansion of the Brand can Help the Business to Respond to Market Changes:** If there are significant changes in the market, brand extensions can, literally, save the business. Several interesting lessons can be learned from the responses to the expansion of digital technologies in the 1990s from Encyclopedia Britanica. The neglect of the threat from the CD-ROM and Internet technology in the 1990s from the top management of the encyclopedia Britanica is a textbook example. In its 230-year history the company had not experienced any significant changes in the market, so they were not ready for rapid, extensive changes that have come with the emergence of the digital technology. The sale of the encyclopedia in North America fell from 117,000 units in 1990 to 51,000 in 1994. The appropriate response to this change was a huge challenge, and the company relied on its greatest asset: its well-known brand. Many brand extensions held the business alive, including CD-ROM, DVD and numerous online alternatives (Kapferer, 2008).
- **Brand Extensions Can Enable the Business to Access New Sources of Revenue:** Companies like Unilever and Procter & Gamble have high rates of introduction of new products, using innovation in order to stimulate the consumption of their products. Traditionally, new products were launched with a new brand, but marketing expenses for new products significantly increased, and these companies have decided on a new strategy: concentrated advertising of the renowned corporate brand and launching new products as an extension of an existing brand. Even top professional sports clubs have determined that the brand extensions are a source of additional income (Draper, 2002).
- **The Strength of the Brand Can Sometimes Be an Obstacle for Brand Expansion:** In 1995 Procter & Gamble entered in the cosmetics and skin care market, wanting to announce a turnaround planned for 2001. The response of consumers was not even close to the expected: the company planned 7% market share in the US, and achieved barely 3%. This extension of the brand failed because it was based on the assumption that a strong brand in one business can guarantee success in another (Hadley, 2002).

- **Brand Extensions Can Damage the Basic Position of the Brand:** The same way that brand extensions can be used to "refresh" the brand, there is a risk that they may somehow damage the brand. Businesses working with premium brands that have low sales volume can attempt to profit from the strength of the brand by launching the brand extensions in the lower price category. This is particularly attractive to carmakers like BMW and Mercedes, who are always trying to use their prestigious brands for mainstream audiences. However, the risk of this approach is that it can erode the premium value inherent in the core of the brand. For example, in the 1970s Porsche had identified the need to enter the market of less expensive cars, and in 1977 it launched Porsche 924. All Porsche models were created with an authentic commitment to pure sports car performance and as a result of high quality the brand received its strength. As a model with lower costs (and price), Porsche 924 could not meet the recognized standards. For the passionate lovers of these cars it seemed like the beginning of the ending for the Porsche legend has started. To this, Porsche responded by increasing the quality and price of 924 and until today the official position of the company is that the lowest level of market entry for Porsche is a used Porsche (Knapp and Hart, 2000).
- **Strong, Well-Defined Brands Easily Enter New Markets:** The expansion of the brand into new markets has become the main way in which businesses maintain the growth rate. Significant market shares worldwide are achieved by a small number of brands, mostly of American origin. The release of restrictions in international trade, together with the improved transport logistics and distribution, allow companies to create value by extending their brands abroad. The most frequently mentioned brand on this issue is Coca-Cola, whose global ambitions began to be seriously pursued by the engagement of US forces in World War II. Foreseeing this moment, the company announced that every soldier will be able to buy a Coca-Cola drink for 5 cents anywhere in the world, regardless of the cost. The US government helped the company to build dozens of factories abroad, believing that Coca-Cola drinks would be good for the morale of the soldiers. This is an excellent example of entrepreneurial response from the American business to the World War II. Coca-Cola enjoyed a postwar boom in growth, both at home and abroad (Hill et al, 2001).
- **International Brands are Fairly New:** Thirty years ago, except for occasional ventures abroad, most companies were generally concentrated within national borders. Even Coca-Cola realized more than two thirds of its sales in the United States until the mid-1980s. Far from aggressive expansion to new geographical markets, most brands were preoccupied with the domestic market. Starting from 1985, until recently, businesses have been criticized by observers and experts for their "international myopia": "The resources and efforts devoted to foreign markets are weak and lack the depth ... The reluctance to take serious global management is not just pain for these companies, it also destroys the economy of the country as a whole "(Jatusriptiak and Kotler, 1985, p. 263).The global march of major US consumer brands emerged later, which peaked in the mid-1990s. Those brands which have the greatest global impact - Philip Morris, Coca-Cola, Levis, Budweiser, McDonalds etc. have built their success on the basis of carefully defined strategy.
- **The Country of Origin Plays a Major Role:** Sir Martin Sorrell said, "There is no globalization, there is only Americanization" (Clifton and Simmons, 2004, p. 258). There are comments according to which the success of major American brands is due to their American origin (Riensenbeck and Freeling, 1991). Many major US brands rely on the attractiveness of Americana - although

this seems a shaky strategy, especially with the growing resentment toward the United States in many parts of the international market. Many brands from other countries also use their country of origin. The apparel brand Burberry, with its distinctive plaid landmark, achieved worldwide success, but remains close to its British heritage. Sales reacted well to this approach - there were 711.7 million US dollars in the US in 2011, up from 65.9 million in 2001 (Gregory, 2004). The potential advantage that the country of origin can provide for the brand is so high that many brands "cheat" around the origin. But this can provide only short-term success. It is important to be fair to consumers, wherever they are. For the brand that tries to enter the markets in new countries, the decision on the role of country of origin is crucial. And in this case it should be transparent.

- **The Choice: Local Versus Global:** In the late 1990s, the global expansion of the big brands seemed to be postponed. Local consumers increasingly respected cultural differences and sensibilities. Approaches to international branding become cyclical. At one time, the brand can be managed centrally, and then the focus of activities is transferred with empowerment to the local team in order to animate and attract local customers. Over time, the choice will again return to the first alternative. This model can be seen within many global brands. It is not some kind of endless hesitation, on the contrary, it is an attempt to find a balanced strategy between two conflicting factors: factors for local branding - the variety of customers and markets and factors of global branding - consumer are mobile, media is globalized, and the Internet and the euro has further reduced borders; consumers expect consistency of their brands; the global branding requires a centralized team to take control, thus ensure quality and economies of scale (Harris and De Chernatony, 2001).

THE BRAND EQUITY PROVIDES LOWER PRICE ELASTICITY AND PRICE PREMIUM

The strong brand is able to increase the price of the product / service without big changes in the sales volume. This is known in economics as the price elasticity - the amount by which the quantity will change as a result of the change in price. The brand has low price elasticity if a slight increase in price leads to a slight decline in sales. Of course, all companies would like to work in an environment where price elasticity is low, with price increases, without a significant loss in sales volume - this is obviously good for any business. The brand can help in creating lower price elasticity.[2]

- **Brand Strategy is More Than Volume:** The focus of many brand strategies is the scope. These are brands that have the role of "competing empires" engaged in conquest and defense of market territory. Frequent words such as "acquisitions" and "retention" reflect the stated conclusion, although very often one essential element is overlooked: the price. As Simon Broadbent stated: "The real benefit from branding is not creating volume, but supporting the price the buyer is willing to pay" (Broadbent, 1994, p. 1235). We often believe that the main goal of brand strategy is to increase sales volume. Various marketing activities are constantly being devised in order to maintain / increase the market share. This looks like a relic of honorary expansionist years of marketing, when the main challenge was to win new customers. In fact, branding is the process of adding value, enabling companies to maintain the price level.

- **Brand Campaigns May Reduce the Price Elasticity:** The investments in brand communications can reduce the sensitivity consumers have to changes in the price. A study of campaign by Lurpack, a British company that produces butter, clearly shows the foregoing. The company applies econometric model to estimate the effects of price changes on sales volume or price elasticity, Figure 2. The campaign lasted in the period 2007-2009. The reduction of price elasticity is evident (Miller and Muir, 2004).
- **Some Industries Have Higher Price Elasticity:** How consumers will react to changes in the price depends on the type of goods in question. This reflects an old idea in economics, elasticity is a function of necessity, and it is clearly proven today. If price elasticity is largely determined by factors specific to the industry, then which role can the brand have? Brands create intangible differences between the products. Many studies have been conducted to show that strong brands have lower price elasticity. For example, an econometric study of the British company that produces PG Tips tea showed that a 1% increase in the price of PG Tips tea over competitors leads to a decline in the market share by 0.4 points. The effect of a similar increase in the price of rivals is much higher: 1% increase in the price of Tetley tea caused a drop in the market share by 1.4 points (Cooper et al, 1999). According to economic theory, the key to explaining this phenomenon is the differentiation. If there are many substitutes for a product, the price elasticity is high. If there are no other products which are same or very similar, then the elasticity is lower. The low price elasticity of PG Tips is explained by the fact that consumers prefer this brand and consider it irreplaceable. In tests with branded products, PG Tips was overwhelmingly elected (though in blind tests no one could tell the difference). However, in the mind of the British consumer, nothing is alike a cup of PG Tips (Wilson and Gilligan, 2005).

Ultimately, what matters is the product. Branding can create differentiation where it little exists, and thus achieve lower price elasticity. However, the impact on price only through branding may not be a foolproof strategy; ultimately, the product is the one that counts. When in 1999, Coca-Cola calculated

Figure 2. The brand campaign reduces the price elasticity

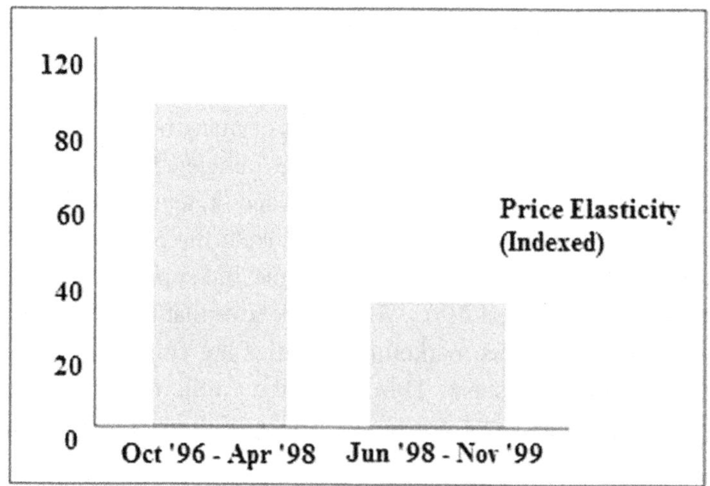

that the price elasticity is low enough to withstand a 5% rise in price; it did not foresee the withdrawal of 17 million consumers in Europe. The company estimated that with a slightly lower volume at a higher price they will achieve an increase in revenues, but in this case, price increases led to a far greater decline in sales volume than expected (Gelder, 2005). This case illustrates a central point in the discussion for the brand: the product is a king. As Bullmore reminds: "You cannot produce a successful brand without firstly producing a good product" (Bullmore, 2000). The surest way to achieve brand differentiation is product innovation. The successful innovation "pulls out" the product from the range of possible substitutes, which reduces the price elasticity - because consumers cannot easily switch to another alternative, they become less sensitive to price changes. Brands like Gillette use product innovation in order to neutralize competitors - for many of its customers; an alternative for the Gillette products is beard. Gillette extensively tested the price elasticity of its Mach 3 razor prior to its launch in 1993 and found out that elasticity was so low that they were able to increase the price up to 35% more than that of its predecessor, Sensor (Checco, 2005). But they simply remained faithful to their customers, thus ensuring long-term success.

- **Strong Brands Have Lower Price Elasticity:** The levels of price elasticity change according to how strong the brand is. For example, a study of prices of consumer goods in the United States shows that customers of brands with high market shares are far less sensitive to changes in the price then consumers of smaller brands (Mulhern and Williams, 1998). This is a kind of effect of "double jeopardy": small brands are punished not only with a smaller market share, but with higher price elasticity.
- **Brands Can Sometimes "Fool" Price Elasticity:** The reaction of people to changes in prices is not always rational and linear, so companies can use it. A series of gradual increase in prices will have a less negative effect on volumes, rather than a large increase, with the same final price. Also, the increase in price can lead to an increase in demand if the price is used as a guide to quality, an issue which is discussed with more details later in the book.
- **The Marlboro Friday Case:** The company Philip Morris has based its success on the strength of the brand Marlboro. The company was convinced that with powerful brand communications the price elasticity can be kept low enough to sustain a prolonged period of gradual increases in price. These increases in price, sometimes as high as 4% above inflation, continued until 1993, when a pack of Marlboro in the US cost more than $ 2, while generic cigarettes were sold for about 69 cents (Beverland, 2009). Philip Morris intended to exert pressure on the price until the limits of the market. In the process, they opened a large gap between them and the end of the price-sensitive market demand, and generic products were there to exploit that gap. As Philip Morris continued to increase the price of its cigarettes, manufacturers of unbranded cigarettes worked hard to increase the quality and ensure good distribution. As a result, they suddenly become a dynamic force in the market, with a jump in the market share from 28% to 36% in just 9 months. On the other hand, Marlboro was losing 0.5 percent of market share every month (Beverland, 2009). It was obvious that a corrective action was required, and when such was conducted, it caused considerable excitement and consternation in the world of management. The report in the Sunday Times described this as a kind of melodrama that circled the Marlboro reaction: "On April 2, 1993, Philip Morris, the largest group with consumer products in the world, took the biggest risk in its business life - it reduced the price of its cigarettes in the United States, Marlboro, for 20% - 40 cents per pack (Beverland, 2009). The decision of Marlboro was later described as a "price earthquake,"

extensively analyzed, now known, somewhat fatefully, as "Marlboro Friday". For many, the price reduction was presumptuous; it seemed, as if to indicate the end of the golden age of branding. One of the strongest brands in the world was "humbled" by several cheap, literally unbranded products. The share price of Philip Morris fell by 23% to end of the day. This was followed by significant declines in many other companies in the consumer products industry. In the Wall Street Journal, Shapiro wrote: "For manufacturers of consumer goods, the action of Philip Morris is a milestone, the most dramatic evidence of fundamental changes in the shopping habits of consumers... More and more consumers leave brands and replace them with cheaper, nameless products... This shows that even the biggest and strongest brands in the world are vulnerable "(Shapiro, 1993, p. 36). With the advantage of hindsight, this is actually an astute strategic move by Philip Morris: the price reduction effectively "froze" the unbranded sector and caused significant difficulties for branded competitors of Marlboro - "Marlboro Friday" was not the judgment day for branding (Feldwick, 1995). In fact, some experts have discovered a real milestone for branding, according to Klein: "The "Marlboro Friday" draw a line in the sand between small price followers and builders of brands with great concept. Builders of brands won and a new consensus emerged: the products that will be developed in future will be those that will be presented not as "commodities", but as a concept: the brand as an experience, as a lifestyle "(Klein, 2001, p. 127).

- **Strong Brands do not Take Customers for Granted:** There is an important lesson to be learned from the story of Marlboro: consumers cannot be taken for granted. Irresistible, but flawed business logic compels companies to achieve as much as possible profit as soon as possible. This logic led Philip Morris (and many others) to increase in price level during the 1980s and early 1990s, but doing so, they gradually lost the support of their loyal customers. Strong brands can indeed have lower price elasticity, but this often encourages self-overestimation. At their peak, strong brands are prone to become victims of their own arrogant assumptions. The low price elasticity should be a reason for caution rather than an occasion for arrogance. As it is said, all empires ultimately fail for themselves. Scot Bedbury, the former marketing doyen of Nike, explains this specific case of Marlboro's imperialism: "For me, the Marlboro men did not fall from his horse because the ultimate revelation of the limits of branding. What drastically pushed him down were two things: the product has lost any real difference - differentiation in the market from other obscure identities of many competitors and their marketing strategy has become entirely predictable "(Bedbury and Fenichell, 2003, p. 76).
- **The Strong Brand is Able to Track the Premium Price Strategy:** Setting a price above the average in the industry can entrust the brand with a certificate of superior quality. This can be a source of real value to the business: by providing a sense of security among consumers about the quality of the product / service brands allow companies to increase their margins by increasing prices. "A premium brand means higher margins, which means you can create a kind of virtuous circle. For us, higher margins mean more money to invest in providing quality experience for customers, which further strengthens our premium brand. "- John Hayes, CEO, American Express (Wheeler, 2006, p.276).
- **Customers Sometimes Want to Pay More:** In many industries, people are not afraid of higher prices, in contrast, the high price serves to assure product quality. In fact, the price can make a real difference in the customers experience with the product. To some extent, consumer satisfaction comes not only from the product itself, but also from the price paid for it - in the eyes of the consumer the price is an important part of the overall product quality.

- **Premium Prices Provide Preferences:** A well-known contemporary example for premium prices comes from the Belgian manufacturer of alcoholic beverages Interbrew, whose beer Stella Artois has established itself as a high-quality light beer, well known in most of Europe, although the beer in its country of origin is considered a fairly standard product. Stella Artois many years promoted its "certainly expensive" brand position, with premium pricing and emphasis on quality in advertising, which dramatized what people would sacrifice to drink this beer. As a result, the brand has dominated the premium position in many markets, especially in the UK. This is a tried and tested formula in many industries, especially in beverages (Shapiro, 1998). Intuitively, it makes sense with the statement that strong brands can support premium price. Empirically, evidences can be forwarded in Table 2, which compares the price index of five key brands of beer in the UK with a measure of the strength of the brand (the connection). As is the case in many industries, the brand with the highest level of connectivity, in this case Stella Artois, maintained the highest price index (Miller and Muir, 2004).
- **Consumers Use Price as a Guide to Quality:** Nowhere price is not so integrated, integral part of the experience with the product as much as in the world of wine; and nowhere the objective assessment of quality is so vague. The ranking of the wine Bordeaux, for example, is made by a jury, which has to evaluate the wine with some "melodic" criteria (Combris et al, 1998). After this, it is no surprise that those with less discernment, but who still want to buy a quality wine will allow the price to be their guide. Many studies show that most people are unable to recognize the wine in a "blind test". Even when in a gathering of the most famous wine tasters a blind test was conducted, initiated by the lover of Bordeaux, billionaire G. Getty, the experts failed to agree on their choice (The Economist, 1999). Price remains to be a guide to quality.
- **Premium Prices are Best in Specific Industries:** The price serves as a guide for quality in the industry where it is considered that there are big differences in quality. For a very long period the basic task of advertising was to convince us that there are big differences in quality between brands, in order to justify the price. Of course, customers realize that large differences in quality may exist in the industries where the product is much more complicated or technical. In reality, the gap in quality between the products is falling in many areas. For example, according to the research by J.D. Power on the standards for the automotive industry worldwide, the following conclusion was adopted: there is no such thing as a bad car. In this industry, the brand has transformed the customers' experience: a driver of BMW, for example, can enjoy a little less if driving the same car branded with the brand Hyundai. Ultimately, almost all car manufacturers have started to provide similar levels of quality, so the challenge for car brands to maintain their premium value has increased significantly (Herman, 2008).
- **Keeping a Premium Price Can Be a Challenge:** Even in industries such as electronics, where consumers are willing to accept premium prices, their maintenance can be difficult. Sony, for example, has long dominated the premium market of electronics, relying on a well-deserved repu-

Table 2. The relation between the price index and connection to some beer brands

	Stella Artois	Budweiser	Guinness	Beck's	Kronenbourg
Price index	1,35	1,28	1,2	1,2	1,19
Connection	18%	12%	5%	4%	3%

tation for innovation and design. However, this dominance was attacked by competitors such as Samsung and LG, which have invested a lot in order to close the gap in quality. During the 1990s Sony survived a slow, miserable decline in the business with goods with low margins – the operating profits fell from 10% in 1995 to 1% in 2005 (Kunii et al, 2005). Although Sony is recognized as one of the strongest brands, it will not help the company maintain its margins while facing the changing market conditions (Yamamoto, 2005).

- **The Road to Premium Value:** The strength of the brand is not a passport to premium price, as the example of Sony showed, but it is certainly a necessary prerequisite. When conditions allow, the price and the brand can enter into a partnership, influencing consumers to feel good that they pay more. Providing an advantage through a strategy of premium price may sound like a dream come true, but really many brands successfully increase market share by charging more for their products / services. Today we all have an open invitation to buy displays of wealth and status. However, many people have become less concerned about showing their money by paying premium prices. Increasingly, people are trying to signal their values through subtle qualities, so the authenticity and originality came to light. The brands that will search for a path to premium value in the future should have this in mind. As the sociologist John Clammer observes: "Shopping is not only the acquisition of things, it is buying identity" (Lewis and Bridger, 2007, p. 115).
- **When Bad News is Good for Business:** Strong brands can sometimes show great resilience in times of change and upheaval. According to Bill Gates, the bad news is good for the business: "You have to constantly be receptive to bad news and then you have to respond to them." According to him, the free flow of bad news is critical for the survival of his company: "Sometimes I think my most important job as CEO is to hear bad news. If you do not respond to them, your people will eventually stop bringing you bad news. And that's the beginning of the end. "(Gates, 2000, p. 74). Why the bad news is so important? Obviously, it is good to have a balanced view of the performance of the company, but there is a bigger picture: the bad news may indicate that the rules of the game are changing. For example, the consumer preferences may be changing or the competitive advantage can be neutralized. Consultants call this a market disruption, defined as "a trend, an event that leads to a transfer of market power from existing to new players" (Bain & Company website, www.bain.com).

THE BRAND EQUITY ATTRACTS QUALITY WORKFORCE

The main and most important audience for any company is its employees. After all, who wants to be ashamed when he/she responds to the question where they work? The better the impression for the employer brand in the outside world, the more likely that good people will want to work there. - Jon Steel, WPP (www.wpp.com)

Recruitment, hiring and training new employees are high direct costs for most businesses. Strong brands can help reduce these costs by improving the profile of the company and increasing the attractiveness as an employer. Moreover, a strong brand can attract the right candidate because he can communicate information about the company's culture. Talent retention is also a strategic priority for the businesses, not only due to avoiding additional costs for new jobs, but also because employees who left the company are likely to join a competitor, and that means taking out valuable organizational knowledge. High levels of "brain drain" could damage relations with customers and suppliers, can disrupt the smooth functioning of the teams and prevent the business form moving forward. Despite these negative effects, the level of employee fluctuations is high in many industries: 30% in advertising agencies in Europe, with similar levels reported by most major consulting firms. Traders with fast food have an outflow of personnel of around 60% (Van Auken, 2003). The cost of re-recruitment is a major factor in schools and hospitals, not to mention the negative effects of discontinuity.

- **Strong Brands Can Help Companies Retain Talented Employees:** The brand may be the articulation of the intention of the company and people more likely would like to stay if they believe in what the company stands for. Strong brands cause a sense of pride and a level of emotional loyalty among employees. As consumers, people use brands as a guide to quality, as store of trust and as a way of building their own social identity. As employees, people use brands as a guide for caliber, stability and job prospects and a way of building their own professional reputation. Companies can use their "employer brand" to attract and retain the best employees.
- **Attracting and Retaining Talent Has Become a Strategic Priority:** In the era of work for a lifetime, companies should not worry too much about attracting and retaining talented employees. They got an annual "dose" from schools and universities, provided through an intensive internship and training programs. Over time, these new employees have progressed in the levels of the company and often stayed loyal until the time for retirement. But things have changed. Then employers were seeking to build stable, long-term labor, and now most companies tend to be lean and mean as the priority are the short-term yields to shareholders. Until the 1970s, most employees expected job security, stable salary and predictable promotion scale. Now most people would not want a job for life, they want flexibility, diversity and independence. With this new, dynamic labor market, attracting and retaining talent is a strategic priority for every business. As McKinsey described, employers are engaged in "a war for talent" (Michaels et al, 2001). In this ultra-competitive environment for recruitment, many successful businesses have begun to actively explore ways in which their brand can play a significant role in attracting talents.
- **Building a Brand Employer:** There has been a change in the world of employment, away from the old approaches to human resources based on lists and charts, which treat employment as a kind of procurement process, to an approach focused more on people which tries to respond to the values and aspirations of potential employees. Given that there is competition for potential employees, it is easy to assume that employment is a kind of marketing rather than a sort of purchase. In line with this, many companies have begun to apply methods inherent for branding when recruiting the best employees. This allows companies to ask questions to potential recruits: What are they looking for from an employer? How do they make the decision on employment? Which role does the work in their lives play? What do they think about? Understanding the target audience is the starting point for any kind of branding. When branding for consumers, the next step is to define the purpose: the target audience is determined, what will be offered? When branding for employees, this turns into a golden rule: be clear in what you are doing.
- **Be Clear About What You are Doing:** This means more than a report on the corporate mission. Let us take, for example, the consulting firms for strategic management - Boston Consulting Group (BCG) and McKinsey. Both companies are very clear about what they do, both very desirable employers. Each attracts different types of candidates: BCG draws people with extensive and diverse experience in business; McKinsey attracts candidates tabula rasa (often recent graduates)

seeking coaching and training (Cappelli and Crocker-Hefter, 2001). This reflects the different approach of the two companies: the clients of BCG expect that each project team will come up with a unique, innovative solution; McKinsey clients expect rigorous application of commercial tools and products. Since both companies have a clear approach to their business, they easily attract the right candidates. Thus, BCG website published: "no two paths to BCG are the same and no two consultants are similar" (http://www.bcg.com/careers/careers_splash.asp), while McKinsey has neat diagram that shows possible career development within the company (http://www.mckinsey.com/careers/). Both companies have strong brands aligned with a strong business model: they don not only attract talent, but the right type of talent.

- **Money Alone is Not Sufficient to Retain Talent:** Factors that attract employees in the company are the reason upon which they determine whether to stay or not. Those employees who are motivated by financial reward will probably be attracted by better offers; even the most generous "golden handcuffs" can be compensated by signing the bonuses. The company that has a clear sense of identity - a strong brand for employees is more likely to retain its best staff.
- **Details Should Not be Overlooked:** Let us consider the approach to retaining talent acquired by United Parcel Service (Cappelli, 2000). The company discovered a significant problem with the retention of their drivers, and they are essential for UPS, because of their detailed knowledge of local roads and clients. With the investigation, the problem was located as "boring and exhausting" tasks for loading vans before starting deliveries. The company simply solved the problem by assigning this task to the employees in the warehouse and outflow of drivers dramatically decreased (Pounsford, 2007). UPS is a strong brand with a proud heritage, and their drivers can enjoy their vintage trucks, but the solution is more than moving boxes, it is a movement of brand perceptions.
- **Combining Marketing and Human Resources:** In terms of communications, the growth and development of branding employers led to the need for harmonization between the internal and external environment. Michael Pounsford from Banner McBride, an agency for internal communications, describes the need for "a consistent approach to customers and employees", while Mark Ritson from the London Business School calls for a "rare reunion between marketing and human resources" (Ritson et al, 2002, p. 65). This is an interesting question: In the company, who exactly is responsible for the talent? If it is necessary the brand to generate value from both, the customers and the employees, then an integrated approach is needed.

THE BRAND EQUITY PROVIDES LOYALTY AND TRUST

Consumer loyalty has become something like a holy grail in marketing management, based on the belief that building a strong brand can deliver higher levels of repurchase. In order to understand this belief, below is a brief elaboration of its origin.

- **From Customer Satisfaction to Emotional Loyalty:** By 1980, most people believed that the key to maintaining customer loyalty is their satisfaction. This was questioned by the historical ideas of Edward Deming: "The consumer who is satisfied today, may have a different set of needs tomorrow" (Deming, 2000, p.108). Since then, a lot of research and analysis are made in order to prove that the results for the level of satisfaction alone cannot actually predict how customers will behave. Of course, satisfaction is needed to maintain the loyalty of customers, but it is not always enough: studies of many brands, including: British Airways, American Express and IBM, have shown that satisfied customers are often not loyal (Jones and Sasser, 1995). Quickly a new perspective emerged. The results of the level of satisfaction measured the rational, functional aspects of the consumer experience and could not "hunt" the buyers' emotions. An extensive research to determine the importance of measuring what is called emotional dynamics was conducted. Studies have shown that the cost of acquiring new customers is five times greater than the cost of servicing the existing - with the clear implication that building loyalty should be a strategic priority for any brand (Applebaum, 2007).

- **Brand Loyalty is Correlated With the Brand Power:** The emphasis on loyalty was further enhanced with the research from Hallberg, according to him, every brand has a core of loyal valuable consumers - they are the engine of the financial value of the brand (Hallberg, 1995). Thus, building loyalty is incorporated as a key marketing objective for all companies: the strong brands are expected to provide loyal customers. Building a strong brand on the one hand supports the increase of the market share, and on the other, consumer loyalty - this relationship can be found in many markets. Using data from WPP Brandz ™, correlations between the strength of the brand and consumer loyalty for seven randomly selected markets and industries were measured. To assess the strength of the brand, results from the size of the market share and the "binding" (which is a measure of the emotional attachment consumers have to the brand) were used. The results in Table 3 show that the correlations between the strength of the brand and consumers loyalty tend to be high (Miller and Muir, 2004). In this regard, small brands suffer from "double jeopardy" - they are penalized twice for being small: they have fewer customers, and these customers are less loyal.

The levels of loyalty are declining. People are becoming less and less loyal to brands they buy. Studies reveal declining levels of loyalty over the long term, shown in Figure 3. A mix of factors contributes to this (Miller and Muir, 2004):

1. Consumers are becoming more confident and aware of their options, and as a result are more likely to seek their merit in any transaction.
2. The comparison of the bids from the competitors became incredibly easier, especially with the expansion of the Internet, and it allows consumers to seek the best offer each time.

Table 3. Correlation between the strength of the brand and the brand loyalty

Industry	Country	Correlation
Airline	US	0,927
Brewery	UK	0,902
Mineral water	France	0,773
Cars	Germany	0,882
Hair care	Japan	0,903
Banking	Mexico	0,967
Newspapers	Canada	0,984

Figure 3. Decreasing levels of brand loyalty

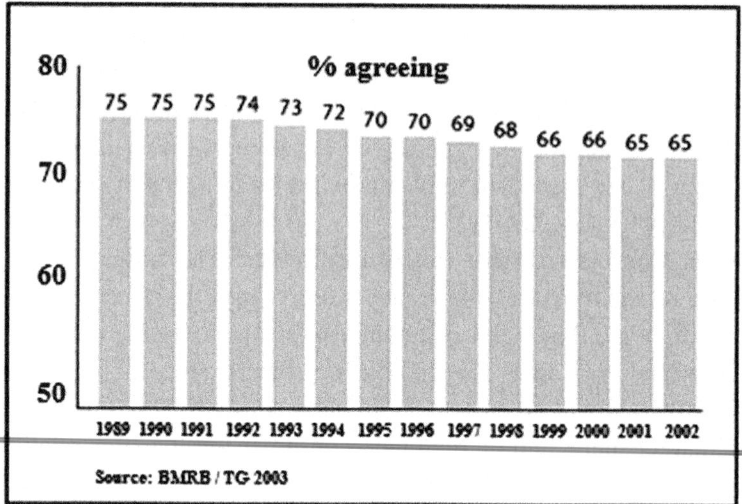

3. For many consumers, loyalty cards encourage the mentality of "discount shopping", and that such consumers are the most promiscuous of all kinds.
4. More people are seeking diversity, willing to try new brands of products; thresholds of boredom crumble and consumers want to get rid of the old routine, and this has a strong negative impact on loyalty.

The road to loyalty. Generally speaking, there are two ways to foster loyalty:

1. **Pledging for Something:** Why the brand Apple inspires a "dedicated core" of profitable customers? What excites people about Apple is the company's intention: enthusiasts really feel that the company is committed to developing technology to unleash creativity in all of us. If consumers can accept the meaning of the company's purpose it is more likely that they will be tied emotionally to the brand. This also applies to employees, it is essential to ensure that the company delivers more than the consumers' expectations.
2. **Delivering More – Constantly:** Authentic emotional loyalty is generated when a company consistently delivers more than the best expectations of the consumer. For example, American Express provides occasional unexpected benefits to holders of their club cards, such as 10% discount for members who shop at Harrods (De Chernatony et al, 2003).

It was the President of Unilever, Niall Fitz Gerald, who described the brand as "a repository of trust" in a statement for The Economist: "The brand means more and more as the choice expands. People want to simplify their lives (The Economist, 2001). This is a source of value for business: if people trust the brand, they are likely to buy the product / service, and even more importantly, is prepared to pay more. The link between consumers' feelings for the brand and their behavior is clear. The study of Henley Centre, shown on Figure 4, reveals the level of trust in brands from various industries.

Figure 4. People have more trust in "their" brand

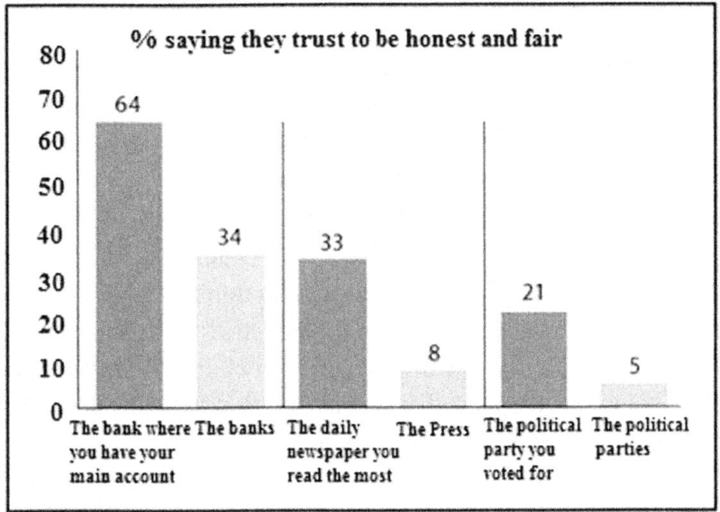

- **Brands are a Guarantee of Quality for Consumers:** The brands were launched as a direct guarantee of quality and consistency, and for this, of course, consumers are willing to pay more. Brands are the first type of protection for consumers – they know where to go if they need to complain. History shows that the unbranded production leads to deterioration in quality. Trust explains the price premium achieved with brands such as: American Express, IBM, BMW and Apple: people are willing to pay more, because they are sure that they will receive a certain level of quality. An interesting illustration comes from eBay, which encourages customers to evaluate (rank) the service they receive from vendors. Research has been done on the prices achieved by well-rated sellers on eBay, compared with the same products offered by the vendors with a weaker rank. After analyzing 2.000 transactions, it was found that a well-ranked vendor is able to charge 7.6% higher price (Powell, 2006).
- **Brands Help Consumers to Reduce their Risk:** When economists write about trust, it is often associated with risk. For example, "trust includes action in which there is a vulnerability or risk of side effects" (Korczynski, 2009, p. 59). So, it makes sense to talk about trust in Visa, Hilton or Johnson & Johnson, because the failure of these brands to fulfill their promises can be disastrous. Similarly, when the product is technical or complex, such as computers or audio gear, trust is also important, because people want to minimize the risk of rapid deterioration of the product. In a sense, this works the same way as our payment of an insurance premium to recover the number of different risks. It seems that people would pay more for brands, if the risk of disappointment is perceived as lower. Thus, the brands help the consumers manage the risks involved in their various transactions.
- **Trust has Become a Scarce Resource:** Many of the ideas for branding emerged in the 1950s and 1960s. Consumers in this period faced postwar shortages, when people were grateful to buy anything they have access to. This, coupled with the propagation of the so-called "paternalistic diet" by the public sector, created generations of dissatisfied consumers. However, people increasingly preferred to place their trust in brands, since they have become increasingly suspicious and

critical. Academics such as Robert Putnam and Francis Fukuyama attributed the fall in the level of trust to the disappearance of the social capital: "The fall of a wide range of social structures, neighborhoods, churches, trade unions, clubs and charities; and the general opinion about the lack of shared values and unity with those around them "(Fukuyama, 1995, p. 75). As many economies in the world are converted into societies with low level of trust, a new generation of consumers who check the labels, compare prices and analyze propositions emerged. In this environment, the brand with high level of trust is a real competitive advantage.

- **The Importance of Trust Depends on the Industry:** Numerous studies show high level of trust for brands like Samsung, IBM and Colgate (Reader's Digest Trusted Brands Survey, 2003). But when people say "I trust Samsung", what do they really think? The clarification lies in the fact that confidence surveys always concentrate on certain industries such as air transport, pharmaceutical industry and credit cards. Clearly, it will be bizarre to claim "I have trust in Johnny Walker." It seems that trust is somehow associated with the function, as indicated Earls, complaining on a British research, which allegedly proved that people have more trust in Tesco supermarkets than in the police (Earls, 2002). When discussing trust in brands, it is important to clarify the role and importance of trust: What does the brand do to be trusted?
- **Trust Comes From Proximity:** People have trust in things that are familiar. A study of six markets in different countries, confirms that people are more likely to trust the companies from their own country, rather than multinationals, Figure 5 (Miller and Muir, 2004). The feeling of closeness seems to be an important part when building trust.
- **The Path to Trust:** In fact, there is no easy guide with a few steps to build consumer trust; real trust comes with the formulation of a clear brand strategy and its continuous execution over time - consistency and transparency. "Trust cannot be built with a single advertising campaign. Trust is built over a long period, not on the basis of communication, but on action. And then again, once established, trust can be lost for a moment - one bad note and it disappears forever" (Fitz Gerald, 2007, Address to the Advertising Association).

Figure 5. People have more trust in domestic companies

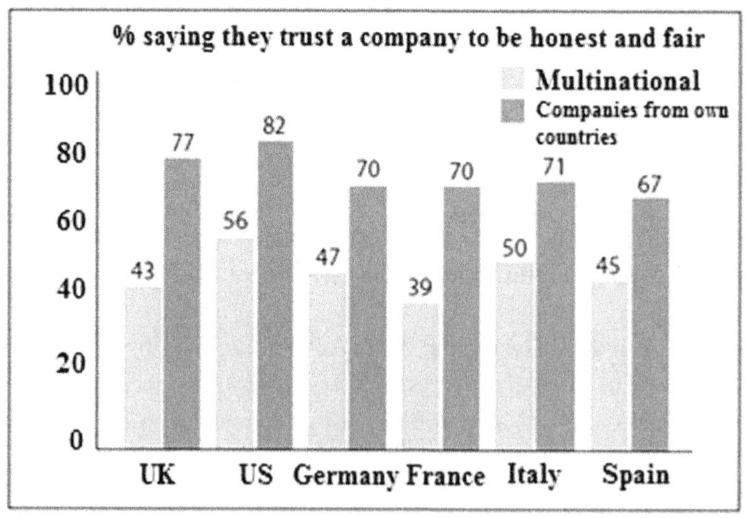

THE BRAND EQUITY STIMULATES INNOVATION

This is the holy grail of business: to make this new product that can change the whole business; or that revolutionary service that will "knock out" the competition. Numerous studies have demonstrated the link between the efficient research and development (R & D) and the measures of the performance of the business, such as sales growth, stock prices and yield to shareholders (Davis et al, 2002). The results of the survey on companies with high quality R & D operations in the UK showed that the share prices of these companies are significantly higher than the share prices of other companies that form the FTSE index on the London Stock Exchange - Figure 6 (Miller and Muir, 2004).

- **Innovation is the Ultimate Source of Value for the Business:** In fact, its importance is obvious. Several perspectives according to which innovations add value to business are identified:
    - They create new products / services and thus new markets.
    - They create improvements to existing products / services, and thus are a source of differentiation and competitive advantage.
    - They may be the only way for business growth, when existing markets are saturated.
    - They are able to stimulate demand by creating novelty and excitement, and this supports the volume and / or value of sales.
- **Strong Brands Provide Purpose for Innovation:** For innovation to be successful, it must be accepted by the company, the employees and, of course, by consumers. Here, strong brands can play an important role: a clear concept of the brand can symbolize the aspirations of the company, and thus provide direction for the activities of research and development. Apple, every ones favorite example of an innovative company, has a clearly understood brand with a clear goal: development of technologies that allow people to have fun. Apple strives for excellence in design and

Figure 6. Companies with intensive R&D activities exceed the average companies

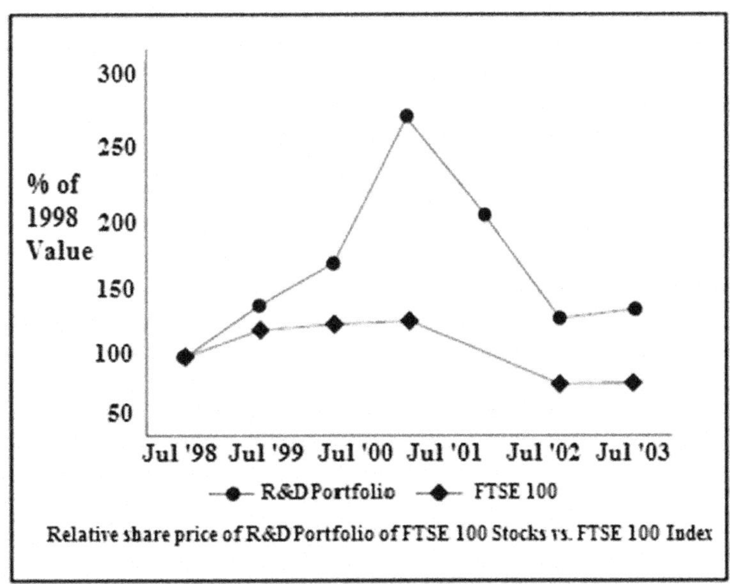

innovation in technology. Apple's brand is clearly understood and favorite among employees and consumers alike. This gives Apple a key advantage: people working on new products have a deep understanding why consumers love Apple. They know what people expect from the company, and even what they do not expect, but would like, anyway. In other words, the power of the brand Apple gives the company a built market orientation. This expands the company, giving a sense of purpose to the innovative activities of the company (Hollis, 2010).

- **Brands Provide Integrated Market Orientation:** Market, contrary to the product orientation is a key component of success. Often, the process of innovation is a painstaking destination through "mountains and seas" of quantitative research and many working hours for the teams. The results of these approaches are mostly in the form of incremental improvements to existing products and they rarely achieve a new breakthrough. As the comments of Stephen King: "Everyone hopes of a nice, neat, rang-list of innovations that can be focused directly on products and advertising" (King, 1993, speech at MRS Conference). Strong brands can provide a better approach to market orientation, encapsulating a deeply rooted understanding of consumers and a well-developed attitude towards them. Snapple and Ben & Jerry's constantly innovate and their efforts are constantly in the spirit of their brand. The impressive assortment of the Dove brand extensions comes from the consistent and well understood brand position. The market research has the role to stimulate innovations, but not to lead them.
- **Innovating the Business Model:** Henry Ford, in fact, did not invent the automobile, but invented the process of mass production that revolutionized manufacturing. Sometimes these innovations are the most powerful of all. If you compare, for example, Apple and Dell, despite their record of innovation, Apple is continuously squeezed out of the market that the company itself has created. Converting innovation into cash is not easy for the company: in 2003 when its iTunes were greeted by Time magazine as the "coolest" invention of the year, Apple's operating profit fell by insignificant 0.4%, but down for 20% compared with the results from 1981. Unlike Apple, Dell does not innovate the product, but the business model. Dell has not done anything to make computers faster, smaller, more powerful and better looking. The great innovation of Dell is its distribution, enabling them to offer a wider range of products at lower prices, to a wider audience. As a result, Dell sells more units than Apple (Berry, 2004). Some companies, however, are able to provide both - product and business innovation.
- **Innovation May Be Coincidental:** Some ideas are random, unintended consequences of solving another problem. Pringles had begun its existence as an idea of using potato paste as a by-product, and now is a market leader with full rights (Clark, 2004). Pizza, shepherd's pie and gazpacho were once ways for poor families to use the food remains and now are an integral part of many international cuisines.
- **Innovation Can Be Devastating:** Some innovations have significant effects on their markets. Certainly, the evidence suggests that it is more difficult for larger companies to introduce radical innovations because they can cannibalize the existing products or services. As a result, despite the hazardous R&D budgets, large companies are struggling to push through an idea that can shake the market. As noted by Baker: "They often start with the process, in order to obtain large, radical idea and end up with something very partial and incremental" (Baker, 2003, p. 78). The devastating innovations are often ammunition for the "hungry" challenging brands. When the online lender of DVDs, NetFlix.com, announced late in 2003 that it has almost 1,300,000 subscribers, an increase of 71% from the previous year, it was clear that their innovative model for video rental

has changed the industry forever. Existing companies, like Blockbusters, had to find a way to respond properly or to face the declining market share (Adamson and Sorrell, 2007).

- **Wealth Favors the Prepared Mind:** This thesis began with the conclusion that there is no formula for innovation. No A-B-C process ensures creating successful new product or service. But also, innovation is not a question of divine inspiration, something that inadvertently comes to creative types (as Mark Earls says: "As an artistic gastro-enteritis."). "Eureka" moments are very vague. The Archimedes' discovery was not an unexpected bolt from the blue. He was preoccupied with thoughts of weight and volume as silently entered his bath to solve the problem. In a sense, he was drawn to the idea: the wealth favors the prepared mind, as Louis Pasteur famously said. There may be no formula for innovation, but new ideas are more likely to occur within the prepared minds. Strong brands can play an important role here. The strong brand needs to implement the company's aspirations. It needs to harmonize the efforts of people within the company, with the tastes and needs of consumers. If employees have this frame of reference, they can easily perceive new opportunities. Strong brands provide a sense of purpose for the company or, rather, a sense for the future. Without this sense, it is harder to recognize opportunities and innovation becomes impossible. As Arie de Geus writes: "We will not perceive signals from the outside world, unless it is a relevant option for the future that we have already worked up in our imagination. The more "memories of the future" we develop, the more open and receptive we are to signals from the outside world "(Earls and Baskin, 2002, p. 82).

CONCLUSION

The brand equity can create value for the business in different ways - from maintaining and increasing market share, to attracting and retaining talented employees. There are several potential sources of business value that can be provided by strong brands:

- Brand equity provides market share. The strength of the brand is correlated with the market share, and this is closely linked to profitability. Furthermore, brands allow self-reinforcing of the market share.
- Brand equity creates barriers to entry for competitors. The brands may have a defensive role: the costs related to the establishment of a strong brand in a particular industry can often deter potential competitors wanting to enter the market.
- Brand equity can expand the business into new areas. Brands provide opportunities for business growth through brand extensions. This can open up access to new sources of revenue or to assist the business in response to market changes.
- Brand equity can provide entry into new markets. Foreign markets can be an important source of potential revenue for strong brands, ensuring proper balance between global consistency and local sensitivity.
- Brand equity provides lower price elasticity. Brands can support the price the buyer is willing to pay – a strong brand can increase the price of the product / service with no significant loss in sales volume.

- Brand equity can make a price premium. Brands can enable companies to charge a premium; sometimes customers want to pay more - a higher price creates a reassuring sense of superior quality.
- Brand equity can deal with market disruption. Brands can help companies to keep their performance in time of uncertainty, if they accept a flexible and open approach to the future.
- Brand equity can attract and retain talent. The brands create competitive advantage by attracting and retaining talented employees. This can also reduce the significant costs associated with recruitment and re-recruitment.
- Brand equity is a source of trust. Brands can foster trust between stakeholders - ultimately it is the source of real value to a company. True confidence comes from having a clear brand strategy and its continuous compliance over time.
- Brand equity stimulates innovation. Brands can create new ideas for products and services, providing the research and development activities of the company with an integrated market orientation.

When analyzing the successful brands, the coherence between: what top managers want to achieve in the future (their strategic vision), what has always been known, or what the company's employees believe in (embodied in the culture) and what the external stakeholders expect or want from the company (their opinion for the company, i.e. the company's image) is revealed. The central message of this thesis is the basic principle of compliance in the model vision - culture - image combined with the concept of radical transparency: the greater the coherence, the stronger the brand.

REFERENCES

Adamson, A., & Sorrell, M. (2007). *Brand Simple: How the Best Brands Keep it Simple and Succeed.* Macmillan.

Applebaum, A. (2007). The constant customer. *Gallup Management Journal, 16*, 562–577.

Baker, S. (2003). Where have all the ideas gone? *Brand Strategy, 15*, 74–86.

Bedbury, S., & Fenichell, S. (2003). *A New Brand World: Eight Principles for Achieving Brand Leadership in the Twenty-First Century.* Penguin Group, New York.

Berry, J. (2004). *Tangible Strategies for Intangible Assets.* McGraw-Hill.

Beverland, M. (2009). *Building Brand Authenticity: 7 Habits of Iconic Brands.* Macmillan. doi:10.1057/9780230250802

Broadbent, S. (1994). Diversity in categories, brands and strategies. *Journal of Brand Management., 2*(1), 1226–1241. doi:10.1057/bm.1994.26

Bullmore, J. (2000). *WPP Annual Report & Accounts.* WPP.

Cappelli, P., & Crocker-Hefter, A. (2001). Distinctive human resources are firm's core competencies. *The War for Talent, 20*, 455–473.

Checco, L. (2005). *Branding For Success!* Trafford.

Clark, K. (2004). *Brandscendence: Three Essential Elements of Enduring Brands*. Dearborn Trade Publication.

Clifton & Simmons. (2004). Brands and Branding. *The Economist,* 256-272.

Combris, P., Lecocq, S., & Visser, M. (1998). Estimation of a Hedonic price equation for Bordeaux wine: Does quality matter? *The Economic Journal*, (107): 390–402.

Cooper, C., Cook, L., & Jones, N. (1999). *How the chimps have kept PG Tips brand leader through 35 years of intense competition*. IPA.

Davis, S., Dunn, M., & Aaker, D. (2002). *Building the Brand-Driven Business: Operationalize Your Brand to Drive Profitable Growth*. John Wiley and Sons.

De Chernatony, L. (2010). *From Brand Vision to Brand Evaluation: The strategic process of growing and strengthening brands*. Butterworth-Heinemann.

De Chernatony, L., McDonald, M., & Wallace, E. (2003). *Creating Powerful Brands*. Butterworth-Heinemann.

Deming, E. (2000). *Out of the Crisis*. MIT Press.

Draper, P. (2002). *Uncommon Practice*. Prentice Hall.

Earls, M. (2002). *Brand New Brand Thinking*. Kogan Page.

Feldwick, P. (2002). *What is Brand Equity Anyway*. World Advertising Research Center.

Fukuyama, F. (1995). *Trust: the Social Virtues of the Creation of Prosperity*. The Free Press.

Gates, B. (2000). *Business @ The Speed of Thought*. Penguin Books.

Gelder, S. (2005). *Global Brand Strategy: Unlocking Brand Potential across Countries, Cultures & Markets*. Kogan Page Ltd.

Gregory, J. (2004). *The best of branding: best practices in corporate branding*. McGraw-Hill Professional.

Hadley, R. (2002). Over-stretching the brand. *Brand Strategy*, *56*, 238–251.

Hallberg, G. (1995). *All Consumers Are Not Created Equal*. John Wiley&Sons.

Harris, F., & De Chernatony, L. (2001). Corporate branding and corporate brand performance. *European Journal of Marketing*, *35*(3/4), 441–457. doi:10.1108/03090560110382101

Herman, D. (2008). *Outsmart the MBA Clones: The Alternative Guide to Competitive Strategy, Marketing and Branding*. Paramount Market Publishing.

Hill, S., Lederer, C., & Keller, K. (2001). *The Infinite Asset: Managing Brands to Build New Value*. HBS Press.

Hollis, N. (2010). *The Global Brand: How to Create and Develop Lasting Brand Value in the World Market*. Macmillan.

Ind, N. (2007). *The Corporate Brand*. Macmillan Business.

Jones, T. O., & Sasser, E. (1995). Why satisfied customers defect. *Harvard Business Review*, *75*, 385.

Kapferer, J. N. (2008). *The New Strategic Brand Management: Creating and Sustaining Brand Equity Long Term* (4th ed.). Kogan Page.

King, S. (1993). *MRS Conference Speech*. San Francisco: MRS.

Klein, N. (2001). *No Logo*. Flamingo.

Knapp, D., & Hart, C. (2000). *The Brand Mindset: Five Essential Strategies for Building Brand Advantage throughout Your Company*. McGraw-Hill.

Korczynski, M. (2009). The political economy of trust. *Journal of Management Studies*, *35*, 56–68.

Kunii, I., Edwards, C., & Greene, J. (2005). Can Sony regain the magic? *Business Week,* (3773).

Michaels, E., Handfield Jones, H., & Axelrod, B. (2001). *McKinsey Quarterly* (Vol. 79). Harvard Business School Press.

Miller, J., & Muir, D. (2004). *The Business of Brands*. John Wiley & Sons.

Mulhern, F., Williams, J., & Leone, R. P. (1998). Variability of brand price elasticity across retail stores: Ethnic, income, and brand determinants. *Journal of Retailing*, *74*(3), 224–259. doi:10.1016/S0022-4359(99)80103-1

Porter, M. (1996). What is Strategy? *Harvard Business Review*, *56*, 167–185. PMID:11143152

Post, R., & Post, P. (2007). *Global Brand Integrity Management: How to Protect Your Product in Today's Competitive Environment*. McGraw-Hill.

Pounsford, M. (2007). Winning the war for talent. *Strategic Communications Management*, *20*, 72–84.

Powell, A. (2006). *Putting a dollar value on a good name*. Harvard University Gazette.

Randall, G. (2006). *Branding: a practical guide to planning your strategy*. Kogan Page Ltd., London.

Reader's Digest Trusted Brands Survey. (2003). Author.

Riensenbeck, H., & Freeling, A. (1991). How global are global brands? *The McKinsey Quarterly*, (4): 63.

Ritson, M., Bergen, M., Dutta, S., & Zbaracki, M. (2002). Capability. *Sloan Management Review*, *93*, 61–76.

Schmitt, B., & Simonsen, A. (2009). *Marketing Aesthetics*. Simon & Schuster.

Shapiro, B. P. (1998). The psychology of pricing. *Harvard Business Review*, *62*, 189.

Shapiro, G. (1993, March 23). Cigarette burn: Price cut on Marlboro upsets rosy notions about tobacco profits. *Wall Street Journal*, p.10.

The Economist. (1999, December 18). The Price Puzzle. *The Economist.*

The Economist. (2001, September 6). Who's wearing the trousers?. *The Economist.*

Van Auken, B. (2003). *Brand Aid: An Easy Reference Guide to Solving Your Toughest Branding Problems and Strengthening Your Market Position*. AMA Press.

Wheeler, A. (2006). *Designing Brand Identity: A Complete Guide to Creating, Building, and Maintaining Strong Brands*. John Wiley and Sons.

Wilson & Gilligan. (2005). *Strategic Marketing Management: planning, implementation and control* (3rd ed.). Elsevier Butterworth-Heinemann.

Wreden, N. (2005). *Profit Brand: How to Increase the Profitability, Accountability and Sustainability of Brands*. Kogan Page Ltd.

ENDNOTES

1. Definition from *The American Heritage Dictionary of the English Language*. (2000). fourth edition, published by Houghton Mifflin Company
2. The notation that strong brands can better increase the prices without a significant loss in volume is widely recognized. It is often suggested that the price elasticity should be taken as a measure of the strength of the brand, examples found by Paul Feldwick, 'What is brand equity, anyway?' WARC.

Chapter 4
How Radical Transparency Can Turn the Brand Equity Into a Basis for Sustainable Competitive Advantage

ABSTRACT

This chapter begins with the analysis of the question whether the real sources of sustainable competitive advantage derive from the strengthening of the companies' internal strengths and eliminating internal weaknesses or are they the result of a successful manipulation with the opportunities in the environment and the avoidance of external threats. Despite the efforts of many authors to summarize the first with the latter, modern scientific thought in the field of strategic management underlines the first variant. As a logical sequence, the analysis of the intangible resources of companies and their (im)mobility follows as a necessary condition for sustainable competitive advantage. The authors analyze the idea of the brand equity as a resource which summarizes all typical resources and capabilities of the company creating and maintaining the desired competitive advantage. Finally, the analysis of the brand equity through the prism of the VRIO model is a further proof for the brand equity role as a source of sustainable competitive advantage.

INTRODUCTION

This chapter begins with the analysis of the question whether the real sources of sustainable competitive advantage derive from the strengthening of the companies' internal strengths and elimination of internal weaknesses or are they the result of a successful manipulation with the opportunities in the environment and the avoidance of external threats. Despite the efforts of many authors to summarize the first with the latter, modern scientific thought in the field of strategic management underlines the first variant. As a logical sequence, the analysis of the intangible resources of companies and their (im)mobility follows as a necessary condition for sustainable competitive advantage. Here we analyze the idea of the brand

DOI: 10.4018/978-1-5225-2417-5.ch004

equity as a resource which summarizes all typical resources and capabilities of the company, creating and maintaining the desired competitive advantage. Finally, the analysis of the brand equity through the prism of the VRIO concept is a further proof for the brand equity role as a source of sustainable competitive advantage.

The company's resources include all assets, capabilities, organizational processes, company's attributes, information and knowledge that the company owns and controls which enable it to define and implement strategies that improve its efficiency and effectiveness. With the language of traditional strategic analysis, company's resources are the advantages that the company can use in the selection and implementation of the strategy.

Many authors suggest a long list of companies' characteristics that allow the implementation of strategies that create value. Numerous possible resources are conventionally classified into the following three major categories (Williamson, 1992):

- **Physical Capital:** Includes technology in physical form used by companies, the buildings, the equipment and machinery, geographical location and access to materials and resources.
- **Human Capital:** Refers to training, experience, assessments, intelligence, relationships, knowledge and understanding of individuals (managers and employees) in the company.
- **Organizational Capital:** Includes formal reporting structure of the company, the formal and informal planning systems, coordination and control, and all the formal and informal relationships between individuals and groups within the company and its environment.

Naturally, all aspects of physical, human and organizational capital of the company are not strategically relevant resources. Some of them may restrict the company in the selection and implementation of an appropriate strategy. Others may lead the company to a suboptimal choice of strategy that reduces the efficiency and effectiveness of the company. However, the goal of this research (and of the companies in reality) is to recognize the mix of resources that can be a source of sustainable competitive advantage. The latter raises the crucial question of what is the basic motive of this book: Which is the role and importance of brand equity in this discussion? Brand equity is a common denominator that summarizes the company's resources. It is a synergistic cause and effect of the company's resources (people, objects, activities and relationships). The brand equity is the result of all relevant activities and links of the company's value chain. As a synthetic resource, the brand equity is the most distinctive source of competitive advantage for companies.

It is said that the company has a competitive advantage when it can implement a strategy that creates value and simultaneously is not implemented by any other current or potential competitor. The company has a sustainable competitive advantage when it can implement a strategy that simultaneously is not implemented by other current or potential competitors and when other companies are not able to replicate the benefits of such a strategy (Porter, 2008). Isn't it what the brand equity allows?

THE SWOT ANALYSIS WITH RADICAL TRANSPARENCY

The analysis of the sources of sustainable competitive advantage of companies turned into the main area of research within the strategic management in the past 30 years (Porter, 1985, Barney, 1996, Rumelt, 1990, Andrews, 1995 and others). Most researches result in a joint statement converted into an axiom in this area: companies gain sustainable competitive advantage through the implementation of strategies that exploit their internal strengths and match opportunities in the environment, while they neutralize external threats and avoid internal weaknesses, Figure 1.

Studies of the sources of sustainable competitive advantage, essentially focused on one of the following alternatives: isolating the opportunities and threats of companies (Porter, 1985), describing the strengths and weaknesses of companies (Hofer and Schnedel, 1988 and Grant, 2001) or analyzing how the first and second alternative to be integrated in order to choose the appropriate strategy.

Although in literature both, the internal analysis of organizational strengths and weaknesses and the external analysis of the opportunities and threats have received proper attention, influenced by Porter and his colleagues, most recent studies focus on the analysis of opportunities and threats of companies in the competitive environment. These papers describe the conditions in the environment that favor high performance of companies. For example, the Porter's model of five competitive forces explains the characteristics of an attractive business, suggesting that opportunities are greater and threats smaller in such industries. Models of competitive advantage based on the environment assume that companies within an industry are identical in terms of strategically relevant resources that they control and the strategies they choose. Second, these models assume that if there is heterogeneity of resources within an industry or a strategic group (for example, with the entry of a new competitor), it will be exceeded in short time, because the resources used by companies to implement their strategies are highly mobile.

The strategic analysis of resources substitutes these with two other assumptions for a proper analysis of the sources of competitive advantage. First, it is assumed that companies within an industry or a strategic group can be heterogeneous in terms of the resources they own and control. Second, it is assumed that the resources may not be perfectly mobile among companies, so heterogeneity can be long-lasting. The model based on the company's resources examines the implications of these two assumptions in order to appropriately analyze the sources of sustainable competitive advantage (Stern and Deimler, 2006). These studies paved the way for recognizing the importance of the brand equity as the most specific corporate resource that offers the choice and implementation of a strategy that is difficult to be replicated by competitors. This means that the brand is nothing but a source of sustainable competitive advantage.

Figure 1. The relationship between SWOT analysis, resource-based models and models for industry attractiveness

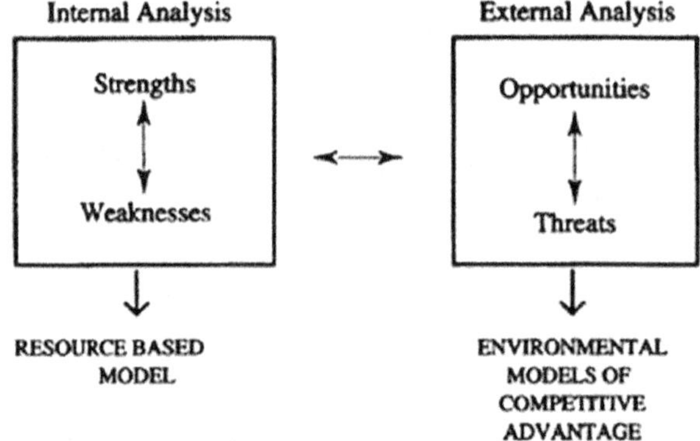

The increased focus on the company's resources as a source of competitive advantage is due to the dissatisfaction with the static, balanced framework of industrial economics and organization. This renewed interest in the old theories on profit and competition is associated with the works of David Ricardo, Joseph Schumpeter and Edith Penrose (Ricardo, 1891, Schumpeter, 1934, Penrose, 1959). The promotion of such thoughts happen several times: at the level of corporate strategy - the interest of the economies of scale and transaction costs reiterated, which raised the question of the role of companies' resources in the establishment of industrial and geographical area of companies' activities of (Teece, 1980); at the level of business strategy - the analysis focused on the relationship among resources, competition and profitability, including competitive imitation (Rumelt, 1982), the adequacy of the return on innovation (Teece, 1988), the role of asymmetric information in the creation of differences in profitability between competing companies (Barney, 1986), and the ways in which the accumulation of resources leads to competitive advantage (Ingemar and Cool, 1989). These observations led to the formation of an integrated model based on resources which later proved to be very good in terms of the inclusion of the practical implications of the theory of competitive advantage based on company's resources. Therefore, this model, shown on Figure 2, can be used to verify the importance of brand equity as a source of competitive advantage. When analyzing it, all relevant internal stakeholders should be involved, not just the top management, because an accurate and consistent execution and location of responsibility for every activity in the company can be achieved only with empowerment, awareness and transparency.

The model is a five phase process of strategic analysis that includes: analysis of the resource base of the company, identifying the capabilities of the company, evaluating the profit potential of the company's resources and capabilities, proper selection of a strategy and an expansion and improvement of the company's resources and capabilities (Grant, 1991). Using the technique of expansion, individual components

Figure 2. An approach to strategic analysis based on resources: a practical framework

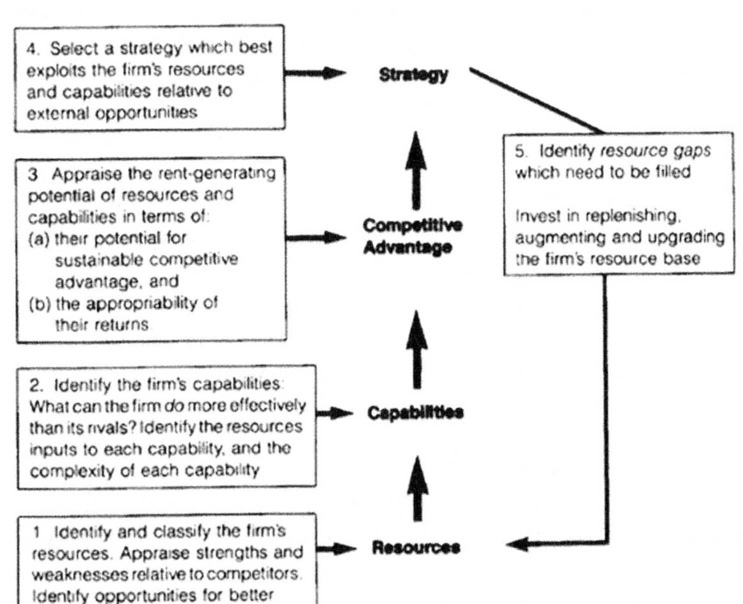

of the model can be discussed, in order to modify the variant that is most suited for the company and helps recognizing the way the brand equity can be used as a source of sustainable competitive advantage.

This analysis reinforces the argument that resources and capabilities of the company are a basis for its strategy. The approach of using the resources and capabilities as the base of the long-term company's strategy is based on the following two premises: first, resources and capabilities provide a guideline for the company's strategy and second, resources and capabilities are the primary source of profit for the company (Rouse and Daellenbach, 2001).

The Resources and Capabilities as a Guide for the Company's Strategy

When defining the strategy, companies often start by establishing the identity and the purpose of the company's existence, usually in the form of a report on the company's mission which answers the following questions: What does the business do? In which markets it performs? Which are its customers? Which are their requirements and needs that need to be served? But in a world where consumer preferences and identity are extremely volatile, and technologies that serve consumer demands are continuously being improved, externally focused orientation is not a reliable basis for formulating a long-term strategy. When the external environment is constantly changing, resources and capabilities of the company can be a much more stable basis for defining its identity. Thus, the definition of the business in terms of what it is capable of doing is a more durable basis for strategy than the definition based on the consumers' needs the business wants to meet.

The decision of Levitt (1986) to the problem of external changes suggests that companies should define markets they serve much wider, instead of narrower: for example, a company from the rail transport should view itself as a company that deals with transport and not specifically with rail transport. But such a broad definition of the market is of little importance if the company cannot acquire and develop the necessary resources and capabilities to serve customers' demand in a wider front. Whether, for example, the railway company is able to develop a business unit for air transport, freight and passenger transport? Perhaps the resources and capabilities of the railway company are more suited for the development of a business unit for real estate or construction and operation of a pipeline. Practice shows that servicing broadly defined consumers' needs is a quite difficult task. The attempts by Merrill Lynch, American Express, Sears and Citicorp are just a few examples which prove that "to meet all the consumers' needs" within the industry creates serious problems in the company. And the intention of Allegis Corporation to meet the travel needs for its customers by combining the services of United Airlines, Hertz and Westin Hotels ended in a costly failure. In contrast, companies whose strategies are based on development and exploitation of clearly defined internal resources and capabilities can successfully adapt to external changes. For example, the focus of Honda in improving the technical performance of the engines for their cars and motorbikes eventually resulted in a successful introduction of a product line of motor oils and related products. The experience of the company 3M in adhesives and adhesive technology has spread into a dedication for developing new products that enable profitable growth of the company's product portfolio, which is always spreading.

The Resources and Capabilities as the Basis for the Company's Profitability

The company's ability to earn a certain rate of return above the cost of capital depends on two factors: the attractiveness of the industry in which the company operates and its ability to gain a competitive advantage over competitors (Porter, 2001). Industrial economy and organization underlines the attractiveness of the industry as a primary reason for the superior profitability and the implications would be the focus of strategic management to hunt for an industry with favorable environment, locating attractive segments and strategic groups within a particular industry and mitigating competitive pressure by influencing the structure of the industry and the behavior of competitors. However, empirical findings still fail to firmly support the link between the structure of the industry and the profitability of the company. Studies show that differences in profitability between companies in one industry are more important than differences in profitability among industries (Schmalensee, 2001). It is not difficult to determine the reasons: international competition, technological change and diversification of companies crossed the industries' borders, causing the former "paradise for profitability" to turn into vigorous competition.

Thinking that the competitive advantage, rather than the external environment, is the primary source of profitability for the company draws the attention of companies to sources of sustainable competitive advantage. An equally important issue in strategic management as the choice between differentiation or cost leadership, or wider or narrower market range, is the resource position of the company. For example, choosing a strategy of cost leadership implies the existence of: economy of scale, superior process technology, ownership or access to cheap inputs and access to cheap labor. Analogous to this, the advantage of differentiation implies a strong brand, reputation, protected technology, specific channels of distribution and specialized sales and after sales services. In sum, the company's strategy should defocus from the search for monopoly profit (return on market power) and to look more for the Ricardo's earnings (return on the resources that provide a competitive advantage above the actual costs of such resources). When such resources will cease to be a source of competitive advantage (will be copied by other companies) the profit they generate would disappear.

If we go further, the detailed view of the market power and the monopoly profits it offers suggests that it has its roots in the company's resources. The main requirement for market strength is the presence of entry barriers (Baumol et al, 1992). The entry barriers are based on: economies of scale, patents, know-how, the company's brand and similar resources or a combination of the existing resources the companies possess which current or potential competitors acquire very slow and / or too expensively. Other structural sources of market power are also based on the companies' resources: monopoly price depends on the market share, which in turn is a consequence of the consumption efficiency, financial strength and similar resources (Wiggins, 1997). Resources that lead to an increase in the market power can be owned by one or more companies. Regardless of the form of competition, the relationship between resources and profit growth are shown in Figure 3 (Grant, 1991).

STRENGTHENING THE IMMOBILITY OF COMPANIES INTANGIBLE RESOURCES

The analysis of the impact of the heterogeneity of resources and their immobility on the sustainable competitive advantage of companies is inevitable. It can begin by examining the nature of competition when resources are perfectly homogeneous and mobile. This does not mean that there are industries in which this assumption is true. Although this is a purely theoretical assumption, however, it is reasonable to expect that in most industries there is a certain degree of homogeneity or heterogeneity of resources and they are less or more mobile.

Figure 3. The resources as the basis for profit growth

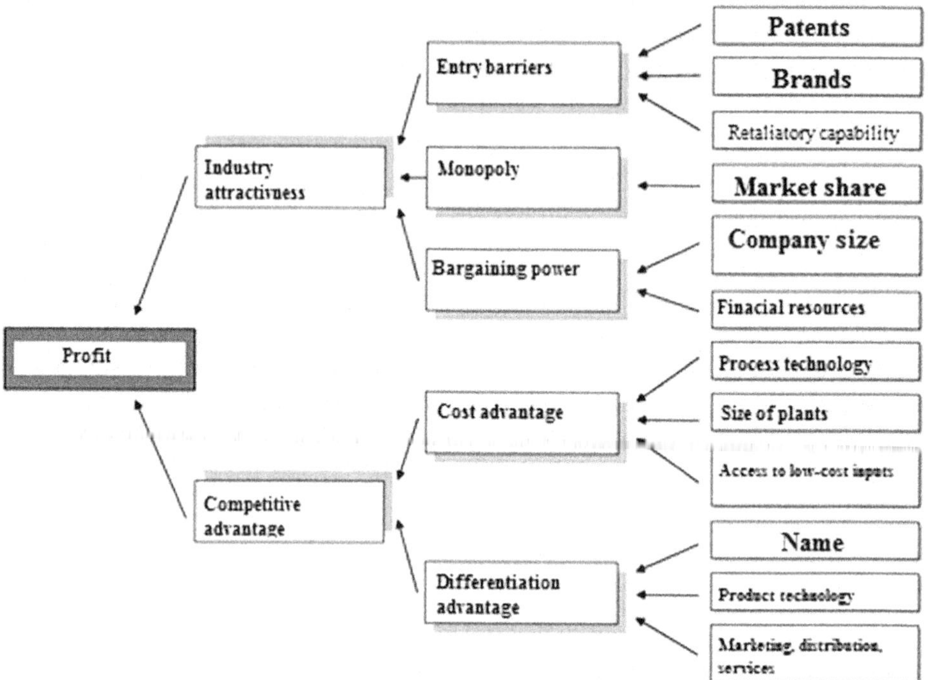

If resources are equally distributed among competing companies and are highly mobile, then can it be expected that gaining a sustainable competitive advantage is possible? Let's imagine an industry in which all companies possess completely same resources. This would mean that all companies have the same volume and the same kind of strategic relevant physical, human and organizational capital. In that case, is there a strategy that one company can choose and implement which will not be chosen and implemented by any other? Of course, the answer is: no. The concept of selection and implementation of the strategy involves the inclusion of various specific resources. If an industry is "inhabited" by the same companies, it means that they implement the same strategies and improve its effectiveness and efficiency to the same level. In this type of industry, it is impossible to gain a competitive advantage (even less a sustainable one). This initiates the analysis of homogeneity and mobility of resources in terms of first movers within the industry; analysis of the impact of resources' homogeneity and mobility to the entry barriers in a certain industry; and an appropriate recognition and development of the resources and capabilities of the company.

The Homogeneity and Mobility of Resources and the Advantage of the First Movers

One objection to the above statement applies to the so-called advantage of the first movers. Under certain circumstances, the first company in the industry that will implement a strategy could gain a competitive advantage. This may be an access to new, different channels of distribution, improved relations with customers or developing a positive reputation before others who later would implement their strategies. So the first mover can gain a competitive advantage.

However, after a good thinking, it is clear that if competing companies are identical in resources they control, then it is impossible to achieve a competitive advantage by a pioneering step. To be the first mover in implementing a strategy ahead of competitors, the company should be aware of the possibilities for implementing such a strategy which other companies in the industry or potential competitors do not have. This original corporate resource (information for opportunity) allows the better informed company to implement a strategy in front of others. But by definition, there are no original resources in the industry (it is comprised by almost identical companies). If a company is able to use some resources to implement a chosen strategy, then, in parallel, it can be done by all the other competitors, because there is no information asymmetry and companies at all times are aware of all the opportunities that can be exploited and do it the same way. This discussion is not aimed to suggest that there is no advantage for the first movers, but for it to exists, companies in one industry need to be heterogeneous in terms of the resources they possess. This is the basic premise on which the essence of branding and the brand equity are based.

The Homogeneity and Mobility of Resources and the Entry Barriers

A second objection to the conclusion that sustainable competitive advantage cannot exist if resources in one industry are perfectly homogeneous and mobile refers to the existence of entry barriers or, generally speaking, barriers to mobility. This argument says that even if the companies in an industry or strategic group are perfectly homogeneous, if there are strong entry barriers and mobility barriers, these companies are able to gain a competitive advantage over companies that are not in the industry (the strategic group). So, this competitive advantage will be reflected in above-average economic performance of companies that are protected from the new competitors' entry or mobility barriers.

A major handicap in the identification and exploitation of the resources of the company is the fragmented and incomplete picture of the company's resources. The financial statements are inadequate because they neglect the intangible resources that are actually the most important assets of the company. Table 1 shows that the highest rates of companies' value are found within companies with famous brands and those who have owned a patent or technology (Business Week Top 100, 2001, (http://www.businessweek.com/).

The main objective of the approach of formulating a strategy based on the company's resources is maximizing the profitability in the long term. Therefore, it is necessary to examine the relationship between resources and profitability because it opens important issues for the strategic management (Grant, 1991): Which options for saving with the use of resources through radical transparency exist? The ability to maximize productivity is particularly significant with material resources such as facilities, the equipment, finance and people. It can refer to engaging lower volume of resources in order to achieve the same level of business operation or using the current volume of resources to achieve higher performance.

Which are the possibilities of using existing resources more intensively, or to ensure their profitable engagement with radical transparency? Most of the take-overs in the world are based on the assumption that the resources of the company can be used more profitably. The returns form diverting resources towards a more productive use can be quite significant.

Table 1. List of companies with the highest ratio market capitalization / book value of the company

Company	Industry	Coefficient
Coca - Cola	Beverages	8,77
Microsoft	Computer software	8,67
Merck	Pharmacy	8,39
American Home Products	Pharmacy	8,00
Wal-Mart	Retail	7,51
Limited	Retail	6,65
Warner Lambert	Pharmacy	6,34
Waste Management	Utilities	6,18
Marrion Merrell Dow	Pharmacy	6,10
McCaw Cellular Communication	Telecommunications	5,90
Bristol Myers Squibb	Pharmacy	5,48
Toys R US	Retail	5,27
Abbot Laboratories	Pharmacy	5,26
Walt Disney	Entertainment	4,90
Johnson&Johnson	Health care	4,85
MCI Communications	Telecommunications	4,80
Eli Lilly	Pharmacy	4,70
Kellogg	Food	4,58
Heinz	Food	4,38
Pepsi Co.	Beverages	4,33

Identifying and Developing the Skills of the Company

The capabilities of the company are a result from the combination and joint functioning of the various resources of the company. There are numerous attempts to define them. For example, according to Snow and Hrebiniak (1980) skills are directly related to ten functional areas in the company. For most companies, the most important capabilities are those resulting from the integration of individual capabilities in the company. For example, the 3M Company possesses above-average functional capabilities within: product development, market research, human resources management, financial control and management of operations. The integration of these functional capabilities that shape the incredible consistency of products and services of 3M worldwide is the key for the company's success.

Hamel and Prahalad (1994) use the term "key competencies" to describe the most important intangible resources of the company. They represent the "collective knowledge of the company, especially the one concerning the coordination of various manufacturing skills and the integration of multiple flows of information through modern technologies." Examples of key competencies or capabilities are: (Hamel and Prahlad, 1994)

- The integration of computer and telecommunications technology of NEC;
- Philips experience with optical media;
- The Casio's harmonization of knowledge and experience for miniaturization, micro processing, material science and incredible precision in operations;
- The integration of optical, mechanical and microelectronic technology into Canon's products etc.

The concept of organizational routines helps to uncover the inherent relationships between resources, capabilities and competitive advantage (Grant, 1991):

1. **The Relationship Between Resources and Capabilities:** There are no predetermined relationships between resources and capabilities in a company. The type, quantity and quality of available resources have a strong impact on what the company can achieve, because they determine the scope and quality of organizational routines. The key "ingredient" of the relationship between resources and capabilities is the willingness of the company to achieve cooperation and coordination between them, as well as consistency and transparency. This means that any company should motivate their employees in a way that will cause a better execution of all functional routines. Organizational values, tradition and the leadership style are key factors for cooperation and employees' dedication and loyalty. Such relationships are seen as invisible resources through which a significant competitive advantage can be created.
2. **The Trade-Off Between Efficiency and Flexibility:** Routines are property of the company, such as skills are property of the individual. Just as the people's skills come to the fore semi-consciously, so organizational routines are the result of thoughtful knowledge and spontaneity, which ultimately determines to what extent will the capabilities of the company be articulated. Just as individuals "rust" when they rarely apply a certain skill, the companies can be "stuck" when it comes to irregular activities. This means that the efficiency and flexibility of each company come into a mutual compromise. Limited routines can be practiced very effective, near to perfect coordination (without any intervention from management and control), but the same company will not be able to respond quickly and adequately to new situations. Conversely, when flexibility as ability to respond quickly to changes is high, then the effectiveness of a wide range of activities in the company decreases.
3. **The Complexity of Capabilities:** Organizational capabilities differ in complexity. Some capabilities result from the contribution of a single resource. The successful development of several cardiovascular drugs from Du Pont is primarily due to the leadership of their main research pharmacologist Pieter Timmermans (Barney and Hesterly, 2007). The success of Drexel Burnham Lambert in the sale of "junk" bonds in the 1980s was almost entirely based on the skills of Michael Millken (The Economist, 2010). Others routines may include numerous interactions between different resources in the company. The ability of Walt Disney for "drawn engineering" is a result of integrated ideas, skills and knowledge derived from experience in making cartoons, psychology and the wide rank of technical disciplines (Christensen, 2001). However, the complexity of capabilities is particularly important for the sustainability of competitive advantage.
4. **Evaluating the Potential for Long-Term Profitability - Sustainable Competitive Advantage:** The utilization of company's resources and capabilities in the form of higher yields depends on two factors (Grant, 1991):
    a. The sustainability of the competitive advantage;
    b. The company's ability to keep these sources and the effects from them in its possession.

The approach to competitive advantage based on resources suggests four key features of resources and capabilities that determine the sustainability of the competitive advantage. They are: durability, transparency, transferability and replicability (Grant, 1991).

Durability

The durability of the competitive advantage of the company depends on the rate at which resources and capabilities depreciate or lapse and become insignificant. The durability of resources varies significantly depending on the degree of technological change. Such changes may shorten the life of equipment and other technological resources. On the other hand, abilities and intangible resources of the company have a greater potential for durability. For example, the company's reputation and brand equity have greater relative durability compared to investments in fixed assets. Most brands which today enjoy the highest level of customer loyalty are market leaders in their industry for almost a century (Coca-Cola, Unilever, GE, Kellogg's etc.). The increased turbulence in the environment reduces the lifespan of most resources, and when it comes to the brand, quite the contrary, it causes the effect of enhancing its value.

The greater consistency of capabilities and intangible resources compared to other resources is due to the possibility of the company to maintain capabilities through the replacement of certain resources. The ability of Rolls Royce to produce handmade luxury cars and the ability of 3M to introduce new products is maintained through several generations of employees. Such longevity depends, above all, on the management of such intangible skills and resources by ensuring their maintenance and renewal. Perhaps one of the most important roles of the organizational culture is providing support for retaining capabilities as a source of sustainable competitive advantage through the socialization of new employees (Barney, 1986).

Transparency

The company's ability to maintain its competitive advantage through time depends on the speed with which other companies can mimic its strategy. The imitation requires the competitor to overcome two problems. The first is the information problem: Which is the competitive advantage of the successful rival and how is it achieved? The second problem concerns the possibility of its imitation: How can a future direct competitor acquire the resources and skills necessary to imitate the successful strategy of a competitor (Dess et al, 2009). The information problem is a consequence of the imperfect information for two sets of relationships: 1) if a company wished to imitate the strategy of its rival, it must provide the capabilities that are the basis of the competitive advantage of the rival and then determine the resources needed to replicate these capabilities. This reveals the aspect of the competitive advantage transparency. In this sense, it is easier to identify and imitate a competitive advantage that is based on one superior capability, which itself stems from one variable, compared with the competitive advantage that comes from several interdependent capabilities resulting from several variables, such as the brand equity. For example, the superior performance of IBM (compared to other IT companies in the US) is multidimensional and difficult to understand. It is particularly difficult to recognize and separate the relative contributions to the success of IBM: the ability to research and develop product, the economies of scale, the vertical integration backwards, the excellent service for customers through quality sales and after-sales services and technical support etc.; 2) It is more difficult to copy a capability that requires complex coordination of many different resources than a capability based on the exploitation of one dominant resource. For example, the ability to deliver the consignment in one day by Federal Express involves close cooperation between a large number of employees, aircraft fleet, vehicles, tracking system and equipment for automatic sorting of shipments - all integrated into one system. In contrast, the position of the low-cost supply of gas in California by Atlantic Richfield is only due to its access to crude oil in Alaskan. The imperfect transparency is the basis of the so-called theory of uncertain imitability of Lippman and Rumelt: the greater the uncertainty in a market for what do successful companies do, the more it prevents the entry of new competitors and the higher the level of profit among existing competitors within the industry (Lippman and Rumelt, 1982).

Transferability

Having determined the sources of superior performance, their imitation requires an extensive employment of resources and capabilities required for a competitive challenge. The primary source of resources and capabilities are the markets for these inputs. If companies can provide the necessary resources and capabilities to imitate the competitive advantage of the successful opponent, then that competitive advantage will be a short-term advantage. However, most of the resources and capabilities are not easily transferable between companies, meaning that future direct competitors are not able, at least not on an equal basis, to gain the resources needed to imitate the competitive advantage of existing competitors. The inability to transfer resources and capabilities stems from several reasons (Grant, 1991):

1. **Geographic Immobility:** The high costs for relocation of equipment and specialized employees put companies into a position of competitive weakness comparing to the company that owns such specific resources.
2. **Imperfect Information:** The accurate estimation of the value of each resource is hindered by their heterogeneity and incomplete knowledge of the potential productivity of each resource. The already established ability of the company to acquire information through time over the productivity of its resources provides a superior knowledge against any future purchaser of the resources in question. Input markets' imperfection results in an overestimation or underestimation of the value of resources, and the latter increases the difference in profitability between companies in one industry (Barney, 1986).
3. **Specific Resources:** Regardless of transaction costs arising from resources' immobility and asymmetric information, the transfer of a resource or a combination of resources can cause a decrease in its value due to a decline in its productivity. The value of the brand equity is so associated with the company that created it, that even a change in the company's ownership can erode its value. For example, when Rover, MG, Triumph and Jaguar merged into British Leyland, the value of these brands dropped significantly (Gregory, 2004). And employees can also suffer a drop in productivity because of an internal transfer. If employee productivity depends on situational and motivational factors, then it is not reasonable to expect that a very successful employee in company can replicate his / her performance in another company. Some resources cannot be replaced (replicated), such as the famous brand as a source of sustainable competitive advantage of the company and the only way to acquire it is to buy the company. However, numerous examples from practice show that the change in ownership could affect the depreciation of the most valuable resources of the company.
4. **The Immobility of Capabilities:** Due to the complexity, the transferability of capabilities and intangible resources is far more difficult than that of material resources. To recreate a capability

elsewhere, it is not enough to transfer all the necessary resources, it is necessary to replicate the whole nature of organizational routines, including the necessary tactical knowledge and conscious and unconscious coordination. The re-creation of a new corporate environment is very uncertain. Providing equal conditions to develop the desired capability may not be impossible, but is, certainly, expensive.

5. **Replicability:** The inability to transfer resources and capabilities is a major constraint for companies that want to imitate somebody's success. The second way to acquire the necessary resources and capabilities is through private investment in them. Some resources can be easily imitated through replication. For example, in retail, the competitive advantage that comes from: electronic system for recording goods, club card for discounts or extended working hours can easily be overcome by copying competitors. In financial services, new product innovation (swaps, stripped bonds, options, futures, etc.) are easily recognized and imitated by competitors. But the resources and capabilities that are based on complex organizational routines are more difficult to be replicated. IBM's ability to motivate its employees and the incredible efficiency and flexibility of Nucor in steel production is a combination of complex routines that are fused through the corporate culture.

Evaluating the Potential for Long-Term Profitability: The Ownership of Competitive Advantage

The return on resources and capabilities of a company depends not only on the sustainability of the competitive advantage in the long run, but also on the ability of the company to keep such assets and returns in its possession (Barney, 2006). This question of ownership refers to the allocation of profits when proprietary rights are incompletely defined. If we go a step beyond the financial and physical assets in the balance sheet of the company, ownership becomes blurred. The company may possess intangible assets such as brands, patents, licenses, trade secrets, etc., but the scope of proprietary rights lacks a precise definition. For example, in the case of the skills of employees, two main problems can occur: the lack of a clear distinction between the company's technology and human capital and the limitations in the employment contracts regarding the services provided by employees (Jensen, 2000). The mobility of human capital shows that it is a risky strategy for the company to depend on the specific skills and knowledge of several key employees. These employees have a strong bargaining position which can be used to offset their contribution in the process of creating value in the company.

The process of strategy selection and implementation should result in a selection of a strategy that most effectively utilizes the key resources and capabilities. Let's take for example the incredible twist that Harley Davidson made in the late 1980s. The recognition by the top management that the most durable, non-transferable and irreplaceable resource is precisely the brand equity of Harley Davidson and its loyal consumers was fundamental. In virtually all other aspects of competitive performance: production cost, quality, production and processing technology and performance on the global market Harley Davidson was significantly inferior to its Japanese rivals. The only possibility of survival of Harley was by implementing a strategy that is based on the advantage of its brand image, while minimizing the weaknesses in other aspects. The new models of Harley Davidson that were sold in this period were based on the traditional design and features of Harley, and the marketing strategy concerned the extension of the image of individualism and strength which was typical for previous customers. In addition, the brand name was protected through a strong control of the dealer network. Certainly, the radical improvements in production efficiency and quality were necessary components of the strategy turnaround, but the strengthening and enlargement of the Harley Davidson image was the main driver of the increase in the market share from 27% to 44% in the US in the period 1984-1988, followed by an increase in net profit from 6.5 to 29.8 million US dollars (Hoskinsson et al, 2008).

The ability of resources to support a sustainable competitive advantage is essential for determining the time frame in the process of strategic planning. If the resources of the company lack durability or they are easily transferable and replaced, then the company should either accept a short-term strategy of "harvesting" or needs to invest in developing new sources of competitive advantage. When the company's resources are easily transferable or replicable, sustainable competitive advantage is possible only if the market is considered small and unattractive or if the company is able to hide its competitive advantage.

Transferability and replicability of resources is a key issue in strategic management. For example, numerous studies show that the advantages of Western companies in the distribution and sales of services were quickly adopted by Japanese companies, while Japan's commitment to quality and the development of new products have proved to be particularly difficult skills for adoption by companies from the Western world.

Identifying the Resource Gaps and Developing the Resource Base

The analysis of the company's resources leads to a conclusion that the resource base of the company is determined and that the main objective of the company's strategy is to use it in the name of profit maximization in the long term. But the approach based on resources does not focus only of the use of existing resources, but also of the development of the resource base. This means investing in the maintenance of the resources volume and its increase in order to strengthen the competitive advantage and expand company's strategic opportunities. This task is often called: filling the resource gaps (Stevenson, 1986).

The sustainability of competitive advantage against the competition and the growing consumer demands require companies to constantly develop the resource base. Such "upgrading" of competitive advantage is the central issue in the Porters analysis of the competitive advantage of nations (Porter, 1990). According to his analysis, the ability of companies and nations to establish and maintain international competitive advantage depends critically on the ability to continuously innovate and transfer the sources of competitive advantage from "basic" to "advanced" factors of production. An important feature of such advanced factors of production is that they offer a sustainable competitive advantage, as they are more specialized, meaning less mobile and difficult to be imitated.

The key to a successful application of the approach based on resources when selecting and implementing the company's strategy is the understanding of the relationship between resources, capabilities, competitive advantage and profitability, in particular, the understanding of the mechanisms by which competitive advantage can be sustained in the long term. This involves designing strategies that ensure maximum effect of the company's unique features, which exactly, the brand equity unites.

THE BRAND EQUITY THROUGH THE PRISM OF THE VRIO MODEL

In order to understand the sources of sustainable competitive advantage, it is necessary to build a theoretical model based on the assumption that companies' resources are heterogeneous and immobile. Of course, all the company's resources do not have the potential for sustainable competitive advantage. To have this potential, the resource should have the following attributes (Barney, 1991):

- It must be valuable in terms to exploit opportunities and / or neutralize threats in the company's environment;
- It must be rare among current and potential competitors;
- It must be difficult to be imitated and replicated by competitors who do not possess it;
- There should not be strategically equivalent substitutes for the resource that is valuable, rare and difficult to imitate.

These resources' attributes should be treated as empirical indicators for evaluating the heterogeneity and immobility of companies' resources in order to determine how much these resources are useful to generate sustainable competitive advantage. In fact, these essential features of resources form the basis of the so-called VRIO model used for the analysis of potential resources to generate sustainable competitive advantage and they are discussed in more details below.

The VRIO model was created to easily and better identify the strengths and weaknesses of companies by analyzing the internal factors - resources and capabilities. The concept is structured in a series of four questions about the activities carried out in the company (Barney, 2009): the question of the value (Value); the question of rarity (Rarity); the question about the possibility of imitation (Imitability); and the question of organization (Organization). The answers to these questions determine whether a resource or capability of the company is its advantage or weakness. Table 2 presents the four basic questions of the VRIO model.

Valuable Resources: The Question of Value

The company's resources can be a source of competitive advantage, but only if they are valuable. They are considered as such when they enable the company to select and implement strategies that improve the efficiency and effectiveness of the company. The traditional SWOT analysis (Strengths - Weaknesses - Opportunities - Threats) suggests that companies can improve their performance when their strategy exploits opportunities and neutralizes threats. The company's attributes can meet the conditions to qualify as sources of competitive advantage (e.g., rare, difficult to imitate and substitute), but such attributes are converted into valuable resources only when they enable exploitation of opportunities and offset the threats in the environment.

The question of value is: Does the resource or capability enable the company to respond adequately to a particular external threat or opportunity? Every company wants to have as many positive responses as possible. To be an organizational advantage, the brand equity as the common denominator of resources

Table 2. The VRIO model for internal analysis of company's strengths and weaknesses

1. The question of value: Does a certain resource enable the company to respond adequately to some external threats or opportunity? Does the brand equity provide such support?
2. The question of rarity: How much certain resources are rare, i.e. how many companies possess them? How much the brand equity is seen as rare and unique?
3. The question of imitability: Do competitors which do not have a particular resource have a cost-weakness in the acquisition and development of such a resource? How much does the creation of a similar competing brand cost?
4. The question of organization: How much the company is organized to take a full advantage of the competitive potential of its resources, and the potential of its brand?

and capabilities, should enable the company to exploit a particular opportunity or neutralize a certain threat. Resources or capabilities that prevent the company from exploiting a particular opportunity or avoid a threat are considered as weaknesses. So, the question of value links the internal analysis of strengths and weaknesses with the external analysis of opportunities and threats. Obviously, it cannot be expected that the resources and capabilities that currently have value, or that synthesize the value of the brand will always have value. Like everything else, they are subject to change. What is important is the change to move in the direction of reducing costs or increasing willingness of customers to pay a higher price (the main purpose of branding).

Company's resources must be valuable to be considered a potential source of competitive advantage, and this shows the significant complementarities between the models of competitive advantage based on the environment and models based on resources. Combined, these models make it possible to isolate the attributes of the company that are able to exploit opportunities and / or neutralize threats, which specifies them as valuable company's resources. Furthermore, the model based on resources suggests which additional features the resources should have in order to generate sustainable competitive advantage.

Rare Resources: The Question of Rarity

By definition, the valuable resources that are possessed by a relatively larger number of existing and potential competing companies cannot be a source of competitive advantage, even less a sustainable competitive advantage. The company enjoys a competitive advantage when it implements a strategy that creates value and that is not simultaneously implemented by another competitor. If a valuable resource is owned by a number of companies, then each of them has the opportunity to use it the same way, implementing a common strategy that does not provide a competitive advantage for any of the companies.

The same analysis applies to the sum of the company's resources when selecting and implementing a strategy, as is the brand equity. A strategy requires a particular mix of physical, human and organizational capital for its implementation. One specific resource required for the implementation of any strategy and which makes a set of resources to be specific is the managerial talent. If the sum of the company's resources is not rare, then many companies are able to implement the same strategy, so it will not lead to a competitive advantage, even though it comes from valuable resources.

This statement raises the second question: How much certain resources are rare, i.e. how many companies possess them? The resources with value but common representation do not create a competitive advantage, but they prevent a competitive weakness. Undoubtedly, the brand equity as a synthesis of the company's resources has a high potential value and rarity, simultaneously.

To have a resource that has value, but is also shared by competitors, is not a source of competitive advantage. The resources that have value but are generally available only lead to competitive parity (Porter, 1998). This means that if the valuable resources of the company are not rare, it should not be assumed that they are not important resources for the company. Rather, such resources ensure the company's survival when used for gaining competitive parity in the field. In terms of competitive parity, although no company achieves competitive advantage, companies increase the likelihood of further economic survival and gaining a competitive advantage in future.

It is difficult to answer how rare should a valuable resource of the company be in order to have high potential to generate a competitive advantage. It is not difficult to see that the valuable resources of the company that are absolutely original (such as the brand equity) will generate, at least, competitive advantage, and have the potential to create a sustainable competitive advantage. However, a small number of companies within a specific industry possess a valuable resource or a combination of resources that lead to a competitive advantage. In general, as long as the number of these companies is less than the number of companies needed to create a perfect competition in one industry, their resources have the potential to generate competitive advantage.

Resources Difficult to Imitate: The Question of Imitability

It is not difficult to see that valuable and rare resources of the company can be a source of competitive advantage. In fact, companies with such resources are strategic innovators frequently, so they would be able to select and implement strategies that other competitors would not be able to select or implement because they lack relevant resources. The observation that the valuable and rare resources can be a source of competitive advantage is a way of describing the advantages of the first movers in the industry.

However, valuable and rare resources can be a source of sustainable competitive advantage only if the companies that do not own them cannot gain them. Valuable and rare organizational resources and capabilities are a temporary source of competitive advantage that exists under the condition that those competitors which do not have such resources and capabilities have a cost- weakness in their acquisition and development. These resources and capabilities are considered difficult to imitate. The company's resources can be difficult to be imitated because of one or a combination of the following three reasons (Lippman and Rumelt, 1982):

- The company's ability to acquire a resource depends on unique historical circumstances;
- The relationship between resources owned by the company and its competitive advantage is often unclear;
- Generating a competitive advantage through company's resources is a complex social phenomenon.

The Question of Organization

The companies' potential to create a competitive advantage is based on the extent of the value, rarity and imitability of their resources. However, to fully realize this potential, the company should be well organized. These considerations lead to the fourth question of the VRIO concept: How well the company is organized to take a full advantage of the competitive potential of its resources? Numerous elements of the organization of the company are relevant to the answer of this question, including the formal organizational structure, authority, responsibility and empowerment, the system of management and control, the system of paying and rewarding employees etc. These elements are often considered to be complementary resources, because their individual importance for creating a competitive advantage is limited. The proper combination can ensure a full utilization of the potential of the company to create a competitive advantage. To fulfill this role, until now, there has not been a better "glue" then the brand equity. Nurturing the vision and values of the brand itself, dictates the level of organization aimed to realize the promise of the brand, which means that all the company's resources are integrated around a common purpose.

Assembling the VRIO Model

The questions of value, rarity, imitability and organization can be consolidated into a single framework through which the potential of any company's resource or the brand as a synthesis of resources and capabilities can be analyzed. The full content of the VRIO model is shown in Table 3.

If the brand is not valuable, then it does not allow the company to implement a strategy based on the use of a particular external opportunity or neutralization of an external threat. The utilization of this kind of brand increases the company's costs and reduces the willingness of customers to pay a set price. This combination of resources is a weakness of the company, so it should either correct it or avoid it. If the brand is valuable, but it not rare, its use in the implementation of the strategy leads to a competitive parity. But its non-utilization leads to a competitive weakness. In this sense, valuable, but not rare brands are considered an organizational advantage. If the brand is valuable and rare, but easy to imitate, its use leads to a temporary competitive advantage. The companies with such resources are considered the first movers on the market. In the period between the acquisitions of such resource by the first company to the point of imitating it by other competitors, the first mover achieves a superior performance. Consequently, these brands are considered unique organizational advantages. If the brand is valuable, rare and difficult to imitate, its utilization generates a sustainable competitive advantage. In this case competitors are facing a cost-weakness to imitate such a brand. Resources in symbiosis create the brand equity that that is considered a sustainable unique organizational advantage. This is, actually, its exalted role. The organization appears as a factor for adjustment within the VRIO model. If the company owns valuable, rare, and difficult to imitate resources, i.e. specific brand equity, but it is not sufficiently organized for his full exploitation, then part of its competitive potential will be lost.

- **Interchangeability:** The last condition for a resource or a combination of resources to be a source of sustainable competitive advantage is that no other strategically equivalent valuable resources which are rare and difficult to imitate exist. Substitution can occur in at least two forms. First, although it may not be possible for a company to fully replicate the resources of another company, it may be able to substitute a similar resource that allows it to select and implement the same strategy. Second, many different resources can be strategic substitutes. For example, employees in a company can have a very clear vision for the future of their company, because of the charismatic style of their leader, while employees in another competitive company may, also, have a very clear vision for the future of their company resulting from the systematic and comprehensive process of strategic planning of the company.

Table 3. Relations between the VRIO model and the strengths and weaknesses of the company

Is the Resource / Capability / Brand...				
Valuable?	**Rare?**	**Hard to Imitate?**	**Exploited by the Company?**	**Advantage or Disadvantage**
No				Disadvantage
Yes	No			Parity
Yes	Yes	No		Temporary advantage
Yes	Yes	Yes	Yes	Sustainable unique advantage

The relationship between resources' heterogeneity and immobility, their value, rarity, imitability, organization and interchangeability and the competitive advantage is summarized in Figure 4 (Barney, J., 1998).

This model can be applied in the analysis of the potential of a wide range of resources and their combinations as a source of sustainable competitive advantage. This analysis not only theoretically specifies the conditions under which a sustainable competitive advantage can be obtained, but also suggests some empirical questions to be answered in order to understand the relationship between a particular resource or a combination of resources and the competitive advantage they can generate.

The literature on various aspects of strategic planning and how to generate a competitive advantage, day by day, is growing more and more. Formal systems of strategic planning lead to a detection of the suitable sources of competitive advantage. Formal systems of strategic planning enable companies to identify and exploit the resources that have high potential as a source of competitive advantage. In this sense, they fulfill their role in the search for sustainable competitive advantage. Apart from the formal, there are informal, casual and self-contained processes through which companies can choose and implement its strategy. It cannot be concluded that they, themselves, are a source of competitive advantage, but practice shows that there are companies that rely on these informal processes and succeed to generate competitive advantage. Regardless of the effectiveness, their main application as an organizational resource is to enable recognition of other resources of the company that would meet the conditions of the sources of sustainable competitive advantage.

Having in mind that the focus of this book is the brand equity as a source of sustainable competitive advantage, the purpose of the strategic planning would be to combine and integrate the company's resources that will contribute to increase the value of the brand, because the latter means higher profitability and value for shareholders in the long term.

CONCLUSION

The literature on various aspects of strategic planning and how to generate competitive advantage through radical transparency in each operation is growing day by day. The practice starts to follow the scientific

Figure 4. The relationship between resources' heterogeneity and immobility, their value, rarity, imperfect imitability, organization, interchangeability and competitive advantage

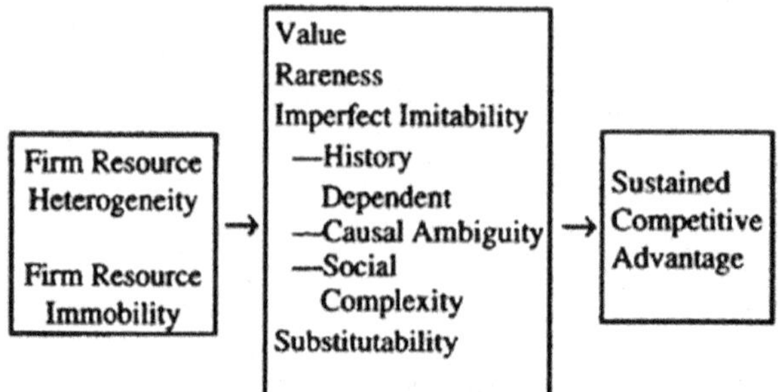

thought. It is reasonable to expect that formal systems for strategic planning and their consistent application can lead to discovering a suitable source of competitive advantage.

Studies of the sources of sustainable competitive advantage, essentially focused on one of the following alternatives: isolating the opportunities and threats of companies; describing the strengths and weaknesses of companies; or analyzing how the first and second alternative to be integrated in order to choose the appropriate strategy. Although in literature both, the internal analysis of organizational strengths and weaknesses and the external analysis of the opportunities and threats have received proper attention, influenced by Porter and his colleagues, most recent studies focus on the analysis of opportunities and threats of companies in the competitive environment. These papers describe the conditions in the environment that favor high performance of companies. For example, the Porter's model of five competitive forces explains the characteristics of an attractive business, suggesting that opportunities are greater and threats smaller in such industries. Models of competitive advantage based on the environment assume that companies within an industry are identical in terms of strategically relevant resources that they control and the strategies they choose. Second, these models assume that if there is heterogeneity of resources within an industry or a strategic group (for example, with the entry of a new competitor), it will be exceeded in short time, because the resources used by companies to implement their strategies are highly mobile.

The strategic analysis of resources substitutes these with two other assumptions for a proper analysis of the sources of competitive advantage. First, it is assumed that companies within an industry or a strategic group can be heterogeneous in terms of the resources they own and control. Second, it is assumed that the resources may not be perfectly mobile among companies, so heterogeneity can be long-lasting. The model based on the company's resources examines the implications of these two assumptions in order to appropriately analyze the sources of sustainable competitive advantage. These studies paved the way for recognizing the importance of the brand equity as the most specific corporate resource that offers the choice and implementation of a strategy that is difficult to be replicated by competitors. This means that the brand is nothing but a source of sustainable competitive advantage.

Thinking that the competitive advantage, rather than the external environment, is the primary source of profitability for the company draws the attention of companies to sources of sustainable competitive advantage. An equally important issue in strategic management as the choice between differentiation or cost leadership or wider or narrower market range is the resource position of the company. For example, choosing a strategy of cost leadership implies the existence of: economy of scale, superior process technology, ownership or access to cheap inputs and access to cheap labor. Analogous to this, the advantage of differentiation implies a strong brand, reputation, protected technology, specific channels of distribution and specialized sales and aftersales services. In sum, the company's strategy should defocus from the search for monopoly profit (return on market power) and to look more for the Ricardo's earnings (return on the resources that provide a competitive advantage above the actual costs of such resources).

The sustainability of competitive advantage against the competition and the growing consumer demands require companies to constantly develop the resource base. The ability of companies to establish and maintain international competitive advantage depends critically on the ability to continuously innovate and transfer the sources of competitive advantage from "basic" to "advanced" factors of production. An important feature of such advanced factors of production is the offer of a sustainable competitive advantage, as they are more specialized, meaning less mobile and difficult to be imitated.

The key to a successful application of the approach based on resources when selecting and implementing the company's strategy is the understanding of the relationship between resources, capabilities, competitive advantage and profitability, in particular, the understanding of the mechanisms by which competitive advantage can be sustained in the long term. This involves designing strategies that ensure maximum effect of the company's unique features, which exactly, the brand equity unites.

The relationship between resources' heterogeneity and immobility, their value, rarity, imitability, organization and interchangeability and the competitive advantage can be summarized in one model. This model can be applied in the analysis of the potential of a wide range of resources and their combinations as a source of sustainable competitive advantage. This analysis not only theoretically specifies the conditions under which there a sustainable competitive advantage can be obtained, but also suggests some empirical questions to be answered in order to understand the relationship between a particular resource or a combination of resources and the competitive advantage they can generate

If the brand is valuable, rare and difficult to imitate, its utilization generates a sustainable competitive advantage. In this case competitors are facing a cost-weakness to imitate such a brand. Resources in symbiosis create brand equity that is considered a sustainable unique organizational advantage. This is, actually, its exalted role. The organization appears as a factor for adjustment within the VRIO model. If the company owns valuable, rare, and difficult to imitate resources, i.e. specific brand equity, it has to be sufficiently organized for their full exploitation; otherwise part of the company's competitive potential will be lost.

Because the focus of this book is building brand equity as a source of sustainable competitive advantage, the purpose of strategic planning should be open, responsive and consistent combination and integration of the company's resources that will contribute to increase the value of the brand, which means higher profitability and value for shareholders in the long term.

REFERENCES

Barney, J. (1986). Organizational Culture: Can It Be a Source of Sustained Competitive Advantage? *Academy of Management Review*, *11*(3), 656–665. doi:10.2307/258317

Barney, J. (1986). Strategic Factor Markets: Expectations, Luck and Business Strategy. *Management Science*, *32*(10), 1231–1241. doi:10.1287/mnsc.32.10.1231

Barney, J. (1986). Strategic Factor Markets: Expectations, Luck and Business Strategy. *Management Science*, *32*(10), 1231–1241. doi:10.1287/mnsc.32.10.1231

Barney, J. (1991). Firm Resources and Sustained Competitive Advantage. *Journal of Management*, *17*(1), 99–120. doi:10.1177/014920639101700108

Barney, J. (2006). *Gaining and Sustaining Competitive Advantage*. Addison Wesley Publishing Co.

Barney, J. (2009). *Gaining and Sustaining Competitive Advantage*. Pearson, Prentice Hall.

Barney, J., & Hesterly, W. (2007). *Strategic Management and Competitive Advantage*. Addison Wesley Publishing Co.

Baumol, W., Panzer, J., & Willin, R. (1992). *Considerable Markets and the Theory of Industrial Structure*. Hartcourt Brace.

Caves, R. (1981). International Corporations: The Industrial Economics of Foreign Investment. *Economica, 38*(149), 1–27. doi:10.2307/2551748

Christensen, C. (2001). The Past and Future of Competitive Advantage. *MIT Sloan Management Review, 42*, 356–371.

Dess, G., Lumpkin, T., & Eisner, A. (2009). *Strategic Management: Creating Competitive Advantage*. McGraw-Hill.

Grant, R. (1991). The Resource – Based Theory of Competitive Advantage: Implications for Strategy Implementation. *California Management Review, 33*(3), 122. doi:10.2307/41166664

Gregory, J. (2004). *The best of branding: best practices in corporate branding*. McGraw-Hill Professional.

Hamel, G., & Prahlad, C. (1994). *Competing for the Future*. HBS Press.

Hoskinsson, R., Hitt, M., Ireland, R., & Harrison, J. (2008). *Competing for Advantage*. Thomson South-Western Co.

Ingemar, D., & Cool, K. (1989). Asset Stock Accumulation and the Sustainability of Competitive Advantage. *Management Science, 32*(12), 1504–1513.

Jensen, B. (2000). *Simplicity: The New Competitive Advantage in a World of More, Better, Faster*. Perseus Books.

Leavitt, H. (1986). A Note on Some Experimental Findings about the Meaning of Price. *The Journal of Business, 27*(3), 205–210. doi:10.1086/294039

Lippman, S., & Rumelt, R. (1982). Uncertain imitability: An analysis of interfirm differences in efficiency under competition. *The Bell Journal of Economics, 13*(2), 418–438. doi:10.2307/3003464

Penrose, E. (1959). *The Theory of the Growth of the Firm*. John Wiley&Sons.

Porter, M. (1990). *The Competitive Advantage of Nations*. Free Press. doi:10.1007/978-1-349-11336-1

Porter, M. (1995). *Competitive Strategy: Techniques for Analyzing Industries and Competitors*. Free Press.

Porter, M. (1996). What is Strategy? *Harvard Business Review, 56*, 167–185. PMID:11143152

Porter, M. (1998). *Competitive Advantage: Creating and Sustaining Superior Performance*. Free Press. doi:10.1007/978-1-349-14865-3

Porter, M. (2001). From Competitive Advantage to Corporate Strategy. *Harvard Business Review, 73*, 258–271. PMID:17183795

Porter, M. (2008). *On Competition*. HBS Publishing.

Ricardo, D. (1891). *Principles of Political Economy and Taxation*. G. Bell.

Rouse, M., & Daellenbach, U. (2001). Rethinking research methods for the resource-based perspective: Isolating sources of sustainable competitive advantage. *Strategic Management Journal, 20*, 118.

Rumelt, R. (1982). Uncertain Imitability: An Analysis of Interfirm Differences in Efficiency under Competition. *The Bell Journal of Economics*, *23*, 418–438.

Schmalensee, R. (2001). Industrial Economics: An Overview. *The Economic Journal*, *98*(392), 643–681. doi:10.2307/2233907

Schumpeter, J. (1934). *The Theory of Economic Development*. HBS Press.

Snow, C., & Hrebiniak, L. (1980). Strategy, Distinctive Competence and Organizational Performance. *Administrative Science Quarterly*, *25*(2), 317–336. doi:10.2307/2392457

Stern, W., & Deimler, M. (2006). *The Boston Consulting Group on Strategy: Classic Concepts and New Perspectives*. John Wiley & Sons Inc.

Stevenson, H. (1990). Defining Corporate Strengths and Weaknesses. *Sloan Management Review*, *18*, 51–68.

Teece, D. (1980). Economies of Scope and the Scope of the Enterprise. *Journal of Economic Behavior & Organization*, *1*(3), 223–247. doi:10.1016/0167-2681(80)90002-5

Teece, D. (1988). Capturing Value from Technological Innovation: Integration, Strategic Partnering and Licensing Decisions. *Interfaces*, *18*(3), 46–61. doi:10.1287/inte.18.3.46

The Economist. (2010, October 21). Drexel Burnham Lambert's legacy: Stars of the junkyard. *The Economist,* p. 32.

Wiggins, R. (1997). *Sustaining Competitive Advantage: Temporal Dynamics and the Rarity of Persistent Superior Economic Performance.* A.B. Freeman School of Business.

Williamson, O. (1992). Markets, hierarchies, and the modern corporation: An unfolding perspective. *Journal of Economic Behavior & Organization*, *17*(3), 335–352. doi:10.1016/S0167-2681(95)90012-8

Chapter 5
Combining Radical Transparency With the Brand Pentagon

ABSTRACT

This chapter completely covers the process of building and managing the brand through the concept of radical transparency. If it is more than certain that the brand equity is a source of sustainable competitive advantage, than it is important to find the best way to build and manage it. This chapter includes each phase of the model named as the brand pentagon: birth, definition, articulation, measurement and expansion of the brand. The model is a compilation of recognized models from world-famous authors, globally validated by major corporations worldwide. The detailed analysis presents the importance of each stage in completing the mosaic called the brand. The brand birth is the initial stage, directly related to the vision of the brand, and the brand-dependent areas: the environment in which the brand is developed. Next, the brand definition analyzes the brand reasons, through positioning and mapping. In the brand articulation phase the ways of brand communication are discussed. The brand measurement and expansion are elaborated in the fourth and fifth stage. The process of building and managing the brand is summarized with a discussion over the need to create a separate culture of nurturing the brand and living for the brand, by building a so-called brand culture and brand company.

INTRODUCTION

This chapter completely covers the process of building and managing the brand through the concept of radical transparency. If it is more than certain that the brand equity is a source of sustainable competitive advantage, than it is important to find the best way to build and manage it. This chapter includes each phase of the model named as *the brand pentagon*: birth, definition, articulation, measurement and expansion of the brand. The model is a compilation of recognized models from world-famous authors, globally validated by major corporations worldwide. Through a logical sequence, gradually systematized and analyzed, all the activities complete the process. The detailed analysis presents the importance of

DOI: 10.4018/978-1-5225-2417-5.ch005

each stage in completing the mosaic called the brand. The exercise of the previous forms the foundation for the next phase. The brand birth is the initial stage, directly related to the vision of the brand, and the brand-dependent areas: the environment in which the brand is developed. Next, the brand definition analyzes the brand reasons, through positioning and mapping. In the brand articulation phase the ways of brand communication are discussed. And as the name suggests, in the fourth and fifth stage the brand measurement and expansion are elaborated. The process of building and managing the brand is summarized with a discussion over the need to create a separate culture of nurturing the brand and living for the brand, by building a so-called brand culture and brand company.

Regardless the state – a developed economy or a developing economy, each brings specific challenges and opportunities. The issues the companies face are somewhat different, but one thing is common to all: it is necessary to develop and then implement a suitable model for building the brand that will satisfy the specific requirements for each individual example. Most of the world recognized and applied models for building brands were developed and refined through the American and/or European perspective. These models include: the process of brand management by David Arnold, the strategic brand management by Kevin Lane Keller, the guide for building brands by David Aaker and the brand program of Jean-Noel Kapferer. The aforementioned models will be briefly explained, followed by a detailed elaboration of the model named the brand pentagon that represents a sublimation of the above models, with the intention to involve all key elements of the process of building the brand, of course, with the necessary adjustments in a particular case. What is crucial for the success of the new business model is the transparent approach in the planning and execution of each element of the process of building and managing the brand, because it is the only way to reverse the mistakes and shortcomings in the process. With a proper involvement of all key internal stakeholders - managers and employees in the process of building and managing the brand through radical transparency, the ultimate goal of any business - creating a brand company can be achieved.

- **The Process of Brand Management by David Arnold:** This model is designed with the intention to serve existing brands as a way to check the current situation and support the transition to a higher level (Arnold, 1992). The first stage is the market analysis. Market analysis should consist of: analysis of sales volume, the value of sales, geographical analysis, seasonality, etc. Further analysis should refer to customers: the range of use, frequency of use, the differences among consumers and so on. The next stage is the analysis of the brand situation, where the brand is analyzed through these issues: growth, efficiency, benefits, attributes, positioning, packaging, price level and the like. This stage is not relevant in the case of creating a new brand. The third phase concerns targeting the future position, so, for example, how will a manufacturer of shampoos attract the largest number of new customers: if the brand relates to hair conditioner or shampoo for dandruff? Will it be in the premium category or an ordinary shampoo, and can it be two in one - a shampoo and conditioner? This phase defines the answers for such issues. In the fourth stage, the positioning and the offer developed in the previous phase are being tested: how this offer will operate in the market. Testing is mainly delivered through simulations or test operations on the market. Often, both are applied, in order to minimize potential risks and negative effects on the company. The fifth or the last stage is the brand introduction or its commercialization and the start of the formal planning and the evaluation process. This model helps managers and employees to easily plan and realize the launch of the company's brand. In real terms, the process is repeated annually, in order to provide "the good brand health".

- **The Process of Strategic Brand Management by Kevin Lane Keller:** This model with four steps begins with a request to identify and establish the position of the brand and its values TKeller, 2007). The focus at this stage is placed on identifying and establishing the position of the brand and its values. The next phase consists of planning and implementation of the marketing programs for the brand. Once the brand position and values are identified and established, the next task is to convey an appropriate message to customers through a combination of marketing activities. The third stage relates to the measurement and integration of the brand performance. This phase includes monitoring the brand through: sales, market share, its reputation and market growth. The performance of the brand can be influenced by several factors, so the main task at this stage is to identify the elements which support and those which harm the process. The last stage refers to increasing and maintaining the brand equity. How can the brand continue to grow and stay relevant among consumers? Today we ignore yesterday's conditions, because the market is constantly changing - consumers are constantly changing. Then how can the brand grow in a market that is constantly changing? Should the brand expand into new markets? How to maintain the brand equity? This model allows the company to set a standard that leads to building a strong and consistent brand.
- **The Guide for Building Brands by David Aaker:** This model includes ten guidelines for building strong brands (Aaker, 1996):
    - **Brand Identity:** Each brand should have its own identity;
    - **Value Proposal:** The value proposal should be determined and well known for each brand, because it is one of the key factors in creating value;
    - **Brand Positioning:** The brand should have a clear position, which will be a guideline for the implementation of communications;
    - **Brand Execution:** It is necessary to realize brilliant and long-lasting communication programs;
    - **Brand Consistency:** Consistency is needed among the brand identity, position and performance over time;
    - **Brand System:** Synergy of activities around the brand should be ensured;
    - **Brand Leverage:** Brand expansion to new products and markets;
    - **Brand Equity:** Tracking brand equity over time through awareness, perceived quality, associations and loyalty;
    - **Brand Responsibility**: Setting persons responsible and in charge of the process of building and managing the brand;
    - **Brand Investments:** Continuous investments in the brand.

These guidelines represent a template for building / managing the brand.

- **The Brand Program of Jean-Noel Kapferer:** Professor Kapferer presents the brand program in 9 steps (Kapferer, 1997):
    - Why should the brand exist? What would the consumer lack if the brand does not exist?
    - Rostrum. From which position is the brand "talking"?
    - Vision. Which is the vision that exists for the brand and for the business or the products and services it covers?
    - Values. Which are the core values of the brand?

- ◦ Mission. Which changes does the brand want to make in the lives of consumers?
- ◦ Territory. Where is the brand legitimate in achieving its mission?
- ◦ "Anchor of activities and products." Which products or activities are best suited for the mission and value of the brand?
- ◦ The style and language of the brand. Which elements in terms of style and language are typical for the brand?
- ◦ The imaginary brand client: Not the targeted, but the reflected consumer.

These guidelines, applied with an appropriate depth, are used worldwide as a guide in building the brand.

- **The Brand Pentagon:** Building the brand is more than choosing a product or service, name fixing, price fixing and market offer. This model assumes that in the center of each activity for building the brand are the primary variables that describe the core of the brand. the brand attributes, the price level, distribution, packaging and profit (Parameswaran, 2006). These variables cannot be drawn from a hat juggler. They need to be developed systematically and be flexible enough to properly react to potential changes in the conditions under which the brand is functioning, Figure 1.
- **The Proposed Model:** The brand pentagon consists of five successive phases, all of which are directly related to the core - the brand performance. The company exists to achieve the expectations of itss shareholders, so the brand exists in order to generate long-term profits. Therefore, the core of the brand covers the Philip Kotler's 4P, adding packaging, service and profit / loss evaluation. These seven variables adapt, as the brand is built through the individual phases.

Figure 1. The Brand Pentagon

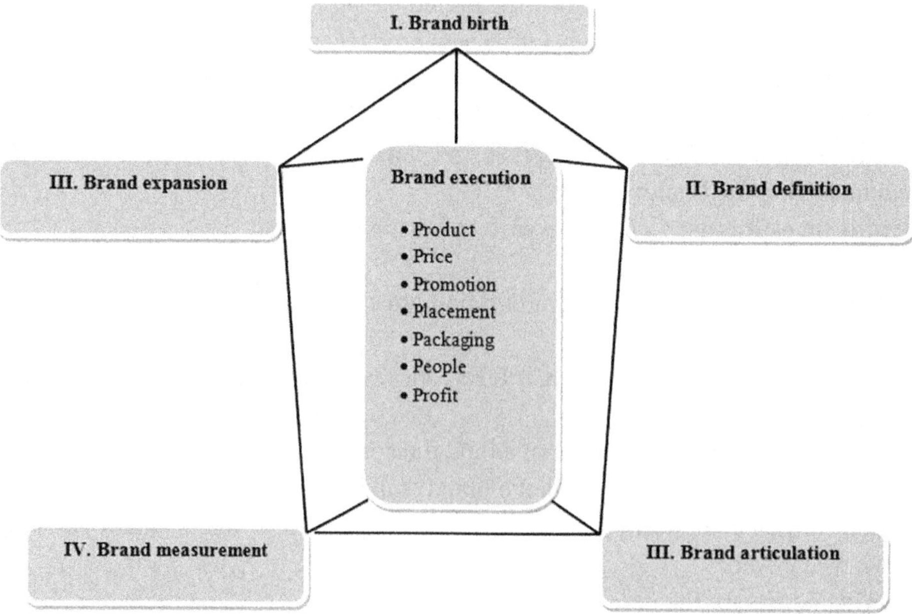

The first phase in the brand pentagon is the brand birth stage. The key question that needs to be answered at this stage is whether there is a market for the products / services of the company. A frequent comment in the marketing circles is that there is a "hole in the market," but what is important is whether there is a market in the hole. For example, there are people who drink the coffee warm; there are some (less) who want to drink cold coffee. They represent the gap in the market. The question is whether the number of fans of cold coffee is large enough to ensure profitable functioning of a brand for cold coffee. The fashion industry, which is the eternal pursuit of creativity, properly uses the market gaps. The first stage is critical because it is the moment when the company must decide whether to continue further or to leave the idea for the brand.

The second stage refers to the brand definition. Once you identify the possibility, for example, consumers do not want big cars, but small, the next step would be a definition of the new car. How small should the car be, which value for the money will be offered, which performances will it have? The brand definition refers to the brand offer which includes rational and emotional significance for consumers. There are several models for defining the brand that will be analyzed in-depth later in this chapter.

The third phase is the brand articulation, that is, how the brand will be expressed to the target consumers? Which will be the name of the brand and why? Which will be the packaging and graphic design? Which will be the positioning? Which role will the other elements of the marketing program have? The brand articulation is about developing a way of presenting the "face of the brand" to customers.

The next stage is the brand measurement, or the way the brand performance is monitored. Once you identify the possibility to define the brand and develop its expression, comes the phase of launching the brand and the measurement of its performance. The brand measurement includes an established system of measures that will follow the progress of the brand on a monthly, quarterly or annually basis.

The fifth stage relates to moving the brand forward through the brand expansion. Once the brand "starts", the next step is to provide a way for it to stay ahead of competitors. Should the brand expand to other products and markets?

Through the five stages of the brand pentagon, the process of building the brand is associated with the central core - the brand execution. The brand execution is refined through the progress from the brand birth, through the definition, articulation, measurement and its expansion. In this way, the brand pentagon leads the company, step by step, through the process of branding products / services or businesses. This chapter will further analyze each phase of the model in detail.

BRAND APPRAISAL

The first phase of the brand pentagon, the brand birth refers to the research of: the possibility of branding, the potential for a new brand, the possibilities for the "tired, old" brands, the way to get to a strong brand. The brand birth phase can be divided into five components, equally important to build a complete picture of the brand potential (Parameswaran, 2006). In fact, this stage is a structural analysis of the brand area or the brand surrounding. The market analysis refers to the recognition of: the market size, its growth, segments, geography, seasonality and distribution issues. The competitors analysis includes analysis of: key market players, i.e. competitors in the industry, including those that produce complementary and supplementary products / services. The consumer analysis includes detailed analysis of customers:

numbers, habits and behavior or analysis all factors that affect the consumer and his/her purchase decision. The capabilities analysis should be an objective look at the capabilities, knowledge and skills within the company, including: technology, research and development, know-how, sales and distribution force. And last but not least, the PEST analysis is an analysis of the board external environment, government regulations, macroeconomic implications, sociological changes, technological developments and global trends. The five components of the phase of the brand birth enable the company to learn more about the opportunities to create a strong, pulsating brand.

Market Analysis

The first step in the brand birth stage is to examine whether there is an opportunity in the market, as defined. Market definition varies from industry to industry. In some cases, an appropriate definition of the market size may lack, and then it is determined by surrogate sizes. The estimation of the size of the market is not enough, you need more than checking numbers to examine the characteristics of the market, such as: volume, value, price segments, seasonality, the growth in volume compared to the increase in value, geography and so on. Assessing the scope of the market and its growth is important, but insufficient to conclude the attractiveness of the market. It is equally important to assess the magnitude of value and its growth, as well as the price segments of the market. For example, in some industries at a certain point a trend of increasing the volume of sales may occur, but with a decrease in value due to a significant decline in prices. In addition to the analysis of value / volume and their growth, market analysis should serve as a compass to identify the segments and their further analysis. A decline or a very small growth may occur in the market as a whole in a particular category, except for one segment where volumes and values may behave quite contrary (significant increase). A typical example is the previously mentioned market for passenger cars. Its growth over the past decade is almost imperceptible, but analyzed separately; the segment of small passenger cars for city traffic experienced a growth that offset the decline in the other segments in the industry.

Viswanath and Mark (2007) argue whether thc large market share guarantees high profits. According to them, the profit of the brand depends on both the relative market share (RMS) and the premium status in the category (price level). Based on this assumption, a double-factor matrix is built, shown in Figure 2.

Figure 2. Brand share versus brand profit

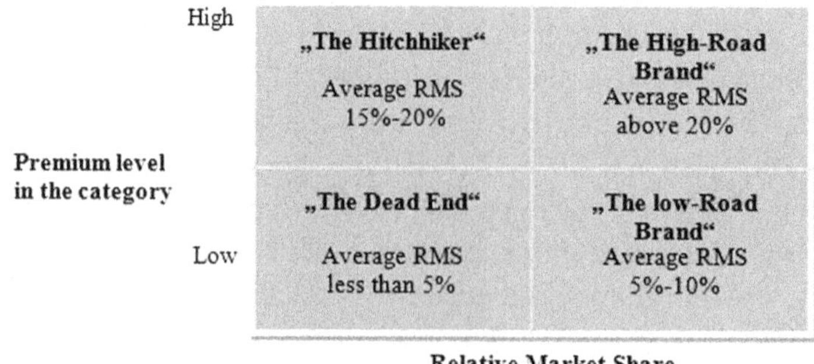

By analyzing the pattern, it can be clearly recognized that the brand with a relatively small market share, but with a premium level can achieve higher profitability from the brand with significant market share, but with a low-price level.

Another important variable for the market analysis are the geographical segments. Even in smaller countries, there are different regions that are specific and vary according to the consumers' characteristics, their preferences and requirements. The geographical distribution is particularly important for companies that are participating in the large, diverse markets and the importance of this issue for companies that are found in many international markets is more than obvious.

The analysis of the seasonal nature of demand in a particular category helps in understanding the differences in the market size through the months. There are seasonal trends affecting the fluctuations in sales during the year, including: holidays, marriages, flu and colds, the beginning and end of the school year, religious holidays and so on.

The market analysis should include the analysis of the distribution dispersion. How much of the market share is spread by a particular distribution channel? Do you need a retail network or it can be circumvented through direct sales? For example, Dell has created a whole new system of selling computers, when they started to use the Internet for consumers to self-configure their PC and order it by themselves.

Market analysis can go in several directions, depending on the company, its product / service, but it should not cause confusion and congestion with information. The data from the market analysis should be systematized in order to draw the most important conclusions of the gaps in the market and the potential of its segments.

Consumer Analysis

The consumer analysis usually follows after the market analysis, but in the case when the market is not well defined, it is good to start with the consumer analysis. This analysis is essentially based on the number of customers belonging to the targeted potential and their behavior (Rust et al, 2000). The analysis of consumers' needs to take into account the socio-economic classification (SEC) combined with the consumers' education and occupation, and the level of a household income. So if the idea of branding refers to a company that produces expensive mobile phones, the analysis focuses on the higher, urban classes from SEC, while the branding of a producer of salt, should take into account all classes, urban and rural.

Another dimension of analyzing the number of consumers is through the product penetration on the market. A very small number of products have high market penetration (90% and more), primarily products for mass consumption. Most products rarely reach the market penetration of over 60% (Kapferer, 2008). When analyzing luxury products, then this percentage falls to 10%. The danger that lies behind these figures is the potential error in assessing the level of acceptability of a particular product / service. For example, if we analyze the penetration of high-class cars on the market as a whole, its penetration is only 10%, but in high SEC class the presence of a luxury vehicle in the households is far greater. Further analysis within the penetration of the product includes the frequency of purchase, i.e. use. This is especially important for products for final consumption. Which average amount of a product is used per household per month? The success of Coca-Cola and the world famous brewers such as Heineken and Budweiser depend on the answer to this question.

The consumer analysis for new product concepts is more complicated because of the lack of information. It is therefore necessary to develop hypotheses and to estimate the number of potential consumers in the targeted segment. But you need to consider that these hypotheses go together with the mistakes. The consumer analysis is not only the estimation of the number of potential consumers, but also the assessment of their purchase behavior (Keller, 2007), shown in Figure 3.

The understanding of the consumers buying process is a critical factor in shaping the brand offer. How important are the various benefits offered? How important is price? Who can influence the purchase decision?

The consumer analysis should result in the estimation of the number of targeted customers and their behavior. If an existing brand is in question, then the estimations are relatively reliable, but if it is a new concept, then the consumers' analysis are based on round estimations, by using surrogate data, including the likelihood of errors.

Competitors Analysis

This analysis should reveal the key market players. In this part of the phase of brand birth competing brands within the industry are being analyzed. Such analysis includes existing rivals, marginal and potential competitors. Today we live in an open world with a huge flow of information. If someone investigates

Figure 3. The consumers buying process

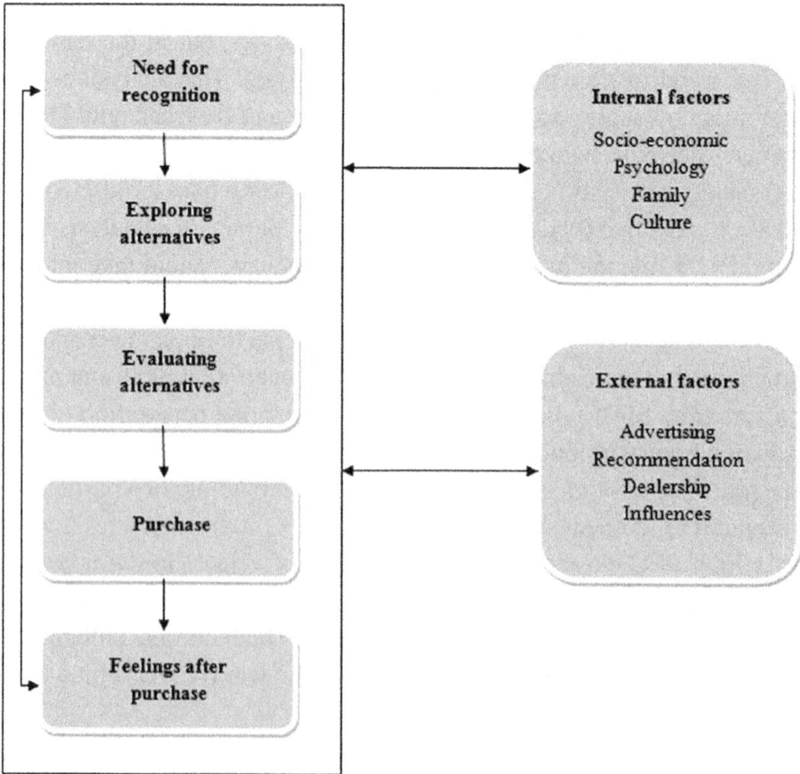

thoroughly enough, he/she can assume what existing and potential competitors prepare. Further analysis includes the analysis of the supplementary and complementary products. The competitors analysis should start with the biggest, direct competitors in the market. This analysis includes consideration of: the history of sales performance in terms of volume and value, pricing strategy, promotional strategy, inputs, distribution, consumer perceptions and so on. In addition, the analysis of the competitors' capabilities and their specifics, marketing skills should be added, the value of competing brands and of course, their profitability. However, the analysis of major competitors is not enough. Often marginal, small brands are converted to triggers, and then leading brands over time. Of course, all begin as small brands, facing opportunities and threats from global trends. Competition may come from companies with complementary products. The manufacturer of toothpaste can turn into a manufacturer of toothbrushes. While scanning the environment, the company should take into account the manufacturers of complementary products that can be transformed into direct competitors. Manufacturers of supplementary products can be converted into strong competitors with small changes in the market conditions. For example, portable computers can entirely substitute desktops with the additional decline in the price of laptops. Scanning competition should also take into account the supplementary products, because what is an appetizer today can be the main meal tomorrow.

Capabilities Analysis

The birth of the brand should include a significant amount of introspection. This is realized through the analysis of the capabilities, which is the analysis of the strengths and weaknesses of the company (Davies, 2003). Before boarding the ship, the company should examine whether it has a "good belly" to file navigation. Capabilities analysis should begin with the company's finance. How are the revenues doing and are they rising? Which is the profitability and its dynamics? Which resources are the key generators of revenue? Which are the reserves in the balance sheet and so on? After the financial analysis, an analysis of what Michael Porter has defined as key capabilities of the company should follow. How relevant are these capabilities for the company's brand? Technological capabilities should not be neglected in the analysis. For example, companies like BMW and Audi have the technological capacity to produce nearly the perfect car, but whether Fiat can make it? But technological advantage is not enough to win the race. Today the market is finicky from offers. If the company or its employees do not have the adequate marketing skills, then it can be a "curse" on the success of the brand. The employees' skills are vital to the success of any brand. The company is obliged to assess the skills and abilities of its employees, in order to assess their internal potential. Outsourcing can be used for certain activities in a predefined period of time, but in the long term the company should have the strings in its hands for all relevant activities that create brand value and profit for the company. The company, also, needs to develop skills for managing relationships with third parties: associates who can provide technology, associates providing production capacity, associates who will perform distribution etc.

The comprehensive analysis of capabilities should include all the above aspects. The results should contribute to the subsequent response to the question: whether the company can face the challenge of branding? The brand may require a longer period of investment in it; does the company have strong financial statements which prove that it can stand it? The brand may require a significant technological breakthrough, does the company have internal experience, skills and abilities to achieve it or buy it at a reasonable price? The brand may require a special system of distribution and sales, is the company flexible enough to implement such a novelty? Capabilities analysis is a company's exercise in "soul searching" before it can venture into the challenges of branding.

PEST Analysis

The phase of the brand birth has five separate steps, and the most neglected of all is usually the fifth step. Most of the companies omit this macro analysis, considering that they have no influence on these factors, or they believe that the brand acts locally, so it does not feel the impact of the socio-economic milieu. This analysis, besides the economic trends, covers the sociological and cultural complexity. In addition, we will briefly describe the trends that influence the brands most intensely.

- **GDP Trends:** What kind of a relationship exists between the growth of the gross domestic product and the branding strategy of the company? The increased GDP at a slower population growth, results in a higher income per capita, which increases the demand for more and better products / services. Better products are branded products. Thus, GDP growth means greater potential for branding, although once (or somewhere) with a low starting base.
- **Sectorial Trends:** The economy and economic growth are determined by three sectors: agriculture, industry and services. Global trends go in favor of strengthening the service sector at the expense of agriculture and industry, regardless of the national economy concerned. This means that agricultural economies turn into economies based on services. This favors the strategy of branding.
- **Urban-Rural Trends:** The distribution of population in urban or rural areas also has a significant impact on the potential for branding companies and their products / services.
- **Educational Trends:** The increasing level of education as a global trend is in favor of developing brands.
- **Occupational Trends:** In most national economies, the service sector begins to dominate. The development of information technologies and outsourcing of business - processes signalize the development of new sectors in the economy. Most of the new jobs did not exist fifteen years ago, and today consumers with such a profile are the most sophisticated lovers of brands. Companies need to track changes in the trends of professions in order to detect potential market opportunities.
- **Changes in the Socio-Economic Classification (Table 1):** Consumers are categorized into classes from A1 to E2, depending on the level of education and profession. In the past twenty years there is a steady upward trend of moving consumers from SEC E through D in SEC C around the countries in the world. The original SEC scheme had the appearance of a pyramid, and now gradually changing, with the expectation that in the next decade it will turn into a diamond. According to the expected direction of the trends in socio-economic classification, the sophistication of the demands and preferences of consumers from the dominant SEC B and C classes will further increase, which is a distinct possibility for developing premium brands.
- **Family Structure:** The increase in the number of households with one or two, rarely three or four members is a global trend and such changes and its effects should be included in the company's future scenarios.
- **Religious Change:** In recent years, a greatly intensified trend among global consumers, besides modernization and Westernization, was the desire of consumers to connect with their religious

Table 1. Matrix of socio-economic classification

Occupation	Basic Educat.	High School	College	Faculty	Master Studies	PhD Studies
Unqualified worker	E2	E1	D	D	D	D
Qualified worker	E1	D	C	C	B2	B2
Retailer	D	D	C	C	B2	B2
Small business owner	D	C	B2	B1	A2	A2
Medium business owner	D	B2	B1	A2	A2	A1
Corporate shareholder	B2	B2	B1	A2	A1	A1
Self employed	B1	A2	A2	A1	A1	A1
Services	D	D	B2	B1	A2	A1
Administrative worker	D	D	C	B2	B1	B1
Low level manager	D	C	C	B2	B1	A2
Medium level manager	C	C	B2	B1	A2	A2
Top management	B1	B1	B1	A2	A1	A1

roots. Companies need to be sensitive to this change and be alert to the religious specifics and possibilities and threats stemming from them.

- **Media Representation:** The Internet and television overshadowed magazines and newspapers. Considering this, companies need to prepare appropriate brand communications in order to reach the targeted consumers.
- **Aging Population:** The increase in the average age of the population, especially in developed countries in Europe and the United States paved the way for developing sequence-specific corporate brands.
- **Changes in the Saving Habits:** In the late 90's and the beginning of 2000 people intensively invested in mutual funds as a way of saving. The average marginal tendency to save in Europe was around 25% (Gorman, 2004). After the financial and economic crisis in 2007-2009, the marginal tendency to saving dropped significantly, but this did not cause an increase in consumption (the fall was due to the decrease in average revenue per customer). At the end of 2009 the stabilization started, with a relative increase in the marginal propensity to spending, which the supply side greeted with open arms. In any case, most dominant economies in the world depend on consumption and stimulate it, which leads towards the process of branding.
- **Population's Credit Indebtedness:** In addition to the analysis of the previous trend, the internal debt of the population in the countries around the world is growing more and more. 40-90% of the durable consumer goods and real estate in different countries are bought on credit. As long as the credit (and payment) ability of consumers worldwide persists, the brands will work, but the risk is looming in several countries.
- **Recycling:** The trend of "green thinking" - the growing concern for the environment, the limitation and renewability of resources in the world opens the way for the development of successful "green brands".

- **Government Policies:** regulation of imports and exports, monetary and fiscal policies, taxes and tax rates, labor relations, protection of property rights and many other issues that are subject to state regulation are affecting the companies or brands. Companies should consider the opportunities and limitations arising from this segment of the environment.
- **Obsession With Value:** Today's consumers, regardless of their income, status, education, profession and other characteristics, require maximum value for the money they are willing to spend. This motivates companies to invest in better, more sophisticated products and continually improve the brand offer.

The brand birth and the situational analysis raise the brand in the context of potential brand in the market, taking into account: competition, customers and capabilities of the company, as well as macroeconomic trends. The brand birth is the stage which supports the need to review the progress of existing brands and the possibilities of brand expansion. This is also the first step undertaken to examine the potential for a new brand in the market. The brand birth can be used in the following situations: the possibility of introducing a new product; the opportunity for improving the product; branding opportunities for the company; opportunities to strengthen the brand; opportunities to expand the brand etc.

The brand birth is a crucial phase of the brand pentagon. In the past two decades we have witnessed the "sprouting" of various brands in many industries like mushrooms. Probably, the most of the above analyzed questions have been asked and answered before making the branding decision. If they have not been asked and answered, they will be. The sole development process of the brand will ask for an analytical and systematic approach to its construction and management. Undoubtedly, the brand birth and its five steps are one of the building blocks in this process. The overcoming of the obstacles in this phase paves the way for the second phase of the model – the brand definition.

BRAND DEFINITION

The brand birth was a phase that identifies the possibility of launching a new brand or renewal of an old one. At the end of this phase, the company has a clearer understanding for the branding decision regarding the question whether there is potential for the branded offer. The brand definition is the next step towards developing a description of the brand offer. Which is the reason behind the brand? What will it mean in the minds of consumers? Which will be the personality of the brand?

The phase of brand definition starts when the company investigates why a consumer would buy the product / service (reasons, positioning) and why consumers would continue to buy the brand (positioning, personality). The phase of brand definition consists of the following four steps, shown in Figure 4 (Parameswaran, 2006):

1. Brand reasons;
2. Brand positioning;
3. Brand personality / image and
4. Brand mapping.

Although each step of this phase will be explained individually, they are often interwoven and take place simultaneously.

Figure 4. Brand definition

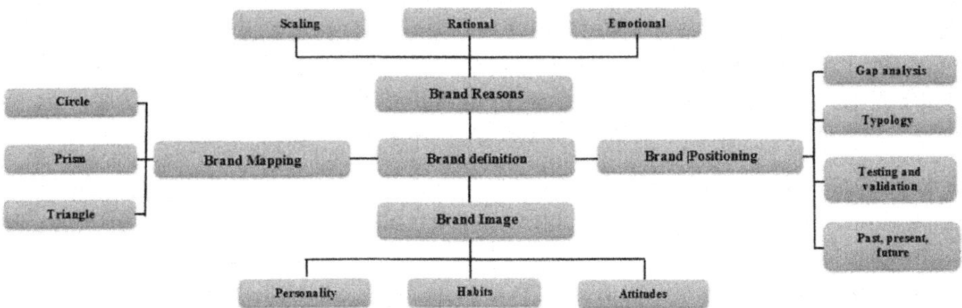

Brand Reasons

Why consumers would buy the brand? Each product or service they buy is a combination of rational and emotional reasons behind the purchase decision. If a consumer buys a brand only for rational reasons he/she will never be happy. If he/she buys it for only emotional reasons, he/she will never be satisfied. If, for example, we want to brand a company that produces soft drinks, one of the first tasks will be to establish the rational reasons (ingredients, taste, cost, quality) and the emotional reasons (freshness, fun, excitement) that would motivate the consumer towards the purchasing decision. The successful definition of the brand is a combination of these two categories.

Rational Reasons

In today's world of nanoseconds, the rational reason could be a difference only for a week or a month. However, the brand cannot function without any rational reason. The primary set of rational reasons refers to how the product is made, ingredients, technology, design and layout, price, packaging and so on. Very often, a specific rational reason is a particular ingredient such as: saffron sauce, toothpaste with bleach, cosmetics with vitamin E and coenzyme Q10, softener for clothes with perfume etc. Today's challenge is to find such a compound that will be unique to the product / service in a particular industry. Brands consist of elements, ingredients, attributes, but consumers buy benefits. The aim is to make the actual connection. For example, Apple once experienced resurgence with its new design and fresh colors. Apple's products look different and cause consumers to perceive the brand offer as "different and cool."

There are several rational reasons for buying a particular product. Thus, several elements which consist the brand offer are formed. The aim is to achieve diversity for the following elements: Price: Can the price be higher or lower? Distribution: Can the product be delivered in a different way? Service: Can we provide a better service? Packaging: Should the packaging be small or large? How to design it? Maintenance: Can maintenance costs be kept to a reasonable level? (Kapferer, 2007).

In a world dominated by brands, rational reasons are often ignored. Most managers assume that all products are the same, that the ingredients are the same, that technologies are the same. Perhaps this is true to the macro level, but there is always a possibility to make a "zig" while all others make "zag". Often, the success of manufacturers from the automotive industry is due to clear rational reasons: great design, comfort, value for the price. When searching for the rational differences, we need to "dig deeper".

Emotional Reasons

Consumers buy something because of rational and emotional reasons, if the rational reasons are known, then which are the emotional? There are nine universal emotions: happiness, anger, embarrassment, fear, sadness, courage, compassion, curiosity and humility. The brand needs to connect with consumers through a combination of them. For example: Whirlpool offers a wide range of products - home appliances. The brand is an emotional benefit to consumers, considered as "the best maker of homes in the world" (Chasser and Wolfe, 2010, p. 202). The basic challenge in this issue is to connect the rational and emotional reasons. The link should be really strong, otherwise some of the reasons would be just an empty promise. When seeking after an emotional reason, care should be taken that it is not ordinary. For example, in the late 90s Samsung was among the first manufacturers of flat-panel TVs. Their TVs looked very "comfortable" compared to the "boxes" of the other brands. The company had inserted a sense of envy for the good design of their TVs in their communications, creating an iconic brand.

How can emotional reasons be discovered? It requires a full analysis in which the consumer behavior is the starting point. The analysis is completed using the conventional "ladder" technique. This technique causes the company to consider more than the ordinary set of rational reasons and to develop a system of "why" questions. The answers to these questions lead to breakthroughs in various directions. For example, a drink for improving the health may consist of 23 vital ingredients. But why a mother would buy it? For her children. Why? To be healthy. Why? To be good at school. Why? To be successful in life. Why? So she would be proud of them. Through this set of questions, different directions are opened. Some may be very absurd, but some may lead to an answer in the search for emotional reasons. The ladder technique should be carried out for different scenarios, including the consumers, in order to discover the hidden emotions that the brand can touch.

Brand Positioning

Positioning is a "mental position in the minds of consumers occupied by the brand" (Trout and Ries, 1972, p. 455). There is no exactly defined time for determining the position of the brand. Optimally, if the positioning of the brand is determined before choosing the brand name and the definition of the promotional campaign, it is considered the right choice. For example, the brand positioning for Honda is "cars with high efficiency" which let to the famous advertising campaign of Honda which still echoes the familiar message "Fill it. Close it. Forget it." (Clark, 2004).

In what positioning differs from establishing the rational and emotional reasons? In a narrow sense, the brand positioning is strengthening the reasons behind the brand. For example, the car rental company, Avis, has positioned itself as: "We are second in the market. We try more." The brand used the emotional situation of defeat and everyone liked it.

Gap Analysis

How to identify the brand position? The gap analysis is a very useful technique. Combined with in-depth data from the market research, it turns into a very powerful tool. Gap analysis illustrates the different brands in a specific industry in a matrix for identifying and locating the positions that brands have in the minds of consumers. The matrix axes may vary in number depending on different factors, Figure 5.

Figure 5. Gap analyses – a matrix for brand positioning

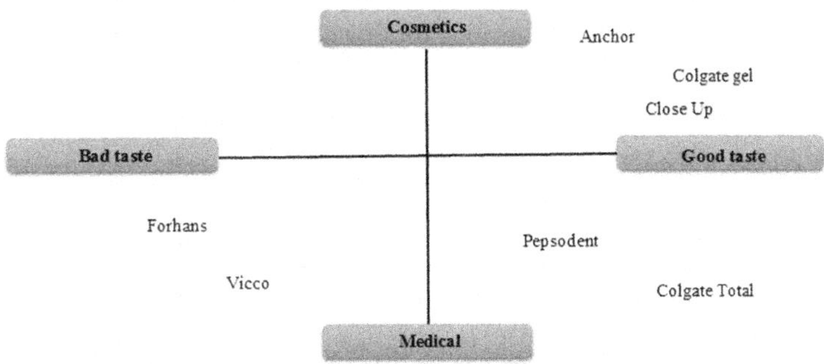

The next stage is to define the desired benefit from the product. If we analyze, for example, the production and sale of toothpaste, variables that would be taken into account, would be: fresh breath, prevent of cavities, taste, teeth whitening, price and so on. Certain brands of toothpaste are reflected in the graph to portray the mental space they occupy. In a hypothetical analysis of the gap in the brand positions for toothpaste, it is likely a free position for toothpaste with good taste and high medical value to appear. If we switch the factors on the axes, for example, medical value and price, we can identify individual gaps and choose the appropriate position for the brand. For example, the brand Colgate Total experienced a global success as it offered 24 hour protection from dental problems, which is a unique position which was not occupied by any other brand, at least at the beginning. The promise was also supported by the original ingredient which actually prevented the occurrence of dental problems. With a detailed analysis of the market, it is possible: to identify gaps within the existing market structure, or to create a new definition of an existing dimension.

Points of Parity and Points of Difference

The concept for developing brand prepositions is based on the points of parity and difference in relation to competitors (Keller, 1998). The brand should have certain points of parity (POP) compared to other brands in the industry. So, if it comes to toothpaste, then the brand is: clean, frothy, has a fresh smell. But the critical task is to identify the points of difference (POD). Through them, we need to determine the way the brand will differentiate from the other brands in the industry, Table 2. Sometimes it is necessary to establish a certain trade-off to come to a point of difference. The company may need to sacrifice certain claims, in order to point out a relevant diversity.

Typology of positioning. Various analytical methods should help to determine the position of the brand. We should constantly bear in mind that the selected position should be relevant, unique and believable (RUB: Relevant-Unique-Believable). The position should be relevant for the consumer, original and he/she should believe in it. The following are several typologies of brand positioning (Aaker and McLoughlin, 2010):

- **Based on the Composition:** This position is usually used for health food products and cosmetics.
- **Based on the Benefits:** This position is exploited by brands from pharmaceutical and IT industry.
- **Based on the Use:** A common position of producers of milk and dairy products and soft drinks.

Table 2. POP-POD of brands

Category	Brand	POP	POD
Toothpaste	Colgate	Whiteness, taste	24/7 protection
Cars	BMW	Design, interior	Power, comfort
Motorbikes	Honda	Price, power	Design

- **Based on the Features:** A typical example of such positioning is for brands for cars and consumer durables.
- **Based on the Users:** This category includes brands for restaurants and cafes and the like.
- **Based on the Price:** The brands that are leaders in costs usually occupy this position, regardless of the industry.
- **Based on Value:** This is a position that is chosen for brands that offer maximum value for the price. Common examples are the brands from the Asian countries.
- **Based on the Tradition:** Some manufacturers of healthy foods and beverages chose the position of roots and tradition with the intention to leave an intense trace in the minds of consumers.
- **Competitive Positioning:** Some brands are positioned in relation to the leading brand in the industry (Avis vs. Hertz, Pepsi vs. Coca-Cola).
- **Based on the Technology:** Today technology is omnipresent. Brands from all industries, from computers to cosmetics claim to be based on technology. However, the original position of Intel is not found in every brand which claims that everything it does is technology.
- **Based on the Design:** Aesthetics is the next new brand. The position of some brands is only due to the design. Examples: the iPod from Apple and the "Beetle" by Volkswagen.
- **Based on the Country of Origin:** The brand can use the country of origin to build an original position in the minds of consumers. Smirnoff does it, using Russia. Bacardi – the white rum from the Caribbean, referring to the free spirit of the Caribbean, does it, and became the largest brand for alcoholic drinks in the world.

The above positioning typologies are not only a list from which you should choose the position of the brand, but represent a starting position and direction for developing the appropriate platform for brand positioning. Certain authors (Prahalat and Hamel, 1999) discussed that these positioning typologies fit only for the brands of products, while corporate brands can choose from three broad options for positioning: based on innovation (Sony), based on the value (Hyundai), or based on the consumer (IBM). These positions do not mean that a particular brand is underperforming in consumer service or is not innovative. This is just tightens the focus of the company - where to spend the most time, energy and money.

- **Testing and Validation:** The options for brand positioning are usually developed through brainstorming techniques, so it is necessary to test and verify their validity for consumers. The testing and validity need to answer the following two questions (2D test): Desirability: Is the option for positioning desired by consumers? Does it correspond to the requirements and unmet needs? Does it create a new need? The possibility of delivery: Is the brand offer able to achieve the positioning? Is it important from the consumers' perspective? According to Procter & Gamble, the brand should generate a score higher than 51% of consumers' preference on the blind tests over the competing bids in order to be ready for launching (Harris and De Chernatony, 2001). All companies are not able to deliver superior performance of the brand in terms of all attributes, but within a particular positioning option, does the brand deliver what it promise?

- **Past-Present-Future:** The brand positioning is a developmental phenomenon in all markets worldwide. Many brands have achieved success based on solid primary position, but the big question that arises is whether such position is sustainable in the long term. The option of positioning should "live" in the constellation with the market dynamics and the competitive pressures. Trends related to consumers are the main obstacle to the development of brands. Market conditions and relationships are not given once and for all, but are constantly changing. The brand should be ready to follow the changes in the requirements and behavior of consumers. The position today is global. Coca-Cola, Levis, MTV, Nivea and many other brands have global positions. However, the relevance of such positions should be maintained. The strategy of positioning can be "knocked out" by a significant change in, for example, government policies. Positioning should withstand the changes in technology. Finally, the brand position should be easily sold - it should provide a sufficiently large number of consumers. Simply, the positioning should be a promise that can be leveraged over the years and over the activities.

Brand Personality and Image

When is the right time to define the personality and image of the brand - before or after the brand name? The elements of brand personality and brand image will be defined and explained in detail in the next, third phase of the brand pentagon. At this stage, it is useful to specify these concepts and to bear in mind the agenda, until their finalization.

Brand Personality

It is the articulation of personal characteristics the brand owns; therefore it is an assumption of which human characteristics the brand would have if it was a human being. People have developed a long list of words that describe someone's personality: shy, funny, charming, calm, patriot, etc. The brand could be young or old, male or female, college girl or a housewife. It may be an American, Japanese, Indian or British, and can be international or global. It can be conservative or liberal, outgoing or shy. When developing the brand definition, it is useful to take into account the desired personality of the brand. This leads to the appropriate branding decision.

The personality of the brand evolves over time. For example, the brand for cars, Seat, before its rebirth was described as a common brand for average cars, and today it is considered to be dynamic, fast, young and fashionable. While the company tirelessly builds the personality of its brand, its market entry affects the personality of other brands. All questions about the brand personality should be closely monitored throughout the process of brand development, individually at all stages.

Brand Image

The ranking of the brand image is the standard which defines the brand performance through various measures. Brand image consists of: benefits, image for the usage, image of the user and experimental areas. The brand image measures the result of the brand in relation to specific benefits. For example, if it is a cosmetics brand, how good are the ingredients, which is the smell, the costs etc. The brand also needs to measure the people who use the brand: are they rich, poor, sophisticated, loving, men, women, family, children and so on. Brand image should assume the opportunities for using the product / service of a particular category. For example, health drinks can be consumed by sick or healthy individuals, younger or older, male or female, etc. So you need to determine which image will be associated with the brand. When developing a new brand, it is especially important to consider the desired future brand image. It is obvious that the image is determined by the consumers, but the company should plan it in the early stages of the brand building process.

- **Measurement Tools:** There are several techniques for measuring the brand image and brand personality. Foote Cone & Belding, one of the largest marketing agencies in the world, has developed two interesting techniques that cause consumers to articulate the brand's image and personality attributed to the brand (Barich and Kotler, 1991). These tools use visual stimuli to get rich and different responses from consumers. Visual Image Profiling (VIP) is based on a set of 30 or more pictures of different people from which consumers should choose the image that suits the brand. Such images can be adapted to certain racial or national characteristics, depending on the country in which the brand operates. Among the images are encountered: a priest, a business woman, a housewife, student, military man, vendor, model, doctor, engineer, nurse, teacher, etc. Image Configuration (ICON) is another visual technique for measurement which uses a set of 20 photos depicting different emotions. Consumers are asked to select some of the pictures depending on the feelings the brand causes. These images are calibrated to specific emotions that lead to a diagnosis of what constitutes the brand in an emotional sense. VIP and ICON are just two of the many techniques for determining the brand image, the essence is not behind the technique, but the purpose.

In the phase of brand definition, the company is still hesitant whether it has a concept that will win. Perhaps the use of all these analyzes acts a little in vain, but their application allows the creation of a clearer picture for the brand and the competitive brands, which can give the brand an opportunities for differentiation over the competition. Small differences at this stage can mean a big advantage in the next phases.

Brand Mapping

When the rational and emotional reasons for the brand are developed, the brand position determined, and even a profile for the brand image and personality planned, we need to "catch" these variables in a template that will be easy to understand and interpret. The models for mapping the brand by Aaker, Kapferer and Keller significantly help the brand definition.

- **The Model for Branding by David Aaker:** Aaker suggests the brand should be viewed as a whole which consists of three fundamental components, shown in Figure 6 (Aaker, 1996):
  - Expanded identity,
  - Core identity and
  - Brand essence

Figure 6. A model for branding by David Aaker

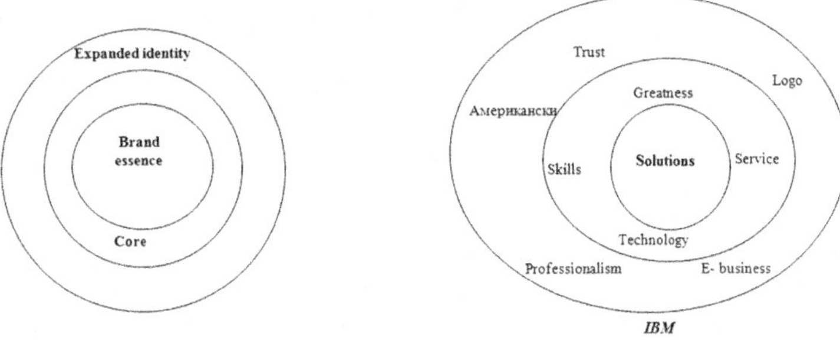

The expanded brand identity consists of a description of: the product (quality, value, usage etc.), the company as a brand, the culture, the values, the brand personality and the brand as a symbol, visual image and heritage. The core identity of the brand refers to the brand offer in terms of quality, relationships and price / value ratio. In the center of the model is the brand essence, which is the only thing to which the brand is committed. It may be premature to think of a complete model for building and developing the brand, when the company is still creating the brand, but it is wise to visualize what would the brand be several years ahead.

- **The Prism by J. N. Kapferer:** Kapferer offers an interesting model for branding which overlooks the interception between the consumer and the brand in a complete way. The model represents a prism of 6 components, shown on Figure 7 (Kapferer, 2008):
  - Personality. For which personality the brand strives?
  - Culture. Which values and beliefs come together with the brand?
  - Picture for yourself. What do customers feel about themselves when they use the brand?

These three components are referred to as components of internalization.

1. Physical appearance. The physical attributes of the brand.
2. Relations. The relations brand-customer.
3. Reflection. A projected image of the user.

Figure 7. The prism by J.N. Kapferer

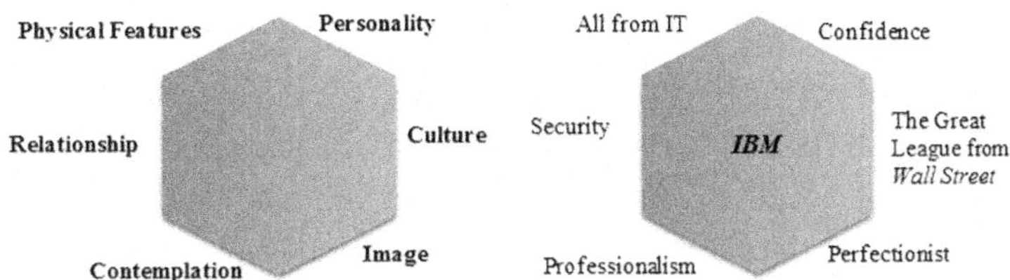

The latter three components are treated as factors for externalization. These six factors that form the prism help the company in defining the brand as a whole, starting with the physical attributes of the brand, the relationship with the consumers and so on. Kapferer analyzes the mentioned dimensions from two different views: the image of the sender and the image of the receiver. To apply this model to a completely new brand is a particularly difficult task, while the use on the existing brands leads towards the discovery of new dimensions and ideas about the brand.

- **The Brand Pyramid by Kevin Lane Keller:** The brand starts with building significance in the minds of consumers by creating brand awareness and then creating a point of difference, apart from the points of parity within the industry, Figure 8 (Keller, 2007). Today's consumers are extremely dedicated to value in their purchasing decision. Thus, it is possible to achieve brand relevance and acceptability. But to be able to charge a premium price, the brand should be perceived as valuable. At this stage, the brand turns into a resource and forms a link with the consumers.
- **Methodologies for Mapping the Brand:** Many multinational corporations have developed their own models for mapping the brand. For example, Unilever has a model that clearly incorporates all brand dimensions of the brand. Numerous marketing agencies around the world as well develop their own models. For example, Foote Cone & Belding have developed a model called *the significance of the brand* that looks at the brand as a: function, character and connectivity (Ind and Bjerke, 2007). In the earlier phases of the process of brand building, the time and effort are more devoted to configuring the brand, the offer, determining the price level, etc., and less to something esoteric, as the model for the brand. But if the issue is completely ignored, the brand may later face significant difficulties so, it would be a wise step to consider this issue, maybe not in great detail, but with enough analysis to avoid the long-term consequences.

Mapping the brand is not a one-off task. The definition of brand may undergo significant changes with the entry of new competitors. The trends related to consumers can move the brand from its fortress. The same can be done with the globalization, as well as with the government policies. The optimal use of brand mapping considers a regular renewal of the circle, the prism and the pyramid of the brand per year. So, the company can see the new opportunities or threats in the environment that, normally, every successful brand exploits or exceeds.

BRAND ARTICULATION

Once it is clear that there is an opportunity to introduce a new brand to the market, as evidenced by the first and the second phase of the brand pentagon, the third stage called brand articulation follows. For example, if the company discovered an opportunity to brand the chain of coffee shops, the next question would be what would the brand name, identity and communications be? The phase of brand articulation explores various facts through which the brand presents itself to consumers. There is not a fixed order for conducting the activities in this phase, but it is good to respect a certain logical and spatial distribution. Neglecting this phase can lead to failure, although there might be a great opportunity for the brand. Many brands are successful because of the careful plans for brand articulation, Figure 9. In order to understand the way of articulating the brand, this stage is separated into three steps (Parameswaran, 2006):

Figure 8. The brand pyramid by Kevin Lane Keller

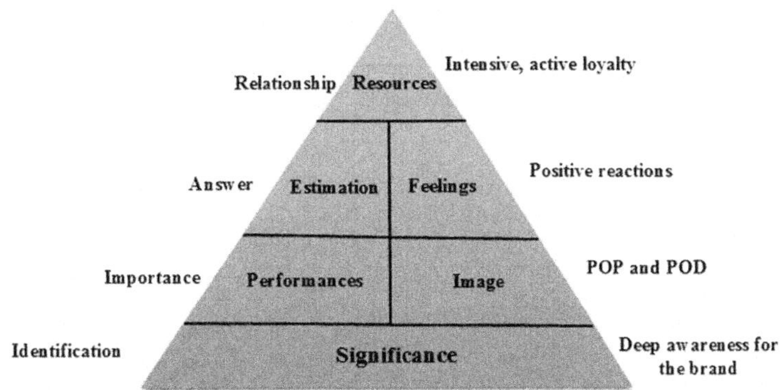

1. Brand identity;
2. Brand communications and
3. Brand service.

The articulation of the brand refers to how the brand presents itself to consumers, how it articulates its offer and how it connects to customers. This stage is divided into three steps (Aaker, 2004). The three steps are not a necessary succession, and they should be viewed as a continuum. Any action from the brand articulation phase needs to be prepared and performed with the attention from all the stakeholders involved. This requires transparency, openness, consistency and cooperation - the fundamentals of the new business model for the long-term success of companies. This approach should not be practiced only in the stage of articulation, although here it is the most apparent, but at each stage in the process of brand building. The isolated application can adversely affect the successful implementation of the concept of building the brand equity with radical transparency and limit its full potential.

The phase of brand identity explains the importance of the brand name, the colors, the design and the logo / symbols. The communications phase explores the various features of what today is called integrated marketing communications. The brand communications include: advertising, direct marketing and all other aspects of communications, including public relations, promotions, events, interactions, etc. But brand communications usually begin with the packaging, its design and graphics. The third phase of the brand articulation is widely defined as brand services. This is the human aspect of the process of branding that is often ignored. The brands from the service sector should pay detailed attention to this stage, but this does not exclude the brands for consumer durables, because exactly through the service, the brand can gain a significant competitive value.

- **Brand Identity:** Which is the brand identity which refers to new products / services? Which should the name, colors and logo be? The brand identity should be easy to remember, important and to mark the beginning. The name should be easily entered into the collective consciousness of consumers. It is also important the brand identity to be portable, adaptable and protected. It is true that a rose would smell as sweet, regardless of its name, however, the good identity, name and

Figure 9. Brand articulation

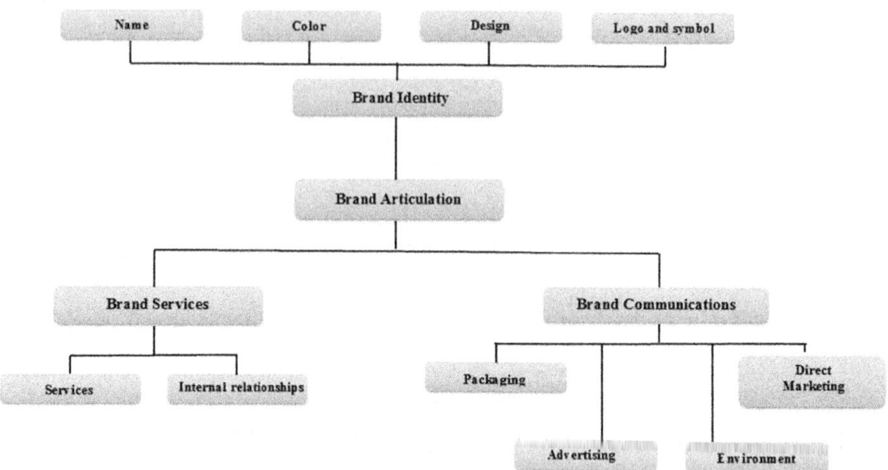

design, can help greatly. The section dedicated to the brand identity explores the different ways in which the brand can present itself to consumers.

- **Brand Name:** With this high-intensity globalization that we are facing today, it is difficult to create a name that has the same meaning everywhere. However, care should be taken at least not to have the wrong meaning. A typical textbook example that is often found in books about branding is the intention of a car manufacturer to launch a line in Latin America under the brand Nova, and later to find that in Spanish it means "does not go" (Wheeler, 2006). The brand name should be easily recognizable. Very often specific symbols and graphics are being added to the brand name in order to support its recognition. The brand name should be easy to pronounce and easy to remember. Brand names are generally classified into three groups: descriptive, suggestive and independent. Combinations can be found within each of these groups: (Sandrop, Rownthree), classical names (Hamam) or symbolic (Apple).

The descriptive names for brands seek to describe the composition, use, process or feelings the brand is trying to evoke, for example, Fair and Lovely – a cream that makes you gentle and beautiful. The suggestive names represent the brand sign or suggestion about the promise of the brand, and, unlike the descriptive names they have an indirect route. For example: Visa – a credit card that will take you anywhere, Real - fruit juice made from real fruit, Indica - a car made for Indians. Contrary to the descriptive and suggestive names of the brand, the third group of brand names has no connection with the brand offer and therefore these names are classified as independent names. A typical example is the brand Canon. Independent names do not necessarily have to be created words, but they may be names that have no connection with the business. For example, Apple has no relation to technology and so on. Independent brand names can be detected by analyzing the company's founder, history, important acronyms etc. These names often create the possibility of forming a complete brand identity around the name. For example, the brand Orange, the famous mobile operator is represented through an orange square.

The brand names are an extremely powerful tool for entering the memory of consumers, and often the most obvious names are the easiest to store, such as Amazon and Hotmail etc. But the danger with the ordinary names is that they are easily forgotten, because the brand name should be unique. The brand names are telegraphic messages stored in the minds of consumers – it is important that these names can tell a story which consumers will remember. For example, Head & Shoulders is an antidandruff shampoo. So, the brand name should tell a story. Another important aspect which is critical for the long-term success of the brand is the issue for brand name registration and protection. However, when choosing a brand name, a dose of logic, emotion and belief should be applied.

- **Brand Design:** In today's open world, the design or appearance of the brand is becoming increasingly important. The most typical example of how design can step out is the company Apple. Perhaps no one pays so much attention to the design as carmakers do. Followed by the brands in the fashion industry (textiles, shoes and accessories), and then electronics manufacturers. Most likely, the brands for products for final consumption (food, beverages, cosmetics etc.) pay at least attention to the brand design (they pay attention only to packaging and ergonomics). It is also possible to use more creativity and innovation in this industry (examples by Nivea). The design of the brand is also important for brands in the service sector. It is important how the stores will look, which graphics and posters will be used, and even how they smell.
- **The Colors of the Brand:** Coca Cola = red, Dove = white, etc... We are surrounded by colors and nature has a way of encoding colors. The colors of the brands strive to reflect the symbolism that nature expresses. For example, many brands that relate to food use red, yellow and green colors. Pharmaceutical brands as well as brands from the financial sector often use the blue color that symbolizes stability and security. Sometimes, some colors have different meanings in different countries (white and black). The sensitivity of the colors is critical for the success of the brand.
- **The Brand Logo and Symbol:** What does the brand need to trigger instant recognition among consumers? Original name, original way of writing the name, symbol, color, design or identity. Nike has a unique brand image that sounds original; it is written with special letters and has a clear symbol. All these elements make the complete identity of Nike. But the greatness of this strong brand is that each of these elements is sufficient for brand recognition. Mercedes-Benz is a global leader in luxury cars. The brand name is always spelled with capital letters forming the logo of this brand. The symbol of the brand is the three-side star. Brands often use certain symbols for easier communication and recognizable brand promise: for example, the apple of Apple, the circles of Audi, the golden arches of McDonald's, the Adidas' triangle and many others.

Used together, the brand name, colors, logo and symbol are a very powerful weapon for brand articulation and communication. Almost everyone remembers the golden arches of McDonald's, the red waves of Coca-Cola and the Nike's heel. Defining the brand identity as part of the brand articulation phase Is about making the look and feeling for the brand. The defined elements of the brand identity do not have to be perfect and are not defines once and for all. They are developed over time.

Brand Communications

How will you communicate the brand with its target consumers? The integrated marketing communications represent all aspects of communications and how all the individual activities are integrated to provide a unified feeling for the brand. The activities which are part of the integrated marketing communications include (Schultz and Tannenbaum, 1993):

- Advertising (TV, newspapers, magazines, radio, outdoor);
- Public relations (press, television appearance or Internet);
- Interactivity (using the Internet for information and services);
- Events (sponsorships, parties, shows, etc.);
- Retail (store and partners);
- Promotion (consumer, price, sales);
- Direct marketing (an electronic mail, telephone, Internet).

All these elements are tasked to convey the key promise of the brand. If the brand stands for sophistication, all these elements should reflect it. The quality plan for integrated marketing communications should answer the following questions (Cooper, 2007): Who are the target customers? Which is the current disposition of consumers? What does the brand offer that is different from others? Which is the reason behind the brand offer? Which should be the tone and manner of the communication? Once you draw this so-called briefing plan of integrated marketing communications, the compliance and adherence to it follows. For example, if the brand Strepsils offers an immediate relief from sore throat, then the elements of IMC (Integrated Marketing Communications) should be formulated with an appropriate tone and manner around the brand promise. This does not mean that all messages of the brand should include doctors and laboratories, but the basic offer - quick relief from sore throat should to be achieved.

- **Advertising:** The plan for the integrated marketing communication usually leads to the development of advertising because it is usually the most expensive component of the IMC plan. Advertising should answer the following key questions: Which is the role of advertising in the industry? What can be achieved through ad? Advertising has a different meaning in different industries, but (as explained by the FCB matrix presented in Figure 10) the functioning of advertising depends on two variables: how involved consumers in the appropriate category are and how the consumer makes the purchase decision - through thinking (rationally) or by feeling (emotionally)?

For products / services that require high involvement of customers in the process of making the purchase decision and thinking (the first quadrant), advertising plays the classic role - to create awareness, knowledge, desire and action. This group includes: cars, appliances, televisions, electronic devices and so on. For products / services that require high involvement of customers in the process of decision making and feeling (the second quadrant), advertising would create a positive feeling which leads to knowledge and action. Cosmetic products are in this group.

For products / services that require low involvement of customers in the process of decision making and thinking, advertising would create an awareness which leads towards testing the product, which in turn leads to a positive feeling. Cleaning products and hygiene products, which are sold based on the promise of performance, belong to this group. For products / services that require low involvement of customers in the process of decision making and feeling, it is all about creating a pleasant feeling for the brand, which leads to testing and usage. Soft drinks and clothes are in this group.

Once you peel away the mystery "how the advertising works," the task of formulating a comprehensive strategy for advertising begins. The advertising strategy depends on the objectives of advertising: whether to increase the trial, reuse, to change opinions, to create a sense of pride of ownership and so on. The advertising strategy requires a review and integration of the elements of the IMC plan. The advertising

Figure 10. FCB matrix

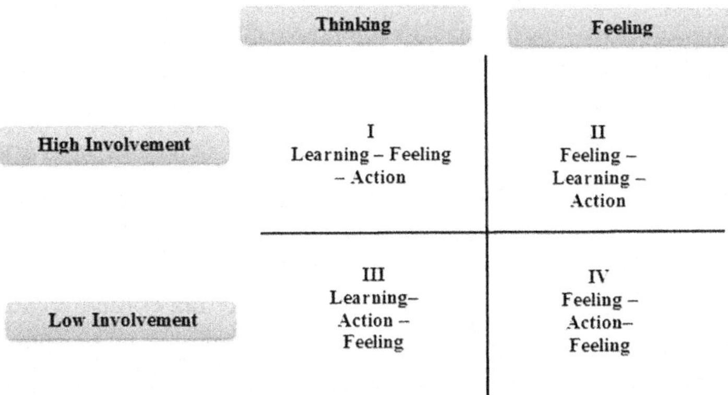

strategy has two main components: creative strategy: creative idea and how it will be implemented; and media strategy: the mechanism of the creative solution delivery.

- **Packaging:** When is the best time to discuss the product packaging? Packaging and its role vary depending on the product category. For example, the packaging is almost non-existent in services and within durable consumer goods acts as protection. Packaging is critical to the success of products for final consumption. And in the case of products such as perfumes and spirits, the packaging is just as important as the product itself. Then, which are the roles that the packing should play? We can freely call it the 4P of packaging (Parameswaran, 2006): protection, portability, pickability and pricing. The packaging has a set of roles for producers and very different role for consumers. This is a key medium for communication - packaging can enhance the story behind the product and can influence the consumer's choice. Packaging can play a promotional role. The packaging managed to experience the development form a material for protection of finished products to a message that is crucial for the purchase decision. Packaging is expected to be a powerful tool for attracting and retaining customers.
- **Direct and Interactive Marketing:** Direct marketing refers to establishing and maintaining a direct contact with the end consumer and gaining his/her trust and loyalty. Dell has managed to create a revolution, using the phone, then the Internet, to help end users to configure their computers and make orders. Direct marketing can begin before the launch of the brand. The first step in developing a program for direct marketing is building a customer base. The next step is to establish a channel of communication from producer to consumer. The third step is rewarding consumers. The next step is gaining loyalty. Gaining loyalty is a key goal in the direct marketing. The fifth step in this program is gaining referrals for sale. At the heart of the direct marketing is the database. It is critical to regularly update and expand it. With the enormous growth of the Internet worldwide, the direct marketing will become increasingly digital. A recent study in the US found that 30% of car buyers in this country have made their choice through the Internet without visiting a single dealer (Nash, 2000). It is expected the next decade to be crucial to the success of programs for direct marketing for a large number of brands worldwide. The success of direct marketing depends very much on the type of the product, but in any case, it is a powerful tool for the development of

relations between the brand and consumers, gaining commitment and, perhaps most importantly, customer loyalty. As it is said in the circles of direct marketing: It is 6.5 times cheaper to preserve a consumer than to acquire a new one (Nash, 2000). Through direct marketing and the elements of its program, the brand can achieve this goal.

- **Promotions:** Promotions, specifically sales promotions are considered to be separate activities that are undertaken for purely tactical reasons, such as deterring new competitors, increasing sales, capitalization of seasonal demand. The promotions can be an integrated part of IMC plan, if well thought out at each stage of the model. The promotions come in different types, aimed at: consumers, retail distributors, intermediaries (agents), and even to employees of the company, while the promotions that are part of the integrated marketing communications, are primarily intended for final consumers. Classic promotions are used for tactical reasons and planned strategic promotions contribute to increase the percentage of trials, usage and help build the brand image. The promotions are mostly produced in the following forms: discounts, competitions and contests, free samples, schemes for collection and branded packaging. Regardless of the format, promotions should be moderate and controlled and they should not result in a regular offer of an additional incentive for consumers. Promotions contribute significantly in brand communications, in particular, to increase the percentage of trials, usage, and gaining commitment from customers. But care should be taken that they are not used just to motivate sales because they can harm the long-term reputation and brand value, which can be a tragic loss of a remarkable tool for building the brand.
- **Retail and Point of Purchase Play a Significant Role in the Integrated Marketing Communications Efforts:** The method of exposing the products for final consumption in retail facilities, under the circumstances of almost unlimited offer, is a very important factor for the success of the brand. In the case when it comes to consumer durables, exposure should additionally contribute to the attractiveness of the brand. Brand communications should use the strength of retail, understanding its role, location and involvement. There will always be a compromise between value and cost, but innovative techniques and ideas for merchandising can be an incentive for the brand where it is needed the most - at the point of purchase.
- **Events:** Demonstrating the brand is the mantra of the new millennium. Consumers want to connect with their brands in many different ways and brands that offer it provide space in the minds of consumers. This form of communication includes customers by holding different events. Brands use events to increase the trial rate by consumers. The rewards are multiple: brand associations, loyal customers or VIP clients, media coverage, publicity and, perhaps above all, oral advertising within important groups. The planning of an event related to the brand needs to be part of the IMC plan. Usually, the publicity and advertising of the event are the most expensive part. But without publicity and exposure to the public, the event cannot be an event.
- **Public Relations (PR):** Companies and corporations need PR. It is important to be written about their financial results, the opening of a new factory, new product introduction, etc. Public relations are any form of unpaid exposure of a company or a brand to the public through the mass media. They all require information of interest, so why write about brands? True, not all brands can provide PR coverage. One way is through achieving a celebrity status: an event that appears in Hollywood cannot be forgotten. But this is an expensive alternative. For example, a launch of a new car model, irrespective of the brand, is always followed by visits to the plant, test drives, media exposure and more. PR is a strong tool for building the brand, which should be planned and incorporated in the IMC efforts, not just an occasional joy to information published by the media.

Brand Services

Does the brand presentation refers only to the brand identity and its communication? In terms of secondary discoveries, changes and upheavals, brands should "hug" their customers – they should connect with them on countless different ways. A pioneer in providing additional services to consumers is the company Johnson & Johnson, which has spent millions of dollars and hours worldwide for popularizing their products for hygiene (Schmit, 2009). For example, during their market entry in India, the company was not able to take an advantage of the advertising message in which it explained the use of their products, so they hired thousands of local women as agents who went from house to house and conveyed direct demonstration, leaving free samples and discount coupons. Although initially the move was considered quite risky, Johnson & Johnson won the market in India and up to this day it is one of the leading brands in this business. Such examples of experimental marketing were the pioneering efforts of companies which sell new products and services. The popularity of personal computers rose through cyber cafes, sponsored by computer manufacturers. But do old established brands need these experimental efforts and whether they have a measurable return on investment? Among one of the most successful attempts for care centers is the one from Nestle in Europe. The European giant is dedicated to children care. They sponsor the designated centers located throughout Europe on significant crossroads and highways. These centers provide opportunities for mothers to feed and maintain the hygiene of their babies and young children. The project has experienced extraordinary success, but how to measure the return on investment for this effort? The answer lies in the minds of mothers and their decisions to purchase Nestlé's products.

There are many opportunities in which the brand can offer an extra service for its customers. Their success is justified by a rise in the sales and improvement in the brand image. For example, Colgate regularly sponsors inspection of the dental health of children in primary schools. The positive feedback from parents results in loyal customers that directly affect the stable value of the brand. Within the brands in the service sector: airlines, hotels, IT services, telecommunications and so on, it is all about the service. Often, a familiar story for a rail transport company that wanted to hire a marketing agency to improve its image is retold. The meeting was scheduled at 9 am on an ordinary working day. Top managers of the railway company arrived at the agency exactly at 9 am and at the entrance they noticed an empty reception, dirty chairs, a table filled with used glasses and ashtrays filled with cigarette butts. No one was there, only the cleaning lady that slowly worked its work. The team waited until 9:15 pm when a young officer appeared who apologized and took them in the meeting room, where they again faced with dirty tables, ratty chairs and carelessness. At 9:30 appeared the director of the agency again apologizing to customers who were on the verge of exploding emotionally, with the comment that the experience they have experienced this morning at the agency is what the users of the railway transport experience every day: dirty wagons, full ashtrays, scattered cups and a slow cleaning lady (Schmitt, 2009). The moral message of the story is that the brand image cannot be improved by advertising if the underlying service is poor.

Jan Carlzon, the former CEO of Scandinavian Airline, talks about the need for authorization of the staff to make decisions at a critical moment when the consumer is facing a trial (Carlzon, 1989). If the airline staff contends better with the problem, the consumer will remain for a lifetime. This is the "moment of truth". The waiter, who runs to reach the consumer to return petty pennies, achieves this moment, just like the stewardess is trying to help the traveler who does not feel well. Such employees acquire lifetime customers for companies. Unfortunately, in the domain of the service sector throughout the world there are companies which limit the quality of service. Enormous opportunities are waiting to be used by service brands. In the literature, this issue is often mentioned as the so-called "Lufthandza effect", a term coined when the German airline made efforts to improve its image after the German skies were opened to new competitors. The company improved several parameters in services that allow them to keep their market position (Donnych and Myat-Hsu Ysuke, 2010). Today, most brands in the service sector control their image through a research on the level of consumer satisfaction. These companies take into account the performance of their services in the eyes of consumers.

B2B Sales and Services

B2B activities are probably the largest sector in an economy. Brands play a key role in forming the first impression. But this is coupled with the need to keep consumers in the long run. Companies participating in the segment of industrial consumption categorize their sales' efforts to the following steps (Parameswaran, 2006): Suspect - A company that is new, with the potential to become a consumer; Prospect - Suspicion turns to expectation, if a need is identified and if the first contact is not finished with a negative feedback; Actual demonstration - At this stage the brand is demonstrated to the potential customer or a contract for a site visit is made; Negotiation - The customer company shows interest for purchase and is ready to negotiate; Close - Negotiations are completed and closed; Order – An order is realized by the consumer. Usually, the sales team of the company leads the customer company through all the steps in the SPANCO cycle, but the last step is often withdrawn. Successful B2B vendors continue the sales process even after the order or after the delivery. Some companies classify these activities into the following stages: presales, sales and after sales. The phases of presales and sales are important, but even more important, is the after sales, when consumers go through a post sales dissonance. Satisfied customers come back with new demands.

Once the first three phases of the brand pentagon are completed, the brand comes to the point of market testing: the phase of measurement and monitoring. Which is the brand performance? Which aspects require improvement? These and other questions will be analyzed in detail in the next phase of the brand pentagon: brand measurement.

BRAND MEASUREMENT

The task of the company is not only to create and launch the brand (many managers make the mistake of thinking that the main task is the brand creation) but to follow the brand in real market conditions. The market changes instantly and a new brand launch causes a chain of reactions. The brand measurement, if systematically and transparently implemented, can provide timely alerts that can be crucial to the success of the company. It is true that it is impossible to completely predict what competitors will do, but to neglect them is naive, so the brand measurement helps the company to understand which is the position of the brand in the market; which are its strengths; and which are the potential threats it faces. The process of measuring the brand is based on a time series of data upon which certain parameters that determine the health of the brand are calculated. The brand measurement includes the calculation of the following measures practiced on a monthly, quarterly, semiannual or annual basis: sales (value and volume) - geographically, market share - geographically, customer loyalty, distribution - depth and width, price level - competitors and substitutes, image, etc. (Cohen, 2005). All these indicators can be calculated on a monthly basis. Some are calculated quarterly and others annually. In order to better plan the brand measurement, it is good to classify these activities into three phases: brand audit, brand track and brand board (Parameswaran, 2006).

The brand board is a calculation of the brand performance, using data for the sales of the company, the monthly market share and similar reference data. The brand track is a regular short-term analysis of the health of the brand, and additional parameters that are calculated in this phase, in addition to sales and market share are: brand awareness, usage and image. The measures for the brand track require a certain consumer research and are typically calculated on a quarterly basis. The brand audit is a long-term analysis of the health of the brand. Certainly, the trend of sales and market share has its role, but the brand audit is more focused on the examination of the performance of the brand in the long term vis-a-vis its competition, consumers and the market in general. A detailed analysis of the company and its customers is essential for a good brand audit. Used in combination, these three processes of brand measurement help the company to recognize the vital signs of the brand on a regular basis.

When it comes to well-known and established brands, the starting point of the pentagon for building the brand may be exactly the phase of brand measurement. The audit indicates that the fashion brands such as Van Heusen and Louis Philipe are taking into account the consumers from the middle class. Is this enough? The brand audit indicates that viewers of MTV and VH1 consider that some novelties should be introduced. What can be changed with these brands? The brand measurement can come up to brand expansion, a new analysis of the brand and everything back from the beginning (Hubbard, 2010).

Brand Board

The brand board is the monthly calculation for monitoring the vital statistics of the brand. In most companies, in accordance with the management culture, the CEOs are expected to have a "black book" which is a fast access to all the most important information about the brand. Just as the board in the car provides critical information needed for driving, the brand board provides critical information about the brand, which is a form of instant access to the most important indicators. The brand board offers enough accurate information on a monthly basis for the manager to make key decisions about the brand. Are the revenues from the brand at the planned level? Is the growth of the brand as expected? Is the market growing? Are marketing costs under control and is the brand profitability on track? All these questions need to be answered by the data that constitute the brand board (Salinas, 2009).

- **Sales Board:** The first number that should light up the brand board is sales in volume and value. When it comes to products for final consumption and durable consumer goods, sales figures are calculated on a monthly basis, while in services they are usually calculated on a daily basis. Depending on the size and scope of the sale of the brand, the board should cover sales within: value and volume, geographical distribution, realization by distribution channels and by product (Salinas, 2009). The sales board is the starting point for a good brand management and many other indicators derive from it.
- **Marketing Inputs Board:** Which inputs are required during the month? Does the brand receive support with advertising? Was the brand backed by some event or a PR? Based on a monthly basis, the marketing inputs board should follow: costs and inputs for advertising – the media plan and used creative elements, PR input - Press reports and all forms of public relations, events - sponsorships and direct - interactive inputs. In addition to the marketing inputs in terms of advertising,

efforts to follow the inputs and marketing costs related to sales promotion should be made, as well as for the distribution schemes etc. (Chernev, 2010).

- **Board for the Competition:** Even the best plans can fail due to lack of information about competitors. The sources of such information may include: reports from the media, distribution network, sales personnel and other partners. This board must display the key activities of competitors regarding: the opportunities to launch new products, advertising campaigns, merchandising, sales promotion, distribution and price changes (Knox and Maklan, 1998). Much of the information is available on the market. The sales staff should be trained to become "the eyes and ears" of the company. They should cherish the philosophy: no information is irrelevant to be noted and conveyed. Key stakeholders should be prepared to respond to any information obtained. In this way, the potential of competitors to jeopardize the success of the brand can be observed.
- **Board for Profit – Loss:** All companies take into account the profit or loss of the company on a regular basis. But they do not make it particularly for the profitability of the brand. The common excuses are the difficulties with the allocation of revenues and costs, seasonal fluctuations, etc. The model of building the brand recommends a monthly analysis of the profitability of the brand through the board for profit - loss. The board for profit - loss represents the brand net realization (sales revenue minus production costs, minus marketing costs, minus the cost of capital) (Salinas, 2009). Brands do not have to be profitable every month. For example, in the months of significant investments in advertising and promotions, profitability may decline. Also, seasonality of demand can affect the monthly profit – loss status. The board for profitability is a sensitive way of taking care of the brand health. In the case of the brands in the service sector, it is more difficult to prepare the board for the profit - loss of the brand, so it can be made on a quarterly basis.
- **Market Share Board:** The market share of the brands is calculated on a monthly basis but with inputs from a period of two to three months earlier. For example, if you calculate the market share of a brand for May, it is necessary to have the data on the market share in April and March. The market share of the brand should be followed both in volume and in value. A common complaint about this indicator are the oscillations in the value of the market share of the brand. But over time, the monthly value of this indicator is a realistic portrayal of the trend of the brand market share. This measure provides meaningful information about the growth of the market (in volume and value, market participation of relevant brands, as well as penetration of distribution). All these measures are part of the board for the market share of the brand (Berry, 2004).

Another indicator of the health of the brand on a monthly basis is the board of consumers (Keller, 2001). It provides information on the level of the usage of the brand in certain segments, but it also shows a synthetic data for the profit - loss on the market. For example, which brands gain share at the expense of others. The board for the market share and the board for consumers, in combination, are key measures of the brand health.

The brand board can be expanded to include more or less information depending on the needs. But care should be taken to avoid overcrowding which can lead to confusion (the panel should not look like a cockpit in the plane). The challenge is to formulate a simple, elegant but very useful picture of the health of the brand on a daily, weekly and monthly basis.

Brand Track

If the brand board is a quick report on the health of the brand prepared on a monthly basis, the brand track is a more complete monitoring of the brand which is conducted quarterly or in semesters (3-6 months). The brand track is not only the analysis of the income, but goes a step further than these figures. The essence of the brand track is to "capture" what the brand board may have missed. The brand track actually measures the attitudes and behavior of consumers which influence the purchase of the brand and the consumers' loyalty. Additionally, the competitors' moves are followed, not only in terms of sales but also in terms of consumer behavior. This phase should also include an attempt to track the changes in the marketing inputs, sales promotion and distribution activities (Parameswaran, 2006).

- **Sales Tracking:** Tracking the brand sales is a slightly more comprehensive trend analysis of the brand sales, in other words, instead of a month view, analysis are prepared, let us say, quarterly in order to verify certain observations that may have been missed. Tracking the brand sales can be made in the range of a city, municipality, region, nationally, regionally, and globally. It is significant because it easily detects the changes in competition and its impact on the brand. The ill-health of the brand which is manifested as a short-term damage can be seen precisely in the period of 3-6 months. Seasonal trends may affect the sales, so this should be taken into account in the analysis (Salinas, 2009).
- **Market Share Track:** The brand board provides information on the market share of the brand at local or national level on a monthly basis. But deeper analysis are usually more difficult and require an extended period of time. Thus, the quarterly track of the market share includes the following additional analyzes: geographical coverage: urban / rural area, inhabitants classifications, large / small cities, the comparison between quarters and alike (Berry, 2004). Similarly, you can analyze the panel of consumers: use, regular use and profit / loss (Keller, 2001). When it comes to products for final consumption such analysis would provide a richer profile of the changes in the market share. Among durable consumer goods, where the decision-making process is slower, the monthly market share affects the short-term tactics of the brand. Thus, in the case of consumer durables the quarterly indicators are a much more stable measure of the changes in the market share.
- **Marketing Inputs Track:** This element is a quarterly analysis of: the advertising, promotions, PR and other inputs behind the brand and their comparison with those of the competitors. With spiral media expenses, most brands today have a "campaign" usage of the media. This means that in the 52 weeks of the year the company would have 3 ad campaigns with an average duration of 8 weeks. This means that 24 weeks of the year are covered by intensive advertising, and 28 weeks are in total silence. Such occasional "flights" can "be captured on the radar" only with a periodic monitoring. Similarly, sales promotions have an average duration of 8 weeks and after a short time the effect fades. Therefore, their monitoring is conducted in the longer period. One of the goals of this type of brand monitoring is to make a comparison with competing brands. Key stakeholders should obtain information on: the schemes of dealers and distribution techniques for motivating dealers, materials used for display, templates for retail and exhibition etc. (Chernev, 2010).

- **Tracking Distribution:** The purpose of this monitoring is to determine the depth and width of distribution (Van Auken, 2003). The width of the distribution is measured as the ratio between the distributors who want to distribute the brand in relation to all distributors in the industry. Depth is measured as volume of goods distributed calculated by the ratio of turnover of inventory, i.e. the smaller the number of days of tying up inventory, the greater the depth of distribution. With the advancement of technology, opportunities for monitoring the depth and width can be monitored on a daily basis, but a better picture is obtained when it is done within a few months. When it comes to competition, tracking the distribution should include: breadth of distribution, national, local, according to the characteristics of the population, urban / rural, by product, by type of distribution etc. (Arnold, 2003). All these dimensions are also calculated for the depth of the distribution. Through such brand tracking, critical market changes are more easily noticeable.
- **Tracking Prices:** Tracking the price level of the brand is not applied in isolation but in comparison with competitors. Deep analysis is needed to forecast future price movements. Most companies practice the cost plus method for pricing their products / services, considering that the determination of the price is intrinsically linked to the cost of the product / service. But for proper monitoring of prices, they need to analyze both the national and global level. The monitoring of prices should be performed on products and their variants, including substitutes and complementary products.
- **Tracking Consumers:** The main objective of the brand monitoring is to go a step further than the amount of sales in order to discover the reasons for each situation. The critical factor affecting sales is consumers' behavior, attitudes, opinions, and the image of the brand from their perspective. The monitoring of consumers applies the measurement of these parameters on a quarterly, semestral or annual basis (Chernev, 2010). Tracking consumers is usually part of a system of market research involving interviews with consumers in two or more markets. Most of the leading marketing agencies have developed specific methodologies for calculating these parameters. For example, if the intention is to measure the image of the car maker Audi, it is necessary to check the views of relevant consumers from a large / small town to a larger / smaller state, i.e. economically more / less powerful environment.

Tracking consumers consists of measuring: the level of brand awareness, the level of use and the brand image (Parameswaran, 2006). These dimensions are also followed for the rival brands. Considering the costs for implementing the necessary market research, tracking consumers is restricted to semestral or annual basis. The data from a panel of consumers provides information on the current level of use and continued use of the products / services of the brand. But through it we cannot obtain the information about the level of consumer awareness for the brand and for the motivation for purchase that causes the trial or usage (Keller, 2001). However, the purpose of the consumers track is to exceed the actual figures and to dive into the reasons behind them. Even more important is that the consumers track rates the image of the brand relative to competing brands.

- **Tracking Consumer Awareness:** On average, consumers list up to three brands within a particular business or product category. The first suggestion is the brand with "first in mind" awareness, the second and third choice usually represent the unsupported level of awareness, followed by the level of supported awareness (Aaker, 1991). The first on mind awareness is the strongest indicator of the health of the brand and is usually strongly correlated with the market share. Unsupported awareness is also a good indicator through which one can predict the brand's rank. Consumers' awareness of the brand was previously described in detail in Chapter 2. The monitoring of brand awareness in a longer period of time becomes obvious as the results initiate changes in the health of the brand.

- **Tracking Usage:** Do you use toothpaste? Which brand of toothpaste do you use? Have you ever used a Colgate toothpaste? The answer to the first question reveals the usage of the brand. The answer to the second question provides information on the current level of the brand use, while the answer to the third question is the level of brand trials. The brand with a high level of current use, and lower brand trial is a healthier brand from the opposite - the one with low current use and high level of trials. The level of brand use can be calculated from the data from a panel of consumers, but monitoring consumer goes deeper than the differences between a consumer that tries the brand and a consumer who uses the brand. For example, the brand can have 5% current use by consumers and 45% of trials by consumers, which initiates that many customers have tried the products / services of the brand, but dropped from further use (Keller, 2001). Tracking consumers can find the cause. Whether it comes to quality, price or perhaps the brand image? The detailed tracking of consumers can take account of the use of the brand in certain segments. The monitoring of the brand use is trying to give a clear picture of the customers and the extent to which they use the brand. Also, it acquires knowledge of the exact level of brand awareness, i.e. how many consumers are aware of the brand and buy it, and how many are aware, but do not buy it.
- **Brand Image Track:** Brand image consists of rational, emotional and experimental factors. The brand image track is trying to measure the image of the brand from the perspective of consumers and compare it with other competing brands. The brand track measures the brand image through several parameters: product quality, the benefits that the product offers, the ratio price - value, the images evoked, the image of the user, the circumstances for using the brand, the dimensions of the personality of the brand and so on. (Dowling, 2001). By monitoring the brand image, the differences in the image between individual product categories or sectors can be noticed, and with the combination of the results we can get the answers to questions such as: Why consumers stopped buying the products / services of the brand? Is brand awareness at an appropriate level? Which are the strengths / weaknesses of the dimensions of the brand image? Does the increase in brand awareness affects the sales? What causes the changes in the brand image? Are there differences in the perceptions of consumers? (Vaid, 2003). Consumers track is a platform for analyzing the awareness, use and image of the brand in the form of a photographic image. This analysis can reveal the reasons for the acquisition and loss of customers which are a key factor for the brand success.
- **Tracking Brand Environment:** We live in a world where time began to be measured in nanoseconds and where the impact of certain events is felt in the distance of thousands of miles. Certainly the macroeconomic and sociological changes are not measurable in the short term, but it is very useful to check them in such a way. What should be taken into account is as follows: Exchange rates – Is the import cheaper? Does competition gain from it? Should we export? And so on. Changes in government policy and regulation - Whether a change in the regulation of market relations can affect the brand? Liberalization and globalization - How these trends will affect the brand? Strategic partnerships or acquisitions and mergers: global acquisitions / brands, mergers of large corporations and their impact on the brands and on competing brands (Nilson, 1998). Most of these trends affect a longer period of time (few to ten years), but with their regular monitoring

we can (at least with a certain level of probability) anticipate potential changes and upheavals. Monitoring the brand environment on a quarterly and semiannual basis is a useful way to develop an early warning system that would help the company to face the future challenges of the brand.

Brand Audit

The brand audit is a complete analysis of the brand health which is conducted annually, covering the macroeconomic picture and the micro detail. The brand audit does not consist only of the elements of the brand board and the brand track, but more than what the brand has to offer, Figure11 (Parameswaran, 2006). The brand audit can start by checking the information gained from the brand board and track. The revision of the brand begins with a compilation of available information about the brand, market, competitors, macroeconomic details etc. All this should be considered and practiced under the principle "audit from beginning" (zero starting point). The first step is to check the data about the company and published studies on distribution, customers and competitors. The next step is a discussion with the experts, both inside and outside the company.

- **Brand Data Audit:** The first data that should be reviewed are those derived from the brand board and track. Sometimes the results of the audit may indicate the existence of missed connections, or information that have been overlooked.
- **Expert Audit of the Brand:** The review of data may reveal specific vulnerabilities. The next step is to talk and discuss with all relevant experts, which include: the marketing team - analysis of the brand opportunities and challenges, competition, market trends; sales team - barriers to sales opportunities, new competitors and new distribution channels; the production department - the process of producing the products of the brand, the development of new practices, the structure of the costs of products, the impact of technological change, the processes of competitors and indirect competition; the department for product development, or research and development - projects for developing products, exploiting new opportunities, technological innovation, competitive environment, investments in research and development; the department of finance - the brand profitability, long-term corporate finance, capital market, future financial trends; the department of logistics - logistics costs of the brand, changes to improve logistics, expected changes in the future; and distribution partners - the health of the brand from their perspective, strengths and weaknesses of the brand, competitive pressures, future trends; suppliers and partners - the health of the brand, the plans of competitors, market trends, complementary / supplementary products; opinions of experts - each industry has its own experts who can predict future trends relatively better than the companies insiders. Discussions with them can give a clearer picture of the brand health. The collection of all this information and its presentation in simple formats lead to conclusions that should prepare the brand to face the future.
- **Brand Consumers Audit:** The audit of brand data and the expert analysis may raise questions that need extra attention, so the next step would be a further analysis of consumer trends associated with the brand. Which are the interactions between consumers and the brand? How can we change it in the future - in the short and long term? While tracking the brand, the focus was put on monitoring the consumer awareness, the usage and the image of the brand and competitive brands. The brand audit covers all this and more. First, the brand track may be conducted in a limited market. The revision of the brand should be a general framework that covers all the markets where the

brand performs. The brand track usually involves only quantitative analysis, and the brand audit refers to quantitative and qualitative analysis simultaneously. The brand track usually follows a format while the brand audit has the freedom to use completely new approaches to understand better the consumers and their behavior. The audit of the brand consumers include: revision of consciousness; audit of the use, testing the depth of use; analysis of the use of the brand within wider geographical coverage and more market segments; analysis of loyalty: which is the index of loyalty of different brands; brand usage in terms of per capita usage, frequency of usage and so on. While the audit of the brand image includes: the brand image through several rational and emotional factors; range of the brand in terms of various attributes of performance; brand differentiation: how similar or different competing brands are, which are the dimensions of similarity, and that of diversity; vitality of the brand, that brand elements that give vitality, energy and youth; brand personality: how does the brand present itself as a person, how is the brand seen against competitors, which are the typical features of the brand personality etc. (Aaker, 2011).

The brand is maintained healthy, prosperous and pulsating if built and controlled at every step. The measurement is not the ultimate goal. It should establish feedback with the activities, inputs and the parameters of the brand.

BRAND EXPANSION

The phase of brand expansion refers to developing a vision for the brand future and a check whether it can be expanded to additional products / markets. Further, this phase includes the appointment of brand extensions and ways in which the brand will be valued. Whether it is a corporate or a product brand, it

Figure 11. Brand audit

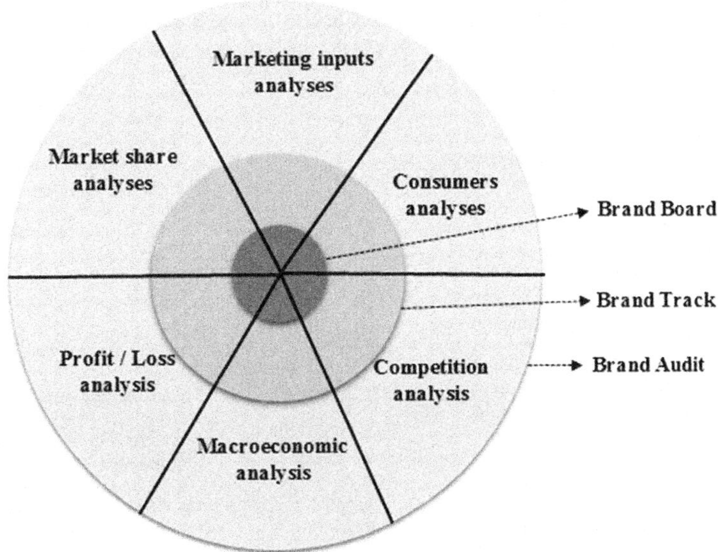

initially covers one or several products in a category, and then begins the cycle of expansion. The brand expansion is exploring the outer limits that the brand can reach. The brand expansion begins with the articulation of the brand vision. What is the essence of the brand and its core values? The brand expansion includes: exploring opportunities to expand the brand, alternatives for their naming, analysis of the brand portfolio and proper valuation of the brand. These are the four main components of the brand expansion (Parameswaran, 2006).

Expanding the Brand

The expansion of the brand is a term commonly used for product brands, but in this case the expansion is analyzed through three different dimensions. The first question is whether the brand can be spread and how much? Some brands cannot cover more than what they already do, but many can be expanded through the range of variants. Variants are the first level of brand expansion, the second is the brand assortment and the extensions are the top level of brand expansion (Berry, 2004).

- **Brand Variants:** They are the basic way to expand the brand concerning the same product and are available in several options. For example, the brand Dove can be found in a variant of a plain moisturizer soap, a soap for skin exfoliation, a soap with extracts with honey, cucumber, etc. Sometimes even an ordinary color change can represent a variety of the product. Most variants offer similar uses for the same target consumers. Their price usually oscillates around a similar price point. They are used to stimulate brand innovations.
- **Brand Assortment:** Compared to variants, the brand range extension refers to adding other products under the brand umbrella. For example, dairy products represent the range that can be covered with a product or a corporate brand. This is similar with a large number of brands for final consumption. The prices of the products in the brand assortment are usually different and address slightly different target customers.
- **Brand Extensions:** When the brand name is used for products that do not belong to the same category, it is considered a brand extension. This is commonly practiced to exploit the strength of the brand or to avail the benefits of a particular technology, a similar profile of target customers or a combination of the both mentioned factors, Figure 12 (Rosenbaum-Elliott et al, 2011).

Figure 12. Technology / consumers matrix

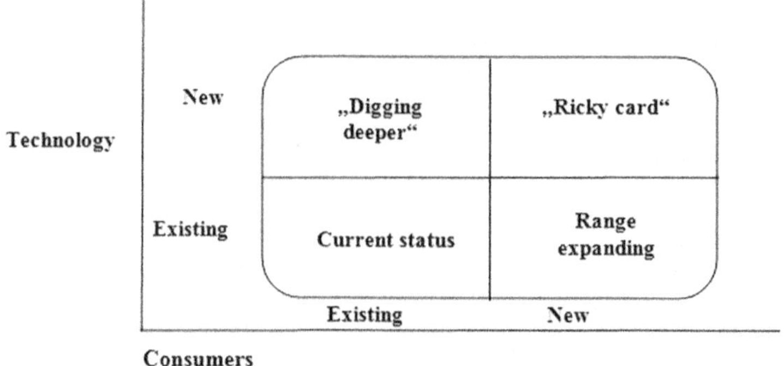

When using existing technology with existing customers, we are making an effort to increase the level of use of the brand - the current status of the brand. Using new technology with current customers is an attempt to dig deep (for example, when HP transferred from printers production to production of PC), which causes a slow acquisition of new customers (Herman, 2008). The application of existing technologies for acquiring new customers is an attempt to expand the scope of the brand, while using new technology to attract new customers is a so-called game of a risky card (the riskiest variant of the available alternatives). The expansion of the brand into new product categories should meet the following two criteria: consumers should be the same or similar and the company should have the technology and ability to enter into a new business (Rosenbaum-Elliott et al, 2011). Brand extensions are not simple; you should choose the appropriate alternative form the matrix technology / consumers. They can be successful only if the company provides the necessary inputs as for an independent brand. So the question is - which are the benefits of using an existing brand? Studies worldwide show that the established brand improves the chances of success for two times more than the introduction of a completely new brand. The error which is usually done is that the average investments in brand extensions are typically 50% lower than those that would be made to introduce a brand new standalone brand (Upshaw, 2005).

Naming the Brand

Several models for conventional brand naming that are called *brand architecture* are developed, Table 3 (Bahamón et al, 2009). The corporate brand is at the macro level. The corporate brand can be the basic brand that encompasses all products and services of the company, but it can also be a quiet brand combined with the brands of products. The brands of products are at the next level related to a certain product category. Furthermore, brands for product lines, separate models, and even a separate product or a specific feature can be introduced. In this way, we form the five levels of branding that make up the brand architecture.

The structure of the brand naming depends on market conditions, or the requirements and behavior of consumers as well as the activities of competitors. For example, if in one industry the corporate brand as the primary brand for all products / services of the company is used, it would be risky to use an entirely new level of brand naming such as a product line brand or a brand for a model. The conventional naming of brands is not considered a rigid, monolithic structure. Sometimes, the break in the rules results in an incredible success. Of course, this involves a certain level of risk and, of course, the company should remain consistent with the business model.

Table 3. Brand architecture

Corporate brand	HP	GM
Product brand	Jet	Chevrolet
Product line brand	Laser Jet	Estate
Brand for a specific model	630 C	X5
Brand for a specific characteristic	Super Color	Large Load

Managing the Brand Portfolio

The most popular model for analyzing the brand portfolio is still the current BCG (Boston Consulting Group) matrix. Depending on the position of the brand, a particular strategy is recommended (Armstrong and Brodie, 2004). Every company should provide answers to the following questions about the brand portfolio: From which brand assets does the corporate arsenal comprise of? Are there opportunities to merge the brands for their mutual benefit? Is there a chance a bigger brand to take over a smaller brand? Which brand should be exploited? What should be done with the excess cash? In which brand to invest and which one to sell? (Henderson, 2013).

- **Brand Valuation:** The valuation of brands is elaborated in detail in Chapter 6.The expansion of the brand is the last, fifth phase of the pentagon for building and managing the brand. The brand that manages to pass through all stages previously elaborated often turns into a successful brand in the market.

BRAND EXECUTION

The pentagon for building and managing the brand consists of five stages through which the brand equity is created, articulated and developed. But, through all the stages it is necessary to reevaluate the brand offer. The legendary 4P from Philip Kotler need to be defined, evaluated and reviewed in each stage. Thus, the performance of the brand consists of (re)defining the 4P elements as well as packaging, people and profits as brand variables (7P) (Parameswaran, 2006). As the idea of the brand develops through the brand birth stage, questions about the elements of the brand performance such as, product features, price, profitability etc. begin to open. In the next phase, when attempts are made to define the brand, it is crucial to retrace the elements of the brand performance: the process of production, the breakeven point in volume and value, the distribution strategy etc. In the phase of brand articulation the name, the graphics, packaging and the marketing communications of the brand are determined. Again, an audit of the brand performance is required. Once you launch the brand, an appropriate measurement system is required through which the progress of the brand will be tracked. Considering the market response towards the brand, a new revision of the elements of the brand performance is required once again. Finally, while studying the brand expansion, you need to check its profitability. It is constantly needed to balance the elements of the brand performance. The brand performance involves commitment of the parameters that form the brand offer. The elements of the performance of the brand vary in importance, depending on the type of product. Certainly the 4P remain important, but people are key to the success of the brand. Trends in durable consumer goods show that this sector increasingly depends on the quality of service (sales and after sales).

- **Product Offer:** Regardless of the category, brands should offer features that have points of parity (POP) within the industry and points of differentiation (POD) compared to competitors. Sometimes a POD may be the price or distribution. However, there are numerous examples of more or less known brands that have made a step forward based on a specific point of differentiation: Honda introduced starting cars and engines by pressing a button, not the key; Barista started selling coffee in the subway in major US cities, Samsung was the first to introduce flat-screen TVs,

Nike made snickers with airbags etc. Examples are numerous, and often the easiest solution is following the tactic "and we, too" - creatively copying a successful innovation. What is important is not to fall into the trap of imperceptible point of differentiation.

- **Price Offer:** The elements of the performance of the brand should be seen as integrated. If the price is used as a point of differentiation, the product offer should be properly aligned. In practice, several ways of pricing are applied: a method of cost plus, a price according to competitors, prices for market entry, setting a premium price and so on. The price offer is combined with the type and size of product packaging, and can be defined depending on the perceived gaps in the market. The determination of price for the brands in the service sector is in the range between the entry price and regular price for the service. The brands for durable consumer goods usually determine the price as a signal of product quality, but in this category products priced from a few hundred to several hundred thousand dollars can be found. The most important issue in this dimension is to achieve balance in terms of value / price, because it is the focus of contemporary consumers.
- **Distribution Offer:** Most of the brands are distributed through the classic channel of distribution. What is important is to find the answer to the question: how distribution adds value to the brand? For example, car manufacturers use a network of dealers to sell cars in the form of a general distributor in a country, which has to meet the necessary conditions. Some of the brands of clothing and footwear use a retail network under its own brand, while others are sold in outlets with more brands. Similarly, the brands for consumer durables are mostly distributed in retail chains with mixed brands, but sometimes they appear in retail outlets under their own, unique brand. The location and layout are crucial for the success of the brands from the service sector. The message of the brand is communicated through the retail stores (hotels, financial institutions, mobile operators, etc.). The decision on the distribution of the brand does not freeze, once adopted, on the contrary, like all other elements of the brand performance, the distribution should be reviewed, depending on the results from the brand measurement.
- **Promotional Offer:** In the brand articulation phase we analyzed the different ways of communicating the brand strategy and build regular marketing communications. The promotion of the brand should be monitored on a regular basis, as soon as the brand is launched. The brand measurement provides results that confirm whether the promotional mix of the brand functions well (Keller, 2007). Changes should not be ad hoc. They should be based on feedback from the system which measures the brand. The brand promotional mix, as well as the other elements of brand performance should be dynamic, but should not be changed without a good reason. The promotional mix that delivers good results does not need change, except perhaps some small experiments with small budgets, just to check that the brand does not miss a great idea.
- **Package Offer:** Packaging is one of the elements of the marketing mix, but many love to say that this is the fifth P element. The brand articulation phase defines multiple dimensions of packaging, such as: size, aesthetics, color, brand communication and so on. Changes in packaging depend on the results from the brand measurement. Thus, we can conclude that a change in the package size, design or brand message is necessary. Unlike advertising campaigns, the decision to change the packaging is relatively difficult. This does not mean you do not need to make the necessary changes. Further attention is needed to assess the rate of product rejection by consumers and to develop an adequate system of exposure in the stores (Chernev and Kotler, 2009).
- **Profit / Loss:** The purpose of branding is to provide a higher return on investment and higher profitability. There are well-developed techniques and systems (analyzed in Chapter 6) to calculate

the profitability of the brand. To allocate the cost of the brand, individual processes and activities in the company should be well known. When it comes to the product brands (products for final consumption and consumer durables) the cost of the brand begins with the cost of production or the cost of the product. This category of costs is often referred to as FDP (Factory Delivery Price). The successful brand requires active marketing. Marketing costs, COM (Costs of Marketing), include the cost of promotion, sales force, logistics and distribution. The basic costs of the brand are FDP + COM. They add certain corporate expenses CC (Corporate Costs). The three groups together, FDP + COM + CC, form the costs of brand COB (Costs of Brand). The product has a retail price, from which a wholesale and retail margin must be deducted in order to obtain the brand net realization NR (Net Realization). Most products for final consumption, have a NP in the interval 50-80% (Parameswaran, 2006). The profitability of the brand is determined by the volume of sales and the difference NR-COB. Amid strong competition, the company may enter the market with the price at which NR is equal to FDP. In this case the company does not calculate the marketing costs, administrative costs and profit in the short term. The aim is to ensure the growth of sales volume, and with the increase in volume, FDP will begin to decline and for a certain period (2-3 years) the company will start to gain significant profitability. In this way, numerous corporate brands have been developed - an initial focus on scale and generating profit at the long run. Sometimes the price level of the brand can be determined at the level NR = FDP + COM, and in rare cases when there is no competitive pressure, NR may be higher than COB and provide a profit even in the first year of brand existence. The selection of the appropriate alternative depends on the company, the industry and the conditions in the environment.

- **Human Factor:** The brand's success primarily depends on people that enable the brand to become reality. Brand management should ensure that everyone is speaking the same brand mantra. The essence is to motivate individuals to internalize the whole concept of the brand. The brand is no longer a luxury in the executive offices and boards of companies. People are transforming the brand into a pulsating, living matter. The brand performance would be incomplete (i.e. impossible) if people do not feel responsible for the future of the brand. The performance of the brand is in the center of the pentagon for building and managing the brand. Each phase of the model is directly linked to the elements of the brand performance, Figure 13.

The model is a contemporary compilation which integrates all the familiar aspects of the brand - from idea to profitable business. The pentagon is a way of creating brand value, which indirectly increases the value of shareholders. Its essence consists of making the brand more important for consumers. The more customers accept the brand offer, the greater the value of the owners of the brand. A win-win situation. So, the pentagon is a systematic way of building valuable brands in the long term.

CONCLUSION

Regardless the state – a developed economy or a developing economy, each brings specific challenges and opportunities. The issues the companies face are somewhat different, but one thing is common to all: it is necessary to develop and then implement a suitable model for building the brand that will satisfy the specific requirements for each individual example. Most of the world recognized and applied models for building brands were developed and refined through the American and/or European perspective.

Figure 13. The brand pentagon – an expanded version

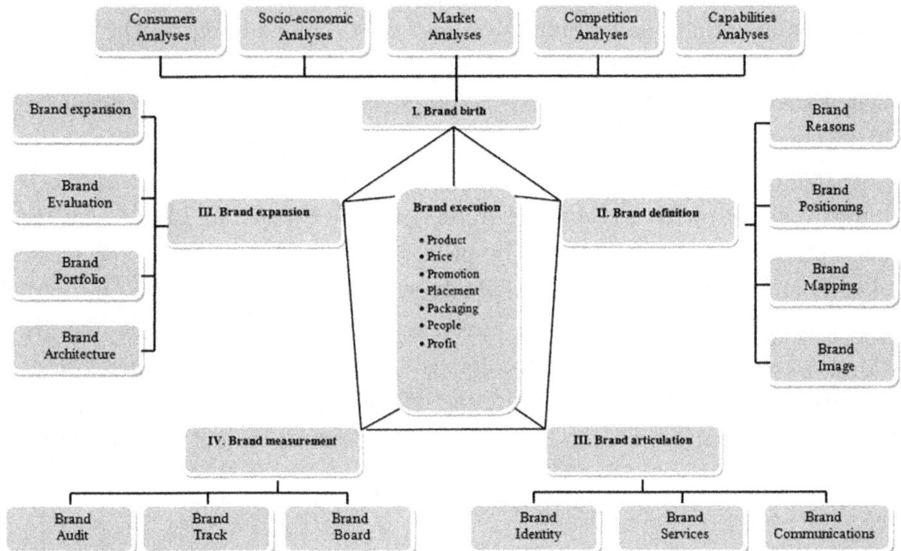

The brand pentagon represents a sublimation of several models, with the intention to involve all key elements of the process of building the brand, of course, with the necessary adjustments in a particular case. What is crucial for the success of the new business model is the transparent approach in the planning and execution of each element of the process of building and managing the brand, because it the only way to reverse the mistakes and shortcomings in the process. With a proper involvement of all key internal stakeholders - managers and employees in the process of building and managing the brand through radical transparency, the ultimate goal of any business - creating a brand company can be achieved.

Building the brand is more than choosing a product or service, name fixing, price fixing and market offer. This model assumes that in the center of each activity for building the brand are the primary variables that describe the core of the brand: the brand attributes, the price level, distribution, packaging and profit. These variables cannot be drawn from a hat juggler. They need to be developed systematically and be flexible enough to properly react to potential changes in the conditions under which the brand is operating.

The first phase in the brand pentagon is the brand birth stage. The key question that needs to be answered at this stage is whether there is a market for the products / services of the company. A frequent comment in the marketing circles is that there is a "hole in the market," but what is important is whether there is a market in the hole. The first stage is critical because it is the moment when the company must decide whether to continue further or to leave the idea for the brand. The second stage refers to the brand definition. Once you identify the possibility, the next step would be to define the offer. The brand definition refers to the brand offer which includes rational and emotional significance for consumers. The third phase is the brand articulation, that is, how the brand will be expressed to the target consumers? Which will be the name of the brand and why? Which will be the packaging and graphic design? Which will be the positioning? Which role will the other elements of the marketing program have? The brand articulation is about developing a way of presenting the "face of the brand" to the customers. The next stage is the brand measurement, or the way the brand performance is monitored. Once you identify the possibility to define the brand and develop its expression, it comes the phase of launching the brand and the measurement of its performance. Brand measurement includes establishing a system of measures that will follow the brand progress on a monthly, quarterly or annually basis. The fifth stage relates to moving the brand forward through the brand expansion. Once the brand "starts", the next step is to provide a way for it to stay ahead of competitors. Should the brand expand to other products and markets? Through the five stages of the brand pentagon, the process of building the brand is associated with the central core - the brand execution. The brand execution is refined through the progress from the brand birth, through the definition, articulation, measurement and its expansion. In this way, the brand pentagon leads the company, step by step, through the process of branding products, services or businesses.

The model is a contemporary compilation which enables integration of the familiar aspects of the brand from idea to profitable business. The pentagon is a way of creating brand value, which indirectly increases the value of shareholders. Its essence consists of creating value for shareholders, making the brand more important for consumers. The more the customers accept the brand offer, the greater the brand value. A win-win situation. So, the pentagon is a systematic way of building valuable brands in the long term.

REFERENCES

Aaker, D. (1991). *Managing Brand Equity*. The Free Press.

Aaker, D. (1996). *Building Strong Brands*. Free Press.

Aaker, D. (2004). *Brand Portfolio Strategy: Creating Relevance, Differentiation, Energy, Leverage, and Clarity*. The Free Press.

Aaker, D. (2011). *Brand Relevance: Making Competitors Irrelevant*. John Wiley and Sons.

Aaker, D., & McLoughlin, D. (2010). *Strategic Market Management: Global Perspectives* (9th ed.). John Wiley and Sons.

Armstrong, S., & Brodie, R. J. (2004). Effects of portfolio planning methods on decision making: Experimental results. *International Journal of Research in Marketing*, *21*(1), 73–84.

Arnold, D. (1992). *The Handbook of Brand Management*. Perseus Books.

Bahamón, A., Cañizares, A., & Corcuera, A. (2009). *Corporate Architecture: Building a Brand*. W.W. Norton & Co.

Barich, H., & Kotler, P. (1991). A framework for marketing image management. *Sloan Management Review*, *32*(2), 94–104. PMID:10111301

Berry, J. (2004). *Tangible Strategies for Intangible Assets*. McGraw-Hill.

Carlzon, J. (1989). *Moments of Truth*. Ballinger Publishing.

Chasser, A., & Wolfe, J. C. (2010). *Brand Rewired: Connecting Branding, Creativity and Intellectual Property Strategy*. John Wiley and Sons.

Chernev, A. (2010). *The Marketing Plan Handbook*. Brightstar Inc.

Chernev, A., & Kotler, P. (2009). *Strategic Marketing Management*. Brightstar Media, Inc.

Clark, K. (2004). *Brandscendence: Three Essential Elements of Enduring Brands*. Dearborn Trade Publication.

Cohen, J. (2005). *Intangible Assets: Valuation and Economic Benefit*. John Wiley and Sons.

Cooper, A. (2007). *How to Plan Advertising*. Cassel Publications.

Davies, G. (2003). *Corporate reputation and competitiveness*. Rutledge.

Donnish, A., & Myatt-Hsu Yule, J. (2010). *Lufthansa Going Global, but How to Manage Complexity?* Eurofound.

Dowling, G. (2001). *Creating Corporate Reputations: Identity, Image, and Performance*. Oxford University Press.

Gorman, A. (2004). *Briefs for Building Better Brands: Tips, Parables and Insights for Market Leaders*. AGCD Books.

Harris, F., & De Chernatony, L. (2001). Corporate branding and corporate brand performance. *European Journal of Marketing*, *35*(3/4), 441–457. doi:10.1108/03090560110382101

Henderson, B. (2013). *The Product Portfolio*. McGraw-Hill.

Herman, D. (2008). *Outsmart the MBA Clones: The Alternative Guide to Competitive Strategy, Marketing and Branding*. Paramount Market Publishing.

Hubbard, D. (2010). *How to Measure Anything: Finding the Value of Intangibles in Business*. John Wiley & Sons Inc. doi:10.1002/9781118983836

Ind, N., & Bjerke, R. (2007). *Branding Governance: A Participatory Approach to the Brand Building Process*. John Wiley & Sons.

Keller, K. (1998). Conceptualizing, Measuring and Managing Customer-based Brand Equity. *Journal of Marketing*, *57*(1), 22.

Keller, K. (2001). *The brand report card*. Harvard Business Press.

Keller, K. (2007). *Strategic Brand Management*. Pearson Education.

Knox, S., & Malan, S. (1998). *Competing on Value*. F.T. Pitman.

Nash, E. (2000). *Direct Marketing: Strategy, Planning, Execution*. McGraw-Hill.

Nilson, T. (1998). *Competitive Branding: Winning in the Market Place with Value-Added Brands*. John Wiley & Sons.

Parameswaran, M. G. (2006). *Building Brand Value*. McGraw-Hill.

Rosenbaum-Elliott, R., Percy, L., & Pervan, S. (2011). *Strategic Brand Management*. Oxford University Press.

Rust, R., Zeithaml, V., & Lemon, K. (2000). *Driving Customer Equity: How Customer Lifetime Value is Reshaping Corporate Strategy*. The Free Press.

Salinas, G. (2009). *The International Brand Valuation Manual: A complete overview and analysis of brand valuation techniques, methodologies and applications*. John Wiley & Sons Inc.

Schmit, B. (2009). *Experimental Marketing*. The Free Press.

Schultz, D., & Tannenbaum, S. I. (1993). *Integrated Marketing Communications: Putting it together and Making it Work*. NTC Business Books.

Trout, J., & Ries, A. (1972). The Positioning Era Cometh. *Advertising Age, 17*, 455–467.

Upshaw, L. (2005). *Building Brand Identity: A Strategy for Success in a Hostile Marketplace*. John Wiley & Sons Inc.

Vaid, H. (2003). *Branding: Brand Strategy, Design, and Implementation of Corporate and Product Identity*. Design Directories.

Van Auken, B. (2003). *Brand Aid: An Easy Reference Guide to Solving Your Toughest Branding Problems and Strengthening Your Market Position*. AMA Press.

Wall Street Journal. (1990, March 23). Ad World Is Abuzz. *The Wall Street Journal,* p.112.

Wheeler, A. (2006). *Designing Brand Identity: A Complete Guide to Creating, Building, and Maintaining Strong Brands*. John Wiley and Sons.

Chapter 6
Evaluating the Brand With Radical Transparency

ABSTRACT

The justification of all the theoretical knowledge in this book is verified through the evaluation of the brand, which is analyzed in this chapter. Gradually, we fully complete the concept: from idea to evaluation of the brand. The valuation of the brand through radical transparency is elaborated through several variants: the brand equity as a measure of the value of the brand, financial approaches to valuation of brands, integration of finance and marketing through the "best practice" approach for brand evaluation and the brand value chain. Thus, we conclude the efforts for the understanding, application and assessment of the brand equity as a source of competitive advantage through the prism of radical transparency.

INTRODUCTION

The justification of all the theoretical knowledge in this book is verified through the evaluation of the brand, which is analyzed in this chapter. Gradually, we fully complete the concept: from idea to brand evaluation. The valuation of the brand through radical transparency is elaborated through several variants: the brand equity as a measure of the value of the brand, financial approaches to valuation of brands, integration of finance and marketing through the "best practice" approach for brand evaluation and the brand value chain. Thus, we conclude the efforts to understand, apply and assess the brand equity as a source of competitive advantage through the prism of radical transparency.

The brand is materialized in several ways. The most immediate and most obvious is through the sale of products / services to consumers. The combination of price, quantity and frequency of purchase creates the volume of sales of a business. This is the basis for the profits and, ultimately, the shareholders' value. The share price of the company moves depending on the expectations for the future ability of the company to generate revenue and to extract profit.

DOI: 10.4018/978-1-5225-2417-5.ch006

The Brand as an Intangible Asset

Intangible assets are turned into a key factor for the shareholders' value. In the past 25 years the average value of the index price / book value of tangible assets calculated for companies whose shares form the S & P 500 (weighted index which is calculated since 1957 from the prices of the 500 most liquid shares of companies with the largest market capitalization in the United States) is about 3.9, which means that investors evaluate these companies almost four times more than their net material assets (Figure 1).

In this context, it is important to note that the index S & P 500 includes a wide range of B2B companies as well as companies from the energy and industrial sectors that traditionally have high material assets in the balance sheets. The analyzed period also includes several business cycles and "bulls" and "bear" stages in the stock markets. The average value of the ratio price / book value of tangible assets of companies in the S & P 500 is gradually increased from an average of about 1.4 at the beginning of the 1980s to an average of about 3.1 in the mid-1990s. The index rose in the late 1990s and exceeded the value of 7 during the dotcom boom of the companies, and returned back to 2.7 in 2008/2009 during the stock market crash (Salinas, 2009).

The long-term value of the index price / book value of tangible assets in the amount of about 3.9 indicates that the material assets of the company represent about a quarter of the value that investors assigned to the company. The remaining three-quarters are related to: patents, business systems, distribution rights, brands, databases and quality of management and employees of the company. Although the book and market value are only partially comparable, share price reflects investors' expectations for future cash flows from the business, so, the ratio price / book value of tangible assets provides a clear indication that investors perceive the value of the company in its intangible assets.

Ultimately, brands represent the relationship between the company and its customers, which are the main generators of revenue. This is supported by the fact that in 2010 the US consumption associated with the brands represented 72% of the US gross domestic product (Quelch and Jocz, 2010). This means that almost two-thirds of the GDP of the world's largest economy is connected with the brands and their value generation.

Figure 1. Value of ratio price / book value of tangible assets of companies in the S&P 500

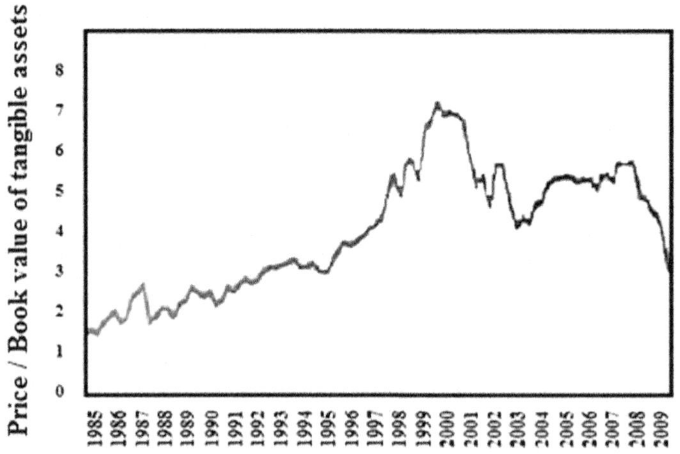

- **Growing Recognition of the Value of Brands:** In 1988, Nestle bought Rowntree for 2.8 billion British pounds, or five times more than its book value, and the following year Philip Morris bought Kraft Foods for 12.9 billion dollars, an amount six times higher than the book value. About 90% of this value was due to the value of the portfolio of product brands of Kraft Foods (Bharadwai, 2008). Such high multipliers of the cost of acquisition demonstrate the importance of brand value and intangible assets against tangible assets. This trend has led to increased interest in the brands, both from professional accountants and the managerial elite. Britain is the first country that responded to this question by introducing Financial Reporting Standard 10 in 1998. In 2001 followed the US Financial Accounting Standard 141, and in 2005 the International Accounting Standard 3 was published, which is an internationally harmonized accounting treatment of goodwill in mergers and acquisitions. Since then, many world famous companies such as: Coca-Cola, Vodafone, AT & T, P & G, Prada, L'Oreal etc. have included the value of their brand in their financial statements (Tollington, 2002). However, the complexity of branding, according to current management thought, does not correspond with the accounting approaches.
- **Brands and Value to Shareholders:** The specific value of brands that contributes value to shareholders is most clearly demonstrated by the survey called "The Best Global Brand", published in Business Week, whose results are published every year, starting from 2001. This ranking has the greatest influence on the boards of directors of companies around the world (Table 1).This research clearly highlights the importance of branding in almost any discussion among executives around the world. According to Business Week publications, brands on average are worth about a third of the total shareholders value (http://www.interbrand.com/en/best-global-brands/2013/Best-Global-Brands-2013.aspx).

Results from similar studies (Milword Brown and Brand Finance) show the same. For example, the value of McDonald's, according to the average value of the brand from the three studies represent 50% of the market capitalization of the company. Ratings clearly demonstrate that the brand contributes significantly to the value of shareholders, irrespective of the market focus. For example, in the case of

Table 1. Value of selected brands according to researches on brand value in 2013

Brand Value in Million US Dollars	Business Week / Interbrand	Millward Brown	Brand Finance	Average	% From Market Capitalization
Apple	98.316	185.071	87.304	123.564	24%
Google	93.291	113.669	52.132	86.364	25%
Coca-Cola	79.213	78.415	34.205	63.944	36%
IBM	78.808	66.662	37.721	61.064	32%
Microsoft	59.546	69.814	45.534	58.298	18%
McDonald's	41.992	90.256	21.642	51.297	50%
GE	46.947	55.357	37.161	46.488	17%
Samsung	39.610	21.404	58.771	39.928	20%
Toyota	34.346	24.497	25.979	28.274	16%
Intel	37.257	13.757	21.138	24.051	19%

IBM brand represents 32% of the shareholders value. For most of the companies, the brand is actually the most important asset of the business.

Studies use the results for the brand value from "The Best Global Brand" publications to show the impact of the brand on the value of shareholders. These studies compare the performance of companies with a strong corporate brand with the performance of the market portfolio consisted of all other shares of companies listed on stock exchanges in the United States. According to the findings, the portfolio which is based on brand value significantly exceeds the market portfolio, both according to the risk and yield. "The brand portfolio" showed monthly yield of 0.64%, or 48% better yield than the market portfolio which included the other companies that were not part of the brand portfolio. At the same time, the brand portfolio weighted by the brand value has had a significantly lower risk than the market portfolio. The value of beta was up to 0.85, or 15% less from the market portfolio (Fehle et al, 2008). This research clearly shows that strong corporate brands support high rate of return, higher from the market portfolio, at significantly lower risk. Similar studies based on the value of brands, also show that the performance of shares of companies with strong corporate brands exceeds the value of the key stock indices (S & P 500 et seq.) (Kalwarski, 2009).

The brand value is associated with the company's market capitalization. For example, the high value of the brand neutralizes cyclical influences in the industry, earnings or negative consequences of periods of recession and weak sales. During such conditions, consumers tend to spend less. So, the limited spending is directed to known and recognized brands and so, sales of their products does not decrease by such dynamics as the industry average. The brand also provides protection from existing and potential competitors, thanks to rising consumer loyalty. In general, companies with strong brands do not suffer much from external threats, and are facing less financial distress.

There are three main reasons why the top management became so interested in the issue of the brand: to manage and improve the performance of the company through increased sales revenues; top management needs to know the exact brand value when it involves in financial transactions; to meet the accounting requirements for intangible assets. (Hollis, 2010).

The History of Brand Valuation

The valuation of brands has emerged as a result of the boom in takeovers in the 80s when with high leverage many undervalued companies were undertaken. Such transactions reached a value of up to several billion dollars and their record in the financial statements was necessary. Adding the brand value in the balance sheet of the individual companies stirred a long debate among key constituents for the treatment of brands and their value as intangible assets. Finally, the debate resulted in changes in the balance sheet and the new accounting standards for recording intangible assets worldwide. More importantly, the financial function within the company was constantly burdened with the question of the valuation of brands from a practical point of view, trying to find common ground between finance and marketing. In the past two decades many approaches and methodologies for valuing brands were developed. Although the debate between the financial and marketing community over the appropriate method for brand valuation is still fierce, we can still draw some general observations and guidance.

There are many approaches and models for determining the value of the brand. However, all relevant approaches, in principle, can be systematized in three categories. The first category consists of models that are based on marketing research in order to measure different dimensions of the brand, and to evaluate the relationship consumers have with the brand. These models are categorized under the term "brand equity" models. All these models provide important insights for the brand value, but no economic assessment of the brand is achieved. The second category of models and approaches to valuing brands consists of purely financial approaches that are designed to provide financial brand value. This category brings together more methods, classified as methods based on income, and comparative approaches. Besides financial value, they provide little information about the relationship between consumer perceptions and intentions and generating non-financial value. The third category combines financial and marketing approaches and models in order to fully understand and assess the value of the brand. These models result in financial sum based on the perceptions of consumers and financial analysis. Only few models systematically integrate financial and marketing analysis. (Lindemann, 2010).

THE BRAND EQUITY AS A MEASURE OF THE BRAND VALUE

At a time when financial markets began to recognize the value of intangible assets, the leading academics from the United States (in the early 90s) tried to conceptualize the brand as an asset of the business. The result was the concept of the brand equity (Aaker, 1996). Despite the use of the term "equity" this framework consists of a combination of measures obtained through marketing research. The model was later expanded by Aaker which has included measures of other models, primarily from Y & R and Interbrand (evaluation of the brand as an asset and assessing the strength of the brand, respectively). The framework for evaluation includes the following indicators: 1. Willingness to pay a premium price; 2. Satisfaction / Loyalty; 3. The perceived quality; 4. Leadership / Popularity; 5. Recognition and respect; 6. Perceived value; 7. Personalities; 8. Trust and admiration for the company; 9. Differentiation; 10. Market share; 11. Differences in price; 12.Coverage / Depth of distribution (Aaker, 2004).

As it can be seen from the list, this model serves more as a transparent guide to the issues and topics that should be taken into account during the brand valuation, rather than a clear quantitative model. Aaker noted that, although all these measures have diagnostic value, the efforts of the management should focus on at least one and up to four relevant indicators. The choice of a relevant indicator requires an educated assessment as weighting factors can be a conceptual and statistical challenge. Aaker suggests that using the same weight for equal weighting of all variables would be a good starting point. As a single measure of brand equity, Aaker (1996) favored the price premium as the most appropriate indicator.

The Aaker's brand equity model is very useful as it provides a list of verified and relevant standards. It also clearly demonstrates the seriousness and complexity of measuring the economic value of the brand. But the model does not include two key elements that are critical for establishing and managing the economic value of the brands. The first element is the relative importance of prioritization of different dimensions. The different dimensions overlap and it is not clear how much they depend on each other. Understanding the relative influence of each element is critical for identifying and managing the creation of brand value. Second, the framework lacks conceptual link to creating financial value. Economic evaluation of the brand is incomplete unless directly related to the financial results of the business. In general, the framework of the Aaker's brand equity model provides useful insights and concepts for evaluating the brand, but cannot provide full economic assessment of the brand.

After Aaker, Keller developed an approach for determining the brand equity in the form of a pyramid. The base of the pyramid is the core of the brand. The next level splits the brand to its rational and emotional aspects that are measured by the performance and image. The next level is about consumers' feelings and estimations of the brand. On top of the pyramid is the brand resonance, measured by the loyalty, interconnection, togetherness and commitment. The relationship between the consumer and the brand can be measured through their position at the pyramid - the level of commitment and affection towards creating a certain rational and emotional connection (Keller, 2009).

While Aaker formulated the brand equity manifest, several companies specialized in marketing research, developed new models that provide an integrated approach to brand equity based on the relative impact of the various dimensions of the brand. One of the most important and frequently used approach is called Brand Asset Valuation (BAV) developed by Y & R in 1993. BAV is a model for measuring the brand equity based on a standardized questionnaire that is used to evaluate thousands of brands in markets around the world. As such, it is one of the largest and most consistent marketing research. The model is based on a questionnaire composed of 32 questions involving four major dimensions of the brand: differentiation, relevance, appreciation and knowledge. Differentiation measures how a brand is different from other brands. The relevance measures how important the brand is for consumers' needs. The appreciation measures the popularity and perceived quality of the brand. Knowledge measures the level of understanding that consumers have of the brand. BAV measures the "health" of the brand by mapping the results of the survey into a two-dimensional matrix called the power network. The X-axis measures the importance of the brand, expressed as a result which multiplies appreciation and knowledge. The Y-axis measures the strength of the brand as a product of differentiation and relevance. Brand equity can be assessed depending on its position in the power network. Because it is a square matrix, the best brands are in the right upper quadrant. Here healthy and leading brands that have high scores in both dimensions are found (Hubbard, 2010). According to studies conducted in 2009, the brands in electronics, including: SONY, LG, Samsung, Duracell and Energizer were commonly encountered in this quadrant. In the lower left quadrant emerging brands appear, which typically have weak position and fail to develop. This quadrant meets: Blaupunkt, Loewe and Technics. The upper left quadrant consists of growing insufficiently differentiated brands, such as: Miele, Dyson and Bang & Olufsen. In the lower right quadrant are popular and well established, but "tired" descending brands, such as: Whirlpool, GE and Toshiba (BAV Electronics, 2006, http://bavconsulting.com/).

BAV is an original study on extensive marketing research which provides interesting insights and guidance. But it does not provide a direct connection with the creation of economic value. This model reveals the importance and differentiation as key factors to increase the value of the brand, and indirectly the value of shareholders. However, high-performance brands according to this model's criteria do not necessarily lead to the creation of financial value. Attempts to incorporate financial data provide additional insights that are still quite common. As such, BAV is usually used to identify and analyze trends, but not to understand and quantify the financial value of the brand.

Another important approach that tries to assess the brand equity, based on marketing research is the BrandZ study by Millward Brown. Similarly to BAV, BrandZ is a quantitative study of the brand equity which is conducted annually, starting from 1998 (www.brandz.com). BrandZ interviews consumers about brands from different industries which they regularly buy. Respondents valued brands over their competitors. According to the creators of BrandZ, this provides important insights because respondents are well familiar with the brands and business they assess. The BrandZ database is quite large and consists of over 650.000 consumer interviews, comparing over 25.000 brands. Through a series of statistical analysis, the study identifies several key parameters for evaluation. The so-called brand dynamics pyramid plays a central role. The pyramid consists of five levels of hierarchy. The lowest level is called *presence* and represents the familiarity of respondents based on historical tasting, presence and knowledge of what the brand offers and promises. The next level is the *relevance (significance)*, which assesses whether the brand is relevant for the consumers' needs, has an appropriate price and can be taken into account during the purchase decision. The third level is *performance*. Here the performance of the product / service is rated - whether the brand is an integral part of the consumers' shortlist. The next level is called *advantage* and is associated with emotional and rational advantage that has been recognized against other brands in the industry. The highest level of the pyramid is called *connectivity* and refers to the rational and emotional ties with the brand that cause prejudice to the other brands in the industry. The higher the level of the pyramid, the stronger the relationship's commitment to the brand. The brand dynamics pyramid is a model which is a hierarchical progression from brand awareness to brand loyalty. The pyramid shows the number of respondents in each level. With additional research, the relationship between the range of respondents and their purchase behavior can be tested and verified. Statistical analyzes support the relationship between the pyramid level and consumer loyalty. Based on these assessments, the likelihood of purchase and re-purchase are determined, depending on the pyramid level. Of course, loyalty increases along with the pyramid level. Also, the volume of spending dedicated to the brand increases with the same dynamics. As respondents are moving to a higher level in the pyramid, the so-called participation in the wallet increases. The BrandZ model is distilling the complexity of the research in one key performance indicator called *brand voltage* which measures the growth potential of the brand. Brand voltage is calculated from the result of the level of connectivity at the pyramid and data for revenues within the industry. The brand with positive voltage has potential for market share growth and resistance to competitors' activities. The brand with negative voltage has a low potential for growth and is much more vulnerable to competitors' activities (www.brandz.com).

The success of the brand valuation and the request for linking branding with the creation of economic value motivated Millward Brown in 2006 to create the approach for brand valuation based on the results from the BrandZ study and to publish it as a response to the study "The Best Global Brand", including the 100 best brands worldwide (Financial Times, 2009). This model follows the established triple analysis that became the basis for all the models based on the brand revenues. First, the total profits of the company is determined and allocated to certain product brands, markets and countries of operation (using publicly available financial data from stock exchanges, Bloomberg, Datamonitor and own research). Second, the portion of earnings which comes directly from the brand equity is calculated according to the brand dynamics pyramid. And the third step, a brand multiplier based on the analysis of the *brand momentum* is calculated. The brand momentum is an index of short-term brand growth (one year) compared to the average rate of growth of all brands that are part of the BrandZ database. The brand momentum index is measured on a scale of 1 to 10, where 10 indicates a brand with the highest potential for short-term growth. It is calculated upon three inputs: the likelihood of an increase in market share, the expected growth of the sector or industry in which the brand operates and the potential growth of the economy as a whole. Finally, the value of the brand is a simple product between the "branded" earnings, the brand contribution and the brand multiplier (http://www.millwardbrown.com/BrandZ/default.aspx).

This model is lacking transparency, for example it insufficiently explains the calculation and assessment of the brand voltage, the brand momentum, short-term growth rates, and the method of weighting and combining all other inputs for calculating the brand multiplier. Thus, the results can be surprising. According to the survey from 2011, Coca-Cola and Philip Morris had a brand momentum of 8 and 9, respectively, despite their position in mature markets with a declining business in some countries. On the other hand, Google and Intel had brand momentum of 3 and 2, respectively, while operating in dynamic technology markets. Since the height of the indicator should represent future cash flows, it appears that the aforementioned examples are contrary to market and industry trends. This causes a lack of confidence and reliability in the results (Financial Times, 2009). From the marketing research perspective, BrandZ study provides interesting insights, as a result of the depth of the research. This model provides an analysis of the brand equity which is useful when evaluating brands. This analysis has similarity with other studies of brand equity based on a survey at a large scale. But as for the other, the results are not so easily turned into an evaluation method through which we can understand, evaluate, and ultimately, create economic value of brands.

The Nielsen Company, in collaboration with Keller, also, developed a model for valuation of brand equity, arguing that it provides a link with the creation of economic value. This model calculates the index of brand equity based on a survey of more than 2.400 different brands. The result for the brand equity is calculated based on respondents' answers to questions pertaining to: favorability, recommendations and willingness to pay a premium price. The index is in the range from 1 to 10 (10 is the maximum score achievable). The approach is relatively simple and contains all major components of the brand equity. The company claims it can correlate the results with the customers' loyalty, but provides no explicit link with the financial results. This model assesses the economic value of the brand based on sales data. Annual brand sales are multiplied by a factor which represents the brand strength (a certain) percentage. The strength of the brand is assessed according to four key indicators. First, the attractiveness of the market has 15% share. This indicator assesses the attractiveness of the market in which the brand operates, depending on the scope and opportunities for growth. The second indicator is the brand acceptance at the market with a weight factor of 35%. This indicator shows how the brand operates on the market, which is its market share and growth rate, in value terms. The third indicator is the consumer acceptability which has the highest weight factor of 40%. Consumer acceptability is measured by brand awareness and brand consideration. The fourth indicator is the distribution coverage and brand availability. The established rates are applicable to normal annual brand sales. The result is called *brand profits power*. It is multiplied with a discount factor which represents the average market yield in order to calculate the brand value. This model assumes an unlimited life cycle of the brand, as well as a constant rate of return (The Neilsen Company, 2006).

The Nielsen approach is relatively simple and can be used on data that is already available for most companies. However, the model is simplified and lacks key elements. The biggest disadvantage are the financial assumptions. To use the assessment of the brand strength in order to determine its profitability does not correspond to any established financial basis and is therefore treated as a hypothesis that requires further examination. The approach does not distinguish the brand from the other assets of the business. It starts with the assumption that the strength of the brand profit represents the financial return of the brand, and everything else relates to other costs and revenues arousing from the remaining assets of the business. This is a questionable assumption. The indicators of the brand strength include some of the most important measures, such as market share, awareness, consideration and distribution. The way they are calculated is somewhat vague, so it is difficult to evaluate them. On this basis, it can be concluded that there is no strong link between marketing and finance. The approach is not suitable for assessing the value of brands.

Another variant of the approach to valuation of brand equity is based on marketing research developed by Pricewaterhouse Cooper (PwC). The key concept is the price premium that consumers are willing to pay more than the lowest price known as the willingness to pay. PwC sees this measure as a final assessment of the brand value. The model is based on an established research technique called trade-off analysis that applies to product development and pricing research. Consumers choose between different offers and different price level. The result is a preference to pay relatively more than the cheapest offer. According to PwC this reflects the preferences of consumers and is therefore plausible economic yardstick. The approach is limited due to the focus on price premium and the lack of visible economic and financial value (Cohen, 2005).

A very simple and understandable method for measuring brand equity is called *net promoter index* introduced by Richheld by Bain & Co. Companies calculate the net promoter index registering the consumers responses to a single issue, ranking them on a scale from 0 to 10. For example, based on the responses to the question: "How likely is it that you would recommend our company to a friend or colleague?" consumers can be categorized into three groups: promoters (range 9-10), passive (range 7-8) and deterrent (range 0-6). Then, the percentage of deterrent is subtracted from the percentage of promoters to get the value of the net promoter index. The result of 75% or above is considered favorable. This approach has become popular because of its simplicity, but it does not offer more than a survey for consumers' satisfaction. The main disadvantage of this model is the fact that the net promoter provides very little information about what impacts the financial performance of the business. Although it can be correlated with a certain latent structure of the brand equity, its superficiality defines it as an inappropriate method for a full assessment of the brand equity and the economic value of the brand, because it is not directly connected with any of them.

Within the models for brand valuation based on the brand equity a visible imbalance between the sophistication of the component relating to marketing research and the simplicity of the financial analysis is perceived.

FINANCIAL APPROACHES FOR BRAND VALUATION WITH(OUT) RADICAL TRANSPARENCY

The financial community "got aware" of the importance of intangible assets and brands in the 80s of the last century, when they realized major financial transactions between well-established brand portfolios. For example, Nabisco, American manufacturer of various food products for final consumption, was taken over by KKR for 31 billion US dollars. This transaction was based on existing cash flows of the brand portfolio of the target company. It was the largest takeover until November 2006, when it merged with a group of US hospitals chain HCA, which was estimated for valuable 33 billion US dollar (Bloomberg, 2007). During the 80s other significant M & A transactions involving companies with strong corporate brands occurred (Investment Dealer's Digest, 2003). These transactions not only show that intangible assets such as the brand are the most important assets of the business, but also pointed out the increase in the gap between book and market value of companies. From the 80s onwards the ratio price / book value of tangible assets of companies from S & P 500 began its long-term growth. For a decade, the ratio increased more than twice - from 1.1 to 2.6. Even in 2008-2009, one of the worst "bear market" in history, the ratio did not fall below 2.7, which means that investors assumed that intangible assets represent around 63% of the shareholders value (Financial Times, 2009). The gap between book and market value of companies showed that investors have recognized the advantage of intangible assets. As long as this gap was relatively small, the financial community has not treated this as an important issue. When the amount of goodwill was minor, this was the way the issue was solved, without significant impact on the balance sheet. But when the large acquisitions of strong brands appeared, the amount of goodwill jumped dramatically to a level that seriously damaged the balance sheet of the aqusitior. The accounting treatment was apparently unsynchronized with the economic reality. These events motivated the emergence of financial approaches for valuing brands which can generally be grouped into three categories: cost methods, market methods and methods based on the cash flow (Lindemann, 2010).

Costs Based Approaches

The cost approach to value an asset is based on the costs of acquisition. There are two types of approaches based on costs (Salinas, 2009). The first is the *original costs approach* that values assets according to the original cost of their acquisition. In the case of the brands, the original amount of the costs would be the sum of all identified investments made directly for the brand. This approach is relatively simple and, if there is accurate documentation it is easy to implement it. Although historical costs are interesting for the calculation of return on investment, they do not provide adequate access for valuing brands because there is no clear link between past investment in the brand and economic benefits they generate. For example, GM has invested a lot of money in manufacturing brands such as Pontiac, Oldsmobile and Saturn. Today these brands are dysfunctional and significantly discounted. On the other hand, the value of the brand Red Bull has exceeded the value of investments in it (Cohen, 2005). The point in having brands as assets is that they create a lot more value than the monetary investment required for them. One significant investment in the brand is the brand concept - the basic idea for the brand, which is independent of the cost, but depends on the creativity of its development. Furthermore, for many long-established brands it is almost impossible to follow and take into account all past investments connected to the brand. For leading brands such as Coca-Cola, Apple and GE it is almost impossible to calculate all brand investments. However, the main reason why the historical costs are not appropriate for valuing brands lies in the fact that there is an insignificant correlation between the money invested in the brand and the economic value that it creates (Tollington, 2002).

Replacement Costs Approach

Another more relevant approach is the replacement costs approach, which values asset on the basis how much it would cost to replace the asset in case it is acquired or created today. Replacement costs can be determined either by analyzing the current prices of assets or by adjusting the original cost with the inflationary factor. The replacement cost approach is economically more relevant because it is based on actual costs required for the acquisition of an asset. This approach is applicable for valuating assets for which the current prices are available and for which the application of the approach is a logical sequence. The method of replacement costs is appropriate for brand valuation in cases when the brand is not represented at the market or the level of brand awareness is negligible, i.e. when its value corresponds to the costs of brand development. This approach is inadequate for active brands because there is no significant relationship between the cost of establishing the brand and its economic value. For example, long-established brands like McDonald's, Nivea or Sony are almost impossible to replace, because of their position in the market (Reilly and Schweihs, 2007). The cost methods are not appropriate for valuing brands because there is no clear link between the cost of introducing and maintaining the brand and the economic value it creates.

Market-Oriented Approaches

The market value approaches operate over the premise that an asset may be valued by the market price for an asset similar to it. In the case of valuation of companies, it can be the listed companies targeted for takeover. The price of the asset is assessed on the basis of a multiplier, calculated from annual income or profits (operating profit or net profit) and the purchase price or market value of the company. This technique is often applied in financial transactions. The relationship between the share price and the company's profits (price / earnings ratio) is often applied to evaluate and compare the value of companies. For all the sophistication of financial modeling, value multipliers are used in most M & A transactions. The main benefit from the market oriented approach stems from the actual prices paid for similar assets. Indeed, the crucial point in this approach is comparability. In order to access this function, there must be a significant number of comparable transactions or listed companies to determine a reliable value. If it is difficult to find comparable companies or businesses, then it is almost impossible to find such brands. The companies with strong brands always involve additional funds. So, this comparative approach "does not get along" very well with the brand valuation. The market approach does not work well for brands because their main purpose is to be different and incomparable. If you take for example the companies Coca-Cola and Pepsi. Their businesses are perhaps the most similar that we can find. The product is almost identical, the companies have the same target markets and consumers, they have a very similar distribution system and charge a similar price for their product. Without the brand, their products would differ very little, but these two brands are very different in terms of image and value. Coca-Cola is the eternal market leader, and Pepsi is the eternal follower and challenger. Coca-Cola has a bigger market share and its average operating margin over the past five years is 8% higher than that of Pepsi. According to the "Best Global Brand" results published in Business Week, the Coca-Cola brand is worth 3.4 times its annual sales versus Pepsi which has a sales multiplier of 2.2 (Business Week, 2014). Coca-Cola has a stronger global press, while Pepsi is more focused on the US market. The example of these two brands demonstrates that brands are incomparable even in the same business. As a result, the market oriented approaches are not suitable for valuing brands because of the lack of comparable transactions and the original nature of brands. If there are comparable transactions and brands, this approach should be used as an additional method for evaluation, not as a first choice for brand valuation.

Approaches Based on Cash Flows

The approaches based on cash flows evaluate the asset according to a net present value of the cash flows which are estimated to occur during its economic life. This is the most widely accepted model and it is in line with the current theory of corporate finance. Thus, the method based on cash flows is the most commonly used method for valuing intangible assets, including brands.

There are several variants of this approach. The main difference between them is the identification and calculation of the specific brand earnings and the discount rate. The following three variants are analyzed:

First, the so-called *method of multiple high earnings* is based on the assumption that the cash flow can be generated from intangible assets only in combination with other tangible or intangible assets. In order to separate the intangible asset to determine its value, supportive inflows of funds are treated as additional costs for the assets. The approach identifies inflows from other assets, later subtracted together with the operating costs from the total revenue stream. So, certain cash flows are assumed to be generated by the intangible asset and are considered the basis for its valuation. The accounting offices often use this approach for evaluating technologies and customer relations. The difficulty with this approach lies in the assumption of the amount of inflows from other assets and their subtraction. Undoubtedly, it is easy to determine inflows from tangible assets, while it is relatively difficult to determine inflows of intangible assets such as the brand. The accounting offices have prepared lists of fictitious costs for such assets. But the validity of some of these flows is uncertain. This approach is commonly used to satisfy the need for determining the value of a wide range of intangible assets and their proper recording in the balance sheet, in order to achieve a correct allocation of the purchase price (Salinas, 2009).

The second approach based on cash flows for valuation of intangible assets is the *method of incremental cash flow*. This method determines the difference between the cash inflow of the company with the relevant intangible asset and that of a fictitious company without the asset. This difference represents the additional cash inflow associated with the intangible asset and its discounting with a specific rate leads to the determination of its rights value. This approach is simpler than the previous version and makes an assumption for the cash flow generated from the specific intangible asset that is valued, rather than for the other assets of the business. This method works on the principle of exclusion, assuming that all earnings which are not a result from a specific intangible asset represent the return from other assets of the business. The approach is usually administered in the form of profit sharing and when the engaged capital is compensated, the remainder is being divided between the valued intangible asset and the other assets. This approach is used by many consulting companies such as Interbrand and Millward Brown, specialized for brand valuation. The validity of this approach depends very much on the quality of the method used to identify the earnings of all acquired intangible assets, as well as the brand (Cohen, 2005).

Another variant of the method of incremental cash flow is the *approach to premium price*. It is based on the assumption that brands can achieve price premium over the generic unbranded offer. This approach compares the revenue from the branded offer and those from the generic product and calculates the net present value of future cash flows arising from the established price difference. As previously mentioned, there are models based on marketing research which assess the brand according to the willingness of consumers to pay a premium price. The approach of premium price is used by many consulting firms, including McKinsey and PwC. This approach is flawed because it focuses on the price premium as the only source of brand value and starts from the assumption that there are comparable branded products and services at the market. In reality there are only a small number of generic products. In contrast, there are almost no generic offers, because all products and services are branded. Even the labels offered by supermarket chains have evolved into a unique brand. The price premium is not the only factor for the brand value, because the scope, frequency of purchase and support costs tend to be equally relevant in the creation of brand value. The premium price approach ignores key factors for the brand value.

The third commonly used method for valuing intangible assets is the *method of royalties*. This method is typically used for valuing brands and patents. It is based on the fundamental premise that external third party would be ready to pay a certain fee to use the brand which it does not possess. In this case, the value of the intangible asset is calculated as the present value of inflows from licenses. This approach is quite popular due to its simplicity and objectivity. However, the approach is another version for valuing intangible assets by comparison. This is a significant disadvantage of this approach, because it relies on the comparability of the rates of royalties. But compared with other methods, data on the height of royalties rates is not affordable. Many royalties agreements are not made public and include several intangible assets under a single rate of royalties. Also, many of the royalty rates which are part of the franchise agreements are related to additional costs that are not part of the calculation. Such hidden income can only be identified by analyzing the entire contract, and most of them are not publicly available. The amount of royalty rates can move in the range of 1-20% of revenues, even within the same industry, they can significantly vary according to geographical areas and types of products. For example, the rate of royalties for a fashion brand for sunglasses and perfumes can be different. The same brand can be charged one rate of royalties in the US and another in China. In telecommunications, for example, royalties rate range from 2-8% (www.royaltysource.com). The diversity of the royalty rates complicates the application of this method. This approach works well in the case of many identified, comparable rates of royalties, but this is rarely the case of brands. This approach faces similar difficulties as the market oriented approach. The originality of brands makes it difficult on comparability. The method can result in underestimation of the value of the brand, because the rate of royalties does not incorporate all the costs for 'renting' the brand. This approach also does not provide specific insights on creating brand value. Based on the stated disadvantages, this method should not be used as the primary method of brand valuation, but in combination with other methods, aimed for checking the results.

Most of the approaches based on cash flows focus on the financial component for valuing brands. The current debate on the valuation of intangible assets such as brands recognize that conventional financial approaches are not sufficient to determine their true value. This is why brands as specific intangible assets should be valued according to the specific progress of the earnings they generate.

THE BEST PRACTICE FOR BRAND VALUATION

Pure marketing research and financial-focused methods fail to provide complete, satisfactory results for assessing the economic value of brands, because the lack of understanding the marketing or the financial dimension. As a result, new approaches to brand valuation that integrate marketing and financial analysis into a complete model for evaluating the brand value are constructed. This method is often referred as the method of economic use. This method values the brand as part of the company and focuses on the added value provided by the brand. The approach appeared as a result of the need to go beyond the mechanical calculation of the financial value and to understand and manage the process of creating brand value. Several world renowned consulting firms have developed their own versions of the method of economic use, including: Interbrand, Brand Finance and Millward Brown.

One of the most famous variants of the method of economic use was developed by Interbrand, a consulting company that is a pioneer in the valuation of brands, since the early 80s. The initial approach was developed for financial goals, to help companies recognize the value of their brands and ensure its accurate measurement in the financial statements. The model is a relatively simple approach to multiplication. The basis for determining the profits arising from the brand is the operating profit of the business. Taxes and a certain rate of cost of capital is deducted from the operating profit to gain the profit from the brand. The multiplier is determined by evaluating the strength of the brand. The strength of the brand is measured on a scale from 0-100. The extremes of the scale are a theoretical concept. A completely unknown brand would score 0, while a perfectly known brand would result 100. The brand with 0 result would have the exact multiplier, so, no value. A brand with a score 100 would have a multiplier 20, which arises from the analysis of price / earnings ratios of companies with strong brands listed on stock exchanges worldwide. Values between the two extremes determine a curve shaped "S", which reflects the relationship between the strength of the brand and brand value, i.e. the stronger the brand, the higher its value and vice versa. The strength of the brand is determined taking into account seven factors. Each one has a different maximum weight and the sum of the weight of all factors is 100. The weight factors are the following (Lindemann, 2010):

1. **Leadership (25/100):** Assesses the extent to which the brand influences the market at which it operates. It is calculated by indicators of price level, depth of distribution and resistance on competitive pressure.
2. **Stability (15/100):** Refers to the loyalty of consumers, i.e. how much the brand is the "creator" of the market in which it operates.
3. **Market (10/100):** Refers to the market where the brand operates. It measures the rates of growth, barriers to entry and the risk of structural change.
4. **Internationality (25/100):** A geographical range of the brand, under the assumption - as many more markets and cultures the brand is able to penetrate at, that much the brand is valuable.
5. **Trend (10/100):** Measures the ability of the brand to be (remain) contemporary and relevant in the market.
6. **Support (10/100):** Measures the amount of marketing expenses, and management of the brand content.
7. **Protection (5/100):** Measures the level of legal protection, including the registration and brand management.

The model which is based on the strength of the brand is one of the most consistent approach to brand valuation used by Interbrand. Although the company each year adjusts the model with the necessary changes, the principles for determining the strength of the brand are basically unchanged. The company so far has made two significant changes to the model. First, they replaced the multiplication by calculating the net present value (NPV) of the specific profit from the brand. Second, they introduced an element of profit sharing called "role of branding," which separates the profit realized by the brand from the profit which is the result of other intangible assets (Perrier, 2008). Replacing the approach of multiplication by calculating the net present value resulted in the use of discount rate, rather than a P / E multiplier in order to calculate the brand strength. The model assumes that the company with the strongest possible brand receives a score of 100 and its risk is similar to that of government bonds. The discount rate varies depending on the brand strength; the weaker the brand, the higher the discount rate, and vice versa (Best Canadian Brands, 2010). With these adjustments, Interbrand defines the basic elements of the method of economic use that values the brand in the context of owner and user. This approach consists of three key elements: financial forecasting of earnings from intangible assets; identification of the earnings from the brand; and assessment of the strength of the brand to determine a specific discount rate. The detailed steps are as follows:

1. **Financial Forecasting:** The company anticipates current and future revenue specific to each brand. Then the operating costs, taxes and certain rate as the cost of capital engaged are subtracted in order to get the economic profit.
2. **Brand Profit Analysis:** This section assesses how much of the profit was realized thanks to the brand. The role of the brand measures the brand influence on the consumers' demand and the point of purchase. With the help of this indicator, the profit from the brand is calculated.
3. **Brand Strength Analysis:** The seven factors for the brand strength set the discount rate used to calculate the NPV of the specific brand earnings.

Based on these three steps, Interbrand calculates the brand value as the net present value of future earnings from the brand.

Another company that has developed a similar method of economic use is Brand Finance. Their approach is very similar to Interbrand, but differs in certain aspects of the brand analysis. Brand value is calculated as the net present value of expected future brand earnings. Their methodology follows the following steps (Lindemann, 2010):

1. **Financial Forecasting:** Brand Finance prepares a five-year forecast of revenues based on data from the company, analysts' estimates and macroeconomic data. The company also calculates a final growth rate as a basis for calculating an infinite flow.
2. **Specific Brand Earnings:** To identifying specific brand earnings, Brand Finance uses the method of royalties. Based on published data, they identify and select rates of royalties for brands that are assumed to be comparable to the brand that is evaluated. A notional commission rate is calculated from comparable royalties rates and used to calculate the brand earnings - their extraction from the total revenues. The potential drawback (trap) in this model is the assumption of comparability, which was previously discussed. In order to create value, brands need to be different, and therefore should not be compared.
3. **The Brand Rating:** Like Interbrand, Brand Finance measures the strength of the brand on a scale of 0-100, depending on a number of attributes, such as the presence of the brand, emotional connection, market share and profitability. The rating of the brand serves as a standard for strength, risk and future potential of the brand in relation to its competitors, and the same is presented on a scale which is graded from AAA to D. The results of the ranking are defined as follows: AAA - Extremely strong brand; AA - very strong brand; A - strong brand, BBB-B - average brand; CCC-C - weak brand; DDD-D - descending brand.

The rating of the brand turns into "beta of the brand", but it is necessary to take into account additional factors such as geographical presence and reputation, which are outside the designated attributes for rating. The brand beta determines the discount rate used in calculations of future brand earnings. The brand value is the net present value of the estimated future earnings. The Brand Finance model relies on the comparability of the rates of royalties in order to determine the specific profit from the brand. However, in many industries, royalty rates may vary with several percentage points, making the final assessment quite subjective.

Another variant of the method of economic use is provided by Millward Brawn, which is based on the BrandZ study to determine the value of the brand equity. This approach was discussed earlier in this chapter. Besides these basic, internationally recognized and applied approaches for brand valuation, there are many more variations on this theme. Several studies have identified over 40 models for valuing brands (Zednik and Strebinger, 2008). Although, in general, most are similar, all claim to use their own tools for research and analysis in order to determine the value of the brand. The methodologies of Interbrand, Brand Finance and Millward Brown became dominant through the rank - lists of brands that these companies disclose on an annual basis. Although there are many other variations of the method of economic use, most of them follow a similar framework. A survey of the range of brands announced by consultancies shows that various methods produce different results for the same brand. Differences in input assumptions and inputs for each model account for the differences in the value of the same brands. These findings have been confirmed by several studies, including a more significant one from a German magazine in 2004. The publication asked nine different agencies for valuing brands to evaluate the fictitious company for retail trade of - chain of gas stations called Tank AG. The results showed large differences in value, starting from 173 million to 958 million, representing a difference of 454% (Markenbewertung - Die Tank AG, Absatzwirtschaft, 2004). However, it would be counterproductive to think that the valuation of brands is not a serious discipline because of differences in individual approaches and the results thereof.

All financial valuations are based on assumptions set in a time interval. The targets for the share price in the next 12 months for stable brand such as the Coca-Cola Company's acquired from 11 top analysts who continually monitor the company had a variance of 30% on 31.08.2009 (Financial Times, 2011). The 2008-2009 showed that the change in conditions can quickly and significantly affect the valuation, especially in the capital markets. The assessment of the value of inputs is of great importance and impact on the results and validity of the evaluation.

The need to establish a common language and to clarify the valuation of brands wake up several initiatives. The German Standardization Office - Deutsches Institut für Normung (DIN) has initiated a working group to create ISO standard for valuing brands (DIN ISO, Project Brand Valuation, www.din.de). There is already such a standard for marketing research. According to them, such a standard would ensure transparency and quality that will raise the reputation of this discipline and will provide relevant valuations of brands.

The "Best Practice" Approach for Brand Evaluation

Between the theory and practice of valuing brands a kind of consensus was "born" that is distilled in a tested and recommended framework for valuing brands. The analysis of the various approaches for valuing brands showed that the appropriate model should integrate marketing and financial analysis, without sacrificing any of them. The approach should keep up with the current theory of corporate finance as well as the practice of capital markets and the industry. The basic model for brand valuation should result in NPV of the expected future earnings of the brand. The approach for brand valuation should focus on assessing the specific process of creating brand value. The utilization of the method of rates of royalties and similar comparative methods can be used to check the analysis, but they are not part of the basic model. The cost methods are useful only when the brand still does not have a significant (measurable) impact on the market. After a thorough analysis of the various models for valuing brands, the approach that follows stand out as the best practice approach for brand valuation (Lindemann, 2010). The model consists of five key steps, presented in Figure 2.

First Step: Market Segmentation

The brand often covers more than one market segment, which is reflected in creating brand value. For example, brands like: Samsung, Siemens and GE produce a wide range of products for many different customer groups. The brand Samsung may have more influence on the consumer's decision to buy a TV, but the impact of this brand on a semiconductor purchase may result in higher financial gain. This is a crucial information for managing the brand because it affects the positioning, communications and investment. The purpose of segmentation is to identify segments relevant to the brand for which there is sufficient marketing and financial data. Once the appropriate segmentation is completed, brand valu-

Figure 2. Methodology for evaluating the brand

First step: Market segmentation

Brands influence consumer choice, but it depends on the market segment.

Brand valuation should take into account relevant strategic market segments (homogeneous groups of consumers).

The criteria for segmentation include: product / service offering, consumers' attitudes, spending habits, distribution channels, geographic differences, existing and new customers, share of wallet and so on.

The evaluation is conducted for each of the identified segments.

Second step: Financial analysis

Based on detailed financial and market analysis, the brand revenues which are expected to be realized in the future are forecasted.

The profits from intangible assets is extracted from the brand revenues as follows:

Revenue from brand
- Operating costs
- Taxes
- Expenses of engaged capital

= Profit from intangible assets

Third step: Brand impact

Dividing the income from intangible assets on part that relates to the brand and part related to other intangible assets.

Identifying and quantifying the factors that influence the purchase decision of consumers and the specific impact the brand has on them.

The brand impact is a percentage of consumers who have chosen the brand, affected by the brand.

The brand profit is calculated as the product between the brand impact and the profit from intangible assets.

The brand profit represents the income which applies only to the brand.

Fourth step: Discount rate

Expected future earnings from the brand are discounted at a rate which approximately reflects their risk.

When calculating the value of the corporate brand, the cost of capital (WACC) represents the most robust and usually reliable rate for discounting the profits from the brand.

The discount rate is used to calculate the net present value (NPV) of the expected total profit of the brand.

Fifth step: Calculating the brand value

The brand value is the NPV of the profits from the brand on each market segment.

The calculation of NPV consists of a period of explicit forecast and afterwards, reflecting the brand's ability to generate future cash flows.

The total value of the brand is the sum of the value of each segment.

ation is carried out in each of the identified segments. The amount of the valuations of each segment represents the total value of the brand (Keller, 2007).

Second Step: Financial Analysis

The brand operates "outside" of the business by attracting and providing consumers' demand. Demand turns into price, volume and frequency. Financial projections assess the revenue that is expected to be generated by the brand in future. The purpose of the valuation of the brand is to determine the useful life of the brand as an asset. In most cases the brand is evaluated assuming a continuum, i.e. the evaluation covers all the expected earnings of the brand in future, if there is no particular limitation (duration of a contract or alike).

In order to prepare the forecast, the first step is to identify past and current earnings that the brand generates, followed by determining the costs and required capital needed to achieve those revenues. When evaluating the corporate brand for companies that do not have special product brands, financial information for the company in general and for the brand are identical. For companies that have multiple product brands, financial data should be identified for each specific brand, and then for the corporate brand as a whole. Although past and current analyzes provide guidance, the main focus should be set on the expected brand performance, based on a thorough analysis of the microeconomic and macroeconomic conditions in which the brand operates. It is always important to compare the final estimation of revenues with historical performance and those of competitors.

Expected demand for the brand products / services is represented by the selling price and volume, converted into an expected revenue stream from the brand. Then, all the necessary operational costs are subtracted in order to get the profit before tax, interest and amortization (EBITA). The calculation continues by calculating the amount of taxes and the cost of capital, which is deducted from EBITA.

The cost of engaged capital is an adequate rate of return needed to compensate the used resources. The weighted average cost of capital (WACC) is considered to be an adequate rate of return for the engaged capital. After deducting the amount of taxes and the cost of capital, the rest is profit from intangible assets. The result of the financial analysis is the forecast of the profit from intangible assets arising from the revenue stream created by the brand. In most cases, the evaluation consists of two periods of forecasting: an explicit and detailed forecast that, on average, applies for a period of 5 years; and an estimated cash flow as an infinite annuity calculated from the net inflow from the last year (in this case year 5), multiplied by the long-term growth rate. Although most of the efforts are dedicated to the preparation of a detailed forecast, the influence of the infinite annuity is much higher and reaches up to 2/3 of the total brand value (Salinas, 2009). Forecasting is not an exact science, in which many economic and financial experts after the crisis in 2008-2009 were convinced. Modeling and subjective assessment should complement each other to achieve the best possible forecast. Financial analysis includes available integrated marketing data in order to avoid separate implementation.

Third Step: Brand Impact

Profits of intangible assets represents the return of all intangible assets of the business. To complete the brand valuation, it is necessary to identify the specific income from the brand. This means that the income from intangible assets should be divided to profit from the brand and profit from other intangible assets. The specific profit from the brand can be identified in different ways, most of which already explained previously in this chapter. A starting point is the identification of the way the brand creates demand and consequently, revenues. This requires analysis and discussion over the consumer's purchase decision (Jacoby, 2001). Modern research techniques can provide a detailed explanation of the reasons for purchase, the selection process and how consumer perception affects them. The latter is a good measure of the relative impact of the brand. To assess how consumers perceive the brand and then how this perception leads to a purchase decision, you need to prepare and analyze relevant data from the market research. Most companies practice various studies and researches on the subject. Research methodologies can be qualitative and quantitative. Ideally, the marketing research is specifically designed to identify and understand the factors that influence the purchase decision and how the brand affects them. However, due to the relatively high costs, many companies use the data from existing researches. In many cases it is quite possible to find a way to incorporate existing data in an appropriate model.

The first step in assessing the impact of the brand on the consumers' purchase decision and the revenue is to identify the reasons why consumers choose to consider, and then buy the product / service of a particular brand. The impact of perceptions on the functional benefits from the brand is very important for B2B brands, where the emotional benefits are significant, but not as much as with the product brands intended for final consumption.

Once you identify the key factors influencing the purchase decision, they should be evaluated according to their relative importance or impact on the purchase decision. Through the process of statistical analysis, the results can be translated into a clearly defined factor influencing the purchase decision. Once you assess the relative importance of these factors, the impact of the brand is determined. It is important to analyze the brand impact on the factors taking into account that they are not isolated - the brand represents all the perceptions for the company and its products / services. The brand is measured by a two-stage approach. First, the percentage of influence of each factor on the purchase decision is determined, Figure 3.

Figure 3. Evaluation of the brand impact

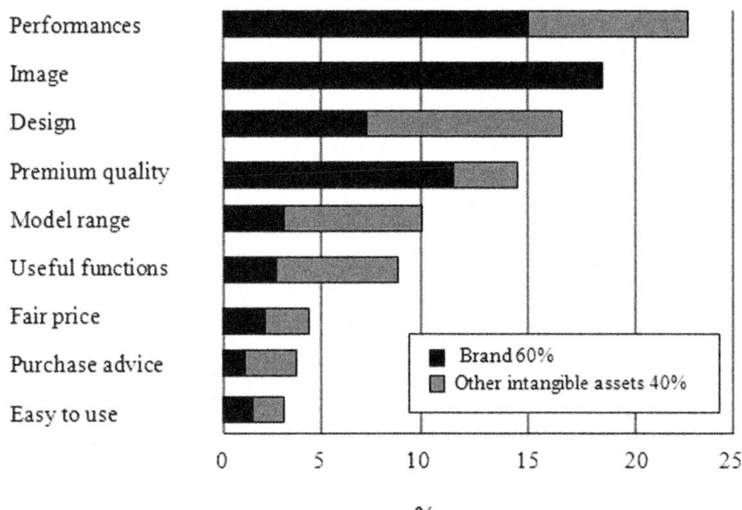

Once you determine the percentage of impact of each factor, the brand impact on each of the factors is evaluated, which is actually a percentage of influence that brand perceptions have on each of the factors influencing the purchase decision. Individual results are summed up to compose the overall brand impact.

The brand impact varies depending on the factors and the brand itself. The greater the impact of the brand, the more the purchase decision depends on the brand. At the market for final consumption and luxury goods, the products have an average brand impact of 60-90%, because most of the purchase factors are influenced by the brand perceptions. The products of Coca-Cola, Louis Vuitton and Nivea are being bought because of the strong influence that brand perceptions have. Although all these products deliver physical value, consumers' perceptions are the cause for a purchase decision. The products have a relatively high quality within their segment, but consumers' demand for these products is created through emotional perception of the brand. Thus, the impact of the brand is very high and dominates the purchase decision. The particular product, service or distribution support the creation and maintenance of brand perceptions. In some industries the range of brand influence is really wide, Figure 4. These include durable goods for final consumption, such as automobiles, electronics and electrical engineering. In these segments, the brand impact can vary between 45 and 70% (Lindemann, 2010).

For brands like: Apple, BMW, Audi, Porsche and Mercedes-Benz, despite the engagement of cutting edge technology, brand perceptions determine the purchase decision. Without the brand perceptions for Porsche, the car would still be well-designed, stylish, with sophisticated engineering, but customers will miss the prestige and status that this brand is presenting.

Most B2B brands have a brand impact between 25 and 50%. Companies in this segment also have high brand impact, because it is difficult to measure the performance that they deliver. These companies operate relying firmly on their reputation which illustrates the impact that brand perceptions have in choosing a suitable supplier. Brands with low brand impact can be found within consumer products and special segments where non-brand factors predominate. Examples can be found within chains of petrol stations where the price and location are key factors and the impact of the brand is below 25%. As previously mentioned, the brand impact varies greatly in different segments, product lines or geographic

Figure 4. Average brand impact in certain industries

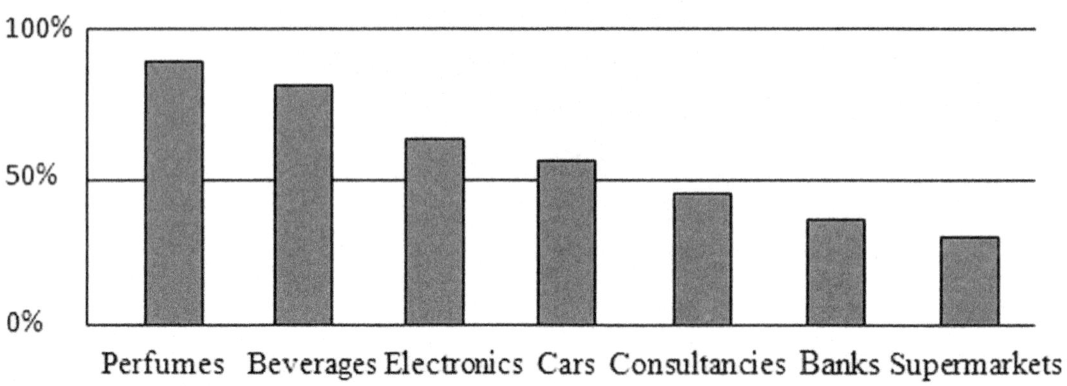

areas. Toyota and Honda have a higher brand impact in Asia and North America than in Europe, where they are bought predominantly due to functional use, with little or insignificant emotional benefits (Lindemann, 2010).

Because the brand impact measures the relative contribution that the brand has in the purchase decision and revenue generation, it is the most appropriate measure for determining the specific income from the brand. The brand profit is calculated as the product of the profits of intangible assets and the percentage of brand influence. The analysis of the brand impact is an important management tool for understanding and managing the creation of brand value. Company's marketing and investment strategies can be optimized through a detailed analysis of the factors influencing the purchase decision and how they affect brand perceptions.

Fourth Step: Discount Rate

Once you complete predicting the brand profits, you need to determine the appropriate discount rate for calculating the NPV of the profits from the brand, which actually represents the brand value. According to CAPM: Capital Asset Pricing Model, the discount rate represents the relationship between the risk and expected return. Potential investors should be compensated in two ways: time value of money and risk. Time value of money is represented by the risk-free rate that compensates the investment of money for a long period of time. The most suitable risk free rate corresponds to the interest rate of government bonds. The discount rate should also reflect the risk of the expected brand earnings, in terms of the risk-free rate. The high discount rate indicates high level of risk that profits from the brand would be realized according to the projections. The higher discount rate results in a lower NPV and vice versa. The discount rate should reflect the likelihood that the brand will deliver the expected income. In the valuation of companies, according to CAPM, the discount rate represents the average cost of capital (WACC). This calculation represents the weighted contribution of all sources of financing. The cost of equity is the risk-free rate plus the risk premium, adjusted according to the specific beta of the company. Most practitioners use a premium in the range of 3.5 to 7 percentage points (Cohen, 2005). The amount of the premium is then adjusted for the company's share volatility relative to the market as a whole, measured by beta. The cost of debt is the effective rate that the company pays on its debt. The problem in using WACC for brand valuation is that it is based on evaluation of all assets of the business. According to some experts is a wide category to be used for valuing brands and does not represent the specific risk of the asset (Salinas, 2009). Basically, this is true because different assets have different risk level. So, it is correct to use different discount rates. This is why many approaches for valuing brands utilize alternative risk assessment which is a hybrid between CAPM and specific models depending on the factors that affect the brand. However, the alternative models for measuring the brand strength and the assessment of risks are the most challenging component of the methodologies for brand valuation. While the CAPM theory and portfolio theory arose from the corporate practice decades ago, starting in the 1920s, the available information and researches on brands are rather weak and difficult to obtain. It is therefore difficult to replicate a comparable level of depth and quality of data. Another thorny issue related to the alternative approaches to risk assessment is the use and validity of a wide range of relevant data converted into one discount rate. However, when valuing corporate brands, the companies' WACC actually reflects the risk of the brand, because it is included in all assets and its application as a discount rate is suggested, in order to calculate the brand profit. Finally, we re-emphasize the need to carefully determine the discount rate because the NPV is very sensitive to it - small changes in discount rate cause significant changes in the amount of NPV.

Fifth Step: Brand Value Calculation

The brand is the sum of the discounted projected earnings from the brand. This value consists of two sets of discounted earnings from the brand. The first set is a detailed forecast, as previously discussed. It usually covers a period of five years, but it can be set in longer time frames. The second set is the value of the brand calculated as an infinite annuity, taking into account the time period after the detailed forecast. The profit in the last year of the detailed projection is the basis for calculating the value of the brand as an infinite annuity, while using a certain constant growth rate that should represent the potential for brand profit growth. This part of the calculation is very significant, because in many cases the value calculated as infinite annuity significantly exceeds the value from the detailed projection. So it is not rare to meet adjustments of the growth rate based on the calculated brand value as an infinite annuity. Finally, the brand value is the sum of the net present value of the detailed projection and the brand value calculated as infinite annuity. In case the use of the brand is limited in time, the brand value is calculated only with the first part of the calculation or a NPV of the brand profit for the entire period of brand exploitation.

ANALYZING THE VALUE CHAIN OF THE BRAND WITH RADICAL TRANSPARENCY

The creation of brand value derives from the brand influence on the customers purchase decision. The manifestation of value the brand creates is the economic value arising from current and future purchases of products / services. In order to maximize the creation of brand value, it is good to understand the cash flows generated by the brand or its impact on the purchase decision. This flow can be described through the brand value chain. There are several concepts that attempt to describe and explain the relationship between the brand, marketing activities and financial results. One of the academic approaches comes from Keller who identified the brand value chain, comprised of four elements: investment in marketing program, the mindset of the consumer, the performance of the brand and the value of shareholders (Keller and Lehmann, 2003). Then this basic concept experienced a transformation into a model that consists of five separate elements: the brand content, customer touch points, customer perception, customer behavior and financial results (Figure 5). The model of the brand value chain is based on the concept of brand value and is the result of numerous theoretical and practical experiences. The rational division of the process of creating brand value in different stages is not a claim for the linear relationship between the phases, but has a purpose to provide a useful logic for identifying, understanding, quantifying and managing the creation of economic brand value.

The brand consists of a set of values and associations through which it can be identified, encoded and managed. The content of the brand consists of all the key elements that create brand perceptions in the mind of consumers, including the name of the brand and its visual forms. This immediately evokes associations. For existing brands these associations are the result of the marketing activities of the company and the experience of consumers with the brand or the products / services that the company sells. Some of the associations for the brand are very different, while others are similar to those of competitors. The interaction of all business activities creates the brand perception. So, the brand is a result of the promise and delivery of an experience. This is why the brand is the most essential component and expression of the business strategy.

Brand Contents

The first element of the brand value chain refers to the brand content which is determined by the positioning statement. At the core of the brand is the DNA of the brand or the so-called *brand platform* consisting of the core brand values from which the key attributes and perceptions about the brand positioning derive. The key values result from the company's history, the company's views for the future of its markets and customers and the company's capabilities to provide diverse and relevant offer to consumers. In order to remain credible in the eyes of consumers and be able to successfully deliver on the promise of the brand, core brand values can be changed only gradually. In this way the damage of the brand value can be avoided. Brands such as: Coca-Cola, IBM and Mercedes are successful examples of continuity and consistency in the values of their brands. Some brand perceptions are a result of the operations and culture of the company that may not have been codified and formalized at the beginning of the business, but became the modus operandi of the company. Microsoft and Google are examples of corporate brands that have developed in this way. The brand content should be codified in such a way that it may be communicated and applied internally as well as externally. Common failures are either too

Figure 5. Brand value chain

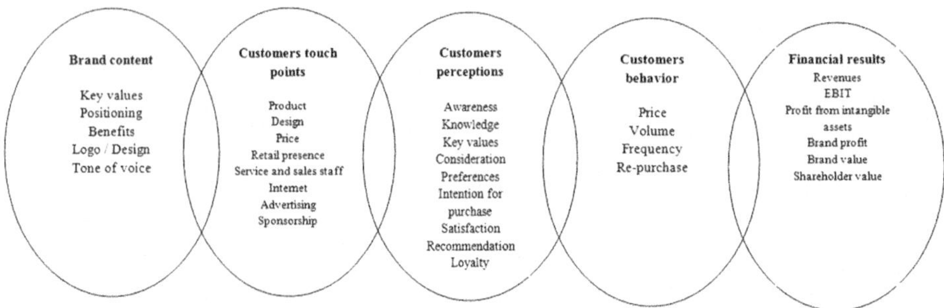

simplified and reduced brand essence or too much elaborated praise that lacks clear definition (Keller, 2007). Useful brand essence combines the various brand associations with the company's ability to deliver them against the consumers' expectations.

The values and their transfer should be adapted to the market conditions. However, the DNA of the product brands (especially for final consumption) is easier to be changed then the DNA of corporate brands, where the whole company has to follow the change through unified communications and behavior. This may change the focus of values and the way they are expressed in communication and behavior throughout the company. For example, the financial crisis in 2008-2009 confirmed that stability and confidence should be among the core values of the brands in the financial sector. Despite been part of the DNA of these companies, they were not highlighted because consumers believed that all banks are secure. But the crisis has significantly changed consumer perceptions, refocusing the attention of financial institutions to communicate confidence and reliability as key values of their brands.

Customer Touch Points

The customer touch points represent all key points of contact between companies and customers. Once you define the brand positioning, the same need to be communicated and delivered through all relevant customer touch points which are the second element of the brand value chain. Management actions should focus brand initiatives and brand investments to these customer touch points. All relevant business functions that have a direct visible effect on the consumers' experience should be united towards the purpose of brand positioning. These include: pricing strategies, advertising, presence on the internet, sponsorships, sales brochures, packaging, distribution, corporate identity, tone of voice, the architecture of the brand and the management of relations between the brand and all other issues related to employees and investors (Kapferer, 2008). If it is a multinational company, it requires coordination and control of activities in each country. In general, the leading global brands are successful because of their consistency in all communications and touch points. Apple, BMW and P&G stand out as brands that achieved to incorporate the above analysis.

The positioning of the brand should also serve as a guideline for the product development and design, as well as for research and development in order to ensure that products or services are reinforcing the core values of the brand. VW's Phaeton model is an example of a product that does not fit into the VW brand values such as simplicity and availability. Not surprisingly, this was the biggest mistake in the recent history of the company. Samsung has a strategic leadership team for research and development in order to ensure that efforts are focused on creating products and services united with the brand. On the other hand, research and development can offer products and services that create leading global brands such as: HP, Intel, Microsoft, Apple and Google.

The brands that have no direct contact with the end consumer should focus on the product, communications and services they offer, because this are the touch points that the company can manage and influence. (Ulrich and Smallwood, 2007). For many B2B and service brands employees are the key touch point with customers. Thus, the CEO of Samsung is rewarded according to how much additional brand value is created (Business Week, 2009). Delivering on the promise of the brand is not limited to the product design, communication and advertising; it also includes activities related to research and development, sales and customers services. Apple and BMW are the best examples of successful application of this integrated approach (Post and Post, 2007).

Customers' Perceptions

The next element in the brand value chain reflects the impact of management actions and the touch points performance on the perceptions of actual and potential customers. The combined touch points can create a vicious circle of: brand awareness, deeper knowledge, integration in the considerations set, purchase, re-purchase and recommendations (Lindemann, 2010). These activities are not linear, but simultaneously appear, making their coordination and consistency even more important. The results are the perceptions and associations consumers have about the brand. The key measure for assessing consumer perceptions are: the level of awareness, knowledge (details regarding the brand offer), differentiation, relevance (price level and offer), performance of core values and delivery, consideration, preferences, purchase intention, satisfaction, recommendation and repurchase intention (Keller, 2000). These so-called measures of brand equity measure and assess consumers' perceptions about the brand and their deliberate behavior when buying. They also assess how close the potential customers are to buying the brand products / services.

Consumer Behavior

Certainly, the brand perceptions are important, but they should convert to purchase, to be commercially relevant and effective. This leads to the next element of the brand value chain, which is consumer behavior. Communications and experience associated with the brand impact consumers' perceptions about the brand and what it offers. These perceptions cause consumer behavior. The higher the relevance and differentiation of the brand, the stronger its influence on consumers' purchase decisions, which then affects the price, volume and frequency of purchase. Consumer behavior materializes at the point of purchase (direct or indirect) through the sales price, volume and frequency, and repeated purchase (Aaker, 2004).

Financial Results

The consumer purchasing behavior produces business income from which the profit is extracted and, ultimately, the value of shareholders. The brand impact is a continuous process which causes the cash inflows. Communications and brand experience ensure that customers buy the brand products / services, again and again, creating a base of loyal customers. At best, the brand perceptions can create a mental monopoly with a broad base of customers that do not take into account any other brand. Then, a sustainable flow of earnings is created. Historical and future cash flows generated from the brand build the basis for an assessment of the share price of the company by analysts and investors. This way, the brand is fulfilling its most important role in creating sustainable value for the stakeholders.

Employees Value Chain

While the core of brand value creation is based on generating revenue from customers, the brand can also be affected by other stakeholders related to the business. Measures of the brand impact on employees are, in fact, the level of employees' qualifications, fluctuation rates, productivity, revenue and operating profit per employee (Business Week, 2009). In order to unite the employees with the brand, companies need to design such corporate values which are communicated and implemented throughout the company, including the recruitment and management. Brand values should be part of the audit of the employees' performance and affect the payment and promotion. However, the brand values need to be relevant. Credibility is fundamental in order to connect employees with the brand.

The Investors Value Chain

Another group that is affected by the brand is investors. But their reliance on the brand works very differently from other stakeholders. Investors recognize that strong brands attract consumers, and the recent generate revenue from which the shareholders value is extracted. This is especially true for companies that manufacture and sell products / services for final consumption, such as: Coca-Cola, P & G, Nestle, Unilever, Pepsi and others. For these businesses the brand is a key factor for financial success. However, when they need to assess the created value and make investment decisions, investors rely on the analysis of financial data. Historical financial indicators are available for all publicly traded companies and can be analyzed through complex statistical models in order to identify future trends. However, the golden rule is that past performance is not sufficient to predict the future.

The investment decision to buy shares from a company is based on the expectations for future value creation, which in turn consists of the appreciation of the share price and the dividend yield. This means that investors rely on the expectations of future cash flows when making the decision to invest. Strong brands support and warrant the detailed analysis of analysts and institutional investors. It is unlikely the shares of companies with strong brands to fail. It is because these companies provide better and more predictable financial results. There are several companies that use the financial value of its brand to demonstrate their superiority to the investors. Samsung, Intel, Philips and Coca-Cola began to cite the value of their brand in the annual financial statements and in communications with all stakeholders to show the strength and sustainability of the company's cash flows (Wreden, 2005). Messages intended for investors should inform on the potential of the brand to support the company's strategy and expected financial results.

The brand is the key asset for the success of the business. The brand has become one of the key indicators in reports for the success of companies. But this is also followed by the limited interest in publishing details about this intangible asset that prevents spilling of sensitive information to competitors. Investors should pay special attention to the value of brands. The published ratings have a direct impact on stock prices. Investors can rely on the belief that brands will provide new and, possibly, increased cash flows in the future. The brands are, still, the most important asset of the business.

CONCLUSION

The justification of all the theoretical knowledge in this book is verified through the evaluation of the brand. Gradually, we fully complete the concept: from idea to brand evaluation. The brand evaluation through radical transparency is elaborated through several variants: the brand equity as a measure of the value of the brand, financial approaches to brand evaluation, integration of finance and marketing through the "best practice" approach for brand evaluation and the brand value chain. Thus, we conclude the efforts to understand, apply and assess the brand equity as a source of competitive advantage through the prism of radical transparency.

Studies use the brand value results from "The Best Global Brand" publications to show the impact of the brand on the shareholders value. These studies compare the performance of companies with a strong corporate brand with the performance of the market portfolio consisted of all other shares of companies listed on stock exchanges in the United States. According to the findings, the portfolio which is based on brand value significantly exceeds the market portfolio, both according to the risk and yield.

There are many approaches and models for determining the value of the brand. However, all relevant approaches, in principle, can be systematized in three categories. The first category consists of models that are based on marketing research in order to measure different brand dimensions, and to evaluate the relationship consumers have with the brand. These models are categorized under the term "brand equity" models. All these models provide important insights on the value of the brand, but no economic assessment of the brand is achieved. The second category of models and approaches to valuing brands consists of purely financial approaches that are designed to provide financial value of the brand. This category brings together more methods, but they are mainly based on income, and comparative approaches. Besides financial value, they provide little information about the relationship between consumer perceptions and intentions and generating non-financial value. The third category combines financial and marketing approaches and models in order to fully understand and assess the value of the brand. These models result in a financial amount based on the perceptions of consumers and financial analysis. Only a few models systematically integrate financial and marketing analysis.

Pure marketing research and financial-focused methods fail to provide complete, satisfactory results for assessing the economic value of the brands, because the lack of understanding the marketing or the financial dimension. As a result, new approaches to brand valuation that integrate marketing and financial analysis into a complete model for evaluating the value of the brand are constructed. This method is often referred to as the method of economic use. This method values the brand as part of the company and focus on the added value provided by the brand. The approach appeared as a result of the need to go beyond the mechanical calculation of the financial value and to understand and manage the process of creating brand value. Several world renowned consulting firms have developed their own versions of the method of economic use, including: Interbrand, Brand Finance and Millward Brown.

Between the theory and practice of valuing brands a kind of consensus is "born" that is distilled in a tested and recommended framework for valuing brands. The analysis of the various approaches for valuing brands showed that the appropriate model should integrate marketing and financial analysis, without sacrificing any of them. The approach should keep up with the current theory of corporate finance. The basic model for brand valuation should result in NPV of the expected future earnings of the brand. The approach for brand valuation should focus on the assessment of the specific process of creating brand value. The best practice approach for brand valuation consists of five key steps:

- Market segmentation.
- Financial analysis.
- Brand impact.
- Discount rate.
- Brand value calculation.

Brand value lies in the brand influence on the customers' purchase decision. The manifestation is the economic value arising from current and future purchases of products / services. In order to maximize the generation of brand value, it is good to understand the cash flows generated by the brand or its impact on the purchase decision. This flow can be described through the brand value chain. There are several concepts that attempt to describe and explain the relationship between the brand, marketing activities and financial results. One of the best academic approaches comes from Keller who identified the brand value chain, comprised of four elements: investment in marketing program, the mindset of the consumer, the performance of the brand and the value of shareholders. Then this basic concept experienced a transformation into a model that consists of five separate elements: the brand content, customer touch points, customer perception, customer behavior and financial results. The brand value chain model is based on the concept of brand value and is the result of numerous theoretical and practical experiences. The rational division of the process of creating brand value in different stages is not a claim for the linear relationship between the phases; it has the purpose to provide a useful logic for identifying, understanding, quantifying and managing the creation of economic brand value.

The brand is the key asset for the success of the business. The brand has become one of the key indicators in reports for the success of companies. But this is also followed by a limited interest in publishing details about this intangible asset that prevents the spilling of sensitive information to competitors. Investors should pay special attention to the value of brands. The published ratings have a direct impact on stock prices. Investors can rely on the belief that brands will provide new and, possibly, increased cash flows in the future. The brands are, still, the most important asset of the business.

REFERENCES

Aaker, D. (1996). *Building Strong Brands*. Free Press.

Aaker, D. (2004). *Brand Portfolio Strategy: Creating Relevance, Differentiation, Energy, Leverage, and Clarity*. The Free Press.

Bharadwai, S. (2008). *The Mystery and Motivation of Valuing Brands in M&A*. Atlanta: Atlanta Knowledge.

Cohen, J. (2005). *Intangible Assets: Valuation and Economic Benefit*. John Wiley and Sons.

Fehle, F., Fournier, S., Madden, T., & Shrider, D. (2008). Brand Value and Asset Pricing. *Quarterly Journal of Finance and Accounting.*, *110*, 203–217.

Financial Times. (2009). Global Brands. *Financial Times Special Report*. NY: Author.

Financial Times. (2011). Global Brands. *Financial Times Special Report*. NY: Author.

Hollis, N. (2010). *The Global Brand: How to Create and Develop Lasting Brand Value in the World Market*. Macmillan.

Hubbard, D. (2010). *How to Measure Anything: Finding the Value of Intangibles in Business*. John Wiley & Sons Inc. doi:10.1002/9781118983836

Investment Dealer's Digest. (2003, February 18). *The Scramble to Brand: Not all Wall Street Banks are Equal – or Are They?* Author.

Jacoby, J. (2001). *Is it Rational to Assume Consumer Rationality? Some Consumer Psychological Perspectives of Rational Choice Theory*. Working paper.

Kapferer, J. N. (2008). *The New Strategic Brand Management: Creating and Sustaining Brand Equity Long Term* (4th ed.). Kogan Page.

Keller, K. (2007). *Strategic Brand Management.* Pearson Education.

Keller, K. (2009). *Marketing Management.* Prentice-Hall.

Keller, K., & Lehmann, D. (2003). How Brands Create Value? *Marketing Management, 116*, 23.

Lindemann, J. (2010). *The Economy of Brands.* Palgrave Macmillan. doi:10.1057/9780230275010

Markenbewertung – Die Tank AG. (2004). *Absatzwirtschaft.* Author.

Perrier, R. (2008). *Brand Valuation.* Premier Books.

Post, R., & Post, P. (2007). *Global Brand Integrity Management: How to Protect Your Product in Today's Competitive Environment.* McGraw-Hill.

Quelch, J., & Jocz, K. (2010). *Keeping a Keen Eye on Consumer Behavior.* HBS Publishing.

Reilly, R., & Schweihs, R. (2007). *Valuing intangible assets.* McGraw-Hill.

Salinas, G. (2009). *The International Brand Valuation Manual: A complete overview and analysis of brand valuation techniques, methodologies and applications.* John Wiley & Sons Inc.

The Neilsen Company. (2006). *The Winning Brands.* Author.

Tollington, T. (2002). *Brand Assets. The Wiley Finance Series.* John Wiley & Sons Inc.

Ulrich, D., & Smallwood, N. (2007). *Leadership Brand: Developing Customer-Focused Leaders to Drive Performance and Build Lasting Value.* HBS Press.

Wheeler, A. (2006). *Designing Brand Identity: A Complete Guide to Creating, Building, and Maintaining Strong Brands.* John Wiley and Sons.

Wreden, N. (2005). *Profit Brand: How to Increase the Profitability, Accountability and Sustainability of Brands.* Kogan Page Ltd.

Zednik, A., & Strebinger, A. (2008). Brand Management Models of Major Consulting Firms, Advertising Agencies and Market Research Companies: A Categorization and Positioning Analysis of Models Offered in Germany, Switzerland and Austria. *Brand Management, 5*, 144–160.

Chapter 7
The 3M Company:
How to Use Radical Transparency to Generate Value for the Company

ABSTRACT

This chapter has a purpose to acknowledge 3M's greatest opportunity to overcome sustainability and transparency challenges which lies within innovation and collaboration. As a science company, 3M partners with its customers and communities to make the world cleaner, safer and stronger. Starting with technology and working toward the improvement of every life on the planet allows the company to think holistically about addressing global challenges. With an eye toward the future, 3M launched their 2025 sustainability goals. These goals range from investing in sustainable materials and energy efficiency to water management and helping the customers reduce their greenhouse gas emissions through the use of 3M products. 3M has also set goals around building a diverse workforce and worker and patient safety in health care and industrial settings. 3M continues to invest in developing products that help its customers reach their environmental goals, as well as increasing its social sustainability efforts.

INTRODUCTION

As the global population marches toward 9 billion people, it is creating an even more urgent need to address sustainability challenges — from air pollution and water shortages to food safety and clean energy. The company's greatest opportunity to overcome these challenges lies with innovation and collaboration. As a science company, 3M partners with its customers and communities to make the world cleaner, safer and stronger. Starting with technology and working toward the improvement of every life on the planet allows the company to think holistically about addressing global challenges. The company's investments in sustainable technologies are guided by the customers' needs. These include glass bubbles that make cars lighter and more fuel efficient, films that make smartphones and buildings more energy efficient, and low global warming potential immersion fluid that cools data centers.

DOI: 10.4018/978-1-5225-2417-5.ch007

Beyond collaborating with customers, 2015 has been a year of many 3M partnerships toward building a better future:

- 3M joined other global companies to help municipalities implement recycling programs through the Closed Loop Fund. This landmark partnership will invest $100 million to protect the environment, generate revenue for cities and create thousands of jobs.
- 3M made an agreement to purchase electricity from a wind farm, helping us work toward our renewable energy goals for 2025.
- 3M announced a revised pulp and paper sourcing policy providing leading-edge protection for forests, critical habitats and forest communities worldwide.
- During 3M's Global Volunteer Day, 3Mers from 80 international locations renovated schools, built outdoor learning centers and engaged thousands of students on the power of science to improve lives. This supports our broader work to encourage young people to enter STEM-related fields.
- 3M Pollution Prevention Pays (3P) program celebrated its 40th anniversary, having prevented over 2.1 million tons of pollution and saving nearly $2 billion (USD) since 1975.

With an eye toward the future 3M launched their 2025 sustainability goals. These goals range from investing in sustainable materials and energy efficiency to water management and helping our customers reduce their greenhouse gas emissions through the use of our products. 3M has also set goals around building a diverse workforce and worker and patient safety in health care and industrial settings. 3M continues to invest in developing products that help our customers reach their environmental goals, as well as increasing its social sustainability efforts as demonstrated by its ongoing commitment to the UN Global Compact and its principles. Moving forward, the emphasis on applying 3M science to improve lives will continue to grow, as will the emphasis on collaboration — with customers, partners and communities.

3M is driven by its Vision: 3M Technology advancing every company, 3M Products enhancing every home and 3M Innovation improving every life. Sustainability is embedded in every aspect of that vision.

Our world is changing more rapidly than ever before and the global community faces evolving challenges of access to clean water; access to education and jobs; access to adequate healthcare; a changing climate; and a demand for raw materials that strains our world's resources. As a company rooted in scientific exploration, 3M is applying technological expertise to help solve some of these challenges that serve as barriers to the improvement of every life on the planet. The people in 3M believe the path to progress begins with a clear purpose and that the best ideas empower people to think, create and live with intent. A sense of purpose is at the heart of how they approach every idea, every product, every life and every community the company touches.

The following chapter invites you to learn more about the progress toward 3M's ambition, as well as its strategy and goals moving forward, outlined in this chapter. It is prepared in accordance with the 3M's Sustainability Report for 2016. And then, everyone can join the journey toward creating a better world. A sense of purpose is at the heart of how 3M approaches every idea, every product, every life and every community. The data provided in this chapter is part of the 3M Sustainability Report that covers 3M's owned manufacturing facilities and leased facilities worldwide, including joint ventures (if greater than 50 percent 3M ownership) and partially owned subsidiaries (if greater than 50 percent 3M ownership) where 3M has full operational control. Acquisitions are included in data sets once legally owned and fully integrated onto 3M systems. All data included in the chapter is global data unless otherwise specified. The data provided in this chapter through facts and figures is based on activities during 3M's fiscal year 2015. For some performance indicators, the previous year's data is provided to allow for annual comparisons.

3M - Improving Lives Since 1902:

- As a signatory member, 3Msupports the UN Global Compact's 10 principles in the areas of human rights, labor, environment and anti-corruption.
- 15%: 3Mers use actual work time to follow their own ideas and insights in pursuit of innovation.
- 89+ thousand: Global citizens living a passion for applying science to life.
- 1.5 billion dollars in cash and product donations invested in 3M communities since 1953.
- 16 times chosen by RobecoSAM to be included in the Dow Jones Sustainability Index.
- 300 + thousand hours volunteered by 3Mers in 2015 alone.
- 3M visionary Pollution Prevention Pays Program has prevented over 2.1 million tons of air, water and waste pollution over the last 40 years.
- You are rarely more than 10 feet away from 3M Science.
- 200 operations in over 70 countries and serving customers in nearly 200 countries.

THE SUSTAINABILITY STRATEGY

Building on its long-standing leadership in environmental stewardship and commitment to customer-inspired innovation, 3M focuses its sustainability strategy on overcoming the global challenges that serve as barriers to improving every life. As a company rooted in scientific exploration, 3M is applying its technological expertise to help solve some of the world's biggest challenges around:

- Raw Materials.
- Water.
- Energy and Climate.
- Health and Safety.
- Education and Development.

Importantly, overcoming global challenges requires recognizing their interdependence: the importance of water access and its impact on health; energy and dependence on raw materials, etc. It also requires a deep commitment across the organization and collaboration with partners, customers and communities. In 2013, 3M created a Sustainability Center of Excellence to integrate Sustainability across its businesses. 3M continues to invest significantly to drive sustainability throughout its operations, product development, marketing and more – working closely with suppliers and customers. 3M now embed sustainability into the strategic planning process for every region, every market, and every business. Internally, 3M is working to create a results-driven culture, as well as a purpose-driven culture. The company's leaders are driving a sustainability culture top-down while supporting and encouraging ideas and commitment from the bottom up. And with its customers and partners, 3M are continuing to demonstrate that it is a unique and indispensable strategic partner; one that can solve business problems using its core strengths and its sustainability expertise. 3M is moving from provider of products to partnering with customers to understand their sustainability goals and challenges and working together to overcome them.

3M Every Life Ambition

3M Every Life ambition is the platform by which the company tells its story and the "north star" toward which it focuses its overall intent. 3M works to imagine a world where every life is improved – where natural resources are reliably available, people have access to education and opportunity, and communities are safe, healthy, connected and thriving.3M aims to help make that world a reality. But an ambition that big won't be easy. So people at 3M pledge the following:

- We will push ourselves to create the science and technology to achieve these goals.
- We will encourage individual passion and curiosity – within the company, with our partners, and within our communities.
- We will acknowledge that we cannot succeed alone and commit to stimulating and supporting collaborations to improve every life on earth.

3M Approach to Goal-Setting

3M 2025 sustainability goals serve as a roadmap for their journey toward improving every life. 3M ambition is to realize a world where every life is improved – where natural resources are reliably available, people everywhere have access to education and opportunity, and communities are safe, healthy, connected and thriving. The power is in partnership. Connection and collaboration is how 3M have operated since 1902. Moving forward, they are increasingly focusing this collaboration on working with their customers and communities to achieve their sustainability goals.3M has been setting global environmental goals since 1990. As a strong part of the company history, these goals have helped dramatically reduce their own environmental footprint and established 3M as a leader in environmental stewardship.

People in 3M are proud to expand beyond their own operations by focusing more on supporting the sustainability goals and needs of the company's customers and our communities. While we recognize the importance of what 3M does in its own operations, and will continue to improve accordingly, we see that far greater impact can be realized with partnership to understand and overcome the challenges we face. In addition to environmental challenges, 3M recognizes the connectedness of social challenges we face in pursuing a better world. Its strategy, goals, and report are organized around these challenges and how the company is addressing them for the sustainability of the business, our planet, and our daily lives.

3M Awards 2015

For the 16th consecutive year, 3M was selected as a member of the Dow Jones Sustainability Index, a global stock index that recognizes and tracks the performance of leading sustainability-driven companies worldwide. As one of the most highly regarded rankings in terms of sustainability performance, this index is created by research analysts who perform an in-depth study of environmental, social and economic performance.

- **The World's Most Ethical (WME) Companies:** The Ethisphere® Institute ranked 3M as one of The World's Most Ethical (WME) Companies® in the Industrial Manufacturing category. This standing recognizes companies that go beyond making statements about doing business ethically and translate those words into action. WME honorees promote ethical business practices internally and exceed legal compliance minimums and shape future industry standards by introducing best practices. The Ethisphere® Institute is an independent center of research that promotes best practices in corporate ethics and enables organizations to enhance relationships with employees, business partners, investors.

- **Eco Vadis Supplier Sustainability Ratings:** Eco Vadis awarded 3Ma Gold Recognition Level for achievements in the top 1% of suppliers assessed in corporate social responsibility (CSR) in global Supply Chains.

Other Featured Awards:

- 3M was ranked 170 out of 500 in the 2015Newsweek Green Rankings;
- 3M ranked in the top 100 on Forbes' inaugural list of America's Best Employers;
- 3M ranked 32nd in Most Reputable Companies in the World;
- 3M ranked 12th in World's Most Respected Companies (Forbes);
- 3M Health Care received the Practice Green Health 2015 "Champion for Change" Award;
- 3M is now in the top 100 of Fortune 500 companies;
- 3M received the Association of Cable Communicators (ACC) Beacon Award for the excellent work done during the Discovery Education 3M Young Scientist Challenge;
- 3M was ranked #24 out of 100 in Workforce Magazine's 2015 list of best companies for human resources;
- 3M was ranked #30 on Corporate Responsibility Magazine's list of 100 Best Corporate Citizens in 2015;
- 3M made Fortune's annual list of the 50 most admired companies in the world;
- The Cause Marketing Forum awarded 3M and DoSomething the 2015 Silver Halo Award for Best Education Campaign;

GOALS AND PROGRESS

Delivering On 2015 Sustainability Goals

Setting goals to drive sustainability progress is nothing new at 3M. The company has been setting global environmental goals since 1990. As strong part of the company history, these goals have helped dramatically reduce the company's own environmental footprint and established 3M as a leader in environmental stewardship. 3M 2015 Sustainability Goals program continued its drive to reduce environmental impacts, but also expanded 3M targets to include social responsibility efforts and economic success factors.

The 2015 Sustainability Goals were:
Environmental Stewardship:

- Reduce volatile air emissions 15% by 2015 from 2010 base year, indexed to net sales;
- Reduce waste 10% by 2015 from 2010 base year, indexed to net sales;
- Improve energy efficiency 25% by 2015 from 2005 base year, indexed to net sales;
- Reduce greenhouse gas emissions 5% by 2011 from 2006 base year, indexed to net sales (this goal was set in 2007);

- Develop water conservation plans in 3M locations where water is categorized as scarce or in a stressed area.
- **Social Responsibility:** 3M successfully achieved environmental stewardship goals on VOC air emission reduction, water conservation planning, greenhouse gas emission reduction and energy efficiency. 3M has encountered multiple challenges in waste reduction, including currency translation issues, and are re-doubling their efforts in this area.
- 3M environmental stewardship goals are indexed to net sales, however internally 3M tracks progress indexed to pounds of production (product output). 3M pounds of production have increased at a faster rate than sales from 2010 to 2015 yielding more favorable results. People in 3M are proud of 3M performance against their Social Responsibility and Economic Success goals as well, and in their 2025 Sustainability Goals, they are significantly expanding their commitments in these important areas:
  - To develop community stakeholder engagement plans at 3M facilities;
  - To promote a road to Environmental, Health and Safety (EHS) Excellence at new 3M Sites.

Economic Success

- Review at least 80% of supplier spending in the following countries: China, India, Korea, Malaysia, Taiwan, Thailand, Brazil, Mexico, Russia, and Turkey to drive conformance with 3M EHS, Transportation & Labor/Human Relations Standards by 2015;
- Enhance the environmental sustainability attributes of new products.

2015 Goals and Results

Goals Achieved:

1. Energy reduction nearly 30% from 2005 ;
2. VOC reduction 31% since 2010 baseline;
3. Pollution prevention pays program celebrated its 40th anniversary in 2015, has prevented 2.1 million tons of pollutants and saved 2 billion USD;
4. Water use reduction 42% since 2005;
5. More than 300.000 volunteer hours from employees and retirees;
6. Supplier collaboration with 98% of production paper purchases on sustainable paper sourcing;
7. Between 2002 and 2015 3M voluntarily achieved a 69% absolute reduction in greenhouse gas emissions;

2025 Goals

Raw Materials:

- Invest to develop more sustainable materials and products to help our customers reach their environmental goals.
- Reduce manufacturing waste by an additional 10%, indexed to sales.
- Achieve "zero landfill" status at more than 30% of manufacturing sites.

Table 1. Social performance and employees

Metric	Metric Units	RY-2011	RY-2012	RY-2013	RY-2014	RY-2015	2014-2015 Annual Change, %	2011-2015 Change, %
Total Global Employees at Year-End(Headcount)	Total Number	84,200	86,600	89,600	90,700	90,400	-0.331	7.36
Total Number Part-Time Employees	Total Number	2,530	2,430	2,580	2,560	2,520	-1.56	-0.395
Total Number Full-Time Employees	Total Number	81,700	84,100	87,000	88,200	87,900	-0.340	7.59
Percentage of Female Employees to Total Employees	%	33.6	33.7	33.7	33.9	33.9	0.000	0.893
Percentage of Female Employees in Management Positions	%	24.0	24.6	25.3	26.1	26.9	3.07	12.1

Table 2. Financial performance

Metric	Metric Units	RY-2011	RY-2012	RY-2013	RY-2014	RY-2015	2014-2015 Annual Change, %	2011-2015 Change, %
Net Sales	Million $USD	29,600	29,900	30,900	31,800	30,300	-4.72	2.36
Operating Income	Million $USD	6,180	6,480	6,670	7,140	6,950	-2.66	12.5
Net Income Attributable to 3M	Million $USD	4,280	4,440	4,660	4,960	4,830	-2.62	12.9
Per Share-Basic	Actual ($USD)	6.05	6.40	6.83	7.63	7.72	1.18	27.6
Per Share-Diluted	Actual ($USD)	5.96	6.32	6.72	7.49	7.58	1.20	27.2
Total Debt to Total Capital (total capital = debt plus equity)	%	25.0	25.0	25.0	34.0	48.0	41.2	92.0
Capital Expenditures	Million $USD	1,380	1,480	1,670	1,490	1,460	-2.01	5.80
Research, Development and Related Expenses	Million $USD	1,570	1,630	1,720	1,770	1,760	-0.565	12.1
Employee Compensation and Benefits	Million $USD	8,060	8,350	8,730	8,840	8,790	-0.566	9.06
Payments to Providers of Capital	Million $USD	1,770	1,800	1,900	2,390	2,700	13.0	52.5
Provision for Income Taxes	Million $USD	1,670	1,840	1,840	2,030	1,980	-2.46	18.6
New Product Vitality Index (NPVI)as Percentage of Net Sales	%	31.7	33.1	33.0	32.8	32.1	-2.13	1.26

Table 3. Community engagement

Metric	Metric Units	RY-2011	RY-2012	RY-2013	RY-2014	RY-2015	2014-2015 Annual Change, %	2011-2015 Change, %
Total Global Giving	Million $USD	66.3	60.3	61.6	81.3	72.8	-10.5	9.76
Total Cash Donations	Million $USD	27.9	30.3	30.3	30.9	34.1	10.4	22.2
Total In-Kind Donations	Million $USD	32.4	31.3	51.0	62.9	38.7	-38.5	19.4

Values presented in this table represent the preliminary values presented to BV at the time of their assurance.

Table 4. Environmental performance

Environmental Management System - Metric	Metric Units	RY-2011	RY-2012	RY-2013	RY-2014	RY-2015		
Total Number of Significant Spills	Total Number	0	0	0	0	0		
		Significant spill, spills included in the organization's financial statement						
Number of Significant Fines	Total Number	1	0	2	1	0		
		Significant fine, fine or penalty over $10,000						
Total Monetary Value of Significant Fines	Million $USD	0.065	0	0.063	0.1131	0		
Total Number of Non-Monetary Sanctions	Total Number	1	0	2	1	0		
Environmental Liability Accrued at Year End	Million $USD	0	0	0	0	0		
Air Emissions – Metric	**Metric Units**	**RY-2011**	**RY-2012**	**RY-2013**	**RY-2014**	**RY-2015**	**2014-2015 Annual Change, %**	**2011-2015 Change, %**
Absolute Scope 1 Emissions (Direct)	Million Metric Tons CO2e	4.06	4.37	5.59	4.39	3.77	-14.1	
Absolute Scope 1 Emissions (Direct)	Metric Tons CO2e	4,060,000	4,370,000	5,590,000	4,390,000	3,770,000	-14.1	
Absolute Scope 2 Emissions (Indirect)	Million Metric Tons CO2e	2.03	2.25	2.36	2.24	1.86	-17.0	
Absolute Scope 2 Emissions (Indirect)	Metric Tons CO2e	2,030,000	2,250,000	2,360,000	2,240,000	1,860,000	-17.0	
*2012-2015 US EPA GHG-MRR/IPCC AR5 based inventory accounting is not directly comparable to 2002-2011 WRI/IPCC TAR, AR4 based GHG accounting.								
*2002 Inventory recalculated according to US EPA GHG-MRR/IPCC AR5 methodology (2.7% Increase in absolute emissions over original reported value).								
Total Scope 3 Emissions (Upstream)	Million Metric Tons CO2e	8.12	10.7	10.6	11.1	9.50		
Total Scope 3 Emissions (Upstream)	Metric Tons CO2e	8,120,000	10,700,000	10,600,000	11,100,000	9,500,000		

continued on next page

Table 4. Continued

Environmental Management System - Metric	Metric Units	RY-2011	RY-2012	RY-2013	RY-2014	RY-2015		
Note: Net GHG emissions based on the categories evaluated. Due to change in boundaries, Scope 3 Upstream emissions should not be compared on a year-on-year basis.								
Total Greenhouse Gas Emissions(indexed to net sales)	Million Metric Tons per Net Sales	206	221	258	208	186	-10.6	
Total Greenhouse Gas Emissions(Absolute-Kyoto and Non-Kyoto)	Million Metric Tons CO2e	6.09	6.62	7.95	6.63	5.63	-15.1	
Total Volatile Organic Compound Emissions (Absolute)	Metric Tons	6,050	5,980	5,430	5,550	4,770	-14.1	-21.2
Total Volatile Organic Compounds Emissions (indexed to net sales)	Metric Tons per Net Sales	0.204	0.200	0.176	0.174	0.157	-9.75	-23.0
2015 Goal Achieved: Volatile Organic Compound (VOC) Reduction 15% by 2015 from 2010 base (indexed to net sales); baseline year was 0.228 metric tons per net sales (MM $USD)								
Energy - Metric	**Metric Units**	**RY-2011**	**RY-2012**	**RY-2013**	**RY-2014**	**RY-2015**	**2014-2015 Annual Change, %**	**2011-2015 Change, %**
Total Energy Use (Absolute)	MMBTUs	26,600,000	27,700,000	28,700,000	29,100,000	28,100,000	-3.31	5.64
Total Energy Use (Absolute)	MWh	7,810,000	8,110,000	8,400,000	8,520,000	8,250,000	-3.31	5.64
Total Energy (indexed to net sales)	MMBTUs per Net Sales	902	931	930	912	929	1.86	2.99
2015 Goal Achieved: Energy Conservation 25% by 2015 from 2005 base (Indexed to net sales); 2005 baseline was 1320 MMBTU per net sales (MM $USD)								
Total Fuel Oil #1, #2, #6	MMBTUs	549,000	1,490,000	1,490,000	1,630,000	1,330,000	-18.4	142
Total Jet Fuel	MMBTUs	184,000	163,000	143,000	161,000	153,000	-4.97	-16.8
Total Propane	MMBTUs	133,000	132,000	138,000	192,000	201,000	4.69	51.1
Total Gasoline and Diesel	MMBTUs	202,000	226,000	190,000	209,000	269,000	28.7	33.2
Total Coal	MMBTUs	0	0	0	0	0		
Total Natural Gas	MMBTUs	15,100,000	14,800,000	15,500,000	15,900,000	14,400,000	-9.43	-4.64
Total Electricity Consumption	MMBTUs	9,600,000	9,980,000	10,300,000	11,100,000	10,600,000	-4.50	10.4
Total Steam Consumption	MMBTUs	833,000	840,000	902,000	1,010,000	1,130,000	11.9	35.7
Total Heating Consumption	MMBTUs	0	0	0	0	0		
Waste - Metric	**Metric Units**	**RY-2011**	**RY-2012**	**RY-2013**	**RY-2014**	**RY-2015**	**2014-2015 Annual Change, %**	**2011-2015 Change, %**
Total Waste Generated (Absolute)	Metric Tons	179,000	179,000	192,000	205,000	211,000	2.93	17.9

continued on next page

Table 4. Continued

Environmental Management System - Metric	Metric Units	RY-2011	RY-2012	RY-2013	RY-2014	RY-2015		
Total Waste (indexed to net sales)	Metric Tons per Net Sales	6.05	6.00	6.22	6.44	6.95	8.05	15.0
2015 Goal Not Achieved: Waste Reduction 10% by 2015 from 2010 base (Indexed to net sales); 2010 baseline was 6.61 metric tons per net sales (MM $USD)								
Total Hazardous Waste (Absolute)	Metric Tons	41,300	39,700	39,400	41,100	44,100	7.30	6.78
% Data Coverage Total Hazardous Waste(Absolute)	%	96.0%	96.0%	97.0%	98.0%	97.0%	-1.02	1.04
Total Nonhazardous Waste (Absolute)	Metric Tons	138,000	140,000	153,000	164,000	166,000	1.22	20.3
Total Waste Recycled and Reused(Absolute)	Metric Tons	212,000	213,000	229,000	235,000	231,000	-1.70	8.96
Onsite Recycle & Reuse	Metric Tons	47,900	51,100	66,000	69,500	65,400	-5.90	36.5
Historically Offsite Reuse and Onsite Recycle Reuse data included the production of Roofing Granules, but due to the nature of their business, Industrial Mineral Products recycle and reuse number are no longer in the total.								
Offsite Reuse	Metric Tons	34,900	33,800	32,000	31,900	31,800	-0.313	-8.88
Offsite Recycle	Metric Tons	129,000	128,000	131,000	134,000	134,000	0.000	3.88
Water - Metric	**Metric Units**	**RY-2011**	**RY-2012**	**RY-2013**	**RY-2014**	**RY-2015**	**2014-2015 Annual Change, %**	**2011-2015 Change, %**
Total Water Use (Absolute)	Million Cubic Meters	41.1	43.4	43.3	42.5	42.1	-0.888	2.43
Sites located in Water Stress/Scarce Areas; Water sources significantly affected by withdrawal of water with water conservation planning efforts	Total Numbers	18	24	22	27	25	-7.41	38.9
3M uses the WBCSD Global Water Tool to screen site locations for water stress/scarce levels and prioritizes conservation plan development based on internal criteria.								
Total Water Use (indexed to net sales)	Million Cubic Meters per Net Sales (MM $USD)	0.00140	0.00140	0.00140	0.00130	0.00139	6.92	-0.714
Health and Safety - Metric	**Metric Units**	**RY-2011**	**RY-2012**	**RY-2013**	**RY-2014**	**RY-2015**	**2014-2015 Annual Change, %**	**2011-2015 Change, %**
Global Lost Time Incident Rate	Per 100 3M Employees(200,000 work hours)	0.38	0.39	0.34	0.36	0.32	-11.1	-15.8

continued on next page

Table 4. Continued

Environmental Management System - Metric	Metric Units	RY-2011	RY-2012	RY-2013	RY-2014	RY-2015		
Global Recordable Incident Rate	Per 100 3M Employees(200,000 work hours)	1.46	1.42	1.41	1.45	1.22	-15.9	-16.4
Work Related Fatalities - 3M Employees	Total Number	0	1	1	0	0		
Work Related Fatalities - 3MContractors	Total Number	1	1	1	0	0		
Work Related Fatalities - Total Number	Total Number	1	2	2	0	0		
Supplier Responsibility – Metric	**Metric Units**	**RY-2011**	**RY-2012**	**RY-2013**	**RY-2014**	**RY-2015**	**2014-2015 Annual Change, %**	**2011-2015 Change, %**
Total Number of Supplier Reviews	Cumulative Number	1,890	2,510	3,210	3,880	4,570	17.8	142
Review 80% of Supplier Spend in Top 10								
High Risk Countries for Alignment with	%	74	78	80	81	86		
3M Supplier Policy and Standards								

Values listed in the table above have been rounded and therefore do not match the raw values exactly. All calculations on the tabulated data use the full precision of the number. Due to rounding, calculations performed using values from the above table may not match the result of the same calculation performed in the same table.

- Drive supply chain Sustainability through targeted raw material traceability and supplier performance assurance.

Water:

- Reduce global water use by an additional 10%, indexed to sales.
- Engage 100% of water-stressed/scarce communities where 3M manufactures on community-wide approaches to water management.

Energy & Climate:

- Improve energy efficiency indexed to net sales by 30%.
- Increase renewable energy to 25% of total electricity use.
- Ensure GHG emissions at least 50% below our 2002 baseline, while growing our business.
- Help our customers reduce their GHGs by 250 million tons of CO2 equivalent emissions through use of 3M products.

Education & Development:

- Invest cash and products for education, community and environmental programs.
- 100% participation in employee development programs to advance individual and organizational capabilities.
- Double the pipeline of diverse talent in management to build a diverse workforce.

Health & Safety:

- Provide training to 5 million people globally on worker and patient safety.

TAKING ACTION

Taking Action: 3M Materiality Strategy

3Mlooks at sustainability in terms of shared global needs and the future of its business. As the population grows, particularly in emerging economies, challenges like energy availability and security, raw material scarcity, human health and safety, education, and employment must be addressed to ensure people across the globe can lead healthy, fulfilling lives. Sustainability materiality assessments are vital components of a company's sustainability strategy and reporting. For more than 40 years, 3M has been a leader among global corporations in sustainability actions and measures, beginning with the creation of our ground-breaking Pollution Prevention Pays (3P) Program in 1975…and leading to a broad portfolio of sustainable products today. As a global corporation, 3M believes that it has a significant responsibility to society in general, and especially to the communities in which it operates. Fulfilling its responsibility is important both from an environmental stewardship perspective and as a key competitive strategy.

3M has created a robust, stakeholder-driven approach to sustainability materiality that serves as a foundation for its sustainability strategy and reporting. Through understanding the critical sustainability issues from both internal and external perspectives, 3M can deepen its social license to operate and develop corporate strategy, goals, targets, programs, initiatives and a stakeholder engagement strategy to advance sustainability globally.

The data provided in 3M Sustainability Report includes information on the most material issues identified that have the potential to impact 3M reputation and that are of high importance to internal and external stakeholders. 3M is a diversified company, so several other environmental-related topics and key performance indicators that have relevance and are important to various sectors of the company are also included in the chapter.

Starting in 2013, 3M began a comprehensive sustainability materiality assessment and stakeholder engagement project. 3M commissioned Globe Scan, an independent research consultancy, to assist in better understanding stakeholders' perspectives of key social and environmental issues. In addition, the study assisted in assessing 3M's corporate reputation and leadership opportunities in the area of sustainability. In 2014, the research with Globe Scan concluded, resulting with a key output: the evidence-based sustainabilitymateriality matrix, Figure 1. This matrix plots significant issues related to sustainability along three axes. From this matrix, 3M can understand the degree of importance of stakeholders accord to each issue, the ability of 3M to make a positive difference on these issues and the level of impact

Figure 1. 3M Sustainability Materiality Matrix: View of customers, external and internal stakeholders

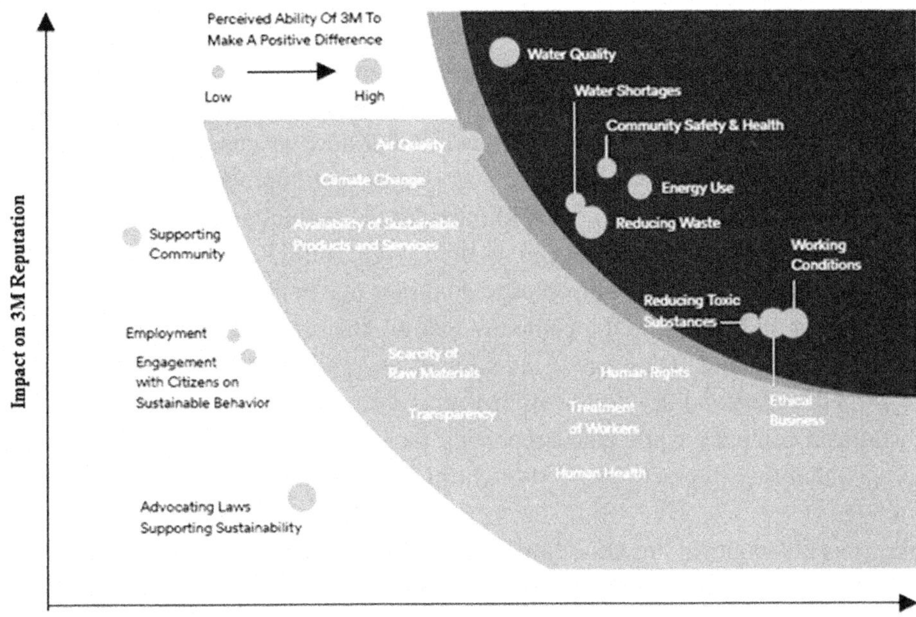

these issues may have on 3M reputation. The matrix is evidence-based, as each point on this matrix is determined from quantitative measures gained from an online survey as described below.

We identified and evaluated relevant aspects of 3M's sustainability performance as defined by internal and external stakeholders. Materiality with respect to sustainability reporting, as defined by the Global Reporting Initiative (GRI) guidelines, includes topics and indicators that reflect the organization's significant economic, environmental, and social impacts or would substantively influence the assessments and decisions of stakeholders. The material aspects defined in the Sustainability Materiality Matrix have been identified through the materiality assessment process. The sustainability materiality assessment determined the material aspects for a wide variety of 3M stakeholders outside of 3M. External 3M stakeholders were surveyed with a survey sample that was inclusive across geography, stakeholder type, and function.

Material aspects include**:** economic performance, raw material, energy, water, emissions, effluent and waste, environmental compliance employment, occupational health and safety training and education, freedom of association and collective bargaining, child labor, forced or compulsory labor local communities, anti-corruption, customer health and safety, product service and labeling, responsibility and compliance. In addition to the topics above, and based on insights gained through the materiality assessment process, 3M has continued to increase communication of its sustainability efforts.

Materiality: Today and the Future

3M has a long history of environmental stewardship with proven results that help the company be successful and also provide positive benefits to our many stakeholders. That is why the company made such an active effort to involve stakeholders when it developed the newest set of Sustainability Goals – goals that further advance 3M environmental stewardship efforts and go well beyond to provide profound societal benefits.

3M 2025 Sustainability Goals were developed from the sustainability materiality assessment and with input from governmental regulatory bodies, non-governmental organizations, shareholders, employees, customers, suppliers, academia and many others. 3M looks far beyond compliance and thinks holistically about how its operations and products affect the world and how we can truly use 3M technology and innovation to advance every company, enhance every home and improve every life. 3M 2025 Sustainability Goals reflect 3M's vision, brand and commitment to continuously improve. People in 3M want to let everyone know that the goals they set are both the right thing for the company and for the world.

Stakeholders increasingly expect companies to do things that benefit society in more direct ways and are not solely focused on benefits to the company.3Mtook this to heart and worked to establish wide-ranging goals that do just that. 3M goals focus around: energy and climate, raw materials, health and safety, water and education and development. 3M sets these goals while understanding that they have to be successful as a company while also supporting the communities where they operate. It's a two-pronged approach that is both practical and thoughtful; it's both analytical and filled with the integrity 3M is known for.

Sustainability is all about finding those intersections where goals move 3M forward toward growth and also supports the company's vision to advance, enhance and improve. At 3M, sustainability also includes collaborating to find better solutions for customers. As the world population grows, particularly in emerging economies, global challenges must be addressed together to ensure we can all live healthy, fulfilling lives. That is why 3M are committed to partnering with customers to identify and collaborate on solutions to address their goals.

Taking Action: Product Innovation

3M is accelerating innovation to deliver meaningful sustainability solutions. 3M has a long-standing reputation as a company committed to innovation and continues to dedicate a large percentage of revenue (5.8 percent) to research and development (R&D) around the world. In addition to having extensive resources at its headquarters in Minnesota, 3M has rapidly expanded R&D operations globally and now operates laboratories in 36 countries and 8,300 researchers worldwide. To drive further global growth of the company, a specific Invest in Innovation (I3) program was put in place in 2012 to focus on organic growth through prioritized investments in new-to-the-world platform development areas aimed at new markets for 3M. The increased R&D spending began in 2013 and is projected to stabilize at six percent to sales by 2017. The additional Invest in Innovation R&D funding is aimed at injecting additional fuel to take 3M's organic growth rate to new levels and launch new product platforms to advance3M's commitment to improving the business, the planet and every life.

By leveraging strategic partnerships with several stakeholders, both internally and externally, 3M is enabled to integrate a rich diversity of ideas and creativity into superior technologies, business assets and innovative product platforms. 3M's seven-phase New Product Introduction (NPI) process provides the robust framework for developing products from idea to launch. Many other tools and systems are in place to expand, promote, manage and accelerate the innovation process. These include but are not limited to technical committees, collaborative ideation, tracking systems, and customer interaction and insights processes and forums.

- **3M Tech Forum: Innovation Through Collaboration:** Established in 1951, the 3M Technical Forum is the central organization within 3M for productive technical interaction at the interpersonal grass-roots level. Through the collective knowledge and global relationships of over 11,000 technical employee members and over 40+ technical chapters and committees, this interconnected global network continues to build 3M technology platform knowledge and share ideas and expertise to spark solutions for the customers.
- **Technology Platforms: 3M's Innovation Engine:** A broad base of 46 innovative technology platforms — ranging from adhesives, abrasives and ceramics to fiber optics, imaging, light management, molding, nonwoven materials, polymer melt processing and many more — come together in new and groundbreaking ways for customized solutions. 3M technologies are transformed into consumer brands known and respected around the world, including Scotch®, Post-it™, Scotch-Brite™, Filtrete™, and Command™ etc.

Driving Growth Through Sustainable Product

To further advance 3M's vision and to make a positive difference for an expected growing population of over 9 billion lives by 2050, 3M is focused on purposeful and responsible solutions to contribute to a healthier world while creating new business opportunities. 3M people are committed and inspired to use their core technology platforms, their large-scale manufacturing infrastructure and expertise and their local presence in every geography to enable new and improved solutions. 3M teams are focused on collaborating with customers and developing product experiences that integrate full life-cycle thinking, have net-positive impacts and create more sustainable business practices.

Sustainability, along with understanding, evaluating and minimizing the environmental, health, safety and regulatory (EHS&R) impacts are at the core of 3M's product innovation process. Responsibility for product stewardship at 3M is shared across a matrix of functions positioned within businesses, regions, and corporate staff groups. Together, individuals across this matrix work to support 3M's core value of respect for the social and physical environment.

Product Responsibility Liaisons (PRLs) or Product Stewards, embedded within 3M businesses and countries of operation, act as champions of EHS&R and sustainability. They help assure that 3M products meet or exceed EHS&R requirements stemming from3M policies, governmental regulations and from customers. It is from this place that 3M infuse sustainability into product innovation from concept to launch. They act as the conduit between the Business Teams and the Corporate Staff Groups (Environmental, Toxicology, Industrial Hygiene, and Safety) assuring that appropriate risk assessments are made and improvements are incorporated into product development. PRLs work with the business teams to minimize the EHS&R impacts of 3M products not only as manufactured products, but throughout the life cycle of the product. Their assessment includes the impacts through raw material selection, manufacturing, customer use, and final disposal.

Life Cycle Management and Analysis

3M has multiple programs in place to evaluate life cycle impacts of products. 3M's Life Cycle Management (LCM) process is in place to ensure that the environmental, health and safety opportunities and risks are addressed globally for all 3M products and internal material transfers throughout their life cycle, Figure 2. Regardless of their source, all 3M products – whether 3M-developed, developed jointly

Figure 2. Life cycle management

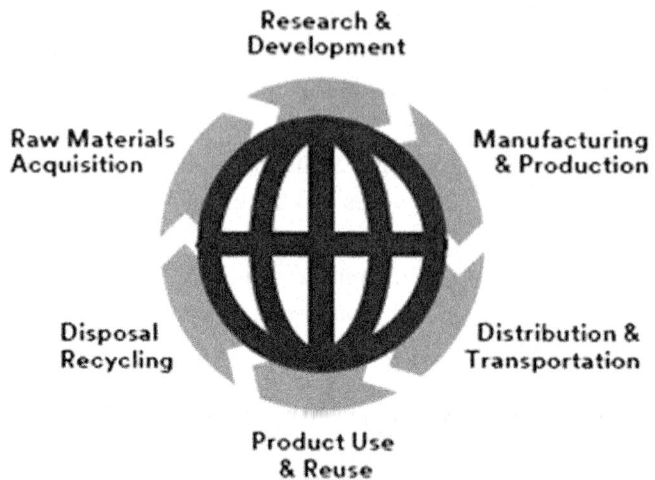

with another company, or acquired from a third party – are subject to review. Any product purchased from an outside supplier for sale as a 3M product receives the same product life cycle consideration as an internally developed and manufactured product. LCM evaluations are a required component of a 3M business unit's new product introduction process.

3M's Life Cycle Management Policy states that LCM evaluations are to be conducted on all new products before commercialization, and on a prioritized basis for existing products. The LCM evaluation helps identify opportunities associated with environmental, health and safety performance and to characterize and manage EHS risks and regulatory compliance throughout a product's life cycle and supply chain. The Electronic Lifecycle Management System (ELMS) is an internal 3M proprietary global database system that standardizes the LCM process and stores product and process EHS&R information and assessments for all stages of a product's lifecycle. In 2015 two new modules (LCM and Hardgoods) were added to seven existing modules in 3M Global Product EHS Self-Assessment Program. Under this Program, each country subsidiary documents and rates their level of expertise in product EHS&R processes against 3M expectations. Based on a Health of the Organization evaluation, a schedule has been developed and implemented to conduct audits against the Product EHS modules.

In addition to the LCM program which applies to all 3M products, 3M also conduct ISO 14040-compliant life cycle assessment (LCA) studies for a number of 3M products. 3M's global strategy for detailed quantitative LCA is first and foremost based on using sound science. In 2014, 3M issued an internal global LCA Standard that defines and outlines how a product life cycle assessment must be conducted if it is to be used for external communication of the LCA data. This includes use in marketing claims, environmental product declarations and regulatory reporting. The Standard requires that all product LCA data (including product carbon footprint assessments) used for external communication be based on sound statistical and scientific principles, follow an international LCA standard and include a quantitative data uncertainty determination. The Standard provides guidance on acceptable international LCA standards and mandates independent internal and third party review prior to external communication of the LCA data.

3Mprimarily completes a cradle-to-gate LCAs as the majority of its products have use and disposal life cycle phases that are difficult to characterize. In addition to product LCAs, 3M has completed cradle-to-gate LCAs representing a number of internal chemicals produced and then transferred to other divisions for further processing. This includes several adhesives that are key components of numerous final products. While it is not possible to complete full LCAs for all 3M products, evaluation of these intermediates allows the company to have a better understanding of the potential environmental impacts of key components and processes.

In 2015, the 3M LCA teams in the US and Europe again received process certifications from The International EPD® System to demonstrate that appropriate procedures are in place to produce scientifically-sound technically-defensible LCAs and Environmental Product Declarations (EPDs). Rather than conduct independent third-party reviews for each individual product LCA or EPD, the teams will continue to undergo an annual recertification process. The underlying management system, along with a selection of LCAs and EPDs generated since the previous accreditation, will undergo an annual third-party audit to demonstrate continued conformance with the program rules and ISO standards. Project-specific independent third-party reviews are also conducted for selected studies. The global certification of the LCA process for multiple parts of 3M organization is thought to be the first of its kind. This certified management system will streamline the LCA/EPD process and reduce the time and cost associated with third-party review of individual LCA studies. This will enable 3M to complete LCAs for a larger portion of its diverse product portfolio.

Deepening Sustainability in Solution Development

3M began a project in 2013 which was piloted in 2015– to build capabilities that further enhance the extent to which new products improve lives in socio-environmental terms. This project will help to educate cross-functional teams on how to think about improving the sustainability attributes and applications of products from before a new idea even gets drawn out on paper all the way through the finalization of the manufacturing scale-up and product launch. Through this new process, the development teams will evaluate their new product and identify opportunities for improvement to create innovative sustainability-focused solutions that impact all phases of a products life cycle from material selection to manufacturing to customer use and end of life. This will build on 3M long-standing Life Cycle Management process and tools for assessment to further integrate sustainability into 3M product development culture and processes, getting to the core of who 3M is.

The company knows that 3M employees care about sustainable product development. A global employee survey conducted in 2013 indicated sustainable product development is the top sustainability-related priority for employees across the company. With over 55,000 products based on various combinations of 3M 46 core technologies, 3M is invigorating its product developers to find new and unique ways to apply technologies and creative product design with customer and consumer insights to help make a positive difference in some of the world's most difficult sustainability challenges. Deepening social and environmental thinking further into solution development will enable 3M customers to advance and help improve lives around the world.

Product Marketing and Communications

3M is committed to compliance with all applicable laws and regulations in the conduct of its business activities, including the environmental, health, safety, and regulatory requirements for hazard communication. Communicating the potential hazards of 3M materials supports 3M core values and is an integral part of keeping stakeholders informed about 3M materials. The means of communicating the potential hazards of 3M materials includes safety data sheets, product labels, product literature, transportation classification documentation, and any other internal and external communication about the potential hazards of a 3M material. Per 3M Policy, each business unit must evaluate the potential hazards of 3M materials and transmit, in the local country language(s), information concerning the potential hazards to employees, contractors, and customers as appropriate to meet all applicable regulatory requirements and 3M standards and guidelines, and to promote informed decisions about the materials' proper and safe handling, use, and disposal. 3M Safety Data Sheets disclose all chemical components of the product down to 1% of mass based concentration, or lower if tied to more stringent hazard-based requirements.

It is3M policy (product representation) to represent 3M products truthfully, fairly and accurately in all sales, advertising, packaging and promotional efforts. Management of every 3M business unit is responsible for ensuring appropriate review of advertising and claims regarding respective business products and services. All environmental product claims must be substantiated and technically accurate to the end user as specified by the 3M's advertising and product representation policy. 3M's *Environmental marketing claims support team* assists businesses in the substantiation of product claims and is comprised of laboratory scientists, legal staff, life cycle management professionals and others with environ-mental marketing and business expertise.

Extensive environmental marketing claim information is provided in 3M's Environmental Claims Guide located on the internal 3M Intranet site. Specifically, the following information is provided for each of more than 50 potential environmental marketing claims (e.g. biodegradable, compostable) that have been identified as relevant to 3M: possible claim terminology, definitions, practical guidance, substantiation necessary, applicable standards, additional external resources and contact information (for questions internally).

3M uses the Corporate Life Cycle Assessment Standard as an additional tool to standardize reports and communicate LCA results to the user/consumer. These communications may be through Environmental Product Declarations (EPD) or other environmental marketing claims. Due to the complexity and broad range of products the company offers, EPDs are not generated for all 3M products. Currently, regional and business strategic decisions are made based on core product volume and market and/or customer demand as to which products will require a Life Cycle Assessment for claims substantiation or to support development of an EPD.

3M 2025 goals are helping to address customer demands regarding sustainability. They are focused on addressing significant global sustainability challenges involving raw materials, water, energy and climate, health and safety, as well as education and development. The goals reflect 3M's expanding sustainability strategy by placing a greater focus on supporting the environmental goals of 3M customers and the communities in which 3M operates.

Sustainable by Design

Design is not only about the products 3M manufactures, but also the way the company expresses who they are as a company; that is where brand design comes in. For over a century, 3M has leveraged multiple creative disciplines of design, including product, packaging, UX, and graphic design, to enhance and deliver innovative solutions to the world. 3M understanding and approach to design has had an impact all across the globe. As 3M evolves, the company wants to bring to life its strengthened, strategic design ethos through core elements of 3M visual identity system such as color, typography, imagery, texture and integration across the global organization. 3M's foundation of science expertise and problem-solving capability can be awe-inspiring, but the power of such impact also relies on 3M ability to creatively communicate its brand identity and connect with its customers to build meaningful relevance.

3M new visual design system brings the 3M brand identity to life first through the foundational strength of the power of three. 3M is a diverse, multi-faceted organization that thrives on a culture both creative and collaborative. Core to its visual system is the integration of triangular shapes, conveying multiple dimensions with a look that is sophisticated and precise in every detail. To mobilize consistency of look and feel around the globe, the new visual identity is designed to be a set of smart tools—not a rigid template system—from a vibrant color palette that represents 3M variety and versatility to dynamic, human-focused photography that reflects the impact of 3M design and innovation on life moments. The company calls this 3M Science. Applied to Life™.

Efficient Packaging for your Favorite Dressing: 3M™ Tegaderm. 3M has made a long-standing commitment to efficient paper and packaging use. The company has reduced designed packaging weight for seven straight years, for a cumulative reduction of ~9,000 metric tons (mT). One example of a recent success story is the redesign of the pouch used for 3M™Tegaderm™ Transparent Film Dressing.

After being challenged to reduce waste on the packaging for this product, 3M came up with an innovative patented process allowing for nesting of the pouch used for each sterile dressing and reducing by 30%the amount of materials needed. The new design is user-friendly, and it even won an award from the 3M pollution prevention pays program. It reduced waste for us at the plant and for our customers in hospitals across the world. The seal adhesive for the pouch is made without natural rubber latex, and the carton used for the box packaging is made from 100% recycled content with at least 35% post-consumer recycled content. At 3M people strive to continually improve what they do. They are proud to put their innovation to use not only on smart product designs but also on solutions for a greener planet.

Taking Action: Responsible Sourcing

3M's approach to sustainability starts with its corporate values, and the same is true for its supplier sustainability programs. To continuously drive supply chain sustainability, 3M strives to partner with its suppliers to understand its collective supply chains, through research, review and engagement in a transparent way. Only then, together, 3m can transform its supply chains to be more sustainable and successful, and assure that its suppliers are continuously working in alignment with its corporate values, just as we do every day in our own operations.

2015 was a pivotal year for 3M supplier sustainability programs. 3M successfully met its 2015 Sustainability Goal (set in 2010) to assess 80% of suppliers in 10 higher risk countries. Then 3M set a new goal for 2025: Drive supply chain sustainability through targeted raw material traceability and supplier performance assurance. As part of this transition, 3M took steps to evaluate the supplier sustainability expectations, and how to communicate and evaluate those expectations throughout its businesses and around the world. Further, since 3M became a signatory to the United Nations Global Compact (UNGC) in 2014, 3M continues to consider ways to extend 3M's sustainability expectations to its "sphere of influence," such as its suppliers.

Also in 2015, 3M conducted extensive benchmarking of peer and leading companies on their supplier expectations, and it commissioned a project by a graduate student in sustainable engineering to help the company evaluate best and next practices in supply chain sustainability. This work culminated in the development of 3M second generation supplier expectations, the 3M Supplier Responsibility Code. This new Code expands on the environmental, health, safety, labor and transportation expectations that 3M had in place for 10 years in its 3M Supply Chain Policies, re-states and provides more detail on the expectations in the area of human rights, and includes additional requirements, such as expectations for business ethics and management systems. Fundamentally, the Code is based on 3Mcorporate values for sustainable and responsible operations, and is also aligned with the UNGC's 10 Principles, which are clearly represented in this new supplier code. The Code also aligns with the Electronics Industry Citizenship Coalition (EICC) Code of Conduct.

3M published its Supplier Responsibility Code in April 2016, and will be communicating these expectations to its supplier community. They are updating their supplier assessment and auditing process to match the revised expectations, and globalizing the supplier engagement process to identify and address varying risks by geography and business type.

Fundamental to 3M supplier expectations is the understanding that a business, in all of its activities, must operate in full compliance with the laws, rules and regulations of the locations in which it operates. Suppliers must maintain compliance systems and be able to demonstrate a satisfactory record of compliance with laws and regulations in the conduct of their business. 3M also encourages suppliers to go beyond legal compliance, drawing upon internationally recognized standards, in order to advance social and environmental responsibility and business ethics.

All 3M suppliers are expected to comply with applicable laws, and those expectations are embedded in 3M contract and purchase order terms. In addition, the supply chain expectations establish a framework that 3M considers important for:

- Maintenance of fair and reasonable labor and human resource practices, including the prohibition of child labor, slavery and human trafficking;
- Safe and healthy workplaces;
- Management of manufacturing and distribution operations to minimize adverse environmental impact;
- Compliance with material content and origin laws;
- Business ethics and anti-corruption.

Due Diligence for Supply Chain Compliance and Risk Mitigation

Supply chain due diligence is an important part of 3M's sustainability initiatives. 3M efforts center on the commodities that can have particular human rights and environmental risks associated with them, namely our use of certain minerals that have the potential to be sourced from conflict areas, and our use of timber-based products and other plant materials.

In August 2012, the U.S. Securities and Exchange Commission (SEC) adopted a rule mandated by the Dodd-Frank Wall Street Reform and Consumer Protection Act to require companies, beginning in 2014, to publicly disclose their use of conflict minerals (tin, tantalum, tungsten and gold, commonly referred to as 3TG) and whether those 3TG may originate in the Democratic Republic of Congo or a neighboring country.

Over the past several years, regulations addressing the harvesting of timber and other plant materials have been established in a variety of countries. Among these are the Lacey Act in the U.S., the European Union Timber Regulation and the Australian Illegal Logging Prohibition Act. Although the specific compliance requirements vary, in general, companies like 3M that use paper or other plant-based materials in products or manufacturing must demonstrate "due care" that these materials were obtained in a legal manner.

In order to comply with supply chain requirements like those described above, and to mitigate supply chain risks and drive sustainability and corporate responsibility within the supply chains, 3M engages in many initiatives. 3M has established a due diligence management system approach for both conflict minerals and legal harvesting compliance, consisting of these elements:

- Establish strong management systems;
- Identify and assess risks in the supply chain;
- Design and implement a strategy to respond to identified risks;
- Audit supply chain due diligence;
- Report on supply chain due diligence activities;
- Develop policies to address the challenges represented by these requirements;
- For existing relevant suppliers, 3M has implemented a prioritized supplier inquiry and verification process;
- Requirements are embedded in 3M Conflict Minerals Policy and other Policies, the Supplier Responsibility Code and expectations for new and existing suppliers;
- 3M established a compliance language in supplier contracts, purchase orders and material specifications as appropriate;
- 3M trains employees who have responsibility for sourcing suppliers and managing supplier relationships on supply chain sustainability, including slavery and human trafficking concerns.

3M sends the CFSI Conflict Minerals Reporting Template (CMRT) to prioritized suppliers to gather information on the smelters and refiners in the supply chains for the 3TG necessary to the production or functionality of our products. 3M supplier requests include links to 3M's conflict minerals website, which includes the Conflict Minerals Policy and 3M training on how to respond to the CMRT. This website also directs suppliers to training resources available through the CFSI.

Figure 3. Supply chain sustainability

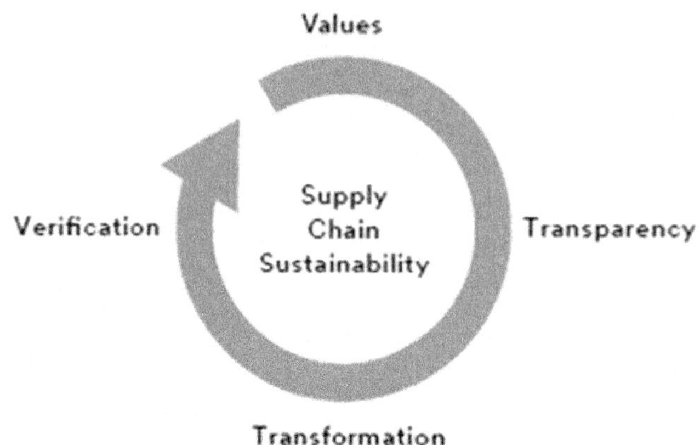

Responsible Sourcing of Minerals

3M deplores the violence that has occurred in the Democratic Republic of Congo and adjoining countries and is committed to supporting responsible sourcing of 3TG from the region. Accordingly, 3M has adopted a Conflict Minerals Policy, as part of 3M's Supply Chain Policies. 3M expects its suppliers to adopt a similar policy and due diligence management system and require the same of their suppliers.

3M is a member of the Conflict-Free Sourcing Initiative (CFSI), an organization established by the Electronic Industry Citizenship Coalition and Global e-Sustainability Initiative (EICC-GeSI), which develops tools and guidance for companies on conflict minerals.3M encourages its suppliers and other companies to participate in CFSI, to advance the conflict-free sourcing of 3TG globally.

CFSI also develops standards for third party audits of smelters and refiners to validate their processes that assure processed 3TG originated from sources that do not fund conflict in the Democratic Republic of Congo or adjoining countries. 3M was an early contributor to the CFSI Initial Audit Fund. The fund supports responsible sourcing of 3TG by providing financial assistance to smelters for first-year independent audits under the Conflict Free Smelter (CFS) Assessment Program, in order to validate conflict-free status according to CFS auditing protocols.

Responsible Sourcing of Forest Products

As part of 3M overall sustainability efforts, the company has had a long-standing commitment to responsible forest management. Recognizing evolving laws and administration efforts, 3M intent is to go above and beyond the "due care" management system necessary to demonstrate compliance with applicable global legal harvesting laws, such as the U.S. Lacey Act and the European Union Timber Regulation. Furthermore, 3M wants to source paper products from suppliers who share 3M values and are committed to protecting the world's forests.

As a diverse global company and sustainability leader, 3M is well-positioned to positively influence practices throughout the paper supply chain. Because 3M does not own forest land (it is a downstream user of paper and pulp), the company developed its Pulp and Paper Sourcing Policy to set standards of excellence for its suppliers and their suppliers through all tiers of supply to the forest.

The 3M Pulp and Paper Sourcing Policy, adopted in the spring of 2015, is designed to assure that the virgin wood fiber used in 3M paper-based products and packaging comes from sources that protect forests and respect the rights of workers and people who live in or may depend on forests for their livelihood. Under the Policy, if pulp and paper used by 3M are made from virgin fiber, they must be traceable to the forest source and must be harvested legally. 3M expects that its suppliers will work to assure and verify that these virgin fibers are also harvested in a manner that is protective of high carbon stock forests, high conservation values, and workers' and indigenous peoples' rights.

3M is committed to working together with its suppliers to help them understand and apply the necessary measures to assure responsible paper sourcing and sustainable forest management. Every six months, 3M reports on its policy implementation progress on 3M's sustainable forestry webpage.

3M is partnering with The Forest Trust (TFT), a non-profit organization with a strong track record in guiding companies on the development and implementation of responsible pulp and paper sourcing and improved forest management across global supply chains. Together, they are engaging with the suppliers, to train them on the forestry issues addressed in the Policy, and support them as they trace 3M materials back through mills to the forest sources and apply their own responsible fiber sourcing programs. Through this collaboration under the framework of 3M Policy, the company is harnessing the power of the supply chain to promote responsible sourcing and sustainability in forest management around the world.

On 3M.com/suppliers, the company has posted training presentations on its Policy and on global legal harvesting laws, a Policy Guidance that provides more detail on key terms in the policy, as well as a template Due Diligence Management System document that its suppliers (or anyone) can use as a foundation for a responsible sourcing program. Overall, 3M goal is to improve the sustainability of the global pulp and paper supply chain by engaging with its current and potential new suppliers to promote performance improvements and their understanding and ownership of sustainable forestry practices around the world.

3M is proud to be an associate member of the World Business Council on Sustainable Development(WBCSD) Forest Solutions Group (FSG), a global platform for strategic collaboration among value chain partners to bring more of the world's forests under sustainable management and expand markets for responsible forest products. As a condition of membership, companies involved in the FSG endorse a set of principles and responsibilities to demonstrate their shared commitment and leadership role in sustainability. 3M actively participates in FSG initiatives, including this year's update of the membership principles and a position statement on deforestation.

In October, 3M hosted a first-ever workshop put on by the World Resources Institute (WRI) and the WBCSD FSG, to promote the Sustainable Procurement Products. This Guide is designed to help companies make informed choices on forest-based products and lays out 10 key challenges that underpin sustainable sourcing and provides solutions to tackle them. WBCSD member companies participated in this workshop, along with 3M supplier representatives based primarily in the US and Europe. WRI and WBCSD representatives led the more than 30 participants through exercises and case studies highlighting the content of the Guide. 3M representatives also discussed the Pulp and Paper Sourcing Policy and implementation activities.

Since 3M issued a new Policy in March 2015 (and even before), it has been working to engage and understand the many tiers of the global forest products supply chain. For each supplier and supplied material, 3M is gathering detailed information to evaluate legality, traceability, third-party certification status, and overall policy conformance. Although complex and time-consuming, this supplier inquiry process provides 3M important information about its supply chain, and helps to identify opportunities for collaboration and improvements in order to advance sustainable forestry.

3M has conducted numerous training and capacity building sessions on responsible paper sourcing and sustainable forestry with 3M personnel and with suppliers. These trainings have been focused on North America, where the majority of paper-based spend is centered, and the Asia-Pacific (APAC) region, which includes high-risk areas for deforestation and other unsustainable forestry practices. All training is conducted in the local language, and in most cases local TFT personnel have participated in or led the sessions, to provide expert perspectives specific to the region. Supplier policy training sessions have been conducted in the US (for US and European suppliers) China (Shanghai), Taiwan and Japan, with more than 80 participants from more than 40 supplier companies. Outside of these more formal training sessions,3Mhas had dozens of one-on-one discussions with suppliers on its policy expectations, particularly in the area of traceability, to come to common understanding of the policy expectations on providing information on mills and forest sources.

3M and TFT conducted three field assessments in China and one in Taiwan. These supplier assessments at the paper mill or converter level aim to verify that there are adequate systems in place for transparency and traceability that allow 3M to know the sources of the fiber and assess them against the policy. The social and environmental performance of the supplier facilities was also evaluated. 3M plans to continue to expand its field assessment work in a prioritized manner, as necessary to ensure its supply chain conforms to its policy requirements.

3M has traced over 50 percent of its annual spend in each commodity category to at least the paper or pulp mill level, and it continues to work with suppliers to gather forest source information. Given the large number of individual forest sources contributing to the global paper supply chain, this remains the most challenging information to obtain, but also the most important to verify that 3M's suppliers are meeting the policy's environmental and social expectations. The key to success on this endeavor is the continuing education of 3M suppliers on the importance of knowing their ultimate forest sources and its policy expectations, in order to mitigate supply chain risks and drive sustainable forestry.

California Transparency in Supply Chains Disclosure. 3M's Supply Chain Policies and the next generation 3M Supplier Responsibility Code apply to the selection and retention of all 3M suppliers and establish a framework for the maintenance of fair and reasonable labor and human resource practices, including the prohibition of slavery and human trafficking. 3M's efforts to eradicate slavery and human trafficking from its direct supply chain for tangible goods offered for sale are described in a disclosure linked from the home page of 3M website, pursuant to the California Transparency in Supply. The California Supply Chains Act (SB 657) disclosure describes 3M systems for verifying and auditing supplier performance in prohibiting slavery and human trafficking, as well as supplier performance in other aspects of 3MSupply Chain Policies. The disclosure also describes 3M commitment to legal and ethical practices through its membership in the UN Global Compact and implementation of 3M's Code of Conduct. Beginning in 2017, 3M will be reporting its activities in response to the UK Modern Slavery Act of 2015.

Assessing Supplier Performance

3M's product supply chain involves suppliers from more than 80 countries classified in over200 sub-categories. There are 10 global commodity teams and numerous sub-teams that work with all client divisions and all 3M factories to assess criticality and develop strategies relevant to mitigating risks and increasing value within all product supply chains. 3M uses a criteria matrix to rank suppliers using multiple factors and critical suppliers are defined within each of the global commodity teams. With its broad global supply chain, 3M are constantly managing changes in supply markets both opportunistically to extract value and defensively where necessary to secure supply.

3M screens 100% of its new suppliers against the labor, human rights, and environmental, health, safety (EHS) requirements of 3M Supply Chain Policies, and going forward will be screening suppliers against its Supplier Responsibility Code. For existing suppliers, 3M periodically monitor their performance against its supplier expectations to limit overall risk exposure. 3M has implemented a risk-based supplier assessment process to help assure that its suppliers meet expectations. The process starts by ranking suppliers using a prioritization matrix tool that takes into account country, type of operations, and annual 3M purchases. 3M may ask suppliers to complete a self-assessment survey (SAS), and the SAS is used to understand supplier programs and whether they meet the intent of 3M expectations. An on-site audit may be conducted, and any deficiencies are ultimately corrected through further communication and follow-up audits.

The supplier audit process covers training, social risks, labor checklists, general working conditions, emergency response procedures, and hazardous materials management - including transportation protocols and employment practices. 3M staff typically conduct on-site audits, but 3M may use third-party auditors as needed. The assessment program has independent oversight from the 3M EHS Advisory Committee. Customer or general public concerns can be brought to 3M'sattention via phone or website, with contact information available online.

3M's complex supply chain requires comprehensive risk assessment mechanisms to identify and mitigate potential sustainability risks throughout the supplier base, especially critical tier 1 suppliers. The focus of 3M risk assessment is on goods-producing suppliers that feed into 3M saleable products. These suppliers represent 24% of almost 24,000 tier 1 production materials suppliers and contract manufacturers. The potentially higher risk suppliers in this group account for 18% of these suppliers.

To date, over 4,500 self-assessments or on-site audits of suppliers have been conducted in prioritized countries, including China, India, Korea, Malaysia, Taiwan, Thailand, Brazil, Mexico, Russia and Turkey over the past eight years. Suppliers reviewed in the last three years represent 86% of 3M's 2015 spend in the listed countries. Most suppliers met 3M's expectations, and those requiring improvement were given specific corrective action in order to retain 3M business. Suppliers with corrective action must pass a 3M requalification assessment after completing the necessary steps. Most suppliers work very quickly to address any 3M findings. Those suppliers unwilling or unable to take the necessary corrective action in a timely manner have been terminated by 3M.

In order to lay a strong foundation for 3M 2025 goal of further driving sustainability into its supply chains, 3M has updated its supplier expectations via a new Supplier Responsibility Code, issued in April 2016, and are updating 3M supplier assessment process to incorporate these revised expectations. 3M are also globalizing the supplier risk analysis and assessment process, and focusing the efforts on key risk areas for each geography and commodity space, such as labor rights, human trafficking, indigenous peoples' rights, child labor, business ethics, workplace safety, and environmental impacts. In addition, 3M are actively seeking out opportunities to collaborate with peer companies, customers, suppliers and other partners to standardize supply chain sustainability and corporate responsibility expectations, so that 3M can realize much greater synergy and progress by working together toward common goals.

Supplier Diversity

Equal access to business opportunities is not just deserved, it's a priority. Regional self-sufficiency is a focus area for 3M, and the company recognizes its importance for business reasons as well as in building connections with local communities. Although 3M collects data around the proportion of spending on local suppliers at its significant locations of operation, this data is business confidential. 3M has a long-standing commitment to sustainable business practices and supporting the economic success of its communities. This includes working with both diverse and small business suppliers. For 3M purposes, a diverse supplier is any supplier who qualifies for one or more of the following classifications: minority-owned business, women-owned business, small business (including HUB zone, woman and Veteran/ service disabled veteran).

3M proactively identifies diverse suppliers to procure goods and services, strongly encourages the use of diverse suppliers across its Sourcing organization, and reaches out through 3M involvement with various organizations, including the National Minority Supplier Development Council (NMSDC), Women's Business Enterprise National Council (WBENC), Metropolitan Economic Development Association (MEDA), Small Business Administration (SBA), and others.

In 2015, 3M spent $1.5 billion dollars with small businesses, representing 27% of its total US domestic spend. 3M also spent $200 million dollars with diverse suppliers, which represents 3.6% of total US domestic spend. 3M continues to reassess elements of this approach, working across the industry to glean best practices.3M remains committed to supporting small business and diverse suppliers and their positive impact on the economic viability of communities.

3M establishes goals and regularly tracks the dollar value of goods and services purchased from small businesses and diverse suppliers in concert with goals set annually with the U.S. Federal Government as part of the Subcontracting Plan for Federal Government contracting. To achieve its goals, 3M is implementing a 4-part strategy aimed to: 1) increase 3M spend with current diverse suppliers by reviewing the existing diverse Suppliers by diversity category; 2) identify additional diverse suppliers in the existing supply base by reviewing the top non-diverse suppliers by commodity team; 3) find "new-to-3M" diverse suppliers; and 4) further disrupt the status quo by working to move some of 3M Tier Two dollars to Tier One and focusing on diverse suppliers in the RFP activity. 3M progress is routinely communicated to leadership across the organization.

Taking Action: Economic Sustainability

Within this part we can learn how 3M technology, products and innovation come together to lead to continued financial sustainability. 3M continues to be inspired and motivated by its corporate vision:

- 3M Technology advancing every company
- 3M Products enhancing every home

- 3M Innovation improving every life

The vision captures the essence of 3M: technology, products and innovation. It describes what 3M does for its customers every day: advance, enhance and improve. It also establishes a stretch goal for all employees at 3M as they have the capability to reach every company, every home and every life all around the world.

Concurrent with the vision, 3M has six strategies that will propel the company forward and achieve its financial goals:

- Expand relevance to customers and 3M presence in the marketplace
- Gain profitable market share and accelerate market penetration everywhere
- Invest in innovation: Invigorate existing market opportunities and focus on emerging megatrends
- Intensify capabilities and achieve regional self-sufficiency
- Build high performing and diverse global talent
- Drive consistent superior levels of operational excellence

2015 Financial Summary

Key Economic Highlights for 2015:

- Earnings per share increased 1.2% to$7.58 per share;
- Operating income margins increased 0.5% points year on year to 22.9%;
- Total worldwide net sales for the year were $30.3 billion, a decrease of 4.7%;
- Organic local-currency sales growth increased 1.3% worldwide: 2.1 percent in the United States, 1.5 percent in Latin America/Canada, 0.9% in Asia Pacific and 0.8% in Europe/Middle East/Africa;
- Currency impacts reduced worldwide sales by 6.8% and acquisitions, net of divestitures, added 0.6% to sales;
- Return on invested capital of 22.5% and free cash flow conversion of 103%;
- $7.8 billion was returned to shareholders through dividends paid and share repurchases;

Three key levers are driving 3M's success, and positioning the company to win in both the short and long term. In 2015, 3M has made significant process on each of these levers.

- **The First is Portfolio Management:** In 2012, 3M began taking action to prioritize, strengthen and focus its portfolio of business. 3M has since realigned from6 sectors to 5 business groups and from 40 businesses to 26. This year, for example, the company combined its dental and orthodontic business within its Health Care business group. Now, through a single and seamless partnership, 3M can offer customers an array of oral care innovations. Combining and realigning businesses is delivering significant benefits, including greater customer relevance, scale, productivity and speed. It is also making the company leaner and better positioned to allocate resource to the best opportunities as it relates to both organic growth and acquisitions. In 2015, 3M also strengthened its portfolio through acquisitions. In particular, the Capital Safety acquisition bolsters 3M already-strong position in the fast-growing personal safety business, and the acquisition of Polypore's

Separations Media business strengthens 3M filtration technology platform. At the same time, 3M divested three businesses that no longer aligned with its strategic objectives, including the library systems business.

- **3M Second Lever is Investing in Innovation:** It fosters a constant stream of unique and cutting-edge products, which drives organic growth. 3M's primary growth strategy is organic, which is why research and development is the heartbeat of the company. In 2015, 3M invested $1.8 billion in R&D, 5.8 percent of sales, while expanding its scientific capabilities globally. 3M opened six customer technical centers around the world, and opened a new state-of-the-art research laboratory in the United States in March 2016.
- **3M is Moving to a More Efficient Business Model Through Its Third Lever Which is Business Transformation:** 3M is committed to business transformation, which will make 3M more agile, more efficient, and most importantly, more responsive to customers. The backbone of this effort is implementation of a global enterprise resource planning system. Business transformation is an important undertaking, with significant long-term benefits.

During the first quarter of 2016, 3M announced its new five-year financial objectives:

- 8 to 11% growth in earning per share;
- 2 to 5% organic local currency sales growth;
- 20% return on invested capital;
- 100% free cash flow conversion;

The company is building, preparing and positioning itself for efficient growth today and into the future.

3M has company-sponsored retirement plans covering all U.S. employees and many employees outside the U.S. The primary U.S. defined-benefit pension plan was closed to new participants effective January 1, 2009. 3M expects to contribute approximately $100 million to $200 million of cash to its global defined benefit pension and postretirement plans in 2016. The company does not have a required minimum cash pension contribution obligation for its U.S. plans in 2016. The increase in U.S. discount rates and other factors resulted in a decreased in the projected benefit obligation (PBO), however the plan's funded status decreased slightly in 2015 as the decrease in the PBO was at a lower rate than the decrease in fair value of plan assets in 2015.

The Company also sponsors employee savings plans under Section 401(k) of the Internal Revenue Code. These plans are offered to all regular U.S. employees. For eligible employees hired prior to January 1, 2009, employee 401(k) contributions of up to 6% of eligible compensation were matched in cash at rates of 60% or 75%, depending on the plan in which the employee participates. Employees hired on or after January 1, 2009, received a cash match of 100% for employee 401(k) contributions of up to 6% of eligible compensation and also received an employer retirement income account cash contribution of 3% of the participant's total eligible compensation. Beginning on January 1, 2016, for U.S. employees, the Company reduced its match on employee 401(k) contributions. For eligible employees hired prior to January 1, 2009, employee 401(k) contributions of up to 5% of eligible compensation will be matched in cash at rates of 45% or 60%, depending on the plan in which the employee participates. Employees hired on or after January 1, 2009, will receive a cash match of 100% for employee 401(k) contributions of up to 5% of eligible compensation and will also continue to receive an employer retirement income

Table 5. Selected financial results

	Dollars in Millions, Except Per Share Amounts				
Operating Results	**2011**	**2012**	**2013**	**2014**	**2015**
Net Sales	$29,611	$29,904	$30,871	$31,821	$30,274
Operating Income	$6,178	$6,483	$6,666	$7,135	$6,946
Net Income Attributes to 3M	$4,283	$4,444	$4,659	$4,956	$4,833
Per Share- Basic	$5.72	$6.05	$6.40	$6.83	$7.72
Per Share - Diluted	$5.63	$5.96	$6.32	$6.72	$7.58
Operating Results	2011	2012	2013	2014	2015
Capital Expenditures	$1,379	$1,484	$1,665	$1,493	$1,461
Research Development and Related Expenses	$1,570	$1,634	$1,715	$1,770	$1,763
Employee Compensation and Benefits	$8,059	$8,347	$8,732	$8,836	$8,791
Payments to Providers of Capital	$1,774	$1,801	$1,899	$2,394	$2,695
Provision for Income Taxes	$1,674	$1,840	$1,841	$2,028	$1,982

account cash contribution of 3% of the participant's total eligible compensation. All contributions are invested in a number of investment funds pursuant to the employees' elections.

Taking Action: Employee Engagement and Recognition

Employee engagement is a priority for 3M. The management knows that employee engagement is good for the company and employees. Engaged employees are more satisfied with their work, tend to stay longer, and are more productive and committed. Employees are encouraged to pursue their ideas with a passion and collaborate with others to make their ideas reality. To facilitate employee engagement, 3M fosters and reinforces behaviors that support engagement using multiple avenues including networking and collaboration, diversity and inclusion, and measurement and feedback on engagement.

Networks and Collaboration

3M has numerous pathways to support organizational communications, learning and knowledge management. There are a variety of corporate and job functional systems to methodically help information and knowledge emerge and flow to the right people at the right time to add value. For example:

- **Formal Learning Networks:** The Learning Solution is 3M's corporate learning management system and is a one-stop electronic learning center that helps employees enroll in, deliver, track and report on learning activities. The Learning Solution serves the learning needs of 3M business units, plants and organizations globally.
- **Intranet Knowledge Platforms Databases:** 3M's intranet site structure is set up so that each employee has a work center as one of the quick-link tabs following login. Each work center is a collection of tools, systems and processes that are used routinely in daily work practices to successfully complete projects and work assignments in an employee's functional work area. Company

news for employees is available on a global news site called Spark 3M News. It enables employees to share news articles, videos and links with others both internally and externally via email and social media.

- **Best Practice Descriptions/Processes:** As a diverse technical company, 3M shares best practices several ways. Three of the most widely used internal organizations are the 3M Technical Forum, 3M Marketing Forum, and the 3M Engineering Technology Organization. These three organizations provide an extensive network of expertise through specialized chapters focused on 3M's core technologies and other emerging markets. Employees in R&D, manufacturing and other parts of the supply chain are able to collaborate and drive innovation globally across the organization.
- **Company Education Facility:** In addition to a variety of general courses, webinars, etc., 3M offers specialized extended courses to increase skills such as the 3M Leadership Development Institute, the 3M Marketing University, compliance courses, the Supply Chain Learning Academy, Harvard Management or, and the General Managers' and Managing Directors' program.
- **Idea Sharing:** Idea management is driven differently across the Company depending on organizational needs and what works best for the area of work. Some platform examples include Yammer, Wiki Enterprise, and various 3M internal and external social media channels. Systems are implemented and available globally to share best practices and ideas. 3M also encourages its employees to spend 15% of their working time sharing and working on their own projects.

Measurement, Feedback, and Action on Employee Engagement

Since 2006, key survey content and follow-up actions have focused on employee engagement. 3M measures engagement and engagement drivers, and provides these results to leaders and their organizations for follow-up. As 3M corporate policy, a standard opinion survey is administered to all employees at locations worldwide once every three years. 3M uses survey results to address employee concerns and identify opportunities for improvement. Summaries of survey results and actions taken are circulated up the management chain to ensure visibility and accountability. 3M also conducts a more strategically-focused survey that includes engagement measures. This survey, the Vision and Strategies Alignment Survey, was last conducted in October 2013.

3M also requires its leaders to actively foster engagement as part of their day-to-day coaching and interactions with others. This expectation is embedded in 3M leadership behaviors, which apply to all 3M leaders and links to their annual performance assessment. 3M supports leaders in these efforts via formal training, videos and on-demand tools.

Results from the Standard Opinion Survey and the Vision and Strategies Alignment Survey indicate 3M's support of employee engagement is strong and continuing to get stronger. Results have improved with each administration, up to 83% favorable in the most recent survey, which is well above the threshold for strength (70% favorable).

Results from 2013 Vision and Strategies Alignment Survey:

- 90% reported they persevere when faced with difficulties, take on new roles and responsibilities as the need arises, and are excited that their work contributes to company success.
- 89% respondents say they feel like they really belong in the company.
- 83% highest worldwide engagement category score since the first survey was conducted.

- 76%reported the people in my work group actively pursue self-development opportunities to meet company needs.
- 72% reported it is very easy to maintain my focus.

Employee Engagement for Sustainability, Rewards and Recognition

3M also has a robust approach to engaging employees in "sustainable thinking" at work and at home. A few key elements include:

- **Global Communications:** Every employee with a 3M email address routinely receives email communications from executive leadership regarding global challenges, environmental days of recognition (Earth Day, World Water Day, International Women's Day, etc.) in an effort to further educate the global workforce on both challenges and ideas for improving how we live and work.
- **Sustainability Week:** In 2015, 3M hosted its third annual "Sustainability Week" celebration – a globally celebrated series of activities including Sustainability brainstorm sessions, a product innovation competition featuring executive judges and global employee voting.

3M uses Sustainability Week, a week-long series of events, to engage our employees in sustainable thinking. True sustainability must be lived daily. But sometimes we all need little reminders to jump start our thoughts and actions. That's why 3M created Sustainability Week, a series of daily events, discussions and communications focused entirely on engaging 3Mers in sustainable thinking. 3M goal is to get the thousands of 3M employees across the globe embraced in the sustainability mindset and participating in activities that make a real impact. From product development competitions to independent research projects, giant brainstorming sessions to discussions at home, this week sharpens 3M focus on using sustainability to improve lives. During the 2015 Sustainability Week, 3M addressed global sustainability challenges we all face every day at home and at work. 3Mers were asked to think creatively, collaborate, and innovate with the shared goal of making life better. 3M built tables for those in need, using construction waste. And it led a Shark Tank-inspired Power Pitch, which allowed teams of employees to suggest business ideas with a sustainability focus to compete for research and development funding with winners chosen through global text voting by their peers. Additional events included a keynote speaker from clothing company Patagonia, events on meditation and mindfulness in effective leadership, and a Bike to Work day.

Hard work and extra effort are rewarded and recognized at 3M through an array of award programs. 3M sponsors many corporate award programs to honor individuals and teams that make significant contributions to the company. In addition, many divisions also have their own specific ways of recognizing and rewarding people. Across 3M, management can choose from a variety of monetary and nonmonetary awards to show appreciation for exceptional contributions. Examples of corporate awards include:

- Awards for specific professionals, such as the Global Marketing Excellence Award and the Circle of Technical Excellence and Innovation Award;
- Awards for cross-functional teams, such as the Golden Step Award;
- Awards focused on employees who improve safety or pollution prevention;
- Two prestigious lifetime achievement awards: the Engineering Achievement Award and the Carlton Society recognition, which honor employees for their scientific achievements.

Taking Action: Engaging 3M Stakeholders

The following part represents how stakeholder-driven approach to sustainability materiality serves as a foundation for 3M sustainability strategy and reporting. As a science-based company, 3M stakeholders include customers and consumers, investors, government agencies, industry organizations, subject-matter experts and academia, non-government organizations, other corporations and more.

Stakeholder engagement can help guide companies on doing business the right way. It can also have a direct impact on a company's financial success (sales, share price and investments), on its operations, and on its reputation. 3M has created a robust, stakeholder-driven approach to sustainability materiality that serves as a foundation for our sustainability strategy and reporting. Through understanding critical sustainability issues from both internal and external perspectives, 3M can strengthen its social license to operate and develop corporate strategy, goals, targets, programs, initiatives and a stakeholder engagement strategy to advance sustainability globally.

Major Stakeholders and Key Actions

Employees:

- Respecting human rights and diversity
- Supporting, optimizing and promoting development and growth
- Ensuring a safe and healthy work environment
- Ensuring equal opportunity
- Providing competitive compensation and benefits
- Attracting and retaining the highest talent by being a company for which employees are proud to work

Investors:

- Delivering profitable returns on investment
- Disclosing timely, concise and relevant information (related to economic, environmental and social issues)
- Responding to inquiries
- Upholding corporate values

Suppliers, Contractors and Industry Associates

- Partnering with suppliers and contractors that meet or exceed expectations
- Supporting collective efforts to deliver business results
- Collaborating to identify, resource and amplify sustainability initiatives
- Respecting human rights for workers across the value chain

Academia and Scientific Organizations:

- Engaging on technical scientific research to develop innovative solutions for society

Nonprofit Organizations and NGOs:

- Partnering to understand societal concerns
- Providing support to advance and solve global issues

Customers:

- Providing diverse innovative product solutions that help our customers deliver on their promises
- Offering a diversified portfolio of products increasingly demonstrating sustainability attributes
- Providing sustainable products to address and help solve global environmental challenges

Government/Regulators:

- Complying with laws, regulations and policies
- Supporting and engaging on development and modification of changes

Local Communities:

- Supporting and engaging in citizenship activities across our value chain
- Providing economic and social value to communities, while minimizing environmental impact
- Supporting safe and healthy communities

Media:

- Ensuring 3M is represented accurately with current information

Memberships and Partnerships

It is through collaboration and partnerships that 3M can accelerate sustainability in the company and in the world. 3M values its partnerships with numerous stakeholders as a way to not only address its sustainability issues, but to help its partners address their sustainability challenges. 3M has joined numerous organizations globally to advance sustainability through collaboration with the organization and its members. Memberships have provided a forum for working on key sustainability issues that are relevant to both 3M and its stakeholders.

Memberships and partnerships help provide 3M with diverse viewpoints on sustainability, a better understanding of the positions of its stakeholders, and a mechanism to learn from the successes and failures of its peers. 3M partners with many organizations. Key engagements include the following listed below.

Employees:

- Committee to Encourage Corporate Philanthropy
- The League of American Bicyclists
- The Science Museum of Minnesota

Investors:

- Dow Jones Sustainability Index
- CDP
- MSCI
- National Investor Relations Institute

Government/Regulators:

- The Commission for Environmental Cooperation
- United Nations & U.N. Global Compact
- U.S. Department of Energy (DOE)
- U.S. EPA Green Power Partnership
- U.S. EPA Energy Star Program
- International Labor Organization

Customers:

- The Closed Loop Fund
- Corporate Eco Forum
- Retail Industry Leaders Association
- Sustainable Brands
- World Business Council for Sustainable Development

Academia/Scientific Organizations:

- Harvard Medical School, The Center for Health and the Global Environment
- Iowa State University. Center for Bioplastics and Bio composites
- University of Minnesota, Center for Sustainable Polymers
- Environmental Initiative
- Intergovernmental Panel on Climate Change
- Society of Environmental Toxicology and Chemistry
- Massachusetts Institute of Technology

Local Communities:

- United Way
- Habitat for Humanity
- American Red Cross
- Feed my Starving Children
- Numerous others local to our manufacturing operations around the world

Industry Trade Associations:

- Air & Waste Management Association
- Alliance to Save Energy

- American Chamber of Commerce (Am Cham)
- American Chemistry Council (ACC)
- American Industrial Hygiene Association
- CAPS Research
- The Conference Board
- The Conflict Free Sourcing Initiative (CFSI)
- European Chemistry Industry Council (CEFIC)
- Green Chemistry & Commerce Council (GC3)
- London Benchmarking Group
- Minnesota Chamber of Commerce
- National Association of EHS Managers
- National Association of Manufacturers (NAM)
- National Climate Coalition
- Pressure Sensitive Tape Council
- Water Quality Association

Labor and Human Rights:

- US Business Leadership Network

Media:

- Sustainable Life Media

Nonprofit Organizations/NGOs:

- Alliance to Save Energy
- Forum for the Future
- Friends of EU Emissions Trading Scheme (ETS)
- TFT (The Forest Trust)
- The Nature Conservancy
- Net Impact
- Practice Green Health
- World Resources Institute (WRI)
- World Skills
- World Wildlife Fund (WWF)

3M's stakeholder engagement strategy continues to evolve. 3M continually look to its stakeholders to help 3M increase understanding, broaden its awareness, seek technical input and expertise and evaluate possible collaborations and strategic partnerships. 3M rely on their counsel and expertise to help guide the company. We believe stakeholder engagement should be based on candid and authentic dialog, grounded in the company's values and should contribute to the evolution of its strategic priorities.

Levels of engagement with stakeholders vary greatly by geography, type and function. For example, 3M employees globally are engaged frequently through sustainability communications and events with diverse topics based on its material aspects, while 3M may engage annually for an industry association meeting. 3M may also have engagements around a specific issue.

In October 2015, 3M hosted the first annual 3M Sustainability in Health Care Summit at the 3M Innovation Center in St. Paul, Minnesota. The goal of the conference was to advance sustainability in health care by sharing challenges and best practices. Executives from over 40 private and military hospitals and non-profit organizations participated, some experts in applying sustainability in their organizations, and some just starting out. 3Mis planning to make this Summit an annual event, to continue to advance sustainability in the health care sector.

In another example, the Commission for Environmental Cooperation (CEC), in collaboration with Natural Resources Canada (NRCan), Mexico's Comisión Nacional para el Uso Eficiente de la Energía (National Commission for the Efficient Use of Energy) (CONUEE) and the US Department of Energy (DOE), is partnering with private sector facilities in Canada, Mexico, and the United States to promote the adoption in North America of the ISO 50001 international energy management system (EnMS) standard. The CEC's North American Energy Management Pilot Program provides partner companies with increased capacity to implement and become certified to ISO 50001 and, possibly, the Superior Energy Performance™ (SEP) program managed by the DOE. Three 3M facilities are participating in this project: San Luis Potosi, Cottage Grove, and Brockville.

3M also receive stakeholder input via shareholder inquiries and proposals, as well as general outreach.

To help 3M think more broadly about its humanitarian impact, in both 2014 and 2015, 3M used the Net Impact Conference to start and encourage a dialog around the idea of social sustainability and 3M's ability to "improve every life" in partnership with others. In early 2016, 3M continued to expand this conversation by creating an art exhibit at South by Southwest that posed the question of what everyone can do to address the global challenges ahead as we look to a growing population. 3M continues to push this conversation and gain insights from stakeholders using a robust sustainability-focused social media and online strategy. 3M look forward to continuing to learn more about this topic from a variety of thought leaders in the years ahead.

Businesses today are operating in a new landscape where broad sets of stakeholders expect an increased level of transparency, access and engagement. To further facilitate this process 3M hired a full-time professional to manage global stakeholder engagement. It is part of the company effort to strengthen 3M by better communicating with its customers, consumers, investors and other stakeholders around the world. A dedicated, full-time focus will allow them to have a more strategic and proactive approach to engagement on a variety of topics, which will keep 3M well-connected and ahead of issues that could affect the business. It is through this position that 3M will facilitate consultation between stakeholders and the board on economic, environmental and social topics. 3M engaged with many external stakeholders in setting the new 3M 2025 Sustainability Goals. These goals are aligned with the key global challenges, as well as the United Nations 2030 Sustainable Development Goals. As such, they present unique opportunities for partnerships and collaboration, which 3M is actively seeking out.

Taking Action: Collaborating With the Communities

3M partnerships with diverse organizations around the world lead to better sustainability solutions. 3M improves lives through innovative social investments in Education, Community, and Environment. 3M goal is to create a better world for everyone, and 3M approach includes annual social investments in its global communities. Through these investments, 3M strives to increase access and student achievement in STEM (science, technology, engineering and math), improve standards of living in communities where 3M operates, and build environmentally sustainable communities.

Improving Lives Through 3Mgives

In 2015, 3M aligned activities to harness the power of its business expertise and employee resources to maximize its impact on 3M communities. It was a landmark year for 3Mgives with investments and programs that aligned community outcomes to business strategies.

3M began the year with 3M chairman of the board, president and CEO, Inge Thulin, leading the Greater Twin Cities United Way Centennial Campaign. Under his leadership, 3Mers across the country invested $6.1 million and the company matched those dollars resulting in 3M giving a total of $15 million to more than 2,500 agencies and projects – record results for the community. The impact was tremendous – more than1 million lives in 150 communities were improved.

3M's community impact is global. The company expanded its Global Volunteer Day to 88 international locations in 2015. More than 16,000 3M volunteers helped to improve the lives of young people from Beijing to Brussels to Buenos Aires through pre-school to high school projects. 3M furthered its reach into diverse communities particularly through the leadership and community engagement work of 3M Employee Resource Networks, including the Women's Leadership Forum. For example, 3M's Latino Resource Network and the African American Network mentored students from a St. Paul high school and hosted a career awareness event at 3M Headquarters. The Military Support Network distributed3M products to veterans who are homeless and 3M's Native American Network packed school supplies for the American Indian School in St. Paul.

3M continues to enhance employee engagement by leveraging the skills and passion of 3Mers around the globe. In 2015, 3M invested in the 3M Catalyst Leadership Way program to send 3M senior executives to engage their professional skills to support community sustainability initiatives in Mumbai and Chennai, India.

The company is also encouraging greater giving around the globe to align community investments with 3M's global operations. In 2015, 3M developed the International Giving Fund in partnership with United Way Worldwide to facilitate investments in community organizations outside of the United States. These investments include funding STEM education projects with 3M Mexico, 3M Argentina, and 3M Brazil; environmental sustainability projects with 3M Canada; and supporting projects that help meet basic needs for children of migrant workers near 3M China.

In addition to financial resources, 3M leveraged its diverse product portfolio to support the communities – in 2015, 3M invested more than $36 million in product and services (Fair Market Value) to strategic community partners. For example, as founding partner with a $5 million commitment, 3M gave more than $1.6 million worth of products at Fair Market Value to help construct and enhance the visitor experience at the National Museum of African American History and Culture on the National Mall in Washington, D.C. The museum is scheduled to open in the fall of 2016.

3M has identified game-changing social programs by building upon new models of investments with innovative and effective organizations. For example, the company invested in the Closed Loop Fund, a collaborative social impact fund that provides municipalities with access to capital to build comprehensive recycling programs. 3M expanded its partnership with DonorsChoose.org, an organization that helps to fund teacher projects in under-resourced schools. Through a partnership with DoSomething.org, 3M engaged thousands of students in STEM in a fun and contemporary way.

3Mgives, the social investment arm of 3M, is governed by the 3M Foundation Board of Directors and Corporate Contributions Committee comprised of senior level executives in the company. The 3M Foundation Board of Directors guides the social investment strategy including giving area, budget allocation and high-level strategy advice for execution by 3Mgives staff.

3M leaders from each region develop and administer programs consistent with the overall 3Mgives strategy and local culture and social needs. For example, in the United States, 18 Community Relations Councils develop regional strategies and direct local social investments in partnership with the 3Mgives team. In addition, 3Mgives regularly convenes a Global Advisory Council comprised of senior leaders from countries around the globe to inform and develop 3M global giving strategy.

Since the inception of the 3M Foundation in 1953, 3M has invested $1.45 billion in cash and in-kind donations in communities around the world. These global investments were bolstered by employees and retirees volunteering millions of hours.

Investing in Resources

K-12 Education. 3M's education goal is to increase student achievement for all students in STEM (science, technology, engineering and math). To that end, 3M has supported innovative and impactful STEM and business educational initiatives for many years. As a company that has thrived on applying science to life, 3M understands the importance of inspiring the next generation of scientists, innovators and inventors. 3M invests in educational initiatives that help young people understand how science impacts their daily lives and encourages and supports interest in science, reflecting the company's commitment to applying science to life. 3M goals are to:

Table 6. 2015 Giving by Focus Area

	Cash	In-Kind	Total	%	Volunteer Hours
Education	$11,518,737	$11,952,525	$23,471,262	33%	96,809
Community	$19,478,865	$24,597,846	$44,076,711	63%	206,701
Environment	$2,757,185	$93,662	$2,850,847	4%	19,460
Total	$33,754,786	$36,644,034	$70,398,820	100%	322,970

Values presented in this table represent the most current values, but are still subject to change.

Table 7. 2015 Global Giving by Region

	Charitable Corporate Cash Donations	Charitable Foundation	In-Kind	Total Donations
Asia -Pacific	$211,874	$16,000	$622,500	$850,374
Canada	$685,597	$0	$298,182	$983,779
Europe MEA	$558,451	$39,413	$88,728	$686,592
Latin America	$2,273,101	$10,500	$136,788	$2,420,389
United States	$12,282,681	$17,677,170	$35,497,836	$65,457,686
Total	$16,011,703	$17,743,083	$36,644,034	$70,398,820

Values presented in this table represent the most current values, but are still subject to change.

- Promote equity by driving quality education to all communities;
- Build a diverse pipeline of talent by increasing student achievement in STEM and business curriculum;
- Support post-secondary programs that attract, retain and graduate high-performing students.
- **3M Science Encouragement Programs:** 3M's STEM support is not new; the company has worked with Saint Paul Public Schools (SPPS) for more than 40 years. Through that partnership, 3M developed several Science Encouragement Programs. One such program is 3M STEP (Science Training Education Program). STEP provides juniors and seniors from SPPS the opportunity to participate in the process of scientific discovery at 3M. Through mentoring and classroom instruction by 3M scientists, and paid summer employment in a 3M lab, STEP students increase job skills, gain insight into scientific careers and enhance their personal development. As of 2015, more than 1500 students have participated in the program. Many have gone on to pursue careers in science and several are working at 3M. In fact, a former STEP student is now a division scientist. 3M strives to help SPPS create positive outcomes and opportunities for students with more than $1 million invested annually and hundreds of eMentors. 3M investments have contributed to great results for all students in SPPS. Student achievement in STEM has increased for the district and more students are pursuing degrees in STEM-related fields while attending top tier schools. 3M believes that all students, regardless of race, gender or any other factor, should have fair opportunities to succeed. In 2015 the disparity between graduation rates for Black and White students decreased three percentage points from 18 percentage points to 15 percentage points. The district also saw graduation rates higher than the state average for American Indian, Hispanic, Black, and English Learners in 2015.
- **DoSomething.org:** 3M partnered with DoSomething.org to develop a fun and contemporary way to engage young people (13 – 18 years old), especially young women in STEM. 3M scientists worked with the DoSomething team to launch Science Sleuth 2.0, an adventure where students use STEM principles to solve a mystery. At the end of the adventure, students had the opportunity to learn more about 3M scientists and to donate $10 provided by 3M to a STEM project in a classroom in need. DoSomething.org enabled us to expose a much broader audience to STEM principles than ever before. 3M goal was to move students from the pre-contemplation level (science is not my thing) to contemplation (science can be interesting and fun). This program also provided an opportunity for 3M scientists to develop a realistic STEM experience and share their personal STEM journey.
- **DonorsChoose.org:** 3M has long recognized the need to support teachers' efforts to make STEM fun and interesting for their students. To do this often requires additional equipment, books, and materials. To help teachers purchase additional STEM teaching aids, 3M started the 3M Ingenuity Grants program in 2003. This program provides grants of up to $15,000 to support STEM classroom projects in 3M communities. 3M has since partnered with DonorsChoose.org to expand its reach into classrooms around the country. In 2015, 3M invested more than $500,000 to support more than 600 projects in 27 states, of which more than 90% were in moderate or high poverty areas.
- **3M Visiting Wizards:** The Visiting Wizards is another 3M Science Encouragement Program developed by 3Mers. This program aims to spark an interest in science in the youngest of learners. 3M Visiting Wizards visit classrooms to share the magic of science with students through science demonstrations and hands-on experiments. The demos and experiments are on topics such

as catapults, energy, and cryogenics. Today, more than 800,000 students have seen how sciences applied to life. These demos are online, and they are accessible to teachers and community leaders everywhere.

- **FIRST Robotics Teams:** 3M is a longtime supporter of FIRST Robotics teams in the U.S. 3M supports nearly 50 teams around the world including teams in Poland and Brazil. In addition to sponsoring teams, 3M provides more than $500,000 in products to the teams. We also have hundreds of employees who volunteer as coaches.

Higher Education

- **3M Frontline Sales Initiative:** Our Frontline Sales Initiative is an innovative, educational partnership with universities, including four Historically Black Colleges and Universities (HBCUs) across the United States. The program was designed to increase the amount of sales education content at universities and elevate sales as a discipline and a profession. By collaborating with universities and faculty, as well as aligning 3M sales leaders and resources, 3M supports the development of professional sales programs. Today, 3M has hired more than 346 students from this program.
- **University of Minnesota:** The University of Minnesota is a key strategic partner with 3M. 3M has donated more than $40 million to support scholarships, fellowships, programs to encourage diversity in the sciences, and more. 3M established the STEM Education Center in 2010 to train elementary and secondary school educators to effectively incorporate evidence-based disciplines into their teaching, and to grow students' interest and competencies in STEM. The 3M STEM Education Fellows Program funds graduate students to work with targeted schools to integrate STEM into their school curricula. 3M's support has allowed the U of M to partner with 200 Twin Cities metro area teachers to increase science and math learning for 15,000 students in the fourth through eighth grades. In addition to supporting science and engineering, 3M also supports business education. The company provides scholarships for students at the University of Minnesota Carlson School of Management.
- **3M Scholarships:** A significant part of building the STEM pipeline is supporting students as they pursue higher education opportunities. 3M provides scholarships to students at the following universities:
    - Georgia Tech,
    - Northwestern University,
    - Penn State,
    - University of Urbana,
    - University of Minnesota, and
    - University of Wisconsin-Madison.

The company also partners with organizations, such as United Negro College Fund (UNCF), to increase higher education opportunities for underrepresented students. In 2015, 3M helped the Twin Cities UNCF raise more than $500,000 for scholarships, earning the UNCF Chairman's Award. In addition, the company supported the Asian and Pacific Islander American Scholarship Fund at the University of Minnesota. 3M also expanded its College/University matching program to include the American Indian College Fund and the Hispanic Scholarship Fund.

3M also recognizes the need to support and encourage students to consider careers in skilled trades. To support the development of a skilled technical workforce, 3M established an initiative that fosters industry-driven partnerships with technical colleges. These partnerships help local community schools to better align curriculum with job skills required for today's technical workforce. The partnership increases awareness of career opportunities by providing internships and mentors in manufacturing. 3M has invested more than $300,000 in support of this initiative.

Volunteerism

3M formalized volunteerism in 1949 as an integral part of 3M's support to our communities. As a result of increased awareness of volunteer activities and implementation of new initiatives, employee engagement increased significantly at 3M. In 2015, the number of volunteers increased 51% and hours grew 11%.3Mgives helps to build sustainable communities through strategic social investments and thoughtful engagement of 3Mers worldwide. 3M volunteers represent the most impactful contribution to communities. Volunteerism is an important part of the 3M's culture – it reflects the corporate vision and supports 3M leadership behaviors.

3Mgives launched an app in 2015 to recruit volunteers. Volunteers are able to sign up for opportunities, upload activity photos and comment on various opportunities.

- **3M Global Volunteer Day:** For the second year, 3M Global Volunteer Day brought 3M employees around the world together to make all of our moments matter for collective impact internationally. This year 3M increased participation at its global locations from 15 to 88—with more than 16,000 volunteers serving in schools and youth organizations from St. Paul to Spain to South Africa.3Mgives promoted diversity and inclusion to support the company's "I'm InVOLved" theme for 2015.
- **3M Volunteer Match:** 3M encourages and supports volunteerism through 3M Volunteer Match, providing $250 matches to eligible organizations for employees who serve 20 hours or more (retirees 25 hours) in a calendar year. Since the inception of the Volunteer Match program in 2001, 3M has donated more than $6.3 million in the names of 25,844 volunteers to over 3,000 organizations in all 50 states. In 2015, 3M donated $562,000, matching 2,241 volunteers to 1,008 organizations in 46 states plus Washington, D.C.
- **Nonprofit Board Service:** To support the hundreds of 3Mers serving on non-profit boards, 3Mgives provides resources to help bolster their impact. Initiated by a 3M Foundation Board member, 3M hosted an "All A-Board Bar-B-Que" where 3M recognized employees for their service at this inaugural 3M Nonprofit Board Service Luncheon. The event provided an opportunity to network and share best practices. 3M's partner, MAP for Nonprofits, compiled a new training on board governance trends to help participants to better serve their organizations. The response to the event was overwhelming and this will be an annual event.

Employee Resource Networks

3M has nine employee affinity groups in St. Paul and the 3Mgives team has connected the networks with volunteer opportunities of interest to each network. For example, members of the GLBT+ Network packed lunches for youth at Face to Face, an organization focused on helping youth who are homeless.

The African American Network was connected with the Martin Luther King Jr. Day Service Coalition, a collaboration of Twin Cities Corporations and, in 2015, painted the after-school youth spaces at the YWCA in St. Paul. Members also led a panel for Twin Cities Rise! Beneficiaries to help prepare them for the future, earning them the Twin Cities Rise.

- **Community Partner Award:** 3M's Native American Network packed school supplies for American Indian Magnet School students, and members of the Military Support Network served at the Minnesota Assistance for Veterans event to help veterans who are homeless. 3M's Women's Leadership Forum volunteers chaired the 3M-sponsored DiscoverE Global Marathon for women in engineering and technology.

3Mgives incorporates insights from 3M employees to inform the development of programs and partnerships. The 2015 research indicates that nearly all 3M employees agree that it is personally important to them to work for a socially responsible company and 87% of 3M employees agree that 3Mgives community investments make them proud to be a 3M employee.

Enhancing 3M Communities

- **3Mgives Campaign in Partnership with United Way:** 3M partners with United Way and non-profit agencies around the country in an annual workplace giving campaign to raise funds and volunteer for local community causes. 3Mers at Headquarters, in plants, and at the one in Austin, Texas office rally together to make a difference for people-in-need in their communities.
- **National Museum of African American History and Culture:** 3M is a Founding 'Cornerstone' Donor of $5 million to the National Museum of African American History and Culture, a Smithsonian organization in Washington D.C. (opening in 2016). In 2015, 3M supplemented cash contributions with innovative 3M products to both provide the foundation for the building and enhance the visitor experience for years to come. The Museum will document and celebrate African American history and culture by giving voice to a story that is quintessentially American -- a story of hope and resiliency, of struggle and pain, of successes and triumphs. This is a story and a museum for all Americans, calling on each of us to examine how our nation has been - and continues to be – transformed by the African American experience. The Museum will broaden the understanding of the greater American story through the lens of the African American experience.

3M was recognized in the Smithsonian's annual report for donating 3M construction materials, safety products and touch screen monitors. In all, 3M donated more than $1.6 million worth of products to help construct and enhance the building. In addition to highlighting 3M's commitment to equity and social justice, this partnership exemplifies the impact of 3M products on the community.

- **Dorothy Day Center:** The Dorothy Day Center serves multiple functions in St. Paul and transforms lives for underserved populations. The Center provides meals, mental health services and medical care, showers, and much more to help people experiencing homelessness. They also provide emergency shelter for hundreds of people each night. 3M committed $750,000 worth of cash and product to the community's new vision for the Dorothy Day Center. This two-building campus is designed to prevent and end homelessness by utilizing an integrated continuum of emergency shelter, supportive services, access to resources and permanent supportive housing. The increase in homelessness is well documented. In its most recent survey, Wilder Research, a leading non-profit research organization based in Minnesota, found a 25% increase in homelessness during the Great Recession and another 6% increase from 2009-2012. The Dorothy Day Center is a visible, daily reminder of the increasing needs in our St. Paul community to prevent and end homelessness.

This project is based on innovative and proven models showing documented success in moving those hardest to serve clients along the continuum from crisis to stability to self-sufficiency. 3Mgives recognizes that the Dorothy Day Center does so much more than providing a shelter – they provide a caring atmosphere to encourage individuals to gain self-sufficiency in the long run. This is a prime example of an innovative investment right in 3M headquarters' backyard.

- **Science Museum Omnitheater Capital Investment:** As a part of a multi-year commitment, 3M invested $500,000 in the Science Museum of Minnesota to replace the theater's current film projection system with a state-of-the-art digital laser projection system that will assure the continued vitality and the cultural and educational programming for the next 10-15 years. This innovative investment is enabling the Science Museum of Minnesota to develop the world's first dual-4K IMAX Laser Dome Digital projection system – ensuring the highest quality of digital programming for students and general visitors to the museum.
- **International Giving Fund – United Way Worldwide:** To enhance 3M's giving around the globe, the International Giving Fund was established with United Way Worldwide to support the company's international community priorities and engage 3Mers in community activities. In 2015, 3M invested $700,000 to establish this Fund through United Way Worldwide. 3M locations across the globe apply for funds as a match for their contributions to signature partners. All funded programs must meet NGO (non-governmental organization) standards of the country and meet compliance standards such as the Foreign Corrupt Practices Act and others. The 3M in-country leader assesses the opportunity for the company and the community. United Way Worldwide vets the organization to ensure compliance with local and international laws.

3Mgives invested, in partnership with United Way Worldwide, in nine initiatives in 2015 – leveraging approximately $768,000 in cash and product contributions from international subsidiaries worldwide. This includes a coinvestment with 3M China to promote preschool readiness among the children of migrant workers by improving the teaching quality of caregivers. 3Mgives is also supporting 3M Canada in efforts to empower youth and educators to create sustainable communities with a $40,000 investment to core national partner, Learning for a Sustainable Future. 3Mgives partnered with leaders in Mexico, Brazil, and Argentina to launch an innovative STEM Science Fair Initiative in partnership with United Way Worldwide, local universities, and other partners. This investment enabled3Mgives to align community investments with 3M's operational footprint.

- **Closed Loop Fund:** 3M committed $5 million to the Closed Loop Fund (CLF), a collaborative social impact fund supported by leading companies that provides municipalities access to capital needed to build comprehensive recycling programs. The fund aims to (1) achieve a reduction of more than 75 million tons of greenhouse gas emissions, (2) divert 27 million cumulative tons of waste from landfills, (3) create 27,000 new local jobs, (4) help municipalities save more than $1.9 billion in waste disposal costs, and (5) provide packaged goods companies with much greater access to recycled materials.

Cities across the nation are spending billions of dollars sending recyclable materials to landfills. These cities are losing revenue from selling recyclables and U.S.-based companies like 3M are missing out on a robust supply of recycled material in their supply chain. This partnership is one of 3M's innovative approaches to strategic social investing – it is the company's first program related investment (PRI) that will actually be paid back to the foundation to recycle funds back into the community in the future.

- **CALSO Social and Technology Accelerator:** 3M invested $91,000 in CALSO for the development of their technology accelerator in Austin, Texas. With this one-of-a-kind accelerator program in the Greater Austin area, CALSO will support technologically innovative startups developing products and services tackling social, environmental or other urban issues. By building a bridge between the technology and social entrepreneurship sectors, CALSO aims to foster technologically innovative solutions for social change. Austin has become one of the most innovative tech cities in the world, providing startups with a unique ecosystem to grow, scale and thrive. However, social entrepreneurs are lacking business support services - this missing link is particularly damaging as the need to develop affordable technologies to address social and environmental challenges is growing.

This new incubator will support seven social ventures for its first year through a yearlong program providing entrepreneurs with a co-working space, classes, workshops, events, mentorship and greater visibility. With this program, 3M aims to pioneer the social and tech revolution in Austin and contribute to designing a favorable local ecosystem for innovation and sustainability. 3Mgives believes that business can be a power for good and this is exemplified most clearly through social enterprises. This innovative investment focuses on developing technologies and social enterprises that can disrupt barriers to economic success and overall well-being for the world's most underserved communities.

- **3M Catalyst Leadership Way Partnership with PYXERA Global:** In 2015, 3M invested in the development of an innovative program with PYXERA Global to leverage the skills of 3M employees to effect social change on a global scale. Many NGOs and governmental organizations around the world have limited resources to focus on capacity development. To address this need and support great partners, 3M created the 3M Catalyst Leadership Way Community Project to utilize the best of what the company has to offer—its people! The 3M Catalyst program provides the opportunity for teams of 3M senior executives to engage their professional skills to support the operations of global NGOs operating in the access to water and water quality sector. Participating volunteers are divided into two teams of 10 for three-week engagements in each location. Each team will be further sub-divided into teams of 3-4 to support a single organization on a demand-driven capacity building project. The initial project is set in Mumbai and Chennai, India in April, 2016. Prior to their international assignments, participating 3M volunteers undergo six weeks of virtual pre-work.

The main goal of this partnership is to leverage the specialized skills of 3M leaders to improve the operational capacity of community organizations. As far as social impact, 3Mgives strives to enable select 3M executives to empower non-profit organizations to report improved operational capacity – enabling these organizations to improve more lives in a meaningful way. In commitment to improving every company, every home, and every life, the 3M Catalyst Leadership Way Community Project is developed to provide leading3M employees with an applied immersive leadership development experience to expand their global mindset. Participants will have the opportunity to work with local communities to build capacity and provide innovative solutions to improve lives.

This investment enables 3M to enhance employee engagement globally by empowering 3M employees to support underserved individuals in Chennai and Mumbai, India. In addition to the tremendous social value, 3M senior executives will get valuable experience, including the following benefits:

- Further develop leadership behaviors.
- Navigate uncertainty, complexity, and ambiguity.
- Expand cultural awareness.
- Develop sophistication in local relations and regulations.
- Observe, interact, & partner with local NGOs / governments.
- Increase global perspectives in a developing market.
- Lead and engage in a multicultural environment.

Taking Action: Respecting Human Rights

A respect for the rights of all humans across the globe guides everything 3M does. The people in 3M believe what the company stands for is just as important as what they sell. For 113 years, 3M has built a reputation for integrity and doing business the right way. 3M expects all employees to act ethically, honor human rights and sustain and advance 3M's global reputation. While 3M has subsidiary operations in more than 70 countries, the company has one Code of Conduct that applies everywhere 3M does business. The Code establishes a consistent standard of conduct for every employee and helps define the ethical decision-making 3M expects its employees to make every day.

3M is committed to respecting human rights in its own operations and in its supply chain. 3M's Global Human Rights Policy Statement was adopted in 2013, and 3M became a member of the U.N. Global Compact (UNGC) in early 2014, thereby committing to align 3M operations and strategies with the UNGC principles on human rights. 3M Global Human Rights Policy Statement includes the following elements: safe and healthy workplace, respectful workplace, workplace security, work hours and wages, freedom of association, child labor, and forced labor.

Within its own business, 3M's approach for managing and ensuring human rights aligns with 3M's Code of Conduct, which recognizes the right of employees to have a respectful workplace. 3M continues to implement its human rights program through its global policy statements, a management system utilizing self-assessments, audits, training, and ultimately, metrics tracking. 3M Code of Conduct Principles are comprehensive, clear, consistent, well-communicated and available to all employees. The Code helps employees and others acting on 3M's behalf take a consistent, global approach to understanding and following fundamental compliance requirements. 3M employees, including supervisors, managers and other leaders, are responsible for understanding the legal and policy requirements that apply to their jobs and, unless prohibited by local law, for reporting any suspected violations of law or these policies.

Upholding 3M's Code of Conduct and values is the responsibility of everyone acting on 3M's behalf. 3M recognizes that reporting suspected misconduct and human rights violations takes courage. 3M employees are encouraged to raise questions or report misconduct or potential misconduct to management, 3M Legal Counsel, the Compliance and Business Conduct Department, their human resources manager, or to 3M-Ethics.com.

In addition, 3M's existing Supply Chain Policies and Next Generation Supplier Responsibility Code set supplier standards and expectations in the areas of environmental, health and safety, transportation, labor, and human resources and supplied materials. The sourcing policies apply to the selection and retention of all suppliers that provide goods or services to3M worldwide.

3M has a global framework around management systems to look at its internal practices and assess human rights violations. 3M internal audit process is truly global, and they are increasing the number of assessments they are performing. This provides 3M with a global perspective on its own internal locations, particularly its manufacturing locations. 3M has now completed a full cycle of internal assessments for all manufacturing locations in Asia. 3M has also done assessments in Latin America, Europe, and the Middle East.

3M support the UN Guiding Principles (UNGP) on Business and Human Rights. 3M human rights management system helps us implement the "protect, respect, remedy" framework. 3M also support the principles of due diligence outlined in the UNGP. And of course, 3M Code of Conduct requires compliance with all applicable laws and respect for internationally recognized human rights in all of its global operations.

3M also respect the ILO Declaration on Fundamental Principles and Rights at Work. Adopted in 1998, the Declaration commits Member States to respect and promote principles and rights in four categories, whether or not they have ratified the relevant Conventions. These categories are: freedom of association and the effective recognition of the right to collective bargaining, the elimination of forced or compulsory labor, the abolition of child labor and the elimination of discrimination in respect of employment and occupation.

Human Rights Elements

- **Safe and Healthy Workplace:** One of 3M's primary goals is to ensure that all employees are provided a safe and healthy workplace. 3M has environmental, health and safety policies and practices that comply with or, in many cases, exceed applicable laws and regulations.
- **Respectful Workplace:** 3M is committed to attracting and retaining a diverse workforce by creating the kind of inclusive work environment 3M employees want and can be proud of. 3M Equal Employment Opportunity (EEO) policies prohibit all forms of discrimination or harassment against applicants, employees, vendors, contractors or customers on the basis of race, color, creed, religion, sex, national origin, age, disability, veteran's status, pregnancy, genetic information, sexual orientation, marital status, citizenship status, status with regards to public assistance, gender identity/expression or any other reason prohibited by law. 3M affirmative action policies and programs are designed to ensure equal opportunities for qualified minorities, women, covered veterans and individuals with disabilities, and also to provide reasonable accommodation to individuals with disabilities.

- **Working Hours and Compensation:** 3M complies with minimum wage legislation globally. In most countries where 3M does business, its compensation exceeds legal minimum wage requirements.3M competitive compensation reflects its practice of establishing competitive salary ranges based on actual pay data from benchmark peer companies. 3M also complies with all applicable laws relating to overtime and breaks.
- **Freedom of Association and Collective Bargaining:** 3M works diligently to create culture that affords all employees the opportunity to work without fear of intimidation, reprisal or harassment, in an environment where employees are able to get their questions addressed in a fair and timely manner. In all locations, the company's relationship with employees, whether union or nonunion, is a key responsibility of all leaders, assisted by human resources representatives. Human resources professionals work with all employees to maintain positive employee relations. 3M recognizes and respects the ability of employees to choose whether or not to join unions and engage in collective bargaining, as permitted by applicable laws in the countries where 3M does business. 3M has identified countries where collective bargaining rights may be at risk, and ensures 3M Human Rights Policies applies to all 3M employees worldwide. Approximately 29 percent of 3M's global workforce is unionized.

3M Human Rights Policy Statement has a specific subdivision on the freedom of association, which ensures that we respect "the ability of employees to choose whether or not to join unions and engage in collective bargaining, as permitted by applicable laws in the countries where 3M does business."

3M is a signatory to the UN Global Compact, which also covers the freedom of association. UN Global Compact Principle 3 states that "businesses should uphold the freedom of association and the effective recognition of the right to collective bargaining." It is of the utmost importance that 3M has a good working relationship with its employees, and 3M spends a lot of time training its leadership to ensure that they foster a positive environment.

3M follows all applicable local laws and regulations regarding notice periods in the event of business operations for both union and non-union employee's changes. 3M's Respectful Workplace Principle states that "everyone is entitled to respectful treatment in the 3M workplace. Being respectful means being treated honestly and professionally, with each person's unique talents, background and perspectives valued. A respectful workplace is free from unlawful discrimination and harassment, but it involves more than compliance with the law. It is a work environment that is free of inappropriate or unprofessional behavior and consistent with 3M's ethics and values - a place where employees can all do their best, and where employees are free to report workplace concerns without fear of retaliation or reprisal." Consistent with major international standards, 3M has similar principles that prohibit the use of forced or bonded labor, and the employment of children under age 16.

As previously mentioned, 3M respects the ILO Declaration on Fundamental Principles and Rights at Work, committing Member States to respect and promote principles and rights in the following four categories; freedom of association and the effective recognition of the right to collective bargaining, the elimination of forced or compulsory labor, the abolition of child labor and the elimination of discrimination in respect of employment and occupation.

- **Child Labor/ Minimum Hiring Age:** 3M complies with all applicable laws relating to hiring minors and applies a global minimum hiring age of 16 even where the law allows hiring workers younger than 16. 3M has those same expectations for all vendors doing business with us.
- **Forced and Compulsory Labor or Human Trafficking:** 3M complies with all applicable laws and employment regulations and does not engage or participate in forced labor. 3M has those same expectations for all vendors doing business with us.

Human Rights Awareness and Training

3M makes available multiple internal resources to which employees may raise their concerns and have them heard and addressed as needed. In most cases, the most effective channel is the employee's supervisor or manager or the assigned human resources or employee relations manager. Employees who are unsure of the identity of their assigned HR/ER manager can reference Identifying Your Human Resources Contact on 3M Source or, alternatively, may report concerns through HR Help. Employees with concerns directly related to 3M's Business Conduct Policies may report concerns electronically or telephonically through 3M-Ethics. HR Help and 3MEthicsPoint accept reports from anonymous callers (as permitted by local law), as well as callers who wish to self-identify. See 3M's Business Conduct policies for more information regarding how to report a concern.

To ensure that employees are aware of 3M policies related to human rights, 3M provides regular training to employees regarding our Business Conduct Policies, including 3M's Respectful Workplace Principle. Employee training regarding our Respectful Workplace Principle includes training on 3M's Human Rights Policy and 3M's commitment to human rights. Current training includes direction on how employees can raise issues for investigation and response. All 3M locations also post information on how employees can report any concerns. The enhanced training will be rolled out to all employees globally, except for production employees outside the U.S. because of translation barriers. 3M will work toward providing training to that population as well in the future. Finally, 3M's website also has information on corporate policies, as well as links and additional information on how to report any concerns.

Human Rights Performance and Assessment

3M's employee relations staff conducts site self-assessments of workplace practices on a biannual basis, which include review of practices related to 3M's Human Rights Policy to ensure that practices are consistent with and reinforce that policy. Various data is tracked through the process to identify potential gaps and opportunities for improvement. To date, approximately 70% of sites have been assessed including self-assessments implemented in 3M operations in the United States, Canada, Latin America, Asia and Europe. In addition, corporate audits are conducted of site workplace and human resource practices. Assessment and auditing of suppliers is also conducted to assure compliance with 3M's expectations related to labor practices. To the best of 3M knowledge, there were no incidents related to the rights of indigenous people in 2015.

3M performs global training to ensure that all 3M employees comply with the law, 3M's Code of Conduct and supporting policies, standards and procedures. 3M Compliance & Business Conduct (C&BC) has created a Compliance Training and Certification Program that ensures all 3M employees are aware of and understand their responsibilities and obligations. C&BC is responsible for the management and administration of the Compliance Training and Certification Program.

3M Global New Employee Compliance Course Program is based on the employee records in the 3M HR system. Employees are assigned courses based on their job function, country location, production/non-production, and supervisor/non-supervisor status. Email notifications are sent to the employee's 3M internet email address informing them of their course requirements and timeline for completion. The new employee courses are due within 60 days of assignment. The "Compliance & Business Conduct Overview" online course is hosted in the Corporate Learning System (LSO). Once the course has been assigned, the new employee can access it from their "My Training Activities" page in LSO. The remaining new employee online compliance courses are hosted on the C&BC Compliance Course site.

Taking Action: Public Policy

3M lives its values and corporate vision through its public policy pursuits. As a diverse global company, developing 3M public policy priorities can be a challenge. 3M manages this by working with local, national and international government agencies and through membership organizations. The public policy issues on which 3M engages extend beyond borders to include promoting international trade, sustainability, respect for intellectual property rights, public health, worker safety, security and international law, and innovation.

In a fast-moving global environment, 3M's public policy values remain consistent even as they address the unique needs of the national, regional and local governments in locations where we operate. 3M reinforces its corporate vision and principles, but they continually identify and re-evaluate their global public policy priorities to address changing circumstances. For example, in the United States, an evaluation process developed by the 3M Government Affairs Department establishes a public policy agenda of issues impacting our businesses. Public policy teams develop a Top 10 list (see below) of Priority Public Policy Issues that serves as a road map for all forms of engagement with federal, state and local governments. Chief among these screens used in determining the Top-10 list are issues with the potential to significantly affect 3M's financial performance and/or 3M corporate reputation. Other screens are the immediacy of impact on the company; situations in which 3M may be uniquely advantaged or disadvantaged; importance based on instinct and/or history; or employee/retiree satisfaction.

Besides linking 3M's vision to the needs and priorities of government officials, the Top 10 list helps ensure the many faces of 3M speak with a single, unified voice. Internationally, 3M managing directors of host country businesses are responsible for evaluating and determining key government issues globally in their respective countries.

3M U.S. Priority Public Policy Issues include:

1. **Tax Policy:** Tax reform is essential to ensuring the long-term competitiveness of American businesses and workers. 3M believes business tax reform should focus on a significant reduction of the corporate income tax rate, transitioning to a competitive international system, and ensuring incentives for U.S.-based IP ownership. In addition, state tax policy should incentivize capital investment and sustainable job creation by rewarding plant expansion and modernization investments, and efforts to increase employment.
2. **Homeland Security/Defense:** 3M believes the nation's homeland security and defense preparedness should be strengthened through improved border and immigration security, improved force protection measures, additional support for first responders, and planning for pandemics or other national emergencies.

3. **Sustainability/Environmental Policy:** 3M's strategies for sustainable development encompass the pursuit of customer satisfaction and commercial success within a framework of environmental, social and economic values. 3M continues to make significant investments to reduce the environmental footprint of its operations; and its sustainable products help customers reduce their environmental footprint and help to meet their sustainability goals. Finally, 3M believes environmental policy and regulations should be guided by science-based decision making.
4. **Patent Protection/Legal Reform:** 3M believes in strongly supporting patent rights for innovators and patent holders across this nation and globally. 3M support efforts to enhance the resources and capabilities of the United States Patent and Trademark Office, improve the quality and transparency of the patenting process, and bring more balance, objectivity and predictability to patent infringement litigation. 3M support efforts, both in the U.S. and in patent offices and courts globally, to enhance the enforceability of patent rights against infringing activities (including bad faith claims of infringement) and the remedies available against infringement. The U.S. legal system is the most expensive in the world, driven often by lawsuit abuse. To ensure the legal justice system is fair, efficient and consistent, we support reforms making liability litigation more equitable, subjecting punitive damages to reasonable caps, and ending destructive practices like indiscriminate screening, venue shopping and case bundling. Such reforms can be achieved while ensuring that those injured by faulty products receive fair compensation proportionate to the injury of the claimant and the fault of the defendant.
5. **Cyber Security Policy:** Because of 3M's commitment to protecting the privacy of personally identifiable data and ensuring business continuity, the company supports legislative efforts that will protect the nation from cyber threats. Recognizing no institution has the resources to respond to global threats or vulnerabilities on its own, 3M supports efforts to facilitate information sharing on cyber threats, coupled with reasonable liability and privacy protections. Data privacy initiatives must recognize that business needs to maintain flexibility to compete in the global economy, and that costly and burdensome regulations will negate the effectiveness of any such activities.
6. **International Trade Policy:** The U.S. economy and American jobs depend on the expansion of free and fair trade through the passage of new trade agreements. 3M supports the Trans-Pacific Partnership and the Trans-Atlantic Trade and Investment Partnership. International trade policy also requires a level playing field, including recognition, protection, and enforcement of intellectual property rights and trading rules.
7. **Health Care Policy:** The U.S. health system should remain market-driven and not weaken the current employer-based coverage system. Within payment programs, reforms should focus on increasing efficiencies within the system as well as improving quality outcomes and patient safety in the areas of complications, readmissions, ER visits, and more.
8. **Regulatory Reform and Economic Development Policy:** The U.S. regulatory environment plays a vital role in advancing the nation's economic security interests. To promote genuine competition, regulatory reforms must include thorough cost-benefit and risk assessments, while preserving the highest standards for safety, quality and efficiency. State government economic development incentive programs are important to 3M's U.S. plants expansion efforts. In particular, tax incentive programs advance competitiveness at a time when there's strong competition among plants for 3M's CapEx dollars; as well, state workforce training programs are important to sustainable job creation.

9. **Energy Policy:** National (and state) energy policy should ensure a continuous, reliable and uninterrupted supply of energy at competitive rates. 3M supports policies that address new sources of energy, alternative energy, faster adoption of technology and improved energy efficiency.
10. **Transportation Infrastructure Policy:** The maintenance and improvement of the nation's transportation infrastructure – which is important to 3M as a supplier of traffic safety and construction products, and as a user of the system – can only be achieved if the Highway Trust Fund remains solvent. 3M believes all highway user fees should be dedicated to the fund.

GLOBAL CHALLENGES

At 3M, people look at sustainability in terms of shared global needs and the future of the business. As the population grows, particularly in emerging economies, challenges like energy availability and security, raw material scarcity, human health and safety, education, and development must be addressed to ensure people across the globe can lead healthy, fulfilling lives. 3M recognizes that its impact includes that of its own operations as well as the far greater impacts 3M can make through its efforts in local communities and for its customers through the products 3M offers.

- **Raw Materials:** The world's population is growing larger, living longer — and consuming more. With this increased pressure on our finite natural resources and materials, we must move beyond low-cost, recyclable materials to renewable products. Companies that address this issue not only help the planet, but they also gain a competitive advantage in the marketplace. 3M has worked on this challenge for decades and will continue to innovate into the future, developing renewable alternatives for impacted resources, revolutionizing recyclable materials and becoming more sustainable.
- **Education and Development:** Global unemployment rates are expected to remain steady through 2017, particularly among youth. Today's job market has fewer opportunities, with most available jobs too specialized for young people and recent graduates. As a technology company, 3M recognizes the importance of well-trained science, technology, engineering and math (STEM) graduates — 3M needs young minds to step into specialized roles and help the company solve future challenges.
- **Water:** People consume it, farm with it and manufacture products with it. Reducing water consumption and improving water quality are important elements of environmental stewardship. Water is our world's most valuable natural resource. Despite water's prevalence, freshwater makes up only 2.5% of our total global water supply. A majority of freshwater is used for irrigation purposes, but nearly 30% of it is used for domestic consumption and industrial functions. Aging infrastructure and increased demand places a premium on clean, accessible water for 3M, its customers and communities around the world. Some of 3M customers are finding it difficult to source or deliver clean, accessible water. 3M can help them solve this problem by developing technology that increases water efficiencies and improves quality.
- **Energy and Climate:** Access to a dependable energy supply directly affects all businesses and communities. Energy usage and climate concerns require systematic change, and we're here to drive that forward. From air emissions to fossil fuels, 3M takes a proactive and collaborative approach to addressing energy demand and climate change — in its operations and for its customers.

3M partners with its customers to understand their needs and address those needs. The issues around effective use of energy resources and climate change are complex and interconnected. At 3M, people are focused on seeking solutions that promote energy conservation, clean energy infrastructure, and reductions in greenhouse gas emissions. 3M already has several products and technologies that reduce the impact of energy use, promote energy efficiency, and help customers reduce their greenhouse gas emissions. 3M goal is to continue developing and implementing global concepts for the greatest long-term impact.

- **Health and Safety:** Global health and safety issues are prevalent in workplaces around the world. Food poisoning and water-borne illnesses lead to the deaths of 3 million people across the globe each year. At the same time, approximately one of every 20 hospitalized patients in low and middle-income countries will contract an infection while under medical care.

Governments, corporations and consumers are driving global demand for safety, protection, healthcare and food safety solutions. Creative innovation, technology, education and collaboration are all critical if we are to tackle the human health and workplace safety concerns. For decades, 3M has had entire business divisions focused on creating products and services for human health, protection, security and safety. At the same time, the company has embraced this commitment in its own operations.

Global Challenges: Raw Materials

The world's population is growing larger, living longer — and consuming more. With this increased pressure on our finite natural resources and materials, we must move beyond low-cost, recyclable materials to renewable products. As competition for nonrenewable materials increases, companies and people have been forced to become smarter and more efficient about resources when designing product lifecycles. To keep pace with today's technology, consumers are upgrading devices at a faster pace and creating a greater need for raw materials to manufacture those products. This puts a strain on the world's resources, and companies that address this issue not only help the planet, but they also gain a competitive advantage in the marketplace. Raw materials are not only used in the production of manufactured goods, but they are also used in a variety of processes and applications. Material diversity and availability based on shifts in supply and demand impact technological, operational and geographic developments across the global economy. Raw material scarcity implies that long-term global demand will exceed world supply.

Efficiencies in product design, and consideration or recovery of alternative material streams are just a few potential solutions that we use to address material shortages impacting 3M's global supply chains. Close cross-functional collaboration is key to strategically unlocking new, improved and unique partnerships.

Maximizing Raw Material Usage

Raw material usage is a measurement of overall product and process yield throughout our manufacturing processes and is a key metric for 3M. It's indicative of operational excellence in our product design and manufacturing processes. 3M raw material usage formula quantifies product output versus "all outputs." All outputs includes everything from the product, the process, and all by-products.

The diversity of manufacturing technologies, processes and products at 3M provides opportunities for creative waste usage solutions for the company. Accurate waste identification is a continuous education process and provides a foundational opportunity to further advance waste minimization and recycling at all 3M locations. One business's by-product may connect as another business's raw material. As 3M continues to grow internationally, integrating consistent, yet resourceful, waste management practices in accordance to 3M standards remains a key objective.

As such, 3M continuously looks for ways to recover, reuse and recycle by-products and other waste material when feasible. And when it's not usable, 3M responsibly disposes of waste materials. The concept of maximizing raw material usage is important both internally and externally to address the global challenge of resource efficiency and scarcity. Improving 3M raw material usage through product design and operational considerations provides cost benefits throughout its supply chain in material use, energy and transportation efficiency.

Waste from manufacturing sites accounts for the majority of waste in 3M's environmental footprint. 3M's waste metrics include 3M manufacturing operations with total output greater than 4.536 metric tons per year, which represents 97 percent of Sales Value of Production (SVOP) of 3M manufacturing sites.

Optimizing Efficiencies in Operational Waste and Recycling

3M's Waste Management Standard applies to all 3M locations and provides a framework for managing all waste types from the time of generation until reused, recycled, treated or disposed. The standard sets a baseline for several core waste program elements and encourages waste minimization and recycling whenever possible. Per the standard, each location assigns a waste management coordinator who is responsible for ensuring that personnel receive applicable waste training. Compliance with all 3M and other regulated waste requirements is evaluated through the internal environmental auditing program.

3M Corporate Environmental Operations identifies and measures efficiency improvement progress toward raw material usage and waste reduction for sites within our global manufacturing footprint. The results and raw data are used to identify, quantify and prioritize projects to improve utilizing Lean Six Sigma Continuous Improvement methodology. Results are reviewed quarterly and annually within regions, businesses and divisions against goals and tracking metrics. Specialized teams within the organization

Figure 4. US engineering historical sustainability trend
(Package Design Waste Reduction in Metric Ton)

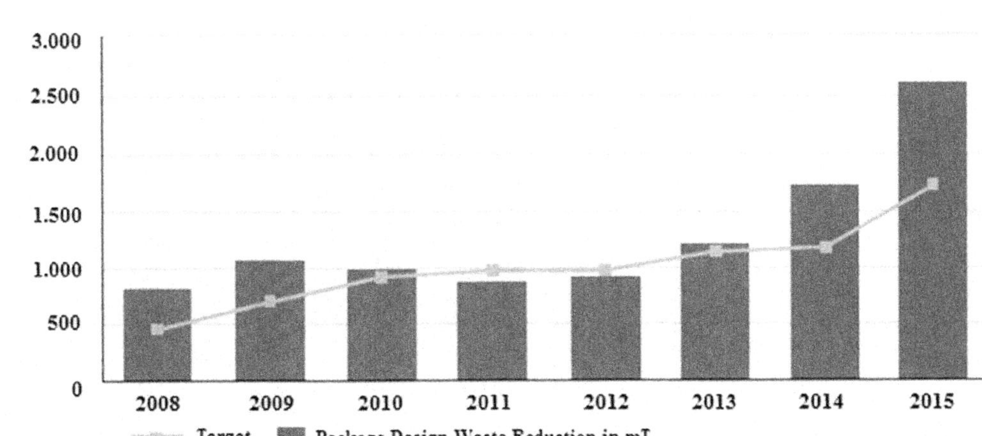

work on a variety of projects and programs, ranging from basic office recycling to more complex projects such as developing and capturing intrinsic waste materials generated off a manufacturing line. Through an evaluation process, all aspects of waste reduction benefits or risk are reviewed.

Some programs have initiated and implemented excellent reuse programs, which are then shared as a best practice throughout the organization for replication. 3M continues to work with customers and manufacturing partners to manage or develop recycling programs to continue to support our community commitment to sustainability.

Many of these specialized projects are a part of 3M's Pollution Prevention Pays (3P) program, which celebrated its 40th anniversary in 2015. Over the last 40 years, the program has prevented over 2.1 million tons of pollutants and saved nearly $2 billion (USD) based on aggregated data from the first year of each 3P project.

In addition to optimizing efficiencies in operational waste and recycling, 3M continues our long-standing commitments to efficient paper and packaging use. 3M has reduced designed packaging weight for eight straight years, for a cumulative reduction of more than 12,000 metric tons (mT). More than half of that reduction (~5,000 mT) was in paper-based packaging. Until last year, 3M only gathered this information in the United States but have since expanded data collection globally.

- **Hazardous Waste:** 3M practices waste minimization whenever practical to reduce the amount and hazards of waste materials generated. Between 2010 and 2015 there has been a 13% reduction in absolute hazardous waste as a percent of total waste. 3M is also dedicated to operating in accordance with all regulations and managing waste materials safely and responsibly. All 3M locations are required to manage all returned, recycled, and waste materials from the time of generation until reused, recycled, treated, or disposed.

When 3M transports hazardous waste, it's for treatment purposes. 3M waste disposal policy requires 3M to evaluate the best possible disposal methods while reducing all potential liabilities.

Figure 5. 3P Global Pollution Achievements: 1975- 2015
First Year Savings Cumulative Totals (Tons)

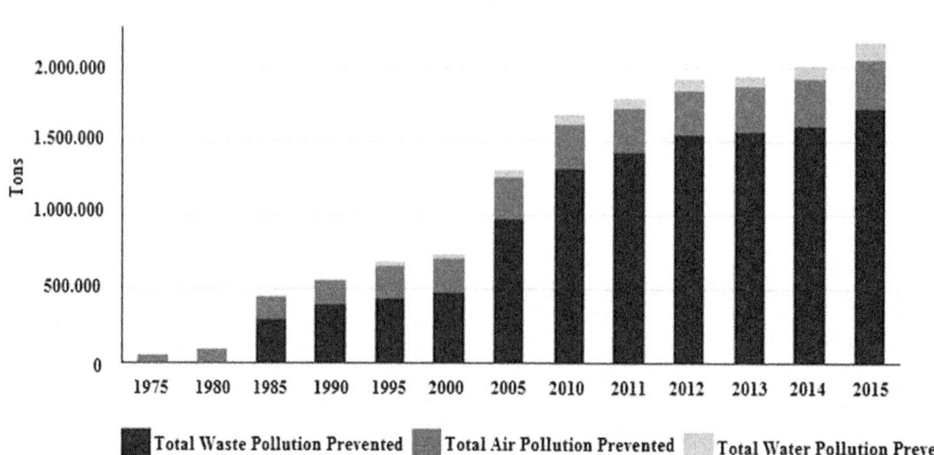

Air Quality Management

An important component to 3M's sustainability strategy is its commitment to improving air quality globally. Air emissions from 3M operations include volatile organics, particulates and substances listed on the U.S. EPA Toxic Release Inventory or global equivalent.

As a company with many solvent-based products, 3M inherently generates volatile organic compounds (VOCs) in many of our manufacturing processes. Emissions of VOCs at many of 3M manufacturing facilities require permits with rigorous tracking requirements. Even where tracking is not required from a regulatory perspective, 3M's manufacturing principles require accurate information on its major sources of emissions to understand the level of emissions and to identify opportunities for reductions. 3M has developed internal programs to minimize its emissions. For these reasons, 3M tracks and reports VOC emissions based on raw material usage and pollution control device utilization.

3M processes do not generate significant amounts of other criteria pollutant emissions (i.e., NOx, CO, SO2 and PM) when compared with many other industrial sectors and utilities and compared with 3M's VOC emissions. For many 3M manufacturing processes, NOx, SO2, CO and PM are created as an indirect by-product or are generated by combustion. In many locations, emissions of these pollutants have been determined to be below thresholds that would require permitting, tracking and reporting. Therefore, 3M has chosen to focus its air quality improvement efforts around tracking and reducing VOC emissions, for which 3M has been very successful.

With the increasing complexity of air quality regulations globally, reductions in actual air emissions and a solid air permit and regulatory approach are increasingly important components of global business growth and long-term sustainability. Air emission reductions are achieved through a variety of methods at 3M and include, but are not limited to, increasing the use of more sustainable raw materials and water-based coatings; improving process and equipment efficiency; upgrading equipment; and implementing and maintaining pollution control technologies. All reduction efforts are integral to the company's overall success and assist the company with the challenge of improving air quality in the areas in which 3M operates.

3M has made efforts to improve its maintenance activities for thermal oxidizers. Thermal oxidizers are the predominant device 3M utilizes for emissions. 3M efforts to reduce emissions through preventative maintenance are leading to real, positive changes. Further, 3M has begun efforts to update VOC standard to ensure a consistent approach throughout the globe.

Implementing and Maintaining Pollution Control

Although 3M has made significant progress in reducing air emissions from our operations through pollution prevention thinking (i.e., elimination at the source) and improving process efficiencies (e.g., Lean Six Sigma), 3M implements and maintains pollution control equipment when necessary. A variety of pollution control technologies are evaluated and utilized to control and reduce its air emissions. These include thermal oxidizers, bag houses, scrubbers and cyclones. 3M maintains rigorous preventative maintenance schedules to ensure proper operation and ongoing air pollution control effectiveness for VOCs, particulate matter and other air emissions. In the future, 3M is looking to expand the use of alternative control technologies to reduce energy and natural resource usage of pollution control equipment, while still providing required air pollution control efficiencies.

- **VOC Emissions:** 3M's commitment to managing and minimizing its volatile organic compound (VOC) emissions is demonstrated by continued results. 3M has had an external VOC emission reduction goal since 1990, resulting in 99 percent reduction in VOCs emitted indexed to net sales. 3M's results have been driven by plant activities, control device installation and lab reformulations.
- **Ozone Depleting Substances:** In order to protect the ozone layer, 3M prohibits the use of highly ozone depleting substances (i.e. Class I ODSs – ozone depleting substances) from all products and manufacturing processes (including raw materials, intermediates, and process aids) worldwide. Hydrochorofluorocarbons (HCFCs), a class of ODSs with lower ozone depleting potential, are in the process of being phased out by regulation. These compounds are referred to as Class II substances in the US Clean Air Act, and as Annex C controlled Substances in the Montreal Protocol. Any use of HCFC (i.e. Class II ODSs) must be thoroughly evaluated via a life cycle management review during the concept phase of new product or process development.

Figure 6. Total Volatile Organic Compounds (VOCs)
(Absolute Metric Tons)

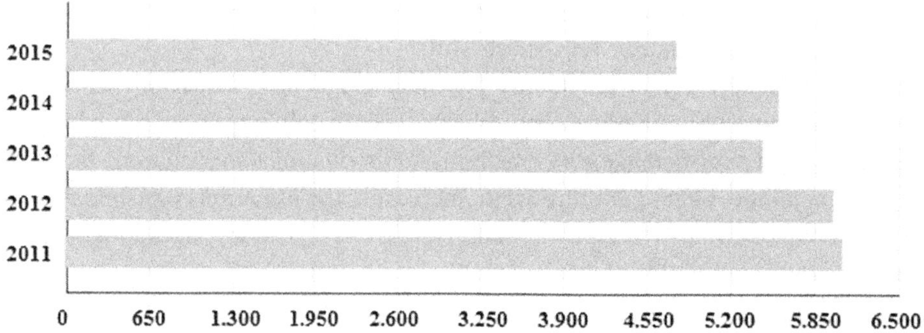

Figure 7. Total Volatile Organic Compounds Emissions Indexed to Net Sales
(Metric Tons/Million USD)

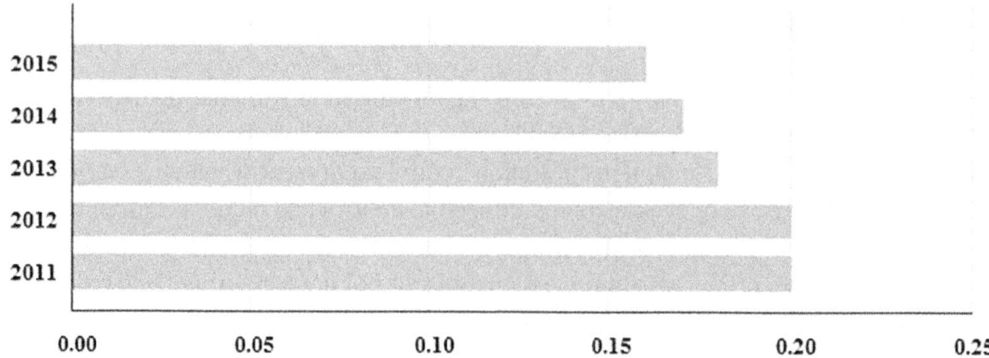

Waste Management

Waste management and minimization is an important component of 3M's environmental stewardship. The 3M Environmental Operations and Resource Recovery organizations provide corporate oversight for global waste management activities. 3M's Waste Management Standard applies to all locations and provides the framework and corporate expectations that are required to manage all waste types from the time of generation until reused, recycled, treated, or disposed. The Standard sets a baseline for several core waste program elements and encourages waste minimization and recycling whenever possible.

3M works closely with the Lean Six Sigma organization to increase waste reduction across all locations. 3M waste reduction indexed to production volume has decreased nearly 5% since 2010. Over 50% of 3M manufacturing plants met their waste reduction goal, and outside of a few isolated incidents, 3M has performed very strongly in terms of waste reduction.

3M did not meet its 2015 waste reduction goal. 3M waste reduction goal was based on 3M total waste indexed to net sales. Roughly two-thirds of 3M's sales are made in foreign currencies but all are reported in U.S. Dollars. When the dollar strengthens, as it has been doing for the past several quarters, it has a

Figure 8. Waste Recycling by Type
(Metric Tons)

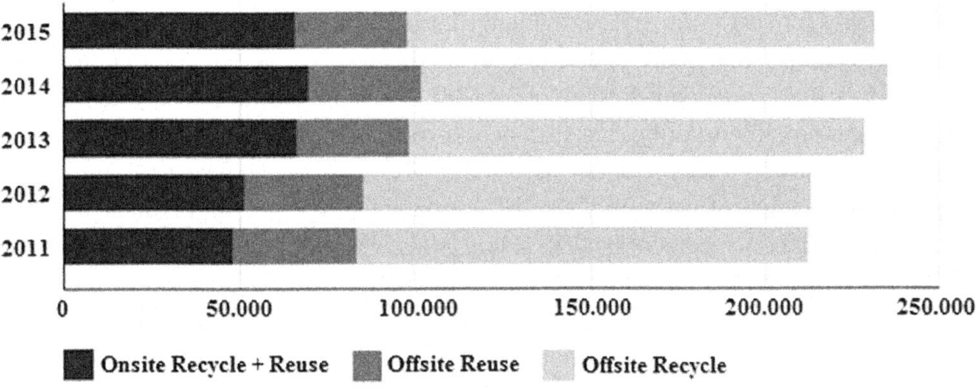

Figure 9. Total Waste Indexed to Net Sales
(Metric Tons/Net Sales Million $USD)

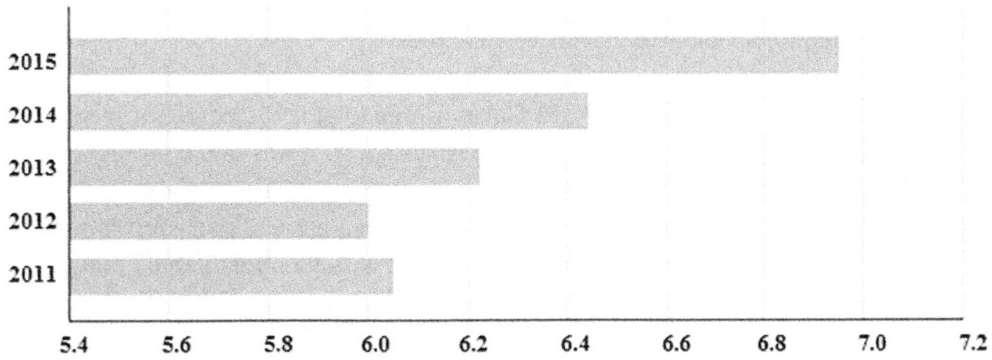

Figure 10. Total Absolute Wastes by Disposal Type
(Non Hazardous and Hazardous-Metric Tons)

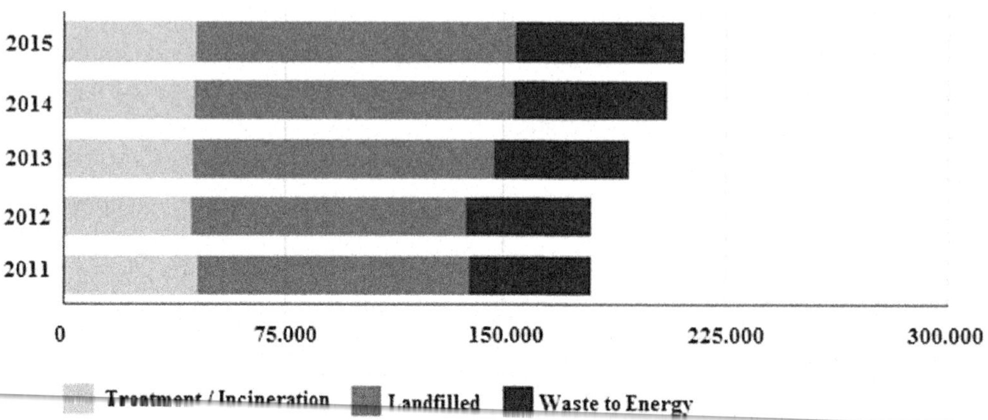

negative impact on 3M reported sales. This then negatively impacts 3M ability to meet its stated waste reduction goal. Other negative impacts include market changes in recycling and recent acquisitions that improved 3M's overall viability as a business.

3M's increase in the production of composite materials such as multilayered films, which provide significant advantages for customers, pose a challenge in the ability to recycle the material using current technologies. 3M continues to explore options for recyclability.

3M also aims to achieve zero landfill status at 30% of our manufacturing sites. Note that zero landfill is not always the best possible solution. For instance, if waste is being transported many miles for processing rather than landfill, this may result in large amounts of waste in the form of emissions. 3Mstrives to encourage the elimination of waste in the most responsible, efficient, and ethical way possible. In addition to its waste reduction and zero landfill status goals, 3M plans to increase repurposing, reusing and recycling of potential waste materials to divert from landfill disposal.

3M Lean Six Sigma program and Pollution Prevention Pays (3P) program are examples of programs that significantly contribute to waste reduction progress. Many successful waste projects under these programs are replicated to varying levels in other facilities. Although 3M continues to gain benefit by continuous improvement at its manufacturing facilities through incremental process improvements in waste reduction, its current and future direction for significant improvements in waste reduction are driven by product and process technology redesigns. These redesign efforts require prioritized focus, resources and collaboration within the business, sales, marketing, engineering and laboratory groups, in addition to the supply chain and manufacturing functions.

- **Protecting the Least Bell's Vireo AT3M Corona:** The least bell's vireo is a species of bird that was designated as federally endangered in1986. Historically, it was found throughout most of the state of California, largely in coastal regions. At the time of its designation 30 years ago, it was found in only 8 counties in Southern California.3M Corona has had a relationship with the Santa Ana Watershed Agency (SAWA) for over 15 years. SAWA monitors habitat and bird counts in the region. For several years, the 3M Corona property had a large number of nesting pairs return each year. Willows are a popular habitat for vireos, and the number of willows on 3M property has continued to increase over the years due to a habitat mitigation project in the late 1990s and early 2000s. In addition to the vireo, 3M Corona has lots of species that call 3M Corona home. Species include bobcats, mountain lions, mule deer, blue and white herons, red tail and Cooper's hawks, falcons, coyotes, rabbits, squirrels, and raccoons, hummingbirds, and a wide variety of exotic birds.

- **It's Time to Make Electronic Devices More Recyclable:** 3M's Thermal Bonding Films and Plastics Bonding Adhesives extend the potential lifespan of mobile devices and make it easier to recycle them. 3M electronics bonding solutions enable faster assembly times and simplify rework by helping manufacturers fix damaged parts and salvage key components.
- **So Much More Than a Floor Cloth:** Contributing to a clean home families can be proud of … and doing so with recycled materials and talented local weavers. Throughout the Indian culture, clean floors are a source of great pride. 3M researchers in India grew up there, and they wanted to create an effective cleaning product at an affordable price. They met with families in their homes to learn more. Then they returned to the lab and created a new kind of cloth with a unique scrubbing corner for tough stains. It was a first for India and a first for 3M; while the company generates 3,000 patents a year, this is 3M's first patent in India. The next challenge: how to make it affordable for families like the ones they visited? What if they could also make the product environmentally friendly … while creating desperately-needed jobs for rural Indians? The 3M team identified leftover threads from the nearby garment industry. Working with a nonprofit group, they found weavers that could recycle the threads into cloth. Producing locally not only put people to work; it also reduced transportation costs and emissions. The end result: an effective, affordable, sustainable product that is helping families, particularly women, with employment in rural areas of India, and with a better, more cost-effective, cleaning solution in urban areas.
- **3M Infection Prevention Solutions is Dedicated to Developing Sustainable Solutions:** To deliver on this promise, 3M challenged o to rethink its surgical drapes–to develop a drape that was better for the planet, for patients and for OR staff. Introducing the improved 3M™ Steri-Drape™ Surgical Drapes, now made with plant-based renewable resources, featuring the same high-quality properties that customers expect: strike-through-resistant barrier, strength, adhesion, drapeability and low linting, plus improved absorption and ease of application.3M™ Steri-Drape™ Surgical Drapes reduce the environmental impact of medical disposables by decreasing the use of fossil fuels and have less CO2 emitted over the product life cycle than our standard polypropylene surgical drape.

What's new:

- Nonwoven layer contains 95% renewable plant-based material.
- 62% of entire fabric made from renewable plant-based material.
- 18% fewer fossil fuel resources used throughout the product life cycle.
- 10% less CO2 emitted during the product life cycle.

3M is on a journey with its customers to develop ingenious, sustainable solutions that help address global healthcare challenges, while protecting the environment and promoting a healthier world.

Global Challenges: Water

People consume it, farm with it and manufacture products with it. Reducing water consumption and improving water quality are important elements of environmental stewardship. Water is the most valuable natural resource for life and thriving ecosystems; therefore, our planet's consumption must be nurtured and thoughtfully managed. 3M recognize that reducing water consumption in its operations and improving water quality are important elements of optimizing environmental stewardship. Quantitatively, the availability of water must meet the needs of current and future consumer demands. In addition, water quality must comply with local regulations and be reliable in the long term.

Water is an important component to the manufacturing and support systems of several of 3M products. Because of this, 3M continues to actively understand, manage and work toward reducing our corporate water footprint while providing innovative solutions to customers. 3M respects its ecological and ethical responsibility and have a vested interest in preserving and improving water availability and quality relative to its operations and the communities 3M serves.

3M's Water Management Standard provides a company-wide framework, including both general and specific elements for water management. The standard requires 3M operations to manage their water resources through understanding the balance of water use, compliance with regulatory requirements, systematic and prioritized conservation practices, and reporting usage. Water resources include water intake, effluent water discharge and rainwater.

To inventory, track and understand water use in 3M operations for improved efficiency, 3M sites are required to report water data quarterly into a corporate tracking system. Additional water source, use and discharge information is collected and provided through an annual assessment and survey process. Aggregated data is evaluated to determine the progress and identify opportunities for increased efficiency in higher-use focus areas.

Water discharges fall under 3M's Corporate Water Standards. 3M operations must manage their water resources through compliance with regulatory requirements, conservation and reuse, and reporting of water usage internally. For unplanned discharges, 3M utilizes WIMS (Worldwide Incident Management System) at its facilities. With regard to direct discharges, all of its facilities have specific internal goals.

3M Footprint

The water data provided below includes manufacturing sites that produce more than4.50 metric tons of product output and accounts for 97 percent of Sales Value of Production (SVOP) of 3M manufacturing sites.

3M 2025 goal is to reduce global water use by an additional 10% indexed to sales. Building upon its previous 40% reduction in water usage between 2005 and 2015 (indexed to sales), 3M will continue to improve in managing and conserving water across our global manufacturing footprint by driving water reduction and conservation process and technology changes within its operations. This is the first-time 3M has had a formal external water reduction goal. 3Mis currently expanding its internal systems to share best management practices in regards to water conservation.

Further understanding of where water is originally sourced for use in 3M operations provides insight into its potential impacts within local watersheds. In 2015, based on 3M's detailed water assessment and survey across sites, results indicate that 19 percent of water is sourced from public/municipal sources, 46 percent is sourced from private groundwater sources, 20 percent is sourced from private surface water sources, and the remaining 15 percent is from storm water, remediation activity and externally recycled sources. Results also indicate a majority of 3M water use in operations is for processing products in manufacturing and heating or cooling of those processes and associated operations. 3M estimates that approximately 26 percent of the total water used was also recycled or reused for secondary use within operations in 2015. 3M continues to improve its data accuracy through monitoring and measurement.

Water conservation efforts have been achieved through recycling, reuse, product redesigns and improvements to its buildings and manufacturing processes. A majority of 3M water-intense manufacturing operations are located in the U.S. and Europe, in areas that are not water-stressed or water-scarce. However, they also contribute significantly to 3M conservation efforts. As the company continues to grow globally, thoughtful consideration is placed on the type of operations and availability of water sources.

To inventory, track, and understand water use in its operations for improved efficiency, 3M sites are required to report water data quarterly into a corporate tracking system. Additional water source, use, and discharge information is collected and provided through an annual assessment and survey process.

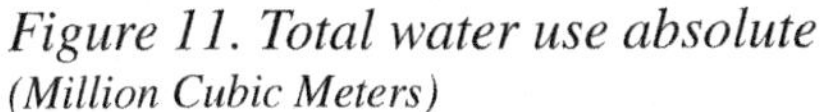
Figure 11. Total water use absolute
(Million Cubic Meters)

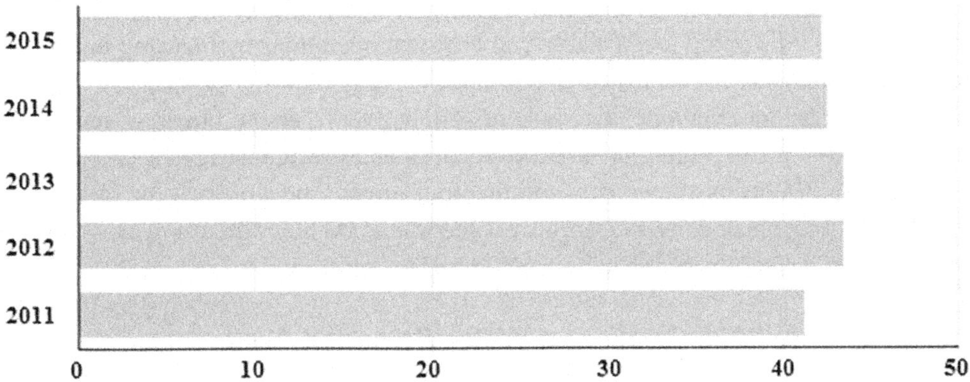

Figure 12. Total water use indexed
(Million Cubic Meters/Million USD)

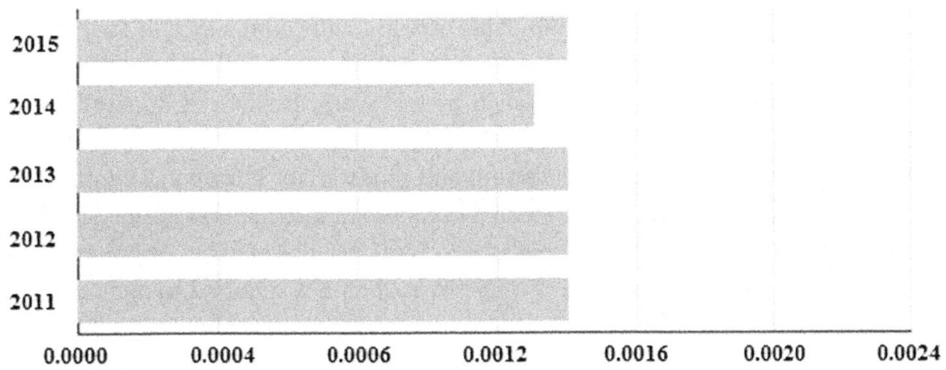

Aggregated data is evaluated to determine 3M progress and identify opportunities for increased efficiency in higher-use focus areas.

Reducing water use and improving water quality are important elements of environmental stewardship. Therefore, 3M continues to actively understand, manage, and work toward reducing its corporate water footprint. 3M's Water Management Standard provides a global framework including both general and specific elements for water management within the company. The standard requires 3M operations to manage its water resources through understanding its water use, compliance with regulatory requirements, systematic conservation and reuse, and reporting of water usage. Water resources include water intake, effluent water discharge, and rainwater.

In addition to corporate goals, internal goals have been developed on a divisional level. For instance, 3M's Materials Resource Division (MRD), a major internal material supplier, is the largest consumer of water resources at 67% of total 3M water resources consumed for the company in 2015. Therefore, 3M has focused on operational efficiencies corporate-wide with additional focused initiatives within MRD for water reduction. 3M's total water usage includes sanitary, process, heating, cooling, remediation, and other miscellaneous sources. Water usage data is tracked and reported annually on a global basis for manufacturing sites that produce greater than 10,000 pounds of product per year. The reporting data accounts for 97% of Sales Value of Production which provides solid coverage of water use considered material to 3M's operational environmental footprint. Overall total water consumption has decreased 40% between 2005 and 2015 indexed to total corporate wide net sales.

Moving forward, 3Mis proud to expand beyond its own operations by focusing more on supporting the sustainability goals and needs of the customers and the communities. For water, 3M goals are focused to promote clean water for everyone, everywhere so that every person, business and community has the water they need to thrive. Aging infrastructure and increased demand places a premium on clean, accessible water for 3M, its customers and communities around the world. Some of the customers are finding it difficult to source or deliver clean, accessible water. 3M helps them solve this problem through its technologies that increase water efficiencies and improve quality.

Goals and Results: 2025 Goals and Water-Stressed Areas

3M has initiated a 2025 goal to engage 100%of water-stressed/scarce communities where 3M manufacturing site uses over 1000 cubic meters of water annually. The intent is to use a community-wide approach to water management. 3Mis making great efforts in partnering with local communities to advance water recycling and conservation. Ultimately, 3M aims to help these communities build and manage their own efforts toward access to clean water into the future. 3Mis currently in the process of pilot projects with three sites to help meet 3M 2025 water goals. This is helping the company build a global framework to develop site community plans and benchmarking with outside corporations on community work.

3M uses the definitions and tools established by the World Business Council for Sustainable Development (WBCSD) to screen the company's various site locations and their affiliated water use with validated WBCSD water availability, population, and biodiversity information both on a country and watershed basis. 3M has identified 25 sites located in water-stressed areas as defined by the an Extremely High Baseline Water Stress (WBCSD-Global Water Tool) that use equal to or greater than 1,000 cubic meters annually. Each 3M site located in a water-stressed area is required to understand its water use, associated business risks and impacts and to work with local water resources to understand potential impacts on the surrounding area. Identified sites are also requested to do water conservation planning, outlining current and future water conservation efforts. Annual stress-level screening evaluations are conducted for global operations using available updates from the WBCSD Global Water Tool, an analysis of site operations and water usage and local conditions.

In 2015, 3M met its water goal of having water conservation plans at all in scope sites located in defined Water Scarce/Stressed Areas. Water conservation planning is a continuous improvement process. 3M continues to work with its sites to assist them in achieving their water conservation goals. With an eye on 3M footprint and the strength of its technologies and collaboration, the company acknowledges it can continue to make a difference in water availability and quality around the world.

Moving forward, 3Mis proud to expand beyond its own operations by focusing more on supporting the sustainability goals and needs of its customers and communities. While 3M recognizes the importance of what they do in their own operations, and will continue to improve accordingly, the company sees that far greater impact can be realized when it partners with others to understand and overcome the challenges we face. For water, the goal is to promote clean water for everyone, everywhere so that every person, business and community has the water they need to thrive.

- **Extracting Water From the Desert:** A team from Oxford University has successfully used 3M™ Novec™ Engineered Fluid in a pioneering field application to assess the quality of water in the Badain Jaran desert in North West China. This geochemical research will play a crucial role assessing the level of pollution from both agricultural and industrial sources in arid regions. It can also be used to monitor rainfall levels and groundwater recharge rates to identify areas likely to

Figure 13. Total global water use by source

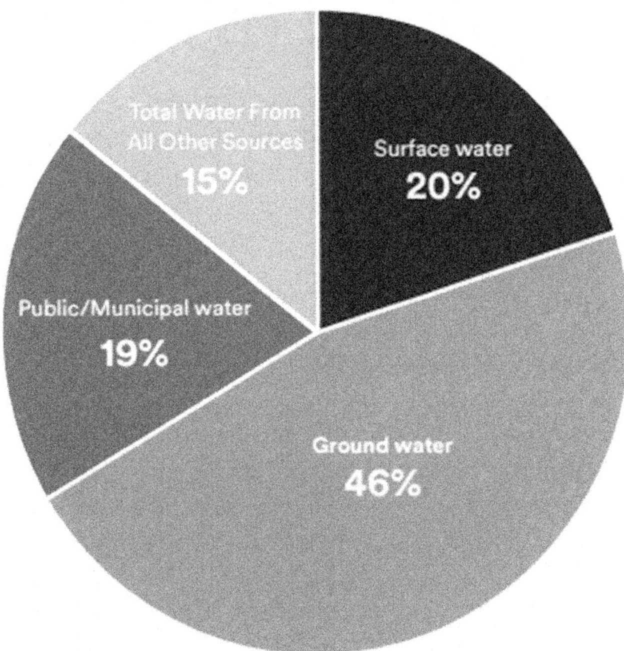

suffer from water shortages in the future. Extracting water from ground samples taken from dry regions is challenging due to the low moisture content, meaning that traditional drainage methods can't be used. A technique using an immiscible displacing fluid that was developed in the 1980s allowed small quantities of water to be recovered, but the chemical was banned a few years later under the Montreal protocol and no suitable alternative has been found until now. Novec has similar physical and chemical characteristics to the banned chemical, but has zero ozone depletion potential and a low global warming potential. The research project was led by the late Professor Mike Edmunds, an expert in groundwater quality, hydrogeo-chemical processes, trace element studies, isotope hydrology and palaeohydrology who taught on the Masters in Science course in Water Science, Policy and Management course at the University of Oxford. Published academic papers on both the use of 3M™ Novec™ HFE-7100 in the new extracting process and the Badain Jaran desert study were co-authored by the professor.

- **Sustainability and Hand Hygiene:** According to the World Health Organization (WHO) and U.S. Centers for Disease Control (CDC), hand hygiene is one of the most important ways to prevent the spread of infections and thereby contributes significantly to keeping patients safe. More than 1 million cases of health care-associated infection exist at any given time; and experts say microbes that can cause infection are most frequently spread between people through contact with unclean hands. 3M has come to the rescue, with 3M™ Avagard™ hand hygiene products that are fast and easy to use. 3M was the first to introduce a waterless, brushless surgical hand scrub designed especially for health care workers. This not only helps increase hand hygiene compliance, it also reduces water usage and material waste. Now 3Mhas gone the extra mile, making a hand soap that doesn't contain triclosan and using plant-based ethanol to make hand hygiene foams and gels more sustainable. 3M even earned the USDA Certified Biobased Product Label on its foam and gel products, verifying that the product's amount of renewable bio based ingredients meets or exceeds levels set by the agency. Sustainable patient safety. That cleans up nicely.

Global Challenges: Energy and Climate

Access to a dependable energy supply directly affects all businesses and communities. Energy usage and climate concerns require systematic change, and we're here to drive that forward.3M has a history of proactive leadership in addressing both the challenges and opportunities presented by climate change and energy conservation. 3M operates under the philosophy that early action is paramount to being a leader in this space, and its programs and results prove 3M success.

This proactive leadership can perhaps best be understood through five areas of action:

1. Executive-level commitment to these important topics and our related principles, commitments and risk-mitigation planning efforts
2. Industry-leading efforts to reduce 3M own greenhouse gas (GHG) emissions
3. Extensive public policy engagement on both climate change and energy conservation
4. A decades-long track record of improving energy efficiency at 3M facilities
5. Serving customers through a wide range of innovative products that help them improve energy efficiency and reduce their carbon footprint

3M Approach: Guiding Principles

For all years of its existence the 3M Greenhouse Gas (GHG) inventory has been generated based on the principles of relevance, completeness, consistency, transparency, and accuracy. The GHG inventory has been calculated from 2002 to the current year by the 3M Environmental Laboratory in accordance with the World Resources Institute (WRI)/World Business Council for Sustainable Development (WBCSD) GHG Protocol Corporate Greenhouse Gas Accounting and Reporting Standard. Additionally, since its promulgation, the inventory has been completed in accordance with the principles of the U.S. Environmental Protection Agency (EPA) Mandatory Reporting Rule (40 CFR 98). The 3MEnvironmental Laboratory maintains an accreditation to ANSI/ISO/IEC 17025 through A2LA, an ILAC MRA signatory, for a number of laboratory methods. Although it is not possible to put 3M's GHG inventory methodology on the lab's scope of accreditation, 3M calculation methodology has been improved by working under a number of the quality system elements required by ANSI/ISO/IEC 17025. Some key quality system elements that have helped improve 3M's GHG inventory include:

- Defined responsibilities and interrelationships of all key staff;
- Documentation of key personnel qualifications;
- Control over quality system documents and procedures;
- Control of records;
- Corrective and preventive action system;
- Internal audit program;
- Documented and approved calculation procedures.

These quality system elements coupled with third party review of 3M emissions have ensured that 3M's GHG inventory is always in line with the five core principles of: relevance, completeness, consistency, transparency, and accuracy.

- **Relevance:** The 3M Environmental Lab's GHG inventory procedures clearly define its boundaries as all GHG emissions from facilities over which 3M has operational control. All GHG emissions from facilities that are under 3M's operational control are included in 3M Scope 1 and 2 GHG inventory.
- **Completeness:** All GHG emissions from facilities that3M has operational control over are either calculated with the best data available or estimated with the most relevant estimation methods. Wherever possible primary data is used to calculate emissions, when primary data is not available, 3M will use appropriate estimations to calculate emissions. As such, because 3M strives to calculate and report all GHG emissions it is responsible for, its de minimis totals constitute less than 1% of the inventory.
- **Consistency:** Every year of the GHG inventory is calculated according to the same approved internal procedures. Additionally, internal audits are performed every year to ensure that the GHG inventory is calculated according to those procedures. Finally, whenever a methodology change is implemented, 3M will, wherever possible, recalculate prior year's GHG inventories to ensure that the GHG inventories are comparable. Where it is not possible 3M will either call this out or ensure that the difference is not material.

- **Transparency:** 3M strives to present all GHG inventory data in as transparent a manner as possible while protecting confidential business information and complying with applicable regulations.
- **Accuracy:** Every year, the accuracy of the numbers as well as the calculations that led to those numbers is thoroughly audited by an internal audit process executed by auditors that are not involved in the calculation of the GHG inventory. Final numbers are not released until the internal audit has been successfully completed and 3Mis confident in its GHG emissions inventory. Additionally, the 3M GHG inventory has been audited by three separate 3rd party auditors; twice by EPA Climate Leader's preferred verifier, CH2M Hill, once by Lucideon, an ANSI-accredited verifier, and once by Bureau Veritas, a CDP verification partner. To date, no material findings have ever been found in our GHG inventory results.
- **Executive Level Commitment:** Climate change and energy efficiency are issues of great importance throughout 3M up to the Corporate Operating Committee and CEO. Top-level executives have empowered the Corporate EHS Committee to take proactive steps and be responsible for all final decisions on climate change and energy strategy. This includes setting company reduction goals and policies.

In addition, for climate change strategy and GHG emission advice, the Corporate EHS Committee has appointed the corporate Climate Change Steering Team. Complementing the efforts of the Climate Change Steering Team, 3M's business continuity planning process and its crisis management program review help manage risks facing the company's physical operations and supply chains (e.g., severe weather events).

To address the issue of climate change, 3M has committed to the following:

- Develop and maintain an inventory of its Scope 1 and 2 GHG emissions;
- Continue to improve energy efficiency in manufacturing and administrative operations, including all aspects of direct and indirect use of fossil fuels;
- Manage GHG emissions to optimize reductions and cost benefits;
- As part of 3M 2025 Goals, increase renewable energy to 25 percent of total electricity use;
- Increase the use of energy efficiency products within 3M operations and encourage their use by 3M suppliers and customers;
- Incorporate an evaluation of environmental and energy impacts throughout the full product life cycle (from raw material acquisition through manufacturing, use and disposal) as part of the Company's Life Cycle Management assessment process;
- Invest in research and development to create new products and technology that will reduce the generation and emissions of GHG;
- Develop partnerships and participate in a positive dialogue with governmental agencies and other organizations engaged in tackling climate change.

Risk mitigation planning. Severe weather and long-term trends could affect 3M's operations and supply chain. To address these and other risks, 3M has developed and maintains a systematic Business Continuity and Planning Process and Crisis Management Program. To implement this process and respond to specific incidents, 3M's Corporate Crisis Management Program coordinates efforts of local crisis management teams maintained at each 3M facility and international subsidiary.

Corporate and local plans take into account natural disaster, infectious disease, employee safety, protection of assets, customer service and the business continuity requirements that may impact specific facilities and businesses. Every year, each local crisis management team must review and update its plan to reflect current conditions. It also performs a tabletop or actual crisis response exercise. 3M Corporate Auditing and Corporate Security monitor facility compliance with the Corporate Crisis Management Program.3M mitigates supply chain risks through a variety of management practices, including multi-sourcing raw materials, pre-qualification of potential outsource manufacturers, maintaining appropriate stocks of raw materials and contingency plans with key suppliers to ensure allocation to 3M in the event of supply disruption.

- **Reducing 3M GHG Emissions:** GHG emission reductions are achieved through a variety of methods at 3M and include, but are not limited to, increasing the use of more sustainable raw materials, improving process and equipment efficiency, upgrading equipment, reducing 3M demand for energy use, increasing its use of renewable energy, and implementing and maintaining pollution control technologies. All reduction efforts are integral to the company's overall success and assist the company with the challenge of addressing climate change. Further details regarding 3M GHG emission reduction achievements can be found in the Goals and Progress section that follows.
- **Public Policy Engagement:** 3M is actively engaged in public policy development to address climate change. One such important direct engagement is with the National Climate Coalition (NCC). 3M is a founding member of NCC, an organization committed to dialogue and policy development with decision-makers in the EPA and many state agencies throughout the U.S.
- **Environmental Investments**: 3M's manufacturing operations are affected by national, state and local environmental laws around the world. 3M has made, and plans to continue making, necessary expenditures for compliance with applicable laws. 3M is also involved in remediation actions relating to environmental matters from past operations at certain sites. Environmental Management System (EMS) framework provides structure and consistency for overseeing daily activities and shifting the environmental focus from reactive to proactive. Implementation of the EMS continues to increase throughout the world and realize reduced costs through operating efficiency, improved environmental compliance, reduced monitoring costs, reduced energy and waste disposal costs, and increased employee activity. 3M's EMS is also expanding its sustainability image around the globe, which has strong financial benefits.

3M approach calls for each site to establish, implement, and maintain documented environmental objectives and targets at relevant functions and levels within the organization. When establishing an EMS plan, each site is called on to consider financial, technological, operational, and business considerations. The objectives and targets should be measurable and consistent with 3M environmental policy, including its commitments to prevent pollution and be compliant with applicable regulations and other requirements to which 3M subscribes.

In 2015, 3M expended about $26 million for capital projects related to protecting the environment. This amount excludes expenditures for remediation actions relating to existing matters by past operations that do not contribute to current or future revenues, which are expensed. Capital expenditures for environmental purposes have included pollution control devices – such as wastewater treatment plant improvements, scrubbers, containment structures, solvent recovery units and thermal oxidizers – at new and existing facilities constructed or upgraded in the normal course of business. Consistent with the company's policies emphasizing environmental responsibility, capital expenditures (other than for remediation projects) for known projects are presently expected to be about $51 million over the next two years for new or expanded programs to build facilities or modify manufacturing processes to minimize waste and reduce emissions. While the company cannot predict with the certainty the future costs of such cleanup activities, capital expenditures or operating cost for environmental compliance, the company does not believe they will have a material effect on its capital expenditures, earnings, or competitive position.

- **Environmental Violations and Liabilities:** Since 2010, all 3M facilities globally are required to internally report environmental exceedances, spills, agency notices and fines through one dedicated system - 3M's Worldwide Incident Management System (WIMS). WIMS has led to continuous improvement related to increased awareness of responsibilities, understanding of the holistic system and more consistent reporting requirements for 3M's 200+ global operations. Further, 3M international auditing program is firmly in place and helps reduce various compliance risks. Each of 3M facilities are audited at least once every three years, and they are audited more frequently if they are determined to be of high risk.

As of December 31, 2015, 3M recorded liabilities of $43 million for estimated "environmental remediation" costs based upon an evaluation of currently available facts with respect to each individual site and also recorded related insurance receivables of $11 million. 3M records liabilities for remediation costs on an undiscounted basis when they are probable and reasonably estimable, generally no later than the completion of feasibility studies or 3M's commitment to a plan of action. Liabilities for estimated costs of environmental remediation, depending on the site, are based primarily upon internal or third-party environmental studies, and estimates as to the number, participation level and financial viability of any other potentially responsible parties, the extent of the contamination and the nature of required remedial actions. 3M adjusts recorded liabilities as further information develops or circumstances change. 3M expects that it will pay the amounts recorded over the periods of remediation for the applicable sites, currently ranging up to 20 years.

In 2015, 3M recorded liabilities of $35 million for "other environmental liabilities" based upon an evaluation of currently available facts to implement the Settlement Agreement and Consent Order with the Minnesota Pollution Control Agency, the remedial action agreement with Alabama Department of Environmental Management, and to address trace amounts of perfluorinated compounds in drinking water sources in the City of Oakdale, Minnesota, as well as presence in the soil and groundwater at the company's manufacturing facilities in Decatur, Alabama, and Cottage Grove, Minnesota, and at two former dispossites in Washington County, Minnesota (Oakdale and Woodbury). 3M expects that most of the spending will occur over the next four years. As of December 31, 2015, 3M's receivable for insurance recoveries related to "other environmental liabilities" was $15 million.

It is difficult to estimate the cost of environmental compliance and remediation given the uncertainties regarding the interpretation and enforcement of applicable environmental laws and regulations, the extent of environmental contamination and the existence of alternative cleanup methods. Developments may occur that could affect 3M's current assessment, including, but not limited to: (i) changes in the information available regarding the environmental impact of 3M's operations and products; (ii) changes in environmental regulations, changes in permissible levels of specific compounds in drinking water sources, or changes in enforcement theories and policies, including efforts to recover natural resource damages; (iii) new and evolving analytical and remediation techniques; (iv) success in allocating liability to other potentially responsible parties; and (v) the financial viability of other potentially responsible parties and third-party indemnitors.

Improving 3M Energy Efficiency

3M has identified a broad approach to managing its energy footprint, which includes evaluating the energy impact of new products and manufacturing processes being developed in its laboratories; new equipment and facilities being designed and built by its engineering staff; and reducing the energy footprint of its manufacturing and administrative facilities. In addition, 3M actively shares information about the energy management program with external stakeholders, such as suppliers, customers and other interested organizations. At 3M, energy management extends beyond energy efficiency efforts in factories and buildings. It is a team effort guided by the global Corporate Energy Policy.

Energy management responsibilities are coordinated by the Corporate Energy Management team, with oversight by 3M's Corporate Energy Manager and Engineering Vice President and with active support from the CEO. The team involves personnel from environmental operations, facility operations, finance, sourcing, engineering, energy management, corporate marketing and public affairs. Each department provides cross-functional contributions, ensuring that:

- Energy-efficient technologies are being used and opportunities are being identified in the design process.
- Renewable energy opportunities are identified and financed.
- Data is tracked routinely and consistently by facilities.

Innovative Products to Help 3M Customers Reduce Their GHG Emissions

Many products 3M brings to market help its customers reduce their GHG emissions. Additionally, 3M conducts product carbon footprint evaluations as part of the product Life Cycle Assessment process on select products and is engaged with key stakeholders to improve and refine common metrics for such analysis. One of the challenges in this area is the wide range of potential approaches and assumptions being used for such calculations. To address these issues, 3M supports further development of common metrics and is working with the World Resource Institute and World Business Council for Sustainable Development, peer companies, governments and environmental organizations. The goal of these efforts is to enable 3M and others to provide cost-effective, accurate and useful information to customers and other stakeholders.

Direct Greenhouse Gas Emissions (Scope 1)

Because overall 3M sales have been reduced as a result of global currency conversions and accounting issues, it is impacting 3M numbers. Fortunately, emissions are dropping and 3Mis hitting its internal milestones and goals. Since 2002, 3M has reduced Scope 1 GHG emission by 77.5%, and it has provided a direct and immediate benefit to the environment. This reduction is even more impressive when one considers it is an absolute reduction (e.g., it occurred even as the company grew sales and production during this timeframe).3M's 2015 Scope 1 emissions are 3,770,000 metric tons CO2e. This is a 14.1%

reduction compared against 4,390,000 metric tons CO2e for 2014. The total GHG Inventory encompasses the company's diversity and complexity. A total of approximately 600 facilities including R&D, manufacturing, distribution centers, and administrative support offices within 3M operational control are accounted for in the current inventory. The total inventory includes both Kyoto and Non-Kyoto classified gases. 3M tracks and reports both absolute and indexed to net sales emission data.

GHG emissions data for 2012-2015 used US EPA mandatory greenhouse gas reporting rule (GHG-MRR)/ Intergovernmental Panel on Climate Change (IPCC) 5th assessment report (AR5) based accounting methods and are not directly comparable to 2003-2011 GHG emissions data, which used WRI/IPCC 3rd and 4th assessment report (TAR, AR4) based GHG accounting methods. The 2012-2015 GHG Inventories are directly comparable. The 2002 emissions inventory was recalculated using US EPA GHG-MRR/ IPCC AR5 methodology to allow direct comparison.

Indirect Greenhouse Gas Emissions (Scope 2)

When 3M thinks about its customers, partners, and communities, and its mutual challenges and needs, it sees a shared opportunity. In addition to environmental challenges, 3M recognizes the connectedness of social challenges that we face in pursuing a better world. 3M ambition, working collaboratively, is to realize a world where every life is improved– where natural resources are reliably available, people everywhere have access to education and opportunity, and communities are safe, healthy, connected and thriving.

In 2015, 3M negotiated a 120MW wind power purchase agreement with Invenergy. Invenergy will provide 3M with renewable energy to help support our operations across North America. The agreement includes the sale of wind energy from the Gunsight Wind Energy Center located in Texas. Energy from the 120 MW project will be delivered into the Electric Reliability Council of Texas (ERCOT) regional electricity grid. This agreement is an important and significant step toward accomplishing 3M goal of increasing renewable energy to 25 percent of its total electricity use by 2025.3M's 2015 Scope 2 emissions are 1,860,000 metric tons CO2e. This is a 17.2% reduction compared against 2,240,000 metric tons CO2e for 2014. 3M continues to be a leader in achieving greenhouse gas (GHG) emission reductions.

3M believes it is paramount that its industry-leading GHG emission reductions achieved to date are duly taken into consideration when evaluating the status of its current GHG reduction goal planning efforts. These reductions have occurred through the hard work necessary to conserve energy, reformulate products, and control high global warming potential emissions. 3M believes that nearly every other company would like to emulate 3M in regard to their own GHG emission reduction achievements. Other companies are setting goals to move closer to the achievements 3M has already realized.

Better Tracking of GHG Emissions from 3M Suppliers and Customers (Scope 3)

3M has been developing its Scope 3 GHG emissions inventory since the publishing of the WRI/WBCSD GHG Protocol Corporate Value Chain (Scope 3) Accounting and Reporting Standard in October 2011. 3M places a high value on sound science and decision-making, so data reported is in accordance to the standard. When the complexity of the supply chain does not allow for direct calculation, an input/model calculation method is used.

For categories 1 (purchased goods and services) and 2 (capital goods), a new model was utilized, based on characteristics of the economy in 2014. The new model reflects the improved carbon intensity, or emissions per dollar, of the economy. Since previous emissions for these categories were based on the model available at the time (based on 2002 economic data), 2015 data is not directly comparable to past years.

3M has expanded its Scope 3 inventory this year by adding emission estimates for categories 5, waste generated in operations, Table 8). Categories 9, 10, 11, and 12 (related to emissions associated with sold products) remain very challenging for 3M, due to the number and complexity of products 3M sells, and the diversity of their uses by businesses and consumers across the globe. Many of its approximately 55,000 product lines are "intermediates" with many potential downstream applications, each with a different GHG emissions profile, making it impossible to reasonably estimate the downstream emissions associated with the various end uses of our intermediate products. However, 3M does offer many products that reduce GHG emissions for its customers – these are detailed in our Climate Change Solutions Catalog. In 2015 alone, about 14 million metric tons of CO2 equivalents were avoided for 3M customers through use of various 3M product platforms as calculated in accordance with the WRI/WBCSD GHG Protocol Project Standard. 3Mis in the process of estimating GHG emission reductions for other Climate Change Solution products, as well as evaluating the emissions impact for the few 3M products that use energy.

With the introduction of Business Transformation to3M, its systems are becoming more unified, and this is providing 3M with better data to more accurately judge and make decisions. It is also helping the company create real, consistent changes throughout its global operations. 3Mexpects Business Transformation to help drive its efforts to reduce all GHG emissions, including Scope 3 GHG emissions.

Setting Energy Performance Goals and Evaluating Progress

As previously noted, 3M has a long history in setting and achieving energy conservation goals. In 2010 as part of 3M 2015 Sustainability Goals, 3M set a global goal to increase energy efficiency by 25 percent by 2015 from a 2005 base year. Finally, energy efficiency and increasing its renewable energy use are key parts of 3M 2025 Sustainability Goals.

3M also identified areas of focus that will make a step-change in the energy and carbon intensity of its operations. The implementation of combined heat and power systems and heat recovery systems at certain 3M locations has a large potential to improve efficiency and reduce carbon emissions. The implementation of advanced energy information systems in 3M manufacturing facilities is expected to give operations personnel information they can use to more effectively manage energy use.

To meet global goals, 3M reviews its Strategic Energy Management Plan annually to prioritize programs. Longer-term action items are added periodically to achieve greater efficiency. The plan uses input from stakeholders, including manufacturing directors, plant managers, operations employees and executive management. The plan aims to continuously improve results; leverage engineering expertise and advances; drive plant-level efficiency improvements; maintain top management support; and protect 3M.

Total Energy Use

3M is a diversified technology company, providing innovative solutions that advance companies and improve people's lives worldwide. 3M strategically manages energy use throughout its global operations by setting aggressive goals and tracking results.3Mis happy to announce that it successfully achieved the 2015 energy conservation goal of a reduction of 25% by 2015 from a 2005 baseline (indexed to net sales).

Table 8. 3M Scope 3 - Greenhouse gas emissions

Scope 3 Category		Metric Tons of CO2e					Boundary
		2011	2012	2013	2014	2015	
Upstream Emissions							
1	Purchased Goods and Services	7.620.000	8.160.000	8.360.000	8.330.000	6.880.000	3M Operational Control
		From Climate Earth using Input/Output Model based on 3M spend					
2	Capital Goods	498.000	584.000	647.000	812.000	577.000	3M Operational Control
		From Climate Earth using Input/Output Model based on 3M spend					
3	Fuel and Energy Related Activities (not including scope 1 or scope 2 emissions)	Partially included in Scope 1 and Scope 2emissions reporting			551.000	621.000	3M Operational Control
4	Upstream transportation and distribution	Not Evaluated	1.510.000	1.230.000	995.000	780.000	3M Operational Control
		Emissions disclosed in previous years were miscategorized as Category 9. Data does not include emissions from transportation of raw materials from suppliers.					
5	Waste generated in operations	Insufficient data				254.000	3M Operational Control
		Environmental Lab calculated from 3M primary data on waste by facility size or number of employees					
6	Business Travel	Not Evaluated	58.600	56.900	61.100	55.800	3M Operational Control
		Environmental Lab calculated from 3M primary data on business travel					
7	Employee commuting	Not Evaluated	352.000	353.000	358.000	356.000	3M Operational Control
		From Climate Earth using Input/Output Model based on 3M employee population					
8	Upstream, leased Assets	Included in Scope 1 or Scope 2 emissions reporting					3M Operational Control
		These emissions are included in Scope 1 & 2, because they are all under 3M Operational Control					
TOTAL Upstream		8.120.000	10.700.000	10.600.000	11.100.000	9.500.000	
		Net GHG emissions based on the categories evaluated					

Because net sales have not been as strong in 2015, this is partially impacting 3M energy numbers and not accurately reflecting the numerous improvements 3M has made in the area of energy conservation.

3M 2025 energy conservation goal is to improve energy efficiency indexed to net sales by 30%. Energy efficiency improvements will address rising energy use, costs and climate impacts. Building on its 50% improvement in energy efficiency between 2000 and 2015, a 30% energy efficiency improvement will keep its global energy use nearly flat over the next 10 years, as the company grows. Specifically, 3M external energy reduction goal is a reduction of 30% indexed to net sales and its internal energy reduction goal is a 30% reduction indexed to output. 3M has also undertaken a 2025 goal to increase renewable energy to 25% of total electricity use. Nearly 800,000 MWh of renewable energy use will be added globally. The primary sources of renewable energy will be wind and solar.

Table 9. 3M Scope 3 - Greenhouse gas emissions

Scope 3 Category		Metric Tons of CO2e					Boundary
		2011	**2012**	**2013**	**2014**	**2015**	
Downstream Emissions							
9	Downstream transportation and distribution	Not Evaluated - see comments		Most of 3M's 60,000+ products are intermediates with many potential end uses. According to the GHG Protocol Scope 3 Calculation Guidance, a company that produces intermediate products with many potential downstream applications, each with a potentially different GHG emissions profile, cannot reasonably estimate the downstream emissions associated with the various end uses of the intermediate products.			
10	Processing of sold products						
11	Use of sold products						
12	End of life treatment of sold products						
13	Downstream leased assets	Not Evaluated	Included in Scope 1 or Scope 2 emissions reporting <1,000				3M Operational Control
		Prior to RY2015, 3M reported facilities leased to 3rd parties under Scope 1 and 2.					
14	Franchises	Not Evaluated	0	0	0	0	3M Financial Control
		No franchises under 3M financial control					
15	Investments	Not Evaluated	0	0	0	0	3M Financial Control
		No investments under 3M financial control					
TOTAL Downstream		-	-	-	N/A	N/A	
		All downstream categories either don't apply or are de minimis					
NOTES							
1	The data reported is in accordance to the World Resources Institute (WRI)/ World Business Council for Sustainable Development (WBCSD) Corporate Value Chain (Scope 3) Accounting and Reporting Standard.						
2	An input/output model calculation methodology based on spend by commodity was used in collaboration with Climate Earth for categories 1 and 2, and based on employee headcount by country for category 7.						
3	A third party audit of the input/output model data in accordance to the WRI/WBCSD Corporate Value Chain (Scope 3) standard was conducted in 2013 to determine the quality of the data reported and the reliability of the calculation method. For Categories 1 and 2, a new model was utilized based on characteristics of the economy in 2014. Since previous emissions for these categories were based on the model available at the time, 2015 data is not directly comparable to past years.						
4	Estimated Scope 3 data uncertainty is ±50% (WRI/WBCSD, GHG Protocol Corporate Value Chain (Scope 3) Accounting and Reporting Standard, 2011)						
5	Values listed in the table above have been rounded to three significant figures. All calculations on the tabulated data use the full precision of the number.						

In 2015, the 3M London Facility in Canada received an EHS achievement award for coordinating eight energy audits and over 40 conservation projects to achieve substantial benefits in energy efficiency and conservation. 3M Science. Applied to Life.™ projects are working toward improving and inventing materials and innovations that will benefit and preserve the environment, and 3M commitment to energy efficiency is exemplified by our EPA Green Power Partnership and the Innovation Center Gold LEED Certification awarded to 3M Spain.

Figure 14. Total energy use
(MMBtus)

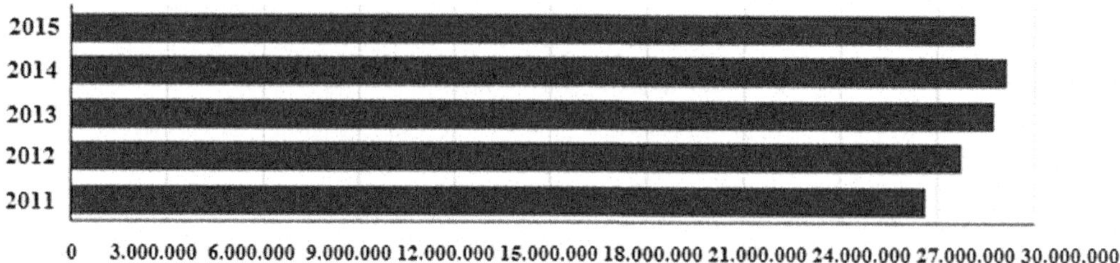

Figure 15. Total indexed energy usage
(MMBtu / Million USD Net Sales)

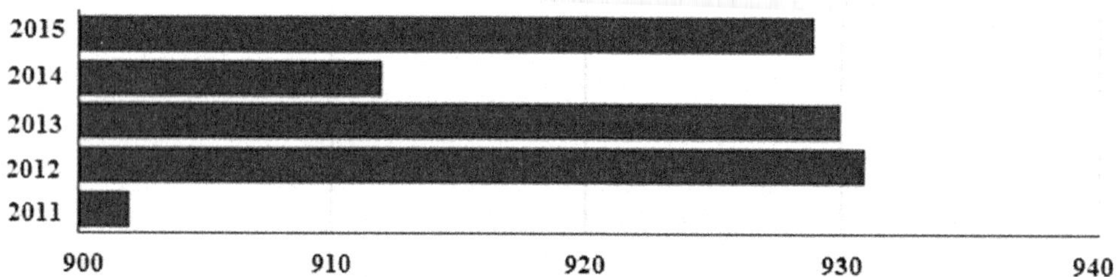

3M presently has 20 sites certified to the energy standard ISO 50001. Two of its sites have undergone a pilot project with sponsorship from the U.S. Department of Energy. In 2015, 3M has 5 U.S. locations undergoing the certification process as a group of cohorts and3 others working individually.

3M are also undergoing the process of becoming certified at the enterprise level, which is a unique and exciting opportunity. It speaks to 3M commitment to energy management. The difference with this certification as compared to individual certifications is that it instills a management aspect to the issue of energy reduction as opposed to just focusing on projects in and of themselves. It will allow top management to review decisions on a quarterly basis and go beyond energy projects into continual energy managing behaviors.

3M collects and analyzes energy-use data and energy efficiency project metrics to: track progress toward corporate energy and greenhouse gas goals; identify opportunities for improvement, benchmark against past performance, and identify best practices that can be applied across global operations. All manufacturing locations and other locations greater than 2800 square meters report energy use and energy costs monthly into an electronic reporting system. Data is analyzed at the facility, division, business unit, regional, country and corporate levels quarterly as part of 3M's EHS Management System Scorecard and Energy Management Dashboard previously described.

Energy efficiency is a social responsibility and a competitive advantage for 3M. Managing its energy footprint reduces operating costs, reduces environmental impact and addresses stakeholder interests in solutions with environmental and energy advantages.

Goals and results. 3M 2025 GHG emissions goal aims to ensure that GHG emissions are at least 50% below its 2002 baseline while still growing the business. 3M is in a leadership position due to its early actions to reduce greenhouse gas emissions more than 10 years ago. Between 2002 and 2015, 3M voluntarily achieved a 69.3% absolute reduction in greenhouse gas emissions. 3Mis committed to continuing that leadership for another 10 years; even as the company grows in order to help its customers address the issue of climate change.

3M has also committed to a 2025 goal to help customers reduce their GHGs by 250 million tons of CO2 equivalent emissions through use of 3Mproducts. While 3M has made significant GHG emission reductions across its global operations, 3M realizes it can make far greater contributions by helping customers reduce their GHG emissions through the use of 3M products. In 2015 alone, about 14 million metric tons of CO2 were avoided for customers through use of 3M product platforms. According to the EPA Greenhouse Gas Equivalencies Calculator this is equivalent to the annual emissions of more than 2.95 million passenger vehicles driven for one year.

Energy Highlights:

- 3M implemented over 400 energy efficiency projects globally in 2015.
- 3M formed partnerships to develop novel solutions for transportation, IT and electronics.
- 3M leveraged grants to advance CO2 recycling, fuel system, battery and solar technologies.
- 3M maintained the Global Energy Data Validation and Utility Review to identify savings within facilities, emphasizing the importance of engaging with supporting utilities to understand and verify data accuracy.
- 3M received recognition from the U.S. Department of Energy for achieving its energy efficiency goal established through the Better Buildings Challenge.

Figure 16. 2002-2015 reductions in absolute GHG emissions

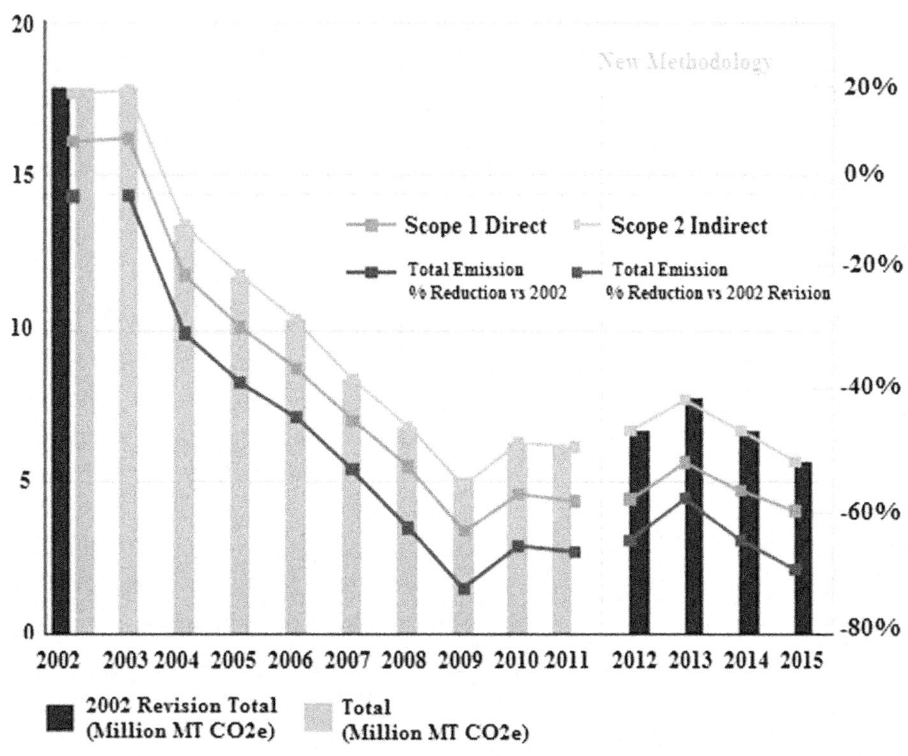

Figure 17. 2002-2015 GHG emissions reductions indexed to net sales

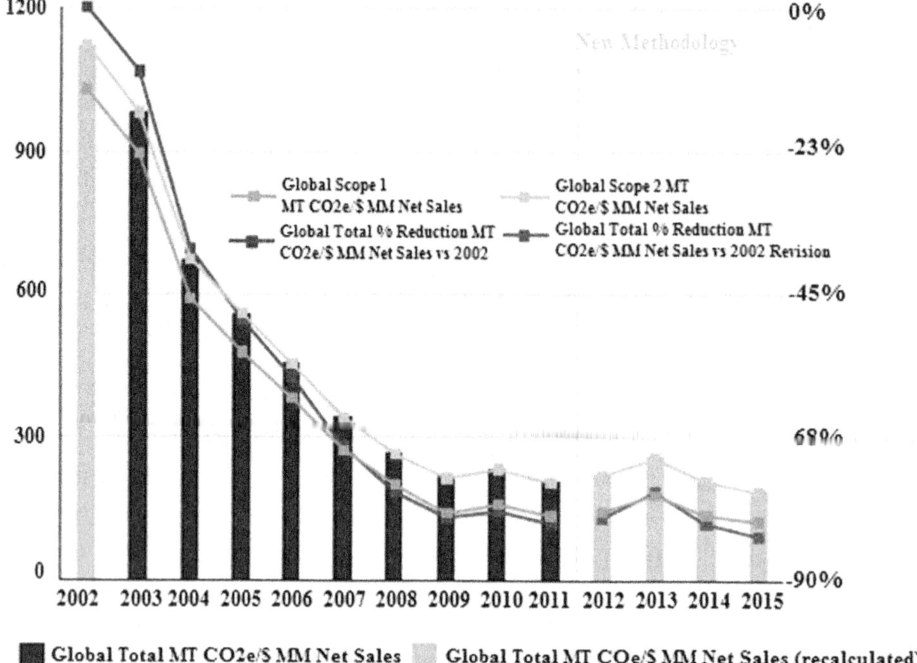

- 3M achieved ISO 50001 certification at 20 sites, and pursuing certification at 8 additional sites.

3M's Environmental Assessment Process. 3M has been completing an environmental assessment process at most locations over the past 3 years with the goal of identifying potential historical liabilities. As a result of these assessments, biodiverse areas may be identified. Where applicable, a public database search is completed, which includes a wetland database. Site visits also identify areas such as rivers, creeks and potential wetlands that are on or near the facility.

Investing in Renewable Energy

3M continues to evaluate, invest in and incorporate on-site renewable energy sources within its own operations where feasible while continuing to expand and collaborate with external partners. 3M estimates that approximately 0.5 percent of 3M energy used today is from renewable sources generated on-site in its own operations. 3M also partners with utility providers that incorporate renewable energy into their own operations, who thereby pass those benefits onto their customers, including 3M.

- **Innovative New Coating for Solar Panels Lets in More Light:** A unique antireflective coating has been developed by 3M and Ducatt to give solar panels a further sustainability edge. The coating works by enabling more light to reach the solar cells, increasing the electricity output of the panels by between three and five per cent. Unlike existing antireflection coatings that use solvents that can harm the environment, the new coating is water-based so no air-polluting elements are released by the coating either during manufacturing or fitting.

A High-Energy Approach to Lowering Energy Use. 3M facilities around the world are committed to reducing the company's environmental footprint by conserving energy. One shining example is the 3M Oral Care facility in Seefeld, Germany, which found ways to improve energy efficiency by 7.5%.In May, 2015, the Seefeld site was awarded its fifth 3M Platinum Energy Award, in recognition of exceptional teamwork on several fronts. The Seefeld team:

- Improved energy efficiency by 7.5%.
- Implemented savings projects accounting for 5.4% of their total energy spend.
- Successfully met the requirements of the ISO 50001 energy management standard

Top Innovation Award for 3M ACCR. The UK's largest electricity transmission network operator, in partnership with 3M and the University of Manchester, received a top innovation prize for its pioneering work on overhead line conductors using 3M ACCR (Aluminum Conductor Composite Reinforced) to improve the efficiency of existing high-voltage transmission infrastructure.3M ACCR lightweight, high temperature, low-sag overhead line conductors are used to replace existing electrical conductors and double the transmission capacity of the line without the need to build new infrastructure. This removes bottlenecks in the system and can also connect other energy sources, such as electricity generated by windfarms, to the grid. The 3M solution is also quieter as the unique aluminum-based material and surface finish of ACCR reduces the corona discharge associated with standard conductors when they are wet or damp, which gives off a fizzing noise.

Global Challenges: Health and Safety

Creative innovation, technology, education and collaboration are all critical if we are to tackle the human health and workplace safety concerns of today— for the sake of tomorrow. Health and safety issues are prevalent, and concerns are growing to ensure safe and healthy workplaces around the world. Governments, corporations and consumers are driving global demand for safety, protection, healthcare and food safety solutions. Food poisoning and water-borne illnesses lead to the deaths of 3 million people across the globe each year. At the same time, approximately one of every 20 hospitalized patients in low- and middle-income countries will contract an infection while under medical care.

3M are always taking steps to protect its most important asset – 3M employees. 3M innovations are only possible with the minds, talent and commitment of all of its employees worldwide. So, 3M puts a lot of thought and effort into keeping them safe and healthy. 3M robust Safety and Health Policy applies to all 3M operations worldwide, including new acquisitions. It is based on its core business values and stems from our Environmental, Health and Safety (EHS) vision for "Safe and Healthy People, Products and Planet." It holds anyone working at or visiting a 3M location to strict safety and health requirements.

3M 2025 goal is to provide training to 5 million workers across the globe on worker and patient safety. Proper use of health and safety products is critical to infection prevention, personal safety and overall health. Building on its existing customer education program, 3M seeks to help educate individuals on worker and patient safety in both healthcare and industrial settings.

Research shows that core body temperature drops rapidly following the induction of general anesthesia, which puts patients at an increased risk for unintended hypothermia, leading to higher mortality rates, longer hospital stays and an increased rate of wound infection 3M™ Patient Warming units are revolutionary forced-air warming systems that help to prevent and treat hypothermia while enhancing patient comfort.

In 1996, a Global Safety & Health Plan (GSHP) tool was initiated for all 3M locations worldwide. It utilizes a well-developed self-assessment process that is categorized into multiple elements addressing various areas and standards related to safety and health. 3M utilizes a variety of tools to manage risks from hazards in the workplace. 3Mhas used specialized tools successfully for a number of years in the areas of Industrial Hygiene, Ergonomics and Process Safety. Each of these disciplines uses a risk management approach to categorize hazard levels and define appropriate levels of control.

Recognizing the need to further minimize the rates of fatalities and serious injuries (FSI), 3M has been engaged in the development of a practical new approach to better managing hazards that have the potential to result in fatalities or serious life-altering injuries. The new approach was implemented in 2013, and includes development of an inventory of FSI precursors— a list of high-hazard activities, operations and situations that have the potential to result in a fatality or life-altering injury. These potential hazards are taken through the risk assessment and reduction process along with all near misses and incidents.

A five-year objective to achieve risk reduction related to high-hazard activities was launched in 2014. The goal for safety and health in 3M is for all sites to achieve100% conformance to six critical GSHP standards related to risk management of high-hazard activities:

- Safety and health hazard recognition and risk assessment;
- Incident and potential hazard reporting, record keeping, investigation and follow-up;
- Powered industrial vehicles;
- Machine guarding;
- Work at height;
- Process hazard analysis.

Employee Health and Safety

The safety of employees at 3M is its highest priority. 3M takes every possible step to actively monitor, measure, and improve leading indicators of performance while simultaneously growing the company. As a result of this efforts, lagging indicators such as worldwide recordable and lost time rates since 2006 has decreased 46% for 3M global employees.

3M also places a lot of emphasis on record-keeping, training FAQs in its newsletters, and providing examples. 3M visits sites and perform audits on record-keeping practices, and it reviews all incident data along with the quality of the investigation, contributing causal factors, and an analysis of corrective actions implemented. Every year, 3M implements incremental upgrades to various elements of its Global Safety and Health Plan. By analyzing its audits and various self-assessments, 3Mis able to create continual improvements. 3M is one of the only companies with a Global Safety and Health Plan that performs self-assessments, and this has been a great calibration for its audits.

Utilizing its Risk Assessment Prioritization (RAP) tools, sites must identify activities that they consider "high-hazard," and focus on how these activities are impacting lost time cases. 3M expects to see a drop in severe cases into the future because of its focus on "high hazards." Since 2013, 3M has documented approximately 17,000 assessments, and these measurements are helping the company lower severe injury rates in the future.

Over 90 percent of 3M sites have people with formal RAP training, and this is a significant increase over past years. Furthermore, in 2015, 3M put a huge effort into providing training sessions for its auditors. 3M now places senior auditors with junior auditors to improve their knowledge and overall skillset. Auditor training has become integrated into 3M employee competency development programs. In 2015, 60 global audits were completed at 3M manufacturing facilities.

3M auditing program has become more developed and global than ever, and the mix of internal and external auditors provides the company with a chance to benchmark its own best practices and create real, substantive changes. 3M global auditing program is minimizing variation from country-to-country and getting everyone on the same page.

In 2015, 3M changed its focus to a layers of protection analysis. This form of analysis, along with its risk assessments and prioritization tools, has driven down fatalities and serious injuries. 3M is heavily focused on not only preventing fatalities but serious injuries as well. 3M tools have been so successful that numerous peer companies are looking to 3M and its health and safety leaders to help advise them on how to improve health and safety. 3M leaders have been invited to speak at numerous international conferences around the globe on their methods.

- **Contractor Health and Safety:** 3M has a long history of ensuring its global safety and health commitment to all employees. 3M Safety and Health Policy apply to all 3M operations, including new acquisitions. It is based on 3M core business values and stems from its environmental, health and safety (EHS) vision for "Safe and healthy people, products and planet."

All visitors, vendors, and contract workers at 3M locations are held to the same safety and health requirements as 3M employees, therefore consistent management systems and evaluation tools are critical to company safety and health success.

3M uses a formal approach to maximize the safe performance of contractors. It begins with a pre-qualification process before granting contracts for work. This process includes getting information such as injury/illness rates, experience modification rates (EMR), and safety program information such as training and activity levels of safety committees. Prior to commencing actual work, formal preconstruction safety reviews are conducted to address potential hazards and controls related to the scope of work. Monitoring of safety performance is frequently conducted throughout the contract term. An assessment of safety performance is conducted at the conclusion of the contract.

3Mcontractor safety standard allows 3M corporate safety group to align its contractor standards with 3Mglobal safety and health plan. Each location has a site contract coordinator. This person is designated for each location to be the main contact for contractor safety. They have the ability to deal with pre-bid meetings and pre-qualifications for contractors. The site contract coordinator is on-site for daily meetings and safety reviews to ensure proper behavior, training, and weekly inspections.

3M are always improving its current systems, and its global safety and health plan has a contract safety element. In addition to the contract safety elements, such as fall protection, confined space entry, and life safety activities, 3M makes sure its initiatives apply to everyone at 3M, including contractors. Contractors and employees are treated the same, so anything that positively impacts employees also helps contractors. As 3M continues to work on global projects, the company is learning from past experiences. 3M seeks to improve contractor safety year-by-year.

3M's Worldwide Incident Management System (WIMS) includes the reporting of all contractor incidents. This includes injuries and contractor worker hours. International locations can now enter contractor worker hours into WIMS. US location hours automatically get entered into WIMS monthly from a file 3M receives from payroll for 3M employees and volt for contingent contract employees. Further, in 2015, 3M has put increased emphasis on contractor health and safety in its audits to get the best data possible. By getting the best data possible, 3M can make the best decisions to ensure the safety of everyone in the 3M community.

3M is excited to announce that in 2015 3M reached the lowest recordable loss rate in company history. All of its big-picture efforts over the years are translating into real results.

Process hazard management. Process hazard management (PHM) is a systematic approach for prevention of process-related fires, explosions and sudden release of toxic materials. 3M PHM employs accepted industry practices and regulations. 3M PHM allows facilities to identify, control and verify that process hazards are understood and managed. The framework for PHM consists of:

- Hazard identification and assessment.
- Hazard reduction and control.
- Control effectiveness verification.

Various tools are being used to ensure the appropriate rigor is being provided to manage the hazards associated with hazardous processes. Risk management of the hazardous process begins with the use of the hazardous process evaluation tool (HazPET), which provides a consistent and simplified categorization of the hazardous processes. Process hazard analysis (PHA) methodologies are used to assess the process hazards and evaluate the effectiveness of existing safeguards.

Recent enhanced PHA requirements will provide a more rigorous hazard assessment methodology. Layers of protection analysis (LOPA) will also be used to analyze the effectiveness of critical safety devices and systems, by providing more attention to independent protection layers.

Comprehensive chemical and noise exposure risk assessment and management. Comprehensive exposure risk assessment and management is a systematic approach for estimating workplace exposures to chemical and physical agents for all materials, processes and employees. Accurate exposure assessments are critical to all exposure management programs and activities. 3M uses the comprehensive approach outlined by the American Industrial Hygiene Association (AIHA), creating an effective and efficient system for assessing and managing all exposure risks.

Over the past decade, over 95% of all chemical agents and noise baseline exposure risk assessments have been completed for all jobs, creating a foundation of exposure assessments used to drive the following:

- Baseline exposure assessments;
- Annual air and noise sampling plans;
- Exposure assessment validation plans;
- Medical surveillance applicability analysis plans;
- Hearing conservation programs including E-A-Rfit training;
- Respirator and personal protective equipment programs;
- As needed, other exposure management programs including administrative, industrial ventilation and isolation controls.

Each year, active qualitative assessments are used to define annual air and noise monitoring and validation plans for each facility around the world. The air and noise exposure monitoring results are then analyzed using statistical methods to determine if any exposure management programs are required. 3M requires each facility where there is potential for significant exposure to chemicals or noise to have annual chemical and noise assessment and validation plans that identify and prioritize processes for exposure assessment, monitoring and statistical validation. The chemical and noise assessment and validation plans enable facilities to prioritize annual activities toward completion of the goal of understanding and managing all workplace exposure risks.

Ergonomics Risk Management. Ergonomic and noise-related injuries continue to be a major topic for 3M, and the company made large strides in these areas in 2015. 3M is placing special emphasis on developing regional leaders for ergonomics at various sites around the globe. At 3M Brazil, for example, 3M has a full-time person that leads Brazil ergonomics and develops projects in this area. 3M are developing similar leaders and programs in places such as Poland, Mexico, India, and Southeast Asia.

3M ergonomic training is available 24/7 to anyone in the world who wants to learn about noise-control, and many company leaders have offered cash-rewards to those who can find ways to limit or reduce noise levels.

Since 2008, 3M has approached hearing loss from three different perspectives:

1. 3M are focusing on proper assessment practices that determine who should actually be in a hearing conservation program.
2. When 3M has hearing conservation programs, it has a hearing loss follow-up tool to ensure proper hearing protection and training is taking place.
3. 3M is engaging people outside of 3M who are world-renowned experts in the area of hearing loss to figure out what 3M can do to make improvements.

Further, 3M recently implemented its dual ear fit program. The new dual ear fit system enables sites to create ear plugs that properly fit each individual's ears. 3M has purchased multiple ear fit systems that are available to sites around the globe.

3M made a number of updates to its manuals including the noise and hearing manual and the chemical exposure manual. These updates, in conjunction with its noise control web courses that are available to anyone around the world 24 hours a day, should help improve its already stellar safety programs.

3M's Noise Control Awards were started about four years ago to recognize the teamwork it takes to make significant improvements in 3M plants. The winners are selected from Engineering Safety Award and EHS Achievement Award submissions and are evaluated by members of the 3M noise assessment and control team. The teams are recognized in their plants, an email announcement goes out, winners are announced during a webinar and they receive hearing protection ear muffs to salute their achievements. Winning projects may also share posters to spread the word about their best practices at the 3M Industrial Hygiene and Ergonomics Conference.

In 2015, 3M had sessions regarding hearing loss with all of its plant managers across the globe. At the Global Plant Manager Conference, 3M had two great seminars on hearing conservation, the "Ears-on Learning" seminar and the "Worldview of Hear Conservation: Requirements and Trends" seminar. 3M huge push around noise control should translate into real results in the future.

Ergonomic risk reduction activities throughout the corporation continue to have a positive impact on illness rates. 3M's ergonomics risk reduction process (ERRP) is a global, comprehensive program.

ERRP integrates ergonomic job analysis, safety and health, and engineering professional development and ergonomics engineering design criteria. ERRP reduces exposure to commonly identify work- related musculoskeletal disorder (WMSD) risk factors and to support operational efficiency throughout 3M.

By offering awards for ergonomic improvements, 3M are driving real, substantive change. The 3M Applied Ergonomics Innovation Award recognizes outstanding efforts focused on ergonomics improvements. It is intended to promote effective application of ergonomics principles and practices that improve the ability of employees to work safely and productively and consumers to use 3M products safely and effectively.

Candidates for this award need to demonstrate considerations and application of ergonomics and/or human factors and other improvements, such as improved quality, lower costs, better efficiency, improved usability, and reduction in risk of injury. Over the 15 years, 3M received 1,100 submissions from around the world focused on reducing ergonomic risks. In 2015 3M had over 100 submissions and granted several awards across 3 categories: (1) Best new ergonomics engineering design, (2) Best ergonomics adaptation of an existing workstation or process, and (3) Best solution for under $1,000.

Auditing and Compliance. To assure that the facility self-assessment and improvement process is effectively being utilized across the company, a risk-based auditing program for safety and health is managed at the corporate level. Audit findings are ranked using the same risk matrix that is utilized for the analysis of potential hazards and incidents. Areas of nonconformance are examined for potential hazards, which can then be investigated for causal factors, risk assessment and corrective action to achieve risk reduction and conformance to established standards. All moderate-to high-risk audit findings are tracked to closure, and are then reviewed and approved by the lead auditor for satisfactory improvement.

Safety and health committees. 3M seeks employee participation at all levels to ensure involvement and ownership of safety and health programs and systems. This involvement is critical to achieving effective, proactive solutions to safety and health issues. Increasing employee ownership and involvement in the safety and health process helps provide a safer, healthier workplace. Emphasis is placed on a cooperative effort between management and employees in achieving these goals. Primary examples of how these efforts align with the risk reduction elements include:

- Job hazard analysis and risk assessments;
- Ergonomics teams;
- Process safety management;
- Potential hazard reporting programs;
- Participation in investigations and prompt follow-up of incidents and potential hazards.

Through this collaborative effort, all employees have the opportunity to be involved in risk assessment activities to then develop action plans and assign responsibilities for completing safety and health-related goals and objectives.

Formal Safety and Health Committees are the most active and visible way that this is demonstrated within 3M. In fact, this aspect is represented by its own standard of performance in the GSHP that requires locations to establish and maintain active safety and health committees. They are defined specifically as an organized group of employees from all levels of the facility whose function is to support the safety and health management system by identifying preventive and corrective measures needed to eliminate or control recognized safety and health hazards. In 2015, 100% of 3M manufacturing facilities worldwide have active employee safety committees.

Goals, Results, and Additional Steps to Protect Employees

Measuring leading indicators of safety and health performance is a key focus for 3M. Aggregated data from all global safety and health plan assessments, audits and incident reporting are evaluated to identify performance status and corporate-wide opportunities. Metrics are tracked and reported for continuous improvement at the facility, business unit, regional and corporate levels. Initiatives such as improving the quality and level of implementation of safety and health management system elements (including preventive measures) at each 3M site results in increased awareness, mature programs, and reduced injury and illness rates. In 2011, 3M set key corporate-wide safety and health objectives to continuously improve related management systems and to proactively reduce negative safety and health impacts. Significant achievement was made in meeting those objectives. Continuous improvement objectives have been identified for achievement by year-end 2018.

3M has been monitoring, measuring and working toward improving leading indicators of performance while simultaneously increasing the growth of the company. As a result of its efforts, lagging indicators such as worldwide recordable and lost time rates have continued to decrease.

3M follows the U.S. Occupational Safety and Health (OSHA) recordkeeping rules and formulas to record and measure injury and illness rates worldwide. All 3M employees and contingent employees, regardless of facility type but within 3M's operational control, are covered by 3M injury and illness recordkeeping rules. In addition, contractors are asked to submit notification to 3M of worker hours and any injuries occurring while performing work in accordance with a 3M contract.

3M has a strong system in place for people who travel to potentially dangerous areas around the globe. When a travel request is placed, 3M employees receive an e-mail on what steps they should take before traveling, such as how to deal with various disease risks. 3M also provides a global traveler's insurance program that ensures 3M employees will be taken care of if a life-threatening event takes place.

Fatal incidents. Injury rates are down at 3M, in fact, they are at an all-time low in 3M and efforts to push them even lower are underway all over the world. Year-end injury and illness results for 2015 have been compiled and there is a trend for lower rates and a reduced number of severe injury incidents. There are indications that this improvement is due in large part to all the work that has been conducted around risk reduction. The cause of injuries due to contact with equipment has decreased sharply since 2013 when the updated risk reduction process was launched across 3M using the risk assessment and prioritization (RAP) tool. The RAP tool is 3M's standardized methodology for risk assessments and is a key part of the analysis of high hazard activities which could result in severe injury or death if safeguards do not effectively control the hazards. Over 40,000 risk assessments have been documented in WIMS since June of 2013 and risk levels were lowered for nearly 12,000 activities as a result of the assessments.

In 2015, an update to 3M Manual 80, A109, guarding floor, roof and wall openings, was released including a reference to 3M's fall protection requirements. This addition helps align 3M's safety and engineering requirements for this topic. Further, a collaborative effort was started between corporate safety and facilities engineering to provide 3M facilities, engineering, EHS, and maintenance staff guidance and direction around anchor points, and protection when working on roofs. 3M also had a half-day fall protection hands-on courses for EHS professionals. This workshop included demonstrations of 3M's fall protection equipment from 3M's personal safety division.

Two new indicators will help track serious injury and fatality rates and how well 3M sites are doing at lowering risk levels for high hazard activities. Both metrics will come from WIMS data. The two indicators are (1) the serious injury and fatality rate (SIF) which measures all injuries that occur in 3M with a severity score of 15 or higher, and (2) the risk reduction report for tracking risk reductions across locations.

3M is always benchmarking its approach with its peers, and believes it has made large strides and improvements in 2015. Many incident management systems focus solely on the severity of the incidents rather than identifying the level of risk associated with incidents, potential hazards or near misses. Requiring incident management system users to identify the most likely consequence from the incident, potential hazard or near miss, and not just the actual severity of the incident, is a critical step to identifying tasks with an elevated potential to result in a serious injury or fatality (SIF).

This new approach was implemented in 2013, and includes the development of an inventory of SIF precursors — a list of high-hazard activities, operations, and situations that have the potential to result in a fatality or life-altering injury. These potential hazards are taken through the risk assessment and reduction process along with all near misses and incidents.

In 2014, 3M initiative to achieve risk reduction related to high-hazard activities was part of a 3M challenge to improve EHS performance at its facilities. Utilizing 2012 as a baseline before program implementation, significant/severe injuries to employees, contingent and contractor workers decreased by 25% in 2015.

Injury and illness rates. 3M global employee incident rates for injuries and illnesses with days away from work have declined 46% since 2006. The most frequent cause of injuries is from contact with objects or equipment. The implementation of the new risk management process is primarily designed to prevent fatal and serious injury events related to certain activities at 3M that have resulted in more frequent injuries than others.

Science inspired by nature. Due to its incredible height, the distance from a giraffe's legs to its heart is twice that of humans, raising blood pressure and putting great stress on the veins. Despite this, giraffes never suffer from swelling or ulcers in their lower legs. Scientists have studied this and determined that the giraffe's tough, non-elastic skin works like the anti-gravity suits worn by astronauts, preventing the stagnation of blood in their lower extremities. That inspired scientists at 3M to create a compression system to help treat a painful human medical condition called venous leg ulcers, which are caused by uncontrolled high pressure in the veins of the lower leg. Venous leg ulcers are extremely common in the United States and affect between 500,000 to two million people annually.

Scientists at 3M figured out that the giraffe's thick and tight skin functions like nature's best compression bandage, and they created a material that reproduces the properties of this skin to help humans. They took the elastic wraps we use when we sprain our ankles or wrists, and modified the material to engineer a leading two-layer compression system that mimics the skin of a giraffe.

Table 10. Fatal incidents

Fatalities	2011	2012	2013	2014	2015
Total Employees **(work-related fatalities)**	0	1	1	0	0
Total Contractors **(work-related fatalities)**	1	1	1	0	0

Figure 18. 3M Worldwide – by region
Lost Time Trends

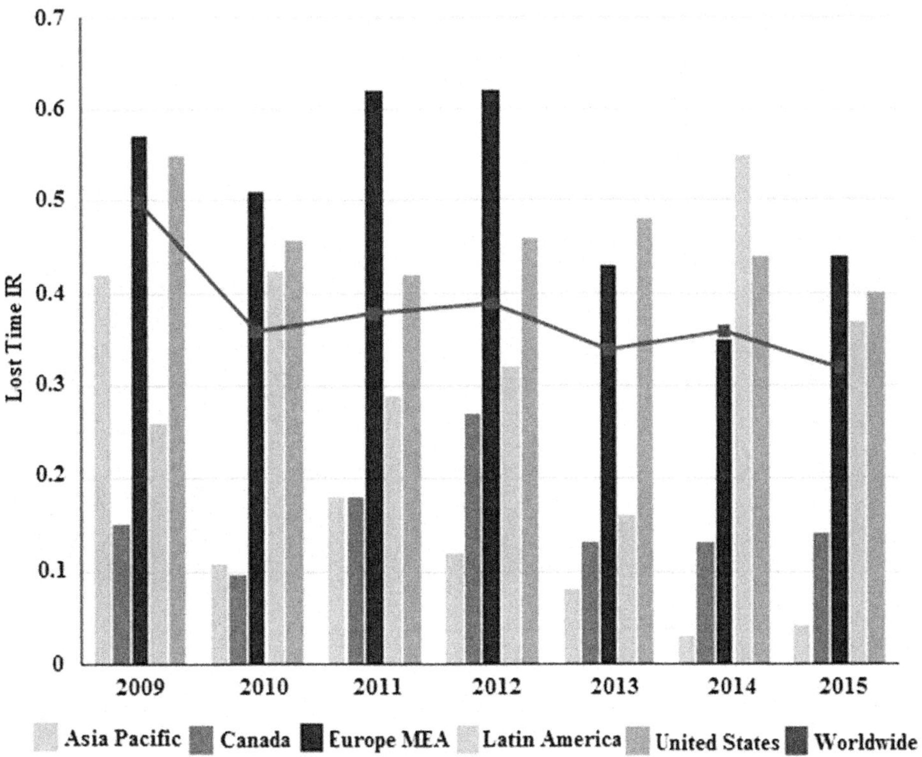

Global Challenges: Education and Development

3M works hard to create a better world for everyone; our sustainability approach revolves around education and development within global communities and our workforce. 3M applies science in collaborative ways to improve lives daily. 3M science not only impacts its customers around the world, but also makes difference in the way the company works. At 3M, people are a collaborative, diverse group whose ideas transform the future. 3M continuously build and enhance its inclusive culture, creating an environment where people feel safe, engaged and free to create.

An inclusive culture at 3M is built on 3M human resources– to respect the dignity and worth of individuals; encourage the initiative of each employee; challenge individual capabilities; and provide equal opportunity. 3M is continuously focusing on building and maintaining an inclusive culture.

Having a diverse global workforce helps us to generate more ideas which yield more innovative solutions. As global markets expand and more than 60 percent of 3M's sales come from outside the United States, 3M relies on employees who understand the needs of diverse customers. 3M goal is to reflect the diversity of its global customers, suppliers and channel partners, and build on each employee's abilities to achieve greater customer satisfaction and accelerated growth.

When 3M seeks and values differences, it is embracing diversity and fostering an inclusive environment that creates opportunities for its people, culture, customers, and communities. These four areas of focus shape 3M actions worldwide.

Figure 19. 3M Worldwide – by region
Recordable Trends

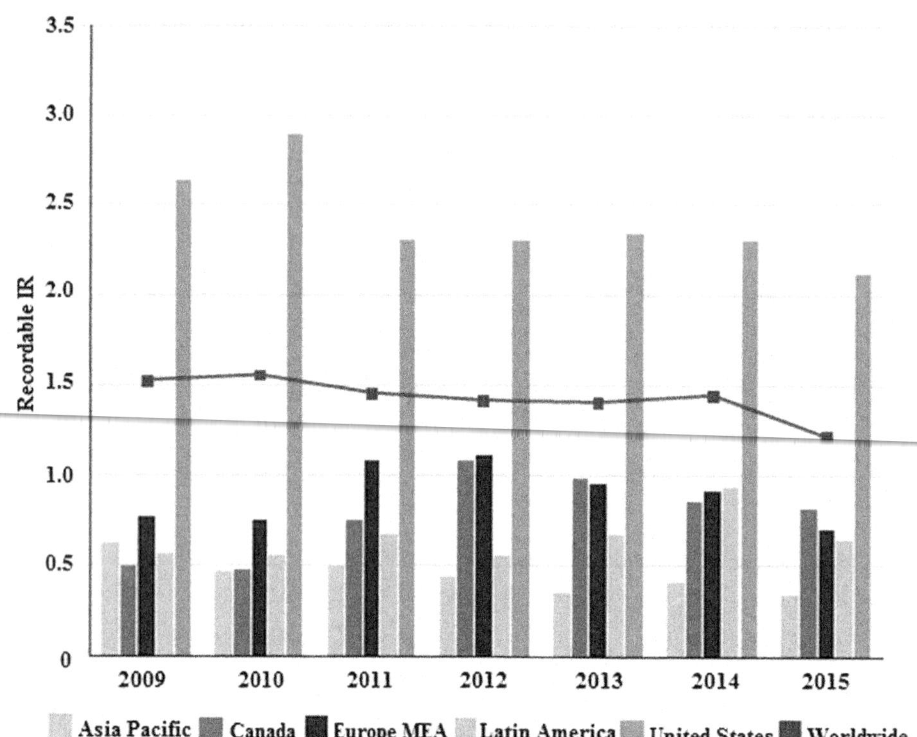

2025 Diversity Goal

3M new 2025 goal is to double the pipeline of diverse talent in management to build a diverse workforce. Increasing women and diversity in every region in which 3M operates is a core part of its sustainability strategy. 3M recognizes that doubling its diverse talent in management will help build a diverse pipeline for executive leadership as well.

People. 3M seeks and values differences in people – in thinking, experience, ethnicity, age, gender, faith, personalities and styles. 3M believes that each individual matters and contributes to growth and success. The different cultures, nationalities, backgrounds, insights, and physical and mental abilities of 3M people power its creativity and ideas. The different skills, experiences and abilities of 3M people are what drive the company forward and keep it relevant and reflective of its customers and markets.

3M continues to position itself as a leading company by ensuring it has a diverse workforce with the right people in the right positions to meet the business needs:

- Seeking and attracting diverse and qualified candidates;
- Building a global pipeline of diverse candidates;
- Strengthening 3M's reputation as a great place for diverse people to work.

Figure 20. 3M worldwide by incident type
Recordable Trends

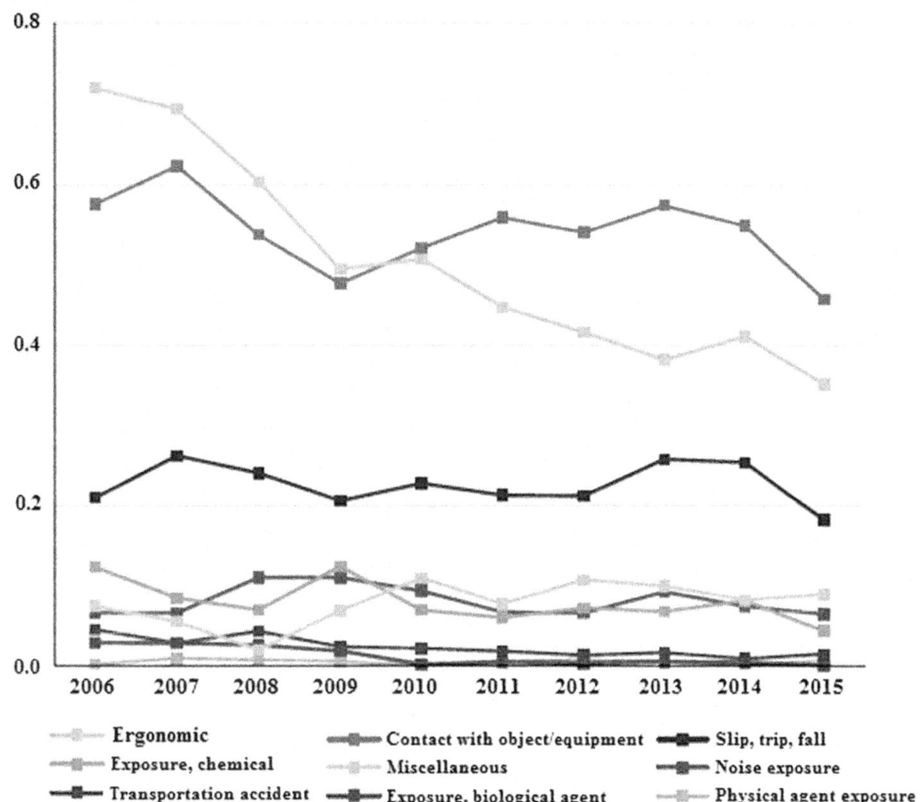

During 2015, in the U.S. alone, 3M participated in several recruiting events to connect with people and talk about employment at 3M, including:

- American Indian Sciences and Engineering Society
- Asian MBA
- Martin Luther King Jr. Day Career Fair
- National Black MBA Association
- National Organization for the Professional Advancement of Black Chemists and Chemical Engineers
- National Society of Black Engineers
- National Society of Hispanic MBAs
- Reaching Out LGBT MBAs
- Society of Hispanic Professional Engineers
- Society of Women Engineers, (National and Regional events)
- South by Southwest
- The Consortium for Graduate Study in Management
- Forum on Workplace Inclusion, hosted by University of Saint Thomas

Globally, 3M hold its "Inventing a New Future Challenge" for students to work as teams on projects finding solutions to problems. In its second successful year, eight countries participated in a local phase of the program, and the top 3 winners came to St. Paul headquarters for the final competition. Some students that applied to the challenge have been offered internships or permanent positions in their countries.

3M has formalized its commitment to diversity by establishing a 2025 sustainability goal to double the pipeline of diverse talent in management to build a diverse workforce. By being more planful regarding the development of 3M future leaders, 3M is creating more robust pools of talented and qualified people to improve the representation of diverse leaders at all levels. This 2025 goal applies to all countries and ensures leadership is accountable for progress.

Initially, 3M is focused on building its pipelines with more women and people with disabilities, and over time it will expand its actions to include other groups of people. 3M will be more successful in meeting this goal as it has a better understanding of its people already working in 3M. In the U.S. and many other countries 3M provides its people with the opportunity to opt-in and provide confidential information about their own disability status, veteran status, race/ethnicity and gender.

3M equal employment opportunity (EEO) policies prohibit all forms of illegal discrimination or harassment against applicants, employees, vendors, contractors or customers on the basis of race, color, creed, religion, sex, national origin, age, disability, veteran's status, pregnancy, genetic information, sexual orientation, marital status, citizenship status, status with regards to public assistance, gender identity/ expression or any other reason prohibited by law.

The Board of Directors values diversity as a factor in selecting nominees to serve on the Board because its experience is that diversity provides significant benefit to the Board and the Company. Although there is no specific policy on diversity, the Committee considers the board membership criteria in selecting nominees for directors, including diversity of background and experience. Such considerations may include gender, race, national origin, functional background, executive or professional experience, and international experience.

Culture. 3M is committed to fostering an inclusive environment where employees thrive, feel safe and respected, involved and valued, and free to be their best selves to create and innovate and contribute. It takes every single person in 3M to use inclusive behaviors to strengthen 3M culture. Inclusive behaviors are included in the descriptors of the Leadership Behaviors and expected of everyone. 3M is providing education to strengthen cultural agility and limit unconscious bias, reinforced by a strong global communication campaign, "I'm in", that has already reached 60 countries and has 75% awareness among 3M people worldwide.

3M is building global fluency through the learning and development of its leaders and people everywhere. Diversity and inclusion topics that resonate worldwide are included in the new 3M Leadership Way programs and enhanced by providing hands-on experiences for greater insight and impact.

One of the ways 3M involves its people in understanding and appreciating diverse perspectives is through participating in communities of interest, also referred to as employee resource networks. In these communities, people can share ideas and work together on common interests. 3M has many communities that support and advance diversity and 3M culture, among which:

3M women's leadership forum. Building on its strong past, the 3M Women's Leadership Forum (WLF) is a community of passionate women and men who realize the business value better gender balance can provide in driving efficient growth. Their mission is to accelerate the inclusion and advancement of women worldwide. WLF chapters and hubs are growing and flourishing in our countries and sites worldwide, and are visibly active in more than 70 locations. These chapters are led by local women and men and supported by their leadership. The 3M WLF is sponsored by a global executive steering team to bridge top-leadership commitment with local leadership responsibility and support and the grass-roots passion of people everywhere.

3M employee resource networks (ERNs). 3M ERNs give employees an opportunity to network and enhance their leadership skills while providing an opportunity to collaborate across cultures, lifestyles and genders. ERNs help 3M recruit, engage and retain more inclusively. They work with 3M businesses to provide relevant customer insights, and sponsor innovative educational opportunities that advance all employees. These networks include:

- A3CTION (Asians and Asian-Americans Coming Together for Innovation and Opportunity Network)
- African American Network
- Disability Awareness Network
- GLBT+ Network
- Latino Resource Network
- Military Support Network
- Native American Network
- New Employee Opportunity Network (NEON)
- Team Austin (a collaboration of our Employee Resource Networks on our Austin campus)
- Women's Leadership Forum

3M's ERNs also partner with 3M businesses to tackle specific business challenges, often with impressive results. Many of the ERNs are able to identify significant market potential in specific customer segments –some of which include millions of current or potential customers. 3M businesses are leveraging ERNs to accelerate growth in emerging markets. For instance, the Industrial and Transportation Business partnered with the Latino Resource Network to understand how to engage and sell to diverse customers using a multicultural business development process.

Customers and markets. To effectively grow the businesses and serve the customers, 3M builds its workforce to reflect the people in the industries and markets who work in them. 3M goal is to reflect the diversity of its global customers, suppliers and channel partners, and build on each employee's abilities to achieve greater customer satisfaction and accelerated growth. With greater insight and understanding of differences, 3M can be more competitive and more relevant in providing breakthrough ideas and approaches to address customers' challenges. 3M's strategy to 'Build high performing and diverse global talent' leverages the strength of its people to implement other 3M strategies, namely 'Gain profitable market share and accelerate market penetration everywhere' and 'Expand relevance to customers and 3M presence in the marketplace'.

3M is using a diversity lens in its business processes, as it gathers insight and inspiration to help solve customers' challenges and expand customer and market opportunities. For example, personal safety products in traditionally male-dominated professions (welding helmets and safety wear) are now available in sizes for women. 3M will continue to explore additional opportunities in product and packaging development and design, service delivery, and supplier diversity, as part of applying greater diversity insight in the marketplaces.

2015 Recognition

- Named as a "Best Place to Work" by the Human Rights Campaign for achieving five years in a row by obtaining a perfect score of 100% on the Corporate Equality Index;
- Among Top 20 supporters of historical black colleges / universities;
- Top 50 employer by the Minority Engineers Magazine – reader's choice;
- 20/20 – 20% by 2020 women on boards;
- Among the top scoring companies in Calvert Investments' Survey of corporate; diversity practices of the Standard & Poor 100. Ranking 90 of 100 points, improving 15 pts. from last survey, which is done every two years.

3M Footprint

The employee metrics below are reflective of employee headcount (total number of 3Mfull-time and part-time employees) not 3M full-time equivalent (FTE) employees. Due to acquisition integration schedules onto 3M's human resources systems, detailed employee information below may differ from employee totals in 3M financial reports.

Investing in People

3M is a company of bright minds collaborating to better the world. Their training is an ever-changing, constantly evolving process. The estimate of 25 hours per FTE of training and development was reached from a formal standpoint, but 3M does not believe it accurately covers the whole picture. 3M utilizes the 70-20-10 development model which indicates that over the course of a career, 70 percent of learning is done on the job, 20 percent comes through other employees, and only 10 percent of meaningful development is reached through formal training. 3M use of Individual Development Plans (IDPs) is an essential aspect of understanding training and development at 3M.

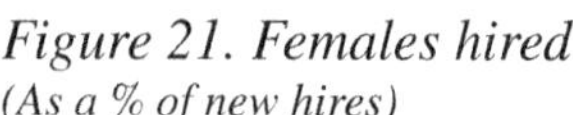

Figure 21. Females hired
(As a % of new hires)

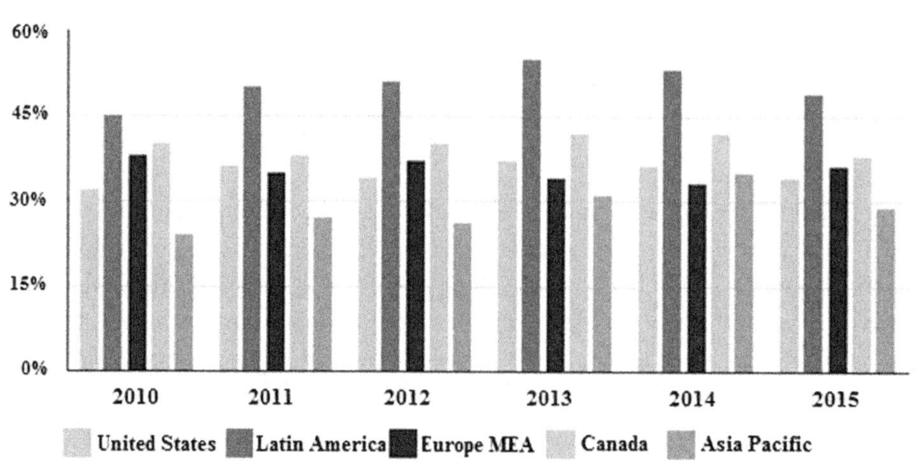

Figure 22. Total 3M employees
(Includes both full-time and part-time employees)

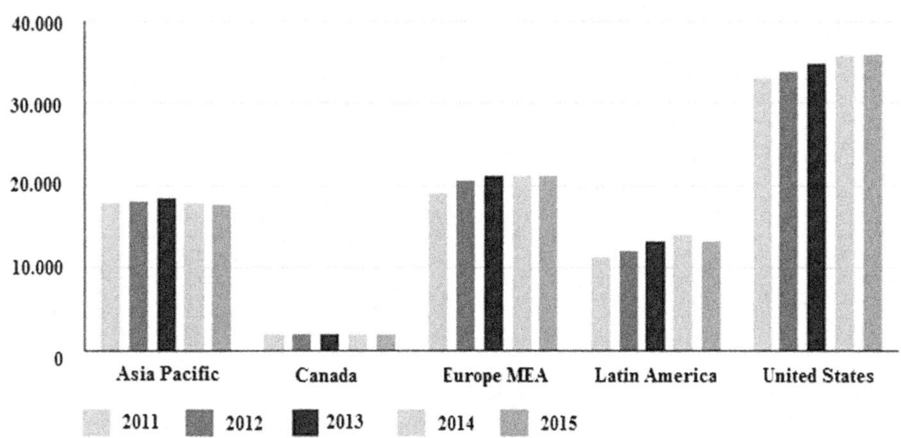

Figure 23. Female employees in management

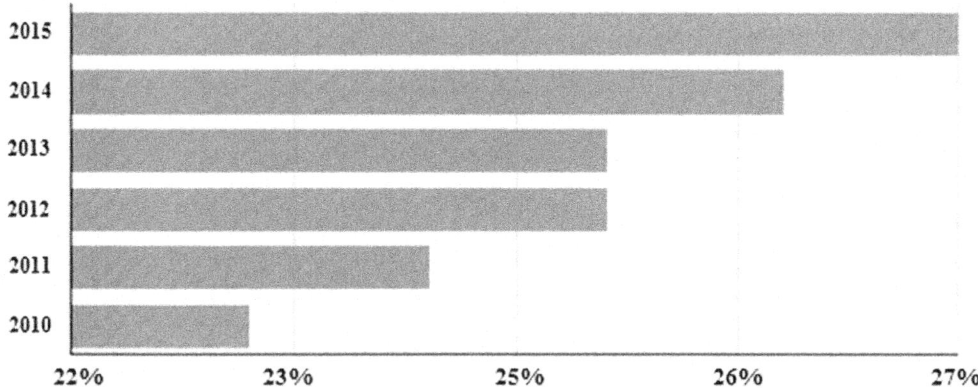

3M strives to have every employee complete a development plan. Around 85% of the professional, non-production population completed an IDP in 2015, an increase of nearly 15% over 2014. This reflects 3M intentional efforts to foster development.

2015 also marked the completion of work to transition to a new technology platform that better supports IDP creation. With the roll-out of the new platform in early 2016, employees will be easily able to link development planning to specific competencies, for which development resources are already available. Aligned with this, 3M has a goal of 100% of professional employees having IDPs.

3M learning orientation and philosophy is results rather than activity-based. Measures such as training hours or costs per employee are not leading human capital performance indicators for 3M. 3M believes indicators that align people results to the success of the company are direct performance indicators of development programs. Leadership and employee engagement, employee retention rates, new product vitality index (a key metric for the company sales percentage of new products introduced in the previ-

Table 11. Percentage of total 3M employees per year

Age Distribution	Percentage of total 3M Employees Per Year					
	2010	2011	2012	2013	2014	2015
Baby Boomers (1943-1960)	**26.60%**	**24.20%**	**22.00%**	**20.10%**	**18.20%**	**16.20%**
Asia Pacific	1.70%	1.50%	1.20%	1.18%	1.05%	0.93%
Canada	0.80%	0.70%	0.60%	0.54%	0.48%	0.47%
Europe/Middle East/Africa	5.50%	5.00%	5.00%	4.43%	4.00%	3.70%
Latin America	1.20%	1.10%	1.00%	0.83%	0.75%	0.57%
United States	17.50%	15.80%	14.20%	13.07%	11.75%	10.00%
Generation X (1961-1981)	**60.20%**	**59.90%**	**60.10%**	**59.30%**	**58.50%**	**58.40%**
Asia Pacific	14.40%	14.80%	14.10%	13.40%	12.60%	12.00%
Canada	1.50%	1.50%	1.40%	1.40%	1.30%	1.50%
Europe/Middle East/Africa	14.70%	14.70%	15.20%	15.00%	14.70%	15.00%
Latin America	8.70%	8.50%	8.50%	8.50%	8.40%	7.90%
United States	20.80%	20.50%	20.90%	21.00%	21.50%	22.00%
Generation Y (>1981)	**13.20%**	**15.90%**	**17.90%**	**20.60%**	**22.80%**	**24.50%**
Asia Pacific	3.90%	5.20%	5.40%	6.00%	6.00%	6.30%
Canada	0.10%	0.10%	0.10%	0.20%	0.20%	0.27%
Europe/Middle East/Africa	2.60%	3.10%	3.60%	4.10%	4.40%	4.80%
Latin America	3.30%	3.80%	4.50%	5.30%	6.00%	5.80%
United States	3.30%	3.70%	4.30%	4.90%	6.20%	7.40%

Figure 24. Employees hired

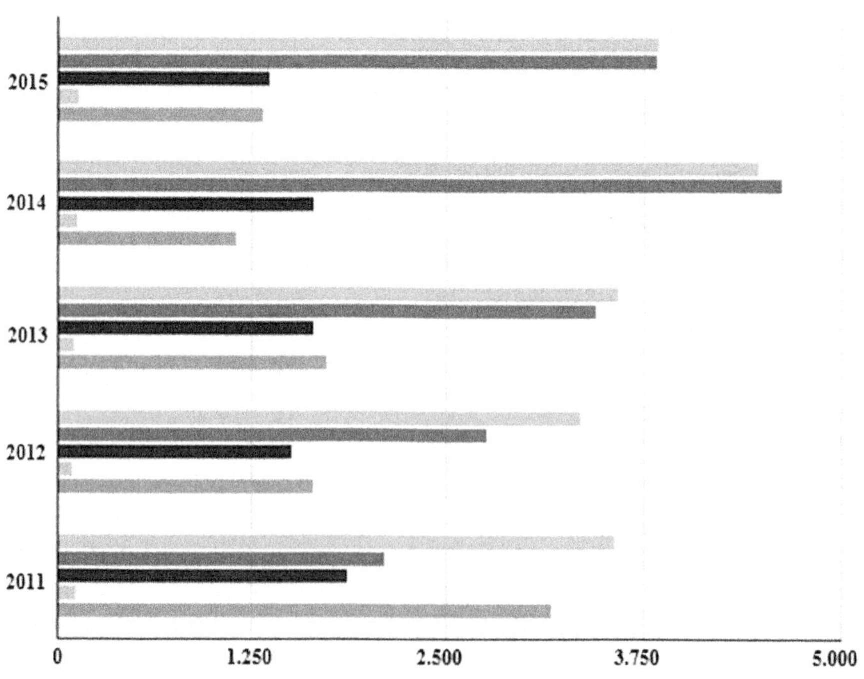

Figure 25. Female employee headcount
(As a percentage of total)

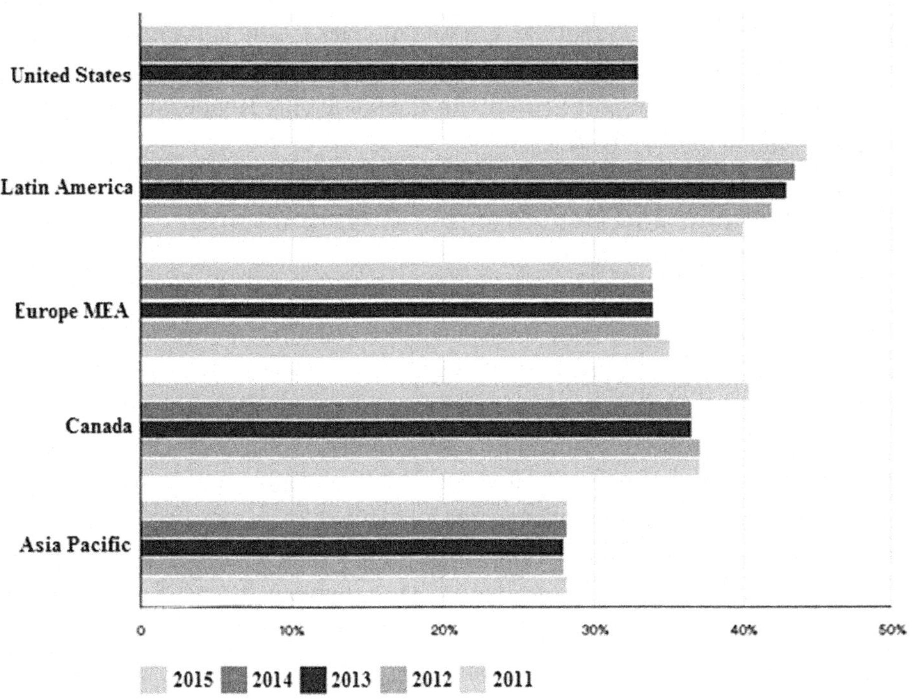

ous five years), brand recognition, acquisition integration milestones, and lean six sigma project value are a few examples of indicators that contribute to 3M's recognition as an industry and global leader.

While 3M can estimate that its numbers are close to averages found in other large manufacturing companies, comprehensive global metrics on training and training investments are difficult to track partially due to 3M's history of decentralized accountability and control over businesses. Business leaders and HR partners in the 3M businesses/functions respond to their marketplaces in terms of meeting those training and development needs. This decentralized, locally accountable approach enables quick reaction and fine-tuning to meet needs of the unique markets and specialty needs of employees serving those markets. However, this approach means that tracking non-corporate/local efforts is difficult because each is adapted to the needs of that unique market and business/function and may not use corporate wide systems.

3M global voluntary turnover rate continues to be under five percent, and this is a source of great pride for our company. Compared to most other companies, 3M employees love working here, and they rarely leave the company. 3M Employee Turnover Rate is an annualized turnover rate that measures employees that have terminated or retired from 3M during the calendar year, excluding foreign service employees and 3M temporary employees. Temporary employees are 3M employees hired temporarily with intent to be employed short-term. They do not include contingent workers (individuals provided by a third-party staffing agency to perform temporary work).

3M calculates voluntary turnover separately from retirements, company initiated turnover, and reductions in force. Voluntary employee turnover is defined as turnover due to employee initiated reasons (e.g., returning to school, going to another job in a different company). Total turnover includes Voluntary turnover and all other forms of turnover (e.g., termination as a result of restructuring, termination for poor performance, retirements).

3M's HR department is unique in that 3M has one global system and process where all of the HR information is tracked. At every 3M location around the globe, HR has instant access to all of the information. 3M uses the QlikView reporting tool – instead of having islands of information, they are all using the same information that can be tracked.

2015 Employee Training and Development Advancements

3M 2025 goal is to have 100% employee participation (production and nonproduction) in development programs to advance individual and organizational capabilities. 3M employees are encouraged and supported to pursue areas of interest and develop career paths and opportunities aligned with those interests. Moving forward, 3M seeks to formalize an individual development plan with every employee.

In 2015, 3M also held area developmental months around that globe. They resulted in an overall increase of course completion; in fact, in 2015 alone, 3M employees completed 1,289,932 courses. 3M placed at #8 on Chally Group's Best Companies for Leaders.

3M new leadership way program was initiated to develop strong leaders. It offers a global, consistent approach that is customer focused and results driven. This approach has been driven by 3M CEO, Inge Thulin, as a method to bring 3M's playbook to life. Four leadership development programs (Catalyst, Amplify, Ignite, and Spark) are part of the leadership way. These programs are targeted for high potential leaders across different career levels. Each program offers participants a blended, multi-channel approach to development. Further, each program recognizes that learning requires both time and practice, and therefore programs are experiential journeys that span months and entail hands-on projects with real deliverables. 3M believes this approach will strengthen 3M's ability to execute against its playbook, and create shareholder value.

Total Rewards

3M total rewards includes a range of plans and programs designed to attract, retain and motivate its high-performing talent. 3M regularly benchmarks its compensation and benefits with those of companies that are comparable in size and scope to ensure that 3M remains highly competitive:

- **Competitive Pay:** Base salary and variable incentive pay linked to company and individual performance.
- **Competitive Benefits:** High-quality medical and dental plan options, savings and retirement plans, and a 3M employee stock purchase plan that helps you become an owner of the company you work for.
- **Innovative Programs and Resources:** Professional and personal growth opportunities, community involvement, and recreational pursuits.

Comprehensive Benefits

3M is committed to providing competitive market pay and comprehensive benefits. In addition to providing a professional work environment that promotes innovation and rewards performance, 3M's total compensation for employees includes a variety of components for sustainable employment and the ability to build a strong financial future. 3M's total compensation program includes the following for all eligible employees worldwide. All regular full-time employees in the US are eligible for these benefits – regular part time employees who work at least 20 hours/week are also eligible. Some programs and benefits may differ internationally due to local laws and regulations.

- **Compensation:** Annual salary, short-term annual cash incentives and long-term equity incentives.
- **Vacation/Paid Leave:** Vacation, holidays and paid leave, including short-term and long-term disability benefits.
- **FlexAbility:** 3M recognizes the importance of helping employees balance their life concerns with their work responsibilities. 3M employees are able to explore a variety of flexible work arrangements with their management, including part-time, job share, flex-time, compressed work week and telecommuting. These opportunities are communicated to employees through management and are administered through 3M internal systems.
- **Life/Disability Insurance***:* Life insurance for employees and their eligible dependents at group rates. Short- and long-term disability benefits offered to help employees who cannot work due to illness or injury.
- **Health Care:** Medical, prescription drug, dental and vision benefits.
- **Health Savings Account:** An employee-owned health savings account that includes an annual 3M contribution.
- **Flexible Spending Accounts:** Tax-free reimbursement accounts for qualified health care and dependent care expenses.
- **Parental Leave:** (U.S. example) To allow parents enough time to bond with their new children, 3M's Family/ Medical Leave Policy offers all regular full-time and part-time employees additional bonding leave for this purpose even if this means they will exceed their 12-week allotment of family/medical leave (stemming from the Family Medical Leave Act) for the year. The additional bonding leave must be taken on a full-time basis and must be completed within 12 months after the birth of the child or placement in the home for adoption or foster care. 3M complies with state laws within the U.S. and with local laws and requirements for operations outside the U.S. While there can be different definitions for "parental leave," in the US during 2015, a total of 722 employees took either short term disability benefits for maternity (paid leave) and/or unpaid bonding leave (includes adoption) (female 497/male 225).
- **Domestic Partner Benefits:** 3M offers same sex domestic partner benefits to employees who meet the requirements of having a domestic partner. Eligible domestic partners and their eligible child(ren) can receive medical and dental benefits, as well as optional life insurance coverage, subject to plans terms and requirements. We also offer retiree medical for qualified domestic partners.
- **Retirement Programs:** 3M Retirement Program provides a solid foundation of retirement benefits, which includes a 401(k) plan with a company matching contribution, employer contributions to a retirement income account, and a retiree medical savings account (RMSA) to help offset the cost of pre-medicare medical coverage in retirement.

- **Stock Ownership/Investment Programs:** After two months of service at 3M, 3M general employees stock purchase plan allows eligible employees to contribute 3-10 percent of after-tax pay to puwonderrchase 3M stock at an option price that is 85 percent of the fair market value of the stock.
- **Dependent Care:** 3M provides a range of resources to assist employees with dependent care, including child care and elder care. 3M offers child care and adult care consultation and referral services through the 3M employee assistance program in order to help employees locate appropriate services for their loved ones across the United States. 3M employees in the St. Paul area also have access to back-up child care, which is available when their regular day care cannot care for their child.
- **Adoption Assistance:** 3M provides financial assistance to eligible employees who choose to adopt children by covering a portion of the eligible expenses associated with the adoption.
- **Employee Assistance Program (EAP):** In 1974, 3Mbegan an employee assistance program that today provides a variety of educational programs, resources and consultation services to U.S. employees and their dependents, and leaders across 3M to assist them in navigating challenging situations. In some locations outside of the United States, 3M offers employee assistance resources at the local level. Resources enhance well-being and effectiveness; prevent problems; or address a wide range of personal, family, work or behavioral health challenges; and are available online, in print literature and other media. In addition, 3M offers U.S. employees legal and financial consultation and referral services through the EAP. Financial issues include debt management and taxes, while legal issues include family, civil, tax or criminal.
- **Corporate-Supported Employee Groups:** Through 3M clubs around the world, 3M encourages employees with shared interests to pursue those interests in a supportive environment. Every country in which 3M does business has a 3M employee club that sponsors special events, activities and sports programs and offers special discounts and privileges in support of exercise, friendship and fun. At 3M Headquarters in St. Paul, Minnesota, the 3M Club of St. Paul goes back to 1963. 3M also sponsors Employee Resource Networks under the direction of 3Mgives.

Additional resources and opportunities offered globally:

- Scholarships for eligible dependents of employees;
- Employee stores for purchase of 3M products online or at many 3M locations;
- Support for community involvement: matching gifts, volunteer match and 3M community giving.

Education and Career Growth

Today's business environment demands that 3M becomes faster and more flexible in anticipating and exceeding the needs of its customers, shareholders and employees. Creating a high-performance culture built on continuous learning helps 3M achieve business growth for the company and professional growth for employees.

- **New Employee Onboarding:** 3M invests in onboarding and developing new employees so that they have the tools, resources and networks they need to succeed. 3M onboarding process begins at the time a candidate accepts a job offer and continues through the first year of employment. In

2013, 3M implemented an onboarding portal via its intranet in more than 60 countries. Countries have customized information available in local languages. In early 2015, 3M deployed a more comprehensive onboarding technology that provides pre-start information delivery and engagement for new employees on the front end and clear metrics, reporting and tracking for 3M on the back end. This investment sets new employees up to be successful and make meaningful contributions from the start. Instituting a 3M-wide onboarding process is also one way we help supervisors and managers support employee growth and achievement consistently throughout the company.

- **Skill Mapping and Contribution and Development Assessment:** 3M has separate processes for employee performance and career development reviews. Each year, all 3M nonproduction employees identify their contributions in meeting their specified goals through an employee performance review system. 3M strives to have 100% of nonproduction employees receiving performance and career development reviews at least annually. In 2015, approximately 95% of global nonproduction employees set up a performance review form and 67% completed the entire performance review process. In addition, employees create or update their development plan that includes goals to elevate individual performance and skills. Additional skill-mapping tools may be used in collaboration with the employee's supervisor to identify long-term desired goals. Contribution and development assessments for production staff follow site-specific procedures depending on local requirements and business-specific needs.
- **Accelerated Leadership Development:** 3M views leadership development as a competitive advantage and is accelerating leadership development across all employee segments by using new technologies and delivery methods to make its programs globally inclusive. There are multiple leadership development programs offered for different stages in employees' career journey. There are business and leadership courses available to employees at any level, including online programs that are free and available to employees in all geographies and cover topics ranging from personal effectiveness to finance. There is also a year-long onboarding program for new supervisors, as well as several programs for leaders as they progress into different leadership roles. 3M is building leadership capability through all its programs by embedding diversity, collaboration and inclusion strategies directly into its programs. 3M has also aligned courses to key leadership behaviors, which are tied to performance assessments and aim to encourage and foster the development of self and others. 3M place great importance on driving engagement of all employees by focusing on their career and development desires.

Since 2012, 3M has embarked on a process to define and communicate global functional competency models which clarify expectations of leaders regarding the knowledge, skills, and abilities to be developed over career within a specific function. Based on shared expectations, career paths are aligned with investment in training and development resources are aligned. Each function with a completed competency model publishes a guide that provides links to relevant training opportunities, as well as development suggestions that can be discussed and agreed on with the employee's supervisor on growing the competency through on-the-job activities or social learning through a coach or mentor. Currently the competency-based resources cover approximately 88% of the non-production employee population.

- **Tuition Reimbursement:** In 3M locations around the world, employees are encouraged to continuously learn and improve their skills. In most countries where 3M does business, it offers, with the management support, tuition reimbursement to encourage employees to upgrade their education to better meet current job responsibilities, prepare for future responsibilities and help qualify for changes in career paths within 3M.

- **Mentoring:** Through the 3M Mentoring Network, the organization encourages self-directed mentoring partnerships. Mentors are identified globally throughout the company utilizing online social platforms, including profile tagging and wikis. An online mentoring program design kit with guidelines for developing and implementing a mentoring program in alignment with strategic business objectives is available to support organizations wanting to offer mentoring programs. An executive mentoring program supports the professional development of high-performing employees. Originally focused on minorities and women, this program was expanded in 2013 to include all high-performing employees.
- **Outplacement Assistance:** 3M offers a range of outplacement services and resources for employees whose positions are eliminated due to business needs. These resources are offered on a worldwide basis to help employees transition to employment in other areas of 3M or outside of the Company and include services such as development of career transition skills and identification of job placement opportunities.

Employee Engagement and Recognition

3M is always happy to report that 3M's turnover rate is far lower than the turnover benchmark rate. 3M takes great pride in this fact, and it's a testament to how much its employees love working at 3M. The company has long been a supporter of gathering a well-rounded view of an individual's performance, and 3M does not use a formal comparative ranking of employees within each employee category.

90% of global salaried, non-production, employees received performance ratings through 3M's Employee Performance Review Process (EPR) in 2015. The reason 3M appraisals apply to 90% of employees, as opposed to 100%) is because there are certain countries that do not require a performance management process for certain salaried production employees.

3M process includes two components: 1) Measurable targets agreed upon by each employee and his/her supervisor; 2) Leadership behaviors ratings, which reflect the extent to which the employee engaged in core behaviors that allow 3M to execute our strategies and meet our objectives. Ratings of achievement of measurable targets impact variable compensation for all employees. Ratings of leadership behaviors impact long term variable compensation for those employees in senior positions.

The performance review process helps hold each of 3M employees accountable for his or her contribution and everyday behaviors in the organization. 3M's performance process aligns personal goals with organizational goals – by guiding behavior, 3M ensures that it achieves its goals in ways that support and strengthen its culture and achieve sustainable growth. In addition, 3M has long prioritized taking a well-rounded view of an individual's performance and ensuring employees are treated in a fair and consistent manner. To achieve this, multiple steps are taken:

- First, performance goals, linked to higher-level organizational goals, are set jointly between the individual and their leader. Tools provided to leaders during 2015 helped to facilitate conversations between leaders and employees to ensure mutual understanding of expectations and desired behaviors.

- Second, feedback on progress toward these goals is provided formally, twice a year, and supervisors are taught and encouraged to provide routine feedback to help employees adjust performance and meet or exceed goals.
- Third, 3M has implemented management team reviews. During these reviews, input from multiple managers, including those not immediately in one's area of expertise, is used to ensure a total picture of the employee is provided. 3M also offers optional tools to gather performance information, such as a client input survey, provide all 3Mers with a uniform set of expectations to drive consistency in ratings across job levels.
- Finally, the management team reviews function not only to provide comprehensive information about an employee, but also to ensure that ratings are consistent across employees within a job. This maximizes fairness by equating ratings for similar performance.

Throughout the year, and in conjunction with performance discussions, employees meet with their supervisor to evaluate progress on current goals and adjust existing goals as need to align to any changes in priorities. As employees meet their goals from their development plan, they are encouraged to update their talent profile and skills profile and review tools that have been developed to capitalize their strengths.

3M is currently in the process of moving its performance management to a new platform that will allow 3M to have more direct linkage between individual performances and objectives. The new platform should be active in 2016, and it will further improve 3M's ability to appraise, improve, and link personal experience, work experience, and leadership behaviors.

Networks and Collaboration

3M has numerous pathways to support organizational communications, learning and knowledge management. There are a variety of corporate and job functional systems to methodically help information and knowledge emerge and flow to the right people at the right time to add value. For example:

- **Formal Learning Networks:** The learning solution is 3M's corporate learning management system and is a one-stop electronic learning center that helps employees enroll in, deliver, track and report on learning activities. The learning solution serves the learning needs of 3M business units, plants and learning organizations globally.
- **Intranet Knowledge Platforms Databases:** 3M'sintranet site structure is set up so that each employee has a work center as one of the quick-link tabs following login. Each work center is a collection of tools, systems and processes that are used routinely in daily work practices to successfully complete projects and work assignments in an employee's functional work area. Company news for employees is available on a global news site called Spark 3M News. It enables employees to share news articles, videos and links with others both internally and externally via email and social media.
- **Best Practice Descriptions/Processes:** As a diverse technical company, 3M shares best practices several ways. Two of the most widely used internal organizations are the 3M technical forum and the 3M engineering and manufacturing technology organization. These two organizations provide an extensive network of expertise through specialized chapters focused on 3M's core technologies and other emerging markets. Employees in R&D, manufacturing and other parts of the supply chain are able to collaborate and drive innovation globally across the organization.

- **Company Education:** In addition to a variety of general courses, webinars, etc., 3M offers specialized extended courses to increase skills such as the 3M Leadership Development Institute, the 3M Supply Chain Academy, the 3M Marketing University and the general managers' and managing directors' program.
- **Idea Sharing:** Idea management is driven differently across the company depending on organizational needs and what works best for the area of work. Some platform examples include Yammer, Wiki Enterprise, and various 3M internal and external social media channels. Systems are implemented and available globally to share best practices and ideas. Additionally, since about 1948, 3M has encouraged its employees to spend 15% of their working time on their own projects and sharing those ideas with colleagues.

Measurement, Feedback and Action on Employee Engagement

3M measures engagement and engagement drivers and provide results to leaders and their organizations for follow-up. As 3M corporate policy, a standard opinion survey is administered to all employees at locations worldwide once every three years. 3M uses survey results to address employee concerns and identify opportunities for improvement. Summaries of survey results and actions taken are circulated up the management chain to ensure visibility and accountability. 3M also conducts a more strategically focused survey that includes engagement measures. This survey, the Vision and Strategies Alignment Survey was last conducted in October 2013.

3M also requires its leaders to actively foster engagement as part of their day-to-day coaching and interactions with others. This expectation is embedded in our leadership behaviors, which apply to all 3M leaders and links to their annual performance assessment. 3M supports leaders in these efforts via formal training, videos and on-demand tools.

- **Survey Measurements on Employee Engagement:** Results from the Standard Opinion Survey and the Vision and Strategies Alignment Survey indicate 3M's support of employee engagement is strong and continuing to get stronger. Results have improved with each administration, up to 83 percent favorable in the most recent survey, which is well above the threshold for strength (70 percent favorable).
- **Employee Rewards and Recognition:** Hard work and extra effort are rewarded and recognized at 3M through an array of award programs. 3M sponsors many corporate award programs to honor individuals and teams that make significant contributions to the company. In addition, many divisions also have their own specific ways of recognizing and rewarding people. Across 3M, management can choose from a variety of monetary and nonmonetary awards to show appreciation for exceptional contributions.

Examples of corporate awards include:

- Awards for specific professionals, such as the Global Marketing Excellence Award, and the Circle of Technical Excellence and Innovation Award;
- Awards for cross-functional teams, such as the Golden Step Award;
- Awards focused on employees who improve safety or pollution prevention;

- Two prestigious lifetime achievement awards: the Engineering Achievement Award and the Carlton Society Recognition, which honor employees for their scientific achievements.

Humanitarian Engagement

3M improves lives through innovative social investments in education, community and environment. 3M goal is to create a better world for everyone, and its approach includes annual social investments in its global communities. Through these investments, 3M strives to increase access to student achievement in STEM (science, technology, engineering and math), improve standards of living in communities where 3M operates, and build environmentally sustainable communities.

- **Engaging Globally:** 3Mgives, the social investment arm of 3M, is governed by the 3M Foundation Board of Directors and Corporate Contributions Committee comprised of senior level executives in the company. The 3M Foundation Board of Directors guides the social investment strategy including giving area, budget allocation and high-level strategy advice for execution by 3Mgives staff.3M leaders from each region develop and administer programs consistent with the overall 3Mgives strategy and local culture and social needs. For example, in the United States, 18 Community Relations Councils develop regional strategies and direct local social investments in partnership with the 3Mgives team. In addition, 3Mgives regularly convenes a Global Advisory Council comprised of senior leaders from countries around the globe to inform and develop our global giving strategy.

Since the inception of the 3M Foundation in 1953, 3M has invested $1.45 billion in cash and in-kind donations in communities around the world. These global investments were bolstered by employees and retirees volunteering millions of hours.

- **Engaging Locally:** The collaboration, discussions and interactions 3M has with its corporate, regional and local stakeholders strengthen the company's connection to the community, help address local challenges and build on relevant capabilities.

As part of 3M's 2015 Sustainability Goals, local stakeholder engagement plans were developed at select 3M manufacturing operations. Work continued in 2015 to enhance the local and regional stakeholder engagement process to further align with corporate strategic focus areas. 270 prioritized manufacturing facilities around the world have completed a stakeholder engagement plan. A framework that enables continuous progress and prioritization was developed with these key features:

- Local stakeholder identification and mapping;
- Local sustainability materiality assessment and alignment prioritization;
- Partnerships and planning;
- Impact measurement for engagement effectiveness;
- Reporting and communications.

A baseline survey regarding stakeholder engagement impact was completed for the sites to use the new framework in conjunction with updated local stakeholder engagement plants. 3M implemented this new framework in 2015 on sites within a select region with the intent to implement globally in the near future.

- **15 Percent Culture: Creativity Needs Freedom:** Since 1948, 3Mers have been encouraged to use 3M resources, to build up a unique team and to follow their own insights in pursuit of problem-solving – and to spend 15 percent of their working time to do it. A core belief at 3M is that creativity needs freedom. That's why, since about 1948, 3M has encouraged its employees to take 3M resources, to build up a unique team and to follow their own insights in pursuit of problem-solving — and to spend 15 percent of their working time to do it.

That initiative is alive and well today, and has led to some of 3M most ingenious inventions, including:

- Automobile window treatment films which enhance comfort, security and privacy in vehicles
- Multi-layer optical film, which reflects 95% of all light. It's likely in your laptop, smart phone and big-screen TV making the screen brighter, while reducing energy use.

CORPORATE PROFILE

3Mcollaborates and applies science in powerful ways to improve lives daily. With $30 billion in sales, its 90,000 employees connect with customers all around the world. Scientists, researchers and marketers work across countries and across subjects to solve challenges big and small in the following business groups: consumer, electronics and energy, health care, industrial, and safety and graphics. These five business segments bring together combinations of 3M's 46 unique technology platforms to produce over 55,000 products, driving innovation and providing for efficient sharing of business resources.

Global operations. Headquartered in St. Paul, Minnesota (USA), 3M has operations in more than 70 countries and serves customers in nearly 200 countries. The company began operations in 1902, and it was incorporated and began selling products outside the United States in 1929. An international operations organization was established in 1951. Types of operations include manufacturing facilities, research and development/laboratory sites, sales and marketing offices, technical centers, distribution centers, and regional headquarters. 3M is a member of the Dow Jones Industrial Average, and is a component of the Standard and Poor's 500 Index.

- **3M Products:** 3M serves customers through five business segments, which increase speed and efficiency by sharing technology, manufacturing, marketing and other resources across all segments.

Industrial business. The industrial segment serves a broad range of markets, such as automotive original equipment manufacturer (OEM) and automotive aftermarket (auto body shops and retail), electronics, appliance, paper and printing, packaging, food and beverage, and construction. Industrial products include tapes, a wide variety of coated, non-woven and bonded abrasives, adhesives, advanced ceramics, sealants, specialty materials, 3M purification (filtration products), closure systems for personal hygiene products, acoustic systems products, and components and products that are used in the manufacture, repair and maintenance of automotive, marine, aircraft and specialty vehicles. 3M is also a leading global supplier of precision grinding technology serving customers in the area of hard-to-grind precision applications in industrial, automotive, aircraft and cutting tools. 3M develops and produces advanced technical ceramics for demanding applications in the automotive, oil and gas, solar, industrial, electronics and defense industries. In August 2015, 3M acquired assets and liabilities associated with Polypore International, Inc.'s separations media business, a leading provider of microporous membranes and modules for filtration in the life sciences, industrial and specialty segments.

Major industrial products include vinyl, polyester, foil and specialty industrial tapes and adhesives; Scotch® Masking Tape, Scotch® Filament Tape and Scotch® Packaging Tape; packaging equipment; 3M™ VHB™ Bonding Tapes; conductive, low surface energy, sealants, hot melt, spray and structural adhesives; reclosable fasteners; label materials for durable goods; and coated, nonwoven and microstructured surface finishing and grinding abrasives for the industrial market. 3M purification provides a comprehensive line of filtration products for the separation, clarification and purification of fluids and gases. Other industrial products include fluoroelastomers for seals, tubes and gaskets in engines.

Major transportation products include insulation components, including Thinsulate™ acoustic insulation and components for cabin noise reduction and catalytic converters; functional and decorative graphics; abrasion-resistant films; adhesives; sealants; masking tapes; fasteners and tapes for attaching nameplates, trim, moldings, interior panels and carpeting; coated, nonwoven and microstructured finishing and grinding abrasives; structural adhesives; and other specialty materials. In addition, 3M provides paint finishing and detailing products, including a complete system of cleaners, dressings, polishes, waxes and other products.

Safety and graphics business. The safety and graphics segment serves a broad range of markets that increase the safety, security and productivity of people, facilities and systems. Major product offerings include personal protection products; traffic safety and security products, including border and civil security solutions; commercial solutions, including commercial graphics sheeting and systems, architectural design solutions for surfaces, and cleaning and protection products for commercial establishments; and roofing granules for asphalt shingles. In August 2015, 3M acquired Capital Safety Group S.A.R.L., a leading global provider of fall protection equipment.

This segment's products include personal protection products, such as certain disposable and reusable respirators, personal protective equipment, head and face protection, body protection, hearing protection and protective eyewear, plus reflective materials that are widely used on apparel, footwear and accessories, enhancing visibility in low-light situations. In traffic safety and security, 3M provides reflective sheeting used on highway signs, vehicle license plates, construction work-zone devices, trucks and other vehicles, and also provides pavement marking systems, in addition to electronic surveillance products, and films that protect against counterfeiting. Traffic safety and security also provides finger, palm, face and iris biometric systems for governments, law enforcement agencies, and commercial enterprises, in addition to remote people-monitoring technologies used for offend-monitoring applications. Major commercial graphics products include films, inks, and related products used to produce graphics for vehicles, signs and interior surfaces. Other products include spill-control sorbents; nonwoven abrasive materials for floor maintenance and commercial cleaning; floor matting; natural and color-coated mineral granules for asphalt shingles; plus fall protection equipment.

Electronics and energy business. The electronics and energy segment serves customers in electronics and energy markets, including solutions that improve the dependability, cost-effectiveness, and performance of electronic devices; electrical products, including infrastructure protection; telecommunications networks, and power generation and distribution.

This segment's electronics solutions include the display materials and systems business, which provides films that serve numerous market segments of the electronic display industry. 3M provides distinct products for five market segments, including products for: 1) LCD computer monitors 2) LCD televisions 3) handheld devices such as cellular phones and tablets 4) notebook PCs and 5) automotive displays. This segment also provides desktop and notebook computer screen filters that address display light control, privacy, and glare reduction needs. Major electronics products also include packaging and interconnection devices; high performance fluids and abrasives used in the manufacture of computer chips, and for cooling electronics and lubricating computer hard disk drives; and high-temperature and display tapes. Flexible circuits use electronic packaging and interconnection technology, providing more connections in less space, and are used in ink-jet printer cartridges, cell phones and electronic devices. This segment also includes the touch systems products, including touch screens, touch monitors, and touch sensor components.

This segment's energy solutions include electrical products, including infrastructure protection, telecommunications, and renewable energy. This segment serves the world's electrical and telecommunications markets, including electrical utilities, electrical construction, maintenance and repair, original equipment manufacturers (OEM), telecommunications central office, outside plant and enterprise, as well as aerospace, military, automotive and medical markets, with products that enable the efficient transmission of electrical power and speed the delivery of information. Products in this segment include pressure sensitive tapes and resins, electrical insulation, a wide array of fiber-optic and copper-based telecommunications systems for rapid deployment of fixed and wireless networks, as well as the 3M™ Aluminum Conductor Composite Reinforced (ACCR) electrical power cable that increases transmission capacity for existing power lines. This segment also includes renewable energy component solutions for the solar and wind power industries, as well as infrastructure products solutions that provide municipalities both protection and detection solutions for electrical, oil, natural gas, water, rebar and other infrastructure assets.

Health care business. The health care segment serves markets that include medical clinics and hospitals, pharmaceuticals, dental and orthodontic practitioners, health information systems, and food manufacturing and testing. Products and services provided to these and other markets include medical and surgical supplies, skin health and infection prevention products, inhalation and transdermal drug delivery systems, oral care solutions (dental and orthodontic products), health information systems, and food safety products. In April 2014, 3M purchased all of the outstanding equity interests of Treo Solutions LLC, headquartered in Troy, New York. Treo Solutions LLC is a provider of data analytics and business intelligence to healthcare payers and providers. In March 2015, 3M acquired Ivera Medical Corp., a manufacturer of health care products that disinfect and protect devices used for access into a patient's bloodstream.

In the medical and surgical areas, 3M is a supplier of medical tapes, dressings, wound closure products, orthopedic casting materials, electrodes and stethoscopes. In infection prevention, 3M markets a variety of surgical drapes, masks and preps, as well as sterilization assurance equipment and patient warming solutions designed to prevent hypothermia in surgical settings. Other products include drug delivery systems, such as metered-dose inhalers, transdermal skin patches and related components. Oral care solutions include restoratives, adhesives, finishing and polishing products, crowns, impression materials, preventive sealants, professional tooth whiteners, prophylaxis and orthodontic appliances, as well as digital workflow solutions to transform traditional impression and analog processes. In health information systems, 3M develops and markets computer software for hospital coding and data classification, and provides related consulting services. 3M provides food safety products that make it faster and easier for food processors to test the microbiological quality of food.

Consumer business. The consumer segment serves markets that include consumer retail, office retail, office business to business, home improvement, drug and pharmacy retail, and other markets. Products in this segment include office supply products, stationery products, construction and home improvement products (do-it-yourself), home care products, protective material products, certain consumer retail personal safety products, and consumer health care products.

Major consumer products include Scotch® brand products, such as Scotch® Magic™ tape, Scotch® glue stick and Scotch® cushioned mailer; Post-it® products, such as Post-it® flags, Post-it® note pads, Post-it® labeling &cover-up tape, and Post-it® pop-up notes and dispensers; construction and home improvement products, including surface preparation and wood-finishing materials, Command™ adhesive products and Filtrete™ filters for furnaces and air conditioners; home care products, including Scotch-Brite® scour pads, Scotch-Brite® scrub sponges, Scotch-Brite® microfiber cloth products, O-Cel-O™ sponges; protective material products, such as Scotchgard™ fabric protectors; certain maintenance-free respirators; certain consumer retail personal safety products, including safety glasses, hearing protectors, and 3M Thinsulate™ insulation, which is used in jackets, pants, gloves, hats and boots to keep people warm; Nexcare™ adhesive bandages; and ACE® branded (and related brands) elastic bandage, supports and thermometer product lines.

3M values. 3M's actions are guided by its corporate vision and values of uncompromising honesty and integrity. 3M is proud to be recognized worldwide as an ethical and law-abiding company. As a company, 3M is committed to sustainable development through environmental protection, social responsibility and economic success.

3M guiding values include:

- Act with uncompromising honesty and integrity in everything 3M does.
- Satisfy customers with innovative technology and superior quality, value and service.
- Provide the investors an attractive return through sustainable, global growth.
- Respect social and physical environment around the world.
- Value and develop the employees' diverse talents, initiative and leadership.
- Earn the admiration of all those associated with 3M worldwide.

Corporate Profile: Corporate Governance

This part includes the Board's leadership structure and responsibilities, the Board's role in risk oversight and the process for stakeholder input. The company believes that good corporate governance practices serve the long-term interests of stockholders, strengthen the board and management, and further enhance the public trust 3M has earned from more than a century of operating with honesty and integrity.

Corporate Governance Best Practices

Board Independence:

- Substantial majority of independent directors – twelve of thirteen directors are independent of the company and management – and all are highly qualified.

- Independent directors regularly meet in executive sessions without management.
- Independent directors have complete access to management and employees.
- Regularly refresh Board; added 6 new directors in past 4 years; average director tenure is 6.8 years.

Board Committee independence and expertise:

- Committee independence – Only independent directors serve on the Board's committees with independent committee chairs empowered to establish committee agendas.
- Committee executive sessions – at each regularly scheduled meeting, members of the Audit Committee, Compensation Committee, Finance Committee, and Nominating and Governance Committee meet in executive session.
- Financial expertise – All members of the Audit Committee meet the NYSE listing standards for financial expertise, and six of the seven members are "audit committee financial experts" under SEC rules.

Stockholder rights:

- Annual election of all directors.
- Majority voting for directors in uncontested elections.
- Proxy access – a stockholder, or a group of up to 20 stockholders, continuously owning for 3 years at least 3 percent of our outstanding common shares may nominate and include in our proxy materials up to the greater of two directors and 20 percent of the number of directors currently serving, if the stockholder(s) and nominee(s) satisfy the bylaw requirements.
- Established policies and criteria for director nominations, including candidates recommended by stockholders.
- No supermajority voting provisions in Bylaws or Certificate of Incorporation.
- Stockholders holding 25 percent of the outstanding shares have the right to call a special meeting.
- No stockholders' rights plan (also known as a "poison pill").
- Established protocol for stockholders to communicate with the independent Lead Director, the chairs of the Audit, Compensation, Finance, and Nominating and Governance Committees of the Board, any of the other independent directors or all of the independent directors as a group or the full Board.

3M Governance Structure

Stockholder outreach and engagement:

- 3M maintains a vigorous stockholder engagement program. During 2015, members of senior management met with a cross-section of stockholders owning approximately 35 percent of its outstanding shares.
- The feedback from those meetings was shared with the Nominating and Governance Committee and the Board and helped inform the Board's decision to adopt proxy access bylaws in November 2015.

Risk oversight:

- Broad risk oversight by the Board and its committees, with committee-level risk analyses reported to the full Board and senior-level internal auditor and Chief Compliance Officer appointed by, and reporting directly to, the Audit Committee.

Board approved long-term strategic plans and capital allocation strategies:

- Each year management presents to the Board, and the Board discusses and approves, detailed long-term strategic plans for the company, the international business, and each of the company's business groups. Each presentation includes an overview of the business group, the financial performance, an assessment of the portfolio for growth opportunities using a SWOT analysis (i.e., strengths, weaknesses, opportunities, and threats); strategic priorities to drive the three key value creation levers—portfolio management, investing in innovation, and business transformation; plans to drive the four corporate fundamental strengths—technology, manufacturing, global capabilities, and brand; and the projected long-term financial performance.
- The Board also approves the long-term capital structure of the company to ensure that there is sufficient capital to invest for future growth. The company is committed to investing in organic growth, most notably through capital expenditures and research and development. The company has invested approximately $16 billion in capital expenditures and research and development to support and fund organic growth over the past 5 years. 3M has opened six customer technical centers around the world, and a new, state-of-the-art research and development laboratory in the United States.
- The capital allocation plans have flexibility to respond quickly to strategic acquisition opportunities that can strengthen the company's portfolio. Over the past 5 years, 3M has invested approximately $6 billion in strategic acquisitions to build upon and strengthen its business portfolio for continued future growth.
- The company has a long history of returning cash to stockholders, having paid nearly $10 billion in dividends over the past 5 years.
- Finally, share repurchases represent the last component of 3M's capital allocation plans. Over the past 5 years, 3M has returned approximately $21 billion to stockholders via share repurchases.

Director orientation and continuing education:

- **Board Orientation:** 3M orientation programs familiarize new directors with 3M's businesses, strategic plans, and policies, and prepare them for their role on their assigned committees.
- Continuing education programs assist directors in maintaining skills and knowledge necessary for the performance of their duties. These programs may be part of regular Board and Committee meetings or provided by academic or other qualified third parties.

Board and Committee evaluations:

Figure 26. An overview of 3M corporate governance practices

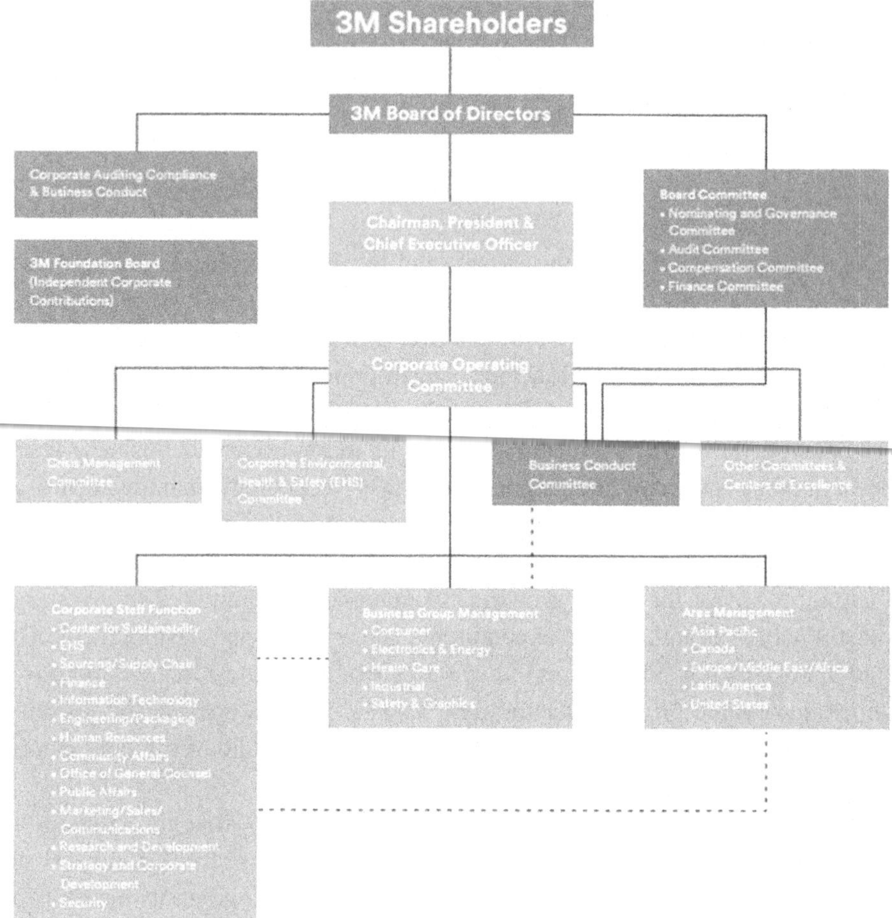

- The Nominating and Governance Committee conducts an annual evaluation of the performance of the Board and each of its committees. The results are shared with the Board and help identify areas in which the Board and its committees could improve performance.
- As part of the nomination process, the Nominating and Governance Committee annually evaluates each of the directors to ensure our directors have the necessary skills and experience to effectively oversee the company.

Compliance:

- Code of business conduct and ethics for directors.
- Code of conduct for all employees, including our Chief Executive Officer, Chief Financial Officer, and Chief Accounting Officer.
- Disclosure committee for financial reporting.
- Disclosure of public policy engagement on 3Minvestor relations web site, under Governance—Governance Documents — "Political Activities and Issue Advocacy," including disclosure of po-

litical contributions and membership in key trade associations where membership dues allocated for lobbying purposes exceed $25,000.

Environmental stewardship and sustainability:

- Long-standing commitment to environmental stewardship and sustainability.
- 2025 Sustainability Goals for raw materials, water, and energy and climate, including increasing wind and solar renewable energy to 25% of total electricity use by 2025.

Executive compensation:

- Annual advisory approval of executive compensation with approximately 96% of the votes cast in favor of the company's executive compensation program in 2015.
- Strong pay-for-performance philosophy.
- Incentive compensation subject to clawback policy.
- Robust stock ownership guidelines for executive officers and stock retention policy for directors.
- Prohibition of hedging or pledging 3M stock by directors and executive officers.
- No employment, severance, or change-in-control agreements with any senior executives, including the CEO.
- Long-term incentive compensation linked to financial objectives of earnings per share growth, organic volume growth, return on invested capital, and free cash flow conversion.

Sustainability Governance

The CEO has been granted, by the Board of Directors, final responsibility for delegating the authority for economic, environmental and social topics from the highest governance body to senior executives and other employees. The authority is spelled out in 3Mmanagement guide. The CEO has been delegated authority in the development, approval, and updating of the organization's purpose, value or mission statements, strategies, policies, and goals related to economic, environmental and social impacts. As a practical matter, issues may initially be raised through a variety of sources (functions, Board, external stakeholders) that might prompt changes in these specific areas, and that may be accomplished through standing functional, business or strategic planning processes. Changes in the company's values, mission, or strategies are routinely reviewed with the Company's Board of Directors.

The company routinely reviews economic, environmental and social topics with the Board of Directors, or committees of the Board to inform or seek their guidance on major topics. The composition of the Board itself also reflects expertise and experience across a broad variety of economic, environmental or social topics. The Board takes an active interest in managing all economic, environmental and social impacts risks. Some are addressed at a full Board level while many others are addressed routinely as part of Board committee activities. The company, through several different functional groups, maintains ongoing consultations with a variety of prospective stakeholders on a diversity of matters, and with the aid of 3rd party external experts has reviewed the company's position on impacts, risks and opportunities. These risk topics are covered as part of the company's enterprise risk management initiative and are routinely reviewed either with one of the Board's committees or, most recently, with the full Board of Directors. Elements of these subjects are covered at each of the eight yearly Board meetings.

The Corporate Operating Committee, which is comprised of the CEO and his direct reports, approves 3M-wide sustainability principles, strategy and goals, as well as any associated major changes. Executive Committees associated with the strategic sustainability functions (composed of cross-functional members) help set and approve relevant policies and provide direction on executing the developed sustainability strategies.

For example, the Environmental Health and Safety (EHS) Committee, appointed by the Corporate Operating Committee, is composed of the following functions:

- Senior Vice President of Corporate Supply Chain Operations.
- Senior Vice President of Research and Development and Chief Technology Officer.
- Chief Sustainability Officer.
- Vice President of Government Affairs.
- Vice President of Medical.
- Vice President of Compliance and Business Conduct.
- Vice President and General Manager of Materials Resource Division.
- Associate General Counsel, Supply Chain and EHS.

3M's Sustainability Center of Excellence, led by 3M Chief Sustainability Officer, collaborates with various other global staff organizations and business units to develop the corporate sustainability strategy and goals. In addition, 3M's corporate staff groups provide technical expertise to assist business groups and area management in implementing and meeting the corporate sustainability strategy, policies and goals. The formation of the Sustainability Center of Excellence in 2013 demonstrates the corporation's commitment to integrate innovation and sustainability for the benefit of 3M operations and customers. The primary role of the Center of Excellence is to develop strategy, set significant goals to advance and track progress and to drive sustainable actions throughout 3M and in collaboration with customers, partners and communities.

Corporate Governance Guidelines

The Board has adopted corporate governance guidelines which provide a framework for the effective governance of the company. The guidelines address matters such as the respective roles and responsibilities of the Board and management, the Board's leadership structure, the responsibilities of the independent Lead Director, director independence, the Board membership criteria, Board committees, and Board and management evaluation. The Board's Nominating and Governance Committee is responsible for overseeing and reviewing the Guidelines at least annually and recommending any proposed changes to the Board for approval. The corporate governance guidelines, the Certificate of Incorporation and Bylaws, the charters of the Board committees, the director independence guidelines, and the codes of conduct provide the framework for the governance of the Company.

Executive sessions. As an agenda item for every regularly scheduled Board and committee meeting, independent directors regularly meet in executive session, without the Chairman/CEO or other members of management present, to consider such matters as they deem appropriate.

The Board's leadership structure is characterized by:

- A combined Chairman of the Board and CEO;

- A strong, independent, and highly experienced Lead Director with well-defined responsibilities that support the Board's oversight responsibilities;
- A robust committee structure consisting entirely of independent directors with oversight of various types of risks; and
- An engaged and independent Board.

The Board of Directors believes that this leadership structure provides independent board leadership and engagement while deriving the benefits of having 3M CEO also serve as Chairman of the Board. As the individual with primary responsibility for managing the Company's day-to-day operations and with in-depth knowledge and understanding of the company, 3M CEO is best positioned to chair regular Board meetings as the directors discuss key business and strategic issues. Coupled with an independent Lead Director, this combined structure provides independent oversight while avoiding unnecessary confusion regarding the Board's oversight responsibilities and the day-to-day management of business operations.

The Board believes that adopting a rigid policy on whether to separate or combine the positions of Chairman of the Board and CEO would inhibit the Board's ability to provide for a leadership structure that would best serve stockholders. As a result, the Board has rejected adopting a policy permanently separating or combining the positions of Chairman and CEO in its corporate governance guidelines, which are reviewed at least annually. Instead, the Board adopted an approach that allows it, in representing the stockholders' best interests, to decide who should serve as Chairman or CEO, or both, under present or anticipated future circumstances. The Board believes that combining the roles of CEO and Chairman contributes to an efficient and effective Board. The Board believes that to drive change and continuous improvement within the company, tempered by respect for 3M's traditions and values, the CEO must have maximum authority. The CEO is primarily responsible for effectively leading significant change, improving operational efficiency, driving growth, managing the company's day-to-day business, managing the various risks facing the company, and reinforcing the expectation for all employees of continuing to build on 3M's century old tradition of uncompromising integrity and doing business the right way.

The Board believes that the company's corporate governance measures ensure that strong, independent directors continue to effectively oversee the company's management and key issues related to executive compensation, CEO evaluation and succession planning, strategy, risk, and integrity. The corporate governance guidelines provide, in part, that:

- Independent directors comprise a substantial majority of the Board;
- Directors are elected annually by a majority vote in uncontested director elections;
- Only independent directors serve on the Audit, Compensation, Finance, and Nominating and Governance Committees;
- The committee chairs establish their respective agendas;
- The Board and committees may retain their own advisors;
- The independent directors have complete access to management and employees;
- The independent directors meet in executive session without the CEO or other employees during each regular Board meeting; and
- The Board and each committee regularly conduct a self-evaluation to determine whether it and its committees function effectively.

The Board has also designated one of its members to serve as Lead Director, with responsibilities (described in the next section) that are similar to those typically performed by an independent chairman.

Independent Lead Director

The Board has designated one of its members to serve as a Lead Director, with responsibilities that are similar to those typically performed by an independent chairman ("Lead Director"). Michael L. Eskew was appointed Lead Director by the independent directors effective November 12, 2012, succeeding Dr. Vance Coffman who had served as Lead Director since 2006. Michael Eskew is a highly-experienced director, currently serving on the boards of The Allstate Corporation, International Business Machines Corporation, and Eli Lilly and Company, and was the former Chairman and CEO of United Parcel Service, Inc. His responsibilities include, but are not limited to, the following:

- Presides at all meetings of the Board at which the Chairman is not present, including executive sessions of the independent directors;
- Acts as a key liaison between the Chairman/CEO and the independent directors;
- Approves the meeting agendas for the Board, and approves the meeting schedules to assure that there is sufficient time for discussion of all agenda items;
- Has the authority to approve the materials to be delivered to the directors in advance of each Board meeting and provides feedback regarding the quality, quantity, and timeliness of those materials (this duty not only gives the Lead Director approval authority with respect to materials to be delivered to the directors in advance of each Board meeting but also provides a feedback mechanism so that the materials may be improved for future meetings);
- Has the authority to call meetings of the independent directors;
- Communicates Board member feedback to the Chairman/CEO (except that the chair of the Compensation Committee leads the discussion of the Chairman/CEO's performance and communicates the Board's evaluation of that performance to the Chairman/CEO);
- If requested by major stockholders, ensures that he is available, when appropriate, for consultation and direct communication; and
- Performs such other duties as requested by the independent directors.

Communication With Directors (Stockholder and Stakeholder Input)

The Board of Directors has adopted the following process for stockholders and other interested parties to send communications to members of the Board. Stockholders and other interested parties may communicate with the Lead Director, the chairs of the Audit, Compensation, Finance, and Nominating and Governance Committees of the Board, or with any of the other independent directors, or all of them as a group, by sending a letter to the following address: Corporate Secretary, 3M Company, 3M Center, Building 220-14W-06, St. Paul, MN 55144-1000.

Director Independence

The Board has adopted a formal set of director independence guidelines with respect to the determination of director independence, which either conform to or are more exacting than the independence requirements of the NYSE listing standards. In accordance with these guidelines, a director or nominee for director must be determined to have no material relationship with the company other than as a director. The guidelines specify the criteria by which the independence of 3M directors will be determined, including strict guidelines for directors and their immediate family members with respect to past employment or affiliation with the company or its independent registered public accounting firm. The guidelines also prohibit Audit and Compensation Committee members from having any direct or indirect financial relationship with the company, and restrict both commercial and not-for-profit relationships of all directors with the company. Directors may not be given personal loans or extensions of credit by the company, and all directors are required to deal at arm's length with the company and its subsidiaries, and to disclose any circumstance that might be perceived as a conflict of interest.

In accordance with these guidelines, the Board undertook its annual review of director independence. During this review, the Board considered transactions and relationships between each director, or any member of his or her immediate family and the company and its subsidiaries and affiliates in each of the most recent three completed fiscal years. The Board also considered whether there were any transactions or relationships between the company and a director or any members of a director's immediate family (or any entity of which a director or an immediate family member is an executive officer, general partner, or significant equity holder). The Board considered that in the ordinary course of business, transactions may occur between the company and its subsidiaries and companies at which some of our directors are or have been officers. In particular, the Board considered the annual amount of sales to 3M for each of the most recent three completed fiscal years by each of the companies where directors serve or have served as an executive officer, as well as purchases by those companies from 3M. The Board determined that the amount of sales and purchases in each fiscal year was below one percent of the annual revenues of each of those companies, the threshold set forth in the director independence guidelines. The Board also considered charitable contributions to not-for-profit organizations with which 3M directors or immediate family members are affiliated, none of which approached the threshold set forth in 3Mdirector independence guidelines.

As a result of this review, the Board affirmatively determined that the following directors are independent under these guidelines: Linda G. Alvarado, Sondra L. Barbour, Thomas "Tony" K. Brown, Vance D. Coffman, David B. Dillon, Michael L. Eskew, Herbert L. Henkel, Muhtar Kent, Edward M. Liddy, Gregory R. Page, Robert J. Ulrich, and Patricia A. Woertz. The Board has also determined that members of the Audit Committee and Compensation Committee received no compensation from the company other than for service as a director. Inge G. Thulin, Chairman of the Board, President and Chief Executive Officer, is considered to not be independent because of his employment by the company.

Board Membership Criteria

3M culture of innovation is powered by the creativity of 3M diverse employees. You can see it in the variety of backgrounds, perspectives, and skills 3M people bring to the collaborative effort of creating world-pleasing products. The Nominating and Governance Committee of 3M Board identifies individuals whom the Committee believes are qualified to become Board members in accordance with 3M Board Membership Criteria contained in the Proxy Statement. Selected individuals are recommended to the Board for nomination to stand for election at the next meeting of stockholders of the company in which directors will be elected.

3M's corporate governance guidelines contain Board membership criteria which include a list of skills and characteristics expected to be represented on 3M's Board. The Nominating and Governance Committee periodically reviews with the Board the appropriate skills and characteristics required of Board members given the current Board composition. It is the intent of the Board that the Board, itself, will be a high-performance organization creating competitive advantage for the company. To perform as such, the Board will be composed of individuals who have distinguished records of leadership and success in their arena of activity and who will make substantial contributions to Board operations and effectively represent the interests of all stockholders. The Committee's and the Board's assessment of Board candidates includes, but is not limited to, consideration of:

- Roles in and contributions valuable to the business community;
- Personal qualities of leadership, character, judgment, and whether the candidate possesses and maintains throughout service on the Board a reputation in the community at large of integrity, trust, respect, competence, and adherence to the highest ethical standards;
- Relevant knowledge and diversity of background and experience in business, manufacturing, technology, finance and accounting, marketing, international business, government, and other areas; and
- Whether the candidate is free of conflicts and has the time required for preparation, participation, and attendance at all meetings.

In addition to these minimum requirements, the Committee will also evaluate whether the nominee's skills are complementary to the existing Board members' skills, the Board's needs for particular expertise in certain areas, and will assess the nominee's impact on Board dynamics and effectiveness.

In 2015, David Dillon was nominated and elected to the 3M Board of Directors. Mr. Dillon retired as Kroger's Chairman of the Board on December 31, 2014, where he was Chairman of the Board since 2004 and was the Chief Executive Officer from 2003 through 2013. From 1995 to 2003, he served as President, and he was elected Executive Vice President in 1990. He also serves on the board of the Union Pacific Corporation.

Diversity

The Board of Directors values diversity as a factor in selecting nominees to serve on the Board because its experience is that diversity provides significant benefit to the Board and the company. Although there is no specific policy on diversity, the Committee considers the Board Membership Criteria in selecting nominees for directors, including diversity of background and experience. Such considerations may include gender, race, national origin, functional background, executive or professional experience, and international experience.

An inclusive culture at 3M is built on 3Mhuman resource principles – to respect the dignity and worth of individuals; encourage the initiative of each employee; challenge individual capabilities; and provide equal opportunity. 3M is continuously focusing on building and maintaining an inclusive culture.

In 2015, there were two women on 3M's Board of Directors: Linda Alvarado and Sandra Barbour, representing 20% of the Board. In the first half of 2016, Patricia Woertz joined as the third woman director. Linda Alvarado is the President and Chief Executive Officer of Alvarado Construction, Inc., a Denver based commercial general contractor, construction management, and development company. In addition to being on the Board of 3M, Ms. Alvarado also serves on the Board of Pitney Bowes, Inc. Ms. Alvarado is the recipient of numerous awards including being named by the Hispanic Business Magazine and Latino Leaders Magazine as one of the "100 Most Influential Hispanics in America" and 2003 Inducted in the National Women's Hall of Fame. Linda Alvarado was not seeking re-election and end her service on the Board on May 10, 2016, when her term expires. Sondra Barbour is the Executive Vice President of Information Systems & Global Solutions at Lockheed Martin Corporation, a high technology aerospace and defense company. Since joining Lockheed Martin in 1986, Ms. Barbour has served in various leadership capacities and has extensive technology experience, notably in the design and development of large-scale information systems. In 2013 she was appointed Executive Vice President, Information Systems & Global Solutions. From 2008 to 2013 she served as Senior Vice President, Enterprise Business Services and Chief Information Officer. Prior to that role, she served as Vice President, Corporate Shared Services from 2007 to 2008 and Vice President, Corporate Internal Audit from2006 to 2007. Patricia Woertz joined the 3M Board in the first half of 2016. She is retired Chairman of the Board and Chief Executive Officer, Archer-Daniels-Midland Company, an agricultural processor and food ingredient provider. Ms. Woertz joined ADM as Chief Executive Officer and President in April 2006, and was named Chairman of the Board in February 2007. She served as Chief Executive Officer until December 2014, and Chairman of the Board until December 2015. Before joining ADM, Ms. Woertz held positions of increasing importance at Chevron Corporation and its predecessor companies. Ms. Woertz served on the President's Export Council 2010-2015 and chaired the U.S. section of the U.S.-Brazil CEO Forum from 2013-2015.In 2015, Kimberly Price joined 3M's Corporate Officers along with Julie Bushman and Marlene McGrath. Kimberly was named 3M's senior vice president of Corporate Communications and Enterprise Services. She joined the company's Corporate Operating Committee and reports directly to President, Chairman of the Board and CEO Inge Thulin. Kimberly has been named as a Centennial Girl Scout Honoree, Minnesota Attorney of the Year, Diversity Journal Woman Worth Watching, one of Savoy's Most Influential Women in Corporate America, STEM Connector 100 Diverse Corporate Leaders and United Negro College Fund Masked Ball Awardee. She helps lead and serves in local, national and international organizations, including the Greater Twin Cities United Way, the Executive Leadership Council and the International Women's Forum.

Board Compensation

3M provides compensation to its executives to recognize their contributions to the success of its business and reward them for delivering performance that meets the growth, profitability, and other objectives of the company. All elements of this compensation are determined by the Compensation Committee, which is composed solely of independent nonemployee directors. In addition, the Committee's decisions concerning the compensation of 3M's Chief Executive Officer are subject to ratification by all of the independent members of the Board of Directors.

The Committee regularly reviews the design of and risks associated with the company's executive compensation program and, with the assistance of its independent compensation consultant, makes decisions concerning changes in the executive compensation program when appropriate.

3M's executive officers assist the Committee with the process of determining the compensation of the Company's executives. In particular, Mr. Thulin, assisted by 3M's Senior Vice President, Human Resources, performs an annual performance evaluation of each of 3M's senior executives whose compensation is determined by the Committee. The results of these annual performance evaluations form the basis for Mr. Thulin's recommendations to the Committee as to the annual merit base salary and target annual incentive compensation increases for such senior executives, as well as the size of their annual long-term incentive compensation awards. The Committee discusses the recommendations with Mr. Thulin at its meetings prior to making its decisions on any change to an executive's annual base salary or target annual incentive compensation or any long-term incentive compensation awards.

The Committee reviews and approves annual performance goals and objectives for 3M's Chief Executive Officer. Acting through its Chairman, the Committee also conducts and discusses with the independent members of the Board of Directors an annual evaluation of the Chief Executive Officer's performance against such goals and objectives. Finally, the Committee, assisted by its independent compensation consultant, annually reviews and approves (based on this annual evaluation), subject to ratification by the independent members of the Board of Directors, the compensation of the Chief Executive Officer.

In May 2015, the Nominating and Governance Committee considered a board compensation study prepared by Frederic W. Cook & Co., Inc. As a result of that study, the Committee recommended and the Board approved to maintain the annual compensation for nonemployee directors of $280,000. The annual cash retainer of $120,000 remains unchanged. Approximately 43% of the annual compensation (or $120,000) is payable in cash in four quarterly installments and approximately 57% of the annual compensation (or $160,000) is payable in common stock after the Annual Meeting.

The chairs of the Finance and Nominating and Governance Committees each receive an additional annual fee of $15,000, the chair of the Compensation Committee receives an additional annual fee of $25,000, and the Lead Director receives an additional annual fee of $30,000. There are no meeting fees. In lieu of the cash fees, a director may elect to receive common stock of 3M. Nonemployee directors may also voluntarily defer all or part of their annual cash fees or stock awards until they cease to be members of the Board.

In 2015, 3M delivered another strong year in terms of both financial performance and returns to its stockholders. 3M remains one of the most successful companies on the planet, and compared to its peers and the median, 3M continues to be one of the top-performing companies. These results reflected the strong performance of the company's leadership team, including the Named Executive Officers, and impacted their incentive compensation.

3M remains committed to executing its playbook, controlling the controllable, and making investments for long-term success. 3M is building the company for efficient growth in 2016 and beyond. As always, 3M executive compensation aligns with how 3M performs.

Stock Ownership Guidelines

The company's stock ownership guidelines apply to all executive officers of the company and are designed to increase an executive's equity stake in 3M and more closely align his or her financial interests with those of 3M's stockholders.

The guidelines provide that the Chief Executive Officer should attain beneficial ownership of 3M stock equal to six times his or her annual base salary, the Executive Vice Presidents and a majority of the Senior Vice Presidents should attain beneficial ownership of 3M stock equal to three times their annual base salaries, and Vice Presidents and the remaining Senior Vice Presidents should attain beneficial ownership of 3M stock equal to two times their annual base salaries. The stock ownership guidelines provide that the number of shares required to be beneficially owned by each covered executive will be calculated based on such executive's annual base salary at the time of initial appointment to a Section

Figure 27. The breakdown of reported 2015 compensation for 3M CEO and the average of 3M other named executive officers as disclosed in the Proxy Statement ("NEOs")

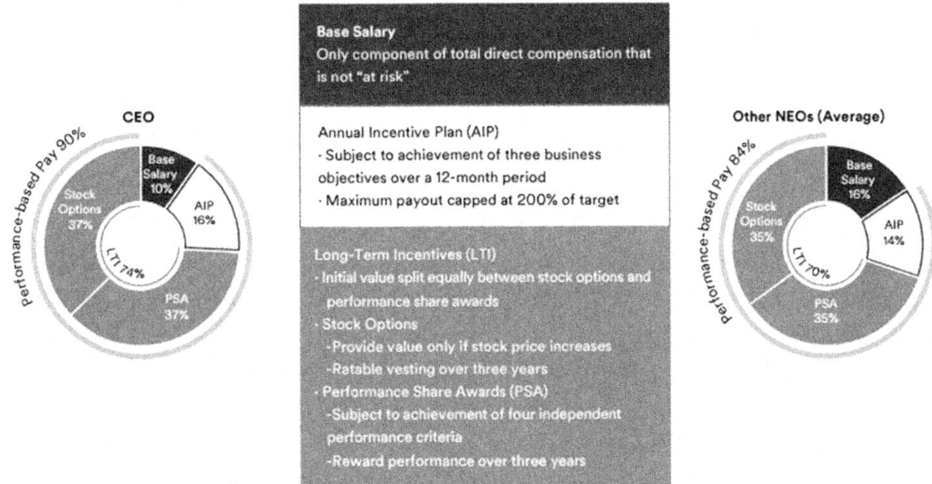

16 position and at the time of a position change from one multiple level to another multiple level, and the fair market value of 3M common stock at that time. Beginning December 31, 2013, and every three years thereafter, the stock ownership guidelines require the company to recalculate the number of shares required to be beneficially owned by each covered executive using their annual base salary and fair market value of 3M common stock at the recalculation date.

The stock ownership guidelines provide that each covered executive should attain the required beneficial ownership of 3M stock within five years of their initial appointment to a Section 16 position or a position change from one multiple level to another multiple level. The guidelines also provide that each covered executive whose required level of ownership increases as a result of a periodic recalculation will have three years from the recalculation date (or the balance of the five-year period since the date of their initial appointment or latest position change, if longer) to attain the required level of ownership. However, if a covered executive is not making adequate progress to meet the required level of ownership within the applicable time period, the guidelines provide that he or she will be required to hold and not sell a sufficient number of the after-tax 3M shares received upon the next payout of performance shares to be on track to satisfy the required ownership level. All of 3M's executives covered by the guidelines either have met or are on track to meet the required level of ownership within the applicable time periods.

- **Prohibition of Hedging and Pledging:** The company's stock trading policies prohibit the company's executive officers from (i) purchasing any financial instrument that is designed to hedge or offset any decrease in the market value of the company's common stock, including prepaid variable forward contracts, equity swaps, collars and exchange funds; (ii) engaging in short sales related to the company's common stock; (iii) placing standing orders;(iv) maintaining margin accounts; and (v) pledging 3M securities as collateral for a loan. All transactions in 3M securities by directors and executive officers must be pre-cleared with the Deputy General Counsel.
- **Policy on Reimbursement of Incentive Payments (''Clawback''):** The company's Board of Directors has adopted a policy requiring the reimbursement of excess incentive compensation

payments made to an executive in the event that 3M is required to make a material restatement of its financial statements. This policy applies to all senior executives of the company including all of the Named Executive Officers. This policy does not require any misconduct on the part of the covered executive whose excess incentive compensation payment is being reimbursed. As long as the company is required to make a material restatement of its financial statements that causes an incentive compensation payout to be higher than it should have been, the company may seek to recover the overpayment from all affected executives irrespective of whether their conduct contributed to the need for the restatement. The company established this policy prior to the passage of the Dodd-Frank Act, which establishes new requirements for such policies. Upon issuance by the Securities and Exchange Commission of final implementing regulations for the Dodd-Frank Act's requirements, the company will make any changes to its existing policy as may be required to comply with those regulations.

- **Factors Creating Alignment Between Pay and Performance and Balancing Risk:** 3M's executive compensation program is designed to maintain a strong alignment between corporate performance and executive compensation by tying incentive compensation to the achievement of performance metrics that increase the company's long-term value. The incentive compensation portion of the program rewards long-term value creation while also protecting the company and its stockholders from inappropriate risk-taking and conflicts between the interests of the executives and the interests of the company and its stockholders. Highlights of the program include:
    - A large portion of each executive's total direct compensation (cash plus long-term incentives) is performance-based, varying from 90% for Chief Executive Officer Inge Thulin to an average of 84% for the other Named Executive Officers;
    - The incentive compensation opportunities provided to the company's executives are based on multiple performance-based metrics, which are focused primarily on growth in revenue and earnings, increase in 3M's stock price, and the efficient use of capital; and
    - Stock ownership guidelines that require covered executives to own amounts of company stock having a value exceeding a specified multiple of their base salary.

Compensation Best Practices

3M compensation program is designed to provide appropriate performance incentives and avoid compensation practices that do not promote the interests of 3M stockholders.

3M does:

- Maintain a strong alignment between corporate performance and compensation.
- Conduct an annual assessment to identify and mitigate risks.
- Have a comprehensive clawback policy.
- Use an independent compensation consultant retained directly by the Committee.
- Limit the number and amount of executive perquisites.
- Prohibit executive officers from hedging or pledging 3M common stock.
- Maintain robust stock ownership guidelines applicable to all of executive officers.
- Conduct competitive benchmarking to align executive compensation with market.

3M does not:

- Have employment, severance, or change in control agreements with any of our executive officers.
- Provide tax gross-ups on executive perquisites.
- Have agreements that would provide automatic "single-trigger" accelerated vesting of equity compensation or excise tax gross-up payments to any of the executive officers in the event of a change in control.
- Provide dividends or dividend equivalents on unearned performance share awards.
- Reprice stock options without the approval of 3M stockholders, except for "anti-dilution" adjustments (such as adjustments for stock splits, spinoffs, etc.)

Benchmarking. In order to provide competitive total direct compensation, 3M annually surveys the executive compensation practices of a large group of comparator companies (approximately 170, although the number and identity of the companies may vary from year to year). Survey data is statistically regressed to recognize the different sizes of the comparator companies (based on annual revenues) as compared to the size of 3M. The survey data is obtained from three consulting firms (Aon Hewitt, Frederic W. Cook & Co., Inc., and Towers Watson). The survey comparator group consists of companies in the Standard & Poor's 500 Index (excluding financial services companies) and/or other companies with annual revenue exceeding $20 billion that participate in the three consultants' executive compensation surveys. By using survey data covering a large number of comparator companies, 3M is able to conduct a rigorous benchmarking process with more complete and reliable data for each executive position benchmarked. The Committee does not review the identity of the companies in this survey comparator group.

In addition, Aon Hewitt and Frederic W. Cook & Co., Inc. provide pay data and information on the executive compensation practices at the companies in 3M's executive compensation peer group. This pay data is used by the Committee to assess the reasonableness of the benchmarking results for each executive position benchmarked, helping to ensure that the company's compensation objectives are being met. 3M's executive compensation peer group consists of the following18 companies (which remain the same as in the previous year), as recommended by the Committee's independent compensation consultant and approved by the Committee:

- The Procter & Gamble Company.
- Johnson & Johnson.
- United Technologies Corporation.
- Dow Chemical Company.
- Caterpillar Inc.
- Honeywell International Inc.
- Deere & Company.
- Medtronic plc.
- E. I. du Pont de Nemours and Company.
- Emerson Electric Co.
- Eaton Corporation plc.
- Danaher Corporation.
- Kimberly-Clark Corporation.
- Illinois Tool Works Inc.
- TE Connectivity Ltd.
- Parker-Hannifin Corporation.

- Tyco International plc.
- Corning Incorporated.

The companies in this executive compensation peer group were selected because (1) their performance is monitored regularly by the same market analysts who monitor the performance of 3M (investment peers), and/or (2) they meet criteria based on similarity of their business and pay models, market capitalization (based on an eight-quarter rolling average), and annual revenues.

Use of benchmarking information. The Compensation Committee considers the pay data from the benchmarking groups when determining each executive's total direct compensation. For executives whose performance meets the company's expectations, the Committee aims to provide them with target total cash compensation that is at or very close to the median of the corresponding target compensation paid to executives in the benchmarking groups, and with long-term incentive compensation delivered through annual grants having values that are within a range of 80 to 120 percent of the median of the corresponding compensation values provided to executives in the benchmarking groups. Executives whose performance consistently exceeds the company's expectations may receive total cash compensation of 120 to 125% of the median of the corresponding compensation paid to executives in the benchmarking groups. Executives whose performance far exceeds the company's expectations may also receive annual long-term incentive compensation grants having values that are within a range of 125 to 160% of the median of the corresponding compensation values provided to executives in the benchmarking groups.

The Committee also uses information on the executive compensation practices at companies in the executive compensation peer group when considering design changes to the company's executive compensation program. Overall, the company believes that use of this information from the benchmarking groups enables the Committee to create better alignment between executive pay and performance and to help ensure that 3M can attract and retain high-performing executive leaders.

Compensation Program Elements

The compensation program for 3M's executives consists of the following elements:

- Base salary;
- Short-term cash incentive in the form of an annual performance-based award opportunity; and
- Long-term equity incentives in the form of annual awards of performance shares and stock options, and in certain circumstances (for purposes of hiring or retaining key talent, for example), grants of restricted stock or restricted stock units.

3M's executives also participate in various benefit plans made available to most of 3M's U.S. employees, are eligible to participate in three deferred compensation plans (which enable them to save for retirement or other financial planning purposes), and receive certain other benefits. The entire program applied to approximately 100 executives during 2015, including all of the Named Executive Officers.

The 2015 total direct compensation of the Named Executive Officers was apportioned among these elements, and how these elements relate to the strategic business goals of the company. This table also reflects the relative balance among the elements as well as the alignment of their compensation with the goal of creating long-term value for the company and its stockholders.

- **Base Salary:** 3M pays each of its executives a base salary in cash on a monthly basis. The amount of this base salary is reviewed annually, and does not vary with the performance of the company. Base salaries are designed to compensate the executives for their normal day-to-day responsibilities, and it is the only component of their compensation that is considered to be fixed rather than variable in nature.

Annual incentive. 3M provides its executives with annual incentive compensation through plans that are designed to align a significant portion of their total cash compensation with the financial performance of the company and its business units. Each executive is assigned a target amount of annual incentive compensation as part of his or her total cash compensation, but the amount of annual incentive compensation actually paid depends on the performance of 3M and its relevant business units as well as their individual performance. For Mr. Thulin, annual incentive compensation represented 61% of his target total cash compensation for 2015. For 3M's other Named Executive Officers, annual incentive compensation represented from 43% to 50%of their target total cash compensation for 2015.

3M's Annual Incentive Plan (AIP) offers eligible employees the opportunity to earn short-term incentive compensation based on three performance metrics, which are weighted as indicated:

- Local currency sales (of 3M or a business unit, as applicable) vs. plan for the current year (50%);
- Economic profit (of 3M or a business unit, as applicable) vs. plan for the current year (20% effective for 2015); and
- 3M economic profit vs. the prior year (30% effective for 2015).

The amount actually paid to an eligible employee for a particular year may range from 0% to 200% of the employee's target amount for that year.

The amount of annual incentive compensation actually paid to an eligible employee may be increased by up to 30% or be reduced by up to 100% based on the employee's individual performance during that year. Individual performance takes into account both quantitative (financial results, for example) and qualitative (market and economic circumstances, for example) factors. In no event, however, may the total amount paid to an eligible employee exceed 200% of the employee's target amount for the year.

While the annual incentive compensation earned by most 3M executives is determined under the AIP, the annual incentive compensation earned by 3M's Named Executive Officers, as well as the other senior executives whose compensation is decided by the Committee, is determined under the executive plan approved by 3M's stockholders at the 2007 Annual Meeting. A total of 18 3M senior executives participated in this executive plan during 2015. This executive plan, which is intended to provide compensation that is exempt from the $1 million annual deduction limit of Section 162(m) of the Internal Revenue Code, provides performance-based compensation for which the performance goal is the company's adjusted net income.

The executive plan does provide the Committee with discretion to determine the amount of annual incentive compensation paid to 3M's Named Executive Officers and its other senior executives. The executive plan establishes a maximum amount of annual incentive compensation that may be earned by each covered executive for a year (a percentage of the company's adjusted net income for such year) and then the Committee utilizes this discretion to pay each covered executive less than this maximum amount based on such factors as it deems relevant. Since the executive plan was first adopted in 2007, the Committee has rarely used this discretion to pay a covered executive anything more or less than the same amount such executive would have received had he or she been participating in the broad-based AIP (including the individual performance multiplier).

In determining the amount of annual incentive compensation paid to a covered executive, the executive's individual performance is considered based upon the annual performance evaluation that Mr. Thulin, assisted by 3M's Senior Vice President, Human Resources, does for each covered executive (other than himself) and the annual performance evaluation that the Compensation Committee acting through its Chairman does for Mr. Thulin. These performance evaluations are done according to 3M's overall performance assessment and management processes, which involve setting annual financial and non-financial goals and objectives for each individual and then assessing the individual's overall performance against these goals and objectives at the end of the year.

- **Long-Term Incentives:** 3M provides long-term incentive compensation to its executives through the long-term incentive plan approved by 3M's stockholders at the 2008 Annual Meeting. This is a typical omnibus-type plan that authorizes the Committee to grant stock options, restricted stock, restricted stock units, stock appreciation rights, performance cash, performance shares, and other stock awards to management employees of the company. The company provides its executives with this long-term incentive compensation based on 3M common stock in order to effectively motivate such executives to build long-term stockholder value.
- **Say on Pay Advisory Approval of Executive Compensation:** As required by Section 14A of the Securities Exchange Act, in 2015 the company conducted an annual advisory vote of stockholders with respect to the compensation of its Named Executive Officers. At the Company's Annual Meeting of Stockholders held on May 12, 2015, approximately 96% of the shares that were voted on this item approved the compensation of the company's Named Executive Officers as disclosed in the 2015 Proxy Statement. While the approval was advisory in nature, the Committee has taken note of this very strong stockholder support and views the outcome as confirmation that stockholders generally believe that the pay of the Named Executive Officers is appropriately aligned with their performance and the performance of the company as well as the interests of 3M's stockholders. As a consequence, the results of this vote have not caused the Committee to make any changes in either the executive compensation program or the compensation of any Named Executive Officer.

Corporate Profile: 3M Board of Directors

- **Inge G. Thulin:** *Chairman of the Board, President and Chief Executive Officer*, Chairman of the Board, President and Chief Executive. Officer of 3M Company. Mr. Thulin served as President and Chief Executive Officer of 3M Company from February 24, 2012, to May 8, 2012. Mr. Thulin served as the Company's Executive Vice President and Chief Operating Officer from May 2011 to February 2012, with responsibility for all of 3M's business segments and International Operations. Prior to that, he was Executive Vice President of International Operations from 2004 to 2011. Mr. Thulin also has held numerous leadership positions in Asia Pacific, Europe and Middle East, and across multiple businesses. Mr. Thulin is on the board of the following public company in addition to 3M: Chevron Corporation. Director since 2012.
- **Linda G. Alvarado:** *President and Chief Executive Officer, Alvarado Construction, Inc.* President and Chief Executive Officer, Alvarado Construction, Inc., a Denver based commercial general

contractor, construction management and development company. In 1976, Ms. Alvarado founded Alvarado Construction, Inc. and has overseen the growth of that enterprise as a commercial general contracting and design/build development firm conducting business across the United States and internationally. Ms. Alvarado is on the board of the following public company in addition to 3M: Pitney Bowes, Inc. Director since 2000. Linda Alvarado was not seeking re-election and ended her service on the Board on May 10, 2016, when her term expired.

- **Sondra L. Barbour:** *Executive Vice President, Information Systems & Global Solutions, Lockheed Martin Corporation.* Executive Vice President, Information Systems & Global Solutions, Lockheed Martin Corporation, a high technology aerospace and defense company. Since joining Lockheed Martin in 1986, Ms. Barbour has served in various leadership capacities and has extensive technology experience, notably in the design and development of large-scale information systems. In 2013 she was appointed Executive Vice President, Information Systems & Global Solutions. From 2008 to 2013 she served as Senior Vice President, Enterprise Business Services and Chief Information Officer, heading all of the corporation's internal information technology operations, including protecting the company's infrastructure and information from cyber threats. Prior to that role she served as Vice President, Corporate Shared Services from 2007 to 2008 and Vice President, Corporate Internal Audit from 2006 to 2007 providing oversight of supply chain activities, internal controls, and risk management. Director since 2014.
- **Thomas K. Brown:** *Retired Group Vice President, Global Purchasing, Ford Motor Company.* Retired Group Vice President, Global Purchasing, Ford Motor Company, a global automotive industry leader. Mr. Brown served in various leadership capacities in global purchasing since joining Ford in 1999. In 2008, he became Ford's Group Vice President, Global Purchasing, with responsibility for approximately $90 billion of production and non-production procurement for Ford operations worldwide. He retired from Ford on August 1, 2013. From 1997 to 1999 he served in leadership positions at United Technologies Corporation, including its Vice President, Supply Management. From 1991to 1997 he served as Executive Director, Purchasing and Transportation at QMS Inc. From 1976 to 1991 he served in various managerial roles at Digital Equipment Corporation. Mr. Brown is on the boards of the following public companies in addition to 3M: ConAgra Foods, Inc. and Tower International, Inc. Director since 2013.
- **Vance D. Coffman:** *Retired Chairman of the Board and Chief Executive, Officer, Lockheed Martin Corporation.* Retired Chairman of the Board and Chief Executive Officer, Lockheed Martin Corporation, a high technology aerospace and defense company. Dr. Coffman served in various executive capacities at Lockheed Martin Corporation before becoming Chairman and Chief Executive Officer in 1998. He retired as Chief Executive Officer in 2004 and as Chairman of the Board in 2005. Dr. Coffman is on the boards of the following public companies in addition to 3M: Amgen Inc. and Deere & Company. Director since 2002.
- **David B. Dillon:** *Retired Chairman of the Board and Chief Executive Officer, The Kroger Co.* Retired Chairman of the Board and Chief Executive Officer The Kroger Co., a large retailer that operates retail food and drug stores, multi-department stores, jewelry stores, and convenience stores throughout the U.S. Mr. Dillon retired as Kroger's Chairman of the Board on December 31, 2014, where he was Chairman of the Board since 2004 and was the Chief Executive Officer from 2003 through 2013. Mr. Dillon served as President from 1995 to 2003 and was elected Executive Vice President in 1990. Mr. Dillon served as a Director of the Kroger Co. from 1995 through 2014. Mr. Dillon began his retailing career at Dillon Companies, Inc. (later a subsidiary of The

Kroger Co.) in 1976 and advanced through various management positions, including its President from 1986-1995. Mr. Dillon is on the board of the following public company in addition to 3M: Union Pacific Corporation. Director since 2015.

- **Michael L. Eskew:** *Retired Chairman of the Board and Chief Executive Officer, United Parcel Service, Inc.* Retired Chairman of the Board and Chief Executive Officer, United Parcel Service, Inc., a provider of specialized transportation and logistics services. Mr. Eskew was appointed Executive Vice President in 1999 and Vice Chairman in 2000 before becoming Chairman of the Board and Chief Executive Officer of UPS in January 2002. He retired as Chairman of the Board and Chief Executive Officer at the end of 2007 but remained as a director of UPS until December 31, 2014. Mr. Eskew is on the boards of the following public companies in addition to 3M: The Allstate Corporation, International Business Machines Corporation, and Eli Lilly and Company. Director since 2003.
- **Herbert L. Henkel:** *Retired Chairman of the Board and Chief Executive Officer, Ingersoll-Rand plc.* Retired Chairman of the Board and Chief Executive Officer, Ingersoll-Rand plc, a manufacturer of industrial products and components. Mr. Henkel retired as Ingersoll Rand's Chief Executive Officer, a position he held since October 1999, on February 4, 2010, and retired as Chairman of the Board on June 3, 2010. Mr. Henkel served as President and Chief Operating Officer of Ingersoll-Rand from April 1999 to October 1999. Mr. Henkel served in various leadership roles at Textron, Inc., including its President and Chief Operating Officer from 1998-1999. Mr. Henkel is on the boards of the following public companies in addition to 3M: The Allstate Corporation and C. R. Bard, Inc. Director since 2007.
- **Muhtar Kent:** *Chairman of the Board and Chief Executive Officer, The Coca-Cola Company.* Chairman of the Board and Chief Executive Officer, The Coca-Cola Company, the world's largest beverage company. Mr. Kent has held the position of Chairman of the Board since April 23, 2009, and the position of Chief Executive Officer since July 1, 2008. From December 2006 through June 2008, Mr. Kent served as President and Chief Operating Officer of The Coca-Cola Company. From January 2006 through December 2006, Mr. Kent served as President of Coca-Cola International and was elected Executive Vice President of The Coca-Cola Company in February 2006. From May 2005 through January 2006, he was President and Chief Operating Officer of The Coca-Cola Company's North Asia, Eurasia and Middle East Group, an organization serving a broad and diverse region that included China, Japan, and Russia. Mr. Kent is a board member and past Co-Chair of The Consumer Goods Forum, a fellow of the Foreign Policy Association, a board member and a past Chairman of the U.S. China Business Council, and Chairman Emeritus of the U.S. ASEAN Business Council. Director since 2013.
- **Edward M. Liddy:** *Retired Chairman of the Board and Chief Executive Officer, The Allstate Corporation.* Retired Chairman of the Board and Chief Executive Officer, The Allstate Corporation, and former Partner at Clayton, Dubilier & Rice, LLC, a private equity investment firm. Mr. Liddy served as a partner of Clayton, Dubilier & Rice LLC from January 2010 to December 2015. At the request of the Secretary of the U.S. Department of the Treasury, Mr. Liddy served as Interim Chairman of the Board and Chief Executive Officer of American International Group, Inc. (AIG), a global insurance and financial services holding company, from September 2008 until August 2009. Mr. Liddy served as Chairman of the Board of The Allstate Corporation, a personal lines insurer, from January 1999 to April 2008, Chief Executive Officer from January 1999 to December 2006, and as President and Chief Operating Officer from August 1994 to December 1998. Mr.

Liddy is on the boards of the following public companies in addition to 3M: Abbott Laboratories, AbbVie, Inc., and The Boeing Company. Director since 2000.

- **Gregory R. Page:** *Retired Chairman of the Board and Chief Executive Officer, Cargill, Incorporated.* Retired Chairman of the Board and Chief Executive Officer, Cargill, Incorporated, an international marketer, processor and distributor of agricultural, food, financial and industrial products and services. Mr. Page was named Corporate Vice President & Sector President, Financial Markets and Red Meat Group of Cargill in 1998, Corporate Executive Vice President, Financial Markets and Red Meat Group in 1999, President and Chief Operating Officer in 2000 and became Chairman of the Board and Chief Executive Officer in 2007. He served as Executive Chairman of the Board of Cargill from December 2013 until his retirement from Cargill in September 2015. Mr. Page is on the boards of the following public companies in addition to 3M: Cargill, Incorporated, Deere & Company and Eaton Corporation plc. Director since 2016.
- **Robert J. Ulrich:** *Retired Chairman of the Board and Chief Executive Officer of Target Corporation.* Retired Chairman of the Board and Chief Executive Officer of Target Corporation, an operator of large format general merchandise and food discount stores. Mr. Ulrich began his retailing career as a merchandising trainee in Target's department store division (Dayton Hudson) in 1967 and advanced through various management positions. He became Chairman of the Board and Chief Executive Officer of Target Stores in 1987 and was elected Chairman of the Board and Chief Executive Officer of Target Corporation in 1994. Mr. Ulrich retired as Target's Chief Executive Officer on May 1, 2008, and retired as Chairman of the Board on January 31, 2009. Director since 2008.
- **Patricia A. Woertz:** *Retired Chairman of the Board and Chief Executive Officer, Archer-Daniels-Midland Company.* Retired Chairman of the Board and Chief Executive Officer, Archer-Daniels-Midland Company, an agricultural processor and food ingredient provider. Ms. Woertz joined ADM as Chief Executive Officer and President in April 2006, and was named Chairman of the Board in February 2007. She served as Chief Executive Officer until December 2014, and Chairman of the Board until December 2015. Before joining ADM, Ms. Woertz held positions of increasing importance at Chevron Corporation and its predecessor companies. Ms. Woertz served on the President's Export Council 2010-2015 and chaired the U.S. section of the U.S.-Brazil CEO Forum from 2013-2015. Ms. Woertz is on the boards of the following public companies in addition to 3M: The Procter & Gamble Company and Royal Dutch Shell plc. Director since 2016.

Corporate Profile: Corporate Code of Conduct

3M maintains a high standard of corporate conduct for all employees. 3M believes what the company stands for is as important as what we sell. 3M has built a reputation for integrity and doing business the right way. 3M expects all employees to act ethically and to sustain and advance 3M's global reputation.

3M's global compliance program is managed and administered by the compliance and business conduct department, led by the Vice President, Associate General Counsel, Compliance and Business Conduct, who is also 3M's Chief Compliance Officer (CCO). The department is staffed with compliance professionals stationed at company headquarters and around the world. The CCO reports to the Audit Committee of the 3M Board of Directors, which assists the Board in oversight of 3M's legal and regulatory compliance efforts. The compliance and business conduct department oversees and administers strategic, systematic and operational components of 3M's compliance program design and implementation.

The compliance program is based on the U.S. Federal Sentencing Guidelines. Its elements include the following:

- A core set of business conduct principles;
- Education, training materials and the schedule upon which compliance training is conducted;
- Periodic evaluations, audits and measurements of the compliance program's effectiveness;
- A 24-hour helpline and website through which employees and others can report concerns and ask questions;
- Programs to conduct appropriate due diligence on business partners, potential and new acquisitions, and candidates for hiring and promoting;
- Investigative expertise;
- Incentives and discipline to address compliance successes and failures.

The compliance and business conduct department collaborates with and is assisted by dedicated compliance organizations and subject matter experts in areas such as corporate audit, corporate security, trade compliance, government contracting, health care regulation, and environmental health and safety. In addition, 3M's business divisions and subsidiaries utilize staff who liaise with the compliance and business conduct department staff in ensuring that their organizations continuously demonstrate legal compliance and ethical business conduct. These staff members assist in business conduct policy training, communications and completion of periodic risk assessments for their organizations.

Continually Improving 3M Compliance Program

In the fast-paced world of global business, it takes more than a written compliance policy to keep a company doing business the right way. Although 3M has subsidiary operations in more than 70 countries, there is one code of conduct that applies globally. 3M code of conduct global handbook summarizes 3M's compliance principles and raises awareness of 3M's core requirement of doing business "the right way, always and everywhere." The global handbook is available in twenty-two languages, and can be accessed electronically and all employees receive a copy of the handbook. Of these twenty-two languages, two were introduced this year in order to ensure that the code and 3M's expectations are understood by all employees, relevant stakeholders and business partners.

The Ethisphere® Institute, the global leader in defining and advancing the standards of ethical business practices, has named 3M as a 2015 World's Most Ethical Company® for the second year in a row. The designation recognizes 3M's impact on the way business is conducted through its efforts of fostering a culture of ethics and transparency at every level of the company.

The code of conduct helps employees and others covered by the code take a consistent, global approach to important ethics and compliance issues. 3M employees, including supervisors, managers and other leaders are responsible for knowing and following the ethical, legal, and policy requirements that apply to their jobs and for reporting any suspected violations of law or the code. Executives and managers are accountable for creating and promoting, through clear direction and leading by example, a workplace environment in which compliance and ethical business conduct are expected and encouraged.

All sections of 3M code, including each principle were reviewed in 2015 and enhancements were identified that will be executed in the upcoming year. Additionally, 3M reviewed and made improvements to underlying policies, standards and procedures. 3M also identified the need for new documents to provide greater clarity to its employees and began the process of creating those documents.

A global communications network was established to standardize, align and share best practices in compliance communications and activities. Newsletters, leadership messages and other compliance communication tools are now available on the internal 3M compliance and business conduct website allowing for efficient global collaboration.

Further, in 2015, six online compliance courses were deployed to the mandatory employee population. The courses included two custom courses and an updated anti-bribery course. Additionally, 3M created a new training presentation to address the risk of conflicts of interest which was specifically designed for managers to discuss with their team. It includes case studies drawn from real life examples.

3M also enhanced its culture of compliance through the requirement that all international subsidiaries implement a local business conduct committee (BCC). A local BCC creates a governance structure to ensure visibility and transparency to the key compliance risk and priorities of a subsidiary. Each BCC meets at least every quarter and includes members of the local senior leadership team. A BCC oversees the local compliance program, establishes priorities for training and communications and drives the development and enhancement of compliance controls to address local risk.

3M recently enhanced integrity assessments system, its online global system for documenting and managing third party relationships. 3M improved it by utilizing a new technology platform, improving the user interface, adding greater functionality and improving overall performance. Post-acquisition due diligence was improved by furthering the effectiveness of 3M compliance integration and post-transaction risk assessment process. This was spearheaded by developing local networks that are responsible for executing various phases of the process.

Business Conduct Committee

The 3M Business Conduct Committee is composed of several senior executives and is chaired by 3M's CCO. The Committee has oversight for 3M's various compliance efforts and, as appropriate, has periodic reporting to the Audit Committee of the 3M Board of Directors and Corporate Operating Committee.

- **Compliance Training and Education:** 3M offers a comprehensive online compliance training program to all employees worldwide. The program's training modules are mandatory for approximately 46,000 global employees, who are required to take modules on a two- or four-year cycle, depending on the course. Modules include data privacy, careful communications, gifts, understanding the Foreign Corrupt Practices Act, environmental health and safety, business conduct and ethics, conflicts of interest, and other key compliance areas. More than 25 courses are offered in multiple languages. The 3M compliance and business conduct website on 3M's intranet offers additional anti-bribery training on 3M's global anti-bribery compliance program. In addition to online training, the compliance and business conduct department, in close collaboration with 3M legal affairs, provides frequent, tailored in-person training to business, subsidiary and staff groups. Some of this training occurs as part of an annual calendar and other training occurs as requested or deemed appropriate.

Commitment to Anti-Corruption

As a member of the United Nations Global Compact, 3M is committed to support Principle 10 on anti-corruption and is working against corruption in all forms. 3M commitment to Principle 10 and involvement in working groups associated with Principle 10 provides opportunity to benchmark and learn best practices from other peer companies and participate in relevant working group opportunities. 3M conducts additional benchmarking with similarly situated companies and take the opportunity to participate in the education of other professionals working on anti-corruption through 3M CCO's and other compliance and business conduct Department professionals' participation in anti-corruption conferences and organizations.

3M's anti-bribery principle requires compliance with all applicable anti-bribery laws, including the U.S. Foreign Corrupt Practices Act, the U.K. Bribery Act and all applicable local laws where 3M operates. The anti-bribery principle applies to 3M employees, as well as to 3M business partners who act on 3M's behalf. In addition, anti-corruption policies and procedures have been communicated to all employees, and "global bribery and corruption awareness" training is required of employees in higher-risk roles, including those in legal, audit, sales, marketing, export and global trading. 3M's anti-bribery principle and 3M-provided training are designed to educate the employees and business partners on recognizing the many forms in which bribes can appear and how to avoid them, even at the risk of losing business opportunities. Furthermore, employee awareness of corruption risk is reinforced through specific anti-bribery certification that is included in the annual code of conduct certification process. Furthermore, the Audit Committee of the Board receives at least quarterly updates from the CCO on the code principles and compliance activities.

3M's commitment to anti-corruption also applies to assessing and mitigating risks of using third-party intermediaries and other business partners. Based upon a risk calibration resulting from an assessment of transaction, geography and other risk factors, 3M conducts reputational due diligence reviews on these third parties (3M's "integrity assessment system.") Depending on the outcome of those reviews, 3M responds to identified risks with training, inclusion of relevant contractual terms and other risk-mitigating controls.

The compliance and business conduct department also collaborates with 3M legal affairs on pre- and postacquisition due diligence processes in the merger and acquisition setting. These processes help identify and assess risks in the target company before acquisition. The pre-acquisition efforts also accelerates our efforts to identify compliance gaps and integrate the acquired company's employees to 3M's compliance program and culture. The compliance and business conduct department is charged to undertake specific, risk-based assessment and if necessary, remediation activities upon the closing of every acquisition, using an established protocol and expert staff.

Reporting Systems

Upholding 3M's code of conduct and values is the responsibility of everyone acting on 3M's behalf. 3M recognizes that reporting suspected misconduct or even asking a compliance question can take courage, but we believe it is the right thing to do. 3M employees are encouraged to raise questions or report misconduct or potential misconduct to management, 3M Legal Counsel, the compliance and business conduct department, or to their human resources manager.

In addition, a 24-hour confidential and anonymous (as permitted by local law) helpline and online reporting system managed by a third party vendor is available internally and externally. Reports are reviewed and responded to by the compliance and business conduct department or other responsible staff departments. The system does not trace phone calls or use caller identification, nor does it generate or maintain internal connection logs containing internet protocol (IP) addresses. Web-based reports are made through a secure internet portal, which does not trace or show user screen names. 3M's employee obligations and reporting principle prohibits retaliation against anyone who raises a business conduct concern in good faith or cooperates in a company investigation. Figure 28 is illustrating a four-year metrics for business conduct related reports raised using 3M reporting tools.

The compliance and business conduct department has the responsibility to review every business conduct concern that is reported. The department determines which reports require investigation and if investigation is needed, assigns the appropriate investigation resource. For concerns that are substantiated, disciplinary action is taken. Discipline comes in a range of forms, from warnings, to suspensions, to termination, consistent with similar past violations. Disciplinary actions may impact one or more persons associated with a single substantiated violation.

Maintaining Business Conduct Compliance

Operating with uncompromising integrity is one of 3M's core values and includes avoiding bribery or corruption in any form. Oversight, monitoring and testing of 3M's corporate compliance program and controls is supported by periodic compliance risk assessments of 3M's businesses, including assessment of risk related to corruption, and specific risk-based compliance and ethics audits performed by 3M's internal audit function. These audits follow a specific audit module that focuses on ethics and business as part of systematic audits of financial and other business controls.

In addition, a dedicated team within 3M's compliance and business conduct department conducts periodic compliance and anti-bribery evaluations in various 3M subsidiaries and operating units each year. These evaluations are selected based on objective and subjective risk factors, and they include reviews

Figure 28. Allegations &disciplinary actions

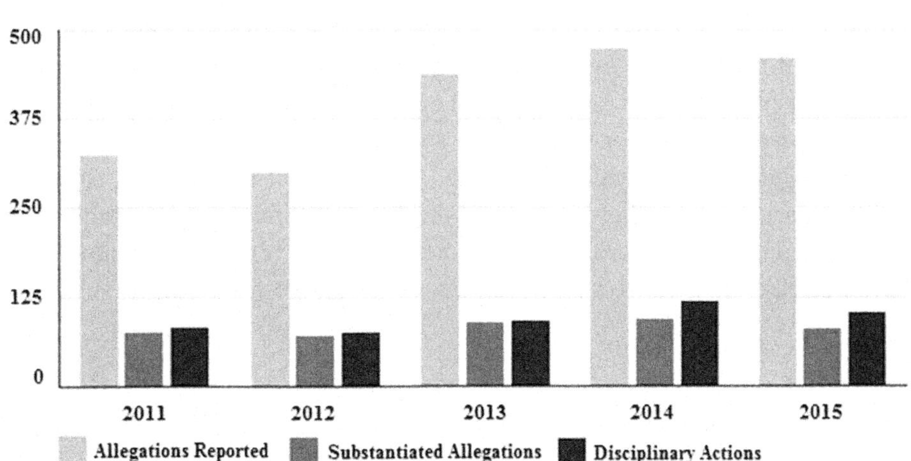

of sample financial transactions, compliance records and interviews with subsidiary and business unit personnel. In 2015, over 500 nonproduction employees were interviewed as part of the evaluation process.

Audits, evaluations and risk assessments are all important activities for the purposes of detecting any opportunities for improvement or even gaps in processes or procedures. Of equal importance, they provide opportunities to reinforce the importance of operating with a compliance and ethical behavior mindset and facilitate the identification of compliance risks. All these outcomes reinforce prevention of future compliance gaps or failures.

As mentioned above, in 2015, 3M enhanced its culture of compliance through the requirement that all international subsidiaries implement a local Business Conduct Committee (BCC). Each BCC creates a governance structure to ensure visibility and transparency to the key compliance risk and priorities of a subsidiary. Each BCC meets at least every quarter and includes members of the local senior leadership.

3M also improved its culture of compliance through there-allocation of resources with respect to compliance responsibility in our international operations. 3M previously staffed two area leadership roles with individuals who had dual functional responsibility (compliance and legal.) These roles were re-allocated, and now there is one employee for compliance and one for legal.

Further, in 2015 as mentioned above, 3M created a global communications network to standardize, align and share compliance communications.

- **Political Values:** To respect 3M employees' right to engage in the political process while also preventing potential corruption, any political contributions outside the United States require approval by the area Vice President and assigned legal counsel.

Corporate Profile: Managing Enterprise Risks and Opportunities

The Board has delegated to the Audit Committee, through its charter, the primary responsibility for the oversight of risks facing the company. The charter provides that the Audit Committee shall "discuss policies and procedures with respect to risk assessment and risk management, the company's major risk exposures and the steps management has taken to monitor and mitigate such exposures."

The Vice President and General Auditor, Corporate Auditing ("Auditor"), whose appointment and performance is reviewed and evaluated by the Audit Committee and who has direct reporting obligations to the Audit Committee, is responsible for leading the formal risk assessment and management process within the Company. The Auditor, through consultation with the company's senior management, periodically assesses the major risks facing the company and works with those executives responsible for managing each specific risk. The Auditor periodically reviews with the Audit Committee the major risks facing the company and the steps management has taken to monitor and mitigate those risks. The Auditor's risk management report, which is provided in advance of the meeting, is reviewed with the entire Board in conjunction with either the Chair of the Audit Committee or the Auditor. The executive responsible for managing a particular risk may also report to the full Board on how the risk is being managed and mitigated.

While the Board's primary oversight of risk is with the Audit Committee, the Board has delegated to other Committees the oversight of risks within their areas of responsibility and expertise. For example, the Compensation Committee oversees the risks associated with the company's compensation practices, including an annual review of the company's risk assessment of its compensation policies and practices for its employees.

The Finance Committee oversees risks associated with the company's capital structure, its credit ratings and its cost of capital, long-term benefit obligations, and the company's use of or investment in financial products, including derivatives used to manage risk related to foreign currencies, commodities and interest rates. The Nominating and Governance Committee oversees the risks associated with the company's overall governance and its succession planning process to understand that the company has a state of future, qualified candidates for key management positions. The Auditor also actively and routinely seeks input from executive Committees with expertise in specific risks. For example, the EHS Committee provides input on risks with environmental or social impacts.

The Board believes that its oversight of risks (primarily through delegation to the Audit Committee, but also through delegation to other Committees, and the sharing of information with the full Board) is appropriate for a diversified technology and manufacturing company like 3M. The chair of each Committee that oversees risk provides a summary of the matters discussed with the Committee to the full Board following each Committee meeting. The minutes of each Committee meeting are also provided to all Board members.

The Board also believes its oversight of risk is enhanced by its current leadership structure (discussed above) because the CEO, who is ultimately responsible for the company's risk management, also chairs regular Board meetings, and with his in-depth knowledge and understanding of the company, he is best able to bring key business issues and risks to the Board's attention.

3M conducts extensive interviews, group assessments and reviews by senior management for completion of risk analysis assessments to provide more customized and useful prioritized results and to incorporate understanding of external factors that could influence the nature and gravity of risk. This process assures that the appropriate risks are properly identified as an enterprise risk, to identify key "failure modes" that could lead to a risk incident, and to review and assess the quality of ownership of the risk and related resources available to ensure proper avoidance, mitigation and response capabilities.

A gap assessment is completed to provide quantification on a common scale of the level of risk and 3M's corresponding capabilities relative to each enterprise risk identified. The outcomes are used to prioritize action plans for each topic.

More detailed quantitative and qualitative sensitivity analyses may be conducted and cover topics such as operational risk (business continuity), raw material sourcing and price fluctuation, compliance, revenue forecasting, climate change legislation, petroleum pricing and strategic planning processes, and many other areas.

The Board of Directors Public Issues Committee reviews public policy issues and trends affecting the company, which inform the Audit Committee's enterprise risk assessment process. The Committee also reviews and approves the company's response to stockholder proposals relating to public policy issues. The Board of Directors has determined that all Public Issues Committee members are independent under the New York Stock Exchange listing standard.

CONCLUSION

The world is facing many global challenges including stressed water systems, inadequate food supplies, pollution, reduced natural resources, lack of access to education and healthcare, and a changing climate. 3M likes to imagine a world where every life is improved – where natural resources are reliably available, people have access to education and opportunity, and communities are safe, healthy, connected and thriving. 3M approach these challenges with a sense of purpose. With a sense of curiosity. 3M aims to help make that world a reality. But an ambition that big won't be easy. So 3M pledges the following:

- 3M will push itself to create the science and technology to achieve these goals.
- 3Mwill encourage individual passion and curiosity both within the company and within its communities.
- 3M will acknowledge that it cannot succeed alone and commit to stimulating and supporting collaborations to improve every life on earth.

Since 1932, 3Mhas been at the forefront of companies adopting programs and policies to ensure environmental protection, social responsibility and economic vitality. Collaboration is an important part of its sustainability strategy. 3M partners with a variety of organizations to gain a diverse set of viewpoints on sustainability, a better understanding of the positions of stakeholders, and a mechanism to learn from the successes and failures of its peers.

3Mlooks at sustainability in terms of shared global needs and the future of its business. As the population grows, particularly in emerging economies, challenges like energy availability and security, raw material scarcity, human health and safety, education, and development must be addressed to ensure people across the globe can lead healthy, fulfilling lives. Every day, 3M innovation aims to tackle some of the world's most pressing areas of concern:

- Raw Materials.
- Water.
- Energy & Climate.
- Health & Safety.
- Education & Development.

3M commitments and goals reflect its focus on helping to overcome these global challenges.

The world's population is growing larger, living longer — and consuming more. With this increased pressure on the finite natural resources and materials, we must move beyond low-cost, recyclable materials to renewable products. Companies that address this issue not only help the planet, but they also gain a competitive advantage in the marketplace.3M has worked on this challenge for decades and will continue to innovate into the future, developing renewable replacements for impacted resources, revolutionizing recyclable materials and becoming more sustainable.

Reducing water consumption and improving water quality are important elements of 3M's environmental stewardship. Energy usage and climate concerns require systematic change, and 3M are here to drive that forward. From air emissions to fossil fuels, 3M takes a proactive and collaborative approach to addressing energy demand and climate change — in its operations and for its customers. The issues around effective use of energy resources and climate change are complex and interconnected. 3Mis focused on understanding those connections and seeking solutions that promote energy conservation, clean energy infrastructure, and reductions in atmospheric greenhouse gases. 3M's goal is to continue developing and implementing global concepts for the greatest long-term impact. Creative innovation, technology, education and collaboration are all critical if we are to tackle the human health and workplace safety concerns. For decades, 3M has had entire business divisions focused on creating products and services for human health, protection, security and safety. As a technology company, 3M recognizes the importance of well-trained science, technology, engineering and math (STEM) graduates — 3Mneeds young minds to step into specialized roles and help the company solve future challenges.

To 3M, sustainability includes collaborating to find better solutions. As the world population grows, particularly in emerging economies, global challenges must be addressed together to ensure we can all live healthy, fulfilling lives. 3M recognizes its customers face those same challenges and share its sustainability goals. For this reason, 3Mis committed to partnering with customers to identify and collaborate on solutions to address their goals. 3Mis always increasing the number of products that address those needs.

Sustainability shouldn't have an expiration date. Life cycle management is a formal part of 3M product introduction process worldwide. 3M considers all the environmental, health, and safety implications of bringing that particular product into the world.3Madopted a new Life Cycle Management Policy in 2001 requiring all of its business units to conduct life cycle reviews for all new and existing products. With hundreds of new products introduced each year, 3M has a continuous flow of opportunities to improve the environmental, health, and safety effects of the things it makes.

As part of 3M's Sourcing Sustainability Standard, expectations are set for suppliers through 3M's Supply Chain Policies: EHS, Transportation, Labor/Human Resources and Supplied Materials. These policies apply to the selection and retention of all suppliers that provide goods and services to 3M worldwide. 3M selectively reviews supplier performance to these policies. Equal access to business opportunities is not just deserved, it's a priority. 3M has a long-standing commitment to sustainable business practices and supporting the economic success of its communities. This includes working with both diverse and small-business suppliers.

Setting goals to drive sustainability progress is nothing new at 3M. 3M has been setting global environmental goals since 1990. A strong part of its company history, these goals have helped dramatically reduce its own environmental footprint and established 3M as a leader in environmental stewardship. Moving forward, 3Mis proud to expand beyond its own operations by focusing more on supporting the sustainability goals and needs of its customers and its communities. While 3M recognizes the importance of what it does in its own operations, and will continue to improve accordingly, 3M sees that far greater impact can be realized when 3M partners to understand and overcome the challenges it faces in partnership with others.

3M approaches its sustainability goals and strategy by:

- Delivering excellence in operations and across its supply chain;
- Innovating to improve lives with its customers and partners; and,
- Enriching the communities where we live and work.

When 3M thinks about its customers, partners, and communities, and its mutual challenges and needs, it sees a shared opportunity. In addition to environmental challenges, 3M recognizes the connectedness of social challenges we face in pursuing a better world. 3M's ambition, working collaboratively, is to realize a world where every life is improved – where natural resources are reliably available, people everywhere have access to education and opportunity, and communities are safe, healthy, connected and thriving. 3M has framed its goals and plans for the next 10 years around shared global challenges, toward realizing that world in the future. Recognizing the interconnections and overlap of the commitments 3M is making and their impact on multiple challenges, 3Mhas organized its efforts by the primary challenge each goal is working to overcome. Unless otherwise noted, all goals are global, have a 2015 baseline, and a 2025 end date.

REFERENCES

The 3M Company. (2016). *3M Sustainability Report*. Author.

Chapter 8
Unilever and Its Supply Chain:
Embracing Radical Transparency to Implement Sustainability

ABSTRACT

The chapter refers to Unilever and its efforts to implement the concept of radical transparency to implement sustainability and it is split into four sections in order to complete its purpose. First, the chapter provides a background on Unilever as a company. Second, the authors discuss several lenses with which Unilever may view their options to find the most optimal starting point or points to enact sustainability measures. The chapter then demonstrates one such tool, Sustainability Stakeholder Rating Tool (SSRT) and discusses how this weighting tool may be applied to three key products including dairy, vegetables, and palm oil. The chapter discusses various ways in which Unilever may encourage sustainable supply chain compliance, verify practices, and drive sustainability down the supply chain via the innovation and still relatively new radical transparency practices of certification, crowd-sourcing, and trust -based networks.

INTRODUCTION

When a company with a well-established supply chain enters the sustainability space, it is understandably with trepidation, and in the best-case scenario, with curiosity and a willingness to experiment. In order to drive sustainability changes, there are a plethora of places to start – from shifting consumer buying patterns, to farmers' production practices, to corporate culture. Commonly, large multinationals rely on multiple product streams going into multiple product lines; the task to 'green' the entire supply chain is daunting, and the process iterative. A company must do two things over and over again. First, the company must find the appropriate tools to help prioritize a starting place. Second, once this prioritization process happens, the company must dig into an evolving toolbox of items which can drive sustainability down the supply chain and ensure compliance in the areas that the company is seeking sustainability. Finally, the company must follow these steps over and over again – capturing learning as the tools are applied – and then re-evaluating its sustainability priorities up and down the supply chain.

DOI: 10.4018/978-1-5225-2417-5.ch008

To assist Unilever with this iterative process, Unilever requested two primary tasks. First, Unilever wanted high-level strategies and frameworks with which the company can make decisions about where to begin implementing sustainability measures across its vast supply chain. Second, Unilever asked for a discussion of ways that the company could drive sustainability down the supply chain and verify supply chain sustainability compliance, particularly in cases where Unilever did not use 3rd party certification schemes. To satisfy Unilever's requests, a supply chain prioritization tool called the Sustainability Stakeholder Rating Tool (SSRT) was developed. Taking into account the complex supply chain ecosystem, the tool is meant to prioritize supply chain actions based on a combination of financial, social, and environmental consideration in various product lines (dairy, oil, and vegetables) from the perspective of Unilever's main stakeholders.

The first part of this chapter which refers to Unilever is reported below and is split into four sections. First, the chapter provides a background on Unilever as a company. Second, this part discusses several lenses with which Unilever may view their options to find the most optimal starting point or points to enact sustainability measures. The chapter then demonstrates one such tool, Sustainability Stakeholder Rating Tool (SSRT) and discusses how this weighting tool may be applied to three key products including dairy, vegetables, and palm oil. Following this, the document discusses various ways that Unilever may encourage sustainable supply chain compliance, verify practices, and drive sustainability down the supply chain via the innovation and still relatively new radical transparency practices of certification, crowd-sourcing, and trust -based networks.

UNILEVER AND SUSTAINABILITY

Unilever, based in Rotterdam, Netherlands, owns many of the leading consumer brands in foods, beverages, cleaning agents, and personal care products. Unilever employs 163,000 people in around 100 countries and their products are sold in over 170 countries around the world.

The top 25 brands in their portfolio account for nearly 75% of their sales. They are the global market leader in all the food categories in which they operate: Savory, Spreads, Dressings, Tea and Ice Cream. They are also the global market leader in Mass Skin Care and Deodorants, and have very strong positions in other Home and Personal Care categories. They have 264 manufacturing sites worldwide, all of which align with their values of safety, efficiency, quality and environmental impacts. Around 50% of the raw materials that they use for our products come from agriculture and forestry. They buy approximately 12% of the world's black tea, 6% of its tomatoes and 3% of its palm oil.

Unilever as company has made a strategic shift towards sustainability, and CEO Paul Polman recently wrote that, "2009 saw the launch of a new vision for Unilever–to double the size of the company while reducing our overall impact on the environment. The commitment presents Unilever with a major challenge… In short, we intend to decouple growth from environmental impact." Unilever's largest opportunities in sustainability are in the expansion in developing and emerging markets and the growing movement of socially conscious consumers. Developing countries face a plethora of issues including major climate change challenges, poverty, and mal-nutrition which may seem daunting for companies to react to. However, large players like Unilever can develop products that meet their functional needs while factoring in the social and environmental challenges. This will allow Unilever to be better positioned to grow in the future compared to those who do not address these challenges.

Another significant opportunity is the growth of the 'conscience' consumer, those who prefer niche products, which has a positive social or environmental impact. While this began as a small consumer group, it has emerged into a broader movement in recent years.

At the same time, Unilever's commitment to sustainability presents a major challenge: incorporating their sustainability impact from the sourcing of their raw materials, to processing and manufacturing, and then all the way to the consumer use and disposal of products. Ironically, Unilever's largest sustainability challenges come from the places it least controls, in the sourcing of raw materials and consumer disposal of products. Unilever must decide where and how to start the prioritization process, while ensuring alignment with thousands of suppliers. As a result, Unilever has relied on a plethora of partners to address sustainable practices at different stages in the value chain over the past 20 years.

Unilever's Sustainable Agriculture Initiative, developed during the 1990's, aims to ensure Unilever's access to key agricultural raw materials and to continually develop market mechanisms that allow consumers to influence the sourcing of agricultural raw materials. The company commissioned two field studies in 1995, one capturing the opinions of leading players and decision makers and another translating the concept of sustainability into a set of operational indicators based on experts for use in Unilever practice. As a result of this theoretical work, Unilever instituted five projects testing their approach to sustainable agriculture. These field projects were used to develop Unilever's ten sustainable agriculture indicators along with the support of farmer groups and various community partners. These ten indicators cover soil loss, pest management, product value, water and the local economy.

In 2005, they embedded their sustainability indicators across product brands using *Brand Imprint*. Brand Imprint provides their brand teams with a 360 degree scan of the social, economic and environmental impact that their brand has on the world. A multidisciplinary team performed a detailed assessment of each brand, looking first at the direct and indirect impacts of our products, or their 'imprint', across the value chain. The team completed stakeholder research and gained insight on various influences on the brand's growth.

More recently, Unilever developed a Business Partner Code to ensure their suppliers meet their expectations on social and environmental impacts. At the same time, Unilever's Sustainable Agriculture Initiative considered how to make their corporate activities more visible to their consumers. They partnered with organizations to educate consumers on how to reduce their environmental footprint. They also began to assess their environmental impact across the supply chain from sourcing raw materials to production, distribution, consumer use, and disposal, developing:

- In 2008, a set of metrics for the environmental impact areas: GHG emissions, water, waste, and sustainable sourcing.
- In 2009, a social impact metrics in order to track performance across the portfolio, allowing them to show consumers the broad scale impact of their purchases; and
- In 2010, the Sustainable Agriculture Code, a 70+ page document codifying sustainability benchmarks across ten areas.

Future Goals in Sustainability

Moving forward, Unilever's goals for sustainability are vast. As described by Paul Polman, CEO of Unilever's vision in 2009 is, "to double the size of the company while reducing our overall impact on the environment by 2020."Unilever's sustainability goals include both business operation improvement and the broader impact associated with the total lifecycle of their products. The company has already taken the lead in many areas. In palm oil, they have bought Green Palm certificates covering 15% of their volumes. In addition, Unilever founded the Roundtable on Sustainable Palm Oil (RSPO) helping to move the industry to sustainable palm oil and have set their own target to be 100% sustainably sourced by 2015.

DECISION MAKING FRAMEWORKS FOR SUSTAINABILITY PRACTICES: SUPPLY CHAIN MAPPING

In order to meet their sustainability goals, Unilever's first objective is to provide Unilever with a high-level framework for thinking through where to begin transitioning to more sustainable practices. The company has a clear picture of the supply chain from the point of the distributor forward through to Unilever, but significant gaps in knowledge exist regarding how products move down the supply chain from farm to distributor.

Consequently, the first step in identifying key pressure points where Unilever can best improve its sustainability practices is to fill these gaps via research to create a complete map of the supply chain from farm to Unilever. Once the supply chain is clearly illustrated, Unilever can identify key pressure points or hot spots to begin making changes. Most companies choose to begin change in places that produce the most change for the least amount of effort. This is the proverbial "low hanging fruit," which is easiest to pick. Several factors contribute to determining what constitutes the lowest hanging fruit.

First, there is the financial cost. Obviously, that which costs the least in both time and effort is generally cheaper to implement. However, there may be instances when actions with the lowest cost or the least amount of effort may not be the most logical place to start. One instance of this is when efforts cost little but take a very long time to implement. A company may wish for sustainability efforts to take root in a shorter timeframe, even if they cost a more. For example, a change initiative that costs little - but take 10 years to produce visible results - may not be the proper place to start as opposed to an initiative that costs a more but produces faster sustainability results.

Second, company must also then consider the sustainability return on investments (SROI) for themselves and their stakeholders, being patient as change occurs. Sustainable project decisions require more inclusive forecasting of future costs and benefits. These elements are subject to uncertainty and are not typically captured in conventional ROI methods. From Unilever's perspective, calculating an SROI over time includes not just the financial return, but an environmental and social return over a longer period of time which brings Unilever closer to fulfilling the terms outlined in its Unilever Sustainable Agriculture Code. In addition, Unilever can estimate an ROI on investments in a sustainable supply chain by looking at the actual dollar amount in brand damage ameliorated by investing in sustainability. Similarly, from a farmer or supplier perspective, an SROI becomes more realistic when they have a longer timeframe from which to calculate the ROI because they have entered into long-term relationships with the buyer and will see the benefits of their investments.

Third, Unilever should consider if their customers are willing to pay more for a sustainable product. This may vary by product. For example, customers may be willing to pay more for a highly visible whole food product, such as tea, while they may not be willing to pay more for a less visible product such as powdered onions that go into a soup cube. In instances where customers are willing to pay more for a product that is sustainable, Unilever may be able to start implementing sustainability measures without a need to think as much about keeping costs low. In instances where customers are not willing to pay more for sustainable products, Unilever must ensure that the cost of Unilever products remain the same as that of its competitors.

Finally, in cases where customers are not willing to pay more for sustainable products, one strategy for prioritizing which ingredients to target for implementing sustainability measures is to start with products in which Unilever has the ability to change the practices of the industry overall. Unilever may have such a significant market share in global purchasing of that ingredient that it has significant sway in the industry to effect agricultural practices of the entire industry. Or, even for products in which Unilever has small market share in overall global purchasing, there may be an ingredient that has significant momentum around it from pressure groups, with whom Unilever can work to change the industry overall.

This may be accomplished in at least three ways. First, Unilever may enact sustainability measures that cost less or no more than current practices. Second, Unilever may enact sustainability measures that have a return on investment (ROI) on capital cost that over X number of years actually saves money. Third, Unilever may enact sustainability measures that do cost more than current practices, but are adopted across the industry so that the cost of competitors' products remains the same as that of Unilever. Here, having the ability to change the industry overall is an important aspect from the standpoint of competitiveness.

EXAMPLE OF A METRIC: THE SUSTAINABILITY STAKEHOLDER RATING TOOL

Four ways are outlined in which Unilever might think about how to prioritize its supply chain, including financial cost, the SROI, customers' willingness to pay, and Unilever's industry influence. There are invariably more. Added to this complexity is the fact that sustainability covers a wide array of different natural resources (water, chemicals, energy sources, etc.) and processes (planting, growing, harvesting, sorting, washing, etc.). Given that Unilever is part of a complex web of various stakeholders throughout a multi-billion-dollar supply chain, The Sustainability Stakeholder Rating Tool (SSRT) captures both the various parts of this web and thinks through the sustainability dynamics at play throughout the supply chain at the farm level.

SSRT is a qualitative effort to capture:

- Stakeholders' perspectives on sustainability at the farm level;
- Sustainability-related categories;
- The relative importance of each of these categories to the various stakeholders; and
- The way in which sustainability categories may differ across different crop categories.

The stakeholders include:

- **The Consumer:** An "average" Unilever consumer who is focused on price and taste above all else;
- **The Environment:** The various systems that make up the proper functioning of the planet: water, air, and soil;
- **The Farmers:** Those responsible for growing the products;
- **The Suppliers:** Those who purchase the raw product and usually conduct the first (and sometimes) second levels of processing; and

- **Unilever Shareholders:** Taking the corporation to be a profit maximizing entity, this category is most concerned with getting a quality product to its consumers.

The SSRT is an Excel-based tool which helps to expose how various people across the supply chain perceive the relative importance of sustainability categories. Users can "spend" a total of 100 points based on assuming the priorities of various stakeholders. There are no correct or scientifically accurate numbers that must be attached to each of these categories and sub-categories. Rather, the SSRT is most useful when it is used by a number of different stakeholders and the relative point allocations can be compared. This comparison provides a quasi-quantitative demonstration of how important each category and sub-category is to the various stakeholders.

The tool is shown in some screen captures that follow, and points are allocated based on the collective opinions. For example, when considering the importance of nutrient management at the farm level (as opposed to nutrient loss or dilution due to processing or spoilage) it is supposed that the consumer is not aware of nor cares about any of the sub-categories within this category. As a result, the consumer does not "spend" any of their 100 points in this category. The environment spends 15 of the 100 available points given that a high nutrient balance is a sign that the balance of nature has been maintained. For farmers nutrient management is vitally important to the sustained fertility of his or her farm. As such, the farmer "spends" 5 points on preventing soil erosion, 3 point on each of crop rotation, organic fertilizer, chemical fertilizer, and soil and plant testing and measurement. Nutrient management dissipates in importance as we move away from the farm with Suppliers and Unilever shareholders only spending 9 and 8 point, respectively. As the user spends points according to their perception the "Nutrient Management" row will be automatically tallied. The tool is built so that the users only need fill in the subcategories.

The first set of rankings, under the header "Single Weightings" take the exclusive point of view of each of the five stakeholders. The second set of rankings "Combination Weightings" allow the user to assign a weight to each of the stakeholders and the tool will then calculate the relative point allocation. For example, the tool can produce the relative point allocations for a 35% Environment and 65% Unilever Shareholder weighting:

As the SSRT is shown above, in the first column the user has weighted all of the Environment's allocations by 35% and the remainder, 65%, to Unilever shareholders. This weighting shows where the relative "hot button" sustainability areas are if largely taking the Unilever shareholder's perspective into account but tempering this with some concern for the environment. These weightings can be combined and compared across the five different stakeholders.

Table 1. The sustainability stakeholder rating tool

Stakeholders	The Consumer	The Environment	The Farmers	The Suppliers	Unilever Shareholders
Nutrient Management	**0**	**0**	**0**	**0**	**0**
Less soil erosion					
Crop rotation					
Organic fertilizer					
Chemical fertilizer					
Soil/Plant Testing/Measurement					

Table 2. The sustainability stakeholder rating tool – weightings

Stakeholders		Combination Weightings			
		Shareholders& Environment	Shareholders & Suppliers	Shareholders & Farmers	Environment & Farmers
Weightings	The Consumer				
	The Environment	35%			50%
	The Farmers			30%	50%
	The Suppliers		45%		
	Unilever Shareholders	65%	55%	70%	

The final part of the tool is the rankings across the various products. These tabs allow the user to think through how the sustainability categories differ across product groups. As with the other parts of the tool, the user should simply fill out the rankings according to how he or she believes they would differ based on the various product groups. See the *appendix* for rankings of dairy, variables, and palm oil.

While the scores within a Stakeholder column are not precise (a 5 versus a 3 is largely arbitrary) the point distributions are most illuminating across the stakeholder columns. As such, it makes sense that the farmer and the environment have relatively similar scores as nutrient management keeps his or her farm productive and also potentially limits the amount of harmful nitrogen-based fertilizers the farmers will put into the soil and which can run off into the water supply. Similarly, it makes sense that the suppliers and Unilever are approximately equally interested in nutrient management in so far as it has the potential to keep down costs (through the prudent application of fertilizers and soil and plant testing to limit the application of fertilizers when they are not required for plant growth).

By design the SSRT is best used in helping individuals across the supply chain think through the relative importance of those sustainability aspects directly involving the farm. However, this methodology could be easily expanded to include later parts of the supply chain including processing, transportation, packaging, distribution, sales, consumption, and waste generation. This more traditional life cycle analysis may help uncover where, across the entire lifecycle of various products (onions, tea, tomatoes, etc.) have the most impact on the environment.

RADCIAL SUPPLY CHAIN TRANSPARENCY

After identifying which crops, products, or brands to start with by using a prioritization tool like the SSRT, Unilever needs to then ensure compliance to its Sustainable Agriculture Code in some way. Supply chain transparency encourages compliance down the supply chain, and is certainly one way for producers in one region to encourage other producers through value alignment and pressure to adhere to sustainability measures. This section is called 'radical' transparency because, despite the entire buzz around certifications, most companies still do not engage in any form of supply chain transparency, do not know where their raw materials inputs originate, and definitely do not make this information available to the general public. Transparency means that the supply chain is visible to Unilever, but it also means that the supply chain is visible to farm producers, suppliers, Unilever customers, and pressure groups. Supply chain transparency about Unilever products may help pressure groups to identify and participate in key points of intervention. Unilever can see what is going on in their supply chain if they institute radical supply chain transparency. Three tools to create radical supply chain transparency are certification, crowd sourcing, and networks.

Third Party Certification Schemes

There are a plethora of third party certifications that have emerged over the past 30 years to address the needs to verify sustainable practices in the supply chain. Below is the list of major certifications for food products for the supply chains analyzed (dairy, oils, vegetables, and tea) which the marketing company BBMG listed in 2009 as the top consumer-recognized food certifications in the United States.

For the certification question, the most important place for Unilever to start is to ask itself is "What do we need to prove about our supply chain, and to whom?" Certification plays a very different role whether you are trying to prove something about the way that farmers are paid and your primary audience is the US consumer, than to demonstrate compliance with ILO child labor laws according for a government regulatory agency. Certification should be seen as a tool in a large toolbox in which different items play different roles to demonstrate sustainability along the chain.

It is important to note that in demonstrating these five certification schemes below the priority for certification for Unilever is that it is first and foremost meant to be a consumer guarantee, so the consumer is the primary audience (and not just for Unilever internally, a government, another manufacturer, etc.)

It is also interesting to note that BBMG demonstrated 13 top certification marks (food and nonfood) to consumers, finding that the top three are all run by the US government and have benefited greatly from *prominence* and *exposure*, two factors that seem to go a long way toward cultivating trust, regardless of aesthetics or even the actual standards behind the mark. Of the food marks listed above, just one is government-sponsored, and the rest are privately run.

Third party certification may be thought of as a type of command and control supply chain management strategy. However, there may be instances when third party certification is not the most optimal mechanism for ensuring compliance. One reason that third party certification may not be the most optimal is cost. Third party certification can be expensive, particularly for small producers. Another instance is when Unilever does not have to prove to its customers or outside pressure groups that a product is produced sustainably. Finally, third party certification is often seen as another form of auditing for compliance, and it has yet to be seen whether monitoring schemes and a 'check-list' approach to sustainability are truly the best ways to engender sustainability practices. However, there are important networks that emerge out of certification and non-certified, trust-based schemes (agroecology, fair trade crafts) which are particularly interesting to consider for the development and sustainability externalities that they provide.

The question then becomes in instances where third party certification is not the mechanism with which Unilever chooses to ensure compliance, how can compliance be accomplished? Several case studies and academic research papers point to long-term relationship building and supply chain transparency as good strategies for encouraging compliance down the supply chain. Shifting core values of suppliers and producers is also a successful mechanism. Supply chain transparency reinforces core value shifts and core value shifts allow more willingness to make supply chains transparent.

Table 3. Certifications for food products for the supply chains

Certification	Background	Farm Size	Public Perception	Critique	Process	Unilever
Organic (under IFOAM global umbrella)	Environmental movement, established in (1972, France)	Large and small, all types of food products	Large volumes sold, largely trusted	Critique that the certification has become watered down from initial	Audit	Y
Trade Guarantee	Whole Foods private label program – launched in 2007, aims by(year) to have	Large and small– verified by partner certification(incl. fair trade, rainforest alliance, and IMO)	Trusted by Whole Foods customers, applies to private label products. Donates 1% of WTG sales to microcredit programs	?	?	N
Fair Trade Labeling Organizations International (FLO)	Movement established as solidarity / third world (first as crafts, then food products) in '60s. Certification launched in (1988 in the Netherlands)	Different standards by product – some just from cooperatives, others include plantations	Some companies want audit disclosure of ft. purchases and publish themselves online	Issue regarding Sourcing(plantations vs. coops/small farmers) Not strong enough on environmental standards	Audit	Y
Rainforest Alliance	Founded in 1986 as response to rainforest crisis	Large and Small	Has a whistle-blower program for reporting violations	Not strong enough on the social/labor standards	Audit – on a scale	Y
Certified Humane	Founded in the US in 2003	For farm animals on large and small farms	Decertify farms who don't meet criteria, backed by 10 animal welfare groups	?	Audit	?

Trust-Based Networks

One way to shift core values is to work with and encourage trust-based networks. Corporate utilization of trust based networks is new, but the experiences suggest that trust based networks may actually be more effective at ensuring supply chain quality than monitoring schemes and third party certification. This is because trust based networks, such as agroecology, create a shift in producer and supplier values. Instead of shifting to sustainable practices just to meet a checklist on the day when the monitoring party comes through, a producer or supplier wants to comply with sustainability standards because they have internalized the standards as part of their core values. The trust-based networks then build reinforcing loops, where 'compliance' is not audited but ensured via producer-to-producer, producer-buyer, and/

or buyer-buyer relationships. Those who do not comply are can essence be 'shunned' from the network and their reputation damaged.

However, trust-based networks require a shift in core values, which can be a long road. To bring producers and suppliers along in a more rapid fashion, a shift in incentive structure can be of great assistance. Under normal circumstances, a producer or supplier is trying to provide a product for the least cost possible. So too is a purchasing company such as Unilever searching for the lowest cost product possible, within their parameters for quality. For most companies, this means switching from supplier to supplier depending on who is offering the best price. However, this creates short term and unstable relationships between suppliers and the purchasing company. The incentive structure here for suppliers encourages them to procure products for the least costs. Suppliers have no incentive to comply with sustainability standards.

Furthermore, companies that convert to sustainability practices often experience a worse before better cycle, where they actually see profits dip before they see profits rise or rebound. A supplier with a short term relationship with a purchasing company has no incentive to go through the "worse" portion of the worse before better cycle. If, however, Unilever creates long-term relationships with a handful of suppliers through long-term contracts and trust-based relationship building, suddenly, suppliers have an incentive to go through the "worse" part of the worse-before-better cycle because they have the incentive of gaining a long term relationship with Unilever and are virtually guaranteed that they will reap the benefits of the "better" part of the cycle. Both Wal-Mart and Patagonia have used long-term relationship building with suppliers as a strategy for driving sustainability compliance down the supply chain.

Crowdsourcing

Several examples of online tools to facilitate supply chain transparency exist or are in the pipeline. These tools include World of Good, Good Guide, and Source Guide. Source Guide is an open source tracking tool that creates supply chain transparency through crowdsourcing. Wikipedia defines crowdsourcing as, "a neologistic compound of "crowd" and "outsourcing" for the act of outsourcing tasks, traditionally performed by an employee or contractor to a large group of people or community (a crowd), through an open call." Corporations are beginning to turn towards crowd sourcing solutions for their design needs. Some examples of crowd sourcing are Next Stop Design, Future Melbourne, and Motors. Crowdsourcing is also on the horizon for supply chain transparency. Something that is co-created by so many parties could have the potential to be respected as more valid than something that is coming unilaterally from a single company such as Unilever. Unilever could sponsor an open source tracking tool which non-profits, customers, academics, and lay people could help to flesh it out.

While it seems risky for a company to allow random strangers to post seemingly unreliable data about their company online, the fact of the matter is that open source crowdsourcing is coming down the pipeline in this arena and companies will be better off utilizing open source supply chain tracking and providing accurate information than not. For example, Wikipedia is an open source platform that contains crowdsourced information about Unilever.

Combining Crowdsourcing and Radical Transparency: The Sourcemap

Sourcemap is the first open source supply chain network founded by Leo Bonanni at MIT Media Lab. This open source project is free and volunteer driven, with a mission to empower sustainability at a social and environmental scale. Sourcemap is a collective tool for transparency and sustainability.

Businesses can insert data on sourcing and supply to share with buyers, thus gaining a marketing and online media advantage. Sourcemap has the potential to share both the product source and environmental footprint to inform a consumer's decision. Its open source platform provides opportunity to solve issues arising from rapidly changing supply chains, while it is also critical that these inputs are properly verified and reviewed.

A mock up demonstrating a Unilever product may be found by searching for "*Ragu Tomato Sauce*," on the source map website. Ragu tomato sauce is made up of ingredients from across the world such as tomatoes, spices, celery, carrots, and onions. Sourcemap highlights the location, quantity in product, embodied energy in kg/CO2 per unit, transport in km, and transport type of each ingredient. In this mock-up, we chose locations for ingredients based on generic food hubs in certain areas. The Unilever Ragu plant is based in Owensboro, KY. Across the US, major hubs for ingredients include: tomatoes in central California, onions in Vidalia, GA, black pepper in India, sugar in Brazil, spice mixtures in Maryland (McCormick Spices). The embodied energy and input count for the Unilever mockup are entirely estimated, but some of our estimates were supported by information from Footprint USA, which is a research database focused on reduction of climate footprint. SourceMap can be used in Google Maps and Google Earth and aggregates the carbon footprint of each level in the supply chain.

Next Stop Design "is an example of crowdsourcing in planning. Citizens submitted designs which were discussed and voted on to select one for a bus stop in Salt Lake City, Utah." Future Melbourne, "allowed citizens to help write the city plan for the city of Melbourne, Australia." Local Motors, "is the world's first crowdsourced car. The overall aesthetics was selected by a design competition among submitted entries. The company's fan community then collaborated on designs for smaller details while the company procured a high-quality engine and electronics, an approach that Wired argues "allows crowdsourcing to work even for a product whose use has life-and-death implications."

THE COSTS AND BENEFITS OF THE TOOLS IN THE SUSTAINABILITY TOOLBOX

Each of the tools for radical supply chain traceability comes with a cost-benefit. What can be seen through a qualitative cost-benefit analysis is that in order for Unilever to really work towards its Supplier Code of Conduct, the tools will work best in combination with one another rather than in isolation.

Certifying the Way to Sustainability

Costs: Certification is mostly static, meaning standards tend to be a checklist and there is not often a dynamic set of improvements for participants to strive for which drive evolving sustainability efforts.

Companies cannot control the 3rd party certification standards to align with their core company values because they are pre-written. There are too many certifications in the marketplace, and their meanings often get muddled for consumers and farmers alike. And lastly, certifications bear a financial cost, which can shut out farmers who want to participate but cannot afford to comply.

Benefits: Certification outlines clear standards and a value proposition for farmers, companies, and consumers that are involved. It is very clear as to how to comply, and what participants who comply are doing. There is an incentive structure for participants, as certification has tended to mean greater market access for participants and a demarcated, differentiated product for consumers. There is a network effect embedded in the well-established certification schemes; in other words, once a farmer gets approved, s/he could enter into a national or global network of NGOs, consumers, aid agencies, activists, and companies looking for their products. There is a movement of consumers who care about certain certified products and identify with those product values, such as organic or fair trade. It is clear who pays money for the scheme. And finally, certification means a third party, independent audit of the supply chain.

Crowd Sourcing the Path to Sustainability

Costs: Structures need to be created, as it is not clear now who pays for crowdsourcing, nor who sets up the infrastructure and regulates it. Because anyone can participate there is a question about if third party certification or verification is needed to guarantee the claims of participants. Furthermore, enough supply chain actors need to care and have access to internet-enabled devices to input their information into the system. Consequently, it is not clear whether crowdsourced supply chain transparency is scalable. Moreover, crowdsourcing does not guarantee sustainability at all as there is no set of standards attached to it. Lastly, it is intimidating for a company to let its supply chain go and to allow information to become public on the internet.

Benefits: there is the first mover advantage of getting supply chain information out to the world in a transparent way. It is cheap and easy, as anyone can participate from any internet-enabled device. Crowdsourced supply chain transparency is also a way to earn the trust of customers, as they can virtually interact with the supply chain. Possibly the most interesting benefit of all to Unilever is that crowdsourced supply chain transparency reveals people's opinions and tells Unilever what their customers care about. Consequently crowdsourced supply chain transparency is a cheap way for companies to datamine to understand their customers' values and beliefs.

Networks/Trust-Based Sustainability

- **Costs:** It is not clear who pays for a network, or how to quantify the costs of that network. Networks are self-regulated. As in crowdsourcing, there is a need to define what is being measured in a 'network' of sustainability, and how progress is determined. Beyond what is being measured, what are the clearly defined values of a network, and who defines these values?
- **Benefits:** Participants share the costs of developing the network. Participation can be determined based on collective values (ex. agroecology), but those values need to be somehow codified or made explicit. Networks can cause value realignment of producers and suppliers which can encourage supply chain compliance.

CONCLUSION

The tools offered in this case study are meant to be used in combination to achieve supply chain sustainability. Each company must understand the ever-evolving tools available to them to guarantee sustainability in the supply chain, prioritize their actions along the chain by product, or category, and then apply the appropriate tools to that category. The tools are not mutually exclusive, and are meant to be used synergistically. An effective company will understand its supply chain priorities and the tools that it can use to guarantee sustainability in different sectors.

Therefore, the recommendations are three-fold:

- With so many consumer-facing products, Unilever must develop some standard prioritization process (like the SSRT, and beyond a 4-box matrix) to prioritize its sustainability actions in its supply chain;
- Unilever should speed up the sustainability process via disruptive technologies which demonstrate radical supply chain transparency;
- The company must work in networks and dedicate both its own resources (time, $, HR) and those of its network partners (certifiers, creative technology providers, NGOs, farmers movements, etc.) to this effort.

In conclusion, this chapter suggests that Unilever takes the following steps as it rolls out its sustainability measures. 1) Fully map the supply chain from farm to supplier. 2) Use the SSRT to gain a deep understanding of how much weight Unilever gives to various aspects of sustainability including the environment, farmers, the bottom line, and customers. 3) Use the supply chain map and the results of the SSRT exercise to identify key points to start making sustainability changes. 4) Drive sustainability down the supply chain using radical supply chain transparency. Radical supply chain transparency includes (but is not limited to) third party certification, crowdsourcing, and building networks.

REFERENCES

Unilever. (2015). *Unilever Sustainable Living Plan*. Author.

APPENDIX

Using SSRT Metric to Think About Fruit and Vegetables

The fruits and vegetable rankings have been done in two columns so as to capture the differences between the fresh or frozen vegetables and those that are processed into other food goods. As may be expected, the most significant differences between these two categories appear in the *nutrient management and product characteristics*. These differences reflect the assumption that there is a high correlation between the importances the consumer places on the sustainability of the product and the degree to which it is processed. That is, the more processed the product is, especially if it is to be greatly altered from its raw form or mixed with other food stuffs, the less important sustainability is to the end consumer. For example, the consumer is likely more concerned about the sustainability of frozen spinach (Birds Eye) than they are with soup cubes (Knorr). It is important to note that this analysis has been done on an aggregated level and there may be significant differences across specific crops within the fruit and vegetable product group.

The processed nature of the foods aside, the greatest areas of opportunity for sustainability related categories for fruits and vegetables are in *nutrient management, pest management, and farm characteristics*. Given the importance of the seeds in the eventual nutrient needs of the plant, seeds selection should be carefully considered as this early choice has knock on effects. In addition, crop rotation and soil and plant measurement can ensure the minimal need for additional nutrient supplements (whether organic or chemical) during the growing stage. While pest management does present opportunities for increased sustainable practices, such as sowing other plants to draw pests from the crop, given the potentially significant negative consequences pests can have on entire fields, it is difficult to see how this can be easily implemented.

Finally, farm characteristics provide some of the greatest potential. Part of this is simple arithmetic. It is crucial to understand not only which categories could have the most positive sustainability impact but to what extent is there the will at the farmer level to change their practices. Effectively training farmers to be more strategic and long-term focused about how they manage their land and crop selection and growth strategies (crop rotations, soil testing before applying fertilizers or water, etc.) would provide significant sustainability returns. However, these come at a great expense. Moving towards closer ties with farmers to ensure that they are following best practices in these areas should benefit all stakeholders for a few reasons: 1. greater transparency 2. greater economic certainty 3. lower product costs (less water, less fertilizer, less waste in the field). However, the hurdle is the massive amount of investment that will be required to do this with small holdings farmers.

It may make sense to encourage suppliers to rank farmers by the tonnage supplied and put them into quintiles. For the top two quintiles a sustainability representative could work with every 5-15 farms based on acreage, willingness to adopt sustainable practices, and overall percentage of crop supplied. For the next two quintiles of farms, perhaps one sustainability representative per every 25-50 farms. For the remaining farms it would be necessary to contract out the sustainability education and monitoring to NGOs who could be assisted to develop a uniform training program which they could help deliver to farmers with between 2-5 acres.

Unilever buys about 1.5 million tons of palm oil and its derivatives each year accounting for 4% of the world's supply. However, over the past five years Unilever's total amount of palm oil purchased has

Table 4. Using SSRT metric to think about fruit and vegetables

TOTALS	Products		Difference
	Fruits & Veg - Fresh or Frozen 100	Fruits & Veg - Processed 100	
Nutrient Management	**15**	**10**	**50%**
Less oil erosion	4	2	100%
Crop rotation	3	2	50%
Organic fertilizer	3	2	50%
Chemical fertilizer	3	3	0%
Soil /Plant Testing/Measurement	2	1	100%
Water	**4**	**4**	**0%**
Less run-Off	2	2	0%
Less water intensive method	2	2	0%
Pest Management	**10**	**10**	**0%**
Less Pesticide/Fungicide	5	5	0%
Less Herbicide	5	5	0%
Product Characteristics	**29**	**25**	**16%**
Non-Toxic to humans	10	7	43%
Nutrients in food end product	5	3	67%
Yield	7	12	-42%
Appearance (Size, Col or and Shape)	3	1	200%
Taste	4	2	100%
Energy /GhGas emissions	**9**	**17**	**-47%**
Harvesting	2	2	0%
Transportation	3	5	-40%
Processing	4	10	-60%
Social Dynamics	**8**	**6**	**33%**
Farmer Empowerment	2	2	0%
Living Wage	2	2	0%
Working Conditions	4	2	100%
Farm Characteristics	**13**	**16**	**-19%**
Maintaining or improving biodiversity	5	5	0%
Less supply chain distance to Unilever	4	5	-20%
Quality Control /Food Safety at farm	4	6	-33%
"Outside" Pressure	**12**	**12**	**0%**
How much do NGOs demands matter?	2	2	0%
Government Regulation/Food Safety	5	5	0%
Certification Availability	5	5	0%
TOTALS	**100**	**100**	**0%**

Table 5. Using SSRT metric to think about palm oil

	Product Oils
Nutrient Management	10
Water	10
Pest Management	10
Product Characteristics	10
Energy /GhGas emissions	20
Social Dynamics	25
Farm Characteristics	10
"Outside" Pressure	15
TOTALS	100

decreased. Palm oil ingredients are used across their portfolio, mainly in spreads, but also in savory products (soups and sauces) and ice cream. The oil is used in soap bars and is also a key ingredient in laundry and personal care products.

Unilever was one of the founders of the global Roundtable on Sustainable Palm Oil (RSPO) – an industry-led initiative partnering with WWF in 2003. The Roundtable works with plantation owners, manufacturers, retailers, banks and other NGO partners including Oxfam to construct standards for sustainable palm oil production. In 2007, the group developed criteria for sustainable palm oil production which were tested by a group of Roundtable members during 2007. This led to national interpretations of the generic criteria and permitted differences in national legislation in various countries. In November 2007, RSPO launched its certification framework and the first quantities of certified sustainable palm oil reached the market in November 2008.

As the most produced vegetable oil in the world, palm oil produces ten times more oil per hectare than soybean, rapeseed, or sunflower. This leads to *farm characteristics* requiring less land area requirements and less energy. Palm oil also has strong *product characteristics* as one of two of the few highly saturated vegetable fats, which are applied to a variety of food products and food ingredients. However, there is growing concern that the demand for palm oil has major environmental and social consequences.

Traditional practices to establish oil palm plantations lead to considerable *soil erosion*. Erosion occurs during the time of forest clearing when the soil is left uncovered, leading to harsh effects on *nutrient management*. Erosion for palm oil is exacerbated by planting trees in rows rather than on lines around them, and by establishing plantations and infrastructure on slopes of more than 15 degrees. *Water management* is also a critical part of palm oil cultivation, with deficits or overuse of water severely changing the yield of the crop.

There is also major concern that the demand for palm oil and biofuel can lead to poorly managed expansion of palm oil production and larger environmental effects. Palm oil has been known as one of the key drivers of deforestation. Almost 75% of the world's palm oil is grown in Indonesia and Malaysia with expansions onto peat land and into tropical rainforest. The cleaning of forests in Indonesia alone accounts for 4% of the world's *GHG emissions*. As quoted on Unilever's website on sustainability and palm oil," An area the size of Greece is cleared every year. Deforestation accounts for some 20% of all greenhouse gases – making Indonesia the third - highest emitter after the US and China." Unilever must create a market for sustainable palm oil in order to address the tradeoffs between palm oil and climate change.

In addition, the losses of natural habits without agreement or compensation have created *social dynamics* leading to local conflicts among indigenous people. Social NGOs and other *outside pressure* groups have campaigned against palm oil. For instance, Greenpeace, an environmental group, claims that deforestation caused by making way for oil palm plantations is far more damaging for the climate than the benefits gained by switching to biofuel. This expands a risk that the adverse publicity would weigh against the use of palm oil for biofuel. Beyond *outside pressure* groups, some traditional consumers have growing concerns for sustainable palm oil, particularly in food, soap, and detergent.

Based on this analysis, greenhouse gas emissions and social dynamics received the highest ranking of importance in SSRT, while the other categories were evenly spread in importance.

The consolidation of the dairy industry in the United States has contributed to environmental issues in significant ways, and unfortunately the sustainability trends described below are affecting the global dairy industry. The size of dairy farms is growing rapidly, and it is not uncommon to see more than 1,000 cows on a single farm (20 years ago, 500 cows was considered a large herd size). The advent of feedlot farming and CAFOs has also given rise to this concentration. With a large herd size, there are concerns about water quality and the over concentration of nutrients on dairy farm. The rankings for dairy are heaviest related to water and energy/GhGas emissions.

Related to *water and nutrient management*, the manure that is produced by dairy cows is spread over and over again over small tracks of land, leading to a saturation of nutrients like ammonia and nitrogen. In the past, these valuable nutrients were spread less intensively and over larger tracks of land. However now, with an over application of manure, the nutrients leech into the soil, producing a toxic effect on local vegetation, and into local groundwater resulting in algae bloom. Farmers in the US are supposed to register a nutrient management plan with the EPA, which is relatively new and a result of the concentration of farms. The issue of nutrient management and water could be one category for dairy, and have a combined score of 30.

Table 6. Using SSRT metric to think about dairy

	Product Dairy
Nutrient Management	**10**
Water	**20**
Pest Management	**0**
Product Characteristics	**20**
Energy /GhGas emissions	**30**
Social Dynamics	**10**
Farm Characteristics	**5**
"Outside" Pressure	**5**
100	

Also, related to nutrient management is the feed that dairy cows receive. Dairy farming and feed harvesting are now geographically distinct in the United States, with feed coming from the corn belt in the Midwest, and dairy concentrated in the south, west, and east. Feed is transported to the cows, but the nutrients from their excretion are not transferred back to the corn belt to be re-distributed.

The majority of *GhGas emissions* are a result of the gases emitted from cows. In fact, agriculture is responsible for 32% of the global methane emissions and of that, 48% come from ruminant animals.

One source said that "In other words, ruminants (domesticated) on Earth emit more greenhouse gasses than all possible means of human transportation (cars, trucks, locomotives, boats of all kind, airplanes, spacecraft, and don't forget those lawn mowers) that burn hydrocarbons."

The social aspects of dairy farming, although not as widely discussed, are important to mention. Regarding labor and *social dynamics* on the farm, the large feedlots have been accused of hiring migrant workers who work long hours and are not treated or paid well. However, dairy farming is not seasonal but happens all year round, and so it can offer consistent jobs with higher wages because a more skilled labor force is required. Cows are a huge, very valuable asset to farmers, and investing in workers also means investing in your assets.

Furthermore, *"outside pressure"* related to food safety is important for the US consumer and government. The issue of the recumbent Bovine Growth Hormone (rBGH) was very visible in the news a few years ago, and many companies (I.e. Starbucks) began to advertise selling rGBH-free milk after being the target of several public consumer advocacy campaigns. Contamination of milk and other dairy products in the *farm characteristics* category, particularly with the outbreaks related to feedlot farming, is of concern to consumer advocacy groups.

Chapter 9
Henkel:
Radical Transparency and Sustainability

ABSTRACT

This chapter analyzes how Henkel aims to create sustainable value with everything they do – together with employees, partners and stakeholders. The company holds leading positions with its three business units in both industrial and consumer businesses thanks to strong brands, innovations and technologies. Henkel also takes responsibility for the safety and health of its employees, customers and consumers, the protection of the environment and the quality of life in the communities in which it operates. In conducting its business, Henkel wants to create sustainable value through innovative solutions. The findings reveal that Henkel creates more value for its customers and consumers, for the communities it operates in, and for the company – at a reduced environmental footprint. Henkel's 20-year goal for 2030 is to triple the value it creates for the footprint made by its operations, products and services - this is an ambition to become three times more efficient. Looking ahead, Henkel intends to continue developing innovations that combine performance, environmental compatibility and social responsibility in equal measure.

INTRODUCTION

Henkel at a glance 2015 –Highlights:

- 139 years of brand and technology success
- 49.450 employees
- €18.1 billion sales
- 125 nations represented by Henkel people
- 43% of sales generated in emerging markets
- 33% of managers are women
- 61% of sales generated by top 10 brands
- More than 3.400 social projects supported
- 38% increase in overall efficiency from 2011 to 2015

DOI: 10.4018/978-1-5225-2417-5.ch009

Figure 1. Henkel around the world: regional centers

Henkel operates worldwide with leading brands and technologies in three business units: Laundry & Home Care, Beauty Care and Adhesive Technologies. Founded in 1876, the company is headquartered in Düsseldorf, Germany. With production sites in 55 countries, Henkel promotes economic development as a local employer, purchaser and investor.

The value-added statement shows that most of the generated sales flow back into the global economy. The largest share of the value added – 52.8 percent – went to the employees in the form of salary and pension benefits. Central and local government received 11.8 percent in the form of taxes; lenders received 1.3 percent as interest payments. Henkel paid 11.1 percent of the value added as dividends to shareholders. The value added remaining in the company is available for investments in future growth.

HENKEL SUSTAINABILITY STRATEGY

Which are Henkel sustainability aspirations? Henkel is committed to leadership in sustainability – this is one of its core corporate values. As pioneers in this field, Henkel wants to drive new solutions while developing its business responsibly and in an economically successful manner. Which strategy is Henkel pursuing? Henkel ambition is to achieve more with less. This means Henkel creates more value for its customers and consumers, for the communities it operate in, and for the company – at a reduced environmental footprint. Which targets has Henkel set? Henkel 20-year goal for 2030 is to triple the value Henkel creates for the footprint made by its operations, products and services. Henkel summarizes this ambition to become three times more efficient as factor 3.In pursuing this goal, Henkel concentrates its activities along the value chain on six focal areas that reflect the challenges of sustainable development as they relate to our operations.

Table 1. Henkel indicators

Economic Indicators		
	2014	**2015**
Sales in million euros	16.428	18.089
Adjusted 1 operating profit (EBIT) in million euros	2.588	2.923
Adjusted 1 return on sales (EBIT) in percent	15.8	16.2
Adjusted 1 earnings per preferred share (EPS) in euros	4.38	4.88
Dividend per ordinary share in euros	1.29	1.45
Dividend per preferred share in euros	1.31	1.47
Environmental Indicators		
	2014	**2015**
Production sites	169	170
Production output in thousand metric tons	7.867	7.940
Energy consumption in thousand megawatt hours	2.219	2.288
Carbon dioxide emissions in thousand metric tons	649	667
Water consumption in thousand cubic meters	7.438	7.190
Waste for recycling and disposal in thousand metric tons	138	142
Employee Indicators		
	2014	**2015**
Employees 1 (as of December 31)	49.750	49.450
Trainees in Germany	484	508
Proportion of female employees in percent	33.2	33.6
Average number of training days per employee	1.5	2.1
Participation in employee share program in percent	30.1	29.7
Occupational accidents per million hours worked	0.9	0.8
Social Indicators		
	2014	**2015**
Donations in million euros (financial and product donations, not counting paid time off from work)	8.2	8.3
Number of projects supported	2.265	3.431

For 2020 Henkel has set new interim targets (base year 2010):

- + 75% overall efficiency.
- +22% more net sales per ton of product.
- +40% safer per million hours worked.
- - 30% less water per ton of product.
- - 30% less waste per ton of product.
- - 30% less energy / CO2 emissions per ton of product.

Figure 2. Value added statement 2015 (in million euros)

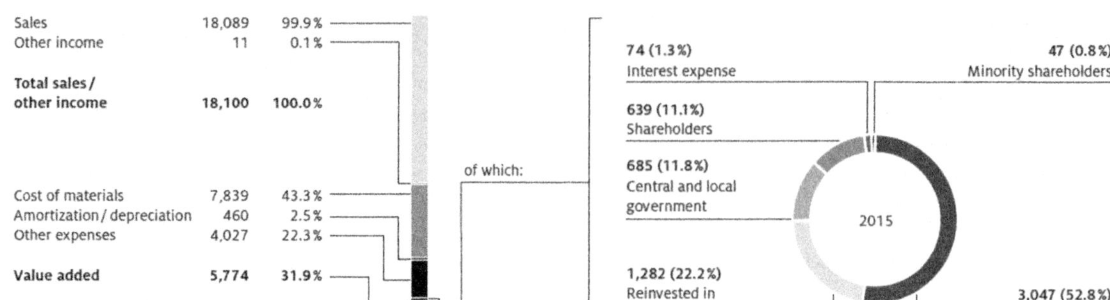

Figure 3. Henkel six focal areas that reflect the challenges of sustainable development

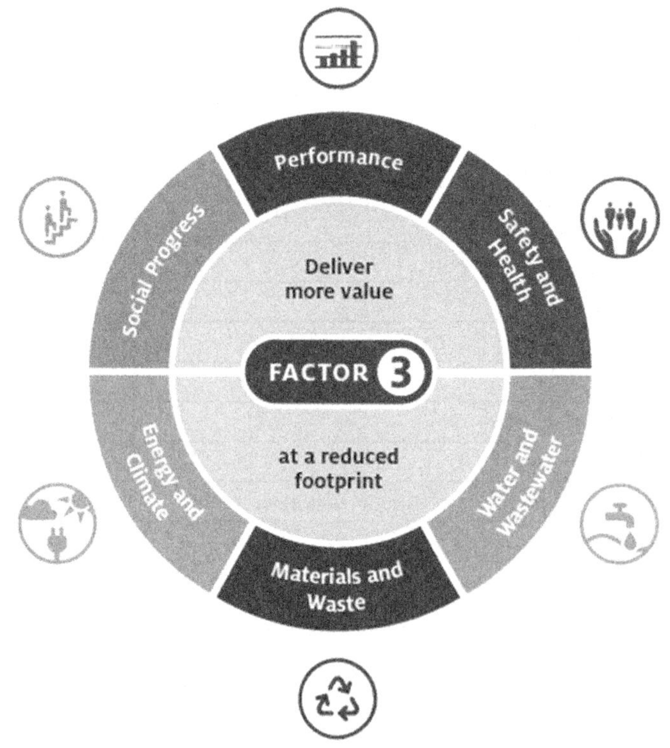

How is Henkel implementing its strategy? To successfully implement its strategy and reach its targets, Henkel rely on its products, cooperation with partners, and the dedication of the people:

- Henkel products - deliver more value at reduced environmental footprint.
- Henkel partners are key to driving sustainability along its value chain.
- Henkel people make the difference – with their commitment, skills and knowledge.

What Henkel Has Achieved

To reach its long-term goal of becoming three times more efficient by 2030 ("Factor 3"), Henkel had set concrete interim targets for the five-year period from 2011 to 2015, which the company achieved. Here is the current status.

Henkel focal areas:

- +38% Overall efficiency (2015 target: +30%).
- + 11 % more net sales per ton of product 2015 target: +10%.
- +33 % safer per million hours worked 2015 target: +20%.
- –23 % less water per ton of product 2015 target: – 15 %.
- –17 % less waste per ton of product 2015 target: – 15 %.
- –18 % less energy / CO2 emissions per t0n of product 2015 target: – 15 %.

Henkel products are systematically assessed according to sustainability criteria throughout the Henkel innovation process. More than 70.000 metric tons of CO2 were avoided by using recycled PET in the packaging for Henkel laundry and home care products.165.000 is the number of product formulas for which Beauty Care has already calculated the carbon footprint.

Henkel partners:

- 18 companies are now members of the purchasing initiative "Together for Sustainability," tripling membership since 2011.
- More than 2,000 audits and assessments have been performed by Henkel at its suppliers since 2012.
- More than 2,200 participants have been able to communicate directly with Henkel experts during webinars offered on the Food Safe Packaging portal of Adhesive Technologies since 2013.

Henkel people:

- About 6.200 - Henkel employees have been qualified as sustainability ambassadors so far.
- Around 63.000 - Schoolchildren have been reached by sustainability ambassadors through Henkel program.
- More than 5 million people around the world have been supported over the past five years by Henkel social engagement activities.

2015 was an important milestone on the path toward Henkel's long-term sustainability goal, "Factor 3." By 2030, Henkel wants to triple the value it creates for the customers and consumers for the communities it operates in and for the company – compared to the environmental footprint of its operations, products and services. Henkel has made great progress in fully integrating sustainability into the business processes. Henkel achieved its interim targets for the first five-year period: With an overall efficiency improvement of 38 percent for the period up to 2015, Henkel is well on track toward its long-term goal. Now, Henkel has defined its targets and ambitions for the next five years: Henkel aims for an overall efficiency improvement of 75 percent by 2020 compared to 2010.

Henkel has another reason to be proud – it has now published its 25th Sustainability Report. It published its first Environment Report ahead of the United Nations Conference on Environment and Development in Rio de Janeiro in 1992. That report reviewed the progress Henkel had made and showed future challenges. Convinced that growth, economic success and environmental compatibility are not irreconcilable, Henkel wanted to demonstrate its commitment to sustainable development.

Henkel approach to sustainability continued to evolve in the following years, becoming more systematic and addressing an increasing number of environmental and social challenges along its value chain. For Henkel – as well as many other businesses around the world – there is no question: Business has to be part of the solution and the sustainability agenda.2015 was also an important year charting the road ahead on major global challenges: The United Nations agreed on the Agenda 2030 for Sustainable Development and its respective goals, and a global climate agreement was reached in Paris. This common understanding of the global priorities will facilitate cooperation and drive progress. With Henkel proven track record in sustainability and its clear strategy, Henkel will be supporting the achievement of these goals. Its commitment to leadership in sustainability is anchored firmly in the company values.

Henkel continuously work to improve all products across its entire portfolio. This enables the company to offer customers and consumers more value and better performance at a smaller environmental footprint. Cooperating closely with its customers and business partners in retail and industry, Henkel is able to leverage its experience in order to optimize logistics, increase the efficiency of production processes, develop more sustainable products and foster sustainable consumption. And it is Henkel people who make the difference. Their understanding of sustainability and its relevance for their respective businesses and areas of responsibility is the foundation for Henkel progress.

Henkel is convinced that sustainability is becoming increasingly important for its business success, supporting its growth, improving its cost efficiency and reducing risks. At the same time, it is only through sustainable business practices that Henkel can maintain the basis for a livable society and a robust economy. Henkel wants to anchor its understanding of sustainability more broadly across society. As part of its Sustainability Ambassador program, Henkel employees also conducted a lesson on sustainability with schoolchildren in Shanghai in 2015. Henkel has now reached around 63,000 children in 43 countries through the program.

Sustainability Strategy and Management

Henkel wants to contribute so that, in 2050, nine billion people will be able to live well and within the resource limits of the planet. Contributing to quality of life and reducing resource consumption through its sustainability strategy, Henkel contributes both to sustainable development and to its company's economic success. Henkel aims to pioneer new solutions while continuing to shape its business responsibly and increase its economic success. As the basis for its strategy, Henkel has adopted the Vision 2050 of the World Business Council for Sustainable Development (WBCSD), whose aspiration is that, in 2050, nine billion people live well and within the resource limits of the planet. For Henkel, this means contributing to quality of life by generating value while using less resources and causing less emissions. Henkel sees sustainability as a shared responsibility for all of society. Its intention is not only that Henkel is a company that creates more value with a reduced environmental footprint, Henkel also wants to inspire others – for example, its suppliers, customers and consumers – to make their own contributions to sustainability.

This is also the intention behind the schools project included in Henkel Sustainability Ambassador Program. Henkel employees receive training so that they are able to explain the importance of sustainable behavior to others, including young children. The significance of sustainability changed over the years. Today, sustainability is more important than ever for Henkel business success. Over the past decades, Henkel has worked intensively on all the dimensions of sustainability. As a result, it succeeded in reaching its interim targets for the past five years. But there are still many challenges ahead. Henkel must continue to set ambitious targets and work purposefully to achieve them. This includes anchoring sustainability even more firmly in its business operations. Each employee must be able to understand the relevance of sustainability to its business success – and convey this to customers, colleagues or business partners. Henkel Ambassador Program encourages its people to engage actively with the challenges of sustainable development. They then pass on that knowledge to others, including schoolchildren. People need this kind of personal engagement to drive sustainable development on all levels in the future.

Henkel's ambition - Commitment to leadership in sustainability is one of Henkel core corporate values. Through its sustainability strategy, Henkel contributes both to sustainable development and to the company's economic success. As sustainability leaders, Henkel aims to pioneer new solutions while developing its business responsibly and increase its economic success. This ambition encompasses all of its company's activities along the entire value chain. Henkel is convinced that sustainability will become increasingly important for its business success in the future. By 2050, the world's population is expected to grow to nine billion. The accompanying acceleration in global economic activity will lead to rising consumption and resource depletion. The effect of increasing pressure on available resources is becoming more noticeable around the world.

Henkel strategy is based on the Vision 2050 of the WBCSD. For Henkel as a company, this means contributing to quality of life by generating value while using less resources and causing less emissions. We want to create more value – for its customers and consumers, for the communities Henkel operates in, and for its company – while reducing its environmental footprint at the same time.

Focal Areas and Strategic Principles

Henkel concentrates its activities on six focal areas that summarize the main challenges of sustainable development as they relate to its operations. In each of these focal areas, Henkel drives progress along the entire value chain through its products and technologies. Henkel has subdivided the focal areas into two dimensions: "more value" and "reduced footprint." In order to successfully establish its strategy and reach its goals, both of these dimensions must be ever-present in the minds and day-to-day actions of all Henkel employees and mirrored in its business processes. Henkel relies here on the contributions made by its products and technologies, collaboration with its partners, and the commitment of its people.

The Sustainability Council is consisted of: Dr. Nicolas Weber, Michael Olosky, Thomas Gerd Kühn, Dr. Andreas Bruns, Bertrand Conquéret, Dr. Thomas Förster, Prof. Dr. Thomas Müller-Kirschbaum, Kathrin Menges (Chair), Carsten Tilger, Dr. Peter Florenz, Marie-Eve Schröder, Georg Baratta-Dragono and Nicolas Krauss. They represent the business units and all corporate functions responsible for putting Henkel sustainability strategy into operational action. The Council steers the development and implementation of Henkel global sustainability strategy.

If Henkel is to work in harmony with its limited resources in 2050, it must become five times more efficient. By 2030, therefore, Henkel wants to triple the value it creates through its business operations in relation to the environmental footprint of its products and services by comparison with the base year 2010. Henkel can achieve this goal, its "Factor 3," in different ways: Henkel can triple the value it creates while leaving the footprint at the same level. Or it can reduce the environmental footprint to one third of today's level while delivering the same value.

To reach its goal by 2030, Henkel will have to improve its efficiency by an average of 5 to 6 percent each year. Henkel had therefore set interim targets for its focal areas for the five years from 2011 to 2015. With improvements of 18 percent in energy efficiency, 23 percent in water use, 17 percent in waste volume, 33 percent in occupational safety, and 11 percent in sales, Henkel reached these targets. By the end of 2015, Henkel had thus improved the relationship between the value it creates and its environmental footprint by 38 percent overall.

On the road to its long-term goal of "Factor 3," Henkel intend to improve its performance in these areas still further over the coming years. To do this, Henkel has defined new interim targets: By 2020, Henkel wants to further reduce the direct and indirect carbon dioxide emissions from its production sites, its water use and its waste volume, in each case by 30 percent per ton of product relative to the base year 2010. Henkel wants to improve its occupational safety performance by 40 percent and its sales by 22 percent per ton of product.

To reach its goal of becoming three times more efficient by 2030, Henkel will have to improve its efficiency by an average of 5 to 6 percent each year. For the five years from 2011 to 2015, Henkel had set concrete interim targets aiming to increase efficiency by 30 percent. Henkel achieved these targets. With its 20-year goal in mind, Henkel has set new interim targets for its focal areas for 2020.

Through these new interim targets, Henkel intend to improve the relationship between the value it creates and its environmental footprint by 75 percent overall (relative to the base year 2010) by the end of 2020.

How Henkel Implements Its Strategy

To successfully implement its strategy and drive sustainability along its value chain, Henkel relies on its products, its partners, and its people. In a comprehensive process, Henkel assessed its footprint and impacts, identified the options for improvement, and defined the main areas for action for the period up to 2020. Here are some examples:

Henkel products:

Figure 4. Henkel 2030 targets

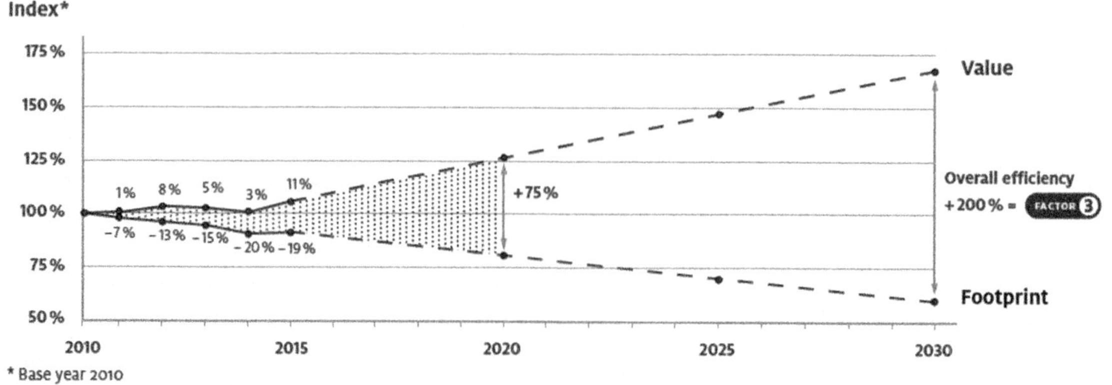

Figure 5. Henkel 2020 targets

- Each new product must continue to make a contribution to sustainability.
- Henkel intends to enhance the transparency on the substances used in its products and their safety on a global scale.
- Henkel wants to reduce the volume of packaging relative to net sales by 20 percent.

Henkel partners:

- Together with its partners, Henkel wants to improve workplace conditions for one million employees in its supply chain.
- Henkel wants to help its customers and consumers to save 50 million metric tons of CO2.
- Henkel wants to educate 300 million consumers about recycling options and inspire them to participate.

Henkel people:

- Henkel wants to mobilize all of its employees to continue working to advance sustainability.
- Through its social engagement activities, Henkel wants to contribute to the quality of life of 10 million people.
- Henkel wants to reach 200,000 children with its education initiatives.

Measuring, Assessing, and Managing Progress

Henkel first published an Environment Report in 1992. It reviewed its achievements, product improvements, and the progress made in the area of environmental protection at its production sites. Henkel subsequently began preparing an annual report on the company's major sustainability activities. In 2015 Henkel collected data on 170 sites, representing 100 percent of its global production volume. To assess its footprint along the entire value chain, Henkel uses representative life cycle analyses that cover around 70 percent of its sales across all product categories. Henkel also assess data on the raw ingredients and packaging materials Henkel uses and the transport operations. Henkel are currently using the knowledge it has gained to further improve its assessment and measurement systems to allow Henkel to make an integrated assessment of its progress toward its 20-year goal for 2030 across the entire company and its value chain. In 2015, Henkel work was mainly concentrated on improving the data basis for the raw ingredients and packaging materials it uses; updating the emissions factors for the energy usage figures for its sites worldwide; and further developing its computing models for logistics emissions.

Henkel works with various measurement methods to optimize the "Value" and "Footprint" dimensions. These allow the actions to be identified that have the greatest effect on sustainability along the value chain. Considering its portfolio as a whole, it is evident that improvements in the raw materials and the use phase have a significant impact on the water and carbon footprint. The various instruments are summarized in the Henkel Sustainability#Master®. Its core element is a matrix that can be used to assess changes in both the "Value" and the "Footprint" dimensions. Henkel uses the results to develop innovations with improved sustainability performance. Only by considering the entire life cycle can Henkel ensure that the action taken will improve the overall sustainability profile of its products. In line with its ambition that each new product must make a contribution to sustainability, Henkel assesses its products systematically throughout its innovation process. To make it easier to optimize its products while they are being developed, Henkel integrates the environmental profiles of possible raw ingredients and packaging materials into the information systems of its product and packaging development departments. This allows the footprint of a new formulation to be computed as early as the development phase.

From its vision and values, Henkel has formulated globally binding behavioral rules which are specified in a series of codes and corporate standards. These apply to all employees worldwide, in all business areas and cultural spheres in which Henkel operates. The Code of Conduct contains the most important corporate principles and behavioral rules. It is supplemented by guidelines for dealing with potential conflicts of interest. These guidelines are a key element of Henkel preventive measures against corruption. Further corporate standards address specific topics such as compliance with competition and antitrust laws; safety, health, environment and social standards; human rights; as well as public affairs. The codes and corporate standards also provide the basis for implementing the United Nations Global Compact, which Henkel joined as early as 2003.

Henkel Compliance organization has global responsibility for all preventive and reactive measures. It is supported by integrated management systems and an organizational structure with clearly defined responsibilities. The Chief Compliance Officer reports directly to the Chairman of the Management Board. He is supported by the Corporate Compliance Office, Henkel interdisciplinary Compliance & Risk Committee, and 50 locally appointed compliance officers all over the world. Henkel Corporate Data Protection Officer is also part of its Compliance organization. Together, this team coordinates the flow of information and helps its employees to implement its requirements locally – for example, through specially adapted training courses. The Chief Compliance Officer reports on any infringements, as well as the measures taken to deal with them, to the Management Board and the Audit Committee of the Supervisory Board on a regular basis.

Since Henkel operates on a global scale, its employees find themselves in a variety of legal and value systems. Many of its employees work in countries where, according to surveys by organizations such as

Figure 6. The process applied to define Henkel targets for 2020

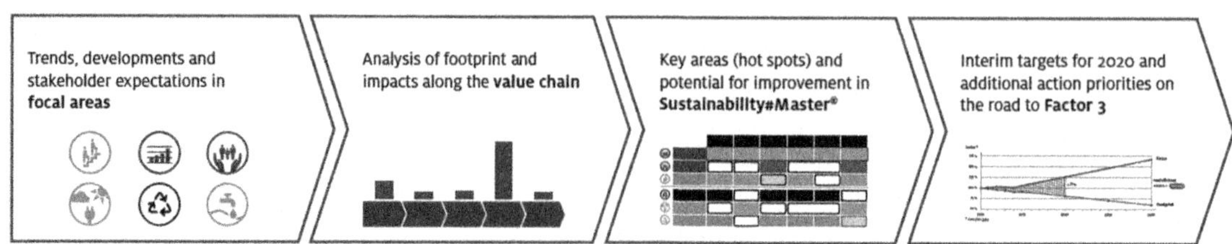

Transparency International, there is a greater risk of encountering corrupt practices. Even in such surroundings, the same applies to all employees without exception: Henkel strictly opposes infringement of laws and standards, and rejects all dishonest business practices. To impart clear rules of conduct to its employees, and especially to avoid any conflicts of interest in everyday work situations, Henkel focuses on regular training courses and communication measures. In 2015, Henkel trained more than 12,000 employees around the world in face-to-face seminars on compliance topics.

Henkel managers play a key role in regard to compliance. Given their position within the company, they bear a special responsibility to set an example for their staff. For this reason, all of Henkel 10,400 managers across the globe must participate twice a year in Henkel mandatory Compliance eLearning program, which addresses many different compliance topics. The main emphasis in 2015 was on antitrust law and data security.

Improper conduct is never in Henkel's interest. The Management Board and senior management circles at Henkel all subscribe to this fundamental principle. Improper conduct undermines fair competition and damages its trustworthiness and reputation. Henkel employees attach great importance to a correct and ethically impeccable business environment. Henkel reacts forcefully to violations of laws, codes and standards. Where necessary, Henkel initiates appropriate disciplinary measures. In 2015, 12 employees received written warnings, and 42 contracts were terminated as a result of conduct violating compliance rules.

Henkel's compliance culture involves continuous monitoring and improvement of the compliance process. As a result, Henkel global Compliance Management System was audited by external auditors in 2013 based on the IDW PS 980 auditing standard with respect to the appropriateness, implementation and effectiveness of the compliance processes in the areas of competition law and anticorruption.

The Head of the Corporate Audit department reports directly to the Chairman of the Management Board. Henkel carries out regular audits based on its risk-based audit planning at its production and administration sites, and at its subcontractors and in logistics centers, to verify compliance with its codes and standards. The audits are a key instrument for identifying risks and potential improvements. In 2015, Henkel conducted 78 audits around the world. In the course of the audits, a total of 2,127 corrective actions were agreed upon. The main emphasis in 2015 was on the following areas: sales and distribution (following the issue of a new corporate standard for this area); finance processes in the shared services; local human resources management; compliance at toll manufacturers and subcontractors; and processes relating to safety, health and environment (SHE). Compliance with the SHE Standards was audited at 117 sites, resulting in the initiation of 478 optimization measures. Maintenance of Henkel Social Standards and its Diversity & Inclusion Policy was examined in 21 audits.

All audit results are included in the Corporate Audit department's annual report to the Henkel Management Board and the Audit Committee of the Supervisory Board. In addition to the regular audits, Henkel also conducted six reviews of internal monitoring systems, mainly for newly acquired entities. These begin with self-assessments by the reviewed Henkel companies, which are then elaborated in more detail with the help of local auditors. Henkel also trained 1,289 employees on aspects of compliance, risk management, and internal monitoring in seminars and during its audits in 2015.

Chaired by a Management Board member and reflecting all areas of the company, the Sustainability Council steers Henkel sustainability activities as a central decision-making body. The business units are responsible for putting its sustainability strategy into operational action. The regional and national companies steer implementation in their respective regions. The corporate functions are responsible for ensuring implementation of our sustainability strategy in their areas.

Figure 7. Main focus of audits in 2015 (Percentage distribution of the2015 Henkel audit program)

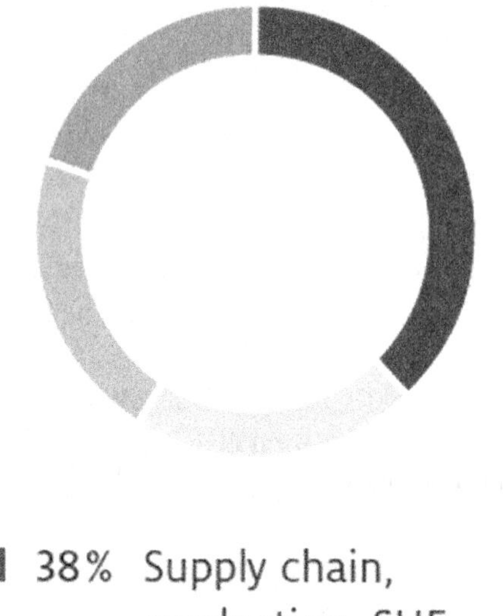

- 38% Supply chain, production, SHE
- 21% Finance, accounting
- 21% Marketing, sales, purchasing
- 20% Information technology, human resources

Figure 8. Henkel organization for sustainability

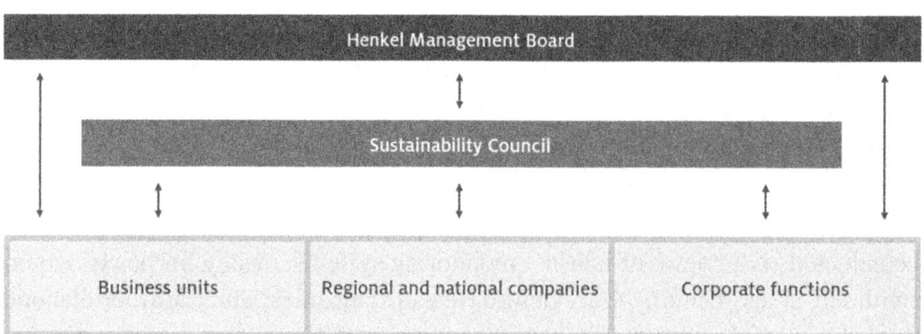

SUPPLY CHAIN

A look back at Henkel targets for the five-year period from 2011 to 2015 shows that the continuous improvements made and the simplification of its purchasing, production and logistics processes have put us in a good position to become three times more efficient by 2030.

Achieving More With Less

Henkel has merged the production, logistics and purchasing activities for all of its business units into a single global supply chain organization. Henkel are working to continuously improve efficiency in all areas while maintaining the high quality of its products.

The production site in Wassertrüdingen, Germany, produces around one-fifth of the products in the Beauty Care portfolio and serves the entire European market – up to 3.3 million units are filled here every day. Since cleaning of the filling lines is a main generator of wastewater, Henkel uses steam instead of hot water to clean and disinfect the equipment. This has enabled Henkel to reduce the wastewater volume per cleaning cycle by more than 90 percent, thus avoiding around 850 cubic meters of waste water per line every year. Another sustainability example is the bundling of single product bottles with film wrapping. This is normally done by shrink wrapping under the application of heat. A new machine now achieves the same effect by mechanically stretching the film, which saves up to 70,000 kilowatt hours of electric power per year. By implementing many such measures, this site has been able to reduce its wastewater footprint by more than 65 percent and its electricity consumption by more than 50 percent per production unit from 2005 to 2015. All of this contributes to achieving its "Factor 3" goal.

Henkel has launched its global supply chain organization under the name of ONE!GSC Horizon. How can this change contribute to more sustainability? Establishing a unified global supply chain is one of Henkel most important strategic projects. It involves a fundamental realignment of its production, logistics and purchasing processes across all business units and functions. The new organization will help Henkel to standardize and harmonize its processes worldwide. It will increase its competitiveness – through faster workflows, better flow of information, more transparency, and greater efficiency overall. This increase in efficiency also plays a key role in reaching Henkel sustainability goals.

In 2015, Henkel again introduced many measures that reduce the environmental footprint of its production operations and boost its efficiency. Henkel strives constantly at its production sites to use even less energy and water and decrease its waste volume, all while still maintaining high quality and continuously improving occupational safety. And Henkel is succeeding: It reached all of the targets it had set for 2015 in these areas.

Standardization of processes also plays a central role in Henkel's purchasing organization. In Henkel purchasing initiative "Together for Sustainability," or TfS, the main objective is to harmonize and simplify increasingly complex, global supplier management processes – not only for the member companies, but also for its shared suppliers. The membership of TfS has already tripled since the initiative was launched in 2011. That shows that the idea works.

Purchasing and Supplier Management

Henkel currently has suppliers and other business partners from around 130 countries. More than 70 percent of its purchasing volume comes from countries that belong to the Organization for Economic Cooperation and Development (OECD). However, Henkel is increasingly opening up new purchasing markets in countries that are not OECD members. Henkel places the same exacting demands on suppliers worldwide. Henkel suppliers are assessed in a comprehensive process that covers sustainability performance and risks as well as key commercial and operating indicators.

Henkel expects its suppliers and business partners to conduct themselves in a manner consistent with its sustainability requirements. In selecting and developing its suppliers and other business partners, Henkel also considers their performance in regard to safety, health, environment, social standards and fair business practices. This is based on its globally applicable Safety, Health and Environment (SHE) Standards that Henkel formulated as early as 1997, thereby demonstrating even then its commitment to assuming responsibility along the entire value chain. Henkel corporate purchasing standards apply worldwide as well, and Henkel supplemented these with a Sustainable Sourcing Policy in 2015.

Compliance with the cross-sector Code of Conduct of the German Association of Materials Management, Purchasing, and Logistics (BME) is mandatory for all of Henkel's suppliers worldwide. Henkel joined the BME in 2009, as its code is based on the 10 principles of the United Nations Global Compact and can therefore be used internationally. The BME code serves as the basis for contractual relationships with Henkel strategic suppliers. This means that they have either recognized the cross-sector BME code – and hence the principles of the Global Compact – or produced their own comparable code of conduct. The BME code has already been translated into 12 languages.

As part of Henkel supplier management activities, the company collaborates intensively with its strategic suppliers. Henkel aims to initiate positive changes throughout the value chain, through joint projects on process optimization, resource efficiency, and environmental and social standards. Furthermore, Henkel has been honoring sustainable innovations by its suppliers for four years. The Laundry & Home Care business unit awarded the biotechnology company Novozymes in 2015 for the development of new, powerful enzymes as the basis for a new generation of innovative formulations. They are used, for example, in the laundry detergents of Henkel Persil ProClean brand in the USA and have been designed specifically to meet the needs of the local market. The Beauty Care business unit recognized Ball Aerocan in 2015 for the joint development of the ReAl can. The technology makes it possible to use recycled aluminum and has been applied to make cans for the deodorant sprays of Henkel Fa, Souplesse and Neutromed brands. The Adhesive Technologies business unit presented its 2015 sustainability award to Covestro Deutschland AG (formerly Bayer Material Science), a supplier of polyurethane technologies. Covestro was recognized for its development of raw materials for Henkel wood adhesives that will allow the company to further expand the business in sustainable wood engineering.

Responsible Supply Chain Process

The results of Henkel assessments and audits from the TfS initiative are a core element of Henkel five-step Responsible Supply Chain Process. This focuses on two main challenges. First, ensuring that all of Henkel suppliers comply with its defined sustainability standards. Second, Henkel aims to purposefully work with its strategic suppliers to continuously improve sustainability standards in its value chain – for example, through knowledge transfer and continued education about process optimization, resource efficiency, and environmental and social standards. This process is performed both at the beginning of its relationship with a supplier and as a regular check of its existing suppliers.

Step 1. Risk Assessment: Henkel uses an early warning system for sustainability risks in global purchasing markets. Henkel begin by estimating the potential risks in a market or a region. In doing so, Henkel concentrate on countries identified by international institutions as being associated with heightened levels of risk. The assessment includes the criteria of human rights, corruption, and the legal environment. Henkel also appraise a second dimension - that of risk value chains. These are industries and sectors that Henkel considers to potentially represent a risk for the company. This helps Henkel to identify countries and purchasing markets that may require special precautions.

Step 2. Assessment: Henkel uses supplier self-assessments based on questionnaires and has them examined as TfS assessments by the independent experts Eco Vadis. These cover Henkel expectations in the areas of safety, health, environment, quality, human rights, employee standards, and anticorruption.

Step 3. Analysis: Based on the risk assessments and the suppliers' self-assessments, Henkel classifies suppliers according to a "traffic light" system. A "red" score always leads to an audit. In the case of a "yellow" score, the areas where improvement is needed are identified and the supplier is audited if necessary.

Step 4. Audit: Henkel works with independent audit companies to audit compliance with the defined standards in TfS audits. Henkel audits include on-site inspections, e.g., at production sites, and discussions with local employees. Follow-up measures after an audit ensure that suppliers implement the corrective actions that have been specified. Repeated serious non-compliance leads to prompt termination of the supplier relationship. In this area, Henkel also actively participate in cross-sectorial initiatives with the aim of improving the transparency and efficiency of supplier audits and helping to establish cross-company standards.

In 2015, Henkel conducted a total of 687 assessments and audits. In the case of repeat audits, 78 percent of the suppliers audited had improved their sustainability performance. Overall, Henkel did not receive any notification throughout 2015 of an infringement by any of its strategic suppliers which would have given cause for terminating its relationship with that supplier.

Step 5. Further Development: As part of its supplier management activities, Henkel works intensively with its suppliers to improve sustainability standards. Henkel strives to initiate positive changes throughout the value chain, through training programs and joint projects. Henkel target for 2020 is to work with its partners to improve the working conditions for one million people employed in its supply chains.

Figure 9. Responsible supply chain process

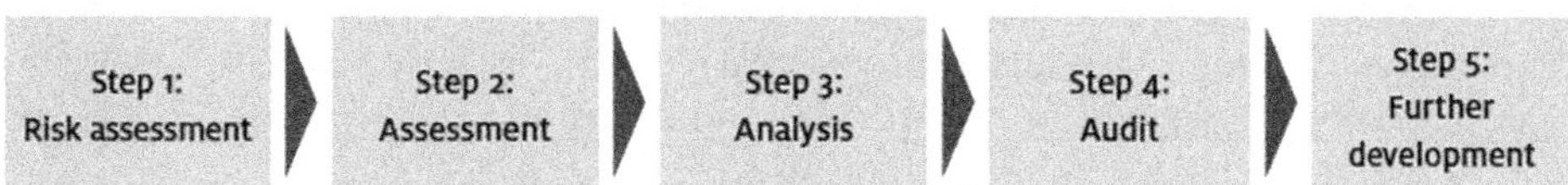

Initiatives for Greater Sustainability

In 2011, Henkel and five other companies in the chemical industry established the initiative "Together for Sustainability – The Chemical Initiative for Sustainable Supply Chains" (TfS). It is based on the principles of the United Nations Global Compact and the Responsible Care Initiative of the International Council of Chemical Associations (ICCA). The TfS initiative aims to harmonize the increasingly complex supply chain management processes with regard to sustainability and to optimize the dialog among worldwide business partners. Above all, synergies are to be created so that resources can be used more efficiently and with a minimum of administrative effort, not only among the member companies but also with all of our shared suppliers.

At the heart of the initiative is the idea: "An audit for one is an audit for all." Suppliers only have to undergo one assessment or one audit. These are conducted by independent experts. An internet platform is then used to make the results available to all members of the initiative for information and approval. Since 2014, TfS has a new legal identity: Through partnering with the Brussels-based European Chemical Industry Council (CEFIC), the initiative now has the status of an independent, non-profit organization. This collaboration will generate even more synergies across the chemical industry.

The TfS grew once again in 2015 and the number of members has tripled from the original six to 18. Last year, the first companies from the USA joined the initiative. Global expansion of the assessment and audit program, driven in part by supplier conferences in Shanghai and São Paulo, was again a main focus of activities in 2015. In addition, the initiative was singled out for mention by the Ethical Corporation: TfS was "highly commended" in the category "Best Supplier Engagement." In 2015, the geographical scope of the TfS initiative was widened once again, particularly in emerging markets. The shared challenges of supply chains in Brazil were discussed at a supplier meeting with more than 300 participants in São Paulo.

Production

Henkel operates 170 production sites worldwide. Henkel works continuously at all of these sites to reduce its environmental footprint while maintaining high quality and safety standards. Henkel has set concrete targets for its production sites to help steer progress toward its long-term "Factor 3" goal. By the end of 2015, Henkel aimed to reduce its energy and water use and waste volume by 15 percent per production unit and reduce its world-wide accident rate by 20 percent (base year: 2010). Henkel achieved each of these four targets: Relative to 2010, Henkel has cut its energy use by 18 percent, water use by 23 percent and waste volume by 17 percent. Henkel worldwide accident rate has dropped by 33 percent versus 2010.

As the next step on the road to its long-term goal of "Factor 3," Henkel has set new interim targets. By 2020, Henkel wants to further reduce the direct and indirect CO2 emissions from its production sites, its water use and its waste volume, in each case by 30 percent per production unit relative to the base year 2010. Henkel has also defined additional priorities for its programs: increasing the amount of renewable energies they use, lowering CO2 emissions during the transport of its products, cutting the volume of waste for landfill, and a stronger focus on saving water in regions where water is in short supply.

Aiming to continuously improve its entire production network, we have begun to introduce the Henkel Production System (HPS). Through this Group-wide optimization program, Henkel wants to systematically identify and eliminate inefficiencies of all kinds along its value chain, such as waiting times, excess production or defects, in order to generate more value for its customers and its shareholders. To this end,

Henkel has set standards for all three business units on the harmonization of production workflows. HPS is based on lean principles and on engaging all employees to ensure that they can implement the new standards effectively while saving on resources. During the transition to HPS, Henkel business units will continue to initiate specific programs for their locations.

The Adhesive Technologies business unit continues to rely on a combination of lean production principles, workshops and structured problem-solving techniques. Through Value Stream Mapping work-shops, Henkel identifies inefficiencies and their causes in order to develop corresponding improvement projects, which often have a positive impact on the sustainability of its processes. In addition to the sustainability workshops introduced in 2014, sustainability scorecards were developed in 2015 to enable better project and investment steering on a quarterly basis.

The Laundry & Home Care business unit is expanding the use of digital technologies in the supply chain. Systematic improvements have been achieved in the areas of safety, environmental protection, and quality through a variety of installed modules. Cameras check the quality of product labels and the accuracy of label positioning as it takes place during the filling process. Sensors monitor work areas near moving machinery parts to make sure that employees will not be put in danger. Consumption data are recorded in real time and continuously evaluated. All of this ensures that its processes run smoothly and efficiently.

In order to continuously improve its workflows, the Beauty Care business unit makes use of the potential offered by digital solutions, among other things. For its Total Productive Management Plus optimization program that has been in place since 2007, a global web-based tool was introduced in 2015 to automate the monthly recording of standardized production and sustainability indicators. This enables real-time performance monitoring and more effective process steering. The expandable modular software system will be rolled out to all sites during 2016.

Standards and Management Systems

Globally uniform standards for safety, health, environment (SHE) and integrated management systems provide the basis for Henkel worldwide optimization programs. The SHE Standards and its Social Standards apply to all sites. Henkel management systems ensure that these standards are implemented consistently across its global production network. Since its employees' behavior plays a key role in this respect, Henkel conducts regular environmental and safety training sessions on a variety of topics at all sites.

Henkel carries out regular audits at its production sites and, increasingly, at its subcontractors and logistics centers to verify compliance with its codes and standards. All audit results, including the monitoring of its SHE and Social Standards, are included in the Internal Audit department's annual report to the Henkel Management Board.

Henkel has its management systems externally certified at the site level wherever this is expected and recognized by its partners in the respective markets. At the end of 2015, around 95 percent of its production volume came from sites certified to ISO 14001, the internationally recognized standard for environmental management systems.96 percent of Henkel production volume is covered by the ISO 9001 quality management standard and 56 percent is covered by the ISO 50001 energy management standard. Furthermore, around 94 percent of Henkel production volume came from sites certified to the OHSAS 18001 standard for occupational health and safety management systems.

Third-party manufacturing is an integral part of Henkel production strategy. For example, Henkel sometimes uses toll and contract manufacturers when entering new markets or introducing new products and technologies. In these cases, the corresponding production volume is often still small. The use of external partners also helps to optimize its production and logistics network and to increase resource efficiency. Currently, Henkel sources around 10 percent additional annual production volume from toll and contract manufacturers.

Henkel requirements regarding quality, environmental, safety and social standards are an integral part of all contractual relationships and order placements. Henkel monitors them using audits carried out by its own staff and, increasingly, by specialized third-party service providers. Henkel aims to establish long-term collaborations with its toll and contract manufacturers. This also includes adding them to its environmental data recording systems.

Occupational Safety

Occupational safety is one of Henkel highest priorities. Henkel remains focused on its long-term objective of "zero accidents." Henkel new interim target is to reduce its worldwide occupational accident rate by 40 percent by the end of 2020 (base year 2010). With this objective in mind, Henkel is working continuously to improve its occupational safety levels through awareness-raising training events; investments to enhance technical safety; and by monitoring the strict compliance with its Safety, Health and Environment (SHE) Standards.

Regular training sessions are held at all sites to raise employees' awareness and enable them to develop safety-conscious behavior. Henkel also conducts training sessions for the staff of contractors working at its sites. The Laundry & Home Care business unit trained its employees using various methods, including seminars by external experts, and by defining global focal topics every two months, on which the sites then conducted a series of events. In addition to the regular safety training sessions, the Beauty Care business unit introduced a new program in Tunisia that is based on recognizing and honoring employees who exhibit outstanding safety-consciousness. The Adhesive Technologies business unit is focusing more strongly on positive dialog on safety in day-to-day work situations. The focus here is on mutual encouragement to develop a safety culture and constructive feedback on unsafe behaviors.

In 2015, Henkel recorded 0.8 occupational accidents per million hours worked. That is an improvement of 33 percent relative to the base year 2010 and means that Henkel exceeded its 2015 target of 20 percent. Despite its continuous focus on health and safety, an employee in Lianyungang, China, suffered a fatal accident in a warehouse. An employee of an external contractor was fatally injured during construction work in Henkel factory in Perm, Russia. These accidents show that Henkel must intensify its global safety training efforts still further.

Logistics and Transport

IT solutions for logistics planning - With the new Transport Management System ONE!TMS, Henkel has introduced a Group-wide IT solution for more efficient handling of its transport planning across all business units and countries. Higher space utilization and optimized routes decrease the transport mileage, reduce fuel consumption and thus diminish CO2 output. In 2015, ONE!TMS was implemented at sites in the Benelux countries, Spain, Slovenia, China and Taiwan. To demonstrate its progress, it is especially important to systematically record the CO2 emissions of its logistics operations. In 2015, Henkel prepared its systems prior to introducing a new instrument, EcoTransIT World, which determines the environmental impact of transports by all transport modes on the basis of the DIN EN 16258 standard. This system will be implemented as of 2016.

In line with its global Supply Chain organization, Henkel has developed programs to reduce emissions that use synergy potentials across business units. Henkel Laundry & Home Care and Beauty Care units, for example, have established a mega warehouse concept in North America, where a few main distribution centers store products until the required quantities are due for on-time delivery to regional warehouses and retailers. This saves 320,000 kilometers in transports and around 380 metric tons of CO2 each year. In another initiative, the two business units began hiring pallets instead of buying them, which resulted in more efficient collection and improved handling of damaged pallets. Laundry & Home Care has rolled out this concept across Europe and is thus avoiding another 480 metric tons of CO2 and 900 metric tons of waste wood every year. Adhesive Technologies is reducing emissions by optimizing express and airfreight services. The resulting improvements along the value chain will save around 1,500 metric tons of CO2 annually as of 2016. Overall, Henkel intend to reduce its logistics emissions by around 5 percent over the next five years. The Adhesive Technologies business unit has initiated a global road safety campaign for its field sales staff. A range of interactive eLearning modules was developed to raise awareness for safe driving. Accessible worldwide, it was used by nearly 1,000 employees in 2015. In safety related team discussions, field sales managers personally convey the importance of this topic to their teams as well. The global training portfolio also includes practical road safety training sessions where needed.

Henkel takes efficiency as well as environmental and safety performance into account when choosing its transport partners. Relevant criteria are included in its request for proposal processes and tenders for the purchase of logistics services. These include energy saving targets and measures for modernizing vehicle fleets.

Henkel's own CO2 emissions are primarily caused by energy generation and consumption. Other CO2 emission sources are not relevant for its business operations. The same applies to emissions of other greenhouse gases. They account for less than one percent of the Scope 1 and Scope 2 emissions. Scope 3 emissions, especially those associated with raw materials and product use, are calculated at the product level.

SUSTAINABILITY STEWARDSHIP

Henkel wants each of its products to make a contribution to sustainability – that means they must offer more value at a reduced environmental footprint. If Henkel is to decouple increased quality of life from resource use, product innovations will play an essential role. Henkel products therefore provide key leverage points for implementing its sustainability strategy. They should offer customers and consumers more value and better performance at a smaller environmental footprint.

For Henkel, this is not a question of developing individual "green" products where only the environmental profile has been improved. Henkel aim is to continuously improve all products across its entire portfolio, taking every aspect into account. A high degree of innovativeness is very important in achieving this. In 2015, Henkel employed around 2,800 people in research and development and invested 478 million euros in these activities. In order to steer product development in line with its sustainability strategy from the outset, criteria for assessing sustainability have been systematically anchored in the Henkel

Figure 10. Product transports per transport mode in 2015

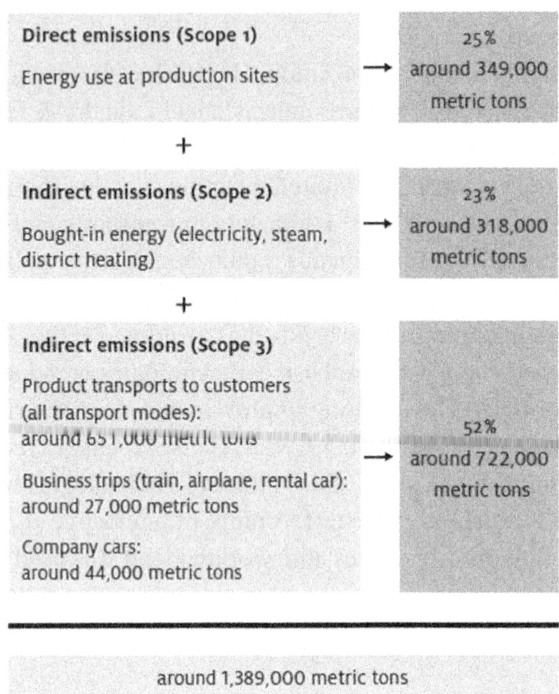

Figure 11. Overall picture: Henkel operational carbon footprint in 2015

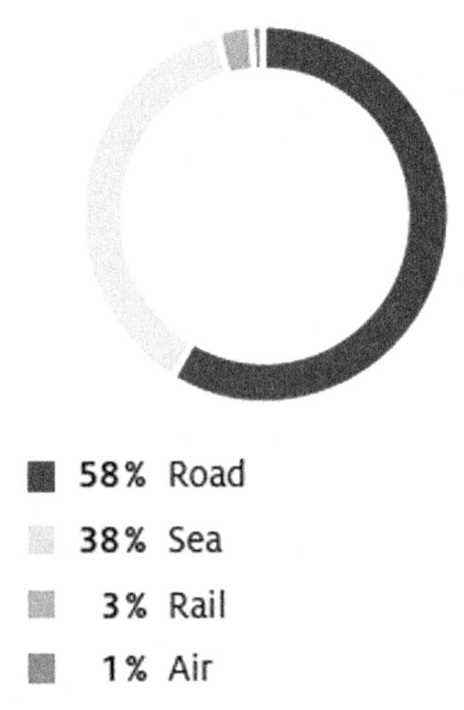

innovation process since 2008. The focus is on innovations that will help its customers and consumers to reduce their energy use and thereby their own carbon footprint.

Product and Consumer Safety

Henkel customers and consumers can be certain that its products are safe when used as intended. All raw materials and finished products are subjected to numerous assessments and tests to ensure a high level of safety during production, use and disposal. This is based on ensuring compliance with legal regulations and farther reaching Henkel standards.

Henkel product developers and experts for product safety assess ingredients according to the latest scientific findings and safety data. They continuously track Henkel products on the market and incorporate the insights gained into the assessments. In addition to considering the basic hazard potential of a substance, Henkel safety assessments focus especially on the actual concentration in the specific formulation and the conditions of use. The use of substances with certain (dangerous) properties is precluded for specific applications from the very start. In other cases, Henkel works to further improve health compatibility by developing alternative ingredients. Since many of its products pass into wastewater after use, their composition has been designed so that their use has the least possible impact on the environment. Wastewater from chemical engineering applications is treated using state-of-the-art technology to remove harmful substances and is then disposed of properly.

In selecting and using ingredients, we also follow controversial discussions in the general public about the safety of chemical ingredients in consumer products. As a rule, we respond by critically reviewing the scientific basis of our assessments with particular care. If there are serious reservations about the continued validity of the scientific data and findings regarding product safety, we either avoid using a substance altogether or restrict its use so that it will still meet our stringent safety criteria. At the same time, it is becoming increasingly important to enable consumers to learn about the ingredients contained in our products. We will therefore enhance the transparency on the substances used and their safety on a global scale.

Figure 12. Sustainability evaluation in the Henkel innovation process

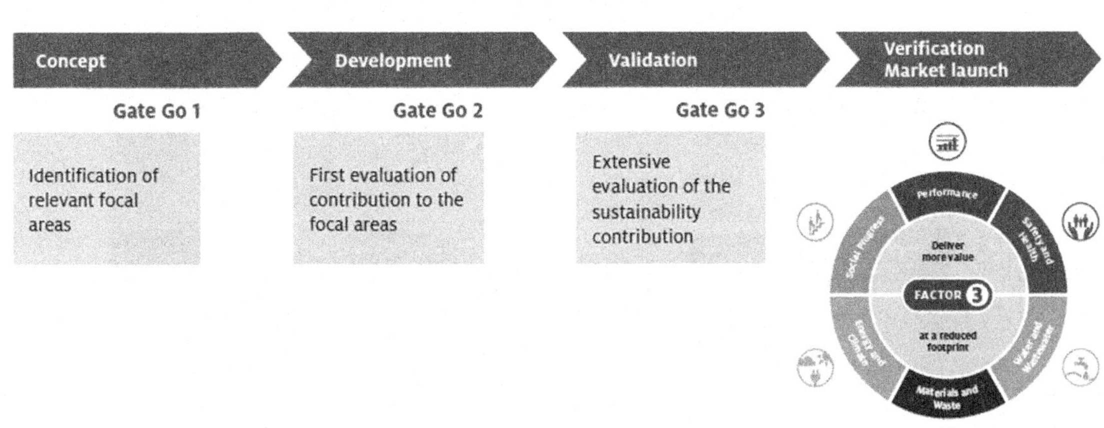

The Henkel focal areas have been systematically anchored into its innovation process since 2008. This means that, at a given point, Henkel researchers must demonstrate the specific advantages of their project in regard to product performance, added value for customers and consumers, and social criteria ("more value"). They also have to show how it contributes to using fewer resources ("reduced footprint"). One of the tools they use to assess the different contributions is the Henkel Sustainability#Master®

The Henkel Sustainability#Master® combines various instruments for measuring sustainability. This evaluation system centers around a matrix based on the individual steps of the value chain and on Henkel six focal areas. The goal is to increase the value of the product and simultaneously reduce its environmental footprint. Hot spots can be identified for every product category on the basis of scientific measurement methods. These are the fields with the greatest relevance for sustainability – this applies to both the "Value" and the "Footprint" dimension. The specified hot spots can also be used to compare the sustainability profile of two products or processes. This allows sustainability profiles to be prepared for each product category. Henkel's researchers use these findings for innovation and continuous product improvements.

Henkel has been carrying out successful research since the early 1980s to develop new methods for testing the safety and compatibility of raw materials and products. Advanced molecular biological methods are used to thoroughly investigate aspects such as the effect of raw materials on human skin cells so that optimized formulations can be developed. This is one of the basic prerequisites for successful product innovations. Henkel goal is to be able to answer questions about the safety of its products and the ingredients Henkel uses exclusively without animal testing. As a matter of principle, Henkel only uses animal testing if this is stipulated by legal regulations and there are no accepted alternative test methods available for obtaining the necessary safety data. Henkel naturally comply with statutory requirements that prohibit animal testing, such as the legal provisions on safety testing of cosmetic ingredients in the European Union.

Figure 13. Henkel Sustainability#Master® – sustainability assessment of products and processes

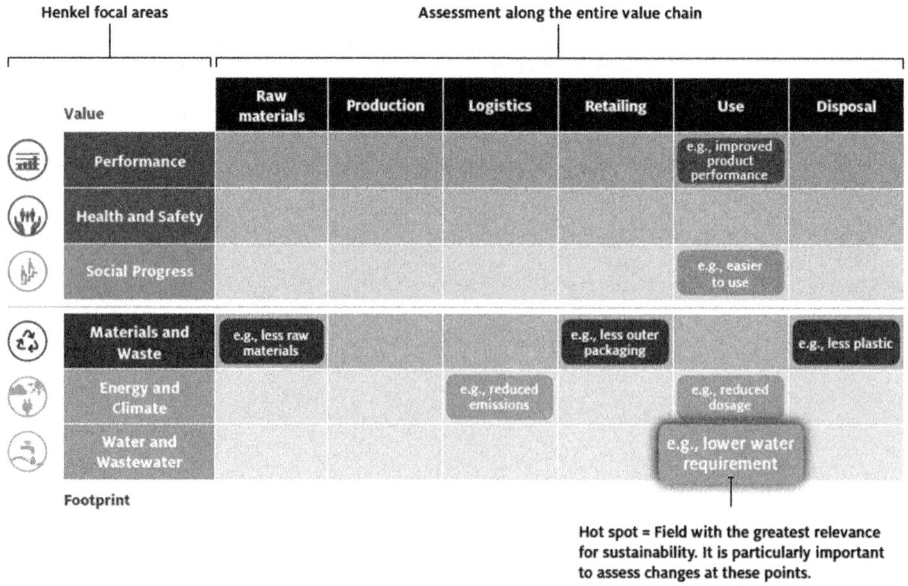

Henkel focal areas | Assessment along the entire value chain

Value	Raw materials	Production	Logistics	Retailing	Use	Disposal
Performance					e.g., improved product performance	
Health and Safety						
Social Progress					e.g., easier to use	
Materials and Waste	e.g., less raw materials			e.g., less outer packaging		e.g., less plastic
Energy and Climate			e.g., reduced emissions		e.g., reduced dosage	
Water and Wastewater					e.g., lower water requirement	
Footprint						

Hot spot = Field with the greatest relevance for sustainability. It is particularly important to assess changes at these points.

Wherever possible, questions regarding the skin compatibility of ingredients are now also investigated with the help of in vitro tests. In vitro tests, such as the skin model (technical name: epidermis model), have been developed by Henkel over the past decades in collaboration with external partners and submitted for acceptance as alternatives to animal testing to the European validation agency. By mid-2016, Henkel made the results of this research freely accessible in an open source model and made the method available free of charge to biologists and lab technicians, for instance, in trade journals. In pursuing this policy, Henkel is making a significant contribution to establishing the use of alternative methods around the globe. Henkel scientists are currently working to make it possible for the skin models, which are as large as a 1cent coin, to be used to research other issues regarding the safety of chemicals.

Responsible Use of Raw Materials

Henkel is committed to responsible management of raw materials, and especially the conservation of natural resources and biodiversity. Henkel uses ingredients based on renewable raw materials to optimize the overall characteristics of its products, wherever this is compatible with environmental, economic and social considerations. Renewable raw materials are already key ingredients in many of its products, such as soaps, shampoos, glue sticks and wallpapering adhesives.

Henkel is aware of its responsibility regarding the purchase and use of ingredients based on renewable raw materials. Henkel is therefore promoting sustainable palm oil production with its partners along the entire value chain. Henkel has adopted the goal of ensuring "zero net deforestation by 2020." This means that palm and palm kernel oil that Henkel uses should not contribute to deforestation of primary or secondary forests with significant ecological value. That includes peat lands and other areas with "high carbon stock." Henkel seeks to drive physical progress in the palm and palm kernel oil supply chain, so as to prevent deforestation. At the same time, Henkel is working with its partners to establish full traceability of palm and palm kernel oils used in ingredients for its products, such as surfactants, by 2020. Henkel aims to ensure that all palm and palm kernel oil that it purchases is being cultivated sustainably. An additional goal is to increase the supply of sustainable oil available on the market by a volume equal to Henkel's demand in 2020. Henkel will thus be making even more targeted efforts to help smallholders and local initiatives in the producing countries. Henkel is working toward these goals by:

1. **Converting to the Mass Balance System for Palm and Palm Kernel Oil:** The vast majority of the palm and palm kernel oil in Henkel products is used indirectly through ingredients based on these oils. Working with its suppliers, Henkel has succeeded in ensuring that to date around 40 percent of the oil is certified according to the mass-balance model (i.e., a controlled mix of sustainable and conventional oil). This exceeds its 2015 target to ensure that at least one-third of the oil was certified according to this model. Furthermore, Henkel intend to increase its purchases of mass-balance-certified oils so that they cover 100 percent of its demand by 2020. By purchasing mass-balance oil, Henkel can contribute more effectively to ensuring that physical sustainable oil enters its value chain. In 2015, Henkel successfully completed the first Roundtable of Sustainable Palm Oil audit of its purchasing operations.
2. **Improving Traceability:** Henkel is establishing pilot projects to trace palm and palm kernel oil that it uses back to the plantations in order to ensure that this oil is being cultivated sustainably. For the raw materials that contain palm or palm kernel oil and for which Henkel worked with its

partners in 2015 to establish traceability, Henkel has achieved a traceability rate of between 67 and 94 percent.

3. **Supporting Plantations and Smallholders:** Henkel is providing targeted support to plantations and smallholders in palm-growing countries to promote sustainable farming practices improve livelihoods and ensure that sufficient volumes of sustainable oil are available on the market. In 2013, Henkel joined together with the development organization Solidaridad and other partners to start a three-year program in Honduras designed to improve the livelihood of 7,500 smallholders and 5,000 workers. Henkel aims to increase its targeted support for small-holders in the future and focus more strongly on other regions, such as Indonesia.

Smart Packaging Solutions

The packaging for Henkel consumer products fulfills many different functions: It ensures the hygiene and intactness of the products, protects them from external influences, provides space for necessary consumer information and often plays an important role in the purchasing decision through attractive packaging design and shelf appeal. In order to minimize the volume of waste, Henkel packaging developers work constantly to design smart packaging that uses the least amount of material possible, and incorporates materials that can be recycled in public recycling systems.

In defining its targets for 2020, Henkel also set targets for packaging. These include a reduction in packaging weight of 20 percent per sales unit as well as increasing the proportion of recycled PET (polyethylene terephthalate) in bottles and recycled aluminum in cans. Additionally, Henkel wants to reach more than 300 million consumers through more targeted information on recycling.

Figure 14. Henkel packaging footprint 2015

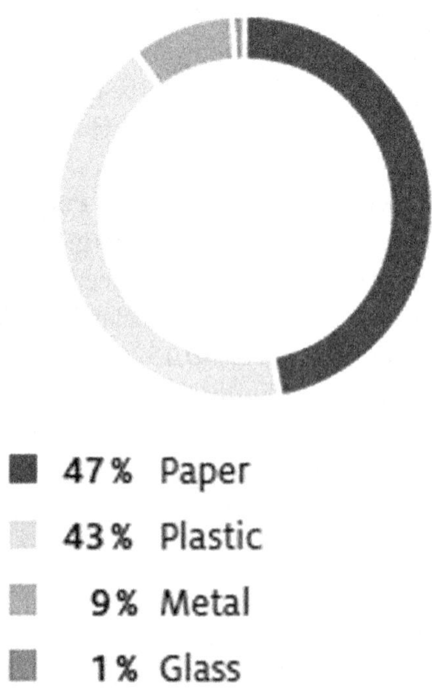

Examples of sustainability in Henkel packaging development:

- **100 Percent Recycled:** In 2015, Henkel introduced polyethylene terephthalate (PET) bottles from the Eco-Bottle series, which are made from 100-percent recycled PET materials. These bottles also fulfilled all of the required optical and mechanical specifications. As a result, up to 500 metric tons of new PET goods can be saved each year.
- **25 Percent Less Aluminum:** As part of its continuous packaging optimization efforts, Henkel has developed an improved conditioner sachet for its hair coloring products. By reducing the thickness of the foil material, Henkel has been able to reduce the amount of aluminum contained in the packaging by 25 percent. This made it possible to reduce the weight per sachet by 5 percent and the CO2 footprint by 25 percent.
- **New Design for Loctite SF 7850:** Redesigning of the primary packaging of the Loctite SF 7850 hand cleanser has made it possible to save 24 percent CO2 and 18 percent weight per bottle. The new design of the 3-liter bottle not only contributes to a more sustainable packaging solution, but also helps to save costs.

Laundry and Home Care

Collaboration with its partners is an important element of Henkel strategy. Together with its partners, Henkel is working to make products that will conserve resources even better, offer improved ease of use, and satisfy the criteria of quality, environmental compatibility and social responsibility in equal measure.

Henkel consumers' expectations mirror its own ambition: Henkel wants its products to satisfy the criteria of quality, environmental compatibility and social responsibility. This is because Henkel views this trio as the driver for innovations and the basis for our future competitiveness. Laundry & Home Care's research and development strategy unites innovation and sustainability to provide resource-efficient technologies and products. Each new product must make a contribution to sustainability in at least one of Henkel six focal areas; partnering with others plays an important role here.

Henkel's ambition – to create innovations that deliver more value for consumers, retailers, the company and society as a whole – is a key pillar of Henkel success. With an innovation rate of over 45 percent, Henkel wants to be an innovation leader, opening up new markets and differentiating it from its competition. Henkel products not only have to deliver first-class performance. They must also always make a measurable contribution to more sustainability.

Over the course of long-standing research cooperation, researchers from BASF and Henkel have jointly developed ingredients for a new generation of premium laundry detergents. They help to remove stubborn stains at significantly lower washing temperatures than is possible with conventional laundry detergents. This new technology is incorporated in the product Persil ColdZyme. If, for example, all Persil ColdZyme wash loads of colored laundry and synthetic textiles were to be washed at 30 instead of 40 degrees Celsius, this would have the potential to avoid around 500,000 metric tons of CO2 every year. This volume would be equivalent to the annual energy demand of 325,000 European households.

How does Henkel generate new ideas for sustainable innovations? This is rooted in close interaction between Henkel research and development and marketing teams. They consider the entire value chain while developing more powerful products that conserve resources even better. Henkel promotes this through its innovation culture and have anchored this approach in its innovation process. Another factor is cooperation with its partners. With BASF, for instance, Henkel conducted a joint project to develop new active ingredients for its premium laundry detergents – for even better cleaning performance at low temperatures.

As a company, Henkel can develop and produce these more sustainable products, but 80 percent of their environmental footprint arises during use. So consumers can make a significant contribution to sustainability, for example by selecting a low washing temperature. This is why Henkel tries to influence consumers' behavior through appropriate communication activities. Henkel retail partners play an important role here, as they are also in direct contact with consumers.

Another important objective is fostering sustainable, resource-conserving consumption. Henkel products are the key here. They are used daily in millions of households and often require water and energy. As much as 80 percent of the environmental footprint of Henkel products is generated during their use. This is why Henkel concentrates on developing products that enable the efficient use of resources such as energy and water.

By using targeted information for consumers, Henkel works to promote responsible-minded behavior while using its products. Through specific communication appropriate for the target group, including on the internet, the company points out the advantages of its products while encouraging resource-efficient use. One example of this is the Persil resource calculator for laundry. Henkel also works hand in hand with our retail partners to advocate sustainable consumption. The Carrefour supermarket chain, for example, teamed up with Henkel employees in November 2015 to inform consumers in the Middle East about sustainable lifestyles as well as laundry and home care products.

Innovations for Laundry and Home Care Products of the Future

The innovation rate at the Laundry & Home Care business unit lies at more than 45 percent. In other words, the business unit generates more than 45 percent of its sales with products that have been on the market for less than three years. Moreover, Henkel has been using ingredients based on renewable raw materials for decades. In 2015, around 25 percent of the organic ingredients in Henkel laundry detergents and household cleaners were derived from renewable raw materials. In addition, by comparison with the previous year, Henkel was able to reduce the carbon footprint of its annual raw material input by 6 percent relative to total sales.

In its innovation management, Laundry & Home Care is focusing increasingly on collaborative research and open innovation, harnessing the capabilities of external innovation partners such as universities, research institutes, suppliers and customers. In order to understand precisely what customers and consumers need and develop first-class innovations; collaboration often begins before the actual product development phase does. As one example of this, Henkel is collaborating with the Rhenish-Westphalian Technical University (RWTH) in Aachen, Germany, to research and develop the laundry and home care products of the future. The new cooperation concept is called "Henkel Innovation Campus for Advanced Sustainable Technologies" – or HICAST, for short. Here, chemists and biotechnologists are working in interdisciplinary teams on breakthrough innovations.

In cooperation with its strategic partner Novo-zymes, Henkel has succeeded in developing new, powerful enzymes as the basis for a new generation of innovative formulations. These also laid the foundation for the successful introduction of its premium laundry detergents under the Persil ProClean brand in the USA. Specifically tailored to the needs of the market there, the patent-pending high-performance formulas develop their full cleaning action even at low temperatures. This performance is also delivered by Persil Power-Mix Caps. These pre-dosed powder-gel capsules unite for the first time the product benefits of a concentrated gel with the whitening-power technology of a powder. This protects laundry especially well against graying.

Many of Henkel laundry detergent products can be used even at low temperatures – with first-class performance – and thus help to reduce CO2 emissions. If, for example, all machine washes with Henkel products for colored laundry and synthetic textiles were to be washed at 30 instead of 40 degrees Celsius, this would have the potential to avoid around two million metric tons of CO2 every year. This corresponds to the amount of CO2 taken up every year by more than 40 million trees.

- **Redyeing Instead of Rebuying:** Under the Dylon brand, Henkel offers textile dyes for dyeing fabrics or reviving their color when washing them either in the machine or by hand. Thanks to Dylon, fabrics can be dyed or their colors revived very easily at home. A powerful dye technology makes it possible to give fabrics a completely new look quickly and easily. Dylon thus helps to prolong the life cycle of fabrics while reducing their footprint. The sustainability benefit lies primarily in reducing the use of water. More than 85 percent of this is accounted for by the water-intensive farming of cotton, above all for irrigation of the cotton fields. Dyeing a pair of jeans with Dylon uses at least 100 times less water than is needed to produce a new pair. That means annual savings of a total of 80 billion liters of water, or the equivalent of the amount of drinking water consumed per person each year by up to 3.9 million people in typical cotton-growing regions.

In the laundry aids category, Henkel introduced color run prevention sheets under the Color Catcher brand in 2015 following the acquisition of the Spotless Group. These sheets offer anti-transfer protection when washing mixed color wash loads. Fabrics with different colors that used to have to be washed separately can now be washed together in one machine load. On average, each sheet eliminates one wash cycle. In terms of environmental footprint, this means above all savings in the areas of energy, water, and materials and waste. The Color Catcher sheets are made of cellulose. They are FSC-certified and can be composted after use. The matrix shows all the hot spots in this product category. These are the fields with the greatest relevance for sustainability.

Figure 15. Henkel Sustainability#Master® – Color Catcher in comparison with competitor products

Value	Raw materials	Production	Logistics	Retailing	Use	Disposal
Performance						
Health and Safety						
Social Progress					Saves time due to less wash loads	
Materials and Waste	100% natural fibers, FSC-certified					Biodegradable and recyclable
Energy and Climate					Less energy due to less wash loads	
Water and Wastewater					Less water due to less wash loads	
Footprint						

Significant improvement

- **Efficient Insect Repellent:** Some insects, such as mosquitoes, are not simply a nuisance; they can also transmit dangerous diseases. The acquisition of the research laboratory for insect control in Barcelona, Spain, in 2014 further expanded the technological expertise of the Laundry &Home Care business unit in the domain of insect repellents. With ZenSect anti-mosquito sticks, Henkel researchers have achieved a first by developing a highly effective mosquito repellent for the European market that is based on a completely new principle. The active agent is derived from natural ingredients and mimics the action of crop plants. It acts on the sensory centers of the insects and suppresses their urge to bite.
- **A.I.S.E. Charter:** Since 2005, when Henkel became the first company to fulfill the criteria of the A.I.S.E. Charter for Sustainable Cleaning, more than 200 other companies have committed to the Charter. All companies that sign the Charter pledge to continuously improve their processes and to report annually on their economic, environmental and social advances, using defined indicators. As part of its further development, the A.I.S.E. Charter was expanded in 2010 to include the key dimension of products. Since then, it has become possible to show not only that a product was manufactured by a company with sustainable business practices, but also that the product itself has an advanced sustainability profile. In the laundry detergents category, for example, four criteria are of particular importance: environmental safety of the ingredients; resource efficiency with regard to dosage and packaging materials; washing performance at low temperatures; and consumer information. Products that satisfy all of the defined requirements may communicate this to consumers on their packaging by means of a new A.I.S.E. Charter logo introduced in 2011. Henkel liquid and powder laundry detergents, fabric softeners, automatic dishwashing products, all-purpose cleaners and special spray cleaning products are now all qualified to bear the logo. Criteria for hand dishwashing liquids and toilet cleaners were additionally finalized in 2015.

Since 2014, Henkel has been supporting the Europe-wide A.I.S.E. online education initiative "Keep Caps from Kids." A video and a website tell viewers why it is so important to keep liquid detergent capsules out of the reach of children. The www.keepcapsfromkids.eu site also provides tips on how to use liquid laundry detergent capsules safely. This online education campaign supplements the voluntary initiative "A.I.S.E. Product Stewardship Programme for Liquid Laundry Detergent Capsules." To add to this, Henkel has offered to make its own knowledge on how to manufacture caps with increased child safety available free of charge to the entire industry worldwide. This involves incorporating a bitter-tasting substance in the soluble film packaging. In the USA, Henkel supports the online education initiative launched in 2014 by the industry association American Cleaning Institute, "Take the pledge – be the key to a safe laundry room and routine," which can be found atwww.cleaninginstitute.org/keypledge.

Beauty Care

Collaboration along the entire value chain is crucial to the achievement of Henkel sustainability goals – from the production of raw materials to the development of sustainable innovations and effective communication with consumers. At Henkel, people are always looking for ways to reduce the environmental footprint of its products. Henkel packaging development plays a key role in the context of product life cycles. Aiming to reduce waste, its developers are working on smart and sustainable packaging solutions.

To reduce the aluminum consumption and thus its energy use and carbon emissions, Beauty Care launched a pilot project with Ball Aerocan in the year 2013 to produce spray cans from 25-percent recycled aluminum. To date, this has helped Henkel lower CO2 output by more than 4,500 metric tons. The recycling process for aluminum requires much less energy than the elaborate extraction of primary aluminum from bauxite ore. In addition, optimization of the alloying elements in the aluminum makes the material more rigid. This makes it possible to reduce the amount of material needed per can. These two effects considerably reduce the carbon footprint per spray can. Since the 2014 market launch of these cans for the deodorant sprays of our Henkel, Souplesse and Neutromed brands, more than 60 million units have been produced. In 2016, Henkel wants to further increase the annual number of cans made of recycled aluminum.

All products must combine consumer appeal and high performance with sustainability. This is also Henkel's ambition within Beauty Care. This approach is integrated deeply in its innovation process – and one Henkel considers to be a competitive advantage. Thanks to its passion for innovation combined with the concept of sustainable development anchored along the entire value chain, Henkel has been able to continuously increase the sustainability contribution that Henkel innovations offer. This enables us to deliver more value to Henkel customers and consumers.

In order to reach its goal of sustainable development, Henkel repeatedly scrutinize its conventional technologies and work on innovative solutions together with its suppliers and partners. These efforts span the entire value chain – from the extraction of raw materials to creative communication with consumers regarding product use. To implement this comprehensive approach, Henkel systematically integrate its sustainability goals in every phase of the product life cycle. In line with its sustainability strategy, we create solutions that generate more value for our customers, consumers, and our company, while reducing our environmental footprint at the same time.

Sustainability is firmly anchored in Henkel's innovation process. This is ensured by integrated systems that provide information in a way that is user-friendly as well as time and cost efficient. Henkel has, for example, systematically determined the carbon footprint for 165,000 product formulas already. Even in the early phase of raw material selection, the intelligent linking of databases permits its product developers to measure and control the effects that ingredients will have on the environmental product footprint. In this way, Henkel purposefully promote the development of formulations with a smaller carbon foot-print or with a higher share of readily biodegradable raw materials.

Environmental compatibility was also a guiding factor in Henkel early decision to stop using solid microplastic particles (these are defined as particles from one micrometer to five millimeters) in the formulations of its cosmetic products. The plastic particles were used in certain rinse-off face care products. Even though cosmetic products account for only a very small percentage of any possible environmental impact, the new products Henkel have launched in Europe since 2014 do not contain any solid microplastic particles. This means that Henkel are ahead of the recommendation adopted in October 2015 by Cosmetics Europe (the European Personal Care Association) that solid microplastic particles should no longer be used in rinse-off cosmetic products from 2020 onwards. As of the beginning of 2016, all new Henkel cosmetic products of this type will be formulated worldwide without solid microplastic particles.

Encouraging Sustainable Lifestyles

One of Henkel goals is to achieve a better quality of life for as many people as possible within the limits of available resources. In addition to providing care for the hair, skin and teeth, Henkel cosmetic products contribute primarily to the social and emotional aspects of quality of life. They help people to look well-groomed, emphasize their personal style and strengthen their self-esteem. Life-cycle analyses also show us that its consumers can influence the carbon footprint of its products to a very large extent as a result of their consumption behavior. More than 90 percent of the energy and water used with its rinse-off products is accounted for in the use phase. To raise its consumers' awareness of this, Henkel makes use of the potential of digital media.

The Henkel Sustainability#Master® reveals the sustainability profile of the new Syoss Renew 7 shampoo. The new platform formula developed for this product permits considerable ingredient savings versus its predecessor, along with improved product performance. It contains 16 percent less surfactants and 60 percent less cationic polymers. At the same time, the formulation has 10 percent more renewable ingredients, enabling the carbon footprint to be reduced by 18 percent overall. Product performance has also been improved, by 75 percent in regard to comb ability and by 80 percent with respect to repairing of split ends – highly relevant aspects for consumers.

For communication with consumers to be as effective as possible, it is also important for consumers to be personally involved. As part of an international online competition, Henkel called on creative talents all over the world to submit short videos with original and entertaining ideas for motivating people to conserve resources when taking a shower. The five winning videos have already been used in the communication channels of a large spectrum of retail partners in several countries. This not only illustrates the relevance of consumer involvement but also the close collaboration with its retail partners, who provide an important communication platform for addressing consumers directly. For instance, Henkel resource calculator allows consumers to find out online just how much their behavior can influence not only water use and the environmental footprint, but also the cost of bathing, showering, drying their hair, brushing their teeth and washing their hands. By providing this transparency, Henkel aims to make sustainable lifestyles more attractive.

- **Taft Ultimate Hairspray:** As part of its commitment to sustainable development, Henkel continuously improve its existing product portfolio. The new Taft Ultimate Hairspray has been formulated with a highly concentrated styling polymer. This means that the amount of product needed for hair styling can be applied with a much shorter spraying time. Less propellant gas and less

Figure 16. Henkel Sustainability#Master® – Syoss Renew 7 in comparison with the predecessor product

Value

	Raw materials	Production	Logistics	Retailing	Use	Disposal
Performance				Strengthening the product category	Improved split-end repair and combability	
Health and Safety						
Social Progress						
Materials and Waste	Renewable ingredients					Less raw materials used
Energy and Climate	Formulation with less CO_2					
Water and Wastewater						Biodegradable ingredients

Footprint

Significant improvement

alcohol are used each time. The result is that the amount of raw material input per application is reduced by 55 percent. In 2015, Henkel achieved a savings potential of 1,500 metric tons of CO2.

- **Dial in the USA:** Studies show that washing one's hands regularly with soap provides an important basis for a healthy life. This is why Henkel Dial brand in the USA supported the Global Handwashing Day for the second time. The idea is to increase awareness of the importance of hand washing as effective and low-cost protection from illness. In addition to this important social aspect, the Dial brand also considers the environment: The Dial Recycling Center shows consumers online which packaging materials are used for Dial products and where they can be recycled.

Henkel also supports its customers in the Hair Salon business in the proper use of its products through in-person training courses and web-based seminars. In September 2015, sustainability topics for the hairdressing salon were added to the advanced vocational training program of the International Schwarzkopf Academy. 25,000 hairdressers have already been reached this way.

Changing lives through the hairdressing trade – this is the idea of the "Shaping Futures" initiative that Schwarzkopf Professional launched in November 2010. In collaboration with the charitable organization SOS Children's Villages, hairdressers and members of the Schwarzkopf Professional staff make it possible for young people all over the world to obtain training in basic hairdressing techniques. Since the initiative was launched, 1,200 young people in 25 countries have been trained through the volunteer engagement of almost 250 hairdressers and employees. In its fifth year, Schwarzkopf Professional also brought "Shaping Futures" to Germany. In collaboration with vocational schools in Hamburg and Nuremberg, young refugees are to be given an opportunity to find out whether hairdressing could be a career for them.

For the 10th year running, Schwarzkopf is an official partner to the "Tribute to Bambi" foundation, which helps children in need. In 2015, the focus of the children's aid projects was also on the well-being of refugee children.

In collaboration with the non-profit organization The Rapunzel Project, Henkel supports cancer patients during chemotherapy through its US-American brand Kenra Professional. The unique Cold Cap technology has been designed to significantly diminish hair loss during chemotherapy. This initiative supplements the "look good feel better" international assistance program for cancer patients, which Beauty Care has been supporting since 2006.The Rapunzel Project promotes the Cold Cap technology, in which a plastic gel cap cooled to minus 30 degrees Celsius freezes the hair roots. This means that patients lose less hair while undergoing chemotherapy.

Henkel comprehensive advice for consumers ensures safe product use. Advice hotlines provide competent, quick and reliable information about product properties or ingredients. They have been set up in most countries where its products are sold. Consumers can also use its social media channels. All told, there were some eight million consumer contacts worldwide in 2015. Product-related feedback is documented in its quality assurance system and channeled into its ongoing product development process.

Adhesive Technologies

Henkel powerful innovations and leading technologies create more value for its customers. Sustainability is an integral part of both its innovation and product development processes. Henkel is the leading solution provider for adhesives, sealants and functional coatings world-wide. Its comprehensive technology portfolio allows experts from its Adhesive Technologies business unit to develop customized solutions together with its customers around the world. One example of this is Henkel long-standing partnership with the Morey Corporation, an electronics manufacturer based in the USA. Henkel experts work closely with Morey to develop solutions to the challenges of the ongoing demand for smaller electronic devices with increased functionality.

Henkel teams are involved as early as the design stage, sharing deep industry knowledge and providing insights into material requirements. Morey uses more than 15 Henkel technologies that enable it to simplify its supply chain, optimize performance and drive sustainability. One of these technologies is the innovative temperature-stable solder paste, Loctite GC 10. It is the first-ever solder paste that can be stored at up to 26.5 degrees Celsius for as long as one year, and at up to 40 degrees Celsius for one month. This cuts energy consumption and reduces waste by eliminating the need to transport or store solder pastes in refrigerated conditions.

Henkel is the global market leader in adhesives. However, it is often not easy to recognize where these products are applied. With Henkel comprehensive technology portfolio, its Adhesives business is the leading solution provider worldwide. Henkel acts as a partner and source of expertise for its customers, and is active in a large variety of markets. These include the packaging, metals, automotive and electronics industries, as well as aerospace applications. Henkel products are included in many things where one might not automatically expect to find them – from packaging, books, cell phones and furniture through to shoes, cars and airplanes.

Henkel aim is to develop innovative solutions that deliver in terms of both performance and resource efficiency. Henkel adhesives help to save energy by making cars and aircraft lighter, as well as by insulating buildings better. Henkel also plays a part in making production processes more efficient. Henkel Loctite GC 10 solder paste is an example of this: It not only creates substantial value for the customers – it also generates significant benefits in terms of energy use, thereby contributing to resource efficiency.

Henkel sees sustainability as a megatrend that will accelerate the development and use of new adhesive technologies, for example in areas such as the automotive industry. Henkel Bonderite brand already enables its automotive customers to achieve major cuts in waste volume and energy use in their manufacturing operations. It is only by introducing innovations like these that Henkel can continue to meet its customers' requirements in the future.

Customized Technologies

Henkel drives powerful innovations and develop leading technologies to create more value for customers and consumers everywhere in the world, with sustainability as an integral part of its innovation and product development processes. Henkel innovations help reduce energy and water consumption, drive down carbon dioxide emissions and improve health and safety in the manufacture and use of objects that touch our lives every day: from automobiles and aircraft through to packaging and cell phones.

Henkel broad technology portfolio places the company in a strong position to adapt its solutions to meet the needs of customers across diverse markets and industries. Henkel experts worked together with Ford to customize its Bonderite M-NT two-step process: a metal pretreatment system that acts as a base for applying paint and protects against corrosion. Henkel customized technology replaces traditional zinc phosphate processes, which require laborious treatment of contaminated wastewater and disposal of sewage sludge containing phosphorus. It makes it possible for Ford to cut waste and reduce energy consumption in its processes and is suitable for use on vehicle chassis containing up to 100-percent aluminum. This opens up new possibilities for increasing the amount of lightweight metals used, reducing overall vehicle weight and cutting vehicle emissions.

Henkel actively supports customers by adapting its technologies for new applications across industries. This same Bonderite process has also been adapted to provide designer garden furniture with long-lasting protection. Fermob, a France-based manufacturer, has recently switched to using Henkel innovative coating technology. Close collaboration with Fermob allows Henkel to understand its specific processes and requirements, and its experts are able to leverage Henkel uniquely broad range of technologies to develop solutions that deliver outstanding performance and improved sustainability.

Technologies from Henkel make it possible for customers to explore innovative new designs and sustainable applications. Henkel Loctite Purbond adhesives for bonding wood support the use of renewable materials in construction projects worldwide. Henkel products are used in the new Arctic observatory in Spitsbergen, Norway, which is part of a global network for researching climate change. The building uses cross-laminated timber (CLT), a wood construction product made by its partner Stora Enso, a global provider to the wood and construction industries. It is made of three or more layers of wood glued together using Henkel adhesives, and offers a positive CO2 balance and excellent durability.

Henkel technologies also enable Bilfinger, a leading engineering and services group, to extend the life-time of its clients' steel pipelines in the oil and gas industry by up to 20 years. Experts from Henkel worked with the customer to conduct collaborative innovation activities. This led to the refinement of Henkel's advanced technologies for repairing pipes that transport gas, water, crude oil and wastewater, which reduces the need to manufacture and install replacement pipes. Henkel Loctite Composite Repair System has the potential for application in over 11,000 petrochemical plants and 9,000 offshore platforms worldwide.

Health and safety is a key concern for its customers: As a global leader, Henkel actively drive standards worldwide by removing critical ingredients from its products. Tangit Rapid, its new solvent-free adhesive for bonding pressure pipes made of poly-vinyl chloride (PVC-U/C), such as those for drinking water, is a key example of this approach. It is the first ever solvent-free adhesive for use on drinking water pipes and offers improved reliability for professional craftsmen while also delivering best-in-class curing time and bond strength.

Henkel completely biostable Bonderite lubricant technologies also support its customers in ensuring the safety of their employees and processes by eliminating the need for storing and applying biocides. Rexam – a leading global beverage can maker – uses these technologies as well as a range of other solutions from Henkel to increase resource efficiency in its processes and improve safety in its plants, helping the business to meet its ambitious sustainability targets. Rexam presented Henkel with its

Tangit Rapid is the first-ever solvent-free pipe adhesive for bonding pressure pipes made of PVC-U/C material that fulfill the European Standards EN 14814 and EN ISO 15493. Its unique formulation not only meets increasingly demanding chemical regulations, but has also received approval for use in drinking water pipes in several countries.

The Henkel Sustainability#Master® assesses Loctite GC 10 based on its value chain and six sustainability focal areas. Henkel innovative temperature-stable solder paste creates the electrical connection between the printed circuit board and the semiconductor components. Its game-changing formula allows it to be stored at room temperature: This removes the need for air freight and eliminates the requirement to refrigerate the solder paste during logistics and storage. In addition, its wider process window and easier handling leads to fewer end-of-line defects. The matrix covers all product category hot spots.

Figure 17. Henkel Sustainability#Master® – Loctite GC 10 temperature-stable solder paste in comparison with industry standard process

Value	Raw materials	Production	Logistics	Industrial processing	Service / Use	Disposal
Performance			Longer shelf life, no need for air freight	Fewer end-of-line defects		
Health and Safety						
Social Progress						
Materials and Waste			Less packaging	Less solder paste waste	Extends product life of devices	Lead reduced to trace amounts
Energy and Climate			Eliminates refrigerated transport	Eliminates refrigerated storage		
Water and Wastewater						
Footprint						

Significant improvement

Collaboration Along the Entire Value Chain

Henkel experts are also a strong partner in joint-engineering projects for customers like FCA US LLC, a subsidiary of Fiat Chrysler Automobiles N.V. A combined team of experts from both companies developed a new technology for sealing welded seams on its vehicle chassis. This eliminates excess emissions that traditional sealants produce during the paint-shop oven phase. This solution, marketed under the Teroson brand, also avoids chemicals currently under discussion and helps reduce vehicle weight. In recognition of this partnership, Henkel was presented with FCA US's award for product-related environmental protection in 2015.

Working together with key suppliers is also an important element of Henkel strategy. Henkel recognizes outstanding supplier performance with three annual awards in the categories of innovation, performance and sustainability. In 2015, the company presented Henkel supplier award for sustainability to Covestro Deutschland AG, formerly known as Bayer Material Science, a supplier of polyurethane technologies. Covestro develops materials that enable us to extend Henkel business in adhesives for sustainable wood engineering. It is also working together with Henkel innovation teams to develop bio-based technologies to support a range of innovative adhesives.

Alongside its high-performance products, Henkel provides customers all over the world with advice, training and service. Henkel maintains a continuous dialog and train them in using its technologies safely and efficiently. Henkel uses its close customer contact to strengthen customers' awareness of sustainability and demonstrate how its innovative solutions can help them reduce their footprint and increase resource efficiency.

Henkel experts provide stakeholders from the food and packaging industry with insights into the current legislation and developments relating to food safety. Henkel Food Safe Packaging knowledge platform offers white papers, webinars, and videos in a range of languages. Henkel's experts help ensure producers are able to offer the highest possible level of safety in their food packaging. Henkel commitment to sharing knowledge by interacting and collaborating with partners along the entire value chain is central to this approach.

A creative new online campaign themed around sustainability invites children, parents and teachers to learn more about the famous Pritt glue stick in a fun and interactive way. Henkel Pritt glue sticks contain 90 percent natural ingredients – water, potato starch and sugar – and are manufactured without solvents and PVCs. This is not only environmentally compatible; it also means these products are harmless in the hands of children.

People

The commitment, abilities and experience of our employees build the basis for Henkel international business success. Essential prerequisites for this are appreciation and further development of its employees. Henkel's diversity is its strength. As a globally operating company, Henkel employs people from 125 nations in more than 75 countries. More than 80 percent of them work outside of Germany. Henkel goal is to create an inspiring, challenging and attractive workplace, where a shared vision and actively lived corporate values serve as a unifying element and a foundation for orientation worldwide. The diversity of its employees and their individual differences, whether regarding their cultural origins, gender, generation, religious orientation or differing values, abilities and experiences, is essential to its strength and innovative capabilities. Henkel promotes individual development worldwide through numerous measures, such as training courses, workshops, and a new, comprehensive eLearning platform.

Henkel 2015 Diversity & Inclusion campaign was designed to further strengthen the understanding of diversity and respectful behavior at Henkel. Selected employees from all regions demonstrated how they initiate change processes and interact respectfully with one another. In 2015, Henkel Diversity Weeks took place for the third time in a row, with numerous activities and events all over the world, making it possible to personally experience the company's diversity and to emotionally involve employees through their engagement.

At Henkel it is considered sustainability to be an opportunity, especially in a world that is constantly changing. Henkel actively lived corporate values help the company to meet the challenges it faces. Henkel managers in particular are asked to internalize the significance of sustainability and set an example through their behavior. This topic is indeed becoming more and more important in connection with employee retention and satisfaction – as well as for attractiveness as an employer. Henkel needs to integrate sustainability in the professional and personal development of the employees – also in the context of their day-to-day work. A good example is the Sustainability Ambassador program. This program includes various initiatives. For instance, Henkel encourages its employees to develop an environmentally conscious approach to their day-to-day professional work.

Diversity in day-to-day work situations and an appreciative corporate culture are of vital importance to Henkel. The company thrives on the individual differences of its employees. In 2015, Henkel conducted a worldwide Diversity & Inclusion campaign to strengthen mutual respect and further foster collaboration.

Henkel Human Resources Management

Henkel success as an internationally operating company in an extremely dynamic competitive environment is based on the achievements of a strong global team. The Code of Conduct provides a framework for how employees behave and act. It helps them to answer ethical and legal questions correctly and appropriately in their day-to-day work and in the course of strategic decision making processes.

Henkel values its employees and their contribution to the company's success. Henkel objective is an inclusive management culture that respects others and appreciates their individual differences. Henkel strives to provide continuing further education for all of its employees as appropriate to their tasks. Henkel wants to create an environment in which all employees can develop and excel. High priority is given to focus further development of its managerial staff and to attracting new talents for Henkel.

Henkel job vacancies are filled based on competence, performance and potential. Henkel aims to increase the share of women in the company at all levels all over the world, and the company also systematically supports the career development of women at all management levels. The share of women in the company was around 34 percent at the end of 2015. Through the measures Henkel has conducted, the company has also been able to increase the share of women in management positions from around 24 percent in 2005 to around 33 percent by the end of 2015.

As digitalization advances, the expectations of both existing and future employees are changing. Henkel response to this is a digitalization strategy that embraces new possibilities in human resources marketing as well as employee recruitment and development. Social media channels such as Facebook and LinkedIn are platforms that are especially well suited for engaging in a continuous dialog with potential candidates in a way that is appropriate for this target group. In addition, LinkedIn makes it possible to directly address candidates for filling specialized job vacancies.

- **Digital Learning:** Learning during day-to-day work and through job rotations plays a central role at Henkel. To implement these measures even more successfully, Henkel has integrated formal learning to a greater extent in day-to-day work and made it available in digital form as needed. For this purpose, the contents of the Henkel Global Academy were combined in a central learning platform in 2015. The system now bundles all available training programs in a uniform format. General in-person training is complemented by more than 500 eLearning modules and around 500 videos and webinars. Business unit specific seminars are also available there. The greater transparency and better presentation of these options facilitate individual selection and flexible use. The system also enables users to repeat partial sequences. The link with the Talent Management System reinforces Henkel understanding of learning as an integral part of the job. The digital learning opportunities also reduce the need for travel and make printed materials unnecessary.
- **Educating for Greater Sustainability:** One of Henkel most important educational initiatives is the Henkel program for Sustainability Ambassadors, which was initiated in 2012 to inspire employees to engage even more intensively with the topic of sustainability. Since then, Henkel has trained around 6,200 ambassadors in 74 countries. As part of their activities, the ambassadors work with elementary school children, to teach them about the responsible use of resources. Henkel has now reached around 63,000 schoolchildren in 43 countries. Added to the program in 2014 was the initiative "(Y)our move toward sustainability," which encourages employees to put sustainability into practice in their day-to-day work, such as in regard to saving energy and eating healthily.
- In 2015, another initiative was added to the program: In "Say yes! to the future," Henkel sales representatives all over the world are being trained on all sustainability topics that apply to sales, going beyond the contents of the Sustainability Ambassador program. They then apply this knowledge in joint projects with its retail customers – in logistics, for example, or in promoting sustainable purchasing decisions. In addition to sales, relevant sustainability matters, the exchange of

international best practice examples for retail collaborations is an important component of the training courses, in order to initiate new forms of cooperation.

- **Work-Life Flexibility:** Henkel has supported flexible working models for years. Through numerous measures, appropriate basic conditions have been created that enable employees to individually meet the challenges of their professional and private lives. Here Henkel attaches great importance to performance rather than physical presence. This has a dual purpose: strengthening our employees' sense of responsibility for working independently and for the results of their work, and encouraging leadership based on trust throughout the company.
- Henkel has further developed this results-based culture continuously since the signing of its global "Work-Life Flexibility" charter in 2012. Uniting family and career often presents great challenges, especially to young parents, due to the necessary childcare. In Düsseldorf, Henkel offers 240 places in three company daycare centers to employees who return to their professions after their parental leave. In 2015, the first Henkel company daycare center outside of Germany was opened in Bratislava, Slovakia. Childcare places for 100 children from two years of age were created here. Henkel also offers various forms of childcare support to its employees in other countries.
- **Focus on Talents:** Qualified skilled personnel expect a simple and rapid job application procedure. This is why Henkel introduced an improved global application process in April 2015. This improvement is the result of one of the largest human resources management projects of the past two years, in which staff from all regions were involved. Based on the Lean Six Sigma methodology, responsibilities of the involved departments were redefined, and the user-friendliness of the IT systems was improved.
- **Developing a Culture of Leadership:** The continuous expansion of Henkel leadership culture is a key element of its corporate philosophy. In 2014 and 2015, top managers took part in a Harvard Business School program that Henkel had developed with that institution. The Henkel leadership principles are the basis of its development programs for top executives: Lead Myself, Lead Team, Lead Stakeholders, Lead Change and Lead Performance. The Lead Myself principle creates a starting point, because only people who can lead themselves can also lead others well. Leading one means internalizing the Henkel values as a guide to one's own actions, considering one's behavior and reflecting on one's leadership role, as well as motivating oneself and setting goals. One of Henkel objectives is to increase the share of managers from emerging markets, in order to illustrate the contribution these regions make to its success. In 2015, about 80 young employees from these regions with high potential for development participated in a special program.
- **Improved Performance Assessment:** Henkel attaches great importance to the development of employees, which at Henkel is mainly the responsibility of their supervisors. In 2015, more than 1,300 employees were promoted within and into the management level. The individual development of its employees is decisive not only for their personal success, but also for that of the company. Based on this conviction, Henkel expanded its Talent Management System for all employees within the management levels and for non-managerial employees with high potential. Even more support is being given to lifelong learning and an active feedback culture. Employees are more closely involved in the development planning: The opportunity to proactively state one's career expectations gives an added dimension to discussions with supervisors. Furthermore, direct access to one's personal learning history and appropriate training options is made available through close linking to the optimized digital learning platform.

- **Performance-Based Compensation:** Recognition of individual performance on the part of Henkel employees through fair compensation in line with market practices is a fundamental component of its corporate culture. There is no systematic difference between the compensation received by male and female employees. To reward personal performance, the salaries of around 10,400 employees in managerial positions worldwide include success-related components. The annual individual performance assessment, which is always done in the context of Henkel vision and its corporate values, has a significant influence on these bonus payments. This includes contributions to the Henkel sustainability strategy and targets, if they fall within the sphere of influence of the employee concerned and have a clear bearing on business performance. The incentive systems for non-managerial employees take local requirements and existing collective agreements into account.
- **Global Health Management:** Henkel cares about the health and performance capability of its employees. Henkel offers targeted health and preventive programs to guard against workplace-related risks that might lead to illnesses. The recently introduced Health Procedure describes the minimum global standards for health protection and health promotion. With its standardized programs for promoting a healthy lifestyle, Henkel wants to reach more than 90 percent of its employees worldwide in the future. In designing these programs, Henkel sites determine different priorities based on local requirements. All Henkel sites worldwide report on four key figures each quarter: availability of first aiders and emergency medical care, the conducting of occupational health exams, and the occurrence of occupational illness.
- **Human Rights and Social Standards:** Henkel is aware of and assume its responsibility to respect and support the protection of human rights within its sphere of influence. As long ago as 1994, Henkel declared in its corporate mission that the company respects the social values of the countries and cultural spheres in which it operates. Henkel under-scored this when it introduced its Code of Conduct in 2000 and when it joined the United Nations Global Compact in 2003.

Henkel Social Standards, which were introduced in 2006, serve as a framework for decision-making within Henkel sphere of influence, also in relation to human rights and fundamental labor rights. They are derived from the guidelines of the International Labor Organization (ILO), the Global Compact, the OECD Guidelines for Multinational Enterprises, and the Social Accountability Standard (SA 8000). Through in-person and eLearning training courses and "local ambassadors," Henkel ensures that its social standards are firmly anchored. Compliance is verified on a regular basis as part of its Group wide audit program.

Social Engagement

Employees, retirees, clients and partners work together with Henkel and the "Fritz Henkel Stiftung" foundation to support social projects around the world. Corporate citizenship has been an integral part of Henkel corporate culture ever since its establishment by Fritz Henkel in 1876. The company's lasting and long-term commitment to social involvement that goes beyond direct business interests was especially evident in the creation of the "Fritz Henkel Stiftung" foundation in 2011. This engagement is supported by the four pillars of its corporate citizenship program: corporate volunteering, social partnerships, brand engagement and emergency aid. In 2015, in view of recent developments, Henkel has

Figure 18. Training categories in 2015

also focused strongly on refugee aid. By 2020, Henkel wants to improve the quality of life of 10 million people through its social engagement.

Since the initiative Make an Impact on Tomorrow (MIT) was launched in 1998, Henkel has supported the volunteer work of its employees and retirees in over 12,100 projects in more than 50 countries around the world. At the same time, more and more employees and retirees are coming together to carry out social projects of a larger scale. One example, which went into its second round in 2015, is the house-building project conducted jointly with the charity organization Habitat for Humanity. Henkel employees demonstrated great social engagement in the course of this "building trip." Within a week, they helped to build a new house for families in need in the Romanian city of Ploiești.

With a fundraising campaign in the fall of 2015, Henkel employees in Germany made sure that children from needy families – including many refugees – have what they need for school.

When emergency aid is needed after a natural disaster, Henkel provides quick and pragmatic assistance through the "Fritz Henkel Stiftung" foundation. In 2015, Henkel supported the reconstruction work following the humanitarian disaster caused by the earthquakes in Nepal. As a first step, the foundation provided the urgently needed emergency financial aid. Now it continues to support volunteer projects of Henkel employees who are assisting with the reconstruction work in the country.

Social Partnerships

Supporting equal opportunity in education is a top priority. In 2015, Henkel continued its partnership with the educational initiative Teach First Deutschland. In this program, university graduates in all fields work as fellows in schools with socially disadvantaged students. With the Light Up project in China, Henkel are promoting the reading skills of Chinese children by donating books and writing materials.

Together with the non-profit organization United Way in Mumbai, Henkel has initiated the Lighting Lives project in India, which is developing solar power in rural regions. In the pilot phase, solar cells have already been installed in three villages in the Palghar district near Mumbai, bringing electricity to the homes of 150 people and to the schools attended by about 1,600 children. The project will be expanded to include other villages and public facilities.

Henkel also provides support for many social projects through its brands. In the fasting month Ramadan in 2015, Henkel initiated the New Beginnings campaign in Saudi Arabia. For every bottle of Persil Abaya, a special laundry detergent for the traditional Muslim outer garment that is usually black, that was sold, a donation was made to the Saudi Arabian organization Al Bir. The campaign supports the Productive Families program, which helps women from low-income families to establish their own microenterprises.

In its fifth year, Schwarzkopf Professional brought the Shaping Futures initiative to Germany. In collaboration with vocational schools in Hamburg and Nuremberg, young refugees are given an opportunity to find out whether hairdressing could be a career for them. The goal is to establish a long-term and permanent educational program. The initiative began in 2010, in collaboration with the charitable organization SOS Children's Villages. Up to now, 1,200 young people in 25 countries have been trained thanks to the volunteer work of almost 250 hairdressers and employees.

Together with Plan International, Henkel and the Pritt brand began a construction and educational project in 2015 in two schools in Brazil. The goal of the two-year project is to break through the cycle of poverty through improvements in the educational situation at two schools in the northeastern part of Brazil. In addition to renovation work and school equipment, the program includes additional measures to improve the quality of schooling – such as workshops for students and their parents.

Stakeholder Dialog

An open exchange of views with its stakeholders provides Henkel with valuable knowledge on trends and risks. It helps the company to align and implement its sustainability strategy responsibly. Understanding the social demands that stakeholders of all kinds place on the company is a key component of Henkel sustainability management. That is why Henkel is open to dialog with all stakeholders, including customers, consumers, suppliers, employees, shareholders, local communities, government authorities, associations and non-governmental organizations, as well as politicians and academia. Henkel discusses concrete questions in a direct dialog with relevant stakeholders, in many multi-stakeholder initiatives, and on dialog platforms on sustainability topics. Numerous internal platforms provide feedback on the insights gained and on opinion formation.

In a comprehensive survey in 2014, Henkel asked its stakeholders what topics have priority for them. Through this Henkel learned how important the integration of sustainability in all of its activities and product life cycles is to its target groups. A second topic its stakeholder groups identified as vital is the targeted influence on consumers to lead more sustainable lifestyles and to use Henkel products responsibly. The results of the survey were taken into account in 2015 in the further development of Henkel strategy and its targets. This regular dialog helps Henkel not only to understand what its stakeholders think of its actions and expect of Henkel in the future. It also enables the company to recognize decisive trends and challenges in good time and to responsibly shape and implement future-oriented sustainability concepts. This is why Henkel participate regularly in scientific and political discussions on future frameworks.

Open dialog helps Henkel to understand which aspects of sustainable development are of interest to individual stakeholder groups. Timely consideration of the views of its stakeholders regarding future environmental and social challenges helps Henkel to set priorities and to adapt its plans and actions in a responsive manner. For instance, Henkel recognized stakeholder concerns regarding the slow progress toward sustainable palm oil early on and considered these while revising its strategy. Stakeholder dialog thus makes an important contribution to Henkel innovation and risk management and helps Henkel to continuously develop its sustainability strategy and reporting. At the same time, this exchange provides a basis for mutual understanding and an opportunity to achieve social acceptance of its entrepreneurial decisions.

Integrated Dialog

All of around 50,000 Henkel employees world-wide are called upon to assume responsibility in their working environment and to base their decisions on the principles of sustainable development. For many of Henkel employees, this includes regular dialog with stakeholders. Experts at its various company sites and in its different business areas engage in discussion with the relevant stakeholder groups on specific local and regional challenges. This enables Henkel to develop strategies and solutions where they are assessed and put into practice. In 2015, as in each year, Henkel employees met with politicians, scientists and scholars, business people and members of the public.

Henkel participates in a large number of initiatives on the local, national and international level, so that it can play an active part in shaping sustainable development in collaboration and through a mutual exchange with other stakeholders. This includes engagement in workgroups and in industrial associations, such as the World Business Council for Sustainable Development (WBCSD), the Consumer Goods Forum (CGF), and the International Association for Soaps, Detergents and Maintenance Products (A.I.S.E.). Here Henkel makes use of its experience and its role as a sustainability leader, for example when helping to shape the discussion regarding solution concepts for sustainable consumption along the value chain.

Under the leadership of its retail partner Wal-Mart Central America, Henkel has come together with 18 other leading companies to create the Central American Sustainability Business Alliance. The goal of this alliance is to collaborate with suppliers, employees, customers and local communities to promote sustainability along the value chain, such as through inexpensive products that reduce water usage and CO2 emissions.

At the fourth Global Footwear Sustainability Summit 2015 held in August in Shanghai, Robert Field-Marsham, Asia Marketing Director Industrial Adhesives, explained the sustainability challenges in the shoe industry and presented Henkel's sustainable adhesive solutions for shoe manufacturing.

The winners of the 2015 Green Talents competition, a program of the German Federal Ministry of Education and Research that has recognized young scientists internationally in the field of sustainable development every year since 2009, visited Henkel in Düsseldorf. They discussed the development of resource-efficient products with Henkel experts.

Henkel's Forscherwelt (Researcher's World) project, in which elementary school children learn in age appropriate lessons how a scientist answers research questions with the help of experiments, was also further broadened internationally in 2015. At the beginning of the year, the project in Russia was expanded to include three new schools, in which more than 100 children took part in the lessons. In April, the first Forscherwelt outside of Moscow took place at the Henkel site in Engels. In Turkey, too, through the collaboration of Henkel colleagues with the local Society for Creative Children and the Turkish Chemical Society, Henkel made it possible for children to participate in Forscherwelt programs.

At the Solutions COP21 exhibition, which offered concrete solutions for climate protection on the periphery of the UN Climate Change Conference in Paris, Henkel France presented the "Lavons Mieux" (better washing) program with its Le Chat Eco Efficacité laundry detergent brand. The objective of the program is to encourage consumers to act more sustainably when washing clothes. Prior to the UN Climate Change Conference in Paris, experts from WWF Germany, the utility company Stadtwerke Düsseldorf and Henkel also discussed climate change at the Düsseldorf site.

Henkel Thailand and the Institute for the Promotion of Teaching Science and Technology (IPST) in Bangkok, which initiated a joint educational project to promote sustainability in schools in 2015, held a national Facebook competition entitled "Thailand's Most Sustainable Family." The aim of the competition was to motivate families to have a more sustainable lifestyle. The winning family had reduced their use of energy and water by more than 22 percent within two months.

Dialog with Politicians and Government Authorities

Policymakers and government authorities often seek out the expertise of companies in their political decision-making processes. Within this context, it is possible for Henkel to describe how political considerations impact Henkel, its employees and business partners and for us to provide pertinent experience-based knowledge. Henkel worldwide "Representation of Interests in Public Affairs" standard provides clear guidance on conduct for this. Henkel also openly provides information about its fields of interest and the scope of its work involving governmental or political affairs through its entry in the Transparency Register of the European Union. At the end of October 2015, the German Federal Government extended an invitation to a nationwide dialog on the further development of the national sustainability strategy. Around 500 representatives from the political world and from companies and associations discussed how the global sustainability goals of the UN could be implemented at the national level. Kathrin Menges, Executive Vice President Human Resources and Chair of Henkel's Sustainability Council, opened the discussion session on the topic of sustainable corporate management.

In order to establish which topics are relevant to its business activities and reporting, Henkel analyzes sustainability challenges using a variety of instruments and processes and assess their significance for the company and its stakeholders. In so doing, Henkel engages in dialog with sustainability focused institutions, international rating agencies and analysts, and academia. Henkel also considers the assessment criteria of various financial and sustainability oriented ratings and the guidelines of the Global Reporting Initiative (GRI). The results of this continuous process are structured on the basis of Henkel six focal areas (Figure 19), in which Henkel aims to drive sustainable development worldwide along the value chain through its business activities.

External Ratings

Henkel assessment and recognition by sustainability experts increases market transparency and provides important feedback on how well Henkel is implementing its sustainability strategy.

Ratings and indices in 2015:

- **FTSE4Good:** Included for 15 years running.
- **London:** Henkel has been named in the FTSE4Good ethical index for 15 consecutive years.
- **NYSE EURONEXT:** Henkel included again.
- **Paris:** Based on a corporate rating by Vigeo, Henkel was again included in 2015 in the Euronext Vigeo World 120, Europe 120 and Eurozone 120 sustainability indices.
- **STOXX:** Listed for the fifth time.
- **Zurich:** In October 2015, STOXX Limited again included Henkel in the STOXX Global ESG Leaders Indices.
- **ETHIBEL:** Listed since 2002.
- **Paris**: In 2015, Henkel was once again listed in the Ethibel Excellence Europe and Excellence Global sustainability indices.
- **MSCI Global Sustainability Indexes:** Listed in global ESG indices.
- **New York:** Henkel is again represented in the sustainability indices MSCI World ESG and MSCI Europe ESG. Companies listed in these indices exhibit strong opportunity and risk management based on environmental, social and governance topics.
- **Global Challenges Index:** Listed since 2007.
- **Hamburg:** In 2015, Henkel was again one of only 50 companies worldwide to be listed in the Global Challenges Index. This index was developed by the Börse Hanover and the sustainability strategy agency Oekom Research AG.
- **SUSTAINALYTICS:** Best in sector.

Figure 19. Identification of key topics for Henkel's sustainability management and reporting

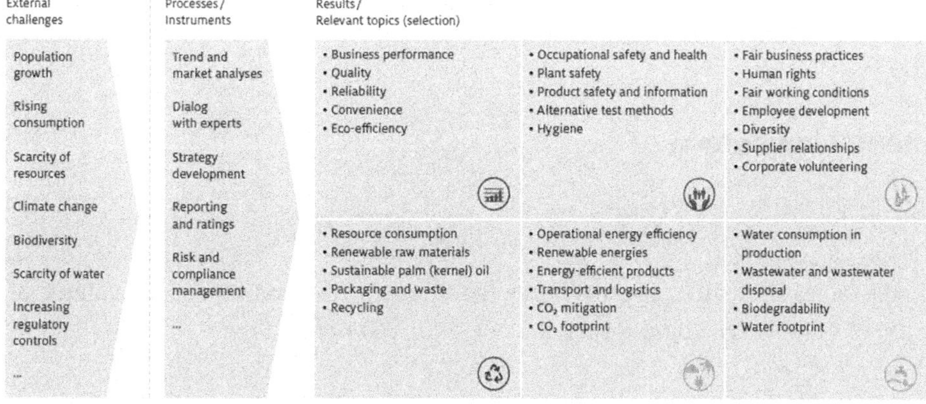

- **Frankfurt am Main:** In the Sustainalytics 2015 sustainability ratings in terms of the environmental, social and governance issues (ESG), Henkel is the world leader in Household & Personal Products com-pared with other companies in the sector.
- **OEKOM RESEARCH:** Prime Status.
- **Munich:** Henkel was again recognized by Oekom Research with Prime Status. With the rating B+, Henkel was among the best companies in the consumer goods sector.
- **World's Most Ethical Companies® Honoree 2015:** Listed for the eighth time.
- **New York:** Henkel has been included in the list of the Ethisphere Institute's World's Most Ethical Companies for the eighth year in a row.

INDICATORS

The indicators Henkel records throughout the company help it to identify potential improvements, steer programs and monitor target achievement. The indicators Henkel records throughout the company offer transparency. Henkel shows the progress of each of its indicators over a five-year period. In the Sustainability Report, Henkel focuses on the publication of its globally relevant core indicators. Henkel provides information on other environmental parameters on the internet.

The production-related data for 2015 were determined at all 170 Henkel sites in 55 countries. Thus, the data represent 100 percent of Henkel production volume. In 2011, the share was 95 percent; it was 99 percent from 2012 through 2014. They are validated centrally for year-end reporting and verified locally within the framework of its internal audit program. Any differences discovered or reported at a later date are corrected retroactively in its reporting system. Since its production structures are constantly changing – due to the start-up of new sites or closure of existing sites, for example – the number of sites contributing data changes accordingly. To ensure the comparability of the annual data, Henkel also shows their progress as an index relative to the volume of production.

Occupational accidents are registered using a globally uniform reporting system. 99 percent of Henkel employees are covered. The published employee indicators also cover 99 percent of its employees. Henkel has been working to increase the efficiency and safety of its production processes for decades. Its sustainability performance over the past 11 years illustrates this very clearly. In all three business units, its optimization efforts focus on improving value creation and occupational health and safety in its production operations while reducing its environmental footprint. Building on the progress achieved, Henkel aims to reduce its energy and water use, its waste footprint, and the accident rate still further.

Environmental indicators per metric ton of output, occupational accidents per million hours worked; base year 2005

Environmental Indicators

Index

The index in the tables shows the progress of the specific indicators relative to the volume of production (per metric ton of output). The base for the index is year 2011 (100%).

Figure 20. Long-term trend: Sustainability performance from 2005 to 2015

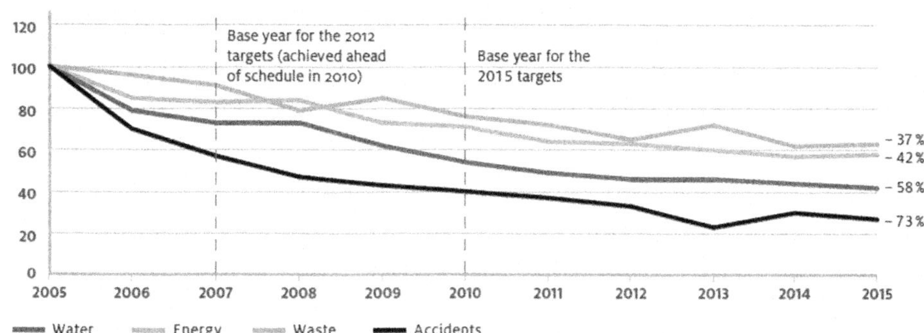

Occupational Safety

Index

The index in the table shows the progress for occupational accidents in relation to hours worked (per million hours worked):99 percent of Henkel employees were covered. The base for the index is the year 2011 (= 100 percent).

Employee Indicators

At 49,450, the 2015 headcount was below the prior year level. This was due mainly to synergies from acquisitions and adjustments in Henkel business units.

The average age of Henkel employees has remained constant over the years. This ensures, in accordance with its diversity strategy, which Henkel's workforce is a good mix of experienced older employees and younger employees whose development Henkel can foster.

The internationality of Henkel workforce reflects its business policy of filling local positions with local employees, and ensuring that Henkel has international teams at its corporate headquarters in Germany.

Table 2. The progress of specific indicators relative to the volume of production

Production Volumes					
In thousand metric tons	**2011**	**2012**	**2013**	**2014**	**2015**
Production volumes	7.498	7.574	7.690	7.867	7.940
Index: Change from 2011 to 2015					+6%
Due to the improved economic situation and increasing global demand, production volumes have been rising again since 2011.					
COD emissions to wastewater					
In thousand metric tons	**2011**	**2012**	**2013**	**2014**	**2015**
COD emissions to wastewater	7.148	6.031	5.746	7.530	6.500
Index: Change from 2011 to 2015					-14%
Chemical oxygen demand (COD): Measure of the pollution of wastewater with organic substances.					

Table 3. Energy consumption

Energy Consumption					
In thousand megawatt hours	**2011**	**2012**	**2013**	**2014**	**2015**
Bought in energy	670	664	648	650	667
Coal	119	112	114	96	127
Fuel oil	167	141	123	113	119
Gas*	1.426	1.428	1.406	1.360	1.375
Total	2.382	2.345	2.291	2.219	2.288
Index: Change from 2011 to 2015					-9%
*Henkel has introduced regional factors for the calorific value of gas and have corrected the figures retroactively. Bought-in energy is electricity, steam, and district heating that is generated outside the sites.					

Table 4. Emissions of heavy metals to wastewater

Emissions of Heavy Metals to Wastewater					
In kilograms	**2011**	**2012**	**2013**	**2014**	**2015**
Zinc	520	375	359	402	351
Lead, chromium, copper, nickel	356	287	260	183	246
Total	876	662	619	585	597
Index: Change from 2011 to 2015					-36%
Particularly hazardous heavy metals, such as mercury and cadmium, are not relevant in Henkel production.					

Table 5. Carbon dioxide emissions

Carbon Dioxide Emissions					
In thousand metric tons	**2011**	**2012**	**2013**	**2014**	**2015**
Henkel's own carbon dioxide emissions*	371	362	353	335	349
Carbon dioxide emissions from bought-in energy*	336	321	309	314	318
Total	706	682	662	649	667
Index: Change from 2011 to 2015					-11%
*Henkel has introduced regional factors for the calorific value of gas and are now using the most current factors for the respective reporting period to calculate the emissions from bought-in energy. The figures have been corrected retroactively. Energy generation accounts for almost all of the carbon dioxide released as a result of Henkel activities.					

Compared with international levels, the total percentage of female employees is good. This applies to managerial staff as well. It is a result of Henkel's consistently applied diversity strategy.

Part-time work models are of relevance mainly in Western Europe and especially in Germany. In emerging markets, such as Asia, Eastern Europe, the Middle East, and Latin America, there is significantly less demand for part-time work models.

An intensive formal and informal dialog with employee representatives has a long tradition at Henkel, even in countries where employee representation has not been established.

Table 6. Waste for recycling and disposal

Waste for Recycling and Disposal					
In thousand metric tons	**2011**	**2012**	**2013**	**2014**	**2015**
Waste for recycling	93	82	88	70	86
Hazardous waste for disposal	15	16	18	17	14
Waste for disposal	45	42	51	51	41
Total	153	140	157	138	142
Index: Change from 2011 to 2015					-13%
Share of construction waste	14	14	30	21	33

Table 7. Water consumption and volume of wastewater

Water Consumption and Volume of Wastewater					
In thousand cubic tons	**2011**	**2012**	**2013**	**2014**	**2015**
Water consumption*	7.954	7.502	7.642	7.438	7.190
Volume of wastewater*	3.560	3.177	3.084	3.004	2.990
Total					
Index: Change from 2011 to 2015			Water consumption		-15%
			Volume of wastewater		-21%
* Henkel has revised the definitions and has corrected the figures retroactively. Because water is lost by evaporation and water is contained in many of the products, the volume of wastewater is smaller than the volume of water consumed.					

Table 8. Emissions of volatile organic compounds

Emissions of Volatile Organic Compounds					
In metric tons	**2011**	**2012**	**2013**	**2014**	**2015**
Emissions of volatile organic compounds	336	336	312	317	328
Index: Change from 2011 to 2015					-8%

Around 11,300 employees in 56 countries purchased Henkel preferred shares under this program in 2015. At year-end, some 14,500 employees held a total of close to 2.7 million shares, representing approximately 1.5 percent of total preferred shares. The lock-up period for newly acquired ESP shares is three years.

Social Indicators

The number of projects supported was significantly higher than the prior year level. This is due to intensive project work for refugee aid. This focus resulted in an increase in the number of people supported. Employee projects required significantly less days off from work in 2015 than the prior year. This is due

Table 9. Occupational accidents

Occupational Accidents per Million Hours Worked					
At least one day lost (excluding commuting accidents)	2011	2012	2013	2014	2015
Henkel employees	1.1	1.0	0.7	0.9	0.8
Employees of external companies who work at Henkel sites and are directly contracted	1.1	0.8	0.5	0.8	0.9
Index: Change from 2011 to 2015			Henkel employees		-27%
			Employees of external companies		-18%
Serious Occupational Accidents					
More than 50 days lost	2011	2012	2013	2014	2015
Accidents during typical production activities	11	7	8	12	13
Accidents while walking or moving around (e.g., stumbling)	7	6	5	5	4

Table 10. Employees

Employees					
	2011	2012	2013	2014	2015
Henkel worldwide (1)	47.250	46.600	46.850	49.750	49.450
Structure of Workforce					
Non-managerial employees	79.9%	79.4%	78.7%	79.0%	77.5%
Managers	18.6%	19.0%	19.8%	19.5%	21.0%
Top managers (2)	1.5%	1.6%	1.5%	1.5%	1.5%
Employee fluctuation worldwide (3)	5.6%	5.8%	4.4%	4.3%	4.5%

1. Permanent staff excluding trainees; figures have been rounded.
2. Corporate Senior Vice Presidents, Management Circles I and IIa.
3. Based on employee resignations.

to a smaller number of team volunteering projects. Generally speaking, employees may request up to five days off from work per year for volunteer activities. Total donations were slightly up versus the prior year.

By joining the Global Compact of the United Nations in 2003, Henkel made a commitment to help achieve the Millennium Development Goals. Through its social engagement, Henkel contributes directly to the attainment of these goals. Henkel does not influence the type of projects proposed under the employee engagement program. Nevertheless, the majority of these projects do indeed contribute to achieving these goals.

Table 11. Age and seniority

Age and Seniority					
	2011	**2012**	**2013**	**2014**	**2015**
Average seniority in years	10.2	10.4	10.3	10.2	10.3
Average age of employees	39.4	39.6	39.6	39.7	39.9
Age Structure					
16-19	18.3%	17.6%	17.8%	18.4%	18.0%
30-39	34.6%	34.5%	34.4%	33.8%	33.4%
40-49	29.4%	29.6%	29.1%	28.2%	28.1%
50-65	17.7%	18.3%	18.7%	19.5%	20.5%

Table 12. Nationalities

Nationalities					
	2011	**2012**	**2013**	**2014**	**2015**
Henkel	125	123	123	124	125
Managers	91	85	88	93	89
At headquarters in Düsseldorf	53	55	56	62	64

Table 13. Percentage of women

Percentage of Women					
	2011	**2012**	**2013**	**2014**	**2015**
Henkel	32.5%	32.6%	32.9%	33.2%	33.6%
Managers	29.5%	30.5%	31.6%	32.5%(1)	33.1%
Top managers (2)	18.6%	18.6%	19.8%	20.6%	21.1%

1. Without acquisitions in 2014.
2. Corporate Senior Vice Presidents, Management Circles I and IIa.

Table 14. Part time employees

Part Time Employees				
	2012	**2013**	**2014**	**2015**
Part-time contracts, global	3%	3%	3%	3%
Western Europe (including Germany)	8%	8%	8%	9%
Germany	10%	10%	11%	11%

Table 15. Personnel development

Personnel Development					
	2011	2012	2013	2014	2015
Internal promotion (managers)	1.387	1.101	1.199	1.154	1.309
International job rotations	475	503	581	666	658
Trainees (Germany)	483	489	487	484	508
Average number of training days (1)	2	2	2	1.5	2.1

1. Training comprises in-person seminars and eLearning modules. Since 2014, Henkel has been focusing more on on-the-job training and job rotations.

Table 16. Employees covered by collective agreements

Employees Covered by Collective Agreements					
	2011	2012	2013	2014	2015
Percentage worldwide	44%	44%	44%	44%	52%
Percentage in the European Union (EU)	79%	79%	79%	79%	78%

Table 17. Employee share program

Employee Share Program					
	2011	2012	2013	2014	2015
Percentage of employees owning Henkel shares	31.3%	28.4%	31.9%	30.1%	29.7%

Table 18. Social engagement

Social Engagement					
	2011	2012	2013	2014	2015
Total number of projects supported	2.343	2.339	2.422	2.265	3.431
Number of people supported	753.629	1.046.321	1.147.483	1.358.108	1.506.525
Time off from work for employee-initiated projects (days)	135	131	51	284	121
Donations in thousand euros (financial and product donations, not counting time off)	6.002	7.302	7.937	8.238	8.316

Table 19. Percentage of projects supported per Millennium Development Goals

Percentage of Projects Supported per Millennium Development Goals					
	2011	2012	2013	2014	2015
1. Eradicate extreme poverty and hunger	30%	11%	13%	12%	10%
2. Achieve universal primary education for girls and boys alike	23%	39%	39%	42%	43%
3. Promote gender equality and empower women	2%	5%	4%	5%	3%
4. Reduce child mortality	14%	8%	8%	7%	5%
5. Improve maternal health	1%	3%	3%	3%	3%
6. Combat HIV/AIDS, malaria and other diseases	20%	3%	3%	3%	3%
7. Ensure environmental sustainability	9%	15%	15%	15%	15%
8. Develop a global partnership for development	1%	16%	15%	13%	18%

CONCLUSION

Henkel can look back on its 140-year history of success with pride. Today, Henkel still aims to create sustainable value with everything they do – together with employees, partners and stakeholders. The company holds leading positions with its three business units in both industrial and consumer businesses thanks to strong brands, innovations and technologies. Henkel also takes responsibility for the safety and health of its employees, customers and consumers, the protection of the environment and the quality of life in the communities in which it operates.

The responsibility that Henkel as a business feels toward the customers and consumers, the people, and society as a whole, has shaped the history of the company. In conducting its business, Henkel wants to create sustainable value through innovative solutions. This conviction is the foundation on which the strong engagement of the people and the long-term successful development of Henkel are built. Henkel's ambition to operate sustainably throughout the company and along its entire value chain boosts its growth, helps to improve its efficiency, and reduces risks. With its global sustainability and climate protection goals, the international community has made enormous progress toward a common understanding of the priorities. Henkel wants to actively contribute to the implementation of these goals. To achieve this, however, sustainability must also be firmly embedded throughout business and society. In playing its part, Henkel is relying on the knowledge and engagement of its people, the strength of its brands and technologies, and partnerships in all areas of its business activities.

Which are Henkel's sustainability aspirations? Henkel is committed to leadership in sustainability – this is one of its corporate values. As sustainability leaders, Henkel aims to pioneer new solutions while developing its business responsibly and increasing its economic success. Which strategy is Henkel pursuing? Henkel's ambition is to achieve more with less. This means Henkel creates more value for its customers and consumers, for the communities it operates in, and for the company – at a reduced environmental footprint. What targets has Henkel set? Henkel's 20-year goal for 2030 is to triple the value it creates for the footprint made by its operations, products and services. Henkel calls this ambition to become three times more efficient: Factor 3. Which are Henkel's priorities for the coming years? Henkel already has a strong foundation with a successful track record. On the road to Henkel's long-term goal, the company intends to further improve its performance over the coming years. Henkel wants to further develop and foster the commitment of its employees to sustainability. Henkel's employees make the difference – with their dedication, skills and knowledge. Henkel wants to strengthen its contributions to addressing major global challenges and maximize the impact it can achieve with its operations, brands and technologies.

We are facing immense challenges: The global environmental footprint of humankind is already greater today than the planet's resources can sustain. For this reason, we need innovations, products and technologies that enhance the quality of life while consuming less input materials. Henkel aims to use its decades of experience in sustainability to develop and implement solutions that are fit for the future together with its partners. To reflect the growing importance of sustainability for its stakeholders and its long-term economic success, Henkel defined three key drivers in 2016 for the coming years: Henkel aims to strengthen its foundation, boost employee engagement and maximize its impact.

To reach the long-term goal of becoming three times more efficient by 2030 (Factor 3), Henkel has set concrete interim targets for 2020 (base year: 2010):

- +22% more net sales per ton of product;
- +40% safer per million hours worked;
- -30% less energy / CO2 emissions per ton of product;
- -30% less waste per ton of product;
- -30% less water per ton of product;
- +75% overall efficiency.

Together with its partners, Henkel wants to improve workplace conditions for one million workers in its supply chains. Henkel wants to help its customers and consumers to save 50 million metric tons of CO2. Henkel wants to reduce the volume of packaging relative to net sales by 20 percent. Each new product must continue to make a contribution to sustainability. Through its social engagement activities, Henkel wants to contribute to the quality of life of 20 million people. Henkel wants to reach 200,000 children with its education initiatives.

Henkel wants its business activities to create sustainable value. This corporate goal connects all employees and goes hand-in-hand with Henkel's corporate values, which guide the decision-making and actions. With their dedication, skills and knowledge, Henkel's employees make their own contribution to sustainable development both in their daily business lives and as members of society. Because of this, Henkel wants to further develop and boost its people's engagement in sustainability.

Henkel wants to strengthen its contributions to addressing major global challenges, and maximize the impact it make through its business, brands and technologies. Against the background of the need to reduce global emissions in order to protect the climate, Henkel has set itself the long-term aim of becoming a climate-positive company. Alongside this, Henkel wants to contribute to social progress and create shared value through collaboration with its partners along the value chain. Henkel anchors environmental and social principles in its supply chains, and work on this together with its partners. This helps Henkel to ensure the quality of its products, avoid risks for its business, and enhance its reputation and brand.

Henkel brands and technologies are used in millions of households and industrial processes every day. For this reason, expanding its contribution to sustainability is important. Henkel puts a clear emphasis on developing pioneering solutions that create more value for its customers and consumers, as well as on providing innovations, products and technologies that deliver even better performance – with a reduced environmental footprint. Promoting sustainable consumption that conserves resources is an important objective within Henkel's strategy. This is why Henkel concentrates on developing products that enable the efficient use of resources such as energy and water. Henkel's aim is to enable its customers and consumers to save 50 million metric tons of CO2 emissions by 2020 – by providing innovative products and sharing its expertise.

With its unique portfolio and innovative technologies, Henkel is excellently positioned to meet environmental and social requirements around the globe – within the company and at its customers and partners. Henkel wants to inspire its customers and consumers with exciting innovations and brands. Beyond that, Henkel also wants to create more value for society. That is why Henkel supports educational projects that help to make people's lives better – especially those of young women. Henkel's strong brands contribute to sustainability. Looking ahead, Henkel intends to continue developing innovations that combine performance, environmental compatibility and social responsibility in equal measure.

REFERENCES

Henkel. (2016). *Sustainability Report 2016*. Author.

About the Authors

Elena Veselinova is an Assistant Professor at the Faculty of Economics at Goce Delcev University, Stip, Macedonia. She is the Head of the Department of Management. Dr. Veselinova has a PhD in Strategy, a Masters Degree in Management, and a Bachelor's degree in Management. She teaches in the areas of strategic management and investment management. Her researches and publications are related to strategic management, brand management, investment management and entrepreneurship.

Marija Gogova Samonikov is an Assistant Professor at the Faculty of Economics at Goce Delcev University, Stip, Macedonia. She is the Head of the Department of Finance. Dr. Gogova Samonikov has a PhD in Finance, a Masters Degree in Finance, and a Bachelor's degree in Marketing. She teaches in the areas of finance and investment management. Her researches and publications are related to finance, investment management and financial aspects of intangible assets.

Index

P

Q

R

S

T

U

V

W

CPSIA information can be obtained
at www.ICGtesting.com
Printed in the USA
BVOW04*0306170717
489205BV00007B/28/P

9 781522 524175